GOVERNING CHINA

ALSO BY KENNETH LIEBERTHAL

Coeditor, with David M. Lampton, *Bureaucracy, Politics and Decision Making in Post-Mao China*

Coauthor, with Bruce J. Dickson, *A Research Guide to Central Party and Government Meetings in China, 1949–1986*

Coauthor, with Michel Oksenberg, *Policy Making in China: Leaders, Structures, and Processes*

Coauthor, with Nicholas Lardy, *Chen Yun's Strategy for China's Development: A Non-Maoist Alternative*

Revolution and Tradition in Tientsin, 1949–1952

Sino-Soviet Conflict in the 1970s: Its Evolution and Implications for the Strategic Triangle

Central Documents and Politburo Politics in China

Kenneth Lieberthal

Governing China

From Revolution Through Reform

W·W·NORTON & COMPANY, INC.

NEW YORK · LONDON

The text of this book is composed in New Baskerville
with the display set in Weiss and Tiger Rag

Composition by Com Com

Manufacturing by Haddon Craftsmen

Book design by Martin Lubin Graphic Design

Library of Congress Cataloging-in-Publication Data
Lieberthal, Kenneth.
  Governing China: from revolution through reform / Kenneth
Lieberthal.
      p.   cm.
  Includes bibliographical references and index.
  ISBN 0-393-96714-X
  1. China—Politics and government—1949– 2. China—History—20th
century.   I. Title.
DS777.75.L557   1995
951.05—dc20   94-40257
                                                                      CIP

ISBN 0-393-96714-X

W. W. Norton & Company, Inc., 500 Fifth Avenue, New York, N.Y. 10110

W. W. Norton & Company Ltd.,10 Coptic Street, London WC1A 1PU

1 2 3 4 5 6 7 8 9 0

TO NAOMI BURD LIEBERTHAL

Contents

Part Two: POLITICS AND POLICIES SINCE 1949   57

CHAPTER 3: The Maoist System: Ideas and Governance   59

The Features of Mao Zedong Thought   60

The Governing System   77

CHAPTER 4: The Maoist Era   83

Wielding Power, 1949–76   85

Conclusion 340

Tables, Charts, and Maps

TABLES

CHARTS

MAPS

Preface

China has captured the world's attention with its explosive economic growth in the 1990s. Newspaper accounts trumpet it as having the most rapidly expanding major economy in the world; 22 percent of the globe's population seems to be adopting market economics with startlingly successful results. The entire region of East Asia has come into its own as an economic entity, fully equal to North America and Europe. Most Asian leaders expect China to provide the engine of growth for the entire region in coming years. Napoleon once reportedly remarked about China, the sleeping giant, that, "When she awakes, she will shake the world." As of the mid-1990s, China is stirring.

But there are lingering questions about the country's future. China's political system has time and again confounded expectations about its strength and stability. Political changes of enormous consequence have punctuated nearly every decade of twentieth-century Chinese history: the fall of the millennia-old imperial system in 1912; the May Fourth movement in the late 1910s; the unification under the Nationalists in the late 1920s; the Japanese occupation of the late 1930s; the Nationalist collapse and communist victory of the late 1940s; the Great Leap Forward and the ensuing famine, perhaps the deadliest in human history, at the end of the 1950s; the ideologically driven, faction-ridden bloodshed of the Cultural Revolution in the late 1960s; the adoption of far-reaching post-Mao Zedong reforms in the late 1970s; and the Tiananmen student protests and resulting massacre at the conclusion of the 1980s.

This long history of periodic political upheaval reflects inherent weaknesses in the Chinese polity. Two stand out. China's leaders have been adept at organizing complex governing bureaucracies, but have not been able to elaborate political processes and institutions to prevent their own power struggles from disrupting the entire system. Despite myriad laws and regulations, therefore, the Chinese system has remained at its apex—among the top two to three dozen officials in the land—essentially lawless and unregulated. Each leader's activities at this level are restricted primarily by the attitudes and resources of the group's other members. But the inevitable conflicts and resulting instability at the apex reverberate throughout the system, disrupting the entire polity.

The Chinese population, in addition, has not been given the opportunity to develop stable means of political participation. The state has for millennia operated on the premise that it must dictate the terms of political activity. It may conditionally entrust the administration of such activities to state-approved organizations such as guilds as long as those bodies stay within the boundaries determined by the political authorities. Chinese state administrations from imperial times to the present have often used ruthless means to suppress groups and organizations seeking to escape this political straitjacket.

The people of China have not, therefore, experienced meaningful, sustained political participation based on stable, autonomous institutions. They have often been mobilized by political authorities to exert themselves for state-directed ends and, in the process, to engage in ritualistic rites of loyalty to state leaders. But truly autonomous political efforts directed toward shaping the policies and/or selecting the personnel of the state have been confined overwhelmingly to illegal underground organizations such as secret societies or to sporadic outbursts of popular protest through demonstrations and street violence. Such protests have occurred repeatedly and make China's leaders feel that radical instability—chaos—always lurks just beneath the surface calm of society.

The outbursts take place either when people sense that paralyzing conflict among the leaders is rendering the state's repressive mechanisms ineffective, or when individual Chinese leaders encourage popular protest to serve their interests in power struggles at the top. The former occurred in the 1989 Tiananmen protest movement; the latter took place in 1978 and 1979, when Deng Xiaoping supported the Democracy Wall movement for a period of months before suppressing it. These outbursts erupt, in short, when the political system gives "space" to the population for such initiatives. Day in and day out, Chinese citizens have not had the opportunity to develop skills in the organization of autonomous groups and associations as a vehicle for political participation. Popular political participation has, therefore, remained sporadic and destabilizing rather than evolving into a conventional means to relieve tensions and mitigate conflict in the system. It would take years to develop the attitudes and skills necessary to enable the latter types of participation to work well.

These weaknesses at the top and the bottom of the political system bode ill for China's future stability. But all long-term observers of this remarkable country know that there are few places in the world for which the phrase *plus ça change, plus c'est la même chose* ("the more things change, the more they stay the same") more aptly applies. Almost all first-time visitors to China marvel at the rate of change they see and hear about, yet the past still weighs heavily on the present in such areas as the organization of the state, basic ideas about the nature of political leadership, and many of the notions regarding the state's relations with society. It is important to understand not only what has changed due to China's many upheavals, therefore, but also what has proved enduring. Ideas and approaches that have evolved only slowly over centuries cannot be jettisoned overnight, regardless of the political rhetoric that might fill the air during times of unrest.

Present-day China is thus a product of its deep imperial past and of its twentieth-century revolutions, both nationalist and communist. It carries forward powerful legacies that inform basic ideas and practices. It also shapes its policies in the crucible of the largest bureaucratic structures in the history of the human race, structures that reflect both the imperial era's legacies and

China's wide-ranging emulation of the Soviet Union in the early 1950s. In the mid-1990s there is again the potential for significant change in China, as the few remaining octogenarian leaders of the communist revolution die and the country pursues a major restructuring of its socioeconomic and political systems. The legacies and institutions of the distant and the more recent past will in varied, cross-cutting ways shape the future.

The challenge of understanding China is heightened by the fact that its experience does not fit neatly into many of the conceptual models of Western social science. It is, for example, simultaneously urban and rural, a member of the industrialized global north and of the unindustrialized global south; even with nearly three hundred million urbanites, it has not yet made the transition away from a peasant society. Over eight hundred million Chinese live in the countryside. Although not very visible to most outsiders, they will affect China's political future in a multitude of ways. Moreover, we are becoming more visible to them, as televisions and VCRs increasingly display the ways and wares of the global north to the Chinese countryside.

The obstacles to understanding China make it tempting to view the country in relatively simple images. In the past four decades, Americans have, for example, variously imagined the People's Republic of China as a communist totalitarian society, a modernizing country, and a utopian revolutionary society. We have at times waxed eloquent over the marvelous similarities between Americans and Chinese, pointing to the shared traits and aspirations that give us a special feeling of friendship for each other. At other times we have regarded the Chinese as "the other"—oriental, strange, and lacking the individualism that defines American character. When the United States reestablished political relations with China in 1971–72, popular images of the Chinese shifted almost overnight from an "army of the blue ants"[1] to what might be termed "eight hundred million protestants practicing their ethic." When China's leaders unleashed their army against peaceful protesters on the streets of Beijing in June 1989, American public opinion toward China veered from positive to negative in the largest single change ever recorded by polling in such a brief period of time.

This fragility in public perception reflects our tendency to focus on immediate developments, which sometimes change very rapidly, rather than on the forces that shape China's long-term evolution. This book is written to take full account of these underlying historical, institutional, and cultural forces, exploring their dynamics and implications in detail. It then applies the insights gained from this effort to the analysis of current issues and challenges. The distant past thus is not presented here as mere description; it is used to provide insight into the present and future.

This volume is organized around the four major components molding China in the 1990s:

□—the legacies of the imperial system and its demise (Chapters 1 and 2);

□—the effects of the particular ways in which the Chinese Communist party developed, including its struggle for power, elite political conflicts, and past policy initiatives (Chapters 2–5);

☐—the organizational structure and operational dynamics of the post-1949 Chinese state (Chapters 6–8); and

☐—the difficult issues facing contemporary China and the political resources available to the state in addressing them. These challenges include sustaining economic growth, coping with environmental problems, and managing relations between the state and society (Chapters 9–11).

The concluding chapter (Chapter 12) focuses on China's relations with the rest of the world and looks ahead at the prospects for change.

I wrote this volume for both students and general readers. I have done my best to avoid jargon and to provide enough background information in each section to enable readers to evaluate the arguments being made. The chapters collectively treat "politics" in broad enough fashion to make this volume pertinent to those interested in Chinese economics, history, and society. The volume has been shaped by the author's experiences both in China itself and in teaching courses on China. Drafts of this manuscript were used in three courses the author has taught, and the current version reflects comments made by my students.

During my various research experiences in China over nearly twenty years I have interviewed people at all levels of the system from Politburo rank, to advisors to the top leaders, to ministers, bureau chiefs, provincial personnel, county officials, city cadres, commune workers, and clerks in local retail outlets, among others. These contacts have included people at all points on the political spectrum from leading reformers to some of the noted conservatives discussed in this volume. Although the identities of these sources must remain confidential, their insights are present throughout this book.

During my more than thirty trips to the PRC, I have conducted research in nearly every major part of the country, as well as in Hong Kong and Taiwan. I have had the pleasure of developing deep personal ties with a number of Chinese in various walks of life. These have not only immensely enriched me over the past two decades; they have also afforded me opportunities to appreciate the long-term perspectives of intelligent Chinese as they have grappled with many of the challenges addressed in this volume. My travels have also permitted me to sample directly the mood of the country almost every year since the late Maoist era. I felt the excitement of the milling crowds and talked with dissidents at Democracy Wall in early 1979, and witnessed the Tiananmen Square protests and the massacre that followed on the night of 4 June 1989. Since my first visit to Beijing toward the end of the Cultural Revolution, China has undergone startling change. My main purpose here is to convey an understanding of the dynamics of change and continuity in the Chinese system.

The end notes serve primarily to guide the reader to the secondary English-language literature on the subjects discussed in the text. Chinese language materials are cited only when they provide the sole source for important information in the narrative. The text employs pinyin romanization, the standard form currently used in China, for transliteration of all Chinese names and terms except a very few for which other spellings are well known (such as Chiang Kai-shek).

To help readers keep track of individuals, a Glossary of Selected Individuals (pages 343–52) provides basic identifying information on the key persons cited. Chinese terms are used only when they provide insight into how China works. The use of abbreviations has been minimized but not eliminated. A list of abbreviations is included in the front matter.

The appendixes in this volume consist of four core Chinese documents. The first two are the current constitutions for the state and the Communist party. They present the system as it is supposed to function. The latter two are documents that mark significant changes in the way the system works. Appendix 3 is the 1956 document "On the Ten Major Relationships." It reflects the pivotal thinking in China's turn away from the Soviet model. Appendix 4 is the November 1993 Central Committee document on forming a socialist market economic structure. It spells out the major policy goals of the coming years, as articulated by the Communist party leadership. These four documents afford an opportunity to read what the Chinese authorities themselves say about their aspirations and means in governing the People's Republic of China.

Acknowledgments

The many opportunities I have had over the years to talk to Chinese about China have improved my feel for the country, added to the joy of studying it, and in important ways affected my judgments about it. I owe them a profound debt. Colleagues and students over the past two decades have considerably sharpened my understanding both of China itself and of how best to teach about it. I am grateful for these experiences and the pleasure they have given.

I want to extend particular thanks to individuals who took the time to read all or part of this book in manuscript and to give me the benefit of their suggestions and corrections. Professors William Kirby (Harvard University), Steven Levine (Duke University), and Andrew Nathan (Columbia University), as well as an anonymous reviewer, carefully read the entire volume; their copious comments and insights have strongly influenced the final presentation. Professors Albert Feuerwerker (University of Michigan), Abigail Jahiel (University of Delaware), Nicholas Lardy (University of Washington), Donald Munro (University of Michigan), Michel Oksenberg (East West Center), Ernest Young (University of Michigan), and Ezra Vogel (Harvard University) read selected chapters and saved me from errors, both conceptual and factual. I very much appreciate the willingness of all these colleagues to contribute their time, energy, and wisdom to this effort.

Another group of individuals played a very important role in producing the final outcome. Dan Lynch and Bettina Schroeder, both doctoral candidates in political science at the University of Michigan, provided outstanding support as research assistants. Kathleen Johnston and Katherine Dietrich did a wonderful job of typing various drafts of chapters, making up the table of contents, and putting up with an author whose sense of humor does not improve as writing deadlines draw near. I thank them all.

I had the enormous pleasure of working on parts of this manuscript for five weeks during the summer of 1993 as a resident scholar at the Villa Serbelloni, the Rockefeller Foundation's study center in Belaggio, Italy. It is hard to convey the quality of the Belaggio experience to those who have not enjoyed it personally. It provided the perfect working environment at a critical stage of this effort. I want to express my sincere gratitude to the Rockefeller Foundation for inviting me to hold this position. I also thank the University of Michigan for granting me leave in the fall of 1991 to begin work on this volume and the University's Center for Chinese Studies for research assistant support.

This book benefited from the deft editorial hand and astute substantive judgments of Steven Forman, my editor at W. W. Norton. He proved to be the ideal editor, knowledgeable about both the subject matter of the volume and the editorial demands of such a project. His contributions have considerably exceeded those of the typical editor, and I feel lucky to have had the opportunity to work with him.

My wife Jane has made many accommodations to this writing effort. I suspect that having the opportunity to share the Bellagio experience made up for some of these, but I am keenly aware of how much I owe her.

Despite the best efforts and strongest admonitions of all of the above individuals, poor judgments and specific errors undoubtedly remain in the text. By appreciation for their advice and help, I do not mean to suggest that any of the above individuals agrees with everything in this volume. For this final text, I assume sole responsibility.

Abbreviations Used in the Text

APC	Agriculture Producers Cooperative
CAC	Central Advisory Commission
CCP	Chinese Communist party
Comintern	Communist International
GATT	General Agreement on Tariffs and Trade
GMD	Guomindang (Nationalist party)
GNP	Gross National Product
IMAR	Inner Mongolian Autonomous Region
IMF	International Monetary Fund
MPR	Mongolian People's Republic
NPC	National People's Congress
NRA	National Revolutionary Army
PLA	People's Liberation Army
PRC	People's Republic of China
SMA	Standard Marketing Area
WTO	World Trade Organization

Pinyin Pronunciation Table

Chinese characters are one syllable long, and the pronunciation of each is made up of "initial" and "final" letters. Pinyin letters generally are pronounced like their English equivalents, with a few notable exceptions. Those that often create difficulties for the native English speaker are the following:

INITIALS:

PINYIN	ENGLISH
c	*ts*
qi	*chee*k
x	*hs*
z	*dz*
zh	*j*ack

FINALS:

PINYIN	ENGLISH
a	f*a*ther
ai	b*ye*
ao	n*ow*
e	b*ut*
i	*see* [*note:* after the initials "ch," "sh," and "zh," the "i" is pronounced "r"]
iu	*yo*
ou	s*o*
u	l*oo*t
ua	tr*ois* (French for "three")

Chinese names: In Chinese, the surname is first, then the given name. In most instances, the surname has one character and the given name has two. English convention provides for capitalization of the first letter of the surname and of the first letter of the first character of the given name. Thus, former Chairman Mao's full name is Mao Zedong.

CONTEMPORARY CHINA

L. Balkhash

Khobdo

Urumqi

Turfan

Barkul

Hami

XINJIANG

Kashgar

AFGHANISTAN

TARIM BASIN

GANSU

Dunhuang

PAKISTAN

Yarkand

CAIDAM BASIN

Xining

QINGHAI

Yangtze R.

New Delhi

XIZANG
(TIBET)

Lhasa

NEPAL

Kathmandu

Thimphu

BHUTAN

INDIA

Dacca

Calcutta

BANGLA-
DESH

BURMA
(Union of Myanmar)

LA

Bay of Bengal

THAILAND

0   MILES   300

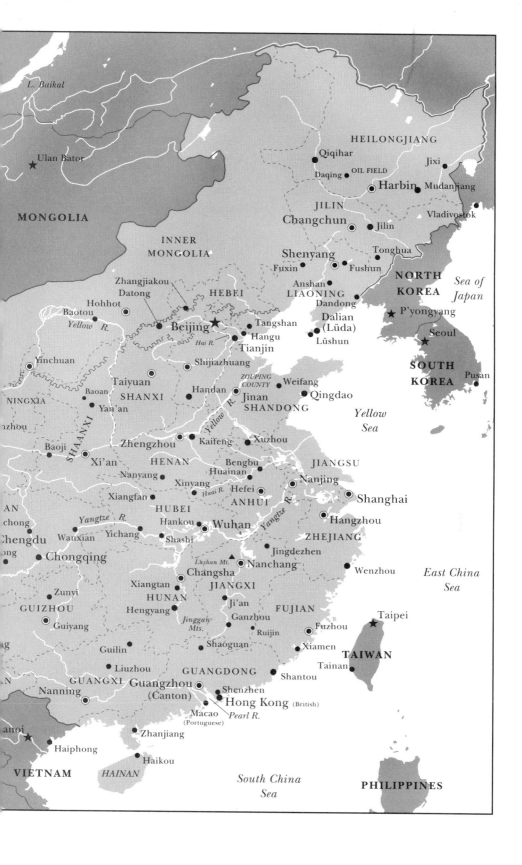

Part One
LEGACIES

1

The Legacies of
Imperial China

The post-1949 Chinese communist state* under Mao Zedong conveyed the impression that it could transform China's society almost at will. It repeatedly convulsed the multitudes with huge political mobilization efforts at the same time it marshaled this agrarian country's scarce resources for a prodigious push toward rapid industrial development. Until the launching of the Cultural Revolution in 1966, the People's Republic of China (PRC) seemed to epitomize worshipful loyalty to Mao, disciplined implementation of political

---

*Throughout this volume, the term "state" is used to include all the governing organizations and the bodies they directly control. When referring to the post-1949 Communist era, "state" thus encompasses the Communist party, the government, the military, and the social organizations that are either owned by the state, such as state enterprises, or under its direct control, such as state-sponsored "mass organizations" like the trade unions and Women's Federation. When only the government or the Communist party is meant, the text uses the terms "government" and "party" rather than "state."

decisions, a pliable population driven by ideological fervor, and disdain for the rest of the world.

Both this image and the more complex reality underlying it reflected the imprint of China's imperial past, a system of rule that began roughly two thousand years ago and evolved gradually up to the beginning of the twentieth century. For example, the imperial tradition nurtured the idea of basing the state system on ideological commitment, strong personal leadership at the apex, and impressive nationwide governing bureaucracies; the assumption in modern China that the government's influence should be pervasive because the government sets the moral framework for the entire society is also a product of the imperial era.

Additionally, the imperial system bequeathed contradictions and weaknesses that bedeviled Maoist China. The very majesty of the emperor's position, for example, produced tensions between the ruler and the bureaucracies of the government administration. The emperor's personal entourage often clashed with bureaucratic officials. Structurally, no national tax collection agency extended into the localities. Rather, taxes were collected by county magistrates, and each governing level (county, prefecture, circuit, and province) siphoned off a certain percentage as these revenues filtered up through the national bureaucracy. The central government's revenue base remained, therefore, sharply constrained. At the village level, moreover, a key stratum of local leaders referred to as the "gentry" divided their loyalties between the state and their own immediate constituencies. While the specifics changed, each of these and other underlying problems of the imperial era found their analogs in the Maoist period.

Within two years of Mao Zedong's death in 1976, Deng Xiaoping began an effort to reform the Maoist system. Deng's own initiatives, though, have also been shaped in many ways by the complex legacies of the imperial era. His post-Mao reforms address some of these, such as the need to elaborate a national tax bureaucracy. But in other areas, such as assuring the loyalty of local officials, the reforms are highlighting the continuing difficulties rather than providing solutions.

Imperial China had a monarchical system of governance and a patriarchal social system. The society was given a very distinctive style and aura by the official ideology of state Confucianism, but in many details it paralleled the multilayered dependent relations, sources of status, and modes of behavior found in Western monarchical societies of the premodern era.[1] The Chinese system distinguished itself from the others primarily by its enormous size, its relatively modern bureaucratic structures of state administration, and its explicit, detailed state ideology. It also lasted an extraordinary length of time. It is almost as if, in Western terms, the Holy Roman Empire had evolved but nevertheless survived into the twentieth century.

This past both shapes and haunts China. Many Chinese observers have blamed traditional ideas for their country's inability to defend itself against foreigners whose military strength had grown along with industrial power. These critics have felt China must reject traditional culture to become a wealthy, strong nation. They argue, for example, that the traditional system discouraged the types of investment behavior and technological change that modern economic growth requires. They have a point. As far back as the Han dynasty (206 B.C. to A.D. 220), Confucian scholars argued that, "When profit is not emphasized, civilization flourishes and the customs of the people improve. . . . To open the way for profit is to provide a ladder for the people to become criminals."[2] This attitude did not prevent the emergence of flourishing commerce in China, but it did sustain a view of commerce as a low-status occupation that alone did not qualify one for prestige or power.

In imperial Chinese society, moreover, the superiority of the civilization eclipsed the idea of nationalism based on ethnicity. The Chinese referred to their empire as *tian xia* ("all under heaven"). *Guojia* ("nation-state") replaced this term only in the modern era.[3] As a consequence, foreigners could gain legitimacy as rulers of China if their actions conformed to the norms of Chinese civilization. When the Manchus conquered China and set up the Qing dynasty in 1644, for example, they started holding the traditional imperial examinations in the Confucian classics the very next year. During its final one thousand years, imperial China was under foreign rule for approximately half the time.

Nationalism has developed as a strong force in the West only since the 1700s. Western nationalists embrace their past as a source of pride, and more than a few have developed myths of a deep past in which they could then root themselves. By contrast, Chinese intellectuals have been wrestling with China's past since the end of the nineteenth century, and many have tried to forge a sense of patriotism by rejecting that past. Tensions over what it means to be Chinese have therefore troubled the country's politics throughout this century; these tensions draw variously on the notions of ethnic, or Han, Chinese, *hua ren* (people who are culturally Chinese), and *zhongguo ren* (citizens of the Chinese state).

The Imperial Chinese System

The traditional Chinese state was an awesome political achievement, the most advanced such governing body in the world. Featuring a centralized bureaucratic apparatus begun over two thousand years ago by Qin Shi Huangdi (r. 221–210 B.C.), the first emperor of the Qin dynasty (221–206 B.C.), China's system of governance evolved through the rise and fall of various dynasties until the early 1900s.

There is no reason to try to capture the evolution of the imperial Chinese system over this period of roughly two millennia. It changed a great deal. But there were fundamental features of that system that provide great insight into contemporary China's style, capabilities, and discontents.

The imperial system in China lasted so long in part because of its own self-confident sense of greatness. The *philosophes* of the European Enlightenment considered China's the ideal system, with rulers chosen for their intellectual strengths and virtue. China's emperors needed no convincing on this score. Their mentality at the height of the last dynasty, the Qing (1644–1912), is captured in a letter written by the Qianlong emperor, who reigned from 1736 to 1796.

The Qianlong emperor wrote in response to an effort by King George III of England to gain China's consent for establishing diplomatic relations between the two countries and for developing trade ties. In 1793 the king sent an extraordinary mission to Beijing, headed by Lord Macartney. The Macartney mission brought England's best manufactures, along with skilled craftsmen and scientists, to impress the Qing court. The Qianlong emperor responded as follows to George III:

> . . . the territories ruled by the Celestial Empire are vast, and for all the envoys of the vassal states coming to the capital there are definite regulations regarding the provision of quarters and supplies to them and regarding their movements. . . . How can we go as far as to change the regulations of the Celestial Empire . . . because of the request of one man—of you, O King? . . . The Celestial Empire, ruling all within the four seas, simply concentrates on carrying out the affairs of government properly, and does not value rare and precious things. Now you, O King, have presented various objects to the throne, and mindful of your loyalty in presenting offerings from afar, we have specially ordered the Yamen to receive them. In fact, the virtue and power of the celestial Dynasty has penetrated afar to the myriad kingdoms, which have come to render homage, and so all kinds of precious things from "over mountain and sea" have been collected here. . . . Nevertheless, we have never valued ingenious articles, nor do we have the slightest need of your country's manufactures. . . . You, O King, should simply act in conformity with our wishes by strengthening your loyalty and swearing perpetual obedience so as to ensure that your country may share the blessings of peace.[4]

The Qianlong emperor had reason to be smug. He was certain that Chinese civilization existed on a higher plane than any other. The Chinese believed that even those who achieved superior military power (such as, at times, the nomadic tribes to China's north) would inevitably adapt to their ways. The erosion of this confidence during the nineteenth century rocked the Chinese society to its foundations.

Overall, the imperial system did a remarkable job of ruling a vast country while employing only a modest number of officials (at the height of the last dynasty, the Qing, about twenty thousand in the formal bureaucracy, supplemented by many staff assistants). To understand the strengths as well as some of the more problematic legacies of this system, five key components warrant more detailed scrutiny: the ideology; the institution of the emperor; the bureaucratic structure; the society; and the economy. It is usually more useful to look first at a country's governing structure and then at the political ideology employed by its leaders to bolster their power, but in China the ideological underpinnings of the governing structure were so fundamental by the time of the Qing dynasty that they must be examined to explain the rest of the system.

CONFUCIANISM AS IDEOLOGY

Confucius (551–479 B.C.) was an itinerant philosopher who lived during the Warring States period, a time of incessant turmoil and warfare. He traveled from state to state, advising leaders how to assure order and prosperity in their realms. Because he based this advice on fundamental precepts he devised concerning human nature, cosmology, rules of correct conduct, and principles governing social relationships, his teachings are called a "philosophy." But Confucianism also became a state ideology and, like Marxism and other political ideologies, it evolved over time in response to the changing political needs of its believers. As political ideology, Confucianism by the late imperial era had three core features.

First, it was a strongly conservative governing ideology. It aimed primarily at preserving order and looked not to the future but to a mythical state in the past to identify the ideal society (it therefore regarded anything "new" or "progressive" as untrustworthy). Long experience was the criterion of worth, and the wisdom of the ancients stood as the highest form of understanding. Confucius proclaimed that wise men "revere the words of the sages." Confucian officials sought to perfect the present by eliminating defects that had crept in since the ancient past.

Second, Confucianism valued hierarchy in both political and social spheres. It assumed that in the political sphere citizens were not and should not be equal. As summed up by Mencius, a disciple of Confucius, those who worked with their minds were fit to rule, and those who worked with their hands were not. Working with the mind required literacy first of all (no mean task itself with a language comprising over forty thousand characters, of which perhaps 10 percent were often used) and then mastery of the Confucian classics. Success required long years of study, and only a small percentage of the population ever succeeded. The ruling group thus remained small, and admission to it required learning a doctrine that justified the right of the few to rule the many. The only democratic component of the system was that, in theory, anyone who could master the ideology could join the ruling elite. Confucianism did not base rule on hereditary factors. But those from elite backgrounds had far greater access to the resources and support necessary to meet this key qualification for joining the political elite.[5]

Confucius taught that social relationships should be hierarchical as well, and that the key to social harmony lay in every person's understanding the mutual obligations that characterized each set of social ties. Typically, the lesser party—son, wife, student, subject—must show loyalty and obedience, while the superior party—father, husband, teacher, ruler—must reciprocate with empathy and acts of assistance.

Third, it was the essence of Confucianism that people should understand the "correct" conduct demanded by each type of relationship and should act accordingly, as this provided the key to a harmonious society. Indeed, although Confucians wanted everyone to understand the bases of the doctrine, they were on balance practical enough to recognize the even greater importance of correct conduct, whether or not it was grounded in profound learning. Following the rules of conduct, including the protocols of speech, became central to social harmony and might, over time, actually nurture correct thinking.

The Confucian emphasis on correct practice led naturally to an emphasis on ritual, the formal expression of the correct way. In the words of one contemporary student of this phenomenon, the Chinese stressed "orthopraxy" (that is, engaging in prescribed practice) over "orthodoxy" (that is, conforming one's thinking to prescribed ideas).[6] Confucians felt that correct practice would itself shape ideas over time. Correct practice, in addition, conveyed one's acceptance of the prevailing official ideology and its associated social theory conveying legitimacy to the government that promulgated and enforced this ideology. One of the six ministerial bodies in the Qing was the Board of Rites.

In China today, mouthing "correct" formulations is still viewed as socially responsible even if all concerned know that there is little relationship between those formulations and the thoughts of the people using them.[7] This situation makes it potentially easier for Chinese leaders to elicit formal support and compliant behavior from the populace; it also makes it difficult for the leaders to know the real state of mind of their own citizens and of their political subordinates.

The superior-subordinate relationships defined in the Confucian doctrine largely stripped youths of initiative and generally placed social power in the hands of the older, more conservative segments of the population. Students deferred to teachers, children to parents, subjects to leaders, and all to the emperor. The emperor, as the key link between heaven and earth, secured prosperity for his country through right conduct toward his[8] subjects and through correct performance of the rites that propitiated heaven. No formal laws could bind the emperor, but, as explained below, most who held this position felt constrained to conform to correct conduct as prescribed by the basic Confucian doctrine. The emperor's virtue in mastering and practicing this doctrine, it was felt, assured the prosperity of the country and thus secured his mandate to rule.

During the imperial age, the Chinese made fidelity to Confucian precepts the defining characteristic of civilized society. Those further from the center of imperial power, who had less regard for Confucian norms, were considered less civilized. The Chinese tried to broker relations with foreign peoples by fitting them into a ritualized system of exchange of goods and pledges of loyalty that Westerners dubbed the "tribute system."[9] This system of diplomatic relations and foreign trade was managed on the Chinese side by the Board of Rites. It was structured so that the conduct of relations with neighboring peoples would utilize rituals that would bolster China's official political cosmology. For example, the kowtow, which was performed by both Chinese and foreigners, required those having an audience with the emperor to kneel down and knock their forehead on the ground three times, and then to repeat this act for a total of "three kneelings and nine knockings of the head on the ground." In this as in other ways in the imperial era, form became as important as substance in maintaining the ideological base of the system.[10]

Confucianism was not the only ideology that influenced China's traditional polity. At various times, Buddhism (which came from India, and reached its golden age in China during the Tang dynasty [A.D. 618–907]), Daoism, and other strands of thought have had significant impact. China's imperial history is also replete with tales of political intrigue, military skulduggery, bureaucratic degeneration, and social upheaval. These phenomena reflect in part another important political and philosophical doctrine called

Legalism. This approach advocated extensive use of material rewards and physical punishments to obtain desired behavior. Legalists premised their approach on the assumption that people are inherently selfish. For much of China's history over the past two millennia, while Confucianism was the official ideology, actual practice also made substantial use of Legalism.

The Legalist philosophy was applied most fully during the reign of Qin Shi Huangdi. One of imperial China's most powerful figures, the first emperor of the Qin dynasty acquired power through astute military campaigns and political treachery. He then established a central bureaucratic state that engendered the imperial Chinese system.

The first Qin emperor's approach to governance differed fundamentally from that of Confucius. The Sage (Confucius) believed that people are educable, and therefore that the state should stress education and rule by example. Qin Shi Huangdi and his notoriously cruel minister Li Ssu, by contrast, adopted the Legalist view that people are inherently selfish and boorish, and respond only to the blatant manipulation of rewards and punishments.

Qin Shi Huangdi's achievements suggest a man larger than life. In his reign there rose major parts of the defensive barrier in the north known as the Great Wall.[11] He oversaw the production of a huge army of nearly ten thousand life-sized terra-cotta figures installed near his massive tomb in Xi'an to protect him in his afterlife. His use of power was as startling in its scope as were all his other activities. He created a society characterized by widespread torture and political knavery. He decreed such excruciating types of execution that it became common for a condemned individual to plead for clemency in the form of a swift death (being beheaded with a broadsword) instead of a slow one (such as being quartered by four oxen pulling one's limbs in different directions).[12]

Qin Shi Huangdi's empire survived his death by less than four years, but his notion of powerful rewards and punishments—of the resort to extraordinary violence to achieve the goals of the state—became an integral part of Chinese governing practice. As a result, China's subsequent political system both extolled rule by virtue and example and made ready resort to cruel punishment. Put differently, the traditional system wedded lofty Confucian ideology and tough Legalist measures into an integral whole.[13] This blend of ideologically defined moralism and hard-edged coercion has long survived the destruction of the imperial Chinese system that spawned it.

THE EMPEROR

The notion that the political system headed by the emperor provided moral guidance for the society was fundamental to traditional Confucian thought. As the "son of heaven" and the "ruler of all under heaven," the emperor assumed responsibility for maintaining "civilized" society and for mediating the relationship between that society and heaven. "Heaven" was not identified with an anthropomorphic deity as in Western religions but rather was more akin to some combination of history and fate.

Confucian principles were not entirely supportive of imperial power, however. These principles envisaged a central role for the emperor; however, in Confucian thought the emperor was accountable for his actions, which would be measured against the standards of the ideology, and those who could claim the most thorough grounding in the ideology were the Confucian scholar officials, not the emperor himself.

On the other hand, the ideology placed such emphasis on obligations to family that these officials were themselves confronted with some daunting dilemmas. Should they criticize the emperor when such criticism might bring great harm in retaliation against their entire clans? How much loyalty should they accord to the emperor and to their bureaucratic duties on his behalf when their families could benefit from a less strict approach to office?

The emperor headed not only the bureaucracy through which he governed but also an extended family and the life of the court itself. The tensions between the bureaucrats (the outer court) on the one side and those involved in the emperor's personal life (the inner court) on the other have been a perennial source of trouble for the political system.[14] Admission to the outer court was based largely on rigorous training in Confucian doctrine. Admission to the inner court, comprising imperial relatives and attendants, was based on blood ties (in the case of relatives), attractiveness (in the case of concubines), and surgery (in the case of eunuchs).

Typically, the early years of a dynasty saw a powerful inner court, as a new ruling house consolidated its power against officials held over from the former dynasty whose loyalty was suspect. The middle years were characterized by the relative flourishing of the outer court, which managed a complex and thriving society. The final decades usually saw the inner court reassert itself. Inbreeding produced weak emperors, and a dissolute life in the imperial palace, the Forbidden City, further eroded discipline. Intrigues among eunuchs, concubines, and court retainers contributed significantly to the decline of a number of dynasties. Overall, the tensions between the leader's personal relations and the formal governmental organs continue to rankle the Chinese system of the 1990s.

Because the emperor was to mediate between heaven and earth (and thus assure heaven's beneficence), the Chinese considered him personally responsible not only for actions under his direct control, such as government discipline, but also for those events over which he exercised only indirect or no control, such as floods and droughts. These latter were taken as signs of imperial incompetence or decay. When the emperor fell short, however, there were no clean political solutions. The emperor's position was so essential to the system (especially in the later dynasties) that no statutory limits could be placed on imperial power.

Among the scholar officials, a particular group, called "censors," was designated to ferret out problems in the political system. These members of the outer court were supposed to call the emperor's attention to poor performance of any officials, including the emperor himself. But since no official had an independent base from which to circumscribe the power and activities of the emperor, criticism had to take the form of remonstrance. The censor could only hope to make the emperor understand his problems and focus attention on correcting them, all the while affirming the emperor's moral superiority. This type of criticism thus bolstered the position of the emperor at the same time that it sought to change his behavior.

Imperial performance so abysmal that nothing could bring improvement occasionally produced large-scale social unrest. Official corruption would bleed the population through excessive taxation, while failure to maintain granaries and dikes would invite disasters. Military forces lost their effectiveness through corruption and sloth, and court rivalries sapped the ability of such regimes to galvanize their energies in support of renewal. Under these circumstances, unrest often began in the peripheral areas of the country, where restless groups threw off the relatively weak yoke of imperial control. That unrest then spread to more central areas, sometimes abetted by strong outside military forces.

The successful overthrow of an emperor was understood as a sign that through poor conduct that emperor had lost the "mandate of heaven." The succession to a new leader and a new dynasty could then be considered legitimate. Should the challenge to the empire fail, however, the emperor retained the "mandate of heaven" in the popular view. Since all failed challengers had defied the most fundamental strictures on obedience and civilization, they suffered terrible retribution.

The imperial system thus left a legacy of strong personal rule at the top, unbounded by formal law or regulation. The emperor's role as propagator and personifier of the official Confucian ideology bolstered the emperor's right to rule. This system was rife with tensions between the emperor and the governing bureaucracies, the inner and outer courts, and those who would reform an emperor gone astray versus those who would let a willful emperor have his way. There was no resolution in this system to the contradiction between a powerful leader whose personal virtue was thought to anchor the entire system and a powerful administrative bureaucracy seeking to enhance its own rights and privileges and to assure stability and prosperity.[15] This contradiction became a crisis when the leader became highly erratic and/or unusually willful. This structural weakness has continued to plague twentieth-century China.

THE BUREAUCRACY

Over a period of centuries, the bureaucratic system initiated by the Qin dynasty took on characteristics that are associated with modern bureaucracy in the West: highly defined offices, merit-based appointments, clearly articulated reward structures, considerable specialization in functions, highly developed formal systems of communications, detailed rules concerning proper lines of authority, regularized reporting obligations, formalized structures for monitoring compliance and deviance, and so forth. Specific codes of dress and conduct reflecting the status of various bureaucratic positions buttressed this system.[16]

In theory, the bureaucracy was to administer the empire so as to assure harmony in accordance with the Confucian precepts. County magistrates, for example, periodically gave public lectures on Confucian morals to the populace.[17] The system thus relied on a strong, ideologically motivated bureaucracy to lay a firm basis for a civilized, harmonious society. Officials might not live up to their obligations under this system, but the remedy would be their removal from office. The classical liberal preference for diffusing power and limiting the "reach" of the government in society is directly antithetical to the fundamental tenets of the traditional Chinese polity.

As in every bureaucratic system, reality departed to some extent from formal prescriptions, but overall the Chinese bureaucratic system was extraordinary in its scope, capabilities, and "modernity." It was a profoundly nonpluralistic system, based squarely on the notions of hierarchy, centralization, and the state as the propagator of the correct moral framework for the society. This centuries-long tradition of centralized bureaucratic rule was one of China's most extraordinary accomplishments. In this sphere, the legacies of China's past remain particularly strong.

Even China's concrete administrative system today bears a strong resemblance to its imperial forebear. During the Qing dynasty, the administration consisted of three hierarchies: the civil, the military, and the censorate. The civil administration in Beijing had six ministries, called boards. These took charge, respectively, of Personnel; Revenue; Rites; War; Punishments; and Public Works. Beneath these there were four levels of administration: counties or cities; prefectures; circuits; and provinces (there were twenty-two provinces in 1899). The total size of the civil administration remained small, however. As noted above, in the 1800s roughly twenty thousand individuals held official positions in the civil bureaucracy, less than 1 percent of the number of officials in 1990. Since the Qing dynasty was ruled by the alien Manchus, each board had both Manchu and Chinese heads and deputy heads.[18]

The military consisted of Manchu troops organized into banners, plus a Chinese professional army called the Army of the Green Standard that was held over from the Ming period and served as a constabulary force. The banner system, so-called because each force had its own pennant, grew out of a Manchu institution from the period before they conquered all of China. The emperor was considered the head of the military.[19]

The censorate attached officials to the six boards and to fifteen circuits in the provinces. Censors scrutinized the administration at all levels and reported problems to the emperor. When censors felt compelled to criticize the emperor himself, they proceeded at enormous personal risk.

Within the ranks of the imperial bureaucracy, mastery of the Confucian classics became increasingly important for admission to and advancement through the official hierarchy. By the later dynasties, the official examinations that largely determined elite recruitment and promotion concentrated overwhelmingly on mastery of the Confucian ideology. This body of knowledge may have had only limited utility for teaching officials how to handle flood control, revenue collection and transfers, and the myriad other duties they would assume when appointed to office. But there were distinct political benefits to making mastery of political orthodoxy the core stepping-stone in a relatively meritocratic bureaucratic system.

The mature Confucian system required that politically ambitious younger people as well as those already in office devote a great deal of time to preparing for the next round of official examinations. People with political ambition, therefore, exerted much of their energies throughout their careers on immersing themselves in the highly conservative ideology that buttressed the regime, and this bound scholars and officials to the state rather than making them independent of it.

The examination system also created a common culture shared by officials who came from diverse parts of a large country. Even the official oral language of Mandarin Chinese, based on the Beijing dialect, added a sense of unity and distinctiveness to the small official class and the larger number of people who aspired to be a part of that class. The larger group of aspirants, moreover, generally assumed informal leadership positions in their local communities and helped to bridge the gap between a distant officialdom and the localities. As of the early nineteenth century, approximately 1.1 million people (out of a population of over three hundred million) had obtained the lowest level official degree and thus formed the lower gentry.[20] Altogether, the examination system was highly effective in indoctrinating the elite and the politically ambitious in the conservative values of the regime. Its legacy is the view that ideological indoctrination of officials is both natural and necessary.

CHINESE SOCIETY

Chinese society displayed the characteristics embraced by Confucian philosophy: it was hierarchical, family-focused, and ritualistic. The overwhelming majority of people made their living off the land, with village size and organization varying considerably in different parts of the country. In south China, single-lineage villages tended to be more common than in the north, and therefore prohibitions on marrying within the village were especially strong in the south. In many cases, clan organizations played powerful roles in the village economy and ritual life.

Since each county had only one official member of the national bureaucracy (the *zhixian*, or county magistrate), the system made extensive use of intermediate elites. The most important group consisted of those who were trained for the official examinations but who currently did not have an appointment to the national bureaucracy. This group included two types of individuals: those who had passed the exams and were awaiting appointment and those who held appointments but were in the midst of the mandatory three-year mourning period for each parent, which required that they stay home without official assignment for that period. Given the often close relationships between such people and the larger landholders in the locale (official office often brought with it the means to obtain land; owning land brought with it the resources to study for the official examinations), this group of trained individuals typically had prestige and power in the villages.[21]

The county magistrate often depended on this intermediate stratum of individuals for advice about local conditions and for assistance in assuring order and managing the economy. These individuals could speak the official language and were literate. They shared the magistrate's training in Confucian political ideology. They identified, on the whole, with the national elite. They thus formed a privileged and important segment of the nonofficial population. At the same time, they were integral parts of their own villages, subject to the strong social expectations of their relatives and friends. They thus had dual roles as informal extensions of the state apparatus and as protectors of their own locales from the demands of the central state.

In a landholding agricultural economy, land ownership formed a major base of social stratification. Studies have made clear, though, that land was considered a commodity and was not held intact from generation to generation. China did not have a system of primogeniture, wherein the eldest son inherited all the land of the father. Rather, the death of a father would trigger a division of the land holdings among the sons. Consequently, there was continuing social mobility, and huge concentrations of land in the hands of particular families tended not to last more than two or three generations.[22]

In this society, women were severely repressed. In the later dynasties a practice called footbinding became popular. When a girl reached about age six her mother would wrap her feet tightly, curling the toes under the ball of the foot. Keeping the feet tightly bound over the ensuing years produced bones that broke and curled under, so that the overall length of the foot ideally would not exceed three inches. The resulting "lily feet" were considered attractive and a sign of status, and only non-Chinese minorities and very poor women who had to work in the fields all day had natural feet. Footbinding was extremely painful, and it sharply limited the physical mobility of women.

Most women were kept out of sight in the women's quarters of the home. Their duties varied with the wealth and status of the family, but they in general were subservient to their husbands and their grown male children. Women were betrothed by their father and typically had barely met their husbands before the marriage. While wealthier men might have more than one wife (or a wife and a number of concubines), a widow was expected to remain chaste after the death of her husband, even if this occurred when she was still very young.

Wives lived in the husband's household and were under the authority of the mother-in-law, which often made for tense, miserable relations. Because women left the household while males brought new people (their wives and children) into the household, there was a very strong preference for male offspring, and female infanticide was not unknown. Women, indeed, were held in such low regard that often girls were not given names (they were merely called "second daughter" or something similar). Grandparents would not count the offspring of their daughters among their grandchildren. As in many patriarchal societies, female suicide was common.[23]

The communists from the 1920s to the 1940s sought to harness female resentment to the cause of the revolution. The slogan they used was that "women hold up half the sky." Gender relations have changed greatly in

China, as elsewhere, during the twentieth century but, as Chapter 11 explains, gender equality is still far from a reality.

The most enduring legacy from traditional society is the pattern of social obligations created by the Confucian value system. As noted above, Confucian doctrine placed tremendous emphasis on knowing the proper behavior—that is, the mutual obligations—attendant on each type of social relationship. The Chinese language itself reflects this emphasis, with its unique nouns to distinguish seemingly marginal degrees of relationship—such as "third cousin twice removed on the maternal side."

The Confucian understanding of human nature and society contrasts strongly with that of the Judeo-Christian heritage. The latter holds that each person owes every other person a general social obligation because of the very humanity shared by all. Underlying this view is the idea that every individual has a soul and therefore some inherent value. Although this tradition has often been more honored in theory than in practice, it has been quite fundamental to the development of Western society and culture.

Confucian society lacks this notion of abstract social obligation. Its obligations are concrete and determined by specific social relationships. An individual, indeed, never stands independently as Ms. Li or Mr. Zhao, but is always part of a web of social relationships: wife, mother, daughter, sister, husband, son, student. One deals with others through these personal connections, and one's social strategy is based to a considerable extent on building supportive webs of personal ties.[24]

This specificity of social obligation helps explain a paradox often observed by Westerners in China. A poor family living at bare subsistence level will take in any distant relative who shows up at their door needing help. The relative may live in the family's cramped quarters, share their food, and eventually find a modest job with their aid. This same family, though, would pass a starving beggar on their street every day and refuse to give him any money. More than that, they would seem amused by his plight, and when they saw him lying dead on the street one day they might crack irreverent jokes.[25] How could the same people appear solicitous in the one instance and callous in the other?

The family's defined social obligation toward the distant relative and lack of obligation toward the begger on the street explain this paradoxical behavior. A stranger without any "connection" (the current Chinese term is *guanxi*) is simply of no concern to the family. His travails are merely a diversion from their dreary everyday routine and the source of some potential interest and amusement.

Such sights remain common in contemporary China, even though Confucian ideology no longer holds sway. A traffic accident quickly draws a crowd, but only police officers help the victims. Others simply enjoy the break from their daily routines. A guide to behavior developed for Chinese visiting the United States in the early 1980s advised the visitors not to stand by and laugh if they saw someone injured in an accident. Rather, the guide explained, Westerners expect you to empathize and to offer help in such a situation. In other cases where Westerners would feel obligated to extend help, Chinese feel no such pressure and, indeed, actually shy away from involvement lest any assistance *create* a relationship with someone whose character is unknown. At the same time, *specific* relationships in China now, as in the past, engender very strong loyalties and powerful displays of mutual obligation.

The fundamental nature of social obligation has been one of China's major obstacles to developing a sense of citizenship. Chinese see themselves more as parts of specific webs of relations than as common members of a single nation. Cooperative efforts at a social level are difficult to extend beyond those who share particular ties, such as in clan and lineage organizations, and larger-scale efforts typically require government intervention to succeed.

The Confucian notion of social obligation shifted attention away from the individual's personal rights and interests as the object of political thought. The pluralist notion of society as an arena of contending groups with social policy emerging from the interplay is fundamentally at odds with the principles and practice of China's historical governance. Rather, in Confucian ideology proper governance maintained harmonious relations through correct policies and appropriate moral guidance. The "natural" state of society is thus one of harmony rather than contention. Since everyone has a common interest in enjoying the fruits of a well-governed, harmonious society, moreover, there are in theory no fundamental clashes of interests between individuals and groups. The basic assumption on which the edifice of representative government rests in the West is completely missing from China's tradition.[26]

Chinese society in the late imperial era was, nevertheless, richly varied. Domestic commerce flourished, and local cultural traditions changed greatly as one traveled around the country. Some regions, such as the lower Yangtze, produced a very cosmopolitan urban life,[27] while others, such as the loess soil region of northern Shaanxi, remained poor and extremely backward.[28] The Qing dynasty, moreover, witnessed a great upsurge of local social and economic activity.[29] This local vibrancy did not, however, produce major changes in the political system itself until the very end of the Qing.

THE ECONOMY

China's economy was overwhelmingly agrarian, characterized primarily by small peasant producers. These farmers showed considerable ability to obtain high yields by careful adaptation to local ecological conditions. Nevertheless, one remarkable feature of the agricultural economy was a lack of technological change in the Ming and Qing dynasties (from the 1300s to the early 1900s). During this long period of basic technological stagnation, agricultural output increased substantially, but this was accomplished primarily by more intensive cultivation, applying traditional inputs, bringing new land under the plow, and introducing new crops such as sweet potatoes.[30]

Two general explanations have been given for this overall dearth of technological development. In one view, China's huge population made the man/land ratio so adverse that there were never sufficient resources to allow for technological experimentation. In addition, the high population density provided very few incentives to find labor-saving ways of increasing output. The other explanation points instead to the role played by extractive elites, who obtained the rural surplus (through taxes, land rents, usurious loans, corruption, and so forth) and then spent this on consumption rather than on investment in improved methods of production.

The discrepancies between these two positions, as is often the case in historical explanation, remain unresolved. There is evidence that the man/land ratio increased over this period, but different scholars[31] disagree over the relevant figures. In similar fashion, there appears to have been a rural surplus that was successfully captured by a small elite (perhaps 4 percent of the population), but explanations of their behavior and of regional variance are very inexact.[32]

Scholars agree that China's economy during the Ming and Qing was highly commercialized, with a substantial portion of farming households producing at least part of their output for the market. An extensive system of local "periodic" markets that convened on a fixed schedule every few days, leading into progressively higher levels of marketing nodes in county towns and larger cities, existed and has been described most thoroughly in the works of G. William Skinner.[33] His research suggests that China by the Qing dynasty consisted really of nine regional economic systems,[34] called macroregions, each of which had its own core and periphery. The nine macroregions were connected to each other by commercial and political ties, but their distinctiveness outweighed their relationships. Each macroregion had its own economic and accompanying social dynamics.

Skinner argues that for most analytical purposes one should think of China more in terms of these regional systems than in terms of the standard administrative divisions of counties and provinces. For the throne, the most important macroregion for revenue purposes was that of the lower Yangtze, with north China the second-most important.[35]

The extensive commercial activity of late imperial China naturally involved a large group of specialized merchants. Although the Confucian ideology assigned high status to farming and low status to commercial activity, in fact commerce provided a major source of individual wealth. Successful merchants often used a part of this wealth to gain respectability and security. They could do so in several ways: purchasing land and becoming an absentee landlord; hiring tutors for their offspring so that they might take the official examinations and enter the government; or directly purchasing a government title and/or office, as at various times the government sold titles and offices to raise money.

Merchants sought security because their interests were vulnerable to state intervention in the economy. Debates over such issues as whether to maintain government monopolies on the salt and iron industries go back to the first century B.C. In economic as in other areas, there were no clear limits to the potential scope of state activity, and during periods of relatively strong governance the bureaucracy's reach extended far into the economy. At the height of the Qing, for example, the government exercised monopolies in the sale of ginseng, the trade with Japan in copper (needed for coins), salt, textiles, porcelains from the imperial factories in central China, and customs bureaus throughout the empire.[36]

The state apparatus, moreover, from early times onward based itself in the major cities and thus rather easily and naturally intervened in urban production and commerce. Indeed, Skinner's research indicates that the Qing administration carefully placed administrative offices in the core city of each macroregion, presumably in order to maximize effectiveness in extracting revenues. But the boundaries of political administrative units (provinces, counties, etc.) partly cut across those of the macroregions, rather than completely conforming to them. This arrangement probably helped prevent merchants from acquiring too much power by making them focus their political activities on units that did not coincide with the sphere of their economic activities.[37] Unlike Europe, where cities grew up largely outside the rural-based feudal system, in China an independent bourgeoisie never had a chance to develop beyond the effective reach of the state.[38]

In sum, imperial China's economy was rural-based, efficient in terms of output per unit of land but not in terms of output per unit of labor, regionally diverse, relatively commercialized, and technologically stagnant. A small elite extracted much of the agricultural surplus and used this for consumption rather than for improving production. While conditions varied greatly across the country, those with adequate property holdings generally became absentee landlords instead of managerial landowners who might seek to increase production so as to maximize profits. The state itself felt free to intervene massively in the commercial sector of the economy.

LIMITS OF THE IMPERIAL STATE

For all its grandeur, the imperial Chinese state undertook a minimal range of functions compared to a modern political system. While it propagated a political ideology that delineated no clear boundaries to the state's intervention in the society, its leaders in fact evidenced more concern over controlling their own administrative apparatus than over expanding the government's roles in the economy and other spheres.[39] Even though China's territory and population grew greatly over the final six hundred years of the imperial system, for example, the authorities kept the number of county-level units at a relatively constant number (about 1,400 to 2,400), thus restraining the size of the formal bureaucracy they had to control.

The imperial government restricted its actual efforts to a few rather circumscribed spheres. These included propagating the ideology, suppressing rebellion (in other words, protecting its own power), maintaining national defense, gathering revenues to sustain itself, selecting its successors, and constructing public works.

China's extensive public works focused on the management of water that flowed from the high western reaches of the country eastward to the sea. The major river in the north, the Yellow River, is highly silted and tends to overflow its banks so often and with such catastrophic results that it is called

"China's sorrow." In the southwest, virtually all water available for agriculture in western Sichuan Province on the populous Chengdu Plain still comes via a remarkable set of water works constructed more than a millenium ago. In southeast China, wet paddy rice cultivation required careful control of water flow for irrigation. Water management was so crucial, indeed, that one school of scholarship portrays the imperial system as shaped primarily by the need to control water resources. Karl Wittfogel called imperial China a "hydraulic society."[40]

Even a state of this great capacity nevertheless falls dramatically short of a modern state that seeks to foster economic development, manage social change, provide for basic welfare, and in myriad other ways penetrate and organize the economic, educational, and social lives of the populace. The imperial Chinese state could be highly successful as long as demands remained limited. When new challenges stemming from the spread of the industrial revolution required such changes as new levels of revenue extraction, new types of economic development, and new approaches to education, this state system proved inadequate to the task and perished as a consequence. But it left enduring legacies for the current Chinese political system.

Imperial Collapse

The imperial system formally ended on 12 February 1912, when the six-year-old Qing emperor Pu Yi abdicated his throne in response to pressures from the republican revolution of the previous year. This marked the end of more than two thousand years of an imperial Chinese system of rule. Previous dynasties had experienced periods of growth and decline with sufficient regularity to warrant scholarly use of the notion of a "dynastic cycle."[41] But only the Qing's dynastic decline produced an actual revolution. Two factors combined to account for this unprecedented outcome: traditional forces of dynastic decline, such as a succession of weak emperors, widespread corruption, frequent floods, and local rebellions, that dominated the situation until the 1890s and substantially weakened the Qing court; and the impact of the industrializing West and Japan, which confronted China with an unprecedented set of demands and resulting crises.

DECLINE OF THE QING

The Qing dynasty reached its peak in the late eighteenth century and then began a gradual decline. Traditional factors contributed to this turn for the worse. Prosperity produced relatively rapid population growth—the population grew from approximately 125 million in 1650 to 225 million in 1750 to 410 million in 1850[42]—but few changes in agricultural technology to expand food production apace with population. The result was a thinner margin to cushion hard times brought on by natural and man-made disasters.

Natural disasters became more deadly as corruption spread in the ranks of the government. Here, the incumbency of Heshen (1750–99), a young aide to the aging Qianlong emperor from 1776 to 1796, marked the turning point. Qianlong put Heshen in charge of revenues and personnel and also assigned him to suppress the White Lotus Rebellion in central and western China. Heshen and his friends siphoned off so much money and so corrupted the bureaucracy that the rebellion continued until after Qianlong's death and Heshen's removal. When the Qianlong emperor's successor, the Jiaqing emperor, forced Heshen to commit suicide and confiscated his estate, Chinese records noted that the estate included sixty million ounces of silver, seventy thousand furs, a silver service of 4,288 pieces, and other items worth more than 1.5 billion dollars.[43] Funds that should have been used to strengthen dikes and ensure the proper management of granaries found other, personal, outlets. The empire was weakened as a result.

Weak successors, some dominated by stronger relatives, followed powerful initial dynastic leaders. Two of the first four emperors of the Qing were towering figures who reigned for sixty years each (the Kangxi emperor, r. 1661–1722,[44] and the Qianlong emperor, r. 1736–96), whereas three of the last four emperors each governed for less than fourteen years (the Xianfeng emperor, r. 1851–61; the Tongzhi emperor, r. 1861–75; and the Xuantong emperor, r. 1908–11). The long ostensible tenure (thirty-three years) of the Guangxu emperor (r. 1875–1908), moreover, was somewhat misleading. He ascended the Dragon Throne at age three, "ruled" under the formal regency of the Empress Dowager Ci Xi until 1889 and under her strong influence through 1897, asserted his own programmatic preferences for only a period of months in 1898, and then suffered effective arrest until his death in 1908.

Weak rulers, corrupt officials, population pressures, thin resources, and other traditional maladies produced unrest first in border areas and then among the disaffected in the more populous parts of China. The White Lotus Rebellion noted above rocked central and western China from 1774 to 1804. During the mid-1800s, four great rebellions—each with its own dynamics— brought the empire almost to its knees. These were the Taiping Rebellion (1850–64), the Nian Rebellion (1853–68),[45] the Southwest Muslim Rebellion (1855–73), and the Northwest Muslim Rebellion (1862–78).[46]

Of these, only the Taiping Rebellion had any real connection with the Western impact on China that would subsequently transform the Qing's dynastic decline into a revolutionary upheaval: Hong Xiuchuan, the charismatic leader of this great rebellion, was a failed degree candidate who, after reading some Protestant missionary tracts, believed that he was Jesus Christ's brother. Nevertheless, even the Taiping, which at one point controlled much of central and eastern China below the Yangtze River, drew basically on indigenous driving forces.

These four rebellions wrought enormous destruction, together causing the deaths of perhaps as many as one hundred million people. To combat them the Manchu-controlled throne encouraged key Chinese provincial leaders to develop provincial armies. As one consequence of the rise of these local armies, China suffered from the existence of personal military forces not fully loyal to an institutionalized central military establishment.[47] The four great rebellions also greatly weakened the fiscal base of the dynasty by taking much land out of imperial control at a time when the land tax provided the largest share of the government's revenue. The court's ideological prestige suffered, too, and this was not helped by the subsequent large-scale sale of government offices and titles to bring in new revenues for reconstruction. Overall, the postrebellion efforts to restore the country's strength failed to address these difficulties adequately.[48]

The factors evident in these events marked the decline of most dynasties. Internal corruption, a breakdown of discipline within the government administration, spreading social unrest, the decline of ideological élan, a growing role for the family members of the supreme leader(s), the elevation of weaker individuals to the top position, and the increasing importance of military versus civilian officials all spelled serious trouble, and sooner or later challengers would link up with sufficient power to overthrow the ruling house. They would then set up their own dynasty, perhaps after an interregnum of years, or even decades, of domestic strife.

Against this background, the Western challenge had begun to affect the Qing by the 1840s, but it did not become central to the fate of the nation until the waning years of the century. The period between the initial recognition of a nettlesome problem (around the 1830s) and the near collapse of the imperial system (in the late 1890s) saw the development of some political and social pathologies that have proven so enduring that they continue in one form or another to plague China in the late twentieth century.

THE WESTERN CHALLENGE

Although China had dealt with the West intermittently for centuries prior to the 1800s, this limited contact posed no serious challenge to China's sense of itself as the Middle Kingdom—the center of the civilized world—as the Qianlong emperor's letter to King George III indicated. Those Westerners who journeyed to China tended instead to be awestruck by the vitality of its economy, the sophistication of its scholars and officials, and the might of its empire. What changed during the course of the 1800s, moreover, was only in part China. The larger change occurred in the West itself—and therefore in the nature of the challenge it posed to Beijing.

The leading nations of the West in the nineteenth century realized the benefits of the revolution in transportation that began in the fifteenth century and the industrial revolution that began in eighteenth-century England. These developments enhanced the military capabilities—and especially the ability to project power—of the newly industrializing countries. More advanced technologies in communications, transport, metallurgy, and so forth effectively shortened distances around the globe. The newly industrializing countries sought to conquer far-flung empires to feed raw materials into their growing industrial plants, to consume the products of their increasingly productive industry, to siphon off their excess populations, and to add to their own sense of superiority.[49]

This new industry-based power produced new perspectives on the international order. The "superior" Chinese culture gradually took on a less lustrous character. British and other traders sought to draw China into the expanding international trading system without, however, fitting themselves neatly into the Confucian cosmology so central to the self-perception of Chinese officialdom.

The Chinese adopted piecemeal responses to the growing pressure to open the country up to the West's traders and products.[50] In the typical pattern, Chinese officials perceived a concrete problem, adopted the minimum response deemed adequate to cope with it, and then encountered two difficulties: their measures produced unintended consequences that created new problems and those measures fell short of addressing the original challenge. In this cumulative fashion, the overall problem moved from periphery to core, eventually undermining the dynasty and the dynastic system itself.[51]

There is little reason to believe that before the 1860s the Chinese saw the Western challenge as anything out of the ordinary. The court tried to prohibit the importation of opium in the 1830s, but in the notorious Opium War of 1839–42 the British successfully won new trading concessions. During the 1840s and 1850s the Chinese tried to fit the pesky Westerners into their system of handling other "barbarians"—that is, to limit their access to China, cloak that access in rituals of the tribute system, and thereby make the necessary concessions in a fashion that affirmed the basic Confucian view of the world.[52] They did this while, in the 1850s, concentrating their attention on the four great domestic rebellions that erupted in that decade.

Western forces, spearheaded by the British and French, continued pressuring the Chinese for greater access to their market and, for foreign missionaries, to their souls. This led to military conflict from 1856 to 1860 and a humiliating Chinese defeat. The West, though, decided that its interests would be best served by a strong government in Beijing that could effectively implement the concessions wrung from it. Some Westerners, therefore, organized an "Ever-Victorious Army" to serve the court in Beijing against the Taiping rebels.[53] This Western approach of supporting Beijing while wringing concessions from it persisted through the latter half of the 1890s.

During the 1860s some Chinese began to understand how dangerous the Western challenge could become. They advocated both learning Western ideas about international relations so as to use the Western conventions to protect China, where possible, and mastering Western military technology in order to use it to ward off Western aggression.[54]

The effort to acquire Western technology, though, produced unintended ripple effects. For example, this policy required that intelligent Chinese go abroad for training in foreign languages and in the pertinent math, physics, engineering, and other subjects. Such travel and intensive training affected the views of many of these individuals in ways that extended well beyond simple weapons manufacturing.[55] In addition, the Qing system could not adequately reward these individuals, whose new careers removed them from the intensive training in the Confucian classics that provided the only legitimate path, via the examination system, to upward political and social mobility. Over a period of decades it became obvious that mastering Western techniques would require changes in core elements of Chinese society itself.

The Chinese thus learned that technology does not develop in splendid isolation. Its use also transmits values, and it has wide-ranging, complex effects on those who seek to absorb and utilize it. China's paramount leader Deng Xiaoping expressed this same observation in the 1980s, saying "When you open the window, inevitably some flies come in with the fresh air." How far to open the window has been an issue of contention in China since the 1860s.

Foreigners sought bases in China from which to engage the Chinese market. They therefore pressured the government to grant them foreign-ruled "concession areas" in or near major cities. These concessions thus became foreign outposts within China itself. Over time, they also became subversive elements in the Chinese system, as revolutionaries could in some cases find security from the Chinese authorities by living in the foreign concessions. Because Chinese law permitted torture of prisoners to obtain confessions, foreigners also sought protection from the Chinese judiciary. The resulting system, called extraterritoriality, allowed for foreign law administered by foreign courts to apply to foreigners in China.[56]

The late Qing attempts to ward off external pressure ultimately proved inadequate. Worse still, Japan worked more effectively to meet the Western challenge, systematically studying Western (especially European) forms of government and ingeniously using strengths in their traditional system to make the extensive modifications necessary to bring about industrial development. By the 1890s they had become stronger in warfare than had their "elder brother" civilization, China.[57]

Japan's decisive victory in the Sino-Japanese war of 1894–95 shocked China far more than anything the West had done to that point. This war revealed that even little Japan had mastered the secrets of Western strength to the point where it could humiliate the Middle Kingdom. Chinese intellectuals and officials directed much of their resulting ire against the Manchu rulers of the Qing dynasty. But some also concluded that the roots of defeat were sunk deep into the traditional system itself. Revolutionary political elites now began to emerge to challenge the Manchus and the entire system. Both the revolutionaries and the Qing loyalists sought desperately to achieve the goal shared by all Chinese: to enable the country to enjoy wealth and power in an age of Western and emerging Japanese imperialism.

THE QING RESPONSE AND COLLAPSE

Three broad strategies to obtain prosperity and security emerged by the end of the 1890s. Remarkably, these three strands of thought have, in shifting balances, dominated the Chinese political debate over the entire century since then. These approaches are not so much totally independent policy packages as points on a continuum that runs from isolationism on one side to all-out modernization on the other. They represent sufficiently distinctive clusters of thought on key issues, though, that they warrant brief individual explanation.[58]

The first approach might be labeled "nativist," although it bears mention that this, as so many terms used by Westerners to describe phenomena in China, has no precisely equivalent Chinese translation. Nativists argue, essentially, that China fares best when it isolates itself from the international arena and finds an ideological basis for binding its massive population together in militant unity. They assert that no country can seriously threaten to conquer and rule another country whose populace is united against the intruders. The key task, therefore, is to find and nurture the ideological basis for unity. Nativists regard influences from the West as divisive. They thus stress the importance of massive popular and elite education in a unifying ideology and active efforts to limit the country's exposure to other ideas and influences. The ideology espoused by different nativists has varied greatly in content from the far left (dogmatic Maoism during the Cultural Revolution of the late 1960s)[59] to the far right (the New Life movement of Chiang Kai-shek in the 1930s).[60] Since the 1910s, though, even the nativists have in general rejected the imperial system as having failed to protect the country from foreign aggression in the 1800s.

The second approach, that of the "selective modernizers," can be summed up in the words of a slogan first used in the 1870s, "Take Chinese learning for the base and Western learning for practical use."[61] This notion seeks to preserve the distinctive, superior qualities of Chinese civilization (supporters of this view differ on what these are) while importing sufficient foreign technology to make China strong enough to ward off external pressure. This idea makes a politically attractive program—it argues that the country can obtain security and prosperity without making fundamental changes. As indicated above, the ripple effects of technology imports have time and again made this approach untenable in practice even as it has remained powerful as a political platform.

The third view, that of the "iconoclastic modernizers," argues that China must become the type of society that can *itself* produce technological innovation. Failure to do this consigns China to perpetual dependency on the decisions of foreigners, who will never permit China to obtain full security. This third platform is "iconoclastic" in that its adherents are in principle willing to change *anything* in order to develop a technologically vibrant society. Few of these individuals favor comprehensive Westernization; rather they envision a distinctive Chinese approach to modernization, but one that is unencumbered by rigid adherence to set traditions or ideology.

China's defeat at the hands of the Japanese in 1895 convinced the major Western powers for the first time that the Middle Kingdom could be conquered in classical imperialist fashion. There followed in the late 1890s the "scramble for concessions" in which various foreign countries sought to, in a phrase from that era, "carve China up like a ripe melon." In response to this suddenly escalating threat to the country, the Guangxu emperor in 1898 launched a brief surge of reforms against the wishes of the Empress Dowager

Ci Xi and her conservative supporters. After one hundred days the Empress Dowager successfully put down the reforms and placed the Guangxu emperor in confinement.[62] Reformist officials who had supported the emperor either fled the country or suffered severe reprisals. In the ensuing conservative backlash a rapidly spreading secret society called the Righteous and Harmonious Fists (dubbed "Boxers" by Westerners), with tacit backing from the Empress Dowager, launched a wave of terror in 1900, called the Boxer Rebellion, against foreigners and Chinese who supported them. In response, a multinational foreign expeditionary force occupied and sacked Beijing and obtained the punishment of conservative court officials who had encouraged the Boxer rampage.[63]

These events convinced the Empress Dowager and many other officials that change would be necessary to strengthen the country and save the dynasty. In the ensuing years Ci Xi implemented a number of reforms, including abolition of the examination system in 1905. But these reform efforts ultimately hastened the decline of the dynasty. The abolition of the examination system, for example, in a single blow cut off access to advancement for the tens of thousands of politically ambitious people who had spent their lives studying for these crucial exams. A policy of sending young people abroad (especially in the early 1900s to Japan) to study modern learning exposed them in addition to revolutionary thinking and anti-Manchu agitation. Other reforms, such as providing greater latitude for local gentry to participate in politics, produced increased political agitation from below and weakened Beijing in relation to the localities. In these and myriad other ways, the reformist medicine finished off the already sick dynastic patient.[64]

The international challenge based on the expanding industrial revolution required that the Chinese government raise far more revenue, change the way it recruited officials, modify its ideology, and adapt its social policies in ways that proved to be beyond its institutional and political capabilities. Chinese failures encouraged additional foreign initiatives. Ultimately, China could not succeed shy of basic changes in a system that had served it well for two millennia. In this sense, the pressures from an industrializing West and Japan provided the catalyst that transformed a typical dynastic decline into a revolution.

The final months of the Qing dynasty highlighted the issues that had assumed a commanding role in shaping modern China—disputes over foreign funding of capital projects, decentralized authority and local resistance to imperial commands, modern military force at the personal command of an ambitious figure, and weak and confused decision-making by the imperial leaders. Specifically, a dispute over funding for railroad development in southwest China, in which Beijing seemed to be preempting foreign loans for the project, led to a revolt by the project's local investors. The revolt quickly caught fire and spread to other provinces, which in rapid order declared their independence from Beijing. The Qing government called on Yuan Shikai, the official who had in the preceding decade built up the country's most modern military force, to suppress the provincial defections. But Yuan instead utilized his own military leverage to bring about the abdication of the emperor, the end of the Qing, and the establishment of a republic with himself as the central figure.[65] The Qing was not so much overthrown as undermined: it simply collapsed. The forces producing that collapse had gradually gathered momentum over the previous decades and would continue to influence Chinese politics throughout the remainder of the twentieth century.

In sum, toward the end of the Qing, for the first time in two millennia, China faced outside forces that were unwilling to conform to the Confucian world order and too powerful to ward off. The Confucian order had provided the bases for social ranking, for career mobility, for conferring prestige, and for shaping attitudes toward authority, education, and history. The loss of faith in this world view thus dissolved the glue that held together the polity itself. Western—and especially Japanese—strength eroded the major premises on which the old Chinese order rested.

2
The Republican Era

The search for a new set of moral principles on which to base the Chinese polity has to date proved unsuccessful. The breakdown of the Qing was so fundamental that it seemed to leave all of Chinese society topsy-turvy. As late as the 1890s Confucianism still dominated the ideological scene, foreign ways were suspect, and a military career held little prestige. By the late 1910s, all of this had changed. The elites debated heatedly the best ideology to utilize, but all the contestants—anarchists, socialists, liberals, democrats, pragmatists, nationalists, and others—were proponents of foreign schools of thought. Those with foreign language skills and foreign educations had great advantages over those who sought to preserve traditional wisdom. Those with military know-how exercised power over those who mastered calligraphy, poetry, philosophy, and the other types of knowledge that formerly had set the political elite apart from mere soldiers and commoners. Chinese elites constantly debated the core question: how best to make the country wealthy and strong? But no single persuasive answer emerged. Ultimately, civil war rather than civil debate decided who would rule the quarter of humanity who called themselves "Chinese."

The Early Republican Era

The demise of the Qing gave birth to the Republic of China in 1912. Sun Yat-sen, the best known of the anti-Manchu revolutionaries, had advocated a republican form of government. Sun, however, had conducted his revolutionary activities primarily from abroad—from such places as Honolulu, San Francisco, and Japan. He learned of the collapse of the Qing while reading the newspaper on a train heading out of Kansas City. After his return to China, he held office in the new regime only six weeks before being ousted by Yuan Shikai. Yuan ruled briefly via a parliamentary government, but by November 1913, after what was termed the "second revolution," he rendered the National Assembly inoperative. In 1916, Yuan tried to establish a new dynasty. The dynastic idea had well and truly died, however, as did Yuan several months later.[1]

The country quickly dissolved into regionally based warlordism. Warlords ruled by virtue of their personal military forces, and they fought each other over lands that could earn them additional tax revenues, which they often collected many years in advance. While some warlords, such as Yan Xishan in Shanxi Province, tried to carry out reforms and promote industrial development,[2] most were determined only to enrich themselves at tragic cost to the population.

Rampant taxation impoverished the countryside and forced many peasant youths into warlord armies. Foreigners became involved, as various warlords competed to obtain the most effective foreign weaponry. Affronts to China's sovereignty thus festered and grew.

Some warlord territories were more important than others. The most important as of the late 1910s was Beijing. Whatever warlord controlled Beijing organized the "national" government. Often the government actually administered little more than the city and its immediate suburbs, but whoever ran Beijing also received all maritime customs receipts from throughout the country. This arrangement extended back to the late Qing when foreigners had taken over management of the customs and had agreed to collect duties on behalf of the national government and to pay the resulting funds only to that government. Because of its great concentration of wealth, Shanghai was the second most important prize in the battle among the warlords.

The national collapse and constant indignities of the warlord period produced anguish among the intellectuals, who heatedly debated about which directions the country should move. These debates proved irrelevant to most Chinese, whose immediate fates were determined by the constantly shifting fortunes of the numerous warlord armies that ravaged the land.

The debates nevertheless had important long-term consequences and they warrant attention. Initially, some leading intellectuals advocated two features deemed central to the success of the West—science and democracy. In pursuit of the latter, Hu Shi (1891–1962), as a student at Columbia University in 1916, began to argue that Chinese intellectuals should write in the vernacular language of ordinary people rather than in the archaic classical form of Chinese. The latter had not evolved over a period of more than a thousand years, yet it remained the language in which all serious tracts were written. Hu argued that adopting the vernacular would make the country's political debates accessible to the common people and could spawn a popular press. He continued to advocate use of the vernacular *(bai hua)* instead of classical Chinese *(wen yan)* upon his return to Beijing in 1917, and the idea soon found sufficient acceptance to create the ground for mass politics. Hu's proposal was officially adopted in Beijing in 1922.

Several developments, nevertheless, discouraged the pursuit of what were termed "Mr. Science" and "Mr. Democracy." World War I produced such slaughter on the battlefields of Europe that it tarnished the allure of Western civilization. China had joined the Allies during the war—promising, among other things, to stop German shipping along its coast—expecting that an Allied victory would end German concessions in the country. Beijing thus expected to reap great benefits from the principles, such as self-determination, articulated by President Woodrow Wilson in his Fourteen Points.

The reality proved deeply disillusioning. From 1900 to 1911 Japan had become a haven for Chinese revolutionaries, as many Chinese students went to Tokyo to study and, while there, converted to revolutionary politics.[3] After the downfall of the Qing and while the West was fighting World War I, Japan took advantage of the power vacuum in East Asia to pressure China. In 1915, Tokyo produced the notorious Twenty-one Demands that would have turned China into a Japanese semicolony had Beijing fully accepted them.[4] The Japanese also pressured each president of China to appoint pro-Japanese cabinet officers. By the late 1910s, resentment of Japan ran high among Chinese intellectuals.

Japan also joined the war effort on behalf of the Allies and signed secret agreements with France and Britain that would turn German concessions in China's Shandong Province over to Japan instead of returning them to China. The Versailles Peace Conference upheld these secret commitments. When word of this betrayal reached Beijing in early May 1919, it touched off an explosion led by students that so rocked the political scene that it is still regarded by many as the birth of modern Chinese politics. The 1919 upheaval, called the May Fourth Incident, gave its name ("May Fourth") to the entire movement of political debate and ferment that engaged China's intellectuals from 1916 to 1921.

THE MAY FOURTH MOVEMENT

While warlords contested for power, the intellectuals sought some new base to reintegrate the society. But the leaders in this effort were not the older scholars whose role had been central to the intellectual life of the Qing. Rather, university-age students and young faculty moved to the fore. Many of these had been trained in missionary schools or had studied abroad, often on money provided by the Qing government as reparations after the defeat of the Boxer Rebellion at the turn of the century.[5]

Because the imperial Chinese state reflected fundamental ideas about the nature of civilization itself, the collapse of the imperial system required reconsideration not only of the form of government but also of the basic ethics and social organization of society. Younger scholars began to attack the ethical base of the strong family system, emancipation of women became one of the political currents among urban youths,[6] the educational system received critical scrutiny, and many schools of "new learning" cropped up around the country.

A movement led by young intellectuals, called the New Culture movement, advocated changes in the organization of Chinese society and politics. New journals began to propagate foreign ideas. Among these, one called *Xin Qingnian (New Youth)*, published at Beijing University and edited by Chen Duxiu, who later became a founding member and leader of the Chinese Communist party, proved especially influential. By the late 1910s, it began publishing articles on socialism. Beijing University, under the influential leadership of President Cai Yuanpei, became a seat for debate among advocates of very different schools of thought.

In response to Chinese capitulation at Versailles, some three thousand students from various universities in Beijing marched around Tiananmen Square to demand that the government fire its pro-Japanese ministers and refuse to sign the peace treaty with Germany. The students burned down the residence of the pro-Japanese minister of communications and assaulted Japan's ambassador to Beijing. A government crackdown led to arrests and bloodshed. In response, a mass movement quickly developed and swept across coastal China.

Hundreds of publications began to appear, as the students tried to turn anti-Japanese feelings into a true mass movement. A boycott of Japanese goods took hold. Demonstrations broke out around the country, and the movement toward embracing modern ideas, including women's liberation, greatly accelerated. The government in Beijing soon found itself confronting a major crisis. It dismissed three of its pro-Japanese ministers and refused to sign the final peace treaty with Germany.

More importantly, though, the May Fourth movement signaled a sharp break with the past and an urgent search to consolidate a new sociopolitical agenda. It created a new form of politics for China—mass politics.[7]

Emerging from the bewildering array of contending interests and factions of the May Fourth movement, two broad political efforts, one led by the Nationalist party or Guomindang (GMD) and the other led by the Chinese Communist party (CCP), came to dominate the Chinese stage from the mid-1920s on. These parties had similar social and political origins,[8] joined in strategic alliances from 1924 to 1927 and from 1936 to the early 1940s, and yet fought each other in bitter, deadly struggles for control of the country's political destiny. As of the mid-1990s the Guomindang is effectively guiding Taiwan, the territory under its control, through a process of rapid modernization and has taken steps toward developing a multiparty democracy;[9] the Chinese Communist party, by contrast, is overseeing rapid economic growth on the Chinese mainland but suffers from waning confidence, widespread corruption, and a failure to build institutions that would insulate it from the harm of factional and generational politics. The Guomindang, though, rules only Taiwan, a small island one hundred miles off the east coast of mainland China, and a few small additional islands, with a total population of little more than twenty million people; the Chinese Communist party, by contrast, monopolizes political power on the mainland, with a population of nearly two billion. Had observers in the 1920s and early 1930s made predictions, they would have bet that these parties' fortunes would be the reverse of what has in fact transpired.

Although in 1924 the GMD and the CCP formally allied and adopted similar Leninist approaches to internal party organization, their styles, experiences, and ultimate priorities differed greatly. Because the CCP won a smashing military victory over the Guomindang in 1949, this volume primarily addresses the development of the Chinese communist movement and its impact on the country. The Guomindang, however, ruled China from the late 1920s to the 1940s and left some enduring legacies. In the 1990s, moreover, it is again a force of importance in the evolution of China's political economy. We begin, therefore, with an analysis of the core characteristics of the GMD's approach to governing China.

THE GUOMINDANG

The Nationalist party formed under the leadership of Sun Yat-sen, the successor to a series of revolutionary political movements he guided since the 1890s. Driven out of power within a year of the collapse of the Qing, Sun had spent part of the 1910s in Japan and part trying to organize a political base on the Chinese mainland. As of the early 1920s he found himself in his native province of Guangdong, where he sought alliances with warlords and sufficient aid from foreigners to permit him to expand his political base.[10]

Sun's political philosophy was summed up in what he termed the "three principles of the people" (sanminzhuyi). He had articulated these in various forms during the decades of his revolutionary activities, first against the Manchus and then against the warlord-dominated governments after 1912. In 1923 he finally summed them up and gave them clearer definition, but each still remained broad and diffuse. The "three principles" became widely known, though, and indicated the three major directions in which Sun thought national policy should go.

The first principle was "nationalism." The term Sun chose for this, minzuzhuyi, connotes putting the country, defined as one nationality, first. Sun had used this term originally as a vehicle for rallying Chinese opposition to rule by the Manchus toward the close of the Qing. By the 1920s, it meant something close to "self-determination" for both the Chinese and for the other nationalities in China. This principle captured the antiimperialist sentiment so powerful in China of that era.

The second principle is usually translated as "democracy," but again the translation misses the essence of the Chinese term Sun used. "Democracy" in the 1990s is translated as *minzhuzhuyi,* which literally means the "doctrine of rule by the people." But Sun instead used the term *minchuanzhuyi,* which means "doctrine of the rights of the people." His explanations of this term made clear that he foresaw a political system that provided for elections, the right of recall, referendums, and so forth. In sum, Sun felt the people should be able to control their own government through various devices. Importantly, he also thought that Chinese were not yet ready for the full implementation of this type of system, and thus he called for a long period of "tutelage" that would prepare the people to assume the duties required by full democracy. The tutelage period would, among other things, establish schools that would raise people's educational level to that required by democracy.

The third principle, "people's livelihood" *(minshengzhuyi),* also lacked specificity. The concrete directions in which Sun seemed to move called for massive projects to build the country's infrastructure, along with efforts to equalize land holdings and develop a just system of taxation. Sun was not advocating a free-market approach to economic prosperity. He felt the state had a determining role to play in creating a just economy.

One reason it is difficult to pinpoint the content of Sun's revolutionary ideas is that he was almost always consumed with the practical tasks of finding allies and gaining support for his next attempt to overthrow the government and seize power. He frequently had to trim his sails in order to firm up support from the United States, Japan, revolutionary Russia, or other sources. Nevertheless, Sun was an excellent orator, and his name and basic ideas became widely known. As of the early 1920s, he probably had more of what in contemporary American politics would be termed "name recognition" than did any other Chinese politician.

In 1923 Sun, whose GMD consisted largely of personal factions organized in almost secret-society fashion, met with a man named Joffe, an agent sent from Moscow by the Communist International (Comintern), which had been formed to promote revolutions abroad without directly embroiling the new Russian state in the resulting problems. Joffe convinced Sun that he should accept Soviet aid, Soviet advice about how best to organize a revolutionary party, and an alliance, brokered by Comintern, with the fledgling Chinese Communist party. Another Comintern agent, a remarkable man named Mikhail Borodin, whose revolutionary career had taken him at various times into the Chicago school system, the European workers movement, and Soviet politics, implemented the ensuing CCP/GMD alliance, which became effective in January 1924. The Guomindang at that time reorganized itself along the lines of "democratic centralism" that Lenin had utilized so effectively in seizing and consolidating power in Russia seven years earlier.[11]

Sun, with Soviet aid, proceeded to develop his armed forces with the object of achieving control over the country through military conquest from the south to the north. His primary training facility, the Whampoa Military Academy near Guangzhou, provided both military training and political indoctrination. Chiang Kai-shek commanded this academy, while Communist party member Zhou Enlai headed up the Soviet-type political commissar system in it. The Whampoa Academy attracted a substantial group of relatively idealistic, strongly nationalistic young men, many of them from rural upper-class families.[12]

In March 1925, Sun died during a trip to Beijing, where he was seeking to broker a political deal with the northern warlords. He left a party that comprised many different types of groups—from communists to social reformers to right-wing nationalists. His successor was Chiang Kai-shek, a former stock broker in Shanghai who had spent years in Japan and had received military training. Chiang headed a very diverse party, however, and his real base of power resided in the bonds of loyalty he had developed with the military commanders he trained at Whampoa. From 1925 onward Chiang never felt secure and unchallenged in his control over the Guomindang party itself. His personal inclinations, moreover, tended toward nationalist antiimperialism but away from radical domestic social reform. His relations with the Chinese communists were, therefore, especially tenuous, but he recognized that he had to maintain this tie as long as he needed Soviet aid.

In 1926 Chiang launched a military campaign to reunite the country, dubbed the Northern Expedition. In this effort, the GMD did not face a unified opposition but rather confronted numerous free-standing warlord armies. In a fateful set of decisions, Chiang set out to negotiate the absorption of these various warlord forces into his own National Revolutionary Army (NRA) rather than risk the destruction of his forces in pitched battles.

The Northern Expedition of 1926–27, which took the NRA from its original base in Guangdong north to the Yangtze, then east and west to Shanghai and Wuhan, and finally north to Beijing, consisted as much of mergers as of battles. Chiang would apply pressure on his warlord opponents and then offer them face-saving compromises, replete with commissions in the NRA and preservation of their forces intact as NRA units. In the early stages of this effort, Communist party agitators helped to soften up the warlord resistance through political agitation in advance of the NRA forces. This combination of outside military pressure and political agitation behind the lines proved effective in bringing nominal success to Chiang's forces. It also meant, though, that the NRA itself became a jerry-built concatenation of largely independent military units, and the GMD became home to the warlords and corrupt officials who had ruled northern China before the Northern Expedition.[13]

In the midst of the Northern Expedition, moreover, Chiang took the fateful step of breaking decisively with the Chinese communists. In the process, he slaughtered upwards of 90 percent of the CCP's members. The initial attack occurred on 12 April 1927, when Chiang linked up with the "Green Gang" and "Red Gang" secret-society forces in Shanghai to ferret out and execute as many communists in the city as could be identified.[14] The second shoe dropped that July, when more leftist members of the GMD who had maintained ties with the communists in the middle Yangtze city of Wuhan yielded to Chiang's blandishments and exterminated the remnants of the CCP there.

Chiang's break with the communists marked a strategic shift in his approach to the international arena, as well. By turning against the CCP, Chiang and the GMD cut themselves off from future aid from Moscow. They could do this because, with CCP help, they had captured the city of Shanghai and the rich lower Yangtze region, which held a large percentage of the entire country's modern industry and wealth. In addition, however, the GMD began to mute what had to date been its very strong antiimperialist thrust and to blunt the social revolution that had been gaining momentum in the country. Relations with the major Western powers would remain tense and uncertain for some years, but the beginnings of a modus vivendi were taking shape as of April 1927. Eventually, foreign aid for Chiang would follow.

In 1927, the GMD shifted the nation's capital to Nanjing (Nanking); their period of rule before the Japanese invasion of 1937 is often called the Nanjing decade. The lower Yangtze region where Nanjing is located is far more business-oriented and naturally well-endowed than is Beijing. The foreign presence in this region—especially that of the British—was also more extensive than had been the case in north China. Reflecting these differences, the political leadership of the Nanjing decade rested in the hands of the newly important forces in Chinese society: those educated abroad, those with ties to commerce and industry, and those with military and/or secret-society bases.[15]

Having ousted the communists and formally unified most of China by late 1928, Chiang sought to consolidate the flimsy structure that had emerged from the Northern Expedition. He relentlessly continued a purge of communist elements and in the process caught many of the country's most politically energetic and creative individuals. Moreover, the absorption of the northern warlords into the GMD toward the end of the Northern Expedition further diluted the party's ideological commitment; the resulting organization became something very different from the disciplined Leninist party that Borodin had counseled to Sun Yat-sen in 1924.[16]

The Nanjing decade saw many substantial economic achievements, and these were especially impressive in view of the global depression of the 1930s. In some parts of the country during this period, the national government bureaucracies reached more deeply into the grass roots than had previously been possible. At the same time, though, because of the overall weakness of the central government, significant experiments in social and economic reform occurred in various locales, especially in some rural counties. More broadly, a huge array of "bottom-up" political and social organizations developed, such as local chambers of commerce and trade unions.[17] China's industrial production expanded significantly, and commerce grew apace. These accomplishments suggest that any government able to impose a modicum of order in China without suppressing all independent and local initiative would have benefited from significant economic growth that had been stunted precisely by a combination of political instability, repression, and internal military strife. China attained its peak levels of output in industry, agriculture, and commerce in 1936—levels that would not again be achieved until well into the communists' first decade of rule in the 1950s.

But internal weakness, domestic opponents, and foreign adversaries limited the GMD's success in this period. All three challenges, moreover, were interrelated.

Internally, the GMD had largely ceased to be an effective party. The absorption of northern warlords and the purge of left-leaning cadres stripped the organization of its ideological aplomb. Three of the worst features inherent in traditional Chinese political culture—nepotism, corruption, and an emphasis on correct speech versus effective action—surged to the fore under these conditions. By the early 1930s it had become common for new appointees to government office to fire virtually all of their subordinates and to replace them with friends, relatives, and politically loyal subordinates. Officials at the highest levels also used their power to have relatives appointed as county magistrates and to other positions that could serve as the source of lucrative graft. The resulting widespread corruption and lack of party discipline gravely harmed the Nationalist movement.

In addition, the GMD embraced the notion that correct speech, not effective action, is of primary importance because it demonstrates correct thinking, and this had pernicious consequences during these years. The GMD held numerous meetings and issued a multitude of proclamations and manifestos. Government organs drew up elaborate plans and high-sounding position papers for any number of projects and initiatives. Generally, however, these pronouncements and documents sought not to solve actual problems but rather to demonstrate the loyalty that participation in the process and adherence to proper forms indicated. In Chinese culture, as explained in Chapter 1, the individual's identity is as part of a group. These rituals of policy-making served to confirm group identity and solidarity. They had the effect of divorcing the policymakers almost totally from the society they governed and from the actions of local officials that affected the lives of the populace.[18]

Chiang Kai-shek had to spend a considerable portion of his time during the Nanjing decade, moreover, engaged in civil wars to maintain his rule. Effectively, the Northern Expedition left Chiang in relatively strong control of the military forces of central and southeast China, but the armies in the north, northeast, northwest, and southwest remained loyal to Chiang's nominal allies instead of directly to the central government. Throughout the Nanjing decade, therefore, Chiang could travel to most provinces outside of the lower Yangtze region only if there had been a prior exchange of hostages.

With depressing regularity Chiang's GMD "allies" teamed up in various combinations to unseat the central government through military challenge. A partial list of the major warlords and their challenges to the central government from 1929 to 1931 illustrates the dimensions of this problem (see Table 2.1).

While Chiang waged almost constant warfare to keep at bay the various warlords who had nominally joined the Guomindang, he focused his primary attention on completing the job that he had begun in April 1927—that is, exterminating the communists. Given the treachery that surrounded Chiang on

TABLE 2.1 *Civil Wars from 1929 to 1931*

DATE	CHALLENGER	LOCALE	NUMBER OF CASUALTIES
Mar. 1929	Li Zongren	Guangxi	Unknown
May 1929	Feng Yuxiung	Henan	Unknown
Oct.–Nov. 1929	Feng Yuxiang	Henan	Unknown
Dec. 1929	Tang Shengzhi	Henan	Unknown
May–Oct. 1930	Coalition forces Feng Yuxiang Li Zongren Tang Shengzhi Yan Xishan	Beijing and elsewhere	230,000
1931	Coalition forces Li Zongren Wang Jingwei	Guangzhou	Unknown

all sides, it is not clear why he harbored such implacable hatred for the communists in particular, but his perseverance in seeking their destruction is remarkable. He once referred to the CCP as a "disease of the heart," which, he said, must be cured before other, more superficial challenges to the body politic (in this case, he was referring to the Japanese!) could command the spotlight.

Chiang effectively destroyed the communists as an urban political force in the late 1920s, and the main body of the movement found refuge in various mountainous bases along provincial borders at that time.[19] Beginning in 1930 Chiang launched a series of "annihilation campaigns" against the communist base areas. Either civil war or Japanese aggression cut short each of the first four of these campaigns. The fifth, carried out with substantial assistance from German military officers, succeeded in routing the final communist base area in the southeast, at Ruijin, Jiangxi, in the fall of 1934. Chiang's army then chased the retreating communist forces across south and southwest China and up into the central region of north China, where the CCP eventually established a headquarters in the small town of Yan'an. In this major year-long retreat, dubbed by the communists the Long March, the CCP again lost nearly 90 percent of its strength but ended up in a part of north China far less vulnerable to Chiang's attack.

Chiang's concentration on the communist threat diverted his attention from the Japanese challenge that grew and became more ominous during the late 1920s. As noted above, Japan had tried to take advantage of Western preoccupation with World War I to force China to accept its Twenty-one Demands in 1915. With the renewal of a Western presence in China after the war, the Japanese focused their efforts more on China's northeast. In 1928 they assassinated Zhang Zuolin, the major warlord of that region, and in 1931 they seized the entire northeast and split it off into a Japanese puppet state named Manchukuo. To head this state they installed Pu Yi, the child emperor whose abdication in February 1912 had marked the end of the imperial era.[20]

In 1932 Japanese militarists launched a brief, violent foray into Shanghai. By 1935 they effectively took over the two northern provinces (including Beijing) that bordered Manchukuo. These activities created growing frustration among Chinese intellectuals that Chiang Kai-shek remained intent on destroying the communists rather than on protecting the country against the Japanese. The Chinese communists lost no opportunity to encourage students and intellectuals to give priority to the growing Japanese encroachments.[21]

In late 1936 Chiang assigned Zhang Xueliang, the son of the assassinated northeast warlord Zhang Zuolin, to lead his Manchurian troops against the communists at Yan'an. Chiang personally went to Zhang Xueliang's nearby base camp at Xi'an to spur them on. But during his stay there Zhang and several of his colleagues kidnapped Chiang Kai-shek and held him captive to force a change in the GMD's policy toward the Japanese. Zhou Enlai, a top communist leader, traveled to Xi'an from Yan'an to participate in the discussions. In what must have been a wrenching assignment, given the massive casualties Chiang had inflicted on the communists over the previous decade, Zhou persuaded Zhang to spare Chiang's life in return for Chiang's promise to lead a national effort that would include the communists and that would give its highest priority to driving the Japanese out of China.[22] Thus began the second united front between the CCP and the GMD—a cooperative effort that began in late 1936 and lasted effectively until the early 1940s (although it did not end formally until after the conclusion of World War II).

The following year Japanese forces launched an all-out attack on China proper, driving the GMD from its base in the rich lower Yangtze region deep into the country's impoverished interior. Eventually the GMD leadership settled in the southwest Chinese city of Chongqing (Chungking) behind the mountainous eastern boundary of Sichuan Province. From 1938 to 1945, Japan occupied the key cities and major communications links throughout eastern China, setting up puppet governments in the areas under its control.

Separated from its natural base in the rich, cosmopolitan lower Yangtze region, the GMD military forces initially put up strong resistance to the Japanese, and sentiments regarding national unity and purpose ran strong.[23] But Sichuan and its surrounding areas as of 1937 were extraordinarily backward places (in neighboring Yunnan the wheel was not widely used before the 1930s!), and as the war dragged on spirits sagged, corruption grew, and factionalism deepened. At some point after the American entry into the war in 1941 Chiang decided that he would count on foreign forces to win the war. From that point on he held his own best troops back to cope with what he was convinced would be an inevitable postwar communist challenge.[24]

The resulting combination of phony war, feudal surroundings, effective isolation, and severe wartime shortages (due in part to America's failure to fully support the Guomindang's war effort) sapped the will and discipline of the Nationalist forces. Inflation became widespread, corruption became endemic, and esprit de corps disappeared. Intellectuals who had fled to Chongqing to fight alongside the GMD began to lose hope.[25]

Against this background, America's unexpectedly rapid defeat of Japan in 1945 with the atomic bombings of Hiroshima and Nagasaki suddenly thrust the GMD back into control of all of China's major cities. With American help, the Nationalists took the Japanese surrender throughout China except in the northeast but muffed their resulting chance in the late 1940s for national renewal. Instead of returning property confiscated by Japan to its Chinese owners, the GMD simply took over that property. After years of privation in the deep interior, Nationalist officers and politicians gorged themselves on the relatively wealthy eastern urban economy, producing levels of corruption that soon undermined popular support. Hyperinflation had become a serious problem in the Nationalist areas in the final years of the war, and gross mismanagement spread this disease to the entire economy in the late 1940s; by the winter of 1948–49 much of China still under Nationalist rule had been reduced to a barter economy.

With the war-weary populace ready to turn against any party suspected of starting a civil war in the wake of the Japanese retreat, the Nationalists and communists initially engaged in half-hearted peace negotiations. General George C. Marshall was dispatched by President Harry Truman to mediate these negotiations, but ultimately they came to naught. Chiang Kai-shek decided to exterminate the communists through all-out civil war starting in the winter of 1946–47.

Strategic errors, military corruption, and factional infighting eroded the capabilities of the Nationalist forces, however, and despite their vastly superior numbers and firepower, they suffered catastrophic defeat.[26] The communists had entered northeast China in force in the wake of World War II. They won their first major battles south of the Great Wall only in January 1949, but they crossed the Yangtze that April, seized Guangdong on the southeast coast in September, and by the spring of 1950 had captured the entire country except the island province of Taiwan and a few small coastal islands. In the final stage of the war, the Nationalist collapse unfolded so rapidly that communist forces had difficulty keeping up with the retreating GMD forces.[27]

So many things went wrong in the final years of Nationalist rule on the mainland that it is difficult to sort out the fundamental from the more marginal causes of the defeat. The GMD never successfully transformed itself into a disciplined political party. With its social bases in the urban Yangtze Delta area, the GMD proved unable to adopt and implement policies that would effectively address the tremendous ills of rural China. Factionalism remained deeply ingrained in party practice, and a major part of the party membership had by the early 1930s lost any commitment it originally had to real public service. The prolonged privation of the war years worsened the tendency toward corruption and malfeasance in the party apparatus. When faced with the communist military threat and the multitude of socioeconomic problems confronting the country at the end of World War II, the GMD simply proved unable to rise to the challenges it faced.[28]

China's society, which in various parts of the country had sprung to life in the 1920s and early 1930s, by 1949 had been brought to its knees. The brutal Japanese occupation, civil war, corruption, GMD and CCP terror tactics, and unbridled inflation weakened the social fabric and left the people disorganized and dispirited; many were eager for a strong state to impose order and provide the populace with a firm sense of direction. While the 1920s and early 1930s had witnessed flourishing development of social, economic, cultural, and religious organizations and spirited debates among intellectuals, by 1949 little of this was left to counter the CCP's efforts at revolutionary social change.

The Communist Rise to Power

The Chinese Communist party arose from the ferment of the May Fourth movement. Radical young intellectuals were impressed by Russia's withdrawal from World War I in the wake of the Bolshevik Revolution and, especially, by Moscow's subsequent disavowal of all Russian concessions that the Tsarist state had wrung from the Qing dynasty. Marxist writings had begun to find their way into China via Japanese translations and articles in *New Youth* and other May Fourth–era journals. They presented a "scientific, advanced" Western theory that predicted the collapse of the Western capitalist system in revolutionary upheaval. To some Chinese intellectuals, a Marxist revolution could catapult the country into the vanguard of civilization as defined by this advanced Western doctrine. Leninism, through its analysis of imperialism as the highest stage of capitalism, also spoke cogently to the conditions in which Chinese found themselves. When Soviet agents of the Comintern added practical advice on revolutionary politics and financial and military aid to this heady mixture, the result was the formation of the Chinese Communist party, which held its first congress in Shanghai in July 1921.[29]

The CCP's victory over the Guomindang in 1949 has had enormous consequences for the subsequent fate of the country. It is, therefore, important to understand the forces that shaped the ideas of the party's leaders and the practices and capabilities of the movement they headed. The Chinese Communist party evolved differently than either its Soviet mentor or the various Marxist parties of Europe. Its distinctive character is in large measure a product of the particular rural, military path to power it pursued. In the process of expanding from the clandestine group of some fifty CCP members who met at the first congress in 1921 to the five million victorious party members at the establishment of the People's Republic of China in 1949, the party acquired outlooks, capabilities, and practices that deeply affected the its exercise of power after 1949.

In part, the CCP's prolonged, rural-based revolution shaped its ideology, giving successful party leaders a distinctly un-Marxist faith in the ability of will and strategy to overcome objective obstacles. In addition, the communists' pre-1949 path to power left the party at the time of national victory with a membership that consisted overwhelmingly of poorly educated peasants, a cohort that continued to exert influence well into the 1980s. This peasant composition of the CCP explains many of the differences between Chinese and Soviet practices in the 1950s and later. This pre-1949 experience also produced means of stimulating change adapted to the poor education and strong commitment of the peasant cadres, including mass mobilization in the form of political "campaigns." The Chinese term for this peculiar type of guided mass action is *yundong*.[30]

Any revolution must go from weakness to strength. All revolutionary forces start out numerically small and on the margins of society. The revolutionary party is thus inevitably shaped not only by its initial energizing ideas but also, profoundly, by the particular strengths and weaknesses of the regime it is trying to overthrow.[31] Almost all revolutionary movements, moreover, fail. The few that succeed typically are influenced by their mistakes and by their defeats as much as by their successes. Mistakes not only curtail particular strategies but also, often, eliminate the leaders who espoused them and the cadres who most ardently supported them. They also leave memories of failure in the minds of the survivors. Therefore, it is important in understanding the molding of a revolutionary party to analyze both its energizing ideas and its various missteps and their consequences.

THE PATHS TO POWER

The CCP's path to power was characterized by uncertainty, experimentation, disappointment, and tenacity. In its early stages it had primarily an urban civilian cast and took its guidance from abroad. Later, it became solidly rooted in some of the poorest regions of this third-world country, and it developed a deeply indigenous, highly militarized identity. Along the way the Guomindang and its allies repeatedly decimated the ranks of the movement, and at two points (1927 and 1934–35) communist losses apparently reached 90 percent of party membership. These changes and the repeated revitalization of the movement toughened and gave confidence to the leaders who survived. Six basic strategies were adoped seriatim in this complex, wide-ranging struggle to achieve national power.

Labor Mobilization (1921–23)

The CCP began with what appeared to be a classic revolutionary strategy for a "communist" party: it sought to mobilize China's nascent proletariat, directing its efforts to arousing the workers to antiimperialist and anticapitalist fervor. In a sense, these early efforts proved successful. The party formed a labor secretariat, and through this vehicle it organized trade union activity in central-south and east China cities and along the major rail links.

The fundamental problem this strategy encountered was the extraordinarily small size of China's proletariat, which was well under 1 percent of the population. Even a militant proletarian organization, therefore, would prove a weak reed in an agrarian country dominated by warlords and their private armies. Events in 1923 drove this fundamental fact home to the communists in particularly brutal fashion.

Early that year, communist organizers precipitated a strike on the Beijing–Hankou railway to improve the lot of the workers. Unfortunately for the CCP, this strike interfered with the plans of one of the major warlord generals, Wu Peifu, to move troops to the north as part of his incessant game of military parry and thrust. Wu, who had previously shown considerable sympathy for the communists, broke the strike by calling in his troops and, in what became known as the February Massacre, slaughtering the railway workers.

Wu's previous support of the CCP made this defeat particularly startling to the young revolutionary leaders of the party. They then took to heart two fundamental truths about gaining power in China of the 1920s: that they would have to find a way to link up with a broader spectrum of the population than the workers alone; and that they would have to secure their ties to supportive military forces in order to avoid being overrun by any warlord they angered.

Shortly after the massacre in 1923, the Comintern counseled the CCP to link up with the GMD, then based in the Guangzhou (Canton) area of Guangdong Province. While it lacked substantial independent military forces, the GMD did have two valuable assets: recognition in China as a party that theoretically represented a broad spectrum of the populace, and a party head, Sun Yat-sen, who conferred legitimacy in that he was widely regarded as the father of the Chinese republic.

As noted above, in January 1924 the CCP formally allied with the GMD. In joining the GMD the communists agreed to give up their independent existence (a pledge they did not honor) and carry out all future propaganda under the name of the GMD rather than their own. With Comintern assistance, the GMD then set up the Whampoa Military Academy. It also set up a Peasant Movement Training Institute in Guangzhou to foment change in the countryside.

United Front with the GMD (1924–27)

The communists sought through the united front with the GMD to gain access to a broader spectrum of the populace, help the GMD ride to national power, and then edge out the GMD leaders and take control. Within the united front, the CCP focused its efforts primarily on political organization in the urban areas, preaching a line of anti-imperialism, rather than of class struggle, to reach their constituency. The CCP also made a side effort in the countryside. Communist party members including future CCP leader Mao Zedong tended to dominate the Peasant Movement Training Institute. The noncommunist GMD concentrated more on training an officer corps capable of leading their anticipated expedition northward to reunify the country. The communists also became involved in political organization within the military, staffing the political commissar system that had been modeled on a parallel apparatus recently developed by Leon Trotsky in Russia for the Red Army.

For a time, the united front proved beneficial to both sides. CCP activities benefited from their identification with the Guomindang, which was recognized internationally and domestically as a force for Chinese nationalism. CCP membership grew rapidly whenever incidents occurred that whipped up antiforeign fervor, and given the large number of foreigners resident in China at the time—and their often high-handed attitudes toward the native

Chinese—such incidents occurred with regularity. For its part the GMD benefited both from Soviet aid and, especially, from the advice on revolutionary
political and military organization provided by Borodin and his colleagues.

Nevertheless, tensions between the CCP and the GMD lay barely beneath
the surface even in the best of times. The Guomindang was itself a loose alliance of individuals with a broad array of political inclinations. Some were virtually identical to the Chinese communists, but other views spanned the spectrum, including the far right. In the jockeying for power that followed Sun
Yat-sen's death in March 1925, the distaste of many GMD party members for
the CCP became quite clear. Nevertheless, over time Chiang Kai-shek gained
primary power in the GMD, and the alliance with the CCP held together. Under these shaky conditions, in 1926 the Guomindang launched the Northern
Expedition to unify the country, as described above.

Fundamentally, Chiang wanted to carry out an anti-imperialist revolution
of national unification. While the CCP sought the same objective, it also
champed at the bit to move on to social revolution. Communist efforts at political mobilization to weaken the rear areas of warlords opposed to the Northern Expedition helped the GMD effort but also rang alarm bells. Often the
communists used class-based appeals to whip up support, and these threatened the social and economic bases of many NRA officers, who disproportionately came from the landed upper classes. They demanded that the communists be reined in, escalating tensions.

As related above, the situation came to a head in April and July 1927,
when first in Shanghai and then in Wuhan the GMD forces and their allies in
the secret societies slaughtered the communists and their supporters. This
turnabout had profound effects on the future development of the communist
movement in China.

By 1927 the CCP had developed two quite different thrusts. Most party
leaders emphasized the urban revolution and regarded Russian advice from
the Comintern as sacrosanct. It was precisely these cadres who were working
in the major cities at the time of the GMD betrayal and repression. Relatively
few of them survived.

The CCP had also developed a rural revolutionary movement, though,
growing out of the Peasant Movement Training Institute and related efforts.
These cadres tended to see the countryside as the real source of China's revolutionary potential. The revolutionary gurus in Moscow, by contrast, viewed
political work among the peasants as important but still basically supplementary to the main revolutionary efforts in the cities.

Mao Zedong was by no means the only important Communist party figure to gravitate to the rural revolution,[32] but his subsequent role as father of
the Chinese communist revolution warrants special attention to his ideas and
activities. Mao had been raised a peasant in the central Chinese province of
Hunan. As a teenager he left his village to go first to the provincial capital of
Changsha, where he enrolled in one of the schools that taught "new learning," and then later to Beijing. There he worked as an assistant at the Beijing
University library, where he gained his first exposure to Marxist thought. His
political thinking went through various phases and ideas, as was true of almost
all those who wound up in the communist movement in the early 1920s.[33]

Once he (and others) founded the CCP, Mao focused primarily on organization work among the peasants.

In early 1927, while working in the Hunan countryside, Mao wrote a report on a violent uprising in the province that resulted in a brief term of political power for the local peasantry before it was put down by Hunanese military forces. Mao's report on that uprising reveals how impressed he was with what had occurred. He declaimed, based on his findings, that

A revolution is not a dinner party, . . . it cannot be so refined, so leisurely and gentle, so temperate, kind, courteous, restrained, and magnanimous. A revolution is an insurrection. . . . In a very short time . . . several hundred million peasants will rise up like a mighty storm . . . and will send evil gentry into their graves. Every revolutionary party and every revolutionary comrade will be put to the test, to be accepted or rejected as they decide. There are three alternatives. To march at their head and lead them? To trail behind them, gesticulating and criticizing? Or to stand in their way and oppose them? Every Chinese is free to choose, but events will force you to make the choice quickly.[34]

Mao considered this report so important that when his official selected works appeared in 1960, this report was the second selection in the first of the four volumes published before his death.

The GMD repression of 1927 killed off disproportionate numbers of communists whose urban priorities clashed with Mao's views. Those left after 1927 were thus far more inclined toward peasant mobilization. It also sowed seeds of doubt about the wisdom of Comintern advice. As signs of impending GMD betrayal had multiplied in early 1927, Stalin had insisted that the CCP firmly maintain its alliance with the GMD. Stalin's advice proved disastrous, although it is not clear that the CCP could have done anything to stave off the GMD's offensive.[35] Survivors like Mao began to question whether the revolutionary leaders in Moscow really understood the conditions the communists confronted in China.

The survivors learned two other lessons. They realized that although the GMD represented many different views, the CCP could not rely on any sector of the GMD to protect it from that party's right wing. The GMD as a whole, in short, could not be trusted. Along with this, the communists realized that they could not seek protection in the military force of an ally; rather, they would have to develop their own army totally loyal to the party. Anything shy of this would lead to disaster in China's violent warlord politics.

Not all members of the Chinese Communist party drew these lessons at the time.[36] Some, including Mao, did, however, and over the ensuing half-decade events made the rest of the party follow suit. Mao's perspicacity did not, though, immediately ensure his leadership over the entire communist movement.

Adapting to the Countryside (1929–34)

The repression of 1927 left the CCP in a shambles, with surviving groups only poorly coordinated and largely working on their own instincts. Late in the year Mao led some forces into the Jinggang Mountains (Jinggangshan) of

Jiangxi Province, a remote area populated primarily by the Hakka, a minority that had formed the major base of support for the early stages of the Taiping Rebellion in the 1850s.[37] Mao there linked up with forces under a colorful, older communist commander, Zhu De. The two men and their troops together fought battles and suppressed attempts to unseat them. Within two years they had established the Jiangxi Soviet in Ruijin, in the western Jiangxi Mountains, where they began to develop the techniques to adapt the communist struggle to a rural base of operations.

The forces of Mao and Zhu were not the center of the communist movement at the time, but their activities warrant particular attention because other efforts by the CCP in various locations failed, bringing the center of gravity to the Ruijin experiment. The Jiangxi Soviet itself was one of a number of communist base areas scattered among the mountains of southeast China. In these remote provincial border areas, a power vacuum existed that permitted the communists to survive and establish local organs of authority. At the same time, the official central organs of the CCP remained in Shanghai and, despite ongoing repression, continued until 1930 to prepare for an urban uprising as the major thrust of the strategy for seizing power. GMD harassment eventually forced this urban remnant to abandon Shanghai during 1931–32 and move to Ruijin.[38] GMD military efforts closed down the other base areas one by one until in 1934 only the Jiangxi Soviet remained as a major communist base in southeast China.

In Ruijin, Mao began to develop his understanding of four crucial issues: how to carry out land reform; how to develop and sustain political activity among peasants; how to govern territory under the CCP's control; and how to develop, train, and utilize military forces in the countryside. In all these spheres Mao's thinking took years to mature, and in each case the rest of the party did not quickly or easily accept the approaches he advocated. At its Jiangxi base during the early 1930s, the party underwent a crucial transition to a rural strategy, but the techniques for winning national power through a rural revolution did not fully develop until a later period, called the Yan'an era, discussed below.

Early in the development of the Jiangxi Soviet, Mao seized upon land reform as a major vehicle for winning favor among the region's Hakka peasants. He was inclined at first to carry out a radical land-reform effort, taking land from all those who could earn a reasonable living from it and distributing it to the landless and the land-poor. This approach quickly established a base of support among the destitute of the region, but it also caused a sharp reduction in agricultural output. Mao's initial foray into the politics of land reform—the crucial socioeconomic issue in the overwhelmingly agrarian China—had not gone well.[39]

Mao subsequently developed an analysis of social groups in the countryside that provided a useful guide to the likely effects of different land-reform strategies. Over the ensuing years he accordingly developed a more flexible rural policy. Under Mao's aegis the party divided the countryside into five classes: "landlords," who could live primarily by land rents rather than cultivation of land with their own labor; "rich peasants," who both worked the land full time and hired extra labor or rented out land because they owned more than they themselves could cultivate; "middle peasants," who worked full time on the land they owned and whose production provided an adequate income to support their family; "poor peasants," who owned some land but still had to hire themselves out because their own land could not provide a subsistence income; and "landless laborers," who lived wholly by hiring out their labor.[40]

Experience taught the party over the years that removing the landlords did not necessarily lessen agricultural output as the most productive farmers were the rich peasants. Indeed, eliminating the landlords enabled the party to strengthen its position in the countryside by replacing them as the major source of rural credit. Removing the rich peasants, though, did adversely affect the harvest. The effects of land reform, therefore, crucially depended on where one drew the line. Attacking rich peasants as well as landlords made more land available for redistribution, but this came at a high price in terms of production. Seizing only the "excess" land of the rich peasants affected output far less than stripping them of all their holdings.

During the Jiangxi Soviet era, Mao and his colleagues also began to develop techniques for achieving sustained peasant political involvement. As Mao indicated in his February 1927 Hunan Report quoted above, peasants are generally quiescent politically; they understand intuitively how much they risk if they challenge authority and lose. However, when aroused, their political activity tends to "rise up like a storm" that unleashes tremendous violence and passion but then quickly spends itself, leaving exhaustion and ennui in its wake. The explosive character of peasant protest activity was not well-suited to a long-term strategy for gaining power through control of rural turf. The CCP had to develop the means to harness peasant political protest, direct it at specific targets, and then consolidate the gains.

To accomplish these goals, the party first sought to package its appeals in terms that spoke directly to the concrete interests of local peasants, rather than in broad abstractions such as "exploitation" or "anti-imperialism." Second, it gained experience in peasant mobilization by launching specific "campaigns" based on fervent but targeted political participation. Third, it elaborated techniques for forming "mass organizations" that would generate some level of peasant activity between campaigns. All of these efforts were continually adjusted as increasingly peasants themselves led the effort to mobilize and sustain the fervor of still more peasants.[41]

In order to control base areas, the CCP had to form actual administrative units to govern territory. Indeed, the Chinese communists accumulated rich experience before their victory in 1949—very much unlike the Bolsheviks who seized power in Russia in 1917 without having ever previously ruled any patch of ground. The CCP began experimenting with different ways of organizing the countryside, recruiting administrative personnel, and combating the natural tendency in China toward elitist, exploitative bureaucratic organizations. They began by drawing on the basic administrative divisions that had characterized the Qing and the republican governments. But later during the Yan'an era, they worked on adjusting these administrative arrangements to new tasks.[42]

Finally, the Jiangxi Soviet period witnessed the first systematic efforts by the communists to recruit and train their own revolutionary army and to develop pertinent military tactics. Since the party's military position throughout this period remained weak, the tactics adopted tended to be more appropriate to fighting an enemy with superior fire power. Mao seems to have drawn heavily from traditional Chinese military thought, especially from his understanding of the fourth century B.C. writings of China's great strategist, Sun Zi. He adapted these writings into principles for fighting a guerrilla war against better equipped forces. The resulting precepts included, eventually, such now famous tactics as trading space for time; luring the enemy in deep; "when the enemy advances we retreat, when the enemy encamps, we harass, when the enemy withdraws, we attack;" concentrating superior force to wipe out an isolated enemy unit, but never engaging in battle where the enemy has superior strength on the spot; developing relations between the troops and the populace as close as those "between lips and teeth;" and using the countryside to surround the city.[43] Much of this can be summed up as giving priority to intelligence capabilities, good relations between officers and men, and tactical advantage in choosing fields of battle.

The impoverished Jiangxi mountain populace did not provide the CCP with recruits of high caliber. However, it may not have been too difficult for the party to establish an esprit de corps among the Hakka minority, who strongly sensed their distinctiveness from the non-Hakka Chinese of the Guomindang.[44] Furthermore, the party honed its techniques for absorbing bandit and secret-society forces, recruiting peasants as an offshoot of the land-reform effort, and using political indoctrination to develop military forces undaunted by the rigors of guerrilla war.

Although the Jiangxi Soviet period proved important for the development of techniques appropriate to rural-based revolution, this period was far less successful for both Mao personally and the immediate fortunes of the party as a whole. Mao had initially developed the Jiangxi Soviet, but Russian-trained members of the CCP continued to hold the top positions in the party. When the party's top leadership moved to Ruijin from Shanghai in 1932, Mao was moved aside, and he did not obtain a leading position in the party again until over two years later at the Zunyi conference on the Long March.

The displacement of Mao also led to the communists' abandonment of his guerrilla strategy to engage the enemy in favor of more conventional, positional warfare under the direction of a Comintern military advisor named Otto Braun and the Soviet-trained Chinese communist leaders. When Chiang Kai-shek's fifth annihilation campaign succeeded in routing the communist forces, Mao subsequently persuaded his colleagues that the major fault lay with the new defensive tactics applied by the Soviet-oriented Chinese leaders.

The fifth annihilation campaign forced the communists to abandon their final base area in southeast China and undertake an extraordinary strategic retreat. The few years of the Jiangxi Soviet's existence had, however, left their mark on the CCP. During these years the party became fully separated from its urban base and increasingly composed of peasant recruits. It had begun to develop its own military arm and had started to learn how to survive and grow in the rural areas. In addition, Mao skillfully used the final defeat of the Jiangxi Soviet to demonstrate that his own brand of Chinese Marxism—what later became known as Mao Zedong Thought, defined by the CCP as "the application of the universal truth of Marxism-Leninism to the concrete conditions of the Chinese revolution"—could provide success, while the advice coming from Moscow led only to disaster.

Strategic Retreat: The Long March (1934–35)

Party legend to the contrary, the Long March was actually a costly strategic retreat. It took the main body of communist forces from Jiangxi in southeast China across to Sichuan in the southwest, and then deep into the interior of north China to Baoan and finally to a new base area centered on the dusty town of Yan'an.[45] It was a searing experience in the lives of the survivors. The going was so difficult that many of the survivors suffered stomach ailments and insomnia for the rest of their lives. Ever after, the CCP has differentiated between those who participated in the march and those who did not. The former, called "Long March cadres," enjoy a prestige and camaraderie that sets them apart even within the ranks of the party itself.[46] It is not an exaggeration to say that Long Marchers have led the Chinese communist movement from the time of the march to the 1990s.

An American journalist, Edgar Snow, captured the spirit of the Long March best in his classic *Red Star over China,* published shortly after the conclusion of the march and based on interviews with communist leaders, including Mao. As Snow wrote,

The Long March had an average of one halt for every 114 miles of marching. The mean daily stage covered was 71 *li,* or nearly 24 miles, a phenomenal pace for a great army and its transport to average over some of the most hazardous terrain on earth. Altogether the Reds crossed 18 mountain ranges, five of which were perennially snow capped, and they crossed 24 rivers. They passed through 12 different provinces, occupied 62 cities, and broke through enveloping armies of 10 different provincial warlords, besides defeating, eluding, or outmaneuvering the various forces of Central Government troops sent against them. They entered and successfully crossed six different aboriginal districts, and penetrated areas through which no Chinese army had gone for scores of years. However one may feel about the Reds and what they represent politically (and there is plenty of room for argument!), it is impossible to deny recognition of their Long March—the *Ch'ang Cheng,* as they call it—as one of the great exploits of military history. In Asia only the Mongols have surpassed it.[47]

The Long March took a devastating toll on the ranks of the CCP. While various sources provide different figures, it appears that 80 to 90 percent of those who began it did not survive to settle in Yan'an. The severe privation of the march sparked sharp disputes among the leaders as to the best route to follow, the appropriate destination, and the composition of the leadership.

The Long March left two legacies for the subsequent development of the movement. Most importantly, early in the march, Mao Zedong achieved primacy within the CCP and leadership of the march itself at a meeting convened in January 1935 at the village of Zunyi in Guizhou Province. The meeting lasted for three days and witnessed bitter polemics. A major issue concerned the route that the communist forces should take and where they should aim to go. This issue became intricately bound up with the question of who should lead the main body of forces on the march.

At the Zunyi meeting, Mao launched a blistering critique of those who had followed the military advice of Comintern representative Braun[48] during the latter part of the Jiangxi period. Mao achieved primacy in the party at this meeting, but for the next seven years he had to fight to consolidate his victory over Wang Ming. Wang had spent the 1930s in Moscow as the leading Chinese representative at Comintern headquarters. He returned to China after the Long March, and it is an indication of Moscow's continued importance to the CCP that Wang immediately became the major rival to Mao's leadership.[49] Mao finally achieved absolute leadership only in the years from 1942 to 1945 in Yan'an. He then retained that supreme position until his death in 1976. During his long reign Mao showed time and again that he never fully forgave many of the individuals who had argued against his taking initial control of the party and the Long March at Zunyi.

Second, the march became the basis for an heroic myth about the CCP that greatly bolstered the party's unity and prestige in subsequent years. The unity of the march veterans did not shatter until about three decades later, when Mao initiated the Cultural Revolution in the 1960s.

The Long March changed the strategic location of the Chinese communist movement. After much debate, the main forces in the march finally decided to head for Yan'an, where a small communist base area had existed for some time under the leadership of Liu Zhidan. This shift took the communists largely out of the range of the GMD's military capabilities. It also, as it turns out, positioned the CCP well to expand its bases in rural north China once the Japanese drove the GMD out of the main cities of that area.

The Yan'an Era (1935–47)

The Yan'an era had a profound effect on the Chinese Communist party and its fortunes. When the communists completed the Long March, the CCP consisted of a relatively small band (10,000 to 25,000) of bedraggled southern troops displaced to a desolate and desperately poor area in the north China hinterland. The GMD, for all its shortcomings, represented in the popular mind the hope for Chinese nationalism.

By the end of the Yan'an era, the CCP's forces had grown to nearly 2.8 million members, the party governed some nineteen base areas that contained a population of nearly one hundred million people, and many, especially in north China, felt that the CCP more than the GMD had acquitted itself well during the prolonged war against Japan. Put differently, during World War II the GMD was driven from its base, degenerated as a resilient political force, and lost considerable credibility with the populace. During this same period, the Chinese Communist party vastly expanded its base, greatly developed its techniques of governance, and significantly enhanced its political prestige.[50] The Japanese invasion thus saved the CCP—although it did so because the communists proved so much better than the Nationalists in learning how to adapt to the new circumstances and gaining through adversity.

When the CCP negotiated Chiang Kai-shek's release during the Xi'an incident in December 1936, the united front against the Japanese on which they insisted contained terms that reflect the lessons the CCP leaders had learned from their earlier bitter experience with the GMD. The communists agreed to incorporate their military forces into the GMD but would do so only on the condition that these forces remained as separate units under direct communist command. The CCP also agreed to stop calling for an overthrow of the GMD and for class warfare, but they demanded that they be allowed to govern their own base areas. On the sensitive issue of land reform, the communists agreed to a mild reform consisting primarily of the limitations on land rents that the GMD itself had adopted in national legislation but had never effectively implemented. Communist propaganda focused on Chinese nationalism and on the need to combat the Japanese. All landlords who would support this cause and agree to the specified rent reductions would be tolerated in the communist base areas. In return for these concessions the GMD made three major commitments: to cease attacking the CCP, to provide the communist base areas with aid, and to fight the Japanese.[51]

In reality, neither the communists nor the GMD faithfully carried out the letter of their agreement, which was hardly surprising given the deep bitterness between them. But each side adhered enough to the spirit of the agreement during the first few years that their cooperation proved reasonably successful. By 1940, however, the spirit of mutual help became frayed on both sides, and within another year the GMD had cut off aid to the communists and was blockading the CCP base areas. The united front had ended in fact if not in name.[52]

The legacies of the Yan'an era proved fundamental to the subsequent history of the Chinese Communist party. Enormous success crowned this period, as the party overcame seemingly insuperable odds to grow and develop. As a consequence, the methods employed in Yan'an acquired a kind of halo about them. In future times of need, Mao showed a strong tendency to revert to the core elements in the heady mixture of success in the Yan'an era.

Party membership was strongly shaped by the devastation of the final battles for the Jiangxi Soviet, the Long March, and the numerous clashes with the Japanese during the Yan'an era. With only very few early members of the CCP surviving to the end of the Yan'an period, the party as of the mid-1940s consisted overwhelmingly of peasants recruited from the base areas of north China. Its leadership, however, reflected the CCP's origins south of the Yangtze, supplemented by intellectuals who trekked out to Yan'an to join the party during the war against Japan.

Many of the policies in Yan'an were a maturing and fleshing out of approaches that had first been tried in Ruijin. The tentative initiatives of the early 1930s now became complete systems of operation along with supporting theoretical rationales. During the early 1940s the CCP paid particular attention, for example, to reducing bureaucratism among its administrative personnel and developing a united-front system of governance that gave non-communists a sense of participation in the communist-dominated base areas. The communists during these years also enhanced their confidence and proficiency in waging guerrilla war.[53]

Several major developments during the Yan'an era bore particularly important long-term consequences. The consolidation, especially from 1942 to 1944, of Mao Zedong's personal rule within the party was one of these. Another was the 1945 adoption of a party constitution that stipulated Marxism-Leninism Mao Zedong Thought as the guiding ideology of the CCP. This move recognized the importance of Mao's major adaptations of the Moscow party line to the specific conditions of China.

To obtain his position of preeminence in the CCP, Mao undertook a "thought-reform campaign" from 1942 to 1944. This effort reflected Mao's desire to eliminate any remnant influence of Soviet-oriented communists, and his understanding that under conditions of separate base areas and incessant warfare he could not rely on discipline alone to ensure obedience in the CCP ranks. The techniques developed to implement thought reform, "washing the brain," as the Chinese also called it, included isolating individuals in "study groups." Under the guidance of a group leader, they studied specified documents to understand key principles. They then had to relate those principles to their own lives in a critical, concrete, and thoroughgoing way. Other members of the group put the individual under extraordinary pressure to examine fully his/her most deeply held views, and to do so in the presence of the group. The individual then had to write a full, self-revealing "confession." Other group members isolated the individual during this process. Only when the confession was accepted would the person be drawn back into an accepted position in the group and in the larger society.

These techniques of pressure, ostracism, and reintegration can be effective in any society. They were particularly powerful in China, where the culture assigns great value to saving face, protecting one's innermost thinking, and above all, identifying with a group. Individuals put through thought reform later described it as excruciating. The resulting changes in views were not permanent, but the experience overall seriously affected the lives of those who went through it. In a milder form, the CCP used these same types of techniques on millions of Chinese after 1949.[54]

Like thought reform, many of the other techniques the communists developed during the Yan'an period reflected the evolving political conditions in which they found themselves. During these years, the CCP followed a strategy of infiltrating behind Japanese lines throughout north China, and by 1945 the communists had established nineteen base areas there. Japanese areas of control, however, divided the CCP base areas from each other, and communications both between and within the base areas were extremely tenuous and primitive.[55] At all times, moreover, many of the base areas were threatened with Japanese military attack, causing the CCP to follow a military strategy of prolonged guerrilla warfare. The Japanese menace on one side and the post-1940 Guomindang blockade on the other severely limited the resources available to the communists in these very poor areas. The demands of guerrilla war placed a premium on developing strong, mutually supportive bonds between the troops and the local populace.

By the end of the Yan'an period, the CCP had developed an operational set of principles and practices that differed markedly from the centralized, functionally specialized, hierarchical, command-oriented approach imposed by Stalin in the USSR. In what some authors have labeled the "Yan'an complex," the CCP stressed a combination of qualities that can be summed up as:

□—decentralized rule, with considerable operational flexibility allowed to local leaders;

□—the importance of ideology in keeping cadres loyal to the goals of the leaders and reasonably consistent in their approaches to problems;

□—a strong preference for officials who could provide leadership in a range of areas—politics, administration, and military—instead of only in a particular, specialized area;

□—stress on developing and maintaining close ties with the local population rather than relying on impersonal commands issued from government offices;

□—a related focus on egalitarianism and simple living among officials as highly preferred ways of keeping in touch with the population.

Although the communist movement fell short of realizing these principles in practice, they nevertheless became deeply held party values.[56] In later years they would become integral parts of the CCP mythology about the success of the Yan'an era.

Another, darker, set of methods also became an integral part of CCP practice during the Rectification campaign in Yan'an. This was the use of false accusations, torture, and "special case groups" to elicit confessions from real and imagined foes within the communist movement. Kang Sheng, working with Mao's support, was the central figure in this effort. Kang had played a key role in the CCP intelligence apparatus in Shanghai in the late 1920s. He then went to the Soviet Union, where he learned the techniques of mass terror and secret police work from Stalin's henchmen. While in the USSR he had strongly supported Wang Ming, and he returned to China with Wang in 1937. Once in Yan'an, however, Kang soon switched his loyalty to Mao Zedong, and Mao brought Kang to the center of power. Kang was a complex man—well-educated, a connoisseur of art, and yet a person with a sadistic capacity to inflict pain and a tendency to see enemies everywhere.

With Mao Zedong's backing, Kang conducted a reign of terror that paralleled the early 1940s Rectification campaign. His actions were so violent that he aroused strong criticism from other CCP leaders, and after 1945 he was removed from intelligence and police work. But his legacy of Stalinist-type methods lived on alongside the better-known Maoist penchant for thought reform. In Mao's later years he brought Kang back to the center of power, and all of China paid the price during the Cultural Revolution that began in 1966 and continued for a decade.[57]

During the Yan'an period, the social composition of the CCP became even more thoroughly peasant. In the context of ongoing guerrilla war, moreover, the party and the military became so intertwined that the distinctions between them were largely artificial. And finally, the leaders of various base areas and military groups became powerful figures with deep personal bonds of loyalty to their immediate comrades. While impressive obedience to central command continued to characterize the movement, decentralization and local initiative became core operating principles.

Fighting a Civil War (1947–49)

After the sudden capitulation of Japan in the wake of the atomic bombings of Hiroshima and Nagasaki, the United States army air-lifted Guomindang troops to China's major cities to take the Japanese surrender. At the same time, in the final weeks of World War II the Soviet Union attacked Japanese forces in northeast China and proceeded to occupy the area that had previously been Manchukuo.[58] Because the Chinese people were by this time thoroughly sick of warfare, neither the communists nor the Nationalists wanted to be seen as the instigator of additional fighting. During much of 1946 an American mediation effort attempted to find a way for the two sides to cooperate. Relations, however, deteriorated and in early 1947 the Guomindang launched an all-out attack to wipe the Chinese communists out of north and northeast China, beginning with the capture of Yan'an itself.

While maintaining control over much of the north China hinterland, the CCP concentrated its efforts on recruiting new supporters among the peasants of the northeast, where it sent many of its forces directly after the Japanese surrender. The communists did their recruiting through a radical land-reform campaign that employed violence in targeting landlords, rich peasants, and a portion of the middle peasants. This campaign produced a flood of new recruits but wreaked havoc with agricultural production in the northeast.[59]

The communists' basic strategy in the civil war was to surround the major cities and cut them off from the hinterland. They also sought to interdict interurban transportation wherever possible. This general approach became famous as the hallmark of the guerrilla, rural-based strategy for revolution. By the end of 1948 the Nationalist garrisons in the northeast had become thoroughly demoralized and could no longer be sustained by the GMD resupply effort. They were withdrawn in the final months of that year.

The year 1949 began with a major communist victory—the largest of the entire civil war—called the Huai-Hai campaign. In this single effort, communist forces wiped out half a million Guomindang troops, dealing a fatal blow to the GMD's hopes for maintaining their position in north China. Tianjin, China's second largest commercial and industrial center, fell after two days of fighting in mid-January, and Beijing surrendered peacefully to the surrounding communist forces at the end of the month.[60]

From February 1949 until their ultimate victory the communist forces used conventional positional warfare rather than guerrilla tactics to uproot the Guomindang. Like the Qing dynasty in the final days of its rule, the GMD after the Huai-Hai campaign proved a hollow shell, and it collapsed more rapidly than either it or the communists had thought possible. Communist armies swept across China in two major thrusts, one down the eastern provinces to Guangdong (captured in September–October 1949) and then to the southwest, and the other cutting straight across central China to the southwest. These efforts routed the GMD forces from the major southwest province of Sichuan in the winter of 1949–50 and secured the surrender of Tibet to Beijing's sovereignty in the spring of 1950.

The shift in late 1948 from a guerrilla war to a conventional war strategy reflected the communists' realization that the fighting would not continue as long as they had initially anticipated. As of 1947, Mao Zedong had commented that he expected to achieve nationwide victory in five years. The party simultaneously began to worry about rehabilitating the devastated national economy and about preventing the flight of urban talent and capital abroad in advance of the communist armies.

In 1948, therefore, the communists shifted their political line. They sharply criticized the radical nature of the land reform that had been implemented in the previous two years and adopted, instead, a far milder version of this effort that would preserve a rich peasant economy. They also began to cultivate the capitalists and intellectuals in China's major cities in an effort to win them over to the communist cause. In so doing, they promised that there would be a long period of "new democracy" before the country would be ready for an eventual transition to socialism.[61]

The rapid collapse of the Guomindang on the Chinese mainland and the organization of the CCP's military forces into different "field armies" meant that various parts of the country came under the rule of particular communist armies and their leaders. These military establishments became the basis for the subsequent civilian administrations that were formed to govern these areas. In most cases, the military commanders who had captured the areas switched hats to become the key local government and party officials.

LEGACIES OF THE CCP'S PATH TO POWER

The CCP enjoyed remarkable success in all its various approaches to mobilizing the Chinese population against the existing system. The communists were successful regardless of the type of appeal they made (class struggle in the early 1920s, anti-imperialism in the mid-1920s, and so on), the groups to which the appeals were directed (workers, various classes of peasants, déclassé elements, intellectuals), or the geographical area in which the political activity took place (southeastern cities and countryside, northern hinterland, northeast countryside). All this demonstrates that from the 1920s to 1940s China's malaise made it an eminently "mobilizable" society. Regardless of issue, target, and locale in this widely diverse and socially stratified country, the feelings of dislocation and discontent ran deep, and revolutionary forces could rapidly gain support.

A second notable element in the CCP's rise to power was that, irrespective of its success in mobilizing support, the party typically failed to translate that support into sustainable political power. The party eventually found that the key to survival lay in seeking out and occupying the interstices of power in the mountainous regions between provinces where no other forces held sway, in desolate parts of north China, or where foreign occupation of cities and transport lines (the Japanese in north China during World War II and the Russians in northeast China from 1945 to 1946) created a vacuum of power in the countryside. From the 1920s to the late 1940s, virtually wherever the CCP faced the GMD head on, the CCP suffered defeat.

This observation raises questions about the many conventional analyses of the CCP's rise to power.[62] According to these standard views, the CCP forced the GMD defeat by astute use of political mobilization to support guerrilla and then mobile conventional warfare. Without doubt, the communists posed problems for the GMD that diverted the Nationalists' attention and resources from other pressing issues. But the major forces behind the defeat of the Nationalists seem, on closer examination, to have been the Japanese invasion, which separated the Nationalists from their natural bases of political power in the lower Yangtze and along the southeast coast, and the related corruption and factionalization of the Nationalist movement, which brought such disaster to China of the late 1940s.

By this reckoning, the CCP's key accomplishment was to find the means to sustain itself as the only viable alternative to GMD rule.[63] But in the final analysis, the GMD collapsed on the mainland primarily of its own dead weight. Indeed, from mid-1949 one of the CCP's main problems became the speed of the retreat of the GMD forces. Those forces in south China often fled so rapidly that the CCP military had difficulty keeping up, and the bandit gangs that took over in the interregnum proved nettlesome for the communist forces when they arrived.[64]

The significance of the strategies the CCP employed in attaining power lies, therefore, in their effect on the dynamics of the communist movement. Regardless of the CCP's repeated disappointments and failures, key elements in their tortuous path to power became integral to the party mystique. The myths concerning the Long March and especially the Yan'an period played powerful roles in shaping Mao's views about how to overcome crises when the CCP encountered them after the conclusion of the First Five-Year Plan in 1957. The years in the wilderness, in short, had stamped the CCP with a distinctive character. The following were some of the most important dimensions of that persona.

Mao Zedong attained a stature in the party that was unchallengeable. Mao had brought the party from the devastation of the failure at Ruijin in 1934 to nationwide victory in 1949. As leading communist officials have subsequently commented, "We felt Mao could see farther than we could see and could understand more than we could understand. Therefore, when we did not understand Mao, we assumed that he was right and we were wrong."[65] The result was what could be termed a bandwagon type of political leadership, in which virtually all top officials tried to sense the direction in which Mao was beginning to move so that they could quickly move in that direction.[66] There were no institutional constraints on Mao's power, and he psychologically and politically dominated most other leading CCP officials.

The consultative leadership style Mao practiced in the late 1940s produced fairly benign informal rules of competition among China's communist leaders. But the Rectification movement of 1942–44 had seen Mao support selective use of another style of rule—a Stalinist approach that centered on witch hunts, false accusations, confessions under torture, and executions. That Mao had shifted his approach after 1945 should not obscure the fact that this more benign late-1940s style—and therefore the system itself—could change at his whim. This core flaw proved highly consequential for the subsequent history of the PRC.[67]

The party membership was overwhelmingly rural in composition, and many in the movement were functionally illiterate. These people tended to be instinctively antiurban and anti-intellectual. They could not handle the paper flows characteristic of large-scale bureaucratic organizations. Yet, they had earned the right to hold positions of importance in the political organs being established to run China. Consequently, many of the characteristics of the PRC's governance—decentralization, mass political campaigns, extensive use of face-to-face meetings, repeated vicious attacks on intellectuals, and so forth—reflect in major part the adaptations of the post-1949 political system to the distribution of capabilities and the attitudes of the peasant cadres who took over the country.

The peasant-based military path to power left a party and army so deeply intertwined as to be virtually indistinguishable as of the late 1940s. The party leadership, moreover, viewed the army as a resource that could serve political as well as security functions. Virtually all party cadres had extensive experience in the military. None viewed the military as a force that should be kept separate from domestic politics. Indeed, as noted above, the pattern of military conquest from 1948–1950 determined which clusters of military/civilian cohorts would hold power over each of the major regions of China in the ensuing decades. Thus, in sharp contrast to, for example, the Russian communist movement when it seized national power, the Chinese communists generally distrusted the cities, regarded the countryside as more revolutionary, and viewed the military as a core force for the revolution. The organization that conquered China in 1949 was more a party army than a political party in the normal sense of the term.

Myths about the governance of the communist base areas during the Yan'an era, which like all myths had a substantial basis in reality but also glossed over much, had already developed and been enshrined in the party's consciousness by 1949. These myths highlighted the party's close relations with the masses, encouragement of spontaneity based on confidence in shared underlying values, utilization of mass mobilization techniques to achieve goals, avoidance of bureaucratic airs that limit contact with—and understanding of—mass sentiment, and cultivation of officials who are expert at political matters, government administration, and military affairs (i.e., who can effectively guide all spheres of work). Enshrined in myth, these approaches took on a sanctity that made them powerful tools in Mao Zedong's hands in the post-1949 politics of China.

Perhaps most important, their pre-1949 experiences convinced the Chinese communist leadership that the proper combination of will and strategy could overcome seemingly insuperable objective difficulties. Time and again the communists faced overwhelming odds and were advised to seek compromise. Time and again they instead shifted to a new strategy and continued their pursuit of ultimate power. Their final success made those who had stayed the course confident that the types of "objective" matters that dominate the thinking of intellectuals and experts could yield to the superior insights and tenacity of the CCP's top leaders and their followers. Nobody believed this more firmly by 1949 than Mao Zedong.

Finally, the Chinese communist leaders had learned to cast a critical eye on Soviet advice, which at virtually every turn had proven inappropriate to the best interests of the CCP. It is this final element that makes so startling the party's virtually total acceptance of Soviet guidance for the first phases of the revolution after 1949. Moscow encouraged the Chinese to establish a system that in almost every major dimension ran counter to the essential qualities of the Yan'an myth, and the CCP responded with remarkable enthusiasm for, and fidelity to, almost all Soviet prescriptions.

The complex legacies of the paths to power, however, eventually weakened the Sino-Soviet relationship, just as these same legacies affected nearly every facet of the PRC's domestic politics from the substance of policy decisions to the means of reaching these decisions and the processes for implementing them.

Part Two

POLITICS
AND POLICIES
SINCE 1949

3

The Maoist System:
Ideas and Governance

By the time Mao Zedong stood with his colleagues atop the gate at Tiananmen on 1 October 1949 and proclaimed the founding of the People's Republic of China, he had already engaged in revolutionary politics for almost thirty years and had headed the Chinese Communist party for nearly fifteen. He had proved that he was a man of tremendous will, tenacity, and skill who was deeply read in China's traditions of statecraft and fully schooled in the realities of power politics and warfare.

Mao, in short, was a strong leader who would not shrink from bloodshed and sacrifice to reach his goals. And his goals were extraordinarily ambitious. He wanted not only to govern China but to change the very nature of Chinese society and culture to eliminate the country's weaknesses and earn it respect in the modern world.

Governance and revolutionary change are, however, mutually antagonistic. Government administration works best in an environment that permits development of long-term programs, staffed by competent individuals, who agree on the basic goals they wish to nurture. For a continent-sized country with a population as of 1949 of about half a billion people, effective government would require the formation of large bureaucracies, with their complex problems of management.

Revolutionary change, by contrast, is by its very nature unsettling. Its adherents must maintain a level of frenetic intensity and passion that rarely is compatible with smooth administration. Revolutionaries tend to view complex administration as an obstacle to their goals, while civil servants often want to temper the enthusiasm and lack of technical expertise that accompany the policy thrusts of revolutionaries.

Mao Zedong and his colleagues were no anarchists.[1] They recognized the importance of developing powerful bureaucracies to govern China. One of their major concerns was to develop—for the first time since the downfall of the Qing dynasty—strong national organizations that would permit the leaders in Beijing to govern the entire country. They also believed that China, too, had to undergo an industrial revolution to gain the economic power that alone would give it both prestige and security in the international arena.

The Chinese Communist party that came out of the poverty-stricken interior ran the administrative apparatus, with the result that critical office holders throughout the system tended to be poorly educated former peasants and soldiers committed to the communist cause. Over the years many better-educated individuals, usually from urban backgrounds, did staff these offices and make them work; while Mao accepted the necessity of tolerating this bureaucratic apparatus, he fought repeatedly against its natural tendency to frustrate the types of revolutionary changes he was determined to make.

Understanding Maoist China thus requires understanding the interplay of the two key elements in the system: Mao's own revolutionary ideas; and the formal administrative system he and his colleagues set up to run the country. That administrative system became so complex that its details are elaborated in Chapters 6 and 7, which are specifically devoted to governing organizations and processes in the PRC. Only a brief introduction to the administrative apparatus is provided in this chapter to provide background for the overview of post-1949 politics in Chapters 4 and 5.

The Features of Mao Zedong Thought

Mao Zedong was a voracious reader and prolific writer. He was also a practical politician who exercised enormous day-to-day influence on the conduct of party, government, and military affairs. As a consequence, he left behind a prodigious and complex record of writings, speeches, and decisions. This record reveals a person who was often inconsistent, who wrestled with ideas, changed his mind, and played practical power politics to the hilt.[2] Mao did not think in terms of Aristotelian logic, and it is hard to find examples of logical reasoning in his writings. He reveled in contradictions and delighted in discerning underlying frictions and countercurrents. For almost any generalization about Mao's ideas, therefore, one can find specific discordant examples or exceptions. Mao's concrete actions, moreover, often cut against the grain of his core principles. Although he promoted a puritanical society, for example, Mao himself was a prodigious womanizer. He stressed the importance of simple living but, unlike such colleagues as Liu Shaoqi, Mao's putative successor until he was purged early in the Cultural Revolution, Mao made extensive use of lavish residences built for his exclusive pleasure around the country.

For all these contradictions, certain fundamental concerns and basic long-term thrusts to Mao's political life stand out. To weigh down the discussion of these with numerous specific qualifications and exceptions is to miss the tremendous impact they had overall in shaping both the history of the PRC under Mao and the legacies of that period for China's subsequent efforts.

Mao's thinking naturally reflected a mixture of influences, including his central China rural background and his subsequent failure to become more than a marginal member of the Beijing intelligentsia in the late 1910s. He regarded himself as well-versed in China's history and culture, but chose a life full of risk and violence. In the most personal terms, for example, he flouted convention and abandoned his first wife, to whom he had been matched in a traditional, arranged marriage. He evidently loved Yang Kaihui, his second wife, but the Guomindang captured her and beheaded her in the late 1920s. His third wife suffered a breakdown on the Long March, and Mao abandoned her to marry Jiang Qing, an attractive Shanghai actress who journeyed to Yan'an to join the fight against the Japanese. Mao's brother, Mao Zemin, was killed while on political assignment in northwest China in the 1940s, and Mao's only mentally and physically capable son was killed by American forces during the Korean War. Some say Mao left two daughters with peasant families while on the Long March. If so, neither was ever subsequently located. His remaining son had, by the late 1950s, developed mental problems and proved incapable of handling official responsibilities. Mao's political career therefore directly cost the health and lives of many of his closest relatives. In the tradition of China's literati, Mao himself wrote poetry and critiqued the essays of his colleagues; he also had nothing but disdain for armchair politicians and specialists who had never put their lives on the line to achieve their goals.

Mao Zedong believed that China's malaise had been caused first of all by the exploitation of imperialist forces, and his reading in Marxism and Leninism provided him with a systematic explanation of this phenomenon. But he also was keenly sensitive to the internal weaknesses that made the country vulnerable to external aggression. These internal problems, Mao believed, were substantially cultural. The Confucian notions of civil identity based on networks of relationships precluded the broader class identity and ardent nationalism that Mao believed were necessary to galvanize the people of the country into effective action. Mao also felt that Chinese in general were too fatalistic and too passive. He attributed this in part to the elitist elements of Confucianism and the sense of dependency that the resulting hierarchical society nurtured.

Mao—like most great leaders—was as much a product of his society as a rebel against it. His attacks on traditional culture and polity, therefore, incorporated some very traditional elements. During the Cultural Revolution of the late 1960s, for instance, he demanded the unthinkable in Confucianism: that youths rebel against their elders. At the same time, however, he promoted his own writings as the revolutionary catechism, which resonated deeply with the tradition of memorizing the Confucian classics as a key to political advancement and social virtue in traditional China. To be sure, Mao stressed activism and rejection of the old (one of his favorite slogans was, "Smash the old, establish the new"), hardly the spirit of the Confucian ideology. But in this as in many instances, Mao was shaped by tradition even as he launched frontal assaults on the legacies of imperial China.

Overall, Mao sought to move China, to wield its people as a powerful tool to shape the country's destiny. Virtually throughout his life he found himself in an objectively inferior power position, and he thus had to appeal to others to act in concert with him. Before 1949, he continuously confronted enemy forces that had far more firepower than he could command. After 1949, he sought to make a place for China in a world dominated by the United States and the Soviet Union. Almost his entire box of political tools, therefore, concentrated on turning weakness into strength in order to overcome the challenges he faced.

China's domestic politics after 1949 formed the one exception, the one arena in which Mao became the center of power. Given his dominant position domestically, Mao became so arrogant that he eventually seemed to lose touch with reality. By the mid-1960s he accepted no other authority, not even that of his doctors regarding his own health.[3] Furthermore, he continued to frame issues and devise solutions in terms he had developed before 1949. These included such approaches as political campaigns, the mass line, the united front, and advocacy of egalitarianism and self-reliance, all of which are described below. But beneath this facade of continuity lay the pathologies of megalomania and, it seems, growing paranoia, which transformed these familiar techniques, devised to change and empower the people and to temper the party, into devices to bend the populace and the party to Mao's personal will. This transition occurred over a period of years. By the mid-1960s, with the launching of the Cultural Revolution, it was complete.

PROMINENCE OF IDEOLOGY

In good Confucian fashion, Mao Zedong believed that right thinking was integral to right conduct. He therefore gave enormous emphasis to matters of ideology and to the importance of ideological education of the people. Put differently, Mao did not use ideology as window dressing to brighten his practical actions with a theoretical gloss; rather, he saw the development and propagation of ideology as central to the success of the movement he led. One of Mao's key sources of power, moreover, was the monopoly he had to determine what would constitute correct ideology for China.

The extent to which Mao lost faith in his own revolutionary ideas and cynically used his ideology as a weapon to deal with his enemies is uncertain. Probably, the reality is more subtle and more tragic than any simple notion of Mao as a tyrant conveys. Mao more likely succumbed to hubris, believing that only he could understand the dangers the country faced and what measures were needed to pull "victory" out of looming defeat. By the end of the 1950s, everyone else was too afraid to tell him the truth. Mao, his colleagues had good reason to think, always asked for the truth but dealt ruthlessly with those who told it. In his increasingly unreal inner sanctum, he resorted time and again to the techniques he had developed before 1949, but as time wore on, the resulting efforts created more bloodletting and tragedy than progress.

No single canon of works was ever designated as the sum and substance of Mao Zedong Thought. The closest Beijing ever came to this was the so-called "little red book" of selections from Mao's works grouped under topical headings that the political wing of the military put out in the early 1960s. It became required reading throughout the country in the late 1960s during the Cultural Revolution. Overall, though, Mao Zedong Thought incorporated the pieces contained in Mao's four-volume *Selected Works* that cover up to 1949, along with many post-1949 texts and political statements by the leader. This was, thus, a living and evolving canon of doctrine. Its very range and lack of precise definition enabled Mao to draw from it to support virtually any direction he wanted to lead the country at a particular time.

Despite this inherent flexibility, the ideology should be taken seriously. Mao believed that it would be impossible in the world's most populous country to lead solely on the basis of formal government administration. He would have to instill in the people certain principles and a commitment to certain types of authority that would enable him not only to remain in power but also to remold the country over which he ruled. In a political system whose technical and human limitations greatly restricted the information available to the leaders and their ability to analyze the consequences of their own policy options, moreover, ideology would be a key tool for ensuring compliance among lower-level officials.

VOLUNTARISM

Marxism propagates a philosophical theory of change called materialism, which holds that the underlying development of the material world—in the case of Marxism, especially of the economic structure of the society—determines human consciousness and therefore the boundaries of major human activity. Lenin took this materialist doctrine and modified it to recognize more fully the potential effectiveness of political agitation and revolutionary efforts to accelerate history. Mao went a large step further. Although he always proclaimed himself a materialist, his lifelong activities were based on the conviction that properly motivated people could overcome virtually any material odds to accomplish their goals. On this basis, for example, during the 1950s he developed advanced socialist forms for governing China even though the country labored under a backward, agriculturally based economy. Also, as we shall see, for a time after 1957 Mao believed that China could "leap" into economic development by the concentrated efforts of its people.

Mao thus ascribed tremendous power to people's volition and considered that the ability to mobilize people to attack problems in a concerted way virtually equaled the ability to solve those problems themselves, a philosophical position called voluntarism. He became convinced of this wisdom through the remarkable survival, growth, and victory of the CCP.

Much of Mao Zedong Thought, therefore, consists of various approaches to molding the will of the people and bringing that will to bear in support of Mao's goals. These approaches include the mass line; campaigns; struggle; and egalitarianism/plain living.

Mass Line

Mao Zedong abhorred the Confucian notion that rulers know what to do because of their knowledge of the classic doctrine and that the poorly educated masses must simply obey their superiors. This idea produced a passive population and a backward-looking leadership, just the opposite of the activist society and dynamic leadership that Mao believed were critical to the success of the revolution. Mao portrayed himself as more of a populist who believed in the inherent wisdom and power of the people. He also permitted no one to question his belief that he better than anyone understood the hearts of the Chinese peasantry, which represented more than 80 percent of the population.

Especially during the Yan'an era the CCP developed a leadership doctrine, dubbed the mass line, that incorporated both the vanguard role of the party and a strong participatory role for the populace. The basic idea was that officials in direct contact with the masses should always remain close enough to the people to understand their fundamental desires and concerns. These officials would report their understanding up the hierarchy to provide the leaders a good sense of what the populace would welcome and implement and what they would not. The top leaders, with their superior understanding of the laws of history and of China's overall conditions, would then reach appropriate decisions that would push forward the revolution in a strong but realistic fashion acceptable to the masses. As the resulting orders for new initiatives were issued, the local officials would try to involve the populace in implementing these directives in order to win popular commitment through popular participation. Mao summed up this whole process in the pithy saying, "From the masses, to the masses."

The mass line was a means to alleviate two problematic tendencies of dictatorships: losing touch with popular sentiment and generating political apathy among the people, who come to believe they cannot influence their own leaders. This technique did not compromise the party's dictatorial rule, because it eschewed any notion that the masses could act against the dictates of higher-level authorities. But it did call for popular political activity, and it demanded that government bureaucrats keep their ears to the ground and regularly get out among the people.

In practice, the political system that developed after 1949 seriously corroded the mass line. Local officials often shied away from accurately reporting the views of the populace for fear of exposing discontent with their own work. People grew hesitant to voice their real opinions to officials who could wreck their lives with virtually a wave of the hand. The lack of informational resources such as a truly independent press meant that the incentives for skewed reporting at each level of the national bureaucratic hierarchy (work unit, township/commune, county, city, prefecture, province, and national ministry) further degraded the information available to those at the very top. At its worst, such pressures led to utter tragedy, as when the top leaders in 1960–61 thought there was a far larger agricultural harvest than in fact existed. They consequently collected far too much grain in taxes—so much, in fact, that nearly thirty million peasants starved to death before the leadership fully realized what was occurring.[4]

Despite these failures of the mass line, the party took the concept seriously as a technique of rule. Chinese bureaucrats were under constant pressure to "go down to the masses" and to "learn from the masses." These efforts sometimes took the form of regular requirements, such as the regulation adopted in 1958 that military officers spend one month each year working in the ranks as common soldiers. Top leaders, moreover, adopted a style of making personal inspections of particular locales to hear directly the views of the people.

Each of the highest leaders tended to develop a few places where he regularly tested the waters on policy directions and results. Liu Shaoqi typically went to Tianjin. In 1949, for instance, he met with a wide range of businessmen in that city to test out the party's united-front approach to winning over business confidence. Liu chose Tianjin both because he had fought in the party underground there and because his wife, Wang Guangmei, came from a prominent Tianjin business family.[5] Chen Yun went to his birthplace, Qingpu County near Shanghai. There he sounded out the peasants at the height of the Great Leap Forward to ascertain their real views of this massive effort.[6] The mass line thus helped convince the top leaders that they remained in close touch with the Chinese people, and few accusations against an official in the political hierarchy were as damning as the declaration that she/he had "lost touch with the masses."

By combining dictatorial leadership with mass participation via the mass line, Mao felt he could mobilize the Chinese people to change the country. The mass line, in short, was critical to Mao's voluntaristic notion that through "people power" (in Maoist jargon, called the "power of the masses") the huge Chinese population could overcome the daunting obstacles that kept the country poor and weak. The mass-line approach, in turn, utilized specific techniques and issues to whip up a mixture of enthusiasm, commitment, and hysteria among the populace. Here the techniques of campaigns and struggle, and the issue of egalitarianism, became lodged in the PRC's political system.

Campaigns

Campaigns, or *yundong*, were concentrated attacks on specific issues through mass mobilization of the populace. Their broad goals were sociopolitical transformation and economic development. Campaigns of the first sort aimed to change the ways people thought about key issues and social relationships; for example, some mass campaigns, such as the Cultural Revolution of 1966–76, sought to arouse real feelings of hatred toward those the regime designated as class enemies. The second type of campaign was utilized to change the basic forms of production—for example, to collectivize agriculture or to socialize industry and commerce—and to convince people to make superhuman efforts to improve their economic performance. Often, especially during the 1950s, these two types of effort merged into a single campaign to change the organization of production in an economic sector, inspire hatred toward the former elites in that sector, and generate enthusiasm for the new system and a willingness to work hard to make it succeed. Such was the case, for example, with the Land Reform campaign of 1950–52, the Agricultural Cooperativization campaign that began in the summer of 1955, and with the Great Leap Forward, which began in 1958. By the 1960s, Mao's campaigns, most notably the Cultural Revolution but also including the Four Cleanups and others, increasingly focused on sociopolitical change and devoted less attention to achieving major increases in production (see Table 3.1).

Over the years, most campaigns conformed to a basic pattern regardless of their goal.[7] This regularity emerged even though the campaign approach was meant to break down the normal bureaucratic control over issues so as to attack them head on. Campaigns typically began with mobilization around

TABLE 3.1 *Major Nationwide Campaigns during the Maoist Era*

YEAR	CAMPAIGN
1950–52	Land Reform
1951	Suppression of Counterrevolutionaries
1951–52	Three Anti Five Anti; Thought Reform of Intellectuals
1955–56	Agricultural Cooperativization Socialist Transformation of Industry and Commerce Anti–Hu Feng Su-Fan (against counterrevolutionaries)
1957	Hundred Flowers Antirightist
1958–61	Great Leap Forward
1963–65	Four Cleanups Second Three Anti
1966–76	Cultural Revolution
1968–69	Shang shan xia xiang (rustication of urban youths)
1973–74	Anti–Lin Biao and Anti-Confucius
1976	Criticize Deng Xiaoping

some broad themes—fighting corruption, promoting agricultural collectiviza-tion, ferreting out those with "rightist" thoughts, and so on. At this early stage, people were given documents to study and were organized to undertake this study in a concentrated, high-pressure fashion. Often, the newspapers, radio, and journals and the officials at every level of the political system whipped up popular fervor, warning darkly (but vaguely) of the enormous dangers to the country's well-being that lurked in society's midst. During this early mobiliza-tion phase, people often neglected their jobs and concentrated all their en-ergy on the campaign. In campaigns of sociopolitical change and structural transformation, the economy typically suffered dislocations during this mobi-lization phase.

At some point, the national authorities would signal the start of the sec-ond stage of a campaign. In their second stage, campaigns became more con-crete, zeroing in on specific individuals and groups as targets of the wrath of the campaign. The targets would suffer severely, undergoing "struggle" ses-sions where they would be subject to overwhelming psychological and physical abuse. They were expected to "confess" their transgressions and to beg humbly for the forgiveness of the masses. During this period of fervor, cam-paigns for organizational changes, such as collectivization of agriculture, would begin to implement them on a trial basis.

In the third stage, campaigns became more clearly coercive, as the targets that emerged during the course of the campaign received formal punish-ment. In many cases, this punishment took the form of long years in prison at hard labor, although it could also assume guises ranging from public execu-tion to simple admonitions to improve one's thought.

Regardless of their specific objectives—and these varied widely—cam-paigns tended to emphasize an interrelated, distinctive set of priorities. In the "high tide" of almost any campaign, antiintellectualism, egalitarianism, and voluntarism surged to the fore as did those cadres who were less well educated but were skillful in political mobilization. While China between campaigns tended to value technical skills, to utilize material incentives, and to stress the need to plan and address objective problems, during campaigns the country turned sharply in the other direction on each of these issues. These huge pol-icy swings were important. Those individuals who tended to stand out during the consolidation phases between campaigns, for example, often fared very badly during campaign periods; similarly, the less educated who became prominent at the height of a political campaign tended to recede during pe-riods of normal politics. The influence of the campaign cycle on career mo-bility tended, over time, to create strong vested interests among some cadres in initiating the next campaign and equally strong interests among others in moving the polity away from utilizing political campaigns as a governing tech-nique.

Campaigns served several purposes in Mao's thinking. By periodically tak-ing issues outside the normal bureaucratic routines, they prevented the bu-reaucracy from becoming too great an obstacle to Mao's more radical goals. Some campaigns, such as the Three Anti in 1951–52 and the Cultural Revolu-tion starting in 1966, specifically targeted party and government cadres. Their use of intense study and of specific social targets helped to "educate" the populace in Maoist values. Based on his experience in Yan'an, Mao believed passionately that tension and struggle were necessary to motivate people and to defeat his enemies. He launched these disruptive, frightening campaigns as a necessary adjunct to the more regularized party propaganda and coercion. This style of addressing major problems also fit well with the political capabilities of the peasant cadres who had joined the party during the days of struggle before 1949. They were, like most peasants, uncomfortable with bureaucratic routines and more at home with politics "outdoors."

Mao made the campaign style a prominent feature of Chinese politics—the country experienced at least one major campaign almost every year until his death in 1976. Many of these campaigns proved so traumatic for participants that Chinese interviewed at the time and later tended to date events more by their relation to the major political campaigns ("just after Three Anti Five Anti," "just before the Four Cleanups," etc.) than by calendar years. A question about what someone was doing in mid-1957 might well draw a blank, but asking about the time of the Antirightist campaign (which began in June 1957) would elicit a clear and precise response. Bureaucrats, too, lived in constant fear another political campaign would begin soon. Mao's extensive use of the campaign technique, developed during the Yan'an era, thus severely impacted on the pace, style, and substance of the post-1949 polity. The campaign form epitomized Mao Zedong's core belief that he could motivate people sufficiently to accomplish almost any goal he set for them.

Struggle

Mao scorned the Confucian ideal of harmony as an absolute social value. Confucius, writing at a time of social and political turbulence, taught that a hierarchical society could maintain stability if every person knew and accepted the rights and obligations attached to his or her place in society. To Mao, this notion assured that China would be dominated by backward-looking elites whose misguided rule would keep the country from surging to the forefront of the world stage in the twentieth century.

Mao did not totally eschew harmony and the gentle persuasion and mediation necessary to achieve it. He did, however, also believe in the absolute value of tension and, a qualitatively more severe phenomenon, of struggle—that is, of direct confrontation that broke previous rules through outrages and violence. Struggle, he felt, built courage and character in a people who, Mao believed, were by inclination and culture too passive and accepting. Through struggle, the Chinese could realize their potential to seize control over their fate. Time and again Mao created situations in which his subjects would have to engage in personal struggle, perhaps even at risk to their lives. While most political leaders around the globe have tried to ensure their people peaceful lives, Mao constantly stirred up the social pot as a calculated part of his rule. Struggle became the linchpin of Mao's voluntarism.

Struggle (*douzheng*) consisted broadly of a politically motivated, direct act against another in massive violation of social conventions. It often entailed bringing down a person who formerly had high prestige and authority. Struggle was not an impersonal administrative process; it was highly personal, direct, violent, and public. Students, for example, who "struggled" against their teachers would face the teachers in front of a school assembly and denounce them, accuse them of specific "crimes," declare that they were no longer hoodwinked by their former mentors, and "draw a clear line" between themselves and their teachers by calling for harsh punishment for the latter. They might also directly slap or beat their teachers, humiliate them by hanging disparaging signs around their necks, torture them by locking them in dank closets for months at a time, and so forth.

The whole object of struggle was to smash prevailing social inhibitions in such a dramatic and traumatic way that the participants (both the activists and the targets) could never again reestablish their prestruggle relationship. Mao made struggle part of a permanent system in which some people became recurring victims, hauled out for new abuse every time the regime wanted to stir up the masses again. Such hapless individuals typically were those given "bad class labels"—i.e., those designated as members of a parish class such as capitalists, landlords, or rich peasants.

Mao utilized struggle in part to give Chinese a sense of empowerment so that they could be mobilized to scale the ramparts of revolutionary change and economic development. But he also made this tool a key weapon in combating the deeply embedded Confucian notion that social identity should be based on an individual's web of social relationships. Mao spent his life fighting to change the type of society that the Confucian legacy had produced, a society in which individuals in different networks found it virtually impossible to work together. This required, Mao felt, welding together large numbers of individuals into broad social groups with which they could identify, groups such as workers, poor peasants, and so forth.

Struggle contributed to this change of social identity. The purpose of struggle was to create major social and political fault lines between people who were typically within the same web of social relationships. Thus, for example, during the land reform of 1950–52 many peasants found themselves struggling against landlords who were also their relatives. The struggle itself, through violence and through violation of other social taboos, weakened the old social network and, Mao hoped, began to create a new social identity in the minds of the participants.

Struggle sessions usually were violent. Over the twenty-seven years that Mao ruled the PRC millions of people died as a direct result of political struggle. Tens of millions of other citizens were tortured, incarcerated, and deeply wounded. Very often, moreover, the close relatives of a "struggle target" would also come under fire unless they "drew a clear line" between themselves and the victim: wives, for example, were expected to divorce their "reactionary" husbands and children to denounce and beat their "backward" parents. Mao did not regard violence and death as experiences to avoid; rather, his own revolutionary experience had taught him that he could vanquish his enemies and China could move forward only on the basis of violence, that the revolution needed a vanguard and a hard leading edge. People learned about life through risk and violence, Mao found, and he did not hesitate to whip up storms of intolerance to destroy those he opposed and to instill in his subjects the priorities he held dear.

Egalitarianism

One of the most enduring substantive themes of Mao's political program was the virtue of egalitarianism, which to Mao meant primarily frugal living. In a desperately poor country such as China, where there was no practical way to raise most people's standard of living, this meant leveling average incomes down to those of the poorer strata. Mao often extolled the virtues of poverty and simplicity. He believed the poor were inherently more willing to build a new society because they had so little vested interest in the old. He constantly exhorted his fellow communists to live simply, both because that would reduce the distance between them and the masses and because poverty itself created a more virtuous person.

In a country of China's size and variety, there is no way to equalize the standard of living in different areas; soil quality, amount of rainfall, state of the infrastructure, access to transport, educational levels, and so forth, varied so widely that major differentials in living standards were unavoidable. In this situation, Mao aimed to develop a society where such local inequalities would be offset by powerful measures to spread egalitarianism within the immediate social environment of each individual. Thus, measures to promote income leveling and prohibit conspicuous consumption kept economic stratification minimal within given villages or work units. Measures associated with the mass line, such as encouraging work-unit leaders to discuss some issues extensively with the employees, were aimed at decreasing the psychological distance between leaders and led throughout the country even in the context of highly stratified political power.

Although Mao himself enjoyed the perquisites of rule, he nevertheless reacted at the gut level against others' extravagance and attachment to physical comfort. Egalitarianism was, Mao felt, essential to the effective implementation of the mass line—and therefore to his entire vision for changing China. Without egalitarianism there could be no full mobilization of the populace, and without mobilization Mao's voluntaristic approach to political change and economic development would fail. Even though Mao lived well himself, therefore, his commitment to egalitarianism greatly affected the lives of his officials and subjects alike.

ANTI-INTELLECTUALISM

Mao Zedong was only marginally an intellectual in the China of the 1910s and 1920s. He had obtained a solid education in both classical and "modern" learning, but he had not achieved high intellectual standing. He worked for a while in the library of Beijing University where he gained access to the leading currents of political thought in the country, but he was not on the level of a student or a professor at this renowned institution. Throughout his life, Mao would engage in some of the practices of traditional intellectuals: he wrote poetry, published his calligraphy, and criticized the writing of his colleagues. He constantly cited ancient history and philosophy as well as more contemporary domestic and foreign thinking in his speeches and texts. Yet throughout his life he detested the Chinese intelligentsia, which included doctors, scientists, engineers, and journalists, as well as scholars and creative writers.[8]

To Mao, intellectuals embodied the traditional ways of China. Their knowledge linked them to past values and practices. More fundamentally, though, Mao disdained intellectuals as people who studied books and then put on airs concerning their purportedly superior knowledge. They thus violated three of the cardinal sins in Mao's political universe: they did not dirty their hands by going out among the people to learn about real conditions; they were nay-sayers who constantly pointed to technical constraints on actions that Mao innately felt the masses could accomplish if properly motivated; and they reinforced social inequality by their air of superiority.

Mao also was well aware of the intellectuals' role in imperial China of protecting the moral code of the society against the vagaries of powerful emperors even as they served those emperors. Mao would not tolerate even this small ambivalence in loyalty in his polity.[9]

Mao's dislike of intellectuals deeply affected the Chinese polity. Intellectuals early on became key targets of struggle sessions. In the course of mass campaigns they were forced to engage in manual labor and in myriad other ways suffered humiliation. Their ideas often were disparaged. As early as May 1958, Mao boasted that he had far outdone the first emperor of the Qin dynasty in his policy against intellectuals: "He buried only 460 scholars alive; we have buried forty-six thousand scholars alive. . . . You [intellectuals] revile us for being Qin Shi Huangs. You are wrong. We have surpassed Qin Shi Huang a hundredfold."[10]

Mao's anti-intellectualism clashed directly with the Soviet model the Chinese imported. That model stressed full utilization of technical expertise while maintaining tight reins on the artistic and creative intelligentsia. During the First Five-Year Plan (1953–57), which was developed and implemented with substantial Soviet support, the Chinese laid stress on technical expertise in very much the Soviet manner. But in the wake of the Antirightist campaign at the end of that plan period, the virulent anti-intellectualism of the Great Leap Forward (1958–61) and murderous repression of intellectuals at the time of the Cultural Revolution (1966–76) virtually eliminated highly trained specialists from most significant decision-making outside of key military projects.

Mao's anti-intellectualism extended to his views on science. He often insisted on "scientific" inquiry, and typically proclaimed that party pronouncements had a "scientific" soundness to them, but there is little indication that he understood the critical inquiry that is central to the scientific method. Mao viewed science as selective empiricism; that is, he believed strongly in trying an idea out in one or a few cases and in summing up the results of those efforts. He regarded that summation and the lessons drawn as "scientific" because they had been "tested" in "practice." This, Mao thought, was preferable to the science espoused by intellectuals, which he believed derived from intellectual gymnastics. Use of the scientific method to constantly question the validity of earlier findings was totally alien to Mao's idea of science. To him, "science" confirmed rather than questioned; he felt most intellectuals used methods that failed to establish "scientific" validity, and he allowed no one to challenge this notion.

In his anti-intellectualism Mao found himself in tune with the party's large peasant cadre. To many of these peasants, intellectuals represented the elitist, urban-based culture against which they had fought the revolution. They were not about to allow these same urban elites to steal the fruits of victory by claiming that the country could develop rapidly only with intellectuals in positions of power and prominence. United-front rhetoric often proclaimed the communists' commitment to good relations with the intellectuals under the slogan, first articulated in 1956 and made the basis for a 1957 political campaign, of "letting a hundred flowers bloom and a hundred schools of thought contend." Nevertheless, intellectuals were despised by both Mao and the peasant ranks of the CCP, and were made to suffer a great deal of hardship as a result.

Repression of intellectuals cost the country dearly in developmental progress. All governments make mistakes in public policy, but few suffer missteps of the magnitude that afflicted China due to its repression of intellectuals. The consequent economic losses and human tragedies assumed a scale that is difficult to comprehend. These disasters stemmed directly from the influence of Mao Zedong Thought.

CONTRADICTIONS AND THE UNITED FRONT

Mao viewed the world as a complex of forces in tension and conflict, with some conflicts being more important than others. An effective leader understood the conflicts underlying events—"contradictions" in Maoist terminology—and adopted a strategy to play off of these. Identifying and addressing the essential conflict at hand was critical to development of an effective strategy.

Mao repeatedly asserted that all efforts should be devoted to identifying and resolving the major contradiction of an existing situation on terms favorable to the communist cause. As soon as that contradiction had been resolved, attention should be turned to identifying the new conflict that was core to the new alignment of forces. Addressing each major contradiction, Mao mobilized all the forces he could muster. Secondary contradictions, he felt, deserve analysis and some attention, but the key always lay in understanding and dealing effectively with the major contradiction.

It was this viewpoint, along with Soviet advice, that led Mao at the time of the Xi'an incident in 1936 to adopt the surprising policy of sparing Chiang

Kai-shek's life and allying with the Guomindang to fight the Japanese. The GMD had been responsible for untold suffering to the communist cause as a whole, and Mao had lost his second wife to a Guomindang executioner. He certainly had more than ample reason to distrust Chiang personally. Yet, at the end of 1936 both he and Moscow saw the contradiction between Japanese imperialism and China's interests as more important than that between the CCP and the GMD. He therefore subordinated the latter to the former. With the defeat of Japan in 1945, the underlying CCP/GMD contradiction again became primary, and Mao shifted tactics accordingly, this time against Moscow's desires.

Viewing politics and life as a perpetual series of struggles, Mao always focused on what divided people and groups from each other so that he could play off those divisions to achieve his ends. He saw the world as one of endless change, in which he could never rest on his laurels. Mao's notion of conflict and struggle, fundamentally at odds with China's Confucian heritage, in fact pervaded every aspect of his political and social thinking. Mao could never be satisfied with the status quo—in this sense, he was a true revolutionary.

The theory of contradictions led Mao to develop a mature set of strategies for marshaling forces to prevail in key conflicts. These strategies were collectively known as united-front work, and in post-1949 China the CCP actually set up a United Front Work Department under the Communist party's Central Committee. The basic idea was a simple one: the communists, themselves always a minority of the population, would have to gain support of many noncommunists to achieve their goals. Having analyzed the key contradiction and the secondary contradictions, therefore, the communists would have to devise a program that the vast majority of people could support to move things toward the desired outcome. This required understanding the attitudes of broad target groups, which in turn depended on the mass line. It also demanded that the CCP cloak its real objectives behind rhetoric designed to win the active support of people outside the movement.[11]

For example, when the Japanese threat posed the key challenge, the CCP, as noted previously, adopted united-front policies that stressed anti-Japanese nationalism and provided for inclusion even of landlords so long as they acted in a patriotic fashion.[12] After the Japanese surrender and the emergence of the GMD/CCP conflict as the key contradiction, the communists launched a land-reform campaign that targeted all landlords as class enemies and dealt brutally with them.[13] While Westerners might view this change as inconsistent and cynical, Mao and his colleagues would view it as natural and necessary. Policy and political commitments were always contingent on the identity of the key contradiction the movement faced.

At all times, therefore, the CCP has pursued a united-front strategy, though the partners in that cooperation and the issues that sustain it have changed greatly over the years. There was a strong philosophical basis in Mao Zedong Thought for this flexibility, but over decades of CCP rule it produced bitterness and cynicism among many in China who found themselves at some point suddenly outside the united front and a target of its often brutal tactics.

CLASSES AND CLASS STRUGGLE

Mao Zedong's notion of contradictions drew partly from Marxist dialectics but also from traditional Chinese philosophy. His ideas concerning classes seem to have originated more clearly in his exposure to Marxism-Leninism, although here too he gave the concept a distinctive Chinese twist.

Marx wrote that society could be analyzed according to the way various groups, or "classes," fit into the production process, given the dominant mode of production (such as feudalism or capitalism) of the period. The motive forces for historical development were the clashes among the major classes brought on by contradictions in the production process. Lenin added a practical political dimension to the Marxist doctrine of class conflict primarily by developing the proletarian party into a disciplined tool for revolutionary struggle.

It is hard to imagine a society less subject to class analysis than was China of the 1910s and 1920s. Capitalism had barely penetrated the country, and feudalism in its traditional European form had long since ceased to exist. Among the key players were regional warlords who had no place in the Marxist analytical scheme. Even Chiang Kai-shek seems to have acted primarily for himself and the GMD rather than in the interests of any of the classes in China at the time.[14] Members of China's urban proletariat were, in most cases, the first generation off the farm and retained strong personal ties to the countryside. In the rural villages, strong ties of kinship cut across supposed class divisions, and clan associations managed the village rituals. With the Chinese understanding of social relationships stressing hierarchical webs of personal ties, class definitions based on relations to the means of production must have struck many Chinese as extraordinarily artificial.

But Marxism-Leninism did make sense to some intellectuals because it provided an explanation for imperialist aggression, and it also explained in "scientific" fashion how China could weaken the imperialist system and become a leading country in the international arena. The prescribed means was struggle, which fit well with Mao's predispositions based on a class analysis of history and China's predicament.

Mao initially embraced class analysis based on people's relations to the means of production; in the countryside the basic productive resource was land. In the urban areas, he not only made a traditional class analysis (identifying, for example, the proletarians and the bourgeoisie), but he also divided the bourgeoisie into those whose interests were harmed by imperialism (the national bourgeoisie) and those whose relationship to imperialism was either more ambivalent (the petit bourgeoisie) or totally supportive (the comprador bourgeoisie).

Some less orthodox aspects of Mao's class analysis in this early period may have been affected by a peculiarity of the Chinese translation for the term "proletariat." While Marx's original use of that term had a distinctly urban meaning, the Chinese translation, *wuchan jieji*, means "the class without property." This difference may have made it easier for Mao to consider himself an orthodox communist in the 1920s while still touting the superior revolutionary virtue of poor peasants—that is, of the rural "class without property."

While translation problems conceivably facilitated Mao's unorthodox interpretations of Marxist class concepts in his early years, by the late 1950s he was using the notion of class analysis in ways that bore little resemblance to the initial Marxist conceptions. The results left a deep imprint on the politics and society of the PRC.

From 1950 to 1952, the period immediately after their victory over the GMD, the communists undertook a series of mass political campaigns (Land Reform, Suppression of Counterrevolutionaries, Thought Reform of Intellectuals, Three Anti Five Anti) in which they determined the class status of each urban and rural inhabitant. These campaigns were the prelude to the collectivization of agriculture and state takeover of the urban economy, both of which were complete by 1956. With private property eliminated, the issue of class identity became potentially murky and confused.

Mao addressed this problem in an un-Marxist fashion. He decided that political attitude (rather than relations to the means of production) could determine class status. For example, during the Antirightist campaign in 1957 he labeled hundreds of thousands of intellectuals as "rightists" based on their behavior during the Hundred Flowers campaign, a label that they retained in most cases until 1979. Mao also held that if political attitude did not change it, class status would be hereditary. Most Chinese who were too young to have received a class status in the early 1950s would inherit their status from their parents, and it would be passed on generation to generation, regardless of wealth or positions. This approach created permanent pariah groups—those people who had received a bad class status (landlord, rich peasant, capitalist, and so on) in the early 1950s, and their descendants.

In addition, the targets of major political campaigns received negative political labels that acquired the quality and hereditary nature of class status. Those targeted during the campaign to suppress counterrevolutionaries in 1951, for example, were thereafter labeled as counterrevolutionaries, which damned both them and their offspring from that point on.

Even though "class" almost completely lost its Marxist meaning in CCP usage, the ideas of class and class struggle remained central to Mao Zedong Thought and the politics of the PRC. In his unique fashion, Mao always viewed enemies and friends in class terms, and he saw society as the battleground for unceasing class struggle. At times when that underlying conflict was not terribly obvious to his colleagues, Mao admonished them, "Never forget class struggle."

Class analysis formed the basis of Mao's theory of struggle, contradictions, the united front, and even mass political campaigns. One result of Mao's ideas on class was the emergence in the PRC of a society based on castes—that is, social orders with permanent, hereditary status that sharply contoured one's life experiences and prospects. Few Chinese considered allowing their children to marry someone of bad class background, since that person was always vulnerable to political attack and personal destruction. The bad classes became permanent enemies in a society that defined progress as requiring unremitting struggle against adversaries. A large portion of the country's creative intellectuals, capable businessmen, and efficient farmers, moreover, fell into this miasma of permanent class oppression. Eventually, class struggle even consumed the political elite, as Mao during the Cultural Revolution turned on many of his party colleagues and branded them as "representatives of the capitalist class."

SELF-RELIANCE

Self-reliance *(zili gengsheng)*, another major theme in Mao Zedong Thought, did not mean that the CCP or the PRC should rely only on their own efforts. Rather, the basic thrust of self-reliance is more accurately captured in another of Mao's admonitions—that one should "keep the initiative in one's own hands."

Mao applied the concept of self-reliance to China as a whole except for the period of maximum Chinese dependence on the USSR, from 1949 until the Great Leap Forward beginning in 1958. China gained enormous benefits from its close relationship with the Soviet Union before 1958. But the increasingly bitter Sino-Soviet estrangement after that year led to a sudden withdrawal of Soviet aid in the summer of 1960. This Soviet turnabout contributed significantly to the dire economic consequences of the Great Leap Forward.

In reaction against what he considered Soviet perfidy and the costs it imposed on China, Mao insisted that in the future China follow a strategy of national self-reliance. In its subsequent foreign policy dealings, the PRC under Mao went to significant trouble to minimize its dependence on any single foreign country. The PRC, for example, obtained supplies of a given commodity from multiple sources whenever possible, even when this raised prices and greatly complicated internal logistics.

In the domestic economy, Mao also viewed self-reliance as a virtue outside of the core economic sectors, such as mining, metallurgy, and railways, where the state exercised tight administrative control through national planning. Especially after 1958, Mao encouraged each section of the country to become self-reliant, and he strengthened government policies in support of this goal in subsequent years. This not only required that each part of the country develop an appropriate array of small-scale industries; it also demanded that every part of China try to grow enough grain to be self-supportive. Given China's varied topography and climatic conditions, this latter policy imposed enormous costs by requiring grain production in areas totally unsuited for it.

Mao's commitment to self-reliance was in part ideological, growing out of his success with this policy during the Yan'an era. In his mind, self-reliance was bound together with such other desirable goals as simple and frugal living, struggling to overcome objective difficulties, gaining confidence through determined efforts, and group effort through common commitment.

Practical and strategic considerations also played into Mao's concern with self-reliance. He felt, for example, that China could best withstand an attack from either the United States or the Soviet Union by retreating into the interior and then wearing down the enemy by launching attacks from secure base areas. This would require that interior areas be able to support both themselves and a war effort without close ties to the coast or to foreign trade. In addition, China's continental size, combined with its poor transportation facilities, weighed against extensive trade macroregions, making some effort to promote the self-reliance of various areas a necessity.

The notion of self-reliance, therefore, had both normative and practical components. Some analysts have mistakenly construed this term to mean "total independence." The real test of self-reliance, however, was whether a community could sustain itself even in adverse circumstances. The ability to "keep the initiative in your own hands" proved to be a major force in Mao's thinking, and over the years many policies in both domestic and foreign affairs bore the imprint of the high value he attached to *zili gengsheng*.

The Governing System

Mao's ideas took effect by means of a massive political administrative apparatus set up after 1949 to govern the country. Here we will merely introduce the names and basic organization of this administrative system. Chapters 6 and 7 provide far greater detail on these structures and their development over time.[15]

The formal Maoist administrative system borrowed heavily from that of the Soviet Union, although it also drew inspiration from China's imperial past, the GMD, and the base area experiences. China's formal alliance with the Soviet Union was forced by the Cold War tensions of 1949, which allowed no room for a neutral stance between the two postwar superpowers; in addition, China's ideological perspective was naturally more sympathetic to that of the Soviets. The Soviet Union had devised the means to use state controls to rapidly produce an industrial base, and the Chinese were anxious to learn how to do this themselves. Stalin, for his part, strongly urged his allies to follow the Soviet model of rule as closely as possible.

Like the Soviets, the Chinese set up parallel national party and government (or state) administrative apparatuses. Thus, at each level of the political system in China—the Center (Beijing), the province, the prefecture, the city, the county, and the locale (township or commune)—there is a full array of party and state organs, with the party in addition having committees, branches, and cells embedded within the state organs. In principle, the party is to make policy and the state is to administer it, but, as we shall see, reality has not been that neat.

With their deep attachments to the military, in which they had all spent decades of their lives before 1949, the CCP leaders set up the military as a third nationwide bureaucracy. On the eve of their victory in 1949, the CCP had pulled all its scattered military forces together and organized them into the People's Liberation Army (PLA), encompassing the army, navy, and air force. The military hierarchy does not completely parallel its civilian counterparts, although the three intersect at key points: most military districts, for example, are coterminous with provinces. To China's top leaders, the PLA has been a major instrument for achieving both international security and domestic policy goals.

The PLA is thus a core component of the Chinese communist system. It has been, moreover, purposely kept beyond the government's jurisdiction. The PLA is assigned a bureaucratic rank equal to that of the State Council, the government's highest level of authority. This means that the government cannot issue binding orders to the military. Rather, the military answers directly to a party body called the Military Affairs Commission, which Mao Zedong personally chaired until his death in 1976 (though it is the vice chairman of the commission who is in charge on a day-to-day basis). This unusual arrangement reflects the fact that the military's first job is to protect the party rather than the government. The party, whose task it is to push the revolution forward, can utilize the military just as for other purposes it might utilize the government apparatus.

China's military operates as a state within the state. At all times in Maoist China, a large percentage of the party's central leadership were military officers. There were complex and subtle connections among the government, party, and military at various levels of the system. Strong personal and career ties bound the military leaders to civilian officials who had previously served with them in communist army units before 1949. In many cases, groups of individuals had fought side by side for one or two decades, and these bonds became an important thread in the tapestry of post-1949 politics. At the end of the civil war these groups controlled various parts of the country, which added a territorial dimension to the situation.

The Chinese communists designed their system with several major features: to be centralized enough to give the top leaders in Beijing the leverage to determine the national domestic agenda; to promote and manage rapid industrial development, in part by obtaining resources from the rural sector; and to bring about guided social change.

At each administrative level (Center, province, and so on) a small party committee exercises ultimate power. At the Center, this body, typically having fourteen to twenty-four members, is called the Politburo, and it has a staff under it called the Secretariat. Mao Zedong served as chairman of the Chinese Communist party, and by virtue of this position he headed the Politburo. The Standing Committee of the Politburo, usually consisting of five or six people, contains the most powerful leaders in the country. Generally, each person in the Politburo also holds at least one other substantive position and has special responsibility in one or another field such as propaganda and education or finance and economics.

The Communist party also established a Central Committee, which had nearly 100 members until 1966, closer to 200 members through the 1970s, and nearly 300 members in the 1980s and 1990s. During the Maoist era, this body held little real power. Membership included those holding some other position of great importance—the head of a province, for example—and those serving some representative function, such as being a model peasant or model worker. Full meetings of the Central Committee are called plenums and are numbered sequentially following each Party Congress, the party organ charged with, among other things, formally electing the Central Committee membership (in reality, these elections are mere ratifications of decisions already made by the Politburo). The Party Congress, which has had as many as fifteen hundred delegates, convenes infrequently; in the Maoist era there were Congresses in 1956, 1969, and 1973 (respectively, the Eighth, Ninth, and Tenth Congresses in the history of the CCP). A Central Committee plenum might, therefore, be called the "tenth plenum of the Eighth Central Committee," meaning the tenth time the Central Committee selected by the Eighth Party Congress convened (see Table 3.2).

While the Central Committee as a body has no real power, there are party departments, called Central Committee departments, that exercise a great deal of power. These have various responsibilities, and include the Rural Work Department, Propaganda Department, and Organization Department (in charge of staff appointments), among others.

The top government body is the State Council, established in 1954 to replace the transitional Government Administrative Council, which had existed since 1949. The State Council is headed by the premier (in the Maoist era, this was Zhou Enlai); there are a number of vice premiers with specific fields of responsibility. The State Council includes commissions and ministries. Commissions generally take charge of major issues that concern a number of ministries. These commissions have included, for example, the State Planning Commission, in charge of long-term and annual plans, and the State Economic Commission, in charge of resolving interministerial problems that cropped up in plan implementation.

A large portion of the ministries work primarily on developing and running the urban economy, while the rural sector has tended to be run more directly by the party bureaucracy. For example, separate ministries have had charge of the metallurgical industry, the electronics industry, the transportation industry, and water resources (primarily, flood-control and irrigation projects). Over the years, the ministries have been merged and split apart by dozens of organizational changes meant to improve effectiveness as the economy and problems of administration changed, and the total number of ministries has ranged from several dozen to more than sixty.

This basic organizational structure, on both the party and the government sides, is largely duplicated at every level of the national administrative system. The terminology changes somewhat as one goes down the administrative hierarchy, but the overall organizational chart of each territorial layer remains quite similar. The leading party bodies below the Center are called committees—the Politburo at the Center becomes the Provincial Party Committee in the province, followed by the County Party Committee, and so forth. The government bodies are called, simply, governments (provincial government, county government, etc.). The party penetrates the government at every level through a variety of means, including having party bodies (committees, branches, cells) in every government organ.

In addition, virtually every ministry, commission, and Central Committee

TABLE 3.2 *Chinese Communist Party Congresses and Central Committee Plenums, 1949–94*

DATE	EVENT
5–13 Mar. 1949	2nd plenum of 7th CC CCP
6–10 June 1950	3rd (enlarged) plenum of 7th CC CCP
6–10 Feb. 1954	4th (enlarged) plenum of 7th CC CCP
4 Apr. 1955	5th plenum of 7th CC CCP
4–11 Oct. 1955	6th (enlarged) plenum of 7th CC CCP
22 Aug., 8 and 13 Sept. 1956	7th plenum of 7th CC CCP
15–27 Sept. 1956	*8th Nat'l. Congress of the CCP*
28 Sept. 1956	1st plenum of 8th CC CCP
10–15 Nov. 1956	2nd plenum of 8th CC CCP
20 Sept.–9 Oct. 1957	3rd (enlarged) plenum of 8th CC CCP
3 May 1958	4th plenum of 8th CC CCP
5–23 May 1958	*2nd session, 8th Nat'l. Congress of the CCP*
25 May 1958	5th plenum of 8th CC CCP
28 Nov.–10 Dec. 1958	6th (enlarged) plenum of 8th CC CCP
2–5 Apr. 1959	7th (enlarged) plenum of 8th CC CCP
2–16 Aug. 1959	8th (enlarged) plenum of 8th CC CCP
14–18 Jan. 1961	9th (enlarged) plenum of 8th CC CCP
24–27 Sept. 1962	10th (enlarged) plenum of 8th CC CCP
1–12 Aug. 1966	11th (enlarged) plenum of 8th CC CCP
13–31 Oct. 1968	12th (enlarged) plenum of 8th CC CCP
1–24 Apr. 1969	*9th Nat'l. Congress of the CCP*
28 Apr. 1969	1st plenum of 9th CC CCP
23 Aug.–6 Sept. 1970	2nd plenum of 9th CC CCP
1972	3rd plenum of 9th CC CCP
24–28 Aug. 1973	*10th Nat'l. Congress of the CCP*
30 Aug. 1973	1st plenum of 10th CC CCP
8–10 Jan. 1975	2nd plenum of 10th CC CCP
16–21 July 1977	3rd plenum of 10th CC CCP
12–18 Aug. 1977	*11th Nat'l. Congress of the CCP*
19 Aug. 1977	1st plenum of 11th CC CCP
18–23 Feb. 1978	2nd plenum of 11th CC CCP
18–22 Dec. 1978	3rd plenum of 11th CC CCP
25–28 Sept. 1979	4th plenum of 11th CC CCP
23–29 Feb. 1980	5th plenum of 11th CC CCP
27–29 June 1981	6th plenum of 11th CC CCP
6 Aug. 1982	7th plenum of 11th CC CCP
1–11 Sept. 1982	*12th Nat'l. Congress of the CCP*
12–13 Sept. 1982	1st plenum of 12th CC CCP

TABLE 3.2 *(continued)*

DATE	EVENT
11–12 Oct. 1983	2nd plenum of 12th CC CCP
20 Oct. 1984	3rd plenum of 12th CC CCP
16 Sept. 1985	4th plenum of 12th CC CCP
24 Sept. 1985	5th plenum of 12th CC CCP
29 Sept. 1986	6th plenum of 12th CC CCP
25 Oct.–1 Nov. 1987	*13th Nat'l. Congress of the CCP*
2 Nov. 1987	1st plenum of 13th CC CCP
15–19 Mar. 1988	2nd plenum of 13th CC CCP
26–30 Sept. 1988	3rd plenum of 13th CC CCP
23–24 June 1989	4th plenum of 13th CC CCP
6–9 Nov. 1989	5th plenum of 13th CC CCP
9–12 Mar. 1990	6th plenum of 13th CC CCP
25–30 Dec. 1990	7th plenum of 13th CC CCP
25–29 Nov. 1991	8th plenum of 13th CC CCP
5–9 Oct. 1992	9th plenum of 13th CC CCP
12–18 Oct. 1992	*14th Nat'l. Congress of the CCP*
19 Oct. 1992	1st plenum of 14th CC CCP
5–7 Mar. 1993	2nd plenum of 14th CC CCP
11–14 Nov. 1993	3rd plenum of 14th CC CCP

department heads its own national bureaucratic hierarchy that extends from Beijing down through the provinces, cities, counties, and so forth. In some instances, these individual bureaucratic empires have been highly centralized, while in other cases the lower level units are made answerable primarily to the local territorial party and government leadership. The distribution of lines of authority has changed often, and each has produced its own peculiar problems.

This complex structure reflected the communists' determination in the 1950s to control all developments in the country from above—party and government units were created to take charge of every type of activity imaginable. Copied from the Soviet system, the governing structure was designed to enable the state to channel resources directly and overwhelmingly to heavy industrial development. The State Planning Commission, along with other bodies, developed plans to be implemented by administrative means rather than the play of economic forces. This involved direct government management of the economy in all its main features and determined government actions to force resources into heavy industrial development.

This system increasingly employed both ideological indoctrination and naked force to whip the population into line. Indeed, the Maoist techniques such as political campaigns and mass struggle often obscured the distinction between indoctrination and terror. Mao excelled at creating a system in which he was able to set Chinese against Chinese to assure the security and promote the goals of the party leadership. An extensive system of forced labor camps awaited millions who fell afoul of the official line.[16]

Although this overall approach to the political organization system was established in the 1950s, the same structures have endured into the 1990s, albeit with many changes in the dynamics of their operations. While this system has afforded the political leadership unchallenged control over the society and economy, it has also produced numerous problems of governance.

First, the structure of the system itself has proved complex and unwieldy. By the mid-1950s, the governing apparatus of the PRC was probably the largest vertically integrated set of bureaucracies in the history of the world. The details of the reporting lines, moreover, gives the system the characteristics of a fragmented authoritarianism: authoritarian in the discipline demanded from subordinates and the lack of real protections for the population or opportunity for them to articulate their interests; and fragmented in that territorial and functional lines of command intersected in hopelessly complex ways.

Mao Zedong regarded this system as endlessly frustrating. In part, Mao simply found abhorrent the habit he saw in Chinese bureaucrats to put on airs, to concern themselves with privilege, and to become petty tyrants. In part, too, he chafed at the ability of the governing bureaucracies to frustrate his policies.

To overcome the natural reluctance of bureaucrats to implement revolutionary programs and to reduce the tendency toward fragmented authority, Mao made major efforts to indoctrinate officials to his own way of thinking. To him, ideology was a major means to bind this system together. In addition, although Mao refused to set up a highly centralized, bureaucratically independent terror apparatus like the one that Stalin had created in the mid 1930s, he nevertheless used powerful weapons such as "struggle" and "special case groups" reminiscent of the Yan'an-era Rectification to assure that officials would comply with his wishes.

Ultimately, though, Mao Zedong never fully resolved the tensions between his impulses toward revolutionary change and the economic need for predictability and reasonably stable administration. His frustrations over this conflict led him in his later years to take initiatives, such as launching the Great Proletarian Cultural Revolution in 1966, that severely damaged the country. Only in the post-Mao era, under Deng Xiaoping, did China finally move fully from revolutionary upheaval to straightforward governance. But even during the Deng era the tensions involved in reforming an authoritarian bureaucratic state have persisted.

4

The Maoist Era

Mao personally and Mao Zedong Thought as an ideology had such a huge impact on China after the revolution that it is appropriate to consider the period from 1949 until Mao's death on 9 September 1976 as the era of Mao Zedong. Mao's unique role in the Chinese political system meant, effectively, that his own ideas profoundly shaped the politics of the PRC.

Mao's stature by the time of victory in 1949 was without equal or challenge. He had led the party from the miserable days of the Long March retreat to victory over both Japan and the Guomindang in a period of fourteen years. Time and again, the broad strategic assessments he made had proved accurate, and his basic tactics had turned out to be effective. He had become the source of ultimate wisdom at the vortex of the greatest revolution in human history. His judgments in the years after 1949 could be discussed to the extent he permitted, but they could not be opposed successfully even by his most powerful ministers.

Mao's prestige within the movement was such in the early 1950s that one foreign scholar has conceptualized the policy-making of the period as an example of the bandwagon effect.[1] That is, other leaders would always try to sense the direction in which Mao was leaning on a particular issue so as to jump on the Maoist bandwagon at the earliest moment possible. The few instances of serious policy disagreements and purges resulted, it appears, from one or another player either misreading Mao's intentions or being purposely misled by the Chairman.[2]

Even Mao's key political position—that of chairman of the CCP—was unique. No other ruling communist party had a chairman above the general secretary (i.e., the chief administrative officer) of the party. In China, the chairman's role was not defined. He was the person to keep the party on the right track and to make broad strategic judgments. As with the emperor in the imperial state, no legal or administrative boundaries limited the power and responsibility of this position. In addition to holding this crucial post, Mao also assumed the leadership of the military (by heading the CCP's Military Affairs Commission) and the symbolic leadership of the state (as president of the PRC until he resigned from this government post in 1959).

Mao used his power to find a path to rapid industrial development, but did so in a fashion that produced massive human tragedies and diminishing returns on the investment he squeezed from the Chinese populace. He modeled the Chinese system on Soviet practice because Stalin had achieved rapid growth of heavy industry in a poor, basically rural country. He then launched the country into first the Great Leap Forward, starting in 1958, and then the Great Proletarian Cultural Revolution, beginning in 1966. These were frenzied, indeed utopian, efforts at economic, social, and political transformation that were entirely delusional and left millions of dead in their wakes.

Mao could stray so far from reality in part because his power drew deeply from the widely accepted tradition of relying on a good leader to produce results, rather than monitoring performance, restricting prerogatives, and limiting tenure. Revolutions in any case tend to put forward charismatic leaders whose power cannot be reined in. Mao Zedong's success before 1949 had been built on his ability to investigate possibilities, consult widely, understand the real prospects that confronted the communists, and act accordingly. Ironically and tragically, he changed fundamentally on all these counts during his twenty-seven years as China's supreme leader. While still espousing the idea that "without investigation, one has no right to speak," he in fact increasingly succumbed to hubris, which allowed him to act in almost total disregard of actual conditions in the country.

In practical terms, Mao used many techniques to assure his dominance of policy-making at the Center. For example, at the major annual communist conclaves called central work conferences, which lasted weeks or even months at a time,[3] Mao reserved the right to sum up the discussions at the end of each meeting. His summation—which at times departed significantly from the thrust of the sessions themselves—became the formal set of conclusions drawn from the conclave. In similar fashion, he issued a directive in March

1953 to the effect that no document issued in the name of the Central Committee of the Communist party could be valid unless he personally had read and approved it first.[4] And in the 1960s he encouraged the development of a cult of personality that made him into a godlike figure.

Naturally, no single individual could monitor closely and make, rather than ratify, decisions on all issues confronting China. Mao did intervene virtually across the board at one time or another on China's national agenda. But he felt himself particularly qualified to make judgments in three issue areas, in each of which his impact was constant and decisive. These were relations with the United States and the Soviet Union, policies to promote the revolution in China (which in turn, of course, connected to many issue areas from culture to economics), and agricultural policy. The arena in which Mao felt least comfortable and that he he understood the least was urban economics, and this policy arena would frustrate him throughout his career.

Wielding Power, 1949–76

China's development under Mao Zedong's leadership was spasmodic, a pattern of lurching from politically induced crisis to crisis. This was not, in short, an ordinary political system seeking to nurture steady development and gradual improvement in the lives of its citizens. It was an extraordinary system of both tremendous strength and startling instability, determined to bring about rapid industrial development, and equally committed to fundamental social change.

The political leadership from 1949 to 1976 made major changes in its strategies every five to ten years, with often startling consequences for the Chinese population. Each strategy, in turn, utilized substantially new tactics to deal with the problems engendered by the previous strategy. Each, therefore, retarded China's progress toward developing stable political processes and governing institutions. This section provides a brief overview of each of the major strategies adopted, the concerns that prompted their adoption, and the results produced.

Any periodization of a span of years is inevitably artificial. Key developments in the economy or in the military, for example, may not coincide with those in elite politics or other spheres. But in China's Maoist years, sharp changes in strategy were sufficiently wide ranging—affecting, for example, economics, military policy, foreign affairs, cultural matters, and social affairs simultaneously—that periodization of this era is remarkably straightforward. The following basic divisions emerge: 1949–56, economic and political recovery and basic socialist transformation; 1956–57, contradictions and rethinking the Soviet model; 1958–61, Great Leap Forward; 1962–65, recovery and growing elite divisions; 1966–69, Red Guard phase of the Cultural Revolution; 1970–76, final phases of the Cultural Revolution and the struggle for succession.

FROM VICTORY, THROUGH RECOVERY, TO SOCIALIST TRANSFORMATION: 1949–56

Mao Zedong declared in March 1949 at the second plenum of the Seventh Central Committee that, looking at the prospect of nationwide victory, "We have taken only the first step in a march of ten thousand *li*."⁵ This was a remarkable statement from the leader of the revolutionary movement, who had already fought for almost three decades across the length and breadth of the country. But it was also a prescient one.

Mao recognized that the CCP had garnered extraordinary experience and skills in rural revolution but that the party's and the revolution's future would be determined by its ability to govern urban China. The cities, though, posed enormous new challenges to the revolutionary movement, which was supported for the most part by peasants, generally illiterate and unfamiliar with urban ways and amenities, who viewed the cities as seats of reaction, the bases of Western imperialism, the Guomindang, and the Japanese.

Thus, China could be captured from the countryside but it could be governed only from the cities, which meant that the experience garnered in previous decades would no longer suffice. The highly decentralized, militarized nature of the communist movement was inappropriate to the task of running the major urban centers and the national economy.

For the CCP as for all revolutionary movements, therefore, victory was a crisis. It shifted the party's tasks from familiar ones to alien ones. The communists had to switch from a strategy of attacking those in power to one of exercising power itself. As the CCP became the "establishment," it faced a host of new and difficult issues.

The Setting

On 1 October 1949, Mao Zedong stood atop the Tiananmen, "Gate of Heavenly Peace," at the entry to the centuries-old Forbidden City and proclaimed the formation of the People's Republic of China. Joined with Mao on top of the Tiananmen rostrum were the other top leaders of the Chinese Communist party, such as Zhu De, Zhou Enlai, and Liu Shaoqi, along with many prominent noncommunist personages lending their support and prestige to the new national government. Mao, who spoke with a heavy central-Chinese Hunan accent, gave a speech that is best remembered for its keynote line. "The Chinese people," Mao proclaimed, "have stood up." Never again, he promised, would foreigners trample on China.

After more than a century of humiliation following the Opium War, and some thirty-seven years after the collapse of the imperial system, the Chinese people were ready to embrace a movement that could bring strong government, national unity, and real independence. Many worried about the communists' programs, and far larger numbers were simply ignorant of them. But most were willing to see whether the CCP could fulfill the promise implicit in Mao's confident assertion that "The Chinese people have stood up." They would sacrifice greatly to make this promise come true, and they would forgive a great deal in the name of creating a strong nation. In the hope all Chinese held for their future, the Chinese communists enjoyed an enormous reservoir of support. The strong governing apparatus they established, in short, faced a pliant society.

But the situation they faced was grim. Urban China's economy was in a shambles. World War II and the civil war had destroyed large parts of the industrial plant and had severely disrupted normal domestic trade patterns. The hyperinflation of the late 1940s had demoralized the population and rendered business virtually impossible. The cities were cut off from their rural markets, and much interurban transportation had been disrupted.[6] The situation was so bad in many cities that, according to a *New York Times* report from Tianjin, local capitalists looked forward to the communist takeover as likely to be good for business.

The urban and rural populations alike were war-weary. After decades of warlordism, resistance to the Japanese occupation, and finally civil war, the populace craved peace and stability. The civil war had, in addition, left millions of men under arms in the GMD and CCP armies, and most longed to return to their farms to begin having families and enjoying the fruits of economic recovery.

Indeed, China's modern history had been so tortured that the CCP "inherited" a society deeply riven in several directions. The Japanese occupation had produced many collaborators who now feared retribution. The rampant corruption of the late 1940s had ruined the lives of many while enriching others. The decades of military conflict on Chinese soil had at one time or another pitted millions of Chinese against each other in deadly combat. Various regions of the country had lived under different political and social systems for much of the previous twenty years. It would take great skill and a very strong hand to pull together this fractious situation and start the country on a clear path to recovery.

The CCP thus faced serious challenges during the initial years after 1949. It had to create political institutions, bring about economic recovery and growth, initiate revolutionary social changes, and establish a secure position in the international arena. Among these, economic recovery assumed initial priority. Nothing could buy the communists support of the urban populace more rapidly than taming inflation and getting the economy going again. The situation placed so many demands on the leaders that in the early years there was a whirlwind of activity in many spheres. The new regime responded to its many challenges with a remarkably strong start.

Gaining Momentum

The Communist leadership moved quickly to organize the population and mobilize especially China's youth to create a sense of a positive new era. In the early years the leaders had four broad substantive priorities: to cement the terms of their relationship with the USSR; to establish a governing apparatus that could rule urban China and unite the country; to restore the urban economy; and to consolidate control over the countryside while paying off a historical debt to the peasantry by instituting land reform on a nationwide basis. Given the pressures from all sides, they had to move simultaneously in all these areas.

The link-up with the USSR was of fundamental importance. China in 1949 faced a bipolar world in which the Cold War had already taken shape. Neither the United States nor the Soviet Union recognized the possibility of neutrality in this international system. Forced to choose sides, China chose alliance with the Soviet Union, and within two months of founding the PRC Mao left China for the first time. His destination was Moscow, where he stayed for nearly three months to hammer out the Sino-Soviet relationship.[7]

The historical record hints that at least some CCP leaders toyed with the possibility of an American option as late as the spring of 1949. But these hints, although tantalizing, are thin, and the political situation in the United States, which was then moving into anticommunist excesses of the McCarthy era, was not conducive to the type of subtle, flexible diplomacy required to develop a healthy relationship with the deeply suspicious leaders in Beijing. In Washington, in any case, the political realities of 1949 demanded continued support for Chiang Kai-shek's forces, which had retreated to Taiwan, until such time, presumably in 1950, when the People's Liberation Army overran Taiwan and brought the Chinese civil war to its conclusion.[8]

The Soviets negotiated hard with the Chinese. They promised a modest amount of financial aid. More important, they dispatched many advisors and, ultimately, numerous blueprints and documents that permitted China to benefit from engineering and technological advances the Soviets had made. They also advised China on governing structures and on techniques the state could use to industrialize rapidly under a planned economy. And Moscow formally entered into an alliance with China that would lend military support should China suffer an attack. But the Soviets also demanded special access to several territories and ports in China, and the right to establish several companies with the Chinese to exploit mineral resources in the PRC. China, in addition, had to toe the Soviet line in all important international matters.

All indications suggest that Mao sincerely wanted all the Soviet advice he could obtain and that he took this advice seriously. Mao had largely made his career in the CCP before 1949 by arguing successfully for a distinctive Chinese road to power. But once he had won nationwide victory, he saw Stalin and his colleagues as the only people who understood how to build a socialist system that worked.

While the Soviet tie put the Chinese communists at odds with the United States, the outbreak of the Korean War with the surprise North Korean attack on the South on 25 June 1950 led to events that made Washington and Beijing implacable enemies.[9] America responded to the North Korean aggression by, among other things, assigning the U.S. Navy's Seventh Fleet to prevent the PLA from crossing the 100-mile-wide Taiwan Strait to finish off the Nationalist remnants on Taiwan. This action signaled Washington's view that the North Korean incursion was part of a Soviet-coordinated series of thrusts to expand communist power. But the result was to place the United States in the middle of the Chinese civil war, a position from which it has never fully extricated itself.

The Chinese early on became worried about a US threat to the security of the northeast, and these fears worsened as the United Nations forces, largely composed of American troops sent to aid South Korea, proved very effective in rolling back North Korean forces in the fall of 1950. American commander General Douglas MacArthur heightened Beijing's anxieties with unauthorized remarks suggesting that UN forces might keep on moving into China to undo the results of the Chinese revolution. As a consequence, Mao Zedong overcame the deep-seated reluctance of almost all other Chinese leaders and dispatched troops into Korea in October, calling them Chinese People's Volunteers to make them seem less official.[10]

From late 1950 until an armistice in mid-1953, Chinese and American forces confronted each other on the Korean peninsula in a bloody conflict that left extremely bitter feelings on both sides. One American reaction to this was to tighten an economic noose around China, cutting off the PRC to the maximum extent possible from trade with the West. This not only set back Chinese economic development but also forced the PRC to lean even more strongly in the direction of the Soviet bloc. In addition, the United States formally recognized the Nationalist government on Taiwan as the sole legal government of all of China, thus blocking the PRC's entry into all noncommunist international organizations including the United Nations and the World Bank. These American policies remained unchanged until the early 1970s.

The CCP acted very quickly in the cities it captured in 1949–50 to bring down inflation and get the urban economy moving forward. The new governing authorities confiscated the enterprises that had been run by the Guomindang and worked to put them back on sound footing. They also generally promoted a probusiness climate to rehabilitate the urban economy and used their influence on the workers to assure labor discipline. They used strong-arm tactics to force hoarders to yield up their hidden stocks of goods, and then dumped these goods on the market when necessary to bring down prices. They held meetings with leading businessmen to assure them of the CCP's understanding and support. And they converted the GMD's virtually worthless dollars into the new "people's currency" (*renminbi*) and then in 1950 used stringent budget and tax measures to withdraw large amounts of currency from circulation.[11]

The net result of these measures was that by the end of 1950 the CCP had broken the back of the inflationary spiral that had left urban-dwellers disoriented and demoralized. The economy would have picked up somewhat in any case simply by the cessation of the civil war and the reestablishment of traditional urban-rural and interurban trade routes. But these concerted measures, developed primarily by Chen Yun and Zhou Enlai, proved a boon to the economy and earned the CCP a reputation as an effective, activist leadership with strong reformist policies. The related sharp decline in corruption as the GMD officials fled and the PLA soldiers took over added to the initial favorable impression.

Against this background, the ability of the Chinese People's Volunteers to fight the US-backed United Nations troops to a standstill in Korea added enormously to the CCP's prestige. This marked the first time in more than a century that Chinese troops had faced those of Western countries and not suffered humiliating defeat. Even though many Chinese were uneasy about the CCP's long-term goals and about the Sino-Soviet alliance, feelings of pride and hope—sentiments long absent from the Chinese scene—by all accounts surged through substantial portions of the urban population by 1951.

Mao and his colleagues had, of course, more than reform on their minds. In mid-1950 they started a drumbeat of mass political campaigns, each targeting a segment of the population, that shortly would change substantially the social, economic, and political lives of China's peasants and urban residents. These campaigns included Land Reform (starting in June 1950); Suppression of Counterrevolutionaries (spring 1951); Three Anti Five Anti (winter 1951–52); Thought Reform of Intellectuals (winter and spring of 1951–52); Agricultural Cooperativization (late 1955–56); and Socialist Transformation of Industry and Commerce (late 1955–56). The first of these paid off the peasants and established a communist power structure in the countryside; the next three softened up urban society; and the final two established a socialist urban and rural economy.

As discussed in Chapter 2, the CCP had experimented with land reform at various times since the Jiangxi Soviet period. Indeed, by the time of the communist victory in 1949 large areas of north and northeast China had already gone through this process. In June 1950 Liu Shaoqi announced adoption of a land-reform law for the rest of the country. This new law aimed to classify all peasants into one or another class and to knock the landlords out of the system. In this way the party would simultaneously replace the old rural elites with a communist power structure in the countryside and settle a profound debt incurred to the peasants during the years of rural-based guerrilla warfare.

The Land Reform campaign of 1950–52 involved some of China's city-dwellers as well as its peasants. The CCP formed land-reform teams of urban youths to go to the countryside to carry out the transformation there, which was often violent. Although figures vary, it appears that at least eight hundred thousand landlords were killed during this period.[12] This direct violence against leading members of village society changed the nature of village social relationships.[13] Even decades later, many peasants in interviews recalled vividly the deep impression this violence had made on them. The resulting land redistribution sought to preserve a rich peasant economy so that agricultural production would not drop (see Table 4.1). Removing the landlords as a class vastly enhanced the CCP's own access to the villages. The related process of classifying each peasant into rich, middle, and poor peasants and agricultural laborers also laid the groundwork for later campaigns to collectivize agriculture.[14]

With land reform remaking rural China, in early spring 1951 the CCP turned its attention to the cities. It launched a Suppression of Counterrevolutionaries campaign that targeted two urban groups: some civil-servant holdovers from the GMD regime (the CCP had kept on many of the former civil servants, especially those in the police forces), and the secret societies that operated in many urban areas. These secret societies were gangs that had

TABLE 4.1 *Regional Landholdings before and after Land Reform*

	BEFORE LAND REFORM			AFTER LAND REFORM				
	CENTRAL-SOUTH	SOUTHWEST	OTHER	CENTRAL-SOUTH	SOUTHWEST	EAST	NORTHWEST	NORTH
Landlords								
Population*	4.20	7.40	7.40	4.30	4.60	4.20	7.40	0.20
Land†	41.40	38.40	29.30	4.30	4.40	3.40	5.60	0.20
Index‡	9.81	5.19	3.96	0.99	0.97	0.82	0.75	1.15
Rich peasants								
Population*	5.00	7.30	3.00	4.80	6.90	4.80	6.60	1.30
Land†	12.10	14.30	6.40	7.00	8.10	8.00	10.10	1.00
Index‡	2.42	1.96	2.13	1.47	1.17	1.67	1.53	0.79
Middle peasants								
Population*	26.30	44.30	38.60	22.90	30.90	40.50	50.70	90.00
Land†	24.80	30.80	42.30	26.10	31.80	44.30	59.00	90.80
Index‡	0.94	0.70	1.10	1.04	1.03	1.09	1.16	1.01
Poor peasants								
Population*	55.60	38.50	n.a.	55.00	50.60	44.60	32.80	8.50
Land†	14.00	8.60	n.a.	52.40	48.10	37.70	24.70	7.40
Index‡	0.25	0.22	n.a.	0.95	0.95	0.84	0.75	0.87
Agricultural laborers								
Population*	0.90	0.60	n.a.	5.20	5.80	3.70	4.20	none
Land†	0.00	0.10	n.a.	4.80	5.80	3.30	3.10	none
Index‡			0.35§	0.92	0.98	0.90	0.74	none

Source Before land reform: Edwin E. Moise, *Land Reform in China and North Vietnam* (Chapel Hill: University of North Carolina Press, 1983), pp. 28–29; after land reform: *ibid.,* pp. 138–39. The data are based on the averages of several surveys and thus do not add up to 100 percent.

*Percentage of total population.

†Percentage of total land.

‡Index: Per capita holdings of each class relative to the average per capita holdings of the rural population as a whole.

§Index includes landholdings of poor peasants and laborers

for years controlled much of the urban transport and intercity transport systems. The Suppression of Counterrevolutionaries campaign used brass-knuckle tactics to root out and destroy its targets. Numerous public executions marked this brief, violent initiative.

For all its drama, though, the Suppression of Counterrevolutionaries campaign seems, on the basis of later interviews, to have passed largely unnoticed outside the specific groups targeted by the effort. This campaign did not involve mass mobilization of the urban populace, and its targets were relatively small, distinct groups.[15] The same cannot be said of the Three Anti Five Anti campaign, which convulsed urban society in the winter of 1951–52 and marked a fundamental turning point in the communists' relationship with the urban populace.[16]

Three Anti Five Anti seems to have been motivated by two elements: the CCP needed additional funds to fight the Korean War and party leaders became worried about corruption seeping into party ranks in the cities. The latter was a natural phenomenon. Mao had warned the party to watch out for the "sugar-coated bullets of the bourgeoisie" in his March 1949 speech to the second plenum of the Seventh Central Committee. He knew that urban China worked primarily by cultivating personal relationships, and that exchanges of gifts and favors were of central importance to this. He also knew that most of the peasant revolutionaries as of 1949 had never been in a city or seen running water or indoor plumbing, and would be dazzled by the material wealth available to them in urban China.

By late 1951 evidence of corruption was sufficient to cause alarm. The CCP therefore launched the Three Anti campaign (against waste, corruption, and bureaucratism) against the cadres at the basic levels of its own urban organization and the Five Anti campaign (against corruption, tax evasion, stealing state property, cheating on state contracts, and stealing state economic secrets) against urban businessmen. Corruption was the issue that tied these two efforts together. The campaign utilized all the techniques developed in the Yan'an era: mass mobilization, study groups and thought reform involving criticism and self-criticism, social ostracism, vague promises of rewards to those who confessed and denounced others and punishment to those who refused to confess, and so forth.

One businessman in Tianjin described this campaign as the most traumatic experience of his life. Before this, he had welcomed the CCP as a positive reformist leadership. By 1951 he had begun to develop ties to the local revenue authorities to avoid tax payments, and had continued to keep two sets of books, as all businesses did. He also had bought and sold gold, a common practice in those days of currency uncertainty. By the end of three months of isolation in a study group during the campaign, he had become a heavy smoker (he had never previously smoked), a habit he was never able to break. He became, he said, a pliant tool in the hands of the communists, recognizing that they were determined revolutionaries and that his life would never again be the same.

During the period the businessman was in the study group, CCP officials had organized his workers into a trade union and recruited one young unskilled worker to become a party activist. After that, the businessman never again enjoyed easy relations with his workers, and everyone feared the young party activist. When the campaign ended, the businessman had to pay a substantial fine for past misbehavior, a sum he had to borrow from the government to pay to the government. His "transgressions" had previously been considered normal business practice, but during the Three Anti Five Anti campaign the CCP declared them to be crimes and applied retroactive penalties.

For the next few years he formally remained manager of this business, but he in fact took his cues from the party activist and never again sought to exercise real authority. When he was given the opportunity to sell the enterprise at a fire-sale price to the government in late 1955, he quickly seized the chance. His experiences were typical of those of China's business class.[17]

During September 1951 through the late spring of 1952, the CCP also implemented the Thought Reform of Intellectuals campaign. This effort mobilized students in universities to criticize their teachers and forced changes in university curricula away from American and European models to the Soviet system and texts. This campaign also used thought-reform techniques, and it traumatized many on the teaching staffs.[18]

The mass campaign approach then eased off for awhile after mid-1952. All sectors of society—peasants, urban cadres, business people, workers, students, and intellectuals—had experienced the traumas of mobilization techniques that purposely violated all the norms of traditional social relationships. Each campaign had forced people to challenge and denounce those to whom they owed deference according to traditional standards: peasants confronted the leading figures in their villages, students confronted their teachers, and workers confronted their firm's owners and managers. Indeed, one hallmark of the campaigns is that they pressured victims to provide information on those with whom they had the closest *guanxi,* thereby transforming the traditional social tie from a secure bond to a source of potential danger. The techniques employed had been honed during the years before 1949, especially in the 1942–44 Rectification campaign in Yan'an. Based on personal experience, by late 1952 virtually all of Chinese society could clearly distinguish between reform and revolution.

The next great effort for the party was the socialist transformation of the economy. In 1952, under Soviet tutelage, the Chinese had established a State Planning Commission, and they were fleshing out the organization of major economic ministries. The Russian advisors then worked closely with Beijing to develop the First Five-Year Plan, which would formally run from 1953 to 1957. A total of almost 150 Soviet-assisted new enterprises constituted the core of this plan. The new state structure would seek to capture resources from throughout the economy and funnel them into investment in these new key enterprises.[19]

Agricultural reform presented a difficult problem. Chinese agricultural production remained poor, and land reform had not provided the basis for major long-term improvements in productivity. In addition, the state did not have adequate means for capturing the agricultural surplus to invest in industrial development.[20] According to Soviet experience, the answer was collectivization of agriculture.

China moved in several stages toward this goal. Beginning in 1953, peasants were encouraged to form Mutual Aid Teams. These generally amounted to pooling labor for some agricultural tasks such as plowing, planting, seeding, weeding, and harvesting; in many cases these teams simply formalized what had long been standard rural practice. Beginning in 1954, peasants were strongly encouraged to enter lower-level Agricultural Producers Cooperatives (APCs). These required a contribution of animals, tools, and land to the cooperative, with people paid from the profits of the cooperative. Half the payment would be based on work done for the co-op, and the other half would be based on the land, equipment, and animals contributed. Not surprisingly, rich peasants tended not to participate, and even many middle peasants proved reluctant to give up clear title to the land the revolution had given them.

In early 1955 the CCP allowed those who wanted to withdraw from the cooperatives to do so, and Beijing was surprised by the number to who took advantage of this opportunity. This sparked a debate over agricultural collectivization at the highest levels of the party. Soviet practice endorsed collectivization as the best way to create large enough agricultural units for the state to be able to take the surplus effectively out of agriculture. Given China's far lower levels of per capita agricultural production, however, Beijing needed to both create a larger surplus and capture a portion of that for urban economic development.[21]

In the ensuing debate, Mao argued that cooperative organizations in agriculture would expand the size of fields and the scale of agricultural activity so that peasants themselves would want to introduce more mechanized farming to meet their new needs. With that mechanization, Mao argued, production itself would go up. More orthodox Marxists, such as Mao's putative successor Liu Shaoqi, suggested that instead the Chinese should introduce more mechanization first. The changes mechanization would produce in farming practices would make the peasants realize the importance of consolidating fields and pooling their labor, and they would then voluntarily enter collective farms. This debate reflected a more fundamental issue of broad importance: Mao felt that political efforts could create the conditions for rapid economic growth, while Liu felt that political efforts should be constrained by the existing types and level of economic production. Mao won the argument.

The issue came to a head in mid-1955. The second session of the First National People's Congress, the nominal legislature, met from 5 to 30 July and adopted a report on the First Five-Year Plan presented by Li Fuchun, the head of the State Planning Commission. This report anticipated gradual collectivization of agriculture. On 31 July, Mao Zedong convened a meeting of provincial, municipal, and lower-level CCP leaders and called for far more ambitious targets. This began the so-called "high tide" of agricultural cooperativization, a surge which put 92 percent of peasant households into collectives by the following spring (see Table 4.2). Within another year, Mao brought about a transformation of lower- to higher-level APCs. The difference

TABLE 4.2 *APCs and Communes* (percent of peasant households)*

YEAR	LOWER-LEVEL APCs	HIGHER-LEVEL APCs	COMMUNES
1952	0.1		
1953	0.2		
1954	2		
June 1955	14	0.03	
Dec. 1955	59	4	
Feb. 1956	36	51	
June 1956	29	63	
Dec. 1956	9	88	
Apr. 1958		100	
Aug. 1958		70	30
Sep. 1958			98

Source Mark Selden, *The Political Economy of Chinese Socialism* (Armonk, N.Y.: M. E. Sharpe, 1988), p. 71.

*Communes were very large rural organizations introduced in 1958.

between the two was crucial: in the higher-level APCs, members were paid only according to the work they did, not according to the capital they had put in. This took away the advantages of the remaining richer strata of the peasantry.[22]

Mao subsequently met often with provincial and lower-level party figures to garner support for ambitious schemes that had generated little enthusiasm among his colleagues in Beijing. He referred to these meetings as his way of getting in touch with those who were close to the front line, and who therefore understood the true conditions in the country. But in meeting with these officials, Mao always had his way. The functionaries stood in awe of the Chairman, and most worked very hard to cultivate their relations with him. By the late 1950s, for example, many provincial party leaders had established palatial estates for Mao's exclusive use. Some reportedly even formed special provincial "cultural troupes" of attractive young women for the Chairman's personal pleasure.[23]

The provincial party leaders were mostly individuals of peasant stock who distrusted the more urbanized and technically proficient specialists at the Center, and had a natural inclination toward decentralization and mass mobilization. Mao thus found an eager audience on his frequent trips to the provinces.

At the same time that agriculture was being collectivized, the Socialist Transformation of Industry and Commerce campaign gave urban capitalists the opportunity to sell their enterprises to the state at bargain prices. After their traumas of the previous few years, most quickly did so. In Shanghai, the owners of the local textile factories actually formed a parade along the Huangpu River waterfront to the municipal Communist party headquarters in the old British Shanghai Bank Building to request that the municipal government take over their businesses. As they marched, they held up banners and heard celebratory gongs and firecrackers along the sidewalks. Many were kept on as managers in their former firms while the communists learned how to run them, but after a few more years, not many remained in positions of authority.

By mid-1956 the Chinese communists had fought the UN forces in Korea to a standstill, rehabilitated the urban and rural economies, embarked on the ambitious First Five-Year Plan, and created socialist-type organizations for both peasants and city-dwellers. No substantial private sector remained in the urban or rural economies. The country had been galvanized, organized, and directed toward a socialist future.[24]

Takeover Politics

The years from 1949 to 1954 also witnessed the transformation of the guerrilla communist army and party into a ruling elite. This involved decisions about appointments to various posts, how to organize the bureaucratic apparatus given differing conditions in various parts of the country, and what to do with the enormous armed forces left over from the civil war.

The basic approach to organizing political power was to establish a moderately decentralized arrangement for a transitional period, with the intention of centralizing this when conditions permitted. The CCP divided the country into six major regions—northeast, north, east, central-south, southwest, and northwest—and it created sets of party, government, and military organs to take charge of each region. Each region initially was put under martial law; as conditions permitted they shifted to civilian rule.[25]

With this organization, the party acknowledged that the timing of policy initiatives would have to vary by region. The Three Anti, for example, began in the northeast in the early fall of 1951, then spread to north and east China early that winter, and then moved to the other parts of the country. Most policies followed roughly this same geographical phasing during these early years.

This system reflected the guerrilla-war and base-area experience of the CCP. Each of the major regions fell under the sway of one of the "field armies" into which the communists had organized their forces during the guerrilla war. Each was led by one or two of the major CCP figures, who typically held a series of posts giving them effective control over all activities in the region. In the important northeast region, for example, Gao Gang, a poorly educated peasant who had risen to the top communist ranks by the late 1940s, simultaneously became the head of the regional party committee, head of the regional government, and head of the regional military organization. Essentially, he was regent for the northeast.

From 1952 to 1954 the CCP gradually shifted people out of the regional political structures, assigning them either to provinces or to the Center. This created jealousies and tensions regarding which individuals would receive high posts in Beijing, and thereby fueled the first major falling out at the top of the party.

Gao Gang was shifted to the Center in 1952 to take charge of the newly formed State Planning Commission, probably because of his close personal ties with the Russians. Gao, however, regarded this commission with some disdain. He felt he should aspire to the premiership, and he believed, mistakenly as it turned out, that Mao Zedong felt the same way. Gao thus began to try to line up the other key players, among them Deng Xiaoping in the southwest and Chen Yi in Shanghai, to support him. He argued that they and he were not being treated well by the clique of those, like Zhou Enlai and Liu Shaoqi, who had been in charge of dealing with the areas outside of communist control, called the "white" areas, during the Yan'an era. The base-area leaders were not faring well in the scramble for positions, and Gao assured the others that they would receive excellent jobs in a Gao administration.

The effort failed. Deng and others informed Mao, and Mao refused to back Gao. Zhou Enlai, Liu Shaoqi, and others then purged Gao and his closest collaborator Rao Shushi, who had been one of the top two leaders in Shanghai, for factionalism. Gao subsequently committed suicide; Rao was imprisoned. The incident was significant primarily for the spotlight it threw on the desire for jobs and the factional identities that grew out of the long pre-1949 experiences of the top CCP cadres.[26]

In broad terms, the political strategy in the early years generally favored the PLA troops and cadres that had captured various regions at the end of the civil war over the local guerrilla forces that had fought in those areas on the communist side for many years. It was felt that the latter had too many close ties in the localities, and Mao was keenly concerned with the need to create a political apparatus that would be loyal to the Center. Much as under the Qing dynasty, a kind of "law of avoidance," in which officials were not allowed to serve in their native locales, came into play. In the vast majority of cases, people were put in charge of areas far from their native places. For decades afterward civilian apparatuses were clearly identified with the various field armies that had swept across China from 1948 to 1950[27] (see Table 4.3).

Also the CCP as a general rule sought in the initial years to recruit leading noncommunist personages to the new government. These individuals brought both prestige and skills to party efforts. The communists promised them that the CCP would delay China's socialist transformation to first rehabilitate the country and put it on its feet. Rarely did such noncommunists acquire real power. The well-known GMD general Fu Zuoyi, for example, had

TABLE 4.3 *Field Armies and Localities*

FIELD ARMY	REGION AT END OF CIVIL WAR
First	Northwest
Second	Central and Southwest
Third	East
Fourth	Northeast and Guangdong
Fifth	North

surrendered Beijing to the PLA in January 1949 without a pitched battle. Fu was rewarded with honors and the portfolio for flood control in the new government, but even in his own ministry he served only as a figurehead. The promises of gradual changes, in any event, proved hollow. The united front soon narrowed significantly.

In October 1954, just five years after the founding of the People's Republic of China, the First National People's Congress convened in Beijing. This meeting formally called the government transition period to an end and established the permanent ruling organs for the new state, to be headed by the State Council. It kept in place the figures who had held the top transitional state positions during the previous years. It also formally abolished the regional government/party/military bodies that had been established in 1949. The Center would henceforth deal directly with the provinces. China had been unified swiftly and successfully, albeit with a great deal of blood spilled in the process. Now the communist leaders would have to determine the long-term path of development to take.

FROM SUCCESS TO CRISIS: 1956–57

The period from 1949 to early 1956 had witnessed missteps and problems along with concentrated violence against target groups. At the end of this period, moreover, material hardship still consigned most of the country's population to severe poverty. It was not until 1956, for example, that every county headquarters in the country had a telephone.[28] But the spiritual malaise that had deepened for a century had in less than seven years visibly lessened.

The new Beijing elite may have broken a lot of eggs to make their socialist omelet, but it was a dish that numerous Chinese found far more palatable than the bitterness they had been forced to eat for many years. In Mao Zedong's own words, China had "stood up" internationally and had recaptured a sense of unity under an ideologically strong government at home.

Political leaders do not change a winning formula without strong reasons for doing so. Yet, by mid-1958, the communist leadership made major alterations in their approach to governing China. This radical turnabout stemmed from four important tensions lying beneath the surface as of early 1956 that, together, sent Mao Zedong and his colleagues off onto an ultimately calamitous course called the Great Leap Forward.

One of these tensions concerned the role of Mao himself in the system. Mao occupied a position effectively unconstrained by law or regulation. He felt most comfortable when dealing with ideology and politics, great power relations, agriculture, and social transformation. He chafed at bureaucratic routine and had little understanding of, or patience for, the details of urban industry and finance. After agricultural collectivization and socialist transformation, though, the focus of government activity shifted to the details of urban economic planning and administration, a forte of the state but not of the party or army. Put differently, the successes of 1949–55 had produced a system that did not *need* Mao, but the Chairman could not find a way to exit from day-to-day leadership—in his terminology, to "retreat to the second line"—and still feel confident about his control of the party and the country.

Another tension involved the social and political results of Soviet-style economic development, which Mao found distressing. The centralized planning system favored top-down command control, regularization of procedures, and specialization of jobs, as well as inequalities in prestige, income, reward structures, and power across economic sectors and geographical areas. In good Stalinist fashion, the system also sought to exploit the "backward" countryside to serve the morally and politically superior urban population. These values, priorities, and work styles contrasted sharply with those developed during the Yan'an era, and they discomfited Mao. He might have kept his unease in check had it not been for the third underlying tension, regarding sources of capital for industrial development.

The Soviet aid program had been crucial to China's economic development. The financial portion of this assistance, however, took the form of low-interest loans rather than outright grants. In 1956 Chinese repayments of these loans began to exceed the value of new Soviet monetary aid. Whereas China previously had been able to rely on the USSR to provide a substantial portion of its net investment capital, after 1956, China would have to rely primarily on itself to generate such capital. This would require new techniques to mobilize domestic capital formation. Eventually, Mao saw this as a looming crisis that demanded radically new approaches to the development process itself.

The fourth tension was between peasant cadres and the urban intelligentsia. Despite intensive political indoctrination, the intelligentsia continued to regard most cadres from the countryside as bumpkins. The peasants, in turn, regarded intellectuals as elitist and "bourgeois."[29] Yet the Soviet model placed a high premium on the administrative and other skills of the urban intelligentsia. This tension between peasants and intellectuals inevitably bound up the fate of the Soviet model with the social cleavages that had fed—and been exacerbated by—the Chinese communist revolution.[30]

With agricultural cooperativization and urban socialist transformation at a high point, Mao decided to resolve the tensions between the intellectuals and the bulk of the communist cadres. Premier Zhou Enlai, the best educated of the top CCP leaders, made the initial speech in this effort at a conference on the working conditions of the intellectuals held in January 1956. Zhou's speech called for better treatment and higher regard for the country's technical and creative intelligentsia.

Developments in the Soviet Union also encouraged party efforts to improve ties with the Chinese intelligentsia. Both the 1955–56 thaw toward Soviet literature and Khrushchev's dramatic de-Stalinization speech at the Twentieth Party Congress of the Communist party of the Soviet Union in February 1956 created ripple effects in China. The former simply made it appropriate for the Chinese to follow the Soviet lead in relaxing pressures on intellectuals. The latter, however, had more profound repercussions.

Khrushchev's blistering attack on Stalin caught the Chinese by surprise and severely embarrassed Mao. Mao had spoken of Stalin with high praise and had published a fawning eulogy to the Soviet dictator upon his death in March 1953.[31] In addition, Khrushchev's address essentially warned against a willful leader's having his way, just after Mao had personally launched the socialist transformation of the Chinese economy.[32] Finally, Khrushchev's speech led to unrest in Eastern Europe and, reportedly, to greater tensions in China itself later in 1956. Mao began to have doubts about Khrushchev's wisdom and leadership qualities.

During March and April 1956, therefore, Mao initiated a searching reevaluation of governing methods and priorities, holding thirty-four special briefings from many departments and State Council ministries and commissions. The result was a framework document entitled "On the Ten Major Relationships."[33] This called, overall, for reduced military spending, much greater decentralization in Chinese administration of the economy, and other changes. In it, one sees Mao beginning to modify the Soviet model to make it more palatable to his own values and priorities.

In September 1956 the CCP convened the first session of its Eighth Party Congress,[34] the first Party Congress since the 1945 Seventh Party Congress had enshrined Mao Zedong Thought as part of the party's official ideology. The Congress adopted new Party Rules, the party equivalent of a new constitution. Almost certainly in reaction to the Soviet de-Stalinization initiative, these rules stated that the CCP took only Marxism-Leninism as its guiding ideology. Mao Zedong Thought was dropped from the formula.

Of greater long-term consequence, Mao sought to address tensions in the party's relations with the intellectuals. The Chairman had always believed in manipulating tension as a way to promote his goals. But Soviet socialist theory had played down the idea that frictions between the party and the "people" could persist once socialism had been achieved. The 1956 uprisings in Poland and Hungary, though, made clear that explosive conflict could erupt in societies ruled by Communist parties.

In late February 1957 Mao gave a talk entitled, "On the Correct Handling of Contradictions among the People,"[35] in which he addressed the issue of conflicts of interest in socialist China. He divided these into two categories: "antagonistic contradictions" and "contradictions among the people." Mao asserted that "contradictions among the people" can be resolved through discussion. He suggested that only a small number of contradictions under socialism are "antagonistic," meaning they cannot be resolved by reasonable discourse. These "antagonistic" contradictions would inevitably be handled through violent struggle, in which the "enemy" would be vanquished.

Mao's speech was intended to energize the intellectuals to address and reduce the "contradictions among the people," but after experiencing the many political campaigns of the previous years, they remained cautious. In the spring Mao strongly encouraged intellectuals to speak their minds, to point out the errors of party officials, and to "let a hundred flowers bloom and a hundred schools of thought contend." By this Mao meant that the communists would not require everyone to accept one orthodoxy in all intellectual matters.

The dam finally broke in May 1957, as the intellectuals unleashed an outpouring of grievances against arrogant and ignorant functionaries. At the same time they raised basic questions about whether China should continue to draw so close to the Soviets, and whether the CCP should maintain a monopoly on political power. In essence, China's intellectuals in May 1957 tried to reclaim a position as loyal guardians of the proper moral framework for the political system. Once started, the momentum of criticism gathered steam, and local party officials found themselves under increasingly severe attack. Workers, too, began to press economic grievances through strike actions and other organized activities.

Mao did not let this stirring last for long. On 8 June 1957, the major party newspaper *People's Daily* ran an editorial that marked the end of the Hundred Flowers campaign. The editorial said that "rightists" had taken advantage of the new freedom in order to attack the party and undermine the revolution. This, according to the editorial, amounted to an antagonistic struggle "between the enemy and the people"—a struggle that could only be resolved through dictatorial force. The Antirightist campaign, under the administrative direction of the party's General Secretary Deng Xiaoping, quickly got underway. It had major, long-term consequences for the PRC.[36]

The Antirightist campaign initially targeted all those who had voiced criticisms during the Hundred Flowers period. It was conducted in such indiscriminate fashion, however, that numerous "rightists" were branded on the basis of anonymous denunciations. Indeed, local officials throughout the country received quotas on the number of "rightists" they were to uncover and denounce in their own units.[37] During the course of the summer and early fall of 1957 roughly four hundred thousand urban residents, including many of the intelligentsia, were branded as rightists and thrown into penal camps[38] or sent to the countryside to do forced labor. Beginning in late summer the brunt of the campaign shifted to the countryside itself, where it targeted those who had voiced any opposition to rapid agricultural collectivization.

There were two important results of the Antirightist campaign. First, by late 1957 it would have taken a very brave person to object to a shift toward radical political and economic policies in Beijing. More importantly, the revolution lost the skills of a significant portion of the engineers, professors, economists, and scientists who arguably were critical to the successful implementation of a Soviet-type development model. These people disproportionately came from the government organs, state enterprises, and universities, and not from the Communist party bureaucracy itself. Mao had turned decisively in favor of the peasant cadres instead of their intellectual critics. Without the latter, the highly centralized, government-administered (as opposed to party-administered) approach to rapid economic development would be hard to sustain.

The effects became obvious almost immediately. At the July 1957 meeting of Communist party leaders at Qingdao, Shandong Province, trends emerged toward greater administrative decentralization and increased party involvement with the economy. A Central Committee meeting that convened in October significantly accelerated these tendencies.

All this took place as China's leaders debated the targets and methods for the Second Five-Year Plan, to run from 1958 to 1962. Mao and his colleagues were determined to continue the rapid expansion of the country's industrial base, with increasing steel production a top priority. But new sources of capital would have to be found, and the level of potential Soviet aid and support would have to be ascertained.

During the latter half of 1957 the increasingly radical political atmosphere created a sense of excitement and held out the possibility of major change. At the same time, the relative ease with which the major socialist transformations had been carried out the previous winter convinced Mao that the general populace strongly supported the party and could become a major resource for accelerated economic development. The problem lay in identifying the key to unlock that energy. The disastrous results of the Hundred Flowers campaign, moreover, had convinced Mao that the intelligentsia were antisocialist and effectively the allies of the now-defunct bourgeoisie. He determined to sharpen the people's vigilance so that they would wage class struggle against these antisocialist elements.

The winter of 1957–58 was a time of experimentation with methods to resolve these new issues on the Chinese agenda. Mao and other leaders traveled to Moscow in November to ascertain among other things, whether the Soviets would commit themselves to major new infusions of aid to China. At the same time, Beijing adopted new administrative regulations that called for major decentralization in management of the economy.[39] Regarding the countryside, a debate raged over how to expand irrigation facilities without large new expenditures of capital. The solution was an enormous mobilization of corvée labor, which in turn created pressures to enlarge and greatly strengthen the APC.

As of November–December 1957 it was not clear where all of this would lead. But the mood among the top party leadership was one of radical renewal, sparked both by the alarming problems growing out of the previous Soviet-led approach and by an increasingly ebullient sense that tapping the latent potential of China's huge population could produce a miracle. This spurred Mao and the party during 1958 to launch the Great Leap Forward, a radically new approach to economic and social development that amounted, in the final analysis, to a tremendous, willful leap away from reality, with tragic consequences that included, ultimately, the deaths of tens of millions of Chinese.

LEAPS FORWARD AND BACKWARD: 1958–61

The Great Leap Forward developed as a set of policy initiatives during the spring and summer of 1958. This extraordinary approach to economic development grew out of the trends noted above: the purge of intellectuals; the surge of less-educated radicals; the need to find new ways to generate domestic capital; the rising enthusiasm about the potential results mass mobilization might produce; and the reaction against the sociopolitical results of the Soviet development strategy.

The Great Leap did not emerge as a full-blown strategy at any specific time. Rather, it was formed out of many initiatives, and it had different effects on the various sectors of society. It is most accurately viewed not as an integrated strategy but as a broad spirit and basic set of priorities.

The fundamental idea behind the Great Leap was that China could leap over the normal stages of economic development through the expenditure of extraordinary effort by the entire society for a concentrated period of several years. This idea rested on the notion that the masses possess great latent productive power and can, by dint of effort and organization, transform their labor into capital.

The Great Leap strategy depended on the mobilization of peasants to provide for themselves without drawing resources from the urban economy and in addition to provide food, industrial crops, and even steel for the urban economy. Thus, the peasants were called upon to increase irrigation, produce farm machinery, develop education, participate in militia activities, and feed themselves without new investment from the national budget. Originally, Mao and his colleagues expected Moscow to provide substantial new assistance that they would use solely to speed urban industrial growth. Although Soviet aid did rise in 1958, increasing Sino-Soviet frictions—in part because of Chinese deviation from the Soviet model—soon made clear that the Chinese could not rely on their Russian neighbors for much additional help. This further increased the burden placed on China's peasants to fund industrial growth.

A strategy that required very extensive mass mobilization was by its very nature more suited to the capabilities of the Communist party apparatus than to those of the government bureaucracy. The Great Leap approach therefore greatly expanded the role of the CCP at the expense of the government—and greatly decentralized policy implementation in the process.[40] China's leaders had assigned the State Council primary responsibility for economic development during the First Five-Year Plan, but they shifted to greater reliance on the CCP itself when they adopted the Great Leap approach to rapid industrial growth.

In January 1958 Mao Zedong criticized Premier Zhou Enlai at a meeting of the top party figures, called the Nanning Conference because it convened in Nanning, Jiangxi Province. Mao's comments highlighted his frustration with the old system. He complained that the State Council experts worked up policy proposals so thoroughly that by the time they got to Mao he confronted two problems: the proposals generally allowed little room for new ideas and they were so technically complex that he could not understand them. He noted that he had responded in recent years by simply approving the proposals without even trying to understand them fully.[41] With a shift to the Great Leap strategy, Mao brushed aside this specialized State Council system and put himself back at the helm in all major substantive matters.

The Great Leap in many ways harkened back to the Yan'an spirit. It stressed egalitarianism, experimentation, ideological fervor, mass mobilization, and the application of organization and will to the accomplishment of technically "impossible" goals. The Great Leap disparaged technical constraints and the experts who warned about them. Its spirit was summed up well in one of its key slogans: "Strive to go all out to achieve more, faster, better, and more economical results." In the final analysis, as later Chinese authors admitted, "better and more economical results" were sacrificed to the goals of "more and faster."

Mao correctly gauged the tremendous response the CCP could generate across the country. The CCP had so effectively cowed all opposition and developed such a strong can-do reputation among the Chinese people that China in 1958 took off into a nationwide frenzy of activity. Previous work habits and even existing bases of social organization changed dramatically, at least for a time.

In August 1958 the Chairman called for the organization of all rural inhabitants into "people's communes" (*renmin gongshe*). These were large, centralized organizations in the countryside meant to facilitate meshing the government administration with economic production in the rural areas. Mao wanted to devise a unit in the countryside that could directly manage the various major tasks there: agricultural and small industrial production and marketing; corvée labor for infrastructure development; health delivery; education; and security. People's communes initially provided the key for this. Although actual conditions varied, the average commune had about twenty thousand members as of 1959. The whole countryside was communized in a matter of months in late 1958. The commune formed the lowest level of state administration in the countryside.

In the communes, huge numbers of people worked incredibly long hours at arduous tasks for months at a time. Indeed, so many new manufacturing efforts such as "backyard steel furnaces" were undertaken that in the fall of 1958 the country actually experienced an acute agricultural labor shortage. Even the most fundamental aspects of peasant daily life changed at the peak of the Great Leap frenzy. People contributed their cooking utensils to be smelted as part of the drive to create backyard steel furnaces, and they ate in communal dining rooms. Some communes debated whether to give up using money altogether. The Great Leap amounted in many ways to the regimentation and militarization of life in the countryside.

The Great Leap's effects were not limited to the agricultural sector. In the military the Chinese decided to abandon Soviet manuals and develop their own; they also sought greater egalitarianism by making all military officers serve as common soldiers for one month per year. The military also became deeply involved in domestic economic construction and in developing extensive militia organizations. In all these ways, the Great Leap moved the PLA away from the trend toward professionalism it had been following since the Korean War in favor of recapturing some of its guerrilla war traditions.[42]

In industry, the Great Leap strategy pushed technicians to the side, and workers ran machinery for long periods of time with no maintenance. Income differentials among workers and managers diminished, and nonemployed urban residents were organized into small production and commercial groups. The educational system admitted large numbers of new students, by organizing part work/part study programs, at the expense of quality.[43] Even government officials became subject to *xia fang*, the policy of sending people in authoritative urban positions "down" to the production front, often in the coun-tryside, to labor among the masses.

Measured by levels of mobilization, the Great Leap succeeded. In one ex-ample, millions of sparrows—scourges of agriculture—were killed in the sum-mer 1958 by people standing on rooftops and making loud noises every time one landed; the sparrows were thus kept airborne until they literally died of exhaustion! In addition, the Chinese made seemingly extraordinary gains in production that year. There were large increases in steel output, one of the core goals of the Great Leap strategy, and substantial growth in other targeted industries. Only later did it become clear that a significant portion of this growth took place because many key Soviet-aided plants, which began to be built from 1953 to 1955, finally came on line in 1958. Unusually favorable weather also helped produce bumper crops in agriculture.

The successes of 1958 induced euphoria in the national leaders. They de-cided, for example, that in 1959 they would leave roughly one-third of the country's arable land fallow, as otherwise they would have trouble handling all the food produced. The top leaders also began to talk confidently of having invented a new strategy for socialist economic development—a strategy that could work far more successfully than that of the Soviet Union.

In late 1958 the leaders did acknowledge that the Great Leap had pro-duced some disorganization and problems; but they remained blind to the magnitude and nature of the difficulties that were developing. By ignoring economic and social laws on a phenomenal scale, the Great Leap eventually created a disaster of gargantuan proportions.

One major problem concerned the people's communes. The communes had the advantage of being able to allocate massive amounts of labor in a planned fashion. These organizations were too large to link rewards closely with labor, however, and they fit poorly with the natural bases of identity among peasants. Peasant life traditionally had revolved around the clan, the village, and the standard marketing area (SMA). The SMA consisted of the various villages (usually more than a dozen) whose people marketed their goods together at the same town every few days. More than economic transac-tions occurred in these market towns. People from different villages got to know each other, exchanged gossip, arranged marriages, and so on. Over many years, SMAs thus became identifiable by the social as well as the eco-nomic connections that people made. The footpaths and cart tracks among villages were visible evidence of the need to funnel the goods of a village into one market town.

The initial communes were so large that each drew together, on average, the people of three SMAs. This created a political, social, and economic unit that differed from any the participants had previously experienced. The party officials in charge of these huge units did not understand the complexities of meshing different SMAs, and soon fundamental problems of administration and morale cropped up.[44]

One reason the leaders in Beijing missed the seriousness of the emerging difficulties was that at the height of the mobilization phase for the mass cam-paigns, there were no incentives for lower-level officials to report the truth to their superiors. Rather, they were expected to provide evidence that the masses had responded enthusiastically to the calls of the leaders and that great results were pouring in. Consequently, officials at every level of the national bureaucratic hierarchy conspired to inflate production figures as they went up the line, with the result that the central officials lived in substantial ignorance of actual conditions in the countryside in the fall of 1958. Hearing about nothing but success—and wanting to believe that they were indeed charting a new, quick path to industrial power and a communist society—they time and again added new demands and new initiatives to the burgeoning Great Leap Forward.

During the fall and winter of 1958 the costs of disorganization began to take their toll. Too many people had been yanked off the fields to permit successful harvest of the fall crop. Steel produced in backyard smelters was of such low quality that it could not be used for much. The transportation system became clogged and disrupted to the point where major urban steel producers could not obtain the coking coal they needed. Poor maintenance practices began to diminish the performance capacity of many machines.

In the early spring of 1959 Mao Zedong began to appreciate the existence of these problems, and he attempted to rein in the excesses of the Great Leap without abandoning its basic strategy. He argued against overcentralization of commune administration, which had produced irrational work assignments and had destroyed peasant incentives to do their work well. He therefore called for the creation of three levels of administration within each commune—team, rising to brigade, and then commune-level—with individuals' incomes and work assignments being decided at the team or brigade level rather than at the commune level. In this and other respects, he sought to tame the tiger he had unleashed in the system. He found it very difficult, though, to convince those lower-level officials at provincial, municipal, county, and commune levels, whose power and resources had grown enormously under the Great Leap decentralization, to heed his suggestions to redistribute power yet again.

This situation came to a head, with a bizarre and fateful twist, at the Lushan conference and Lushan plenum in July and August 1959. These two meetings, held at one of the favorite resorts of the party leadership atop Mount Lu ("Lushan") in Jiangxi Province, convened originally to review the overall situation and to make plans once the spring planting had been completed and the leaders had some idea of the likely size of the fall crop.[45]

At the Lushan conference, Peng Duhuai, who was minister of defense and vice chairman of the Military Affairs Commission, and some others sharply criticized the excesses of the Great Leap strategy and argued that they had resulted from an abandonment of the consultative decision-making process that the leadership had previously used. Peng and his supporters also indicated that they felt the country was rapidly slipping into crisis because of the terrible conditions being created by the Great Leap.

While most of these criticisms echoed those Mao himself had made earlier in the spring, the Chairman nevertheless smelled a rat. He interpreted the actions of Peng and his colleagues as an orchestrated attack on his own position, perhaps quietly inspired by the Russians, who were very unhappy at China's abandonment of the Soviet model. Mao let his critics speak and then, late in the conference, he electrified his audience with a blistering attack on those who had spoken up. He questioned their wisdom and their motives, and he demanded that all top officials attending the conference make a clear choice between Peng and his colleagues or Mao. Never one to miss an opportunity to add extra tension to a situation, Mao proclaimed that if the meeting sided against him he would take to the hills, raise another army, and overthrow the CCP!

Under this pressure, the party leadership sided overwhelmingly with Mao and branded Peng and some others an "antiparty" group. These individuals were purged. By the end of the summer, Peng was no longer minister of defense or vice chairman of the Military Affairs Commission, having been sent to do gardening in a village in the suburbs of Beijing instead. The conference and the succeeding plenum then produced two sets of decisions. One denounced the crimes of the "rightists" who had revealed themselves at the highest level of the party and called for new vigilance against other rightists at all levels of the system. The other highlighted again the excesses of the Great Leap and called for the same types of consolidation measures that Mao had been espousing all spring.[46]

The results of the clash at Lushan proved fateful in several ways. First, Mao's vicious response to Peng's criticism seemed to change the unwritten ground rules of policy debate among the leaders. Before Lushan the leadership at the top conclaves had felt it proper to voice their opinions, within some self-imposed constraints, before a decision was made. The denunciation and purge of Peng suggested this would no longer be the case. Second, Mao chose Lin Biao to replace Peng as minister of defense and vice chairman of the Military Affairs Commission. Lin had long been a favorite of Mao's; Peng had not. Lin then tried to position himself to succeed Mao, and in the process he became a major contributor to tensions and infighting among the top party leadership.

Finally and most importantly, the decisions emanating from the plenum proved contradictory in spirit if not in substance. The attack on rightists undermined the leadership's attempt to draw in the excesses of the Great Leap. Indeed, the opposite occurred: with everyone eager to demonstrate that they leaned to the "left" instead of to the "right," a new upsurge in radicalism took place in late 1959 and 1960. Communes now appeared in many cities, and radical excesses and misreporting of production figures became even more widespread. The system spun out of control in an orgy of mobilization and of "reporting" that proved little better than utopian fantasy. The result was a national tragedy.

The core of the tragedy was the leaders' demand for sufficient food to feed the cities even as agricultural production plummeted from bad policies, mismanagement, confusion, and unfavorable weather. Local officials collected the food because their jobs depended on pleasing those above them, not those whom they governed. As a consequence, China's countryside slipped into famine. The full extent of the famine did not become widely known because officials sought to cover it up and not all areas of the country crossed from hardship into crisis. But demographic figures that became available in the 1980s detail the horrors of 1960–61: roughly thirty million people, primarily the very young and the old, starved to death. Nearly another thirty million who would have been born in this period were either stillborn or not conceived. All the horrors of famine such as cannibalism of children occurred, and in some parts of the country primary schools did not reopen—because no children survived—for years afterward.

The Chinese economy as a whole spun into deep depression. In part, this reflected the economy's substantial reliance on inputs from the agricultural sector, inputs that in 1961 simply dried up. In addition, Moscow had become so unhappy at both Mao's policies and his claims about a new road to socialism that in July 1960 the Soviets abruptly withdrew all their technicians from China and canceled their aid program. This severely affected many of the country's heavy industrial plants. The double blow of agricultural collapse and loss of aid produced a far more pronounced decline in economic output than the United States experienced at the nadir of the Great Depression in 1932.

The Great Leap Forward, born of a sense of growing crisis and harnessed to a fundamental faith in ideology, organization, and the masses, traced an extremely radical, wildly unrealistic approach to economic development and the transformation of social values. It reflected both Mao Zedong's utopian ideas and his virtually unbounded political power. The greatest part of the tragedy occurred, moreover, during the Second Leap, the new upsurge following the Lushan plenum of August 1959. A direct response to Peng Dehuai's supposed challenge to the Chairman's power, the Second Leap resulted from Mao's attempt to wipe out "rightism" throughout the party. He waged this political battle at the expense of consolidation efforts that he knew were necessary. In the years 1960 to 1962, Mao's political hubris, combined with the incentives lower-level officials had to lie to their superiors, resulted in 545 times as many deaths as the United States suffered in the entire Vietnam war.[47]

The Great Leap thus failed because of flaws in its basic policies and the inherent dynamics of China's political system, including the incentives to falsify information from the grass roots. The withdrawal of Soviet aid and three years (1959–61) of particularly inclement weather deepened the failure. As a result, the Communist party, which had previously proved itself to be rough, violent, but above all successful, had now demonstrated that it could err catastrophically. Mao Zedong himself, moreover, bore a large part of the responsibility for the disaster.[48]

INCREASING TENSION AMID RECOVERY: 1962–65

As Beijing's leaders became aware of the extent of the Great Leap disaster, they adopted emergency measures. When urban food shortages became severe, the leaders decided in June 1961 to shift the major part of the burden back onto the peasants. They did this by forcing more than twenty million people who had entered the cities during the Great Leap back to the country-side from 1961 to 1962. This was achieved in large part by the rationing of nearly all urban food and consumer goods. Urban residents received coupons that were valid only for the purchase of specific items, in specific locales, and for specific periods. Peasants, who were not similarly given ration coupons, were thus unable to support themselves in the city.

In the wake of this mammoth resettlement effort, the CCP adopted a series of policies that had the effect of freezing people into their current work units.[49] Workers and staff in state enterprises from then on would be entitled to lifetime employment with benefits, but they lost their right to change places of work without the permission of the management. Enterprises then became all-encompassing units for their employees, providing housing, health care, recreational activities, rationed goods, pensions, and so forth. Political education and other government policies impacted on employees through their enterprises, and thus for urban employees the place of work (called by Chinese the "unit," or *danwei*) became the key interface between the population and the political system. The units became so self-enclosed that most employees retained few contacts with, and had little knowledge about, those outside of their work unit.

The urban unit system combined with strict residence registration requirements in the countryside to prevent further rural-to-urban migration after the early 1960s. This had the effect of formally dividing China into a two-tiered system, with a privileged urban society supported by substantial state subsidies and a highly exploited rural society whose members were denied access to jobs in the urban economy.

The ameliorative policies in the countryside included dividing communes into smaller units that closely approximated the former standard marketing areas and establishing the three-level system (team, brigade, and commune) that Mao had first advocated in March 1959. Related initiatives in other sectors included relaxing policies toward literature and art, inviting many specialists back into positions of authority, and generally undoing the radical excesses of the Great Leap. These new policies began in 1960–61, and by 1962 many officials felt that the next appropriate step would be further decollectivization of agriculture, which had, in any case, occurred spontaneously in various localities that had been particularly devastated by the famine. Mao personally took a back seat as these policies were developed and implemented, but in the summer of 1962, as the peak of the crisis passed and the economy began to recover, he again stepped to the fore.

Mao's summer 1962 resurgence highlighted the disparate lessons that China's leaders had drawn from the devastation of the Great Leap. For many of the top figures including Mao's putative successor Liu Shaoqi and Chen Yun, one of the leading economic officials, the Great Leap demonstrated once and for all that the country should no longer utilize massive political campaigns to accomplish national goals. The society had become too complex for this "primitive" means of policy implementation developed during the party's days in the wilderness.

For Mao the lessons were different. He gave up on the idea of using mass campaigns to achieve major advances in economic development, but he still felt these campaigns had a critical role to play in bringing about changes in values. Mao's faith in the beneficent effects of struggle persisted despite the bitter experiences of the Great Leap.

From 1962 to 1965, therefore, two quite different agendas emerged on the national scene. Most leaders concerned themselves with cleaning up the mess left over from the Great Leap, a job that required pragmatic economic policies and related efforts. Mao and some of his supporters, by contrast, became obsessed by the fear that economic rehabilitation policies would steer the country away from revolution, and they demanded continuing mobilization to attack internal political enemies.

Mao's belief evidently stemmed in part from developments in the Soviet Union under Khrushchev. As the Soviet leader tried to move his system away from its Stalinist heritage, he took measures that Mao regarded as an abandonment of socialism. Khrushchev's decision in 1960 to withdraw aid from China lent further credence, in Mao's view, to the thesis that the USSR under Khrushchev was no longer a socialist society. Mao found this thought deeply alarming; he had never before contemplated the possibility that a socialist revolution could be undone and could degenerate into what Mao regarded as a class-based, exploitative system. He now focused on the possibility that China could follow the same path after his death.

With the Soviet Union's experience very much in mind, Mao took two initiatives between 1962 and 1965. He began to educate the Chinese on the dangers of "Soviet revisionism" under Khrushchev,[50] and he began to look for signs of agreement with Soviet methods among his colleagues. Others—including the defense chief Lin Biao and Mao's wife Jiang Qing—who might benefit from Mao's distrust of many of his colleagues egged him on and fed his darker suspicions.

The resulting mix of policies was schizophrenic. Substantive economic policies stressed material incentives, coordinated development, clear hierarchies of authority, realistic planning, and use of technically skilled personnel. Yet along with these conventional policies the country experienced a steady drum beat of political agitation advocating ideological commitment, denouncing internal enemies linked to the external threats from the United States and increasingly the Soviet Union, and promoting egalitarianism and class struggle. Polemics against "Khrushchev revisionism" poured forth. In 1964 Mao also dictated the start of a huge new program of economic investment deep in the interior of southwest China, the "third line" or "third front," to prepare the country for the possibility of war with the United States should the hostilities in Vietnam continue to escalate.[51] In addition, various intense political campaigns took place: a rural Four Cleanups,[52] a second urban Three Anti, among others.

As Mao became concerned with combating "revisionism" he increasingly relied on the People's Liberation Army, headed by Lin Biao, to achieve his domestic political goals. The government bureaucracies under the State Council had implemented the First Five-Year Plan, while the CCP had run the Great Leap Forward. With Mao doubtful about each of these two nationwide political hierarchies, he turned toward the third pillar of the PRC, the army. Lin's political ambitions led him to pursue a dual strategy within the army based on mass indoctrination in Mao Zedong Thought, which Lin had excerpted and compiled into the "little red book," and development of the atomic bomb. China tested its first nuclear weapon in October 1964.[53]

Lin's skillful handling of politics and high technology in the army seemed to Mao to resolve what the CCP termed the "red versus expert" problem—that is, the problem of combining both political commitment and technical expertise.[54] The PLA seemed to combine technical expertise, organizational discipline, and ideological fervor. Mao thus began to expand the administrative and political roles of the PLA in society. In 1964 Mao called for the population to learn from the PLA, implicitly instead of from the party, a remarkable step in a communist society. He also established political organs staffed by PLA officers in many government offices.[55]

Mao's political apprehensions may have reflected his more general worries about his own mortality. His speeches in 1964 make frequent mention of the inevitability of death. Increasingly conscious that his time was limited, Mao likely felt it urgent to ensure the continuing vitality of the revolution after his death.

The economic policies of 1962–65 brought about a remarkably rapid recovery: the economy regained average 1957 levels of output by 1965. But there remained a relatively tense political atmosphere, with ambitious people like Lin Biao and Jiang Qing trying to secure their power at the top by undermining Mao's relations with other colleagues. This was an unstable mix, and it did not last.

THE GREAT PROLETARIAN CULTURAL REVOLUTION— THE RED GUARD PHASE: 1966–69

Mao Zedong was a political leader of extraordinary daring. In the Great Proletarian Cultural Revolution, he again demonstrated his commitment to revolution, his skill in mobilizing the Chinese against each other, and his readiness to sacrifice the lives of huge numbers of people to achieve his goals. Mao's own character was central to this latest upheaval, because without his actions the Cultural Revolution would not have occurred. Put differently, there was nothing inherent in the PRC system of governance that would have led to the Cultural Revolution had not Mao guided the system in this direction.

Mao Zedong seems to have had four broad goals in the Cultural Revolution.[56] First, he sought to change the succession. As of 1965 his likely successor was Liu Shaoqi, but Mao had come to distrust Liu and the level of his commitment to revolution. Mao wanted both to dislodge Liu and to put another successor in his place, probably Lin Biao. But to remove a figure as deeply entrenched as Liu, who had been Mao's putative successor since the Seventh Party Congress in 1945, would require a major effort to blacken his name.

Second, Mao wanted to discipline the huge bureaucracies governing the country. Always deeply concerned about the inherent tendency of officials to put on airs, to take advantage of their offices for private gain, and to lose contact with the populace, he determined to force them to stand up to the test of mass criticism and potential humiliation. In this way, they would have to prove again their leadership mettle or they would fall. To make sure that officials could not shield themselves, Mao conspired with Lin Biao to have the army— and probably with Kang Sheng, head of the public security (policy) system, to have the civilian security forces[57]—stand aside when the mass attacks occurred in the latter half of 1966.

Third, Mao wanted to expose China's youth to a revolutionary experience to, in his words, "raise a whole generation of revolutionary successors." Acting out of his faith in the experience of struggle as a force in shaping character, he created a situation in which this postrevolutionary generation of youth would have to live by their wits to come out whole. A period of testing and radical uncertainty, Mao felt, would make China's youth develop strength of character and commitment to the revolutionary cause.

Finally, Mao wanted to make substantive changes in various policy areas. Seeking to reduce income inequalities and material incentives, he eliminated wage increases and bonus payments for urban employees.[58] He sought to reduce urban-rural differences by, for example, spreading China's limited health-care resources more evenly around the country rather than permitting them to be concentrated in major cities, where health professionals preferred to work. In the countryside, he also sponsored the training of peasant medics, called "barefoot doctors."[59] In education, he sought to eliminate practices such as university admissions which favored those who scored best on exams. In China as elsewhere, examinations inherently favored those from intellectual and elite backgrounds. He also wanted the educational system to stress ideology and practical knowledge rather than scholarship. In the military, he tried to reduce status differentials by, among other things, eliminating the system of military ranks. Officers subsequently were addressed by their substantive position, such as Brigade Leader Zhang or Division Commander Li.[60] Overall, he sought to minimize the scope of any kind of private activity and to commit the Chinese to a fully collective, materially frugal existence.

At some point between 1965 and 1966—the details are still debated among scholars—Mao decided to take drastic action. The goals outlined above informed the specific efforts he made. Yet, the Cultural Revolution was so base and violent in its focus that one has to ask about the dark emotional elements that may have contributed to Mao's decisions. Within four years of pursuing policies that had produced thirty million deaths and had thrown the country into a deep economic depression, Mao now launched the society on a trajectory toward civil war. He instigated youths to beat and kill their elders,[61] and he had many close colleagues with whom he had worked for more than three decades beaten, tortured, and left to die without medical treatment.[62]

The national response to Mao's call to launch a Cultural Revolution amounted to wild adulation of the leader who had caused such enormous suffering. The school-age generation of China in the mid-1960s had been taught to demonize and dehumanize whole classes of people and to tolerate and celebrate gross violence, even sadism, against them. This system was also characterized by a pervasive Maoist personality cult and bureaucratic repression of anyone stepping out of line. The numerous mass political campaigns over the previous fifteen years had left many personal grievances. These factors combined to produce a massive popular response to Mao's calls for political violence.[63]

Tactically, Mao used his strong ties to Lin Biao to secure the basic allegiance of the military to his demand in 1966 that they stay back from the fray. He also secured the support of Premier Zhou Enlai, who may have felt that it was useless to oppose Mao but possible to influence his policies and their implementation by aligning with him. A less flattering interpretation has Zhou seeing the Cultural Revolution as a vehicle for ousting Liu Shaoqi, with whom he was never close.

Mao used his wife Jiang Qing and her followers as surrogate leaders of the important propaganda bureaucracy once he ousted the officials there. In short, from late 1965 through first half of 1966 Mao put together a coalition of key players that enabled him to launch a frontal assault on the party bureaucracy and on the leadership of many state organs.

Having quietly secured the allegiance of the military, Mao then used the propaganda apparatus to bolster his own prestige among the masses and to demonize his targets. In this, he was helped by the stream of official propaganda that from 1961 to 1965 had consistently portrayed Mao as virtually infallible and had shifted blame for the Great Leap Forward disaster onto hapless lower-level officials. This effort to maintain the legitimacy of the system now came back to haunt those leaders whom Mao wanted to unseat.

In August 1966, having lined up his Cultural Revolution coalition at the apex of the political system, Mao unleashed the Red Guards to attack the party. Most Red Guards were urban high school and college students. Mao ordered the schools closed but did not let the students return home. He encouraged the students to form Red Guard groups and, quoting some of the exhortations of the time, to "make revolution," "do battle with revisionism," "yank out the small handful of capitalist roaders in the party," "overthrow China's Khrushchev [i.e., Liu Shaoqi]," "knock down the number two person in authority taking the capitalist road [i.e., Deng Xiaoping]," "destroy the old and establish the new," and "bombard the headquarters [i.e., the Communist party]." At the same time, he instructed all top leaders not to suppress the Red Guards but rather to face them and answer to them.[64]

Red Guard groups quickly launched a reign of terror in most big cities. They waved the little red book of Mao quotations and engaged in contests to see who could recite the quotations most rapidly from memory. Millions of Red Guards traveled to Beijing to march in parades past Mao, who stood atop the Tiananmen Gate to review them in the late summer and early fall of 1966. The Red Guards also took to the street to, in the slogan of the day, "destroy the four olds." This translated into destroying old culture by raiding houses, burning books and antiques, beating and humiliating people who seemed not to be in the spirit of things, and killing those who tried to resist. In all these instances, the police stood back and let the youths wreak havoc. In addition to causing general mayhem, the Red Guards also attacked officials at all levels of the political system. Through the end of 1966, the military and police permitted this to unfold virtually without interference.[65]

Mao fairly easily overcame opposition at the top of the party to the Cultural Revolution, which, after all, broke almost every innerparty norm about how to address party problems. The Chairman "packed" the eleventh plenum of the Eighth Central Committee in August 1966, allowing jeering Red Guards into the balconies to shout down those who might oppose the Cultural Revolution. He obtained from this plenum a "sixteen point declaration" on launching the Cultural Revolution "with fanfare."[66] In October 1966 the top leadership convened for a major review of the situation (such conclaves, called "central work conferences," occurred several times a year except from 1967 to 1976, during which only a few were held).[67] At this meeting Mao heard bitter complaints about Red Guard behavior throughout the country, and he himself stated that he had been surprised at the power of the movement he had unleashed. He nevertheless decided to let it continue for awhile so as to "further test" his colleagues.

Beginning in January 1967 in Shanghai, Red Guard groups and their counterparts among urban workers, generally called "revolutionary rebels," actually seized power from the local party and government. "Seizing power" literally meant that they stole the seals of office so that neither party nor government could officially receive or send out documents. In reality, the municipal party and government officials were swept aside, and a committee of Red Guard and revolutionary rebel leaders took over and briefly formed what they called a Shanghai commune. This power seizure quickly received the blessing of the Cultural Revolution leaders in Beijing, and it marked the start of a process over the coming two years of power seizures in various provinces and cities and the formation of new "revolutionary committees" to exercise authority.[68]

In February 1967 many of the old marshals, the top leaders of the military, teamed up with a few others (excluding Lin Biao, of course) to challenge the thrust of the Cultural Revolution. They held a series of meetings with the leading radicals who were guiding the Cultural Revolution under Mao's aegis. Zhou Enlai chaired these tense, hostile sessions, and he reported the proceedings to Mao. Mao decided against those who challenged the Cultural Revolution, and this series of meetings then became known as the "February adverse current." The Cultural Revolution continued, becoming more violent and anarchic.

From 1967 to 1968, many shocking episodes of increased Red Guard radicalism and violence alternated with more settled times. Mao instructed the military to "support the left" early in 1967, but did not indicate what that meant in any given situation. During this period, moreover, China shut itself off from the outside world to a remarkable degree. At one point in 1968 the PRC had only one ambassador actually posted abroad, in Egypt. Beijing's relations with virtually all its neighbors except Vietnam also deteriorated, and ties with the Soviet Union became extremely tense.

The spring of 1968 was perhaps the most violent time, although no firm statistics exist to confirm this impressionistic statement. During those months China slipped into virtual civil war, as Red Guard factions turned against each other to do battle for power. Many had obtained guns and explosives, and the skirmishes ranged from melodramatic conflicts between opposing loud speakers to extremely cruel, bloody assaults with automatic weapons and other deadly force. Taking prisoners, widespread use of torture, and other human rights abuses became common practice. The outside world obtained a glimpse of the violence when trussed up corpses, many without heads, began floating down the Pearl River into Hong Kong. Nobody in Beijing exercised close control over this orgy of political violence.

Confronted with this fragmentation of the movement, Mao became frustrated with what he viewed as the self-centeredness of the Red Guards, who seemed incapable of uniting together to cooperate in building a new China. He therefore ordered the army to reestablish order in the cities and to send the Red Guards out to remote rural areas in order to "make revolution" there. Military forces in many cases carried out these orders with relish, suppressing radical Red Guard groups and "convincing" these radicals to resettle in harsh interior and border regions. About eighteen million Red Guards were sent to the countryside in this effort.[69]

When radical Red Guard leaders in Beijing questioned whether Mao supported this military activity, the Chairman convened a meeting with them and announced that, "I am the 'black hand' [who has been ordering your suppression]. If you leave this meeting and try to say something different, I warn you that I am making a tape recording of the meeting and will make it public." The PLA thereupon virtually took over the administration of China, placing military representatives in all major schools, factories, offices, hospitals, theaters, and other urban work units.

Mao's move toward suppression of the Red Guards may have been inspired in part by the Soviet-led Warsaw Pact invasion of Czechoslovakia in August 1968. In the wake of that invasion the Soviet leader Leonid Brezhnev had said that the USSR and its allies were obliged to put back onto the socialist path any country that had strayed from it. Beijing felt threatened by this new Brezhnev doctrine, and for good reason given the rapid buildup of Soviet offensive military forces along the PRC's northern border, which had been taking place nonstop since the beginning of the Cultural Revolution. Mao needed to restore order and prepare the country for possible war.[70]

The Red Guard phase of the Cultural Revolution ended in 1969. In April of that year the CCP convened its Ninth Party Congress, which declared the "victory" of the Cultural Revolution, restored Mao Zedong Thought to the Party Constitution along with Marxism-Leninism as the CCP's guiding ideology, and inscribed in the same constitution the explicit mandate that, "Lin Biao is Mao Zedong's closest comrade in arms and successor."[71] Mao then abolished the special committee, called the Cultural Revolution Small Group, that he had established to run the Cultural Revolution.

SETTLING THE SUCCESSION: 1969–76

Between 1966 and 1969, the Cultural Revolution had destroyed a great deal and produced little of long-term value. It had inflicted enormous violence on the population, especially in the cities, and had left deep scars and social fissures. Although no reliable figures are available, those who suffered incarceration, serious injury, or death certainly reached into the millions. The CCP itself and much of the state apparatus had been paralyzed, with a large percentage of leading figures at all levels humiliated, stripped of power, and forced to do manual labor or to suffer a worse fate. The economy largely stagnated because of disruptions in transportation, decline in worker discipline, and virtual destruction of the central economic statistical apparatus. Worse yet, technological innovation stagnated almost completely,[72] as the nativist impulses in the country surged to the fore. The PLA assumed control over administration of economic, governmental, police, and social units, but this in turn raised tensions and political conflicts at all levels of the military.[73]

The late 1960s phase of the Cultural Revolution shaped a generation of China's youth. These were high school and college students whose institutions shut down in the early summer of 1966 and either remained closed or reopened only in a grossly altered form during the ensuing three years. These millions of students thus spent an important part of their teenage years on the streets, treating social and economic issues as political concerns and resolving political conflict through brutality, intolerance, and fanaticism.[74] This would become a "marked" generation of China, one that would remain a social and political problem for the country in the decades ahead. In 1969 and 1970, however, they were being shipped out the countryside—often to the most isolated and desolate parts of the border regions and interior—by the millions.[75]

With so much disruption and flux, the political succession remained undecided. Lin Biao was the putative successor, but he worried, with good reason, that Mao would abandon him, and his close association with Cultural Revolution violence made him disliked by many. In addition, Lin was in poor health and therefore vested much authority within the military in his wife, Ye Qun, and his son, Lin Liguo. Ye became a member of the ruling Politburo in the wake of the Ninth Party Congress.

The attacks on institutions from 1966 to 1969 threw the top leaders back on their personal resources and networks in the increasingly deadly game of Chinese power politics. Put differently, the intrigues of the "inner court"—the personal relations of top leaders—became so important to politics that the functioning of the "outer court," the bureaucratic machinery of the state, faded considerably in determining political outcomes. The new Politburo membership ratified by the Ninth Party Congress in April 1969 reflected the growing importance of inner-court politics. Mao placed his wife, Jiang Qing, on this Politburo. Lin Biao's wife, Ye Qun, also joined, as did Zhou Enlai's wife, Deng Yingchao.

Within the military, Lin increasingly relied on two very loyal groups: the officer corps of the Fourth Field Army, the group with which Lin had fought for years before 1949,[76] and the air force, which was headed by a close associate and, less formally, by his son Lin Liguo. From 1969 to 1971 Lin tried to secure his own power base, but Mao Zedong and Zhou Enlai gradually undermined him. Mao chastised key Lin supporters and removed them one by one in 1970 and 1971. Zhou sponsored domestic priorities that focused on economic development rather than the more radical policies with which Lin had become associated.[77] It appears that in these strange times even Jiang Qing, the very symbol of radicalism, bided her time and quietly cooperated with Zhou in order to unseat Lin Biao.

These complex machinations came to a head in September 1971 when, allegedly, Lin in desperation tried to assassinate Mao and claim the mantle of leadership for himself. Mao, it is said, learned about the plot in advance and avoided the danger. Lin and his family, excepting his daughter, then supposedly tried to flee to the Soviet Union, but their plane crashed in Mongolia with the loss of all aboard. All bodies were burned beyond recognition. Lin's demise discredited the military itself, since Lin had supposedly orchestrated a military-based coup.[78] Taking advantage of the PLA's disgrace, Zhou Enlai then acted quickly to begin removing the army from civilian administration, a job that took years to accomplish.

More importantly, Lin's death discredited the Cultural Revolution itself and the national leadership in the eyes of many Chinese. When the story of Lin's alleged plot and his fate was relayed to the population in late 1971, many felt that the enormous suffering and bloodshed of the Cultural Revolution had, after all, been imposed on them as a consequence of the game of power politics in Beijing. The people had been mobilized, after all, to fight to the death to defend "Mao Zedong and Mao Zedong Thought," which represented the purity and perfect knowledge of the revolution itself. Mao had fully backed Lin as his chosen successor, the one who best understood and applied Mao Zedong Thought. Suddenly, though, the propaganda organs put out the story that Lin had been a scoundrel all along and that Mao had always understood this. Mao had only *seemed* to back Lin in order to flush him out and expose his true colors, at which point Mao foiled Lin's plot and rid the system of this usurper.

Even people who had been persuaded to regard Mao as virtually a god—and by 1971, Chinese citizens typically bowed three times before Mao's picture each morning and evening, "reporting" the day's events and their thoughts to the Chairman at each evening ablution—did not believe this new story. Lin's treachery, whatever it might actually have been, made cynics of many believers and greatly eroded the credibility of the entire leadership and its policies.

With Lin gone, the tacit alliance between Zhou and Jiang Qing soon frayed, as each maneuvered to gain the succession. In 1972 Mao suffered a heart attack and other severe health problems.[79] Although hidden from the general public, these setbacks must have sharpened intrigue over the succession in China's equivalent of the White House, the Zhongnanhai. The same year Zhou learned he had terminal cancer, adding still more intensity to the succession issue. During 1973 the battle lines over the succession shaped up, and the issue dominated Chinese politics for the ensuing five years.

The remaining three years until Mao's death witnessed a seesaw battle between the "moderates" headed by Zhou Enlai and the "radicals" led by Jiang Qing.[80] Zhou pulled together many former officials whom he managed to rehabilitate from their Cultural Revolution purgatory. In addition, Deng Xiaoping, who had been the number-two target of the Cultural Revolution after Liu

Shaoqi, came back into Mao's good graces during 1973. By 1974 Zhou pulled Deng into his own camp. Jiang Qing solidified a radical group that, at the top, was headed by herself, former Shanghai cultural affairs official Zhang Chunqiao, former editor Yao Wenyuan, and former factory security official and then leading labor organizer early in the Cultural Revolution Wang Hongwen. All had spent important parts of their careers in Shanghai, and all by the early 1970s held important positions in Beijing. After their ouster in October 1976, they were dubbed the Gang of Four.

Like selective modernizers before him throughout the twentieth century, Mao had late in his career turned toward a nativist position out of frustration over the contradictions inherent in the selective modernizer approach. He, like earlier leaders this century, had found that modern technology and the needs of industrial production impact on the structure and values of the society in ways he could not abide. During the 1970s, though, Mao sought again to achieve a balance in which economic development could proceed without doing fundamental damage to his radical social and autocratic political ideas. In this context, the personal tragedy of Mao Zedong in his later years was that he could not find a successor who sought both to spur economic development and to limit the sociopolitical repercussions of that process. Mao therefore intervened periodically in the conflict between Zhou's moderates and Jiang's radicals to tip the scale in one direction or the other, but he never permitted either side to gain decisive advantage.

From 1973 to 1976 the moderates generally controlled the executive organs of the political system, while the radicals had the upper hand in the propaganda and cultural apparatus. The military was not clearly committed and remained an object of concern for both sides. The moderate political platform edged somewhat toward that of the iconoclastic modernizers throughout this century, those who feel China should make whatever changes are necessary to develop modern technology and a modern economy. The radicals, by contrast, typified the nativist belief that China fares best when it isolates itself from the international arena and finds an ideological basis for binding its massive population together in militant unity.[81]

Broadly speaking, the radicals gained the upper hand in late 1973 through the summer of 1974 and again from late 1975 to the summer of 1976. The moderates, increasingly led by Deng Xiaoping as Zhou Enlai weakened from cancer, held the initiative from mid-1974 to the fall 1975. When Zhou Enlai died on 6 January 1976, the radicals soon succeeded in removing Deng from power again. But by the time of Mao Zedong's own death from natural causes on 9 September 1976, several developments had shown that the radicals were widely disliked, although they retained a core of supporters. Most notably, on 5 April 1976, large-scale popular demonstrations ostensibly in honor of Zhou Enlai at Tiananmen Square quickly assumed an antiradical thrust. The radicals successfully suppressed the demonstrations, arresting and beating many people in the process. But popular knowledge of these events weakened the radicals' legitimacy and chances of surviving Mao's death.

As the succession battle raged, the radicals repeatedly used their control over propaganda to stir up mass campaigns to put pressure on the moderates.

The rapid changes in policy lines that these campaigns produced exhausted and embittered the population.[82] Politics had more than ever taken a deadly turn, and most individuals tried to find ways to weather the storm by disguising their real emotions and thoughts even more than usual. The Chinese polity had entered a bizarre period that was brought to a conclusion only by the death of Mao and the arrest, a month later, of the leading radicals.

SUMMARY: THE MAOIST SYSTEM

The Maoist era was a remarkable time for China. Mao led a movement that provided strong central authority in a country that had experienced profound social and political malaise over many decades. He proved his assertion that the people of China had "stood up" in the international arena. One of his last major foreign policy moves was to agree to a limited rapprochement with the United States, inviting President Richard Nixon to Beijing in February 1972. From that moment on, China had a key role to play in what became known as the "strategic triangle" (China, the USSR, and the US).[83]

Under Mao and with help from the USSR in the 1950s, China began to develop a heavy industrial base and imported a great deal of fairly modern technology. It also copied a system of government that produced state ownership of the major means of production, collective ownership under state management of agricultural production, and a Leninist-type political structure that suppressed any truly autonomous social or economic organizations. To be sure, the Chinese system developed a style that differed from that of the Soviet Union. But the fundamental system was Communist party–dominated and Leninist, and this preempted the establishment of vibrant independent organizations as part of the Chinese development model.

Although committed to the rapid development of heavy industry, Mao remained sensitive to the inherent tendency of policies based on the Soviet model to increase inequalities, create a bureaucratic class, and widen the urban-rural gap. He therefore repeatedly intervened in the workings of this system to change its social and political results, primarily toward egalitarianism among those who live and work together, anti-intellectualism, antiurbanism, and antibureaucratism. In this sense, Mao periodically went into battle against his own creation, and in the end the tumult exhausted both Mao and "the system" without producing a clear winner. Both the battles and their outcomes left major footprints on the Chinese body politic.

One of the most notable features of the Maoist system is how powerful Mao himself remained. In a country of such enormous size, with national and provincial leaders who had climbed the rungs of power by dint of courage, skill, and ruthlessness, it is remarkable to note the extent to which Mao was able to overwhelm his colleagues and set the broad agenda. This must in part be seen as a product of China's long tradition of imperial rule.

Mao also combined his control over the prevailing ideology with great tactical political skill, ruthlessness in dealing with enemies, and the power that derived from his personality cult.[84] The bureaucracies and the people of

China did not always respond as Mao wished,[85] but his unique role in the system at virtually all times enabled him to define the terms of battle. That a committed revolutionary remained in a position of exceptional power for twenty-seven years after the CCP's victory in 1949 explains a great deal about the history of the PRC during that period.

Summing up Mao's legacies as of 1976 in the political arena, the balance sheet may read as follows. Mao created massive institutional structures—party, government, army—to run China but severely undermined the integrity and legitimacy of those same structures with the Great Leap Forward and the Cultural Revolution. The structures were too massive to disappear, but they were in such disarray by the time of Mao's death that making them "whole" would consume years and in some ways be impossible. Mao brought to power a very strong group of experienced revolutionaries, but in his later years set them against each other. The scars would prove lasting. Mao's expansion of the educational system during the 1950s had been undercut by his later attacks on intellectuals, and by 1976 China suffered an acute shortage of intellectual capital. Having established a strong, legitimate political system after years of turmoil in China, Mao spent his final decades destroying the effectiveness of that very system.

As a revolutionary who spent over twenty-five years fighting for national power, Mao devoted great attention to raw power as a critical dimension of Chinese politics. He inherited a weak, deeply fragmented society in 1949, a country desperate to regain unity and the belief in some central, energizing idea, and to recapture lost pride and stature. Throughout the remainder of his career, Mao used the goal of unity to goad the populace and his colleagues. Time and again he proved most adept at finding the fault lines in the Chinese body politic and then manipulating and exacerbating them to maintain his control. He thus never fully developed a centralized KGB apparatus like that in the Soviet Union. He relied instead on keeping people divided and off balance and ultimately dependent on him to provide the right way to escape from the country's predicaments. Considering his fondness for division and struggle, it is little wonder that Mao left a country exhausted by social conflict and a bureaucratic system in which mistrust and factionalism had become endemic.

The system Mao created sought to isolate social groups as part of its strategy for limiting potential challenges from below. Numerous policies worked toward this end: peasants could not link up with urban groups; a system of residence registration prevented peasants from moving into cities. Moreover, the state forced peasants to deal with the urban economy only through the mediation of state-run "supply and marketing cooperatives," effectively cutting off almost all nongovernmental urban-rural contact.[86] Within cities, most residents after the Great Leap disaster were locked into their units, the places of employment or study assigned them by the party. These units generally became economic, social, and political cocoons, and contact between units became structurally more and more difficult—to the point where major units maintained "foreign affairs offices" to manage their contacts with other Chinese units. Typically, an urban resident spent his or her entire career in the unit assigned them when they first found employment in the state sector of the economy.[87]

The intelligentsia, normally a bridge between various social groups (disaffected intellectuals, for example, had played key roles in many major peasant revolts throughout Chinese history), became especially isolated. The 1957 Antirightist campaign and the virulent anti-intellectualism of the Cultural Revolution made members of the intelligentsia a despised, outcast group with no social standing. They were by the late 1960s referred to as the "stinking ninth category."[88] In a political system that sought to deny recognition and independence to social groups in general, the intellectuals became a target of especially acute violence intended to grind them down and destroy their cohesion.

Even within the governing bureaucracies, Mao utilized rectification campaigns and other methods to prevent power centers from developing. In the system he sought to create, administration would be decentralized and flexible while power would be highly centralized under his personal control.

Finally, Mao's strong belief in the inherent value of struggle led to policies that subjected the citizenry to extraordinary levels of violence. The overthrow of the initial targets of the revolution—landlords, capitalists, and others—did not end the violence. Intellectuals and other "rightists" came under the gun in the second half of the 1950s, to be followed in the late 1960s by all those who seemed committed to traditional culture, to represent bureaucratic authority, or to be "disloyal" to Mao and Mao Thought.

Perhaps the greatest weakness of the Maoist system was precisely that the Chairman loomed so large in it. In one fashion or another, Chinese politics from 1959 through 1976 centered on the issue of the succession to Mao. Mao's futile attempt to guide his own succession brought suffering to tens of millions. The deterioration of the system in Mao's later years undid some of the major political accomplishments of his first decade: it reinfested the system with acute personal factionalism; it reduced the extent to which military forces answered to national unified commands; and it left the country uncertain of the correct ideology to follow to achieve wealth, strength, and international stature.

Mao Zedong was thus an extraordinarily powerful man who left legacies for China of enormous importance. Had he died in 1956, he would be remembered as a remarkable leader. But by his death in 1976 his impact on the PRC had become disastrous, and Mao's successors have been grappling with his mistakes ever since.

5

The Reform Era

Mao Zedong's death on 9 September 1976 and the coup against Jiang Qing and her key supporters the following month left the Chinese political system in crisis. Mao's last years were especially pernicious for the long-term viability of the CCP's rule. In the mid-1970s, for example, he advanced the thesis that the "capitalist roaders" who wanted to lead the country to "revisionism" were located "right in the Communist party itself," thus dealing a body blow to the CCP's remaining institutional legitimacy. The vicious political infighting of that period totally undermined the normal patChs for making policies and settling disagreements, causing the whole system to suffer a serious decline in capabilities. And the population itself seems to have been exhausted and disillusioned.

Mao elevated his own role to the point where he personally, rather than the Communist party as an institution, defined the prevailing line. Mao became the sole deity in what amounted to a political theocracy, and he left no successor or authoritative high priest in his wake. He purged Deng Xiaoping a second time in April 1976 and had him stigmatized for making a "right devia-tionist attempt to reverse correct verdicts," referring to verdicts on the Cul-tural Revolution and its victims. His own wife was arrested in October 1976 amid charges that Mao for years had not trusted her and had warned her against scheming. From 1973 Lin Biao, dead since 1971, had been castigated as "leftist in form but rightist in essence." In short, Mao's death left a power vacuum and a degraded state system in which those who were politically sainted one day could, the next, be overthrown and dragged through the mud, with often horrendous consequences for their families and major sup-porters.

In some desperation in his last years, Mao had turned to Hua Guofeng as a potential successor. Hua had joined the revolution in the 1940s and found himself in charge of Mao's home town after 1949. He met Mao in the early 1950s and thereafter gradually rose through the communist hierarchy, first in Mao's native Hunan province and then, starting in 1971, in Beijing. With nearly open warfare between Jiang Qing's leftists and the moderates, led first by Zhou Enlai and then Deng Xiaoping from 1974 to 1976, Mao positioned Hua as a compromise candidate who might lead the country when the Chair-man passed away.[1] Hua, however, lacked the stature and the power base in Beijing to consolidate power after Mao's death.

By late October 1976 China's leaders had to figure out how to repair the political system and how to explain to the population what had gone wrong. Initially, they took the easiest path: they rallied behind Hua Guofeng as a "wise leader," blamed all problems of recent years on the underhanded ma-neuvering of the Gang of Four, and attempted to resume the regular central work conferences and other activities that had characterized the CCPs style of governance before the Cultural Revolution.[2] However, the core issues on the immediate political agenda remained: whether to rehabilitate Deng Xiaop-ing; how to resolve the grievances of the tens of millions who had been wronged during the Cultural Revolution, and how to regard both Mao Ze-dong and the Cultural Revolution itself.

Deng Xiaoping's potential rehabilitation faced opposition by Hua Guofeng, who was trying to establish his own legitimacy as China's leader after Mao. Hua's political allies, like Hua himself, had been helped in their careers by the Cultural Revolution, or at least had not suffered grievously because of it. These included Wang Dongxing, a former personal bodyguard to Mao whom the Chairman had made head of the 8341 Division of the PLA (China's equivalent to the American secret service, which provided personal security for the CCP's top leaders); Wu De, the mayor and first party secretary of Bei-jing, who had given the orders to clear Tiananmen Square on 5 April 1976, when there were popular demonstrations there against the Maoist leadership; Ji Dengkui, a poorly educated man who had risen primarily through the in-dustrial bureaucracies; and Chen Xilian, Military Affairs Commission vice chairman, whose political base was in the southern part of northeast China.[3] These and others like them sat on the Politburo. All shared a strong interest in maintaining Mao's good name and in affirming the value of the Cultural Revolution.

Of all the top leaders, Hua had the greatest stake in protecting the reputation of Chairman Mao. In 1976, in the wake of Deng's second purge, the deathly ill Mao purportedly told Hua that, "With you in charge, I am at ease." This quotation alone provided the basis for Hua's initial assumption of the top military, party, and government posts upon Mao's death. Hua had these posts confirmed at the Eleventh Party Congress in August 1977.[4] If Mao were to become less than infallible, Hua's base of legitimacy would quickly erode.

Not surprisingly, Hua sought to maintain his power in part by sanctifying Mao's name and decisions. At a Central Committee work conference in March 1977, he favored a position that became known as the "two whatevers"—whatever Mao had decided would remain valid, and none of Mao's instructions should be contravened. At that meeting he also argued against rehabilitating Deng Xiaoping, a move being advocated by older leaders such as Chen Yun and Wang Zhen.

Deng's rehabilitation was an issue of central importance. Deng had been a major target of the Cultural Revolution during the late 1960s. Rehabilitated in 1973, Deng aggressively and effectively moved the country away from Cultural Revolution radicalism until his second purge in 1976. Hua knew that he could not compete with Deng's competence and political stature. Hua had risen as a product of the Cultural Revolution, while Deng would almost certainly steer China on a very different course. Hua therefore argued that one of Mao's last acts had been to purge Deng, in April 1976.[5]

The effort to maintain his own position allowed Hua little room for change in the face of deep popular disenchantment with the conditions the country faced. He quickly began to give way. In April 1977 Deng wrote a letter to the Central Committee that accepted Hua's leadership, and that summer Hua agreed to Deng's reassuming all the party and military posts he had held as of his purge in 1976: vice chairman of the CCP; member of the Standing Committee of the Politburo; vice chairman of the CCP's Military Affairs Committee; and chief of staff of the PLA.[6] At the Eleventh Party Congress in August 1977 Hua declared an official end to the Cultural Revolution but warned that such political movements would continue to be periodically necessary.[7]

Surveying the crisis-ridden Chinese system in 1977 and 1978, Deng decided that only major reform would permit the CCP to remain in power. The party, Deng felt, would have to improve the standard of living of the populace, and to do this it would have to eschew Maoist egalitarianism and collectivism. Deng, as most other twentieth-century Chinese leaders, sought to make the country prosperous and strong. Unlike Mao in his later years, though, Deng felt this required opening up to—rather than shutting off—the rest of the world.

Deng Xiaoping's Reform Impulse

Under Deng Xiaoping's aegis in the late 1970s, China began the most far-reaching, systematic reform effort that any socialist country had attempted to date. This chapter focuses on the reforms at the apex of the political system, reforms that ultimately decentralized political power, energized and changed the ways the economy and society functioned, and made it necessary to follow far more than politics in Beijing to understand the direction in which China was moving.

Nevertheless, political considerations in Beijing dictated the pace and thrusts of the reform effort throughout the 1980s. The two key players were Deng Xiaoping and Chen Yun, both members of the CCP since the 1920s. Each had allies within their own generation of political leaders, and each had a following among those ten to twenty years younger than they. Deng's most prominent protégés were Zhao Ziyang and Hu Yaobang, and Chen's were Li Peng and Deng Liqun; in the mid- to late 1980s all held dominant positions within the system. Deng's protégés themselves took some initiatives by the mid-1980s, and each finally ran afoul of their patron. The protégés also contended amongst themselves. Ultimately, though, the key political cleavage that developed was that between the patrons, Deng Xiaoping and Chen Yun. Deng at all times remained the more prominent of the two—a result in part of his greater political ambitions and energy. But neither Deng nor Chen ever tried to remove the other, and the political story of the 1980s thus revolves in a fundamental away around their evolving contention over policy initiatives, political power, and official positions for their followers.

It was Deng Xiaoping's commitment to move China in the directions explained below that created the opportunity for major change to take place without mass upheaval. It was Chen Yun's initial support for and then ultimate concerns about the directions of the reforms that substantially explain the major swings in Beijing's policies since 1978.

In many instances, local-level officials and even major segments of China's population took advantage of political initiatives coming from Beijing as well as political disagreements among the leadership to push reforms forward "on the ground," creating new situations that became national policy when leading reformers subsequently endorsed them.[8] In each instance, though, the developments at the apex of the political system—in the form of either policy initiatives or political struggles—created "space" for flexibility and initiative at lower levels. This chapter seeks to explain the ideas and politics at the Center since 1978. The remainder of this volume then considers the linkages between the Center, lower levels of the political system, the society, and the major issues that confront the system.

There was no single blueprint for reform. In many instances the initial reform policies recalled approaches taken in the 1950s and during the recovery period in the early 1960s. In the 1980s the difference was that Deng understood the inadequacies of previous policies and encouraged more significant change as required. The results raised difficult political issues and challenged deeply entrenched interests. Among Deng's greatest accomplishments was his ability in the late 1970s and much of the 1980s to sustain, on balance, proreform momentum in a badly divided political system.

Although the reforms followed a sometimes tortuous course, the outcome was remarkably successful in some key areas, even as they created grave problems with which the system must yet grapple. In the economy, China's real gross national product (GNP) per capita nearly doubled during the first decade of reform, an astonishing feat even from a low initial base (see Table 5.1). At the same time, the political system changed in significant ways, with substantial improvements in information flows, policy process, and flexibility in adapting to local conditions. China's relations with the international economy and with various foreign groups and institutions grew rapidly. But these changes came at the cost of developing any consensus on national values. And major elements of the political system changed little or not at all, and thus became more out of touch with an evolving social and economic milieu. Inflation and corruption also became endemic problems.

At the start of the reforms in late 1978 Deng lacked an overall plan, but he had decided that it was necessary to create an economically efficient society with a capacity for technological change if the PRC were to become prosperous and strong. He also recognized the need to impart legitimacy to CCP rule after the disasters of the late Mao years.

In broad terms, four major conclusions informed Deng Xiaoping's specific reform efforts. These conclusions derived from Deng's own experiences and concerned developments both in China and abroad.

Deng held, first, that on a global scale, the basis for rapid economic growth had shifted from extensive to intensive development. That is, by the late 1970s growth stemmed more from new production technologies than from added production capacity. Deng recognized, however, that China's Soviet-type system performed very poorly both in generating new technology and in bridging the gap between research and development and actual pro-

TABLE 5.1 *GNP per Capita (constant 1987 yuan)*

YEAR	GNP PER CAPITA
1978	529.54
1979	562.14
1980	598.57
1981	617.32
1982	661.06
1983	719.20
1984	812.64
1985	898.53
1986	956.67
1987	1042.53
1988	1136.50
1989	1166.43
1990	1212.87
1991	1284.96
1992	1443.67

Source World Bank, *World Tables 1993* (Baltimore: Johns Hopkins University Press, 1993), pp. 186–87.

duction. The influx of capital, technology, and managerial know-how necessary to overcome these problems was available to those who would participate in the global economy, as the recent experiences of South Korea, Taiwan, Hong Kong, and Singapore had demonstrated; but Deng knew also that the Chinese system was poorly structured to enter the global economy. Moreover, Deng regarded the necessity of keeping pace with the worldwide trends toward technological dynamism and economic efficiency as a matter of China's long-term national security. This conclusion largely matched that of iconoclastic modernizers throughout this century.

Deng was convinced that excessive bureaucratic control stifles change and efficiency. To develop efficiency, it was necessary, therefore, to decentralize power within the state and to permit at least part of the Chinese economy to develop outside the noncompetitive state sector of the economy. The latter would force the state sector itself to become more efficient and dynamic. It would also require far-reaching changes in employment practices, the legal system, property rights, social policy, the incentive system, and so forth.

Second, Deng concluded that after the disillusionment of Mao's last years, ideological exhortations rang hollow, and that the Chinese people sought a higher standard of living. Events during the 1970s had so eroded the legitimacy of the Chinese Communist party that a new source of confidence in the party's right to rule would have to be found. Deng decided that source must be more and better resources for the populace, and argued that the party's only hope was the utilitarian principle that it could consistently "deliver the goods."

Third, Deng felt that even with economic reform and a wealthier society, China would have to be ruled solely by the CCP. Deng had always held deeply authoritarian views concerning China, and believed that anything less than total control by the CCP would produce chaos and violence. The tumultuous years of the Cultural Revolution reminded everyone of the dark potential of social forces in China when they were set free. Many feared that a reduction in party strength would produce an avalanche of efforts by individuals and groups to settle scores from the Cultural Revolution, with the prospect of widespread attendant chaos.

Finally, in the international arena, Deng in the early 1980s concluded that China could obtain a period of peace if it astutely utilized diplomacy to do so. It could then use this temporary respite from military preparation to build up its industrial capabilities to the point where over the longer term the Chinese economy could support a modern, powerful military force. Achieving this would of course require that China actively play the game of US–USSR–PRC trilateral diplomacy to its own security advantage.

Although he had a general notion of the directions he wanted to move the country, Deng did not have a real plan in mind. As his reforms unfolded, there was a great deal of adaptation to the cross pressures created by earlier initiatives. Deng's genius, in fact, lay not so much in his ability to foresee the measures that would be necessary as in his extraordinary political skill in establishing and maintaining the political viability of a wide-ranging reform effort through the twists and turns of Chinese politics starting in the late 1970s.

Managing the Politics of Reform

Once rehabilitated, Deng first had to remove Hua Guofeng and lay the groundwork for major change. He quickly undermined Hua's power. Power in China derives as much from personal resources, such as relationships developed over the years, as it does from formal office. Deng was rich in personal relationships. He began his career in the CCP while working in France in the early 1920s. Back in China, he became a staunch early supporter of Mao Zedong in the hinterland, took part in the Long March, and served for years as a political commissar in one of the major communist guerrilla armies that eventually swept across China in the late 1940s. He ended the civil war in his native Sichuan Province in the Southwest, but within three years was posted to Beijing. In the capital he spent most of the time until 1966 serving as general secretary of the CCP, a post that kept him in close contact with a large number of party officials throughout the country.[9]

Deng's career gave him rich experience in both military affairs and civilian administration before his final purge in 1976. In addition, he had been purged twice (in 1966 and 1976) but never turned against colleagues, which stood him in good stead with the populace and many of the cadres. Deng thus came into office in 1977 with tremendous political resources to work his will.

Deng recognized the widespread desire to move decisively away from Cultural Revolution–type politics, and he acted accordingly. As of 1977–78, even initiatives to restore the pre–Cultural Revolution system seemed bold and reformist, given the decade-long attacks on this system that had torn the country apart. Deng thus was able to unite two groups of officials: those who longed for the days before the prolonged streak of ultraleftism that had begun with the Great Leap Forward; and those who had decided that more fundamental changes were needed to create a more humane political system and market-driven economy.

Both these groups in Deng's proreform coalition were composed of pre–Cultural Revolution officials: some of them had become targets of the Cultural Revolution and had spent many years in difficult political and personal circumstances; others had survived relatively intact but had not been key supporters of the upheaval. The issue that divided Deng's coalition in its early years, though, was fundamental: whether reform should return China to what many felt were the halcyon days of the mid-1950s, or change the way the PRC had been governed at any point since 1949.

Those who adhered to the former position had relatively clear ideas about what they wanted to accomplish. Those in the latter camp generally, as of the late 1970s, had only a vague sense that past methods would not work. At the outset, they lacked the knowledge and skills to develop a picture of the specific alternatives they sought. Nevertheless, they argued for greater experimentation and increased willingness to take risks to find effective policy proposals. During the early and mid-1980s, these more radical reformers gradually moved far enough beyond their more moderate counterparts that eventually serious, open tensions developed.

Importantly for Deng, from 1978 to 1984 these two approaches to reform could be contained within one coalition. The Cultural Revolution had so thoroughly damaged the political system that all agreed that basic steps toward rehabilitation of former institutions and methods of governance would have to come first. Specifically, it was not difficult for Deng to achieve wide agreement among his supporters in favor of:

□—rehabilitating cadres who had been persecuted without good cause during the Cultural Revolution witch hunts;

□—giving priority to economic development, which would require rapid restoration of the country's pertinent institutions to run the economy and abolition of the commune system in agriculture;

□—providing significant resources and incentives to bail out the agricultural sector, which had become a serious drain on the entire economy;

□—moving away from class struggle and mass movements (that is, mass political terror) as methods of policy implementation;

□—breaking out of the rigidities imposed by the dogma of Mao Zedong Thought; and

□—opening to the outside world, meaning the rest of East Asia and the West.

Only in 1984, once major progress had been made on all of the above, did the tensions in the coalition rise to the point where they dominated subsequent policy-making. Before 1984, though, even key figures such as Chen Yun, Wang Zhen, Hu Qiaomu, and Deng Liqun, all moderates in 1978 who in later years came to be regarded as arch conservatives, provided crucial support for the above agenda.

Deng initially pursued his efforts along two major lines: loosening the ideological straitjacket and creating a general sense of new opportunities to generate excitement and support.[10] Among the top leaders, he engaged in intricate ideological gymnastics to demystify the system after the excesses of the Maoist personality cult. He needed to clear away the psychological barriers to wide-ranging changes in the polity, as his emerging program amounted to a fundamental reversal of many of the ideologically derived priorities for which the blood of millions had been spilled during the Cultural Revolution.

Deng began almost at once to tackle the ideological question.[11] His message from the start was that Hua did not really understand the essence of the theology for which he was claiming the position of high priest.

Through 1978 Deng pursued more flexibility in the interpretation of Mao. During that year a discussion began on Mao's notion of "seeking truth from facts." Deng did not initiate this effort, but a key protégé of his, Hu Yaobang,[12] played a major role in promoting it once it began. Hu had become vice president of the Higher Party School in October 1977, and he used his position there to promote publication of this proposal. Deng used the notion of "truth from facts" adroitly to undermine Hua's "two whatevers." This was the centerpiece of an important speech he gave to a political work conference of the military on 2 June. By the end of that year, Deng had garnered widespread support for the idea that the essence of Mao Zedong Thought was that one should always "seek truth from facts, *and make practice the sole criterion of truth.*" Deng added the italic clause to the well-known Maoist dictum, and he thereby created an ideological basis for making reality, rather than Mao Zedong Thought, the test for determining the correctness of policy.

This pragmatic guide to action permitted the leadership to delve into the country's actual conditions and to suggest innovative solutions to the problems they uncovered. Although this may seem an unremarkable situation, in fact it is quite startling that this shift from ideology toward pragmatism had come about within two years of the death of the godlike Mao Zedong.

Deng also quickly signaled his willingness to move policy along rapidly to create new possibilities for major groups in the population. The resulting broad policy initiatives of mid-1977 through the end of 1978 marked dramatic departures from Cultural Revolution orthodoxy. They cascaded from the top echelons of the party with a speed and scope that outraced China's capacity to keep up.

The evolution of policy toward the use of foreign loans and capital offers one example. It went from a strict ban on accepting any loans or investment in early 1977, to a willingness to accept credit in the form of long-term deferred payments for imports as of the spring of 1977, to accepting outright loans from private foreign sources in that summer, to accepting foreign government concessionary loans (i.e., foreign aid) in the fall of 1978, to writing a law to permit foreign direct investment (that is, formation of joint ventures between Chinese and foreign firms) during that winter. By the end of 1978, Beijing indicated that it sought to bring in US $40 billion in foreign investment—an amount that the country had absolutely no ability to absorb and utilize.[13]

Cultural Revolution priorities and restrictions were quickly abandoned in many other fields. In education, for example, the Maoists had abolished examinations for university entrance or graduation, substituting a system of "recommendation" of applicants by work units, which favored those with good political connections and those from disadvantaged backgrounds. This system sharply discriminated against those from "bad" classes. The predictable results included the admission of unqualified students and the erosion of academic standards in the universities. But in the summer of 1977 entrance examinations were reinstated, thus radically shifting the social base of students who would gain admission. By the spring of 1978, the government had introduced tracking systems and key schools that would receive the best students, teachers, and resources. That summer, Beijing decided to start sending students and teachers abroad for advanced training.[14]

This almost bewildering succession of plans and initiatives was too hurried to make much economic or administrative sense. To some extent, it reflected a system lurching toward reform without the information and procedures necessary to fine-tune the efforts. More fundamentally, though, it also reflected a political calculus. Having decided to challenge Hua Guofeng and set the country on a different course, Deng sought to mobilize as much excitement as he could from various quarters.

The slogan that guided this effort was that China must achieve the "four modernizations—that is, the modernization of agriculture, industry, science and technology, and national defense." Zhou Enlai had first used this slogan in late 1964, but it had quickly disappeared. Zhou again raised it in his last official address in January 1975, at a meeting of the National People's Congress. Again, politics aborted the effort to make this a national priority. By 1978, though, the four modernizations had become the touchstone of national policy. There was disagreement, however, about how to achieve them.

At a meeting of the National People's Congress in February–March 1978, Hua Guofeng announced an ambitious "ten-year draft program" formally covering the years from 1976 to 1985. It called for the completion by 1985 of 120 large-scale projects, including the construction of fourteen integrated industrial bases, development of ten new oil fields, and a doubling of steel and coal output.[15] Hua based his ambitious plan on the idea that Maoist types of political mobilization remained an effective tool to achieve rapid economic development. Although Deng supported Hua's ambitious plan when it was announced, during the winter of 1978–79 he moved adroitly to distance himself from it.

In 1978 the gross output data of the economy indicated such rapid growth that in July of that year Hua and the national press began to talk about a "new Leap Forward." But the enormous growth actually stemmed from the return of production factors that had been left idle or were vastly underutilized during the Cultural Revolution and its immediate aftermath. Evidence mounted that this type of crash development program would quickly run into critical bottlenecks and could not be sustained.

In 1978 the United States and Japan stepped into the fray in a fashion that provided support to Deng Xiaoping. In May of that year President Jimmy Carter's national security advisor Zbigniew Brzezinski traveled to Beijing and, in essence, informed the Chinese leaders of the great benefits China could reap if Beijing were fully to normalize its diplomatic relationship with Washington. Many of these benefits would stem from American support of foreign investment in China and of China's greater access to the international economy. Shortly thereafter, the Chinese signed a long-term trade agreement with Tokyo that provided for substantial development assistance in exchange for Chinese energy exports.

As US-Chinese and Sino-Japanese diplomatic and economic contacts intensified, and as signals multiplied in Beijing of departures from Maoist orthodoxy, foreign firms and banking institutions began to flood Beijing with offers of capital and specific projects. This was a time of substantial liquidity in the international economy, which enhanced the attractiveness to the West of the virtually untapped Chinese economy.

In December 1977 Deng Xiaoping placed Hu Yaobang in charge of the CCP's Organization Department, the organ most directly concerned with implementing party control over personnel appointments. In this position, Hu attacked head-on the explosive issue of rehabilitating those who had suffered during the Cultural Revolution. Controversy ensued, some arguing that those who were rehabilitated would inevitably feel deeply aggrieved for their family's suffering and might seek revenge. China's peculiar personnel system, moreover, would typically put these individuals back to work in the very positions from which they had been ousted, thus leaving them to work alongside of their accusers and tormentors. Hu nevertheless insisted that the party correct as many wrongs as possible. He led these efforts energetically throughout 1978. Hu's initiative mobilized important additional support for Deng even as it stiffened the resistance of those who had benefited from the Cultural Revolution.[16]

Deng, in short, pursued a multipronged policy to box in Hua Guofeng and undermine resistance to change. His policy overall included the following elements:

□—Creating flexibility within Maoist dogma. By making "seek truth from facts . . ." the core idea in Maoist ideology, Deng successfully utilized the Chairman's prestige to release China from the shackles of Mao's political dogmas.

□—Providing quick payoffs to supporters. Deng sought both to generate enthusiasm and to create constituencies with vested interests in his success. He therefore reinstated bonuses for urban workers, supported higher procurement prices to peasants for their goods, rehabilitated millions of people who had been attacked, and so forth.

□—Creating vociferous domestic advocates of modernization. Deng in the late 1970s systematically sent central and province-level leaders on trips abroad to see how far behind China had fallen; many came back shocked. He also sent students abroad, promoted the rapid distribution of televisions, and used television to present images of the outside world to China's populace.

□—Disciplining the bureaucracy. Deng supported removal of Cultural Revolution radicals from positions of power, rehabilitation of former officials, development of a "discipline inspection" bureaucracy to enforce orders from Beijing, and other related measures to counteract the results of years of radical Maoist advocacy of rebellion from below.

Whenever the leaders create political "space," China's citizens take advantage of the opportunity to voice their views. Given the PRC's grossly underdeveloped institutional means for the populace to convey views to the leaders, such expressions typically take the form of mass demonstrations and other forms of direct actions such as putting up wall posters and writing petitions. Deng's wide-ranging efforts thus soon produced stirrings on the streets of Beijing. By the late fall of 1978, posters written by workers appeared calling for more rapid reforms. A wall leading to the intersection of Changan and Xidan streets in the western part of the city center became a gathering place for dissidents, who posted their proclamations and sold political broad sheets there. Quickly dubbed Democracy Wall, this area immediately attracted the attention of Western journalists and the Chinese leadership. Posters on

Democracy Wall dealt with many issues and conveyed increasingly fundamental critiques of the situation in China. Most called for further reforms. Many initially denounced Stalin to indirectly criticize Mao Zedong, and some became bold enough to attack Mao Zedong directly.[17] Generally, these posters and proclamations strongly supported the directions in which Deng was moving the system.

At an elite level, the Chinese party leaders convened a month-long central work conference in November–December 1978, followed immediately by the third plenum of the Eleventh Central Committee, which met 18–22 December. At the work conference, Deng and his allies seized the initiative from Hua Guofeng. They pointed to both economic studies and the voices of people at Democracy Wall to argue that serious changes must be made, and finally won the argument that it was no longer tenable to assert that Mao Zedong had always been correct. How would it be possible to rehabilitate many of the people who had been purged while maintaining that Mao had never erred? Declaring Mao's infallibility and placing all blame for Cultural Revolution excesses on the dead Lin Biao and the purged Gang of Four simply would no longer suffice.

The central work conference and the ensuing third plenum turned the tide and set the stage for further changes. Subsequent party histories proclaim that at these meetings the long-term "leftist deviation" in the party, which had started with the Great Leap Forward in 1958, finally ended. These meetings were so consequential that it is worthwhile to review the major issues on which they made important decisions.[18]

The plenum declared that henceforth the top priority goal would be to achieve the four modernizations—in agriculture, industry, science and technology, and national defense—and that the correctness of all policies would be judged in terms of whether they facilitate or hinder achieving that goal rather than in terms of their fidelity to Mao Zedong Thought. The plenum also announced that the campaign to criticize Lin Biao and the Gang of Four had been successfully concluded. Now the goal could shift from carrying out this campaign to nurturing economic development. The plenum also described the "two whatevers" as incorrect and endorsed instead the discussion on "seeking truth from facts. . . ."

Additionally, the plenum mandated significant increases in crop payments to peasants, the protection of peasants' private plots, and the provision of production incentives. It specifically criticized the ideal of achieving egalitarianism. It established a Discipline Inspection Committee to enforce discipline in the party, which was directed against the leftists who had dominated party affairs throughout the Cultural Revolution. It also called for management reforms in state enterprises and for some decentralization of urban economic administration.

In personnel affairs, the third plenum ousted the head of Mao's personal security force, Wang Dongxing, from his major posts, reportedly because he refused to accept the above decisions during the debates at the central work conference. It placed Chen Yun, Wang Zhen, and Hu Yaobang, among others, onto the Politburo. In addition, it announced the political rehabilitations of Defense Chief Peng Dehuai, who was purged in 1959 and died in 1974, and former Guangdong party boss Tao Zhu, economic administrator Bo Yibo, and head of the Central Committee General Office Yang Shangkun,[19] all ousted in the Cultural Revolution.

The third plenum acted on one additional matter: on 16 December, two days before the plenum convened, Beijing and Washington announced the normalization of diplomatic relations between China and the United States. Deng Xiaoping had personally negotiated the key elements in this agreement during the preceding weeks. With the announcement, Hua Guofeng held a press conference in Beijing in which he signaled clearly his skepticism about the deal that had been struck. The third plenum, however, appraised the foreign policy of the time as "correct and successful."

The third plenum thus marked a major defeat for Hua Guofeng in his effort to hold back the tide of movement away from the Cultural Revolution. By the end of the plenum, Deng Xiaoping had the initiative in his hands, and he pushed the country toward greater political stability, openness, and economic development. Deng had not yet thought through the limits of the reforms, but he had gotten things moving in a big way. Difficulties, however, would soon rein him in.

Deng's wide-ranging assault on the Cultural Revolution's legacies in China opened a Pandora's box, and in early 1979 trouble began to appear in various spheres. China's relations with Vietnam had deteriorated sharply in 1978, especially over China's support for the increasingly anti-Vietnamese Khmer Rouge in Cambodia. In late 1978, Vietnam had swept across Cambodia, driving the Chinese-supported Pol Pot regime from power and installing a puppet government loyal to Vietnam. In February 1979 Deng ordered an attack against Vietnam along the Sino-Vietnamese border to "teach Hanoi a lesson." By March, Democracy Wall had become more of a hindrance than a help to Deng's plans. The focus of criticism increasingly shifted from the specific despotism of Mao to the more general issue of dictatorship in China. A courageous dissident named Wei Jingsheng called for China to adopt the "fifth modernization"—that is, democracy—as a necessary step for achieving the better-known original four modernizations.[20] Deng, who has never favored democracy, ordered Democracy Wall shut down. Wei was arrested and sentenced to fifteen years in prison for allegedly revealing state secrets during the Chinese attack on Vietnam.[21] Arrests of other Democracy Wall activists ensued.

During the winter of 1978–79 the evidence quickly mounted that China's plans to absorb huge amounts of foreign investment were simply unrealistic. Lower-level Chinese economic officials, perhaps sensing that their opportunity to acquire direct foreign investment might be short-lived, rushed to sign numerous deals without much attention to their feasibility. The top leaders soon recognized that the current binge of deal-signing might obligate the PRC to take on a far larger hard currency debt than it could manage. Within China, moreover, new studies pointed to severe investment imbalances and other problems reflective of an overheated economy, and fears of inflation grew.

In March 1979 a central work conference brought out admonitions from Chen Yun and other moderate reformers that China would need a period of "readjustment" to dampen down inflationary fires and solidify the leaders' control over the changes occurring in the country. Chen had at other times—in early 1959 and again in 1961–62, for example—played a key role in putting the country back on an even keel.[22] Deng now went along with Chen's cautious call for reducing overall investment levels, shifting the investment mix more toward light industry and agriculture, and imposing stronger centralized monetary controls and limitations on the import of foreign capital. Having achieved political victory at the third plenum, Deng did not oppose some loss of momentum after that victory was sealed.[23]

In the spring of 1979, Deng also responded to increasing concerns about the system's spinning out of control by articulating the "four cardinal principles." These stressed that all future policies must be in conformity with (1) Marxism-Leninism Mao Zedong Thought, (2) the socialist road, (3) continuation of the people's democratic dictatorship, and (4) absolute political dominance by the Chinese Communist party. It subsequently became clear that there was little agreement on the concrete, operational meaning of the first three of these policy tests. But the fourth amounted to a firm commitment that, as political and economic changes reshaped Chinese society, the CCP would suppress any independent political forces that sought to represent new social interests.

Although Deng still had not forced Hua Guofeng's removal, by the summer of 1979, he, along with a broad coalition of older cadres, had gravely weakened Hua and his supporters who, like him, had benefited in career terms from the Cultural Revolution. Most of Deng's key backers at this stage were people who wanted to exorcise the Cultural Revolution from the system but did not wish to change fundamentally the nature of the system itself. Chen Yun typified those who placed priority on economic growth and avoiding the excesses produced by Mao Zedong's revolutionary initiatives.

Chen believed firmly in a planned economy but also felt the state should recognize the limits of the plan. He believed that people are motivated by material incentives and not solely by ideological exhortation, and he therefore supported growth of consumer industries and abandonment of the previous policy of radical egalitarianism. Chen had always felt that obtaining adequate food supplies for the cities was one of the most critical issues confronting China, and he supported reforms in the agricultural sector designed to boost rural production, especially of grain. Chen also advocated ties with the international economy, but he was concerned to limit those connections so that China would not lose control over its own fate.

Chen also felt that the state should occupy a dominant role in the economy to bring about rapid industrial development. Fearing runaway inflation and the social upheaval it might cause, he sought to create an economic policy that would produce managed growth. Chen thus wanted to improve the efficiency of the state sector, strengthen the agricultural sector's ability to supply foodstuffs and industrial crops such as cotton for the urban economy, and utilize market forces to supplement the state economy. This was a far cry from blind belief in the magic of the market, but it nevertheless brought Chen on board for many reforms of the late 1970s and early 1980s.

In addition to people like Chen Yun, Deng's coalition also brought together reformers who, as noted above, were groping toward more radical approaches. Generally, these individuals were more than a decade younger than Deng and his generation of leaders. Zhao Ziyang and Hu Yaobang typified this more adventurous group. Hu had been a close associate of Deng's almost his entire career, rising and falling over the years with Deng's own political fortunes. He had headed the Communist Youth League in the years before the Cultural Revolution. As noted above, Hu became head of the CCP's Organization Department in December 1977. A year later he moved laterally to take over the party's Propaganda Department, where during 1978 he played a critical role in promoting the discussion of "seeking truth from facts. . . ." Then in February 1980 Hu became general secretary of the CCP, and in July 1981 he replaced Hua Guofeng as chairman of the Chinese Communist party. He retained the general secretary post when the chairmanship was abolished a short time later.[24]

Zhao Ziyang's pre–Cultural Revolution career had kept him outside Beijing, and there is no evidence to link him with Deng Xiaoping before the Cultural Revolution. Zhao had served in Guangdong Province, which borders Hong Kong, from the beginning of the 1950s until his purge early in the Cultural Revolution. In October 1975, he had been appointed both governor and first party secretary of Sichuan Province. This landlocked southwest Chinese province, which included Deng Xiaoping's birthplace, had a population at the end of the 1970s of about one hundred million people. Sichuan had suffered grievously from civil strife during the Cultural Revolution,[25] and its economy was in poor shape when Zhao took it over.

Once the winds of change began to blow in Beijing in 1977, Zhao was bold and adept at rehabilitating Sichuan's economy. He loosened the collective agricultural system and increased peasant incentives, and quickly the province reverted to its traditional role as a net food exporter. His experiments with new incentive systems in industry also seemed to work. Deng and other leaders at the Center took note of these developments and began to groom Zhao for responsibilities in Beijing. Zhao worked in Sichuan through 1979, but during that winter he moved to Beijing, and became a member of the Politburo of the CCP in February 1980, vice premier of the State Council two months later, and premier that September. During 1980 Zhao also became head of a commission with substantial authority to develop economic reform proposals.[26]

Between 1977 and 1984 Hu Yaobang and Zhao Ziyang became convinced that China would benefit from relatively bold actions to change the system. Hu focused especially on policies toward intellectuals, while Zhao targeted the economy. Both became deeply involved in expanding China's relations with the outside world, especially with Japan and the West. Increasingly, they came into conflict with the supporters of moderate reform, such as Chen Yun, who wanted to apply the brakes once the system had been cured of its most harmful maladies. Hu, Zhao, and their followers wanted to press forward.

With Hua and his supporters defeated between 1978 and 1981, the decade of the 1980s witnessed a seesaw battle between different sides of the increasingly divided reformist coalition. It pitted advocates of only modest reform led by Chen Yun against those who wanted to move decisively to a market system, led by Deng Xiaoping with Hu Yaobang and Zhao Ziyang as his chief lieutenants. There were tensions within each camp, and from time to time other issues not directly pertaining to economic policy intruded, but essentially the conflict was about the extent of reform in the management of the economy.

The ensuing politics of the 1980s and early 1990s demonstrate the system's failure to institutionalize consensus-building and compromise at the top even after Mao's death. By the mid-1980s both Deng and Chen had developed very different policy packages. Deng stressed marketization and diversification of the economy, the depoliticization of society, opening to the international arena, and higher rates of growth. Chen sought planned growth, greater attention to political ideology, a more limited opening to the outside world, and more modest rates of growth. Because no rules or institutions could limit the activities of these two leaders, no mechanism existed to integrate their programs or balance their powers. Policy, therefore, tended to lurch from one policy package to another. Neither leader sought to knock out the other one; perhaps the bitter memories of Cultural Revolution political battles were too fresh. But this contention imparted instability to politics and policy throughout the 1980s and into the 1990s.[27]

A policy cycle developed that favored first Deng's priorities and then Chen's. Radical reformers loosened up the controls Beijing exercised over the economy. Lower-level officials then quickly took advantage of their new opportunities to bring prosperity to their own localities. This produced soaring budget deficits, rapidly rising inflation, worsening corruption, and rampant materialism among the population. As a consequence, Chen Yun–type reformers, who by the late 1980s had become true conservatives, argued for consolidation, retrenchment, and readjustment. This would entail the reimposition of some administrative controls, a clampdown on increases in the money supply, new drives against corruption, and greater attention to ideological education. This seesaw dynamic produced, in the terminology used by Chinese, alternate periods of "loosening" (*fang*) and "tightening" (*shou*).

The first such cycle took place in 1980. During that year the Chinese economy began to overheat as the early stages of reform took effect. Localities took full advantage of looser controls to increase their rate of investment, and paid out too much money to workers in bonuses. As a consequence, inflation set in, too much currency was issued by the Bank of China, and the central government confronted looming budget deficits. A meeting of provincial party secretaries in September 1980 could not agree on how to respond to this situation, but at a CCP work conference that November Deng yielded to Chen Yun's proposal to initiate a period of retrenchment. The agricultural reforms, nevertheless, continued apace.

In 1981 think tanks established by Deng-protégé Zhao Ziyang in Beijing worked on developing new reform initiatives. The most fundamental reform begun to date had been the initiation of a process that was leading to full de-communization of agriculture and a return to family farming. No other re-form so significantly affected the lives and livelihoods of so many people. The exceptionally good agricultural harvests that seemed to stem from the rapid return to family farming provided support for those who argued in favor of more radical reforms. Agricultural results would continue to provide a major boost to the radical reformers through the bumper harvest of 1984. In the urban economy, the retrenchment continued through 1982.[28] At the end of 1982, however, the Twelfth Party Congress provided a springboard for major new reform efforts.

The Twelfth Party Congress and the first plenum of the Twelfth Central Committee directly following it called for far-reaching rectification of the party apparatus. The more radical reformers hoped to utilize this rectification to weed out opposition to their policy proposals. Hu Yaobang almost immediately began to encourage further loosening up in the ideological realm. He articulated more explicitly than ever before the notion that the CCP continued to have the right to rule China because it could produce improvements in the general standard of living. This rationale played very much to the strengths of the radical reformers, with their concerns for providing individual incentives and for raising incomes.

Zhao Ziyang had spent his pre-1980 career in provincial positions. During 1983, Zhao began forming a reform coalition with coastal provincial leaders and with leaders of the "special economic zones"—coastal areas designated by Beijing in 1980 to provide special incentives for foreign investment. He did so by arguing for decentralization of budgetary authority, which would leave far greater resources in the hands of the leaders of China's wealthier provinces. This fit in with Deng's economic rationale of boosting the national economy by encouraging local initiative. The related political calculus was to build alliances with key provincial and local players in the Chinese system, most of whom were members of the Central Committee of the Chinese Communist party.

The radical reformers' coalition strategy naturally produced opposition from those left out. This included a wide range of important players: leaders of interior provinces, members of such bureaucracies as propaganda, personnel, and security, whose tasks were complicated further and whose prestige was lowered by the reforms, and Chen Yun's group, who feared both the economic and the sociopolitical consequences of the more radical program. Chen's coalition struck back. At the top, his supporters included Song Ping, Li Xiannian, Yao Yilin, Hu Qiaomu, and Deng Liqun, all of whom had strongly encouraged the initial reform efforts in the late 1970s. Hu Qiaomu had served at times as Mao Zedong's secretary and was one of the few well-educated members of the CCP elite; Deng Liqun as of 1983 was in charge of the CCP's propaganda bureaucracies. During the latter part of 1983 Hu Qiaomu and Deng Liqun deftly turned the proreform rectification, an effort to tighten discipline and weed out leftists, into an antireform campaign against "spiritual pollution." At an elite level, they minced few words in blaming Hu Yaobang for what they perceived as a sharp decline in the ethics of the Chinese system.

Hu Yaobang and Zhao Ziyang responded to this challenge by eliciting Deng Xiaoping's support for a major effort to vault China into the ranks of advanced nations through a Chinese technological revolution. Using, among other things, the writings of Alvin Toffler on the "third wave,"[29] they persuaded Deng that the key to China's development lay in rapid expansion of the country's scientific base. This would, in turn, demand greater freedom of education and thinking. Deng came out in support of this initiative in February 1984, and as a consequence the radical reformers were soon able to beat back the "antispiritual pollution" campaign. A Hu Yaobang protégé, Hu Qili, replaced Deng Liqun as the man in charge of CCP propaganda, and Zhao Ziyang increased his control over urban economic policy and over science policy. Political offices are part of the spoils of Chinese politics, and each time a faction surges in power it quickly takes advantage of the opportunity to reward its members with new appointments.

At the third plenum of the Twelfth Central Committee in October 1984, Hu Yaobang and Zhao Ziyang promoted far-reaching urban economic reform. This plenum was symbolically important, given the pivotal role of the third plenum of the Eleventh Central Committee in December 1978. In 1984, the third plenum adopted a document of principles on urban economic reform that pointed the way toward Deng Xiaping's preference for radical reorganization of the urban economy along market lines. This document maintained some role for the planned economy, but it strongly favored market forces to guide most economic outcomes. The constantly improving harvests of 1979 to 1984 lent great credibility to the Deng group's arguments. In the countryside, the reformers had successfully brought about fundamental changes in rural production, shifting from people's communes to family farming, between 1979 and 1984. The results were better than anyone could have anticipated. The radical reformers now asked, essentially, for similar freedom to reconfigure the urban economy.

Deng Xiaoping also mulled over the prospects for long-term peace along China's borders during 1984. By the end of the year he began to call for reductions in the size of the military establishment and for major reforms within the military system, both of which he pursued in earnest during 1985.

The year 1985 began with a new surge of reform initiatives, starting yet another cycle of expansion and retrenchment. This cycle entered a retrenchment phase in 1986, and those opposed to the radical reformers managed in January 1987 to convince Deng to oust Hu Yaobang from power. As Deng had looked to a Hu Yaobang/Zhao Ziyang team to take over for him once he stepped aside, this purge signaled major trouble for the political system. It raised the possibility, subsequently borne out by events, that Deng would, like Mao, be unable to designate successors and then assure a smooth transition of power.

Yet another cycle began in early 1987, as Zhao Ziyang articulated new reform initiatives that were embodied in the decisions of the Thirteenth Party Congress, which convened that fall. But these, too, quickly ran into trouble, and by the summer of 1988 the opposition led by Chen Yun counterattacked. Party decisions late that summer called for retrenchment, but by then the party was so divided that the effort proved half-hearted. This retrenchment really took effect only after the Tiananmen massacre in June 1989, and it lasted for two years. In early 1992 Deng Xiaoping personally intervened to start a new expansionary cycle that, basically, was still in progress as of mid-1994.[30]

Overall, the radical reformers never won a full political victory, and the relations between moderate reformers and their radical colleagues became increasingly embittered as time wore on. Because both sides were led by octogenarian Long March party elders, moreover, both contended over the eventual political succession to this older generation. The unresolved succession thus remained an important ingredient that further limited the ability of the various groups to reach a stable consensus.

Against this background of recurrent cycles, intraelite and state-society tensions associated with the reforms welled up most dramatically in the spring of 1989. The first months of that year witnessed conflicting dynamics. Zhao Ziyang and his radical reform colleagues sought to keep the reform effort moving ahead, and in this they were egged on by an increasingly articulate and bold collection of intellectuals and scientists. Nevertheless, the general thrust of policy at that time was toward retrenchment, and some efforts were made to tighten up, especially in the financial realm. In the midst of this tense political situation, Hu Yaobang died of a heart attack in mid-April. Hu had been purged in 1987, and his death touched off student demonstrations calling for the leadership to recognize Hu's full merits as a reformer. Hu had been an advocate of greater political and intellectual freedom; he thus provided frustrated students and intellectuals a vehicle for their criticisms of the more conservative leadership.

The demonstrations over Hu Yaobang during the ensuing six weeks turned into a fundamental challenge to the regime itself[31]—partly, it can be argued, because the leaders treated it as such. The top leaders responded ineptly when the demonstrations began, perhaps because they initially assumed the guise of mourning rituals for the departed leader. Official missteps enraged the students of Beijing, who expanded their efforts and eventually turned the demonstrations into explicit challenges to the way China was being led.[32] Official corruption and soaring inflation, both closely associated with the reforms, became two of the key targets of the demonstrators. They argued that these and other problems could be resolved if the leaders would permit a freer press and greater democracy. The student movement hence became known in the world's press as a Democracy movement. It focused its activities on the huge urban square that is the physical and political center of Beijing–Tiananmen Square.

The size and dynamics of the Tiananmen movement are testimony to the tremendous changes that the first decade of reforms had wrought in society. The reforms had among other things reduced political repression, encouraged greater freedom of thought, exposed many to foreign ideas and images, and focused people on improving their material standard of living. These changes produced demands by urban Chinese to be treated as citizens and not simply as members of the "masses." Student protest has a prominent history in modern China (recall the student-led May Fourth demonstrations in

1919), and with reforms reshaping society without producing major changes in the political system, tension was bound to erupt into social protest.

The Tiananmen demonstrations began as student actions in Beijing, and they subsequently spread to many other cities. Perhaps even more worrisome to China's autocratic leaders, the protests quickly involved not only intellectuals but also workers, entrepreneurs, and even many communist officials. For example on 4 May the huge crowds cheered when a contingent from the CCP Central Committee Propaganda Department marched into the square holding aloft a banner proclaiming that henceforth they would publish only the truth. Similar contingents came to the square from the major party news organizations, from the Academy of Social Sciences, and from other nonstudent units.

By the end of May many students, workers, and others had formed self-proclaimed "autonomous" organizations to represent their interests.[33] This marked a further challenge to the state. Until that moment, the communists had denied all citizens the right to participate in organizations other than those officially sanctioned by the authorities. Agreeing now to the legality of autonomous organizations would change the very nature of the communist system.

The student demonstrations played into elite politics in Beijing. In the spring of 1989, Zhao Ziyang feared he was close to being removed by Deng as a symbol for the country's economic difficulties. The reformist Soviet leader Mikhail Gorbachev, however, was scheduled to visit Beijing in mid-May for a summit meeting that would formally end the long Sino-Soviet split, and the Chinese did not want to carry out top leadership changes just before the Gorbachev visit. As May arrived with the massive student challenge to the leaders continuing, Zhao knew he was in serious political trouble, but that he would remain in office until at least a decent interval after the Gorbachev visit. In a related development, virtually all the major international media had decided that the Gorbachev visit to Beijing was so important that it demanded priority coverage. A very large number of reporters and cameramen descended on the city from abroad in late April and early May, just as the student demonstrations were gathering steam.

Facing this mix of forces, Zhao decided in early May that he would signal to the students his sympathy for their demands. This marked a considerable turnabout for Zhao. He had associated himself with ideas of greater political democratization in 1987, but more recently his followers had begun to support the idea that the best path to successful reform would be to have a strong, autocratic leader use his power to implement change.[34] This view, called "neo-authoritarianism," was intended to lay the groundwork for Zhao to become an autocratic leader in Deng's wake. Because of this and because Zhao's sons allegedly had become corrupt businessmen in Guangdong Province, Zhao had originally been as much a target of the demonstrators as were the other top leaders.

Zhao Ziyang's sympathetic response to the students was broadcast on the national evening news on 3 May. His remarks made him an instant hero among the demonstrators, and this intensified the sense of crisis at the top of the system. The top leaders felt they could not act decisively to regain control over the situation until after the mid-May Gorbachev visit; in the meantime, the students and their supporters gained center stage and enormous global publicity.

President Gorbachev's visit proved acutely embarrassing. Students staged a hunger strike in Tiananmen Square that garnered widespread popular sympathy. The Chinese government therefore could not hold the usual arrival and departure formalities for visiting heads of state in the square. Directly after Gorbachev's departure there was a showdown among the leaders of China in which the octogenarians, who had formally retired from their executive posts—especially Deng Xiaoping, Chen Yun, Yang Shangkun, Wang Zhen, and Li Xiannian—banded together to make all the key decisions. On 19 May Zhao Ziyang was removed from power and martial law was declared in Beijing. When troops then tried to move into the city, however, they found that virtually the entire urban population turned out to block their paths; they were stymied and eventually had to retreat. The situation then simmered for several weeks in a virtual standoff until, on 3 June, troops reentered the city in force, this time with orders to seize their objectives utilizing "all necessary means." In the early hours of 4 June widespread shooting began, producing a blood bath seen live on television around the world. During the following few days the PLA troops continued to consolidate their control over the city, using much violence and making numerous arrests. Beijing subsequently announced a death toll of 331. Outside observers place the toll between nine hundred and three thousand, but no fully reliable figures are available.

The situation throughout the country quickly quieted down once the top leaders demonstrated their willingness to draw blood to impose order. But while the use of force provided a tactical victory, it also produced a strategic disaster. Global public opinion turned sharply against Deng and his colleagues, who overnight changed in the public perception from reform leaders to retrograde autocrats and killers. Many countries imposed economic and other sanctions on the PRC in the wake of the Tiananmen massacre. Domestically, moreover, the party's use of troops against the population of Beijing produced tremendous revulsion and cost all the top leaders a precious amount of public support. Within the governing bodies themselves, moreover, the Tiananmen incident left a legacy of great bitterness, as many key officials had strongly opposed the use of force and found the students' demands reasonable.

On a popular level, the Tiananmen movement provided China's citizens with a rare opportunity to learn how many people shared their own criticisms of China's leaders. The unit system that Mao had imposed on China had reduced tremendously the amount of "horizontal" communication between people in different units, and thus citizens had no way to find out whether their own views were unique or widely shared. During the demonstrations, people learned that not only other ordinary citizens but also many ranking officials shared their sense of alienation. In the early evening of 3 June just hours before the blood bath, for instance, the normally reserved Beijingers hailed strangers on the street to exchange gossip and views, typically concluding each brief encounter with some sarcastic remarks about the political leadership. In the aftermath of the 4 June massacre, the authorities reimposed the unit system, but the events of April–June made clear how much society had changed and revealed to everyone the extent of popular alienation.

On 9 June, in the wake of the massacre, Deng Xiaoping called for a period of several years of stability.[35] Deng also demanded that the party produce results to rebuild support among the population. With Deng's first two anointed successors, Hu Yaobang and Zhao Ziyang, having fallen, the new people to move to the fore were Chen Yun–protégé Li Peng as premier, Jiang Zemin, former head of Shanghai Municipality, as general secretary of the party, and Deng ally Yang Shangkun, an octogenarian, as vice chairman of the Military Affairs Commission. Since 1989 Li and Jiang have ostensibly shared civilian power. In reality, however, the dynamics of Tiananmen demonstrated to all that the octogenarians were still a decisive force in the political system, and neither Li nor Jiang took any initiatives that might put them at odds with their patrons. Within the group of elders, moreover, the important divisions over the reform effort between Deng Xiaoping and Chen Yun remained. In this situation, Li Peng positioned himself with Chen Yun, while Jiang Zemin took his cues more from Deng Xiaoping. On the whole, the Tiananmen tragedy left the top level of the Chinese political system gravely weakened and in disarray. On balance, the Chen Yun forces had the upper hand in the wake of the purge of Zhao Ziyang and the bloodletting in Beijing.

The Tiananmen repression did not, however, resolve the fundamental debates about the best economic path to pursue, which continued virtually unabated. A new political challenge arose with the unexpected downfall of Communist parties throughout Eastern Europe and the Soviet Union from 1989 to 1991, which produced strong concerns among conservative leaders in the PRC. They reacted by heightening propaganda against what was termed "bourgeois liberalism" and taking new measures to try to limit the "corruption" entering China from the outside world.

The reform decade finally hit a crisis, therefore, in 1989, when the problems created by the reforms and the forces set loose by them combined to create a fundamental challenge to the system. The leaders beat back this challenge with brute force, but the system itself had changed enough to make any effort to turn back the clock impossible. By mid-1989 China had opened to the outside world and had let loose dynamic forces for domestic change. Yet in the wake of the Tiananmen massacre the country faced such major challenges that many observers doubted whether the system itself could survive for long.

Deng Xiaoping had initiated China's transformation, and he for the most part skillfully kept it moving forward. In January and February 1992, at age eighty-eight, he made another bold move to generate momentum for renewed reform. Deng traveled to the Shenzhen Special Economic Zone bordering Hong King and then to other parts of Guangdong Province and Shanghai. In each place he called for the whole country to push ahead with rapid market-oriented changes, emulating the economic development of Shenzhen. He also insisted China open still wider to the international arena.[36]

Deng's "southern journey"—the expression *nan xun,* used in the Chinese press, is reminiscent of the terminology formerly used for tours by the emperor—was part of a strategy to seal the succession and solidify the reforms. The Fourteenth Party Congress was scheduled to convene in the fall of 1992, to be followed by a new National People's Congress the following spring. Deng wanted to see reform-oriented officials secure the top party and government slots at these two meetings, and the Fourteenth Congress to give a firm imprimatur to market reform for the 1990s. Deng seemed keenly aware that this would be the last Party Congress he and the other octogenarians would live to see.

During the spring and summer of 1992 there were numerous indications of a seesaw battle, as reformers and conservatives tried to hammer out a deal that would permit the Congress to convene. Finally the Fourteenth Congress met on 12–18 October, and proved to be only partially successful. Its substantive economic program gave an unrestrained endorsement to market-oriented reform. Politically, however, the Congress produced a far more mixed victory for reformers (the details are analyzed in Chapter 8, on the succession). This disjuncture between the economic and political outcomes of the Congress was repeated at the National People's Congress in March 1993.

Deng's journey through the south touched off an explosion of economic activity throughout China. Local officials seized the opportunity to increase investment and sign deals. Individuals at all levels of the system sought ways to make additional money through entrepreneurial activity. A new expression soon developed for plunging into the market—*xia hai,* literally, "to go down into the sea." The government allowed foreign firms to enter major new sectors of the economy, such as insurance, retail sales, and legal work. Foreign direct investment in the PRC soared to roughly US $20 billion in 1993 alone.

But all of this frenetic activity brought with it the types of problems that cropped up in each of the earlier waves of reform enthusiasm. These included inflationary price increases, growing corruption, and bottlenecks in key goods, especially in the energy, construction, and transportation sectors. As of mid-1994 it is still not clear how—and when—these pressures will be reined in.

The Content of Reform

Having navigated the twists and turns of reform politics we must now look more closely at the substance of the reform policies themselves. These initiatives, as noted above, were not carefully coordinated or fully thought through. But they brought tremendous change to the lives of most Chinese and significantly affected the way the PRC functions, both economically and politically.

The following discussion begins with reforms in two broad social areas: creating a pool of talent and reducing the scope of politics in Chinese life. It then considers the three major areas of economic reform: reforming agriculture and recreating a family farming system; developing a vibrant nonstate sector in the urban economy; and nurturing ties to the international economy.

CREATING A POOL OF TALENT

By the late 1970s Deng was convinced that China needed both technical talent and organizational expertise to develop its economy rapidly. Mao had increasingly relied on motivating the masses to superhuman effort to accomplish key targets. But studies done in 1977 and 1978 concluded that capital/output ratios—the amount of resource investment required for each fixed increment in output—had been rising steadily and were approaching levels that could not be sustained. To change this, China would require skills that are critical to "intensive" development, in which much of the increase in production stems from devising better, more efficient means of producing goods.

Among the implications of a shift toward intensive development were, in the short term, the rehabilitation of cadres and intellectuals who had lost their positions during the Cultural Revolution. The former possessed valuable experience in organizing production, gathering statistics, and in other ways more effectively utilizing the country's very scarce resources, while the latter would provide the best available technical base.

Having rehabilitated a large number of cadres by 1980, though, Deng then began moving them out to make way for younger people who were better qualified for the challenges of guiding intensive development. Many of the rehabilitated cadres were of peasant origin, veterans of the revolution, and poorly educated. Few knew anything about the outside world or the demands of technological change and global production. In the early 1980s, therefore, Deng and his reform group began to stress the importance of cadre retirement and the promotion of a younger, better-educated cohort of officials. But the older generation viewed their positions as a lifetime commitment rather than as a career from which one retires.[37] Moreover the dearth of significant numbers of well-educated younger people made this transition complex and drawn out.

The rehabilitation of intellectuals took place fairly rapidly. In 1979 the CCP declared that, some thirty years after the founding of the PRC, nearly all citizens had finally shed any former hostile class nature and had become a part of the "people." According to this decision, intellectuals and former capitalists should be considered workers, and former landlords and rich peasants should be considered ordinary peasants. Those still in labor camps on political grounds should, by and large, be considered fully reformed and therefore be released. From 1979 to 1981, some Chinese sources indicate that roughly half the four hundred thousand or so arrested during the 1957 Antirightist campaign were released from prison. A few of the remaining two hundred thousand had won release at some earlier time; the others had died in prison. By 1981, many of these individuals began to greet foreign scholars in the guise of researchers at national research institutes or in other similar capacities. In one notable instance, when Deng Xiaoping visited the United States in January 1979 to celebrate the formal establishment of full diplomatic relations with the United States, one of his key advisors had been released from twenty-two years in prison virtually on the eve of the trip!

Deng also promoted policy changes to enable intellectuals to work without substantial political interference and to train younger talent. He argued that quality professional work is itself a reflection of political loyalty, a notion profoundly alien to that propagated by Mao and his more leftist followers, who saw commitment to professional work as a manifestation of social and political elitism.[38]

This shift toward a more meritocratic society to foster intensive economic development encountered serious constraints. China had for so long suppressed its intellectuals that the country basically lacked the teachers and the textbooks necessary to implement this new set of priorities. Moreover, the values and habits of many individuals still in power often permitted students with "good" family and political connections to rise rapidly even if their academic achievements did not warrant it.

Fundamental to Deng's efforts to create a pool of talent was the notion that these individuals should contribute their views and skills to the political leadership without, however, developing a truly independent base or role. Put differently, the new and old cadres were to maintain communist discipline and remain within the political framework articulated by the CCP leaders. The intellectuals, as in the imperial era, were in loyal fashion to limit themselves to giving the leaders their insights when asked. Deng never felt that intellectuals should, as in the West, consider themselves independent critical observers with the freedom publicly to raise any issues that troubled them.

In practice, the overall reform effort created conditions that reduced the sense of discipline among the cadres and nurtured a greater feeling of independence among the intelligentsia than the top political leadership desired. Both these developments contributed to the politics of the Tiananmen tragedy of 1989.

STATE AND SOCIETY

In a totalitarian system, the political sphere becomes coterminous with the society itself. In almost no other society has the personal been politicized to the extent it was in urban China at the height of the Cultural Revolution. The core Maoist priorities were to permeate the public and the private: egalitarianism and frugal living, political purity and class struggle, sexual prudishness and political devotion. But the reformers recognized that "intensive" economic development would require the kind of initiative and independence that were absent in a caste-ridden, ideologically driven society.

Deng thus largely dispensed with ideological appeals and political coercion to motivate people; he chose to utilize material incentives instead. As noted above, in the late 1970s he and his colleagues granted the first pay raises to urban workers in more than a decade, reinstated bonuses, and otherwise provided people with incentives to make greater efforts.[39]

However, monetary incentives would be ineffective without allowing people the freedom to live better and making goods available for purchase with their new wealth. The reduction in the scope of politics was a critical element in meeting this requirement. Once a nonpolitical sphere was officially recognized, people ceased to be afraid to wear more stylish clothes, acquire basic consumer goods, and in other ways to enjoy their income. After decades of Maoist austerity, there was tremendous pent-up consumer demand in China, and the reformers successfully tapped some of this energy in the service of economic development. The government had to shift investment priorities in the direction of increased production of consumer goods.[40]

As with other reform initiatives, these efforts produced ripple effects. With people encouraged increasingly to work for money and material goods, what the Chinese call the "red-eye disease"—jealousy—quickly spread. Virtually every major social group—peasants, workers, entrepreneurs, government officials, intellectuals—soon felt that other groups were benefiting more from the reforms than they were. Social discord increased accordingly.

In addition, desperate to provide immediate material benefits to large segments of the population at the end of the 1970s, the leaders decided to spread rapidly the availability of television sets and of programming via stationary satellites. For the vast majority of Chinese, who had had no previous access to television, this would amount to a significant improvement in the quality of daily life. The leaders did not, however, comprehend the extent to which television would contribute to a revolution of rising expectations by making the people aware of their own relative backwardness.

With propaganda touting higher consumption rather than ideology, the government's base of legitimacy shifted to its ability to continue to improve the standard of living of the population. This policy also created a fertile arena for the growth of corruption and resulting loss of discipline within the state bureaucracies. It largely drained the society of any sense of selfless common purpose. This abandonment of the government's traditional role of providing a moral framework for the society gave the reformers considerable flexibility in choosing new initiatives to pursue. It also, however, made popular support to a considerable extent contingent on maintaining visible economic growth, and no political leadership can provide that consistently. The result was evident at Tiananmen Square in April–June 1989.

AGRICULTURE

Internal government studies carried out in 1977 and 1978 shocked top political leaders by revealing that more than seventy million peasants lived severely deprived existences, while the average peasant fared no better in 1978 than did his counterpart in 1952. For a party that rose to power with the support of the countryside, this presented a sorry record of accomplishment.

Nearly 80 percent of the Chinese population lived in the countryside on the eve of the reforms, and thus changes in agricultural policy were of paramount importance in the overall reform effort. The reformers transformed the agricultural system, and production boomed. Initially, Deng insisted that the urban sector pump more money into the rural economy. This at first took the form of state-mandated increases in the procurement prices the government paid for agricultural output. The state also eased its former insistence that peasants plant grains even where conditions were ill-suited to this. Soon China's peasants gained some power of choice over the crops they would plant.

In the early 1980s, the reformers dismantled the agricultural people's communes that were initially formed during the Great Leap Forward. In their stead, China developed a family-farming system in which each family leased land from the collective.[41] The government eventually permitted leases of fifty years and more that could be inherited, bought, and sold. The leasing system provided a means for reestablishing all the incentives of family farming without turning all the land over to direct private ownership.

The leasing system, in turn, freed up much surplus labor in the countryside; the government accommodated this pressure by easing the residence restrictions that bound the peasant to the land and by allowing peasants to set up small-scale enterprises in services and light manufacturing. Peasants still were barred from establishing permanent residence in the major cities, but the government allowed them to move to smaller towns to set up shop. As a consequence, in the mid-1980s some one hundred million adults abandoned tilling the land and took up other work in the villages and townships throughout China.

All of these changes produced spectacular growth in agricultural output and in peasant standards of living. Peasant demand for consumer goods mushroomed, providing strong market support for increased production in the light industrial sector.

The reforms in agriculture moved China in new directions. Millions of people changed their line of work. Townships grew rapidly and became significant economic and social elements in the Chinese polity. Whole markets opened up and created large new demands for consumer goods. Private and collective enterprises sprang up like, in the traditional Chinese phrase, "bamboo shoots after a spring rain," and began to exert competitive pressure on the sluggish state industrial sector.

Agricultural output, however, did not sustain high growth after 1984, even though the population continued to grow. Fears of peasant migrants inundating the major cities began to spread. Rural irrigation works deteriorated as the state's ability to mobilize collective labor declined. And concerns about the environmental consequences of uncontrolled rural industrial growth became more pressing.[42]

THE URBAN ECONOMY

Deng and his reform-minded colleagues introduced highly significant changes into the urban planned economy, as well. They legalized multiple forms of ownership,[43] encouraging the growth of private and collective enterprises outside the state sector that would pressure the state sector to reform itself. Given the state's former monopoly on controls over the urban population and delivery of urban services, the development of nonstate urban enterprises would eventually raise fundamental issues about the nature of urban governance.

The reformers contracted the scope economic planning. From a plan that listed over six hundred items as of 1978, by the late 1980s the national plan covered about twenty-five items. Some of this planning authority shifted to local levels of government but much of it simply disappeared, to be replaced by other allocation and investment mechanisms.

Of crucial importance, economic administrative powers were decentralized from the Beijing ministries and commissions to major territorial units, the provinces and municipalities, to tap the initiative of these territorial authorities. The budgetary system was adjusted to provide far greater fiscal authority for the provinces.[44] One result was that by the late 1980s, the central government was running a large structural budget deficit while the wealthier, generally coastal, provinces developed large revenue surpluses.[45]

Price adjustments were introduced. During the 1980s the state lifted all administrative price controls on small consumer goods and allowed the market to set prices. For goods still produced at fixed prices under the state plan, moreover, the authorities adopted a "dual price system." This permitted surplus goods—those produced above the plan targets—to be sold at a higher price than the fixed plan price. The higher price was in some cases set by the market; in others it floated between benchmark prices set by the state.

The results were startling. Real standards of living increased at an extraordinary rate, economic decision-making shifted in substantial measure from Beijing to the provinces and municipalities, geographical inequalities grew, and the overall economy became far more lively and diverse. The fastest growing sector of the economy under these reforms was the nonstate sector. The nonstate sector in turn enlivened the urban economy and provided employment for large numbers of peasants who left the land.

However, the economic reforms also caused problems. By the late 1980s inflation produced double-digit price increases that were dampened at the cost of the severe recession induced by the credit squeeze in 1989 and 1990. Growing inequalities in living standards encouraged peasants to drift into major cities along the coast seeking employment, causing increased social disorder. The system of multiple prices for certain industrial goods proved irresistible to those who could engage in illegal "price arbitrage"—that is, who could obtain a product at the low, state-set price and then sell it for the above-plan market price, pocketing the difference. Corruption grew apace.

CHINA AND THE INTERNATIONAL ECONOMY

China's self-imposed isolation during the Cultural Revolution decade came, by chance, at a time when the economies of the other parts of East Asia were just taking off. Japan, South Korea, Taiwan, Hong Kong, and Singapore all used export-led growth strategies and imports of capital and technology to take advantage of rapidly expanding international trade.[46] When Beijing began to emerge from its cocoon in the late 1970s, therefore, it faced a region that had been significantly transformed. In 1965 per capita incomes in most of East Asia were still at third-world levels; by the late 1970s much of the region had modernized significantly.

China's communist leaders had previously viewed the international economy as the almost exclusive domain of the major capitalist countries, all of which it regarded as imperialist powers engaged in a zero-sum struggle with the socialist countries and the third world. It had therefore banned all Western investment in the PRC on the assumption that such investment would be used solely to exploit the country's resources, drain off profits, and subvert the political system. In similar fashion, it had stayed away from the international financial institutions, such as the World Bank and the International Monetary Fund, since it regarded these as dominated by the Western capitalist countries, especially the United States.

The experiences of East Asia outside of the PRC changed the perceptions of China's reformers on these issues. China suddenly found itself in danger of becoming a backwater in the region, a country unable to catch up economically or technologically with its smaller neighbors. The issue of relations with the international economy thus began to be cast in new terms. Rather than seeking the greatest possible protection from the threat of this international economy, Deng Xiaoping and some other Chinese leaders began to ask how the country could reap the benefits—technology, capital, managerial know-how, access to markets—that other countries in East Asia had so obviously garnered from participation in the international economy over the previous decade and more.

The implications of this new approach were far-reaching. In 1979, China passed its first joint venture law, which laid out an initial framework for accepting direct foreign equity investment.[47] Soon thereafter Beijing began to develop special economic zones at selected places along the coast, the most important one being Shenzhen, in Guangdong Province bordering Hong Kong. These zones, utilizing a mix of the models developed in South Korea and Taiwan, offered exceptional tax treatment and other concessions to foreign firms to invest in those areas.[48]

These early steps produced cascading effects, as had been the case each time over the previous century that the country had started to open its gates to the outside world. This time, of course, foreigners participated in China according to rules laid down by the Chinese—the extraterritoriality of a previous era would not appear again.[49] The overall effects of greater interaction with the international arena, though, proved impossible to bottle up in the special zones. A few examples suggest the scope of the changes that international contact either required or encouraged.

Foreign investment demanded that Beijing adopt laws that would define property, govern contracts, stipulate taxes, and in other ways make the economic environment predictable enough for foreign firms to participate in. The United States is more legalistic than any other country, but by the late 1970s even most European and Asian multinational corporations employed numerous lawyers and expected countries to provide certain basic legal guarantees.

China, however, literally had no legal system and no law in a Western sense as of 1977. When the PRC was founded, the party declared all Guomindang laws invalid, and during the early 1950s it began to develop new legal codes to replace the defunct GMD statutes. This effort, however, came to a halt at the beginning of the Great Leap Forward, and it never resumed.[50] As of 1977, therefore, China was governed by decrees, by bureaucratic regulations, and by the personal orders of various officials; it had no codes of law at all. In addition, many of the decrees, regulations, and so on were kept secret. The first foreign firms that sought to invest in the PRC signed contracts subjecting their investments to all pertinent rules and regulations, even though they were not allowed to know what these strictures were!

Beijing soon realized that it would have to start developing a legal infrastructure in order to attract the foreign investments it desired. During the 1980s, therefore, it began to flesh out its legal system and to make more transparent its extensive bureaucratic regulations. The government also paid increased attention to developing a court system with judges knowledgeable about the law and legal procedure. This has been a long, complex effort; in July 1993 Beijing announced that the PRC had only fifty thousand lawyers and would train an additional hundred thousand by the end of the century.

Beijing's desire to join the World Bank, the International Monetary Fund, and the Asian Development Bank to obtain low-interest loans and economic and technical advice also produced important domestic changes. The reporting requirements that these organizations, especially the World Bank, impose on their members are strict. In addition, the World Bank strongly encourages its member countries to analyze their economic situation in categories that are common throughout the system. These employ concepts, such as gross domestic product, that are different from those traditionally used in Soviet-bloc countries.

After considerable internal debate over the issue, China decided to meet the requirements to join the World Bank and other organizations.[51] As a consequence, Beijing became far more open about the Chinese economy, and changed its methods of compiling economic data. In return, the World Bank not only provided extensive loans and project assistance, it also did a series of studies on development strategies for the Chinese economy as a whole and for key sectors individually. The rules regarding the availability of data *within* China changed as well, so that for the first time many Chinese economists obtained data about their own country that previously had been barred to them.

To pay for this increased level of interaction with the international economy, Beijing encouraged a vast expansion of the country's exports. This demanded major improvements in the quality of domestic production in the affected sectors. Under the Maoist system, enterprises followed an economic plan or bureaucratic orders. There was no stress on product style, little attention to innovation, and almost no penalty for work performed poorly or behind schedule.[52] China's major potential exports such as textiles, however, required that producers meet tight production schedules, adapt nimbly to changes in consumer demand, and maintain top quality in order to be competitive.

Before China's opening to the international economy Chinese enterprise managers responded only to production orders, not to consumer demand. This produced much misunderstanding in initial contacts between Chinese managers and Western business people. The latter assumed production to be market-driven, while the former assumed that producers do not have to think at all about the consumers. It took considerable time for each side to begin to understand the assumption the other was making. Gradually, more and more Chinese managers began to take heed of consumer demand, which created new pressures on the organization of production.

Foreign firms also felt that major economies could be achieved simply through managerial reform. Virtually all Chinese enterprises are grossly over-staffed, pay little attention to maintenance, and overstock inventories of production inputs. Foreign investors and buyers pressed the Chinese incessantly to change these conditions to become more competitive, and leaders in Beijing often agreed in principle. But this managerial system had become so intertwined with local social and political practices that real managerial reform might have threatened any enterprise's relations with the community.[53]

Building up foreign trade and importing foreign capital also required that the Chinese grow more knowledgeable about the international arena and acquire modern technical skills. Both these needs prompted increased contact with foreigners who possessed the knowledge needed by China. In the late 1970s, as noted above, the country began to send senior people on trips abroad to make contacts and learn from foreign practices.

Soon students too could go abroad to pursue advanced degrees, primarily in engineering and the hard sciences.[54] Although many of those who left for foreign study did not return home, these efforts produced significant effects inside China. Students abroad maintained contact with their relatives, friends, and colleagues in China, and sent back information that proved startling and unnerving to the recipients. More Chinese began to work hard to develop the skills necessary to obtain an opportunity to go abroad. A craze developed to study English, and then Japanese. The resulting demand for study materials increasingly exposed students to books written in the United States and elsewhere, expanding their intellectual horizons beyond official Chinese orthodoxy.

The Chinese government found itself forced to give up the monopoly it had exercised over the information available to its politically aware, skilled people. Foreigners in China, Chinese traveling abroad, and the growing volume of foreign publications and electronic media that penetrated the PRC all made the country's borders more porous. The ones who benefited most from these developments were people from traditional intellectual and elite families that had been repressed under the Maoist system.

The opening to the international economy thus brought ripple effects into many dimensions of life in the PRC. The complex results have profoundly changed the social life, economic well being, and distribution of power and resources in the Chinese polity.

*   *   *

This chapter set up a basis for understanding the Chinese system by explaining the ideas that energized reform, the politics of the reform effort at the Center since 1978, and the major thrusts of national reform policies. But

China's system consists of far more than elite politics and national policies. The country still boasts by far the world's largest governing organizations, bureaucracies that themselves have grown considerably during the reform era. These bureaucracies, on the whole, generate the information on which the leaders depend and impact strongly on both the development and implementation of national policy. Any analysis of China requires, therefore, detailed examination not only of leadership politics but also of the ways in which politics, administrative structure, and bureaucratic practice interact.

Both the governing bureaucracies and the society itself have evolved greatly under the reforms to the point where the nature and dynamics of basic linkages—between the Center and the provinces, the provinces and the basic levels, and basic levels and the populace—are matters of heated debate among those who follow developments in China. The following chapters focus first on the political apparatus itself from its apex to its foundations to explain both the formal organizational arrangements and the real topography of power. The remainder of the volume then examines the complex dynamics of this state system as it wrestles with the core issues that confront it: political succession, managing the economy, limiting environmental damage, coping with a changing society, and dealing with the global arena of the 1990s.

Part Three

THE
POLITICAL
SYSTEM

6

The Organization of Political Power and Its Consequences: The View from the Outside

As the victorious Mao Zedong approached Beijing from the Fragrant Hills in the western suburbs in March 1949, he carried with him two works of traditional Chinese governance, the *Shi Ji* (Records of the Historian) and the *Cu Zhi Tang Qian* (the General Mirror for the Aid of Government).[1] He intended to draw deeply from the wisdom of his predecessors in developing his techniques of rule. He also sought advice from a quite different source: Stalin's socialist system in the USSR. Mao would wed imperial China to Soviet experience to build his regime in the PRC.

The imperial Chinese and the Soviet systems in fact had a number of points in common. Both stressed centralized control and bureaucratic administration. Both utilized ideology to buttress the legitimacy of the system, and held that the leaders embodied the correct ideology, leaving no room for private, individual interests or for organized opposition to the state. Both consciously fostered competition among various bureaucracies in order to maximize control by the top leaders.[2] Naturally, the overlap was very far from complete: the substance of the respective ideologies differed enormously, for example, and the imperial Chinese system did not seek to maximize economic growth as did the Stalinist system.

From its Soviet-style beginnings in the mid-1950s, the PRC's political system has experienced significant upheaval, including the Great Leap Forward, the Cultural Revolution, and the reforms after 1978. Nevertheless, the decisions made in the regime's early years about the formal structure of the system have endured even as substantive issues, policies, and the allocation of power have changed greatly over time. Individuals who joined the Communist party in the 1920s have maintained control in China ever since 1949. Only with the passing of Deng Xiaoping and Chen Yun, the two most powerful of the survivors of the pre-1949 struggles, might the formal system move into a new stage.

This chapter introduces the political system as it appears to outsiders and is portrayed on the PRC's official organizational charts. As Chapter 3 notes, the Chinese system is divided into three nationwide bureaucratic hierarchies—the party, the government, and the military. Each civilian hierarchy comprises four major territorial entities: the Center, the provinces, the counties, and the cities. In the party and government hierarchies these entities are organized in roughly the same way. This chapter first examines their operation in detail, then presents some of the inherent matrix problems the structure creates, and finally explains the solutions adopted at various times to these and related problems.

A fifth major territorial level of political administration, the prefecture, is not discussed in detail here. China formally treats prefectures as merely "dispatched organs" of the provinces. In reality, the presence and importance of prefectures varies greatly by province. Liaoning Province has abolished almost all prefectures, Sichuan still has some but meshed many into enlarged municipalities in the mid-1980s, while Hunan retains the prefecture as an important operational level of administration. Where they exist, prefectures rank below provinces and above counties, and they serve as coordinating organs between these two administrative levels. In basic organization and function, prefectures are like provinces and counties. Because many localities lack prefectures, the following discussion omits them for the sake of simplicity.[3]

As with all major political systems, the real topography of authority and methods of governance in China differ considerably from the image created by formal organization charts and published rules of procedure. Chapter 7, therefore, explains the hidden parts of the Chinese political system, and how the system looks to the inside participants. The picture given in Chapter 7 is not totally separate from that presented in the current chapter. Organic relationships connect the two. Neither suffices without the other to explain the PRC's past and future.

Formal Organizational Structure

Throughout the PRC era, as in imperial times, four political layers have remained the bedrock of the bureaucratic system: the national, or Center (*zhongyang*); provinces (*sheng*); counties (*xian*); and cities (*shi*). Since 1949 the work unit (*danwei*) has become a fifth core layer of the system (see Chart 6.1). Having delineated these basic administrative layers—in most cases, matching boundaries that existed prior to the founding of the PRC[4]—Beijing then organized party and government structures for each. The party structures always exercise ultimate authority over their government counterparts.

THE ORGANIZATIONAL CHART AT THE CENTER

Because the Chinese political system duplicates itself at each of the territorial levels, this section outlines the structure at the Center in some detail. The province, county, city, and unit levels are dealt with more briefly directly following the discussion of the Center.

Each territorial level of the Chinese system, on both the party and the government sides, has a basic organizational flow. Each has a large congress that meets infrequently but is in theory the most powerful body; a smaller committee that brings together important people and meets somewhat more frequently; and a still smaller committee that brings together the top few people. In theory, the larger the body, the more powerful it is. In reality, the opposite is true—the smallest committee is the most important structure. Under these committees, there are administrative departments that actually run day-to-day the various party and government organs.

At the Center, the major party organs are, in ascending order of importance, the Party Congress, the Central Committee, the Politburo, and the Politburo Standing Committee. There is a Secretariat, for administration, and specific departments nominally under the Central Committee (see Chart 6.2). The *National Party Congress* has the largest membership—recent Congresses have had over fifteen hundred delegates—and it meets infrequently.[5] Meetings of the Party Congress are major events; policy debates among the leaders are often affected by the need to reach a consensus in time to convene the next Congress. Each Congress solidifies the central political tasks for the party. The Twelfth Congress in 1982, for example, anointed the post-Mao reform effort, the Thirteenth Congress in 1987 legitimized nonstate ownership,

CHART 6.1 *Territorial Layers of State Administration*

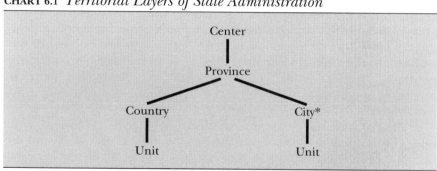

*Cities have various ranks, depending on their size and importance. Three cities—Beijing, Tianjin, and Shanghai—have ranks equivalent to that of the province. These and other large cities have suburban counties under their jurisdictions.

CHART 6.2 *Party Organization at the Center*

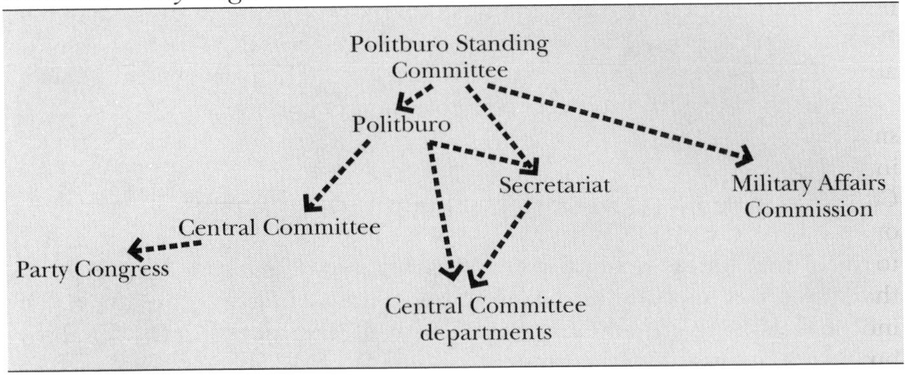

Arrows indicate general direction of authority in practice.

and the Fourteenth Congress in 1993 gave a major political boost to market-oriented changes. Party Congresses also provide the occasion for appointments (or reappointments) to top party posts and to the Central Committee.

But people do not work for the Party Congress—rather, much like an American political party convention, it convenes, hears many speeches, passes resolutions, adopts rules of procedure, and disbands. In theory, the Party Congress is the highest organ of authority, but in fact its large size and infrequent meetings make it a vehicle for announcing and legitimating some major decisions rather than for initiating and deciding important policies.

The *Central Committee* is a smaller body but still, in recent decades, has had several hundred members. Like the Party Congress, the Central Committee convenes infrequently (recently, once or twice a year), and its members all hold other substantive positions. Indeed, many official positions, such as heading the party in the important metropolis of Shanghai, bring with them almost automatic membership in the party's Central Committee. Central Committee members receive a number of special privileges and have access to inside information on party affairs. But with few exceptions the Central Committee meetings (called plenums) discuss and announce policies rather than decide them. Formally, each Central Committee is chosen by a Party Congress. In reality, the Politburo in consultation with others determines the list of nominees to the Central Committee, and only at the Thirteenth Party Congress in 1987 did that list consist of more people than the number of slots to be filled on the Central Committee (the 1987 list had five more people than positions). Meetings of the Central Committee, as explained in Chapter 3, are numbered sequentially until the next Party Congress convenes to choose a new Central Committee.

The *Politburo* also functions as a committee, albeit as a small and powerful one. This is considered the command headquarters of the party, and it typically has fourteen to twenty-four members (and sometimes a small number of "candidate" members). Nearly all members of the Politburo are among the twenty-five to thirty-five people (described further at the beginning of Chapter 7) who form the top power elite. Like the other bodies just discussed, membership on the Politburo is not itself a full-time job. Indeed, usually some Politburo members head distant provinces such as Guangdong and, presumably, miss most Politburo meetings.

The truly powerful inner circle is the *Standing Committee of the Politburo,* a small body with four to six members that seems to meet weekly (these meetings are not announced publicly). Until 1982, the chairman of the Chinese Communist party headed the Standing Committee, and there were typically one to six vice chairmen. When these posts were abolished at the end of 1982 to prevent individuals from rising above the party as Mao Zedong had done, the general secretary became the top bureaucratic official in the party. This individual has the right to convene and to preside over meetings of the Politburo and its Standing Committee. Deng Xiaoping had served as general secretary from April 1954 to 1966, and the wide-ranging contacts with the party bureaucracy that this post required provided a major base of support for him when he sought to begin the reforms in the late 1970s (see Table 6.1).

The general secretary is the formal head of the *Secretariat.* For most of its existence, this body has functioned as the staff support for the Politburo and Central Committee. Its members oversee preparation of documents for Politburo consideration and turn Politburo decisions into operational instructions for the subordinate bureaucracies. The Secretariat's functions have changed quite a bit over time, being very broad and activist during some periods, such as the early Great Leap Forward, and much less so at other times, as in the early 1990s.

The *Military Affairs Commission,*[6] is in charge of the People's Liberation Army. This commission has existed in one guise or another in the CCP since the 1930s. Until the early 1990s only two individuals—Mao Zedong and Deng Xiaoping—had headed this body (with a brief transitional leadership by Hua

TABLE 6.1 *Top Leaders of the CCP (post-1949)*

Chairmen of the CCP	
Mao Zedong	Oct. 1949–Sept. 1976
Hua Guofeng	Sept. 1976–June 1981
Hu Yaobang	June 1981–Dec. 1982
General Secretaries of the Secretariat*	
Deng Xiaoping	April 1954–1966†
Hu Yaobang	Dec. 1978–Jan. 1987
Zhao Ziyang	Jan. 1987–May 1989‡
Jiang Zemin	June 1989–

*The General Secretary was called Chief Secretary from April 1954 to September 1956 and from December 1978 to September 1982.

†De facto, as the Secretariat ceased to function during the Cultural Revolution, which began in 1966.

‡Zhao was Acting General Secretary for January–October 1987.

Guofeng directly following Mao's death). At lower levels of the party there is no equivalent of the Military Affairs Commission. Jiang Zemin heads this body as of 1994.

Central Committee departments at the national level assume responsibility for various issue areas. Those that have existed continuously since 1949 (with some exceptions during the Cultural Revolution) are Organization (personnel appointments); Propaganda (media, education, political study, and public health); United Front (relations with noncommunists); and International Liaison (foreign affairs and relations with other communist parties). In addition, there is a General Office that coordinates many of the administrative details of the central party bureaucracy,[7] a Subordinate Organs Committee to do party work in the organs directly under the Central Committee, and a State Organs Committee, which makes sure the party bodies in the central government organs receive appropriate documents and carry on party activities (such as holding discussion meetings). There has also been at times a powerful Policy Research Office.

On the government side, the basic current structure was adopted in 1954. A new *National People's Congress* (NPC), the putative legislature and government equivalent of the Party Congress, is chosen at most every four years. Since the reforms began, the NPC has convened in plenary session annually, and each meeting in recent years has brought together roughly three thousand delegates. The NPC has a Standing Committee that meets more frequently, and during the 1980s it developed permanent committees that hired their own staffs and began to function on a regular basis. Recent evidence suggests some strengthening of the NPC's role in policy deliberation, as this body has begun to participate in drafting some major policies and has stalled other initiatives desired by leading party officials.[8] The NPC is still only a very pale reflection of an independent legislature. Under Mao Zedong, though, this body had been virtually supine.

The *State Council* is in theory chosen by the NPC (see Chart 6.3.). It is headed by the premier (Zhou Enlai to January 1976; Hua Guofeng to September 1980; Zhao Ziyang to April 1988; Li Peng as of mid-1994), and it serves as the cabinet in the Chinese political system. As explained in Chapter 3, a number of commissions and ministries are subordinate to the State Council. Most ministries and commissions head their own nationwide vertical bureaucratic hierarchies with offices at each subordinate territorial level of administration.

The State Council membership itself consists of the premier, vice premiers, state councillors (equivalent to vice premiers), and virtually all heads of commissions and ministries. But this also has a Standing Committee comprising a subset of these individuals.

The actual organization of the central party and state apparatus is, of course, vastly more complex than the above basic outline conveys. On both the party and government sides, for example, there are numerous additional bodies established for particular purposes. A long-term party body at the Center, for example, is the Central Discipline Inspection Commission, which has the task of ferreting out violations of rules in the party. This has existed in var-

CHART 6.3 *Organization of the Government at the Center*

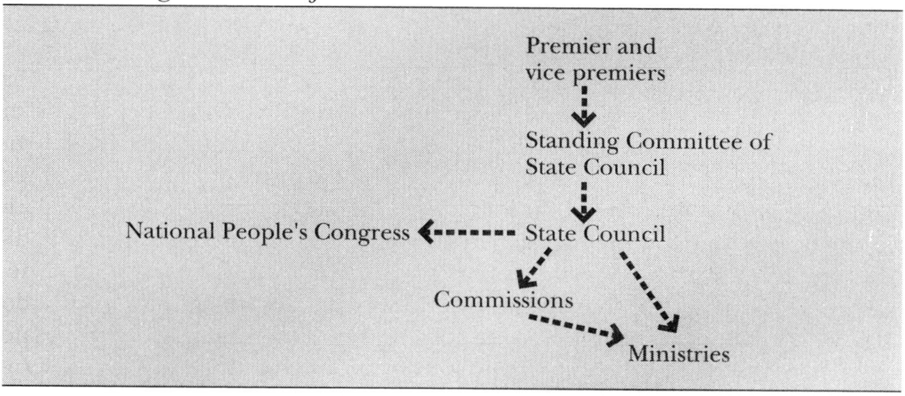

Premier and
vice premiers

Standing Committee of
State Council

National People's Congress ◄- - - - - - - State Council

Commissions

Ministries

Arrows indicate general direction of authority in practice.

ious guises since 1949 except during the Cultural Revolution.[9] Other central party bodies, such as the Central Advisory Commission (which existed only from 1982 to 1992 and was used as a kind of way station for retired leaders), have been the products of specific political needs at particular periods.

The government to a far greater extent than the party has changed its organizations over the years. Relatively few government organs below the level of the premier have avoided mergers, divisions, or other major organizational changes since 1954. The number of ministries, for example, has varied from two dozen or so to over sixty, and reorganizations at this level are common. These amalgamations and divisions of ministries reflect two contrasting tendencies: the desire of specialized bureaucracies to achieve ministerial status; and the desire of the State Council to limit the demands made on it to coordinate lower-level units and resolve disputes among them.

The ministries in charge of petroleum, coal, electric power, and water resources, for instance, have at one time or another stood independently or been combined in every mathematically feasible way since 1949. One high official commented in the late 1980s that the water resources ministry had been forced in the early 1980s to amalgamate with the electric power ministry to form the Ministry of Water Resources and Electric Power because the State Council was tired of having to resolve the constant battles between these two units. The electric power ministry wanted China's water resources used for hydropower generation, while the water resources ministry saw irrigation and flood control as its primary missions. The political rules in China require that the minister present a unified "ministerial" position to the State Council. By amalgamating the two units, therefore, the State Council essentially required that they resolve their differences "in house." This amalgamation did not change much—all but a few of the bureaus of the ministries remained as they were, and the offices even remained in distinct buildings. The forced unification, moreover, did not last long.[10] As of 1994 the State Council had forty ministries and commissions with a total staff of some forty-five thousand administrative, managerial, and technical personnel.

PROVINCES

The Center reaches out to deal with the country through thirty provinces. Provinces vary in their size, wealth, topography, and even dialect and culture. For example, densely populated Guangdong along the southeast coast has become wealthy with the reforms of the Deng era, and its people are well known for their mercantile culture. Most Chinese who have emigrated to other Asian countries and to the United States hail from Guangdong Province. Xinjiang in the far northwest, a huge province dominated by mountain ranges and vast deserts, is sparsely populated—largely with non-Han minorities, many of whom are Muslim. Sichuan in the southwest touches no foreign borders; it has a population of more than one hundred million, most of whom live on the Chengdu Plain, which is surrounded by mountain ranges. Many Chinese attach certain characteristics to people from various provinces—those from Hunan are reputedly hot-tempered, perhaps reflecting the hot peppers they love to eat, those from Beijing are polite, Fujianese are intelligent, Shanghai natives are gauche and sharp with money, those from Guangdong will eat anything and are quick and crafty, those from Hebei are frank and solid, and so on.

Many provinces are separated by natural topographical barriers, and most have names that reflect geographical features. Shandong, for example, means "east [*dong*] of the mountains [*shan*]," Shanxi is "west of the mountains," Hunan is "south of the lake," Hubei is "north of the lake," Shanghai is "on the sea," Sichuan is "the four rivers," and Heilongjiang is "black dragon river." Beijing means "the northern capital."

Provincial borders, moreover, only occasionally coincide with the boundaries of the macroregions analyzed by G. William Skinner. Put differently, provincial boundaries do not necessarily lie along natural economic fault lines; densities of population, transportation links, and commercial activities, with their influences on social identification, dialect, and so forth, do not closely match provincial divisions (see Map 6.1).

Provinces are, nevertheless, an important component of the political system. "Province" itself refers to a rank in the national political administrative hierarchy that is fully equal to the rank of a ministry in the central government. Twenty-two units at provincial rank are actually named provinces (e.g., Guangdong Province, Hunan Province), while three are named metropolises (Beijing City, Shanghai City, and Tianjin City), and five are named autonomous regions (Tibet, Xinjiang Uighur, Ningxia Hui, Guangxi Zhuang, and Inner Mongolia).[11] Because all territorial units with the rank of province are formally equal to each other and to central government ministries, none of these units can issue binding orders to any others. Some provinces, especially those like Shanghai that contribute a great deal of money to central government coffers, are actually more important than others, and their leaders generally are accorded more respect in Beijing than are government ministers. Provincial rank is, therefore, a powerful one in the political hierarchy.

Unlike states in the American system, provinces do not have powers that inherently belong to them by law. Rather, the powers exercised by the province-level units are all delegated to them from the Center. Nevertheless,

MAP 6.1 *Provinces and Macroregions*

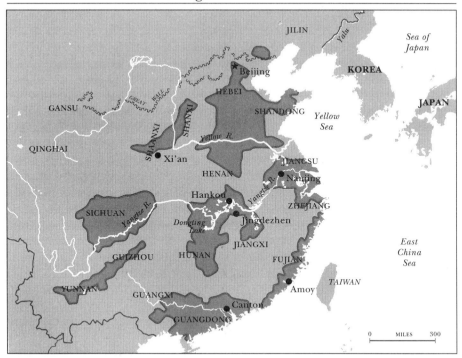

the provinces are very powerful actors in the political system, especially recently. They constantly lobby the Center for resources and greater leeway and exploit the growing flexibility allowed them by the Center. In this effort, they derive leverage from several sources:

□—All major "central" construction projects and enterprises require active provincial cooperation in mobilizing and organizing resources and support services. While the Center knows that provinces cannot simply reject central commands, both sides recognize that provinces can largely scuttle the Center's initiatives through delays and "mishaps." The Center can in theory override this provincial power through harsh penalties (such as purges) for inadequate support, and under Mao this sometimes happened.[12] But over the long run active cooperation works better for both sides than does the Center's use of coercion. The post-Mao reform efforts depend heavily on a cooperative relationship with the provinces.

□—The richer provinces are a major source of funds for the Center, but at least until 1994 provincial and lower units collected all taxes.[13] The Center then bargained with the provinces over the division of funds. Because the reforms have sought to encourage provincial enthusiasm, the strength of the provinces in these negotiations has increased substantially.

□—Many provinces are themselves the size of European countries.

Sichuan has a population of over one hundred million, and Guangdong has some seventy million citizens. These enormous populations require that the provincial political leadership have considerable authority to coordinate the development of goods and services in their territories. Beijing cannot manage a country the size of China without important tasks being performed at lower levels of the political system.

□—The loss of ideological discipline, the officially sanctioned scramble for wealth, and resulting corruption have significantly eroded the leverage of the Center over activities of the provinces. Although Beijing retains important resources to bring provinces to heel, provincial leaders often evade orders that are not quite specific and are not given high priority by the national leaders.

□—Fundamentally, the reform effort seeks to shift power toward territorial units and away from national bureaucracies in Beijing. This fundamental policy approach has greatly strengthened the provincial and lower territorial levels.

□—Certain core features of the political system (detailed in Chapter 7) give the provinces leverage. Since 1984, each province has controlled the appointment of all but the highest provincial officials. The structure of reporting lines for most civilian bodies other than the party committees themselves is quite decentralized, with a powerful role for the territorial party committee at each level. The provincial territorial party committee is thus an extremely important actor in the Chinese system.

As noted above, the political structure at the provincial level largely mirrors that at the Center. This similarity has developed because each provincial organ must deal with its counterpart organ at the Center, and the Center has therefore essentially replicated itself in each province. The typical provincial government has fifty to sixty departments/bureaus and employs roughly ten thousand people.

COUNTIES

Beneath the province, the county is the major unit of political organization. While myriad adjustments are made to the boundaries of counties each year, the overall number of counties has remained between 1,400 and 2,400 for millennia. Indeed, some counties in China trace their continuous histories back two thousand years or more!

As with the province, "county" refers to a rank in the national political administrative hierarchy. As of 1992 the PRC had 1,919 counties and more than one hundred additional units with the rank of county, most of which are either "autonomous counties" or "banners."[14] Both of the latter are designations for county-level units that have large minority populations. County governments, each headed by a magistrate, are usually organized into approximately forty departments and employ up to seven hundred people.

Counties play a strong role in the political administration of China. Typically, orders from above call for implementation of policies that take into account local peculiarities, and thus counties often exercise considerable discretion within the territories they administer. Increasingly, moreover, counties have been given leeway to pursue their own strategies of economic development, and many dynamic county leaders have seized the initiative to transform their localities. Counties derive political power from the same factors that bolster the position of provinces vis-a-vis the Center.

Like provinces, counties contain almost the full array of party and government organs so that they can deal effectively with their counterpart bodies at the level of the province. The bureaucratic system replicates itself yet again at the county level.

Political organization below the county level has changed repeatedly over the years, as the communists have struggled to find the best way to mesh the imperatives of economic administration, social governance, political mobilization, and security. This seemingly ceaseless tinkering with the bottom of the political system reflects the difficulties of linking the state up with a changing economy and society.

CITIES

Cities can plug into the national political administrative hierarchy at any rank, depending on their size and importance. As noted above, for example, three major metropolises—Beijing, Tianjin, and Shanghai—have the rank of provinces. As of 1992, another 447 cities had the rank of county or higher and thus were located directly below the province in the national political hierarchy. China in 1994 has fourteen cities with over one million people apiece.

Each city has a full set of party and government organs that basically parallels that of the Center, province, and county. Headed by mayors, cities are typically organized into about fifty-five departments and bureaus and employ roughly twenty-two hundred administrative and support staff. Deng Xiaoping's reforms have increasingly made cities the key level of organization for the economy. To foster this, the reformers have brought large rural areas around major cities under the administrative control of the municipal authorities to integrate rural development more closely with the urban economy. Many cities, therefore, include suburban counties in their municipal boundaries; Beijing, for instance, encompasses nine suburban counties and Shanghai has ten such counties. Because of this administrative strategy, the number of so-called cities grew from 242 in 1984 to 447 in 1992.

UNITS

China's huge bureaucracy links up with the Chinese citizen at the level of the *danwei,* or "unit." For most, this refers to the place of work—factory, research institute, ministry, and so forth. For students it is the school where they study.

For unemployed urbanites it is the neighborhood "residents' committee." When agriculture was communized, the peasant's unit was the commune. Units in the state and collective sectors are the lowest level of the political system, not independent social organizations. During the famine of the early 1960s, the PRC completed the development of the *danwei* as a major vehicle for controlling citizens' behavior and channeling their efforts.

Urban units became multipurpose bodies that isolated people from those who worked in other units. A major urban enterprise would, for example, be the source of many things for its employees: housing, recreational activities, schooling for the children, health care facilities, and so forth. The *danwei* also provided ration coupons for food, clothing, and furniture, administered the birth-control program, mediated marriage disputes, and provided pensions and burial funds. The *danwei*'s permission was required to get married, obtain a divorce, or change jobs.

The *danwei* also carried out purely political tasks: political campaigns generally were carried out *danwei* by *danwei;* this created lasting cleavages, as campaigns first targeted one group and then another. Mao Zedong utilized these cleavages when he set Chinese against each other. Through this technique of manipulating tensions and creating mutual antagonisms within *danwei*s, Mao largely obviated the need to organize a separate, centralized police apparatus such as the Soviet KGB. The *danwei* also organized compulsory political study, enforced "surveillance" on individuals who had committed "mistakes," and spied for the police via *danwei*-based "order maintenance committees." The rural *danwei* carried out a roughly parallel set of tasks.

Key to the *danwei*'s importance was the fact that very few individuals ever obtained permission to transfer from one *danwei* to another. For peasants, this meant that they could not freely move about the countryside or migrate to the cities. For workers, this tied guaranteed lifetime employment to loss of labor mobility. Each *danwei*, therefore, became a relatively isolated social and political unit, with little communication between members of different *danwei*s. The quality of life of a citizen depended crucially on the resources and leadership of his or her *danwei*.[15]

Each of the pertinent higher-level political units had tentacles that reached directly into the *danwei*. A large urban enterprise would, for example, have a cultural/educational office directly subordinate to the CCP propaganda apparatus, a party committee subordinate to the municipal party committee, and a security section subordinate to the local police apparatus. The head of the *danwei*, therefore, did not fully control the activities in it.[16]

The reforms have impacted significantly on the *danwei* system. They have permitted limited mobility in the countryside and have destroyed the commune. They have also permitted development of joint venture and privately owned enterprises in the cities that are not merely extensions of the government apparatus. They have also created an urban "floating" population[17] of about one hundred million people who are not attached to any urban *danwei*.

The reforms are thus eroding the fundamental link the Maoist system created to handle the relationship between the state and society, and one of the important tasks of the 1990s is to create alternatives to the *danwei* system, which emerged full-blown three decades ago.

As the above overview demonstrates, one of the key characteristics of the Chinese system is the *duplication of both party and government structures* on all levels of the national bureaucracy. This creates an extraordinarily complex matrix of vertical and horizontal authority that results in serious problems of governance.

The Matrix Muddle: *Tiao/Kuai Guanxi*

In a system geared to governing all major aspects of economic and social life, there is virtually no way to rule effectively without both vertical and horizontal bureaucratic domains. The leaders' determination that the Communist party dominate the system adds further complexity to the bureaucratic leviathan. Western scholars of organizational dynamics term this cross-hatching of horizontal and vertical lines of authority a "matrix" problem, and all large-scale organizations must deal with matrix issues. Since China has developed the largest bureaucracy in the history of the world, its matrix muddle is of unprecedented scale.

The Chinese use vivid terminology to describe their criss-crossing jurisdictions: the vertical bureaucracies are called lines (*tiao*), while the horizontal coordinating bodies at various levels are called pieces (*kuai*). The relationships between the vertical and horizontal bodies are called *tiao/kuai guanxi*. And Chinese officials often talk about whether, in a particular instance, the "horizontal serves the vertical" or the "vertical serves the horizontal." What do they mean?

The organizational arrangements delineated above ensure that, despite the highly authoritarian nature of China's political system, actual authority is in most instances fragmented. There are numerous reporting lines throughout the system—through the party, through the government, to the territorial organs, and so forth. As shown in Chart 6.4, for example, the hypothetical energy department under the Zhongshan county government would be subordinate *both* to the Zhongshan county government *and* the energy bureau under the Guangdong provincial government. At the same time, the Zhongshan county government must answer to both the Zhongshan county Communist party committee and the Guangdong provincial government. In addition, the organization department of the Zhongshan county Communist party committee will strongly affect the career opportunities of the leaders of the Zhongshan county energy department, who must also obey party discipline as members of the party committee of the energy department (see Chapter 7 for more information on this).

The simple point is that the officials of any given office have a number of bosses in different places. In this sense the Chinese polity can be considered one of "fragmented authoritarianism."[18] It becomes important in these circumstances to determine *which* of these bosses have priority over others. Typically, the Chinese cope with this in a minimal way by indicating that the primary leadership over a particular department resides either on the vertical line (*tiao*) (i.e., with the Guangdong provincial energy bureau in the above example) or with the horizontal piece (*kuai*) (i.e., with the Zhongshan county

CHART 6.4 *Lines of Authority to the Hypothetical Zhongshan County Energy Department in Guangdong Province*

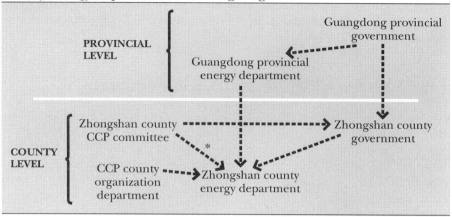

Arrows indicate general direction of authority in practice.
*Party discipline over party members in the energy department.

government itself, in the above example). The one with priority has what is termed a "leadership relationship" (*lingdao guanxi*) with the department in question, while the other one has a nonbinding "professional relationship" (*yewu guanxi*) with it.

But the distinction between leadership and professional relations does not come close to resolving all the problems. As the above overview indicates, many organs can get access to issues that pass through the various departments. And if, as is often the case, a problem is large enough that its solution requires action by not just one department, but also by other departments (such as Construction and Finance, or the energy department of another county), then the lines of criss-crossing authority become exceedingly complex and cumbersome. It may be well-nigh impossible to find one official who has leadership authority over all the pertinent units at any level below that of the Politburo in Beijing. This fragmentation of authority in the Chinese political administrative hierarchy makes it relatively easy for one actor to frustrate the adoption or successful implementation of important policies, especially since units (and officials) of the same bureaucratic rank cannot issue binding orders to each other.[19]

Techniques for Making the System Work

With nationwide hierarchical bureaucratic empires under ministries and Central Committee departments defined by the functions they perform, and with powerful territorial party and government coordinating bodies at multiple levels of the system, the Chinese political system faces potentially severe problems: *overload* at the top, as lower-level officials avoid responsibility by pushing decisions "up" the system; *gridlock* from the fragmentation of power into different functional bureaucracies and territorial fiefdoms; *lack of accurate information* because of the distortions created by multiple layers of bureaucracy and because the CCP has not allowed any truly independent sources of information, such as a free press, to develop; and *corruption* and petty *dictatorship* as officials at each level have the opportunities and incentives to violate rules and cover up their transgressions.

To manage this complex party-state, the CCP has developed various basic operational techniques and principles specifically designed to mitigate some of these problems; virtually all these techniques have evolved significantly during the reform era. None of these remedies has fully resolved the problems, but all have affected the way the system has worked.

IDEOLOGY, DECENTRALIZATION, AND NEGOTIATIONS

As indicated above, one consequence of the structure of the Chinese political administration is that most important issues require the cooperation of officials who are in different bureaucratic domains and who therefore lack jurisdiction over each other. Construction of a major new steel plant, for example, may demand the active support of individuals in the Iron and Steel Ministry, the Finance Ministry, the State Planning Commission, and the local government and party authorities (for road-building, housing construction, sanitation, removing peasants from their land, etc.). If foreign capital is involved, the People's Bank, the Ministry of Foreign Trade and Economic Cooperation, and others will also have to come on board.

For many such issues, the only level of the political system where one body has authority over everyone involved in the project is the Center. There is a thus a natural tendency for the conflicts among the various bureaucracies to be pushed "up" to the Center for resolution. The Center tries to control the types of issues that land on its docket in part by proclaiming that in principle the "importance" of an issue should determine the level of political administration at which it is to be taken up. But there are no hard and fast rules to decide how important an issue is, and importance varies in part according to the priorities of key individuals at the Center at any given time. During one of the periodic drives against corruption, for example, the case against an important county official may be referred all the way to the Center for a decision on publicity and punishment. During more normal times, a county corruption problem would be dealt with by county and, possibly, provincial authorities. Even without hard criteria to determine importance, though, time and again Chinese officials stress that it is the importance of an issue that determines how it is handled.

In practice, the importance principle works primarily to make sure that certain types of issues *are* decided at a high level. It does little to mitigate the problem of too many issues being pushed up the national political hierarchy.

A second widely applied operational principle is, therefore, that a problem should be handled at the lowest level in the system at which consensus can be reached to resolve it.[20] Put differently, in most cases the Center prefers that lower levels manage problems without taking the time and attention of the Center in the process. On the whole, a large proportion of the decisions that affect day-to-day operations of almost every sort are taken at local or middle levels of the political system. Most individuals assert that typically the decisions made at their work unit—be it a government office, a state enterprise, or whatever—affect their lives in far greater measure than decisions taken at the Center.

Naturally, the Center wants lower levels to be guided by broad policy statements from above that articulate policy lines and goals. The pervasive role of ideology during the Maoist era contributed greatly toward achieving this coordination. At that time, officials at all levels were taught to view the Center as the fount of wisdom and themselves as local extensions of the will of the Center. Rigorous programs of ideological indoctrination for officials maintained a relatively high degree of sensitivity to themes and priorities articulated by the Center. The ready recourse to an iron fist for those who deviated reinforced the tendency of officials at all levels to strive to understand and implement priorities directed from Beijing.

The Cultural Revolution and its aftermath did fundamental damage to the use of ideology as a resource of the Center. Officials at all levels lost their innocent belief in the automatic validity of the Center-mandated policies when they witnessed the enormous destruction and waste produced by the ill-conceived policies of Mao and his radical supporters. Deng Xiaoping recognized this sea change in the Chinese political climate when he began to articulate his reform programs.

The reforms have further contributed to the loss of ideology as a resource available to the Center to coordinate and enforce its priorities. This developed naturally from several circumstances: the reforms required a reevaluation of Maoism, thus removing the cloak of official infallibility from the Chairman and tarnishing the CCP, which had so stridently and ruthlessly proclaimed that infallibility for decades;[21] the reforms encouraged people to exercise initiative and make money, all of which made them less receptive to communist ideology;[22] the reforms opened China not only to foreign investment but also to foreign ideas,[23] and these made people recognize that the party had grossly misled them for decades about conditions in the industrialized countries of the world; and the reforms created strong incentives for localities to make money for themselves,[24] which encouraged local officials to differentiate their own interests from those of the Center.

No longer operating as the legitimate source of ideology has been a major blow to the power of the Center. Among other consequences, it has produced a situation in which the normative (that is, value-based) incentives for officials to obey Beijing have diminished considerably. These developments have occurred during a period, moreover, when Beijing has purposely diminished its control over two other potential resources—material and coercive incentives—to encourage local coordination and compliance.

As noted in Chapter 5, Deng Xiaoping recognized the importance of reducing Beijing's direct administrative role in the economy to spur rapid economic growth. The reform leadership thus increased the discretionary budgetary and extrabudgetary funds of provincial and lower-level units. And Deng also recognized that the system would have to become less coercive if the leadership wanted lower-level officials to utilize fully their talents and initiative. The results have been diminished use of the security forces to enforce discipline at lower levels and, to a very limited extent, greater recourse to law instead of political command.

Although the Center's ability to utilize ideology as a vehicle to enhance policy coordination has diminished drastically, Beijing still does make use of broad policy pronouncements to set a general tone and direction that it asks lower levels to support. This tone is usually summed up in several slogans or formulations (*tifa*) that officials at all levels of the system utilize habitually. While these do not in themselves provide much concrete assistance to policy coordination, they do create an atmosphere that affects behavior at all levels of the system. Also, there are always some very particular matters to which the Center gives top priority and for which it seeks direct control.

Because of this general fragmentation of authority in the system, resolving a matter below the Center often requires building a consensus among an array of pertinent officials. This need to construct a consensus generally predisposes officials to negotiate with other relevant officials from an early point. Chinese policy-making is, consequently, characterized by an enormous amount of discussion and bargaining among officials to bring the right people on board.

The resulting bargains are often wide-ranging, complex, and fragile. They may involve personnel assignments, funds, access to goods and markets, or substantive issues concerning a project or policy itself. And officials assume that others will try to "trade up" on their deals as soon as conditions warrant their doing so.

The proposal to build a mammoth dam at the Three Gorges section of the Yangtze River illustrates the bureaucratic deals that must be struck. The dam would provide badly needed electric power to the downstream provinces, especially Hunan and Hubei (see Map 6.2). It would also increase the flood protection afforded these provinces, which would suffer greatly if weather conditions produced simultaneous flood surges on the Yangtze and the Han rivers. But the Three Gorges Dam would displace more than a million people who live above the dam site (primarily in Sichuan Province), and the Sichuanese would receive little of the electric power and none of the flood-control benefits. The dam might also disrupt river traffic along the vital Yangtze artery. But because Sichuan, Hubei, Hunan, and the central ministries involved are all of the same bureaucratic rank, none has operational authority over the others.

Among the trade-offs dam proponents accepted in order to build a consensus on the dam are the following: most important, the dam height will be held to 175 meters instead of the more than two hundred meters originally proposed. This lower height wins over a major constituency in Sichuan Province—the municipality of Chongqing. At 175 meters, the reservoir behind the dam will end at Chongqing Harbor and thus will make that city the major trading center between Sichuan Province and the rich provinces of cen-

MAP 6.2 *Three Gorges Dam Project*

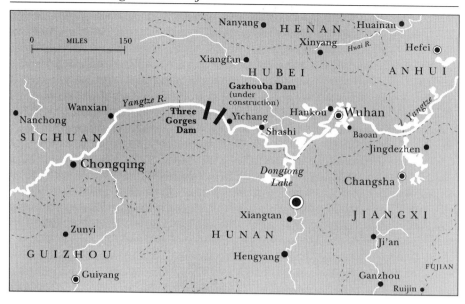

tral China. A greater height would have flooded Chongqing, while a lesser height would have left the smaller and less politically powerful city of Wanxian as the key trading port. The dam is being constructed with an elaborate and expensive ship lift to satisfy the concerns of the Ministry of Transportation. Sichuan Province itself is receiving special investment funds from the State Planning Commission to offset costs of relocation of people displaced by the dam reservoir. The Ministry of Water Resources (whose primary task is flood control) is the key promoter of this dam project, and it negotiated these and additional concessions to other parties in order to win their support, or at least reduce their opposition.[25] Such deals are the basis of much of Chinese political decision-making.

Despite its unitary nature and the general lack of real legal constraints on the activities of the Center, therefore, the Chinese political system is characterized by an enormous amount of negotiations among officials, and many decisions are taken at relatively low levels in the national bureaucratic hierarchy. Given the deflation of the ideological power of the Center, little else would make the system work effectively.

IMPROVING AND CHANNELING INFORMATION

One of the most serious problems of a vertically integrated system like China's is the difficulty leaders have in obtaining accurate information. Most data are reported level by level up the national administration, and typically at each level there are incentives to introduce biases and distortions. For example, a county official interviewed for a scholarly research project in 1990 protested that the county did not have data on the county finances at issue. When the Western scholar noted that the province published province-wide data that must have been aggregated from the county reports, the county official responded, "Oh, you want *that* data! I had thought this was a scientific project that required accurate numbers." In another instance, shortly after the Sino-American rapprochement of the early 1970s the Chinese government asked Washington to provide it with American satellite information on the area under cultivation in China. America did so—and in this way Beijing found out that roughly 20 percent of its cultivated land was not being reported by local officials.

Beijing's determination not to allow people to criticize the government has led to a policy of suppressing all independent sources of information gathering and transmittal, such as a free press. By thus denying themselves the one relatively systematic option for checking the accuracy of the information they receive, the top Chinese leaders have made themselves virtual captives of their own system and of the distortions it inevitably produces.

Leaders have used many methods to circumvent their own officials in order to obtain reliable information. Mao Zedong usually traveled around by train, and he was known to order unscheduled stops so that he could pop in at a nearby village and pump the local officials with questions. (Mao's guards reportedly often beat him to the village, however, and it is unlikely that local people would in any case tell the august Chairman the real story on local conditions.) Mao also selected at least one member of the 8341 Division of the PLA (China's guard regiment for the top leaders) from each county, and he personally debriefed many of them when they returned from home leave. But it was well known among his coworkers that though Mao always sought the truth he rarely liked to hear it, and thus few dared to present him with unvarnished reality.[26] As we have seen, one who did—Peng Dehuai at the Lushan conference in July 1959—paid for it with his career and eventual death during the Cultural Revolution.

Many top Chinese officials have cultivated one or more locales where for particular reasons they know the people well enough to get a straight story from them. For Chen Yun, this is Qingpu County near his native place of Shanghai; for Liu Shaoqi, it was his wife's home town of Tianjin (where Liu had also worked in the CCP underground). They have often used their contacts in these places to obtain feedback on policy implementation or to initiate small experiments that, if successful, might provide the basis for policy advocacy later on. It appears, though, that the post-Mao generation of leaders has not continued this stratagem to the same extent.

China's leaders have traditionally used two major devices to improve the quality of the information they receive, and in recent years they have added a third. The first traditional device is the mode of operations called "democratic centralism," which Beijing learned from the Soviets. The "democracy" element has nothing to do with votes or multiparty systems. Rather, democracy here means consultation. The idea is that before an issue is decided, consultations should occur with all pertinent people. During that period, individuals may express their views freely on the issue so that necessary information is made available to the decisionmakers. Nobody should suffer for the views expressed in this phase of the decision-making process. Once a decision is reached, however, centralism prevails, which means that people must implement the decision regardless of whether or not they agree with it.

Democratic centralism is an attempt to enjoy the advantages of disciplined dictatorship without sacrificing free discussion and the airing of views. It is at best an uncertain technique, as only rarely is there a clear distinction between making one decision and modifying a previous one. More fundamentally, though, in the Maoist era experience soon showed that people were vulnerable for the opinions they had expressed during the consultative, "democratic" phase of this process, and thereafter the quality of information available to the central leaders fell off dramatically. The huge famine of 1961–62 was greatly exacerbated, for example, by the imposition from above of absurdly high quotas for grain procurement. The quotas, in turn, were based on gross misinformation about the true state of affairs in the countryside.[27] As noted in Chapter 4, this set of errors resulted in roughly thirty million deaths.

Deng Xiaoping and the reformers made considerable efforts starting in the late 1970s to rein in the terror and to nurture greater freedom of discussion, especially within the policy-making process. Numerous comments by Chinese officials indicate that these efforts achieved some success and that the system became more effective in gathering and transmitting information during the 1980s.

A second traditional approach to information gathering drew on the meeting system and the document system. The Chinese communists believe in using face-to-face meetings extensively. In the initial years, this may have been encouraged in part by the low levels of literacy among many peasant guerrilla fighters who assumed high office after 1949. Barely able to read documents,[28] they functioned best when they could go over things orally. This style of operation has continued.

Virtually the entire top political elite gathers at least once a year—usually in the summer—at a major resort for an extended meeting that reviews the state of the country and decides on basic priorities for the coming months. These meetings—called central work conferences—typically involve all members of the Politburo, heads of major Central Committee departments and State Council ministries and commissions, all provincial party and government heads, and others, depending on the major topics of the meetings. Such meetings may last for a month or more. They usually involve some plenary sessions, but for the most part participants are divided into smaller groups that meet daily. A fairly elaborate system of reports and bulletins from these groups lays the groundwork for the top leaders at the end of the meeting to pull things together and reach a series of conclusions. The meeting chairman has the formal right to sum up the conclave—a power that Mao Zedong often used to good political advantage.[29]

These long meetings also provide ample opportunity for delegates and their spouses to mix informally. Gossip circulates, news is revealed, and as at Lushan in July 1959, these meetings have been the occasion for many of the political sparks that have flown since 1949. In similar but less elaborate fashion, work conferences are held at all territorial levels of the political system and in the various functional systems (*xitong*s) discussed in Chapter 7.

The meeting system is so elaborate that the Chinese have even put out handbooks on key meeting types and on preparation for various kinds of meetings. Almost any bureaucratic body can convene a meeting, and an official can bring in the people he wants to have participate in the discussion simply by declaring that the meeting is "enlarged" (that is, attended by people who do not normally belong to the group that is meeting). This arrangement gives many officials a legitimate vehicle for testing out ideas with a hand-picked group without being accused of under-the-table scheming.

Although the meeting system is important to the overall political system, firm rules are hard to come by. In some instances of important decisions by central work conferences (e.g., the Lushan conference decisions to purge Peng Dehuai, launch a related Antirightist campaign, and scale back the targets for the Great Leap Forward), a Central Committee plenum convenes immediately afterward to give these decisions formal endorsement. In other instances, such as the August 1958 conference at Beidaihe that decided, among other things, to adopt people's communes as the form of organization for agriculture,[30] Mao Zedong used an enlarged Politburo meeting very much in the way a central work conference would normally be utilized. No Central Committee plenum convened to lend added legitimacy to the resulting decisions. It thus is not clear what the boundaries are on the types of actions these meetings can take. Indeed, there may be no clear boundaries in a political system that is still more responsive to personal choice than to institutional regulations.

The current Chinese political system also maintains an extensive document system that in many ways reflects the imperial Chinese bureaucratic system that came before it.[31] Every ministry has its own in-house document series, as does the Central Committee, the central CCP Secretariat, every territorial government and party committee, and other major bureaucratic bodies. Typically, these documents are numbered sequentially from the first document of each calendar year.

The document system determines the ways various documents are handled. Each document has a label that specifies its type. Specialized personnel sort the documents, and handbooks have been published to guide the document handlers in their work. Document types include the following: an order (*mingling*) must be carried out precisely by the recipient, with no deviation; an instruction (*zhishi*) should be modified to suit local conditions, with approval of the modifications by the next higher territorial level; a circular (*tongzhi*) provides information for reference, with the implication that it would be a good idea to utilize whatever might be appropriate; and an opinion (*yijian*) simply expresses the current views of an official. Many more gradations of literalness fill the gaps between the strict *mingling* and the nonbinding *yijian*.

The Chinese system has been hindered in its ability to collect accurate information by many factors, some of them matters of deliberate choice. Until the 1980s, poorly educated people had a tight hold on the system. Many of these revolutionary cadres discriminated against people who were highly literate. As the administrative system became more complex, this anti-intellectualism imposed increasing burdens on the functioning of the bureaucracy.[32] This was especially true during the Cultural Revolution, with its wholesale attacks on intellectuals and the virtual destruction of, among other things, the state statistical system by know-nothing radicals. Reformers during the 1980s worked hard to bring younger, better-educated individuals into office.

Attacks on individuals for remarks they had made during various meetings in previous years had the effect of producing a bureaucratic apparatus of yes-men, a high price to pay in a system lacking in independent sources of facts. The very degree of domination of the party over the society increased its problems in understanding popular moods and tolerances. The Mao Zedong cult, which grew to gargantuan proportions by the mid-1960s, added another major obstacle to accurate reporting up the national hierarchy.

In addition, the Chinese system developed an extraordinary degree of secrecy. Virtually all documents were classified, and individuals generally saw information strictly on a need-to-know basis. Normally, office workers did not discuss their work with colleagues, as a presumption of secrecy prevailed. Information was thus strictly channeled. Even Politburo members below the very highest level were not allowed to access information freely in spheres outside their designated areas of responsibility. With information scarce, control over information naturally became a type of power in itself. Ministries and other bodies therefore zealously guarded their data, which in turn inhibited consideration of what effect the decisions of one unit would have on the activities and interests of others.[33]

The result was a system forced to work with little reliable information. The system was strongly geared toward transmission of orders downward, with much less sensitivity to the need for a good flow of data upward. Time and again, the Center tried to move an issue along without the data needed for a finely tuned analysis and decision. China paid dearly for this situation.

During the 1980s the reformers took many measures to mitigate the problems in the information system. As previously noted, for example, they greatly reduced the incidence of political persecution of officials for having made suggestions that were not ultimately accepted. They also reduced substantially the degree of secrecy in the system, in part at the urging of the World Bank and other foreign and international financial institutions, and they encouraged the publication of more data and the discussion of more issues in widely circulated journals and other forums.[34]

The reformers also tried a new method to deal with the paucity of data. Zhao Ziyang, in his years as premier, developed a group of State Council think tanks outside the normal bureaucratic system. These think tanks derived their power primarily from the direct access they enjoyed to the premier. Those who wanted to influence policy, therefore, were well-advised to be responsive to the new think tanks when they had requests. The people who staffed these new bodies were generally young reformers who recognized the problems in the extant bureaucratic system. They worked hard to cultivate direct ties with units at all levels of the national administration and to bring the resulting data to bear on policy matters.

The think tanks made considerable progress in improving the information flows to the top, and in some instances lower-level bodies in the provinces and cities made similar improvements.[35] But in the final analysis this structural innovation was gravely weakened when Zhao became party general secretary, which soon took him away from direct responsibility for the economy, and then was purged in the wake of the Tiananmen massacre of 4 June 1989. Ultimately, the think tanks had been Zhao's personal creations and grew out of his personal networking. Some were either dismantled or substantially gutted with Zhao's fall from power.

Overall, therefore, the Chinese have used a variety of means—including advocacy of democratic centralism, formal meeting systems, elaborate document systems, and experimentation with think tanks—to enhance the quantity and quality of information available to policymakers. The reformers have in many ways improved the situation, which in Mao Zedong's later years had seriously deteriorated. Nevertheless, all autocratic political systems have major difficulties in generating good quality information about themselves, and China's geographical size, poverty, and enormous population combine with its highly authoritarian system to limit sharply the national leaders' understanding about what is happening throughout the PRC.

Petty Dictatorship and Corruption

China, like the USSR, set up a system in which every official is highly vulnerable to those above him but is able to act like a petty dictator toward those below. Each official must be sure that his own bailiwick works effectively, and typically each has considerable ability to skew in favorable directions the information that goes to higher levels. Usually, upper levels do not enquire very closely into how things are done—so long as the key priorities seem to be met.[36]

Based on the *danwei* (unit) system, officials in China have an extraordinary degree of leverage over their subordinates. For the most part, they can strongly influence careers, even to holding a subordinate virtually hostage in a meaningless position for years at a time. They also may control the available housing, which is a crucial matter in a country with a severe urban housing shortage. Permission to have a child, permission to marry, permission to divorce, and access to many goods and services can be influenced or determined by the boss at the office or factory. Before the reforms, commune, brigade, and team officials held similar power over peasants.

Such power often breeds despotism and corruption. Ironically, the reforms have encouraged the latter in several ways. Most important, they have occasioned a drastic decline in any sense of ideological élan that might have restrained people from turning their political power to personal advantage. The reforms have also increased the legitimacy of amassing money and material goods—and thus of demanding these things in return for favorable decisions. And the reforms have created many gray areas in terms of what constitutes entrepreneurial activity versus illicit moneymaking through abuse of power.

China's leaders have always recognized the potential for corruption among officials at all levels of the political system, but they have not done well in curbing abuses. The issue badly divided the leadership during Mao Zedong's reign. The Chairman, for example, in the Hundred Flowers campaign and in the Cultural Revolution, proved willing to bring in nonparty people as part of his effort to curb officiousness by cadres. Other leaders, such as Liu Shaoqi, opposed "rectifying" the party by going outside of its ranks.[37]

The Chairman's attacks on the political apparatus during the Cultural Revolution left the party in a shambles. Fully half its membership by 1978 had been recruited during the Cultural Revolution, and most of these individuals had joined because of their dislike of the older party cadres. But in the late 1970s, as explained in Chapter 5, virtually the entire older generation was rehabilitated. The changing policy lines, rapid coming-to-grips with the reality of Mao's damaging policies, internal rifts within the party, and other factors made the party itself a very poorly disciplined and uncertain instrument of rule as of the early 1980s.

At several points during the 1980s the top leadership focused on growing corruption and other problems in the party and tried to correct these. They set up Discipline Inspection Commissions, but these proved wholly inadequate. Indeed, the lines of authority had each Discipline Inspection Commission reporting to the territorial party committee that it was supposed to rectify![38]

The net result of these half-hearted efforts was that corruption and lack of discipline within the party appear to have grown considerably since the early 1980s. Periodically, some lower-level officials are arrested and given exemplary punishment—including, sometimes, execution—with attendant publicity intended to have a deterrent effect. But no high-ranking officials have been arrested for corruption since the reforms began, and many lower-level officials complain privately that the upper levels corrupt the entire system—both by their example and by the payoffs they demand from below. Thus, cynicism over corruption at high levels is pervasive.

State Dominance over Society

The above sections outline the formal organization of the Chinese political system, highlight the resulting matrix muddle, and explain basic attempts to mitigate some of the most severe problems the system confronts. The overall picture presented is of a fragmented authoritarianism that is extremely complex, increasingly decentralized, and suffering from ideological deflation, growing corruption, and petty despotism. This final section briefly introduces the fundamentals in the relationship between this political system and society.

Almost all CCP leaders agree with both their Confucian predecessors and their communist counterparts in other countries that the leadership knows best what is in the overall interests of the society. This basic idea does not absolve the leaders from trying to find out the real state of things, including the attitudes of citizens. But it does make the leaders feel that citizens have no right to demand that the leaders adopt policies the citizens prefer. Rather, the leaders believe that citizens cannot understand what is best for society and therefore do not have the right to promote their own inevitably flawed views on policy.

This attitude has encouraged China's leaders to try to gather information about the objective issues they confront but to suppress any attempts by individuals or groups to promote their own views. Mao Zedong's approach was the mass line, which sought to gather information from the populace but reserved to the leaders the right to make decisions. He believed that actively involving the population in implementation of his decisions increased popular support for those policies. Only very faint echoes of the mass line are still heard in China in the 1990s.

This is, thus, in principle a system in which the state dominates the society. Neither in theory nor in practice is individual advocacy or interest-group activity regarded as legitimate. The political leaders have expended enormous resources—in ideological indoctrination, political coercion, and manipulation through material incentives—to bolster the top-down nature of this system.

In the minds of the CCP leaders, the way to address issues is through the creation of official organizations. For example, many peasants have an immediate interest in flood control. The leaders have created a specialized bureaucracy (the name has changed over the years, but generally it has been known as the water conservancy bureaucracy), one of whose major tasks is to further develop the system of flood control. That bureaucracy is expected to fight hard to protect and expand the regime's work in the flood-control area, and in this sense, the peasants' interest in flood control is "represented" in the system. But if peasants were to organize to demand greater attention to flood control from the authorities, this would be regarded as an insurgency and would be suppressed, violently if necessary. Only the leaders have the right to determine what is in the "real" interests of the peasants and of other groups and to create appropriate official organs and assign appropriate tasks to them.[39]

The regime has utilized an extraordinary array of controls to assert its dominance over the society. All nonofficial organizations exist only at the sufferance of the party, and the CCP has permitted relatively very few of these to form. Even religious and public health organizations, moreover, typically require party approval of their leadership, and when the party senses any domestic political threat, it usually quickly restricts the activities of any independent bodies.

In broadest terms, the state exercises control over society through several basic means. For example, the *hukou* and *danwei* systems tie down most Chinese to specific locales and work places. As explained above, these systems sharply limit contacts between individuals in different work places.

Upon graduation, students are in many cases in a situation analogous to that of workers in state organs and enterprises. Their *danwei*, the school, exercises close supervision over them. The ultimate leverage the state has over students is the assignment of preferred jobs in the state bureaucracy or in state enterprises. A political blemish on the student's record can easily produce a disastrous job assignment that will potentially ruin the student's entire career unless the student "escapes" by finding work in the growing foreign joint venture and private sectors.

Both peasants and urban-dwellers outside the state bureaucracy and enterprises are under less direct control. When peasants lived in people's communes, the local officials who ran the communes exercised considerable leverage over them. But under the reforms local rural officials have lost a significant percentage of their former clout.

Similarly, the increasing development of collective and private enterprises in the cities and townships creates a situation in which more urban residents work in places that lack a Communist party presence and that are outside of the nomenklatura and personnel systems, detailed in Chapter 7, through which the party has maintained much of its leverage over career opportunities.

Therefore, while under Mao the political system dominated—and decimated—the society, the Deng-era reforms have witnessed a conscious reduction in the state's tight control of social and economic activity. The decline of ideology, development of nonstate sectors of the urban economy, conversion to family farming in the countryside, greater use of market forces rather than official orders to determine the allocation of goods and services, emergence of relatively well-off people, increased exposure to the international arena, and purposeful policies of political relaxation have created a situation in which one must ask whether the society is beginning to gel in a fashion that will permit social groups on a regular basis to put pressure on the state itself.

7

The Organization of Political Power and Its Consequences: The View from the Inside

Chapter 6 described the formal organization of the PRC's political system and its consequences. The present chapter focuses on the real configurations of political power and on the behavior of the key individuals within the system, the several million party cadres that govern China. In shifting focus to the actual exercise of power in the PRC, it becomes necessary to draw a distinction between "organizations" and "institutions," for the Chinese political system is strewn with organizations that have not become institutions. "Organizations" are coherent, internally interdependent administrative or functional structures. "Institutions," by contrast, are practices, relationships, and organizations *that have developed sufficient regularity and perceived importance to shape the behaviors of their members.*

Organizations—committees, offices, and their rules—exist in abundance, even at the highest levels of the Chinese system. But in reality the top power elite, the twenty-five to thirty-five individuals who at any given time oversee virtually all sectors of work and politics, personally redefine the real rules of the game on an ongoing basis, and they are constrained only by the views and actions of others within this inner circle. The presence of organizations more than institutions is not limited to the upper echelons; at all levels of the political system the PRC has been a highly personalized system embedded in a complex organizational matrix.

While such things are hard to measure, it appears that the PRC has been far less institutionalized as a political system than was the imperial Chinese government.[1] Even the Republic of China developed more formal civil service requirements in its first decade than the PRC produced in its first forty years in power. The PRC's revolutionary origins as a peasant-based party, its ambitious goals to revamp China's society, and its being ruled into the 1990s by the original party revolutionaries who seized power in 1949 have proven major obstacles to the development of enduring political institutions.

This chapter presents a view from the inside. It first analyzes the way power is actually allocated behind the formal organizational facade among the top power elite. It then branches out to consider how this small group deals with the country's massive bureaucratic apparatus and the configurations of authority within the apparatus itself. It concludes with a consideration of the strategies used by the PRC's political cadres. Chinese officialdom generally tries to keep these key dimensions of the political system—its physiology rather than its simple anatomy—carefully hidden from view.

The Top Twenty-five to Thirty-five

Right from the start the CCP established a basic approach to organizing power at the apex that in its essentials has endured into the 1990s. The key group has been the top twenty-five to thirty-five leaders headed by a core leader who, together, determine the direction of policy in all important spheres.[2]

Naturally, a great deal has changed in the composition and dynamics of relations among the top power elite since 1949. In the early years this group consisted wholly of hardened revolutionaries who had fought for decades to achieve national political power. This was a diverse group of accomplished individuals. In a country where geographical distinctions are sharp, the group hailed from widely differing areas: Mao Zedong, Liu Shaoqi, and Peng Dehuai from the central China province of Hunan; Zhou Enlai from the sophisticated eastern province of Fujian; Deng Xiaoping and Zhu De from the huge southwest province of Sichuan; Chen Yun from the metropolis of Shanghai; Peng Zhen from the north China province of Shanxi; Lin Biao from Hubei; and so forth. They also came from different social classes. Zhu De and Peng Zhen, for example, were from very poor peasant stock, Mao and Deng hailed from relatively well-off households in the countryside, and Zhou came from an elite family. They also had very diverse educational backgrounds. Among the group, only Zhou Enlai acquired an elite formal education. Most had either led or shared the leadership of entire armies or of major underground networks for years before 1949. This was not a homogeneous group of toadies around a single strong leader.

Nevertheless, the extent to which all these individuals paid homage to Mao Zedong is extraordinary. During the revolution, Mao acquired enormous stature among his colleagues as someone who consistently made the right strategic choices in life-and-death situations. After 1949, he bolstered his power through both his ruthlessness and his astute manipulation of the political resources at his command. For example he had the central guards unit under his command provide him with intelligence on the personal habits and activities of his colleagues, and used this information to embarrass a colleague when he wanted to weaken him or throw him off balance politically.[3] At times he took advantage of his control over military appointments to change the garrison commander in the locality where a contentious central meeting was convening, thereby assuring himself of the personal loyalty of the local troop commander. And he made other leaders dependent on him simply by virtue of the importance of his personality cult to the legitimacy of the entire political system.

Undoubtedly, traditional ideas about the strength and power of the first emperor of each new dynasty also contributed to this deference. In the late 1960s, for example, Lin Biao is reported to have declared that, "We may not always understand what Chairman Mao means, but we must always do as he says. The first emperor of each new dynasty is always very strong."

Mao often absented himself from Beijing and allowed many issues to go forward without his active intervention. He would indicate the broad directions in which policy should move but then sit back to see how his colleagues handled the issue. But Mao adopted many measures to make sure that he remained apprised of all important developments. For example, in 1953 he decreed that no document could be issued in the name of the Central Committee until he personally had reviewed and approved it.[4] And, to repeat, he brooked no opposition when he felt strongly about an issue. There are virtually no instances of other leaders directly opposing Mao when he had made his position and feelings clear.

While Mao insisted on having the last word where he had a policy preference, he nevertheless abhorred bureaucratic routine and the details of daily office work.[5] Western scholars have debated whether the best way to think about the Mao era is in terms of "Mao in command" or in terms of Mao as "first among equals." In retrospect, this division seems to have missed the mark, and the Chinese may have found the best terminology in defining the key position simply as that of a "core leader."

Mao's personal style became increasingly despotic during and after the Great Leap Forward. He trusted primarily those in his inner circle—his administrative secretaries called *mishus*, a group discussed below, personal guards under Wang Dongxing, his physician, a few close associates, relatives, and mistresses—and he minimized face-to-face contact with other leading officials. Even those closest to him found themselves constantly vulnerable to his whims, including his penchant for dispatching others to remote rural areas for long periods of time to toughen them. He set his entourage to spying on each other, and he had the last word even on the diagnoses and treatment of medical problems that other leading officials developed. Mao dictated, for example, the timing of operations on Zhou Enlai's cancer in the early 1970s.[6]

Mao's despotism came fully to the fore during the Cultural Revolution, when he first placed under house arrest and then permitted the public humiliation and torture of the majority of leaders who had been in the top power elite of the 1950s. One author who interviewed many of Mao's surviving colleagues states that Mao seemed to enjoy toying with his beleaguered comrades before having them done in. For example, he called Liu Shaoqi in from house arrest and told him that he was pleased with Liu's self-criticism. Liu immediately reported to his family that their troubles were about to end. Instead, Mao almost immediately afterward permitted Liu's public beating and torture, which went on for more than a year and from which he died in 1969. Mao also ordered Liu's wife, Wang Guangmei, thrown into prison, where she languished in harsh conditions of solitary confinement for more than a decade. Liu's children were beaten and scattered around the country.[7]

In similar fashion, former head of the public security apparatus and deputy defense minister Luo Ruiqing was crippled and in 1978 died from the complications stemming from torture;[8] Peng Dehuai also died from torture; Deng Xiaoping fared slightly better, but one of his sons, Deng Pufang, became a paraplegic when Red Guards threw him out of an upper story window. Mao's power was such that even during his final months in 1976, when he lay almost immobile on his bed virtually unable to communicate and largely unaware of his surroundings, every intelligible word he uttered still had the force of law.[9]

When Deng Xiaoping gained the political initiative in 1978, he tried to establish a new set of norms to govern relations among the top power elite. He attempted to give some substance and credibility to the top organizations of the party and government, all of which had been changed at will by Mao in his last decade in power. Deng therefore encouraged regular meetings of key bodies, nurtured more extensive consultation, and stopped Mao's practice of throwing purged leaders into prison or subjecting them to beatings and torture.

The obviously disastrous consequences of Mao's personal rule helped Deng initiate these changes—all of his colleagues could readily see the dangers of granting one leader unbridled power. In addition, Deng personally had not gained his legitimacy as much through revolutionary struggle as had Mao, and therefore he stood on a somewhat more equal footing with the surviving generation of increasingly elderly revolutionary leaders. Yet Deng also faced a dilemma: in wanting to bring about change, he had to seek to maximize his own power to effect reforms at the same time that he sought to circumscribe his power in order to turn the leading political organizations into real institutions.

Deng, far more than Mao, ultimately had to play a game of coalition politics. He was first among equals, at least among the party elders; this was not a "Deng in command" system. Deng made a virtue of necessity by specifically rejecting the trappings of Mao's power: he not only refused to become party chairman, he abolished that post altogether in 1982; he never moved into the Zhongnanhai, the old imperial abode where Mao had made his home in Beijing; and he attempted to build up the prestige of his protégés in the party and the government. In all of this, he had to negotiate with powerful elderly colleagues, most notably Chen Yun, but also Li Xiannian, Bo Yibo, Peng Zhen, and Wang Zhen, each of whom had large factional bases in the party, the government, or the military.[10]

Nevertheless, Deng retained some of Mao's important powers. His high domestic and international prestige as a symbol of China's reforms bolstered his position in the Zhongnanhai, where the top party and government bodies are located. Like Mao, Deng had the critically important right to determine who would belong to the top power elite itself.[11] Leaders of Chinese factions strengthen their positions in substantial measure by providing appointments for their followers.[12] Chen Yun, for example, gave Li Peng a critical boost to his career in 1983, and Li subsequently remained loyal to Chen's policy preferences. Deng took care to consult with his colleagues about these decisions—and he allocated positions with an eye to maintaining coalition support. For example, he left the State Planning Commission in the hands of Chen Yun–supporter Song Ping even when Zhao Ziyang held responsibility for overall economic policy. But the ultimate power stayed in Deng's hands, not by any statute but simply by his prestige and connections in the system.

Deng also injected himself into the policy process to set national priorities. He did this in a detailed fashion in the late 1970s and early to mid-1980s. After that, his involvement became more selective and sporadic, as age slowed him down. As befits the core leader in the Chinese system, Deng's major policy decisions have concerned everything from economic priorities to personnel appointments to foreign policy initiatives to ideological pronouncements to restructuring the military system.

As noted above, when all is said and done the top power elite in China remains an intensely personal arena. The older generation of leaders has known and worked with each other for, in some cases, over sixty years; the younger members of this select group, men generally in their sixties and early seventies who hold key executive offices, are not closely confined by the formal rights and restrictions imposed by the Party Rules or the State Constitution. At this level of the system, politics is informed by small group dynamics more than by formal rules and institutional boundaries.

Nevertheless, it is important to understand the distinctions within this top group and their internal allocation of power. The biggest distinction within the power elite as of 1994 is that between the elders (*yuanlao pai*) and those who actually exercise direct executive power. There is also a third important group at this level of the Chinese system: those who are personal assistants to the members of the power elite.

The *elders* are not engaged in daily management of any issue area. They do not go to the office each day; formally, they are retired, but they are consulted on all serious matters. In the 1950s, given the youth of the CCP movement as a whole, there were few elders, such as Liu Bocheng and Zhu De, and they were not terribly important to the system. In the early 1960s, following the great Leap Forward catastrophe, there were some efforts to encourage Mao Zedong to join the group of elders, which Mao resisted. These efforts contributed to Mao's distrust of Liu Shaoqi and Deng Xiaoping, which in turn propelled him toward the Cultural Revolution.

With the aging of the revolution, the role of elders has become more important. Since the late 1980s, the party elders have decided all important issues themselves, though they are semi- or fully retired. The elders of the 1980s and early 1990s have included Deng Xiaoping, Chen Yun, Li Xiannian (d. 1992), Bo Yibo, and Peng Zhen. All held major positions for decades after 1949, during which they built up extensive networks of followers who have continued to depend on of their patrons even after the patrons retired.

Since the late 1980s, therefore, the elders have been a key component of the political system. But these individuals represent the last of the Long March generation of revolutionaries still active. Their passing in the early and mid-1990s should produce a substantially changed situation. Behind them, there are no individuals of comparable prestige and followings. A stratum of elders will remain, but their role is more likely to approximate that of their counterparts of the 1950s.

The elders of the late 1980s and early 1990s may be seen broadly as the equivalent of a board of directors of a major corporation, "PRC, Inc." Like a corporate board, they set the major directions of the enterprise, and those in daily charge of the enterprise serve only as long as they maintain the elders' confidence. If the elders so choose, they can intervene decisively on particular issues, but overall they focus primarily on broad policy and who should hold the top executive positions under them. By the mid- to late 1990s, this should become a weak board.

The *younger members of the top power elite who hold direct executive authority* are themselves differentiated in two ways: by functional area of work and by degree of specialization. Broadly speaking, the Chinese organize the top executive members of the power elite into major functional areas, which, as explained below, are referred to inside the party as "gateways" (*kou*s). Intermingled with this division of responsibility along the lines of the various *kou*s is a distribution of members into three layers, based on degree of specialization.

The *key generalists* are those at the very top of the system who may be considered the equivalent of the chief executive officer or president of a major corporation. These individuals, including the general secretary of the Communist party and the premier of the government, become involved in many operational issues on a day-to-day basis, and they carry heavy work loads and responsibilities.

The *bridge leaders* are more narrowly specialized than are the key generalists. Each heads either a *kou* or a sub-*kou* (see below, pp. 192–94), and is responsible for helping to develop policy within a certain sphere, coordinating the activities of the bureaucracies relevant to executing that policy, and resolving the differences that crop up between them. Each of these bridging leaders heads a leadership small group that coordinates between the relevant bureaucracies and the top leadership. Typically, these bridge leaders are themselves members of the Politburo and its Standing Committee. Their appointment as of the late 1980s and early 1990s was determined by Deng in consultation with the elders. To continue our metaphor of "PRC, Inc.," these bridge leaders are vice presidents in charge of major functions.

Specialized leaders have control over individual important bureaucracies. They include the heads of the State Planning Commission, the CCP Organization Department, the Ministry of Foreign Affairs, and so forth. The heads of a few key province-level bodies are also at this level in the system. These leaders run the most important bodies in the system. In corporate terms, these are the individuals in charge of top-level departments (strategic planning, finance, etc.) and the heads of the most important operating divisions of the firm.

The above division into *kou*s and layers represents to an important extent how relations among these leaders are structured. To reiterate, though, no formal rules define these divisions. No rules limit the way the top leaders organize themselves or constrain what they are able to do. The only effective check on each of these leaders is the attitudes and actions of the other leaders. Put differently, those at the highest levels of the Chinese system are above the law—indeed, for the most part what they say practically has the force of law.

Despite fifteen years of reforms, this is therefore a realm of Chinese politics where organizational boundaries, tasks, memberships, and identities change often and easily, and they do so at the command of the very top leaders. Actual power depends as much on personal ties with other leaders as on the formal office held. The very longevity of ties among a small group—among the current elders, going back more than sixty years—has given these interpersonal dynamics a special intensity and complexity.

Newcomers to the top, such as Jiang Zemin, necessarily remain somewhat on the periphery, regardless of their formal titles and responsibilities. Jiang, for example, currently heads, among other things, the Military Affairs Commission, which is formally in charge of the military. The PLA's Command and Control Headquarters, which is the communications, intelligence, and combat center for the military, is located in the Western Hills area of Beijing. Access to this site is guarded by the armed personnel of the Military Affairs Commission's administrative bureau. But despite Jiang's formal leadership of this body, even he is denied entry unless he has received prior approval from Deng Xiaoping or from Deng's personally authorized representative.[13]

Surrounding the top leaders, the elders and executive members of the power elite alike, are *personal assistants,* of which the two most important types are the personal secretaries and the personal guards. Regardless of the formal office, each of the top leaders has a personal office and personal body guards. The personal office consists of a group of "secretaries" (*mishus*), the number varying by leader.[14] Mao Zedong usually had at least five *mishus,* for his daily needs, to read to him when he wanted to relax, and for his substantive policy work. Zhou Enlai had more than ten *mishus* at a time. Indeed, long after Zhou's death the Chinese published an entire book on Zhou's *mishus.*

The *mishus* are thus individuals who are close to the top leaders but are not a part of the open bureaucratic system. They can derive great power from their proximity to key leaders—indeed, over time they may become substantial officials in their own right. For example, Chen Boda headed Mao's personal office before 1966; Mao then spun him off into the Cultural Revolution Small Group, the campaign headquarters for the Cultural Revolution, through which Chen wielded enormous power. Other *mishu*s of Mao included Lu Dingyi, who then became head of the propaganda apparatus, and Hu Qiaomu, who later became a Politburo member in his own right. Zhou Xiaozhou, a provincial leader purged with Peng Dehuai at the Lushan conference in 1959, had been a *mishu* of Mao's in the 1940s. Indeed, the cases of Chen Boda and Zhou Xiaozhou suggest that Mao both promoted his *mishu*s into major positions after they left his office and then reacted with a strong sense of betrayal if they subsequently disagreed with any of his policy preferences. This underside of Chinese politics has played a very important—and little known—role in the PRC.

Leaders choose their own *mishu*s, and these typically are not individuals who have worked their way "up" the bureaucratic ladder. But since a *mishu* may have to represent his boss at official meetings and in other official capacities, he is assigned a bureaucratic rank as if he were a part of the formal bureaucracy. Once the *mishu* leaves the office of his patron, he is assigned a formal position equivalent to his rank. Most *mishu*s of the top leaders receive at least the bureaucratic rank of deputy governor of a province or vice minister of the State Council. When they leave the personal office of their patron, and if their patron is still in good standing and they themselves have not made an error—they assume very important positions.

The *mishu* system thus provides a vehicle for factional politics. Top leaders use their ability to recruit *mishu*s, assign them formal bureaucratic ranks, and then after a period of time "seed" them in various official posts as a means of enhancing the leader's own political base at the Center and in the provinces. For example, one very important body at times has been the Policy Research Office of the CCP. Mao Zedong tended either to recruit the head of that body to be one of his *mishu*s, or to make one of his former *mishu*s the head of that body. Zhao Ziyang made Bao Tong, his former *mishu*, both secretary to the Politburo and the head of the major institute charged with developing reforms of the political system. Bao was purged and arrested when Zhao fell from power in 1989.

Via the *mishu* system, moreover, leaders cement their ties with each other by employing the offspring of their colleagues and then placing them into official positions. The *mishu* system thus provides an important vehicle for enabling children of the top elite to enter near the top of the bureaucratic system without having to work their way up through years of service at lower levels.

Finally, as leaders age their *mishu*s have tended to become politically more important in the system. Older people have less energy to meet directly with others and, in some cases, tend to trust fewer people around them. In those circumstances, *mishu*s have acted as surrogates for their bosses to an extraordinary extent. For example, Mao Zedong reportedly in his later years stopped personally attending Politburo meetings, sending one of his *mishu*s in his stead. The older leaders all receive the official notes of important meetings such as Politburo meetings, but they rarely have the inclination to plow through these documents. More often, they rely on the summaries of the meetings provided by their *mishu*s.

Mishu influence can thus be extraordinary. For example, one of Lin Biao's *mishu*s, Zhang Yunsheng, wrote a memoir in which he revealed that Lin during the critical early years of the Cultural Revolution relied on his *mishu* to provide a summary of the documents that came into his office each day, rather than reading the documents himself. Since Lin almost never left his office compound, this *mishu* provided a major part of Lin's links with the outside world when Lin's actions were of critical importance to the development of the Cultural Revolution.

Indeed, Mao Zedong, according to the testimony of his political colleagues, would after the 1950s accept frank criticism only from his *mishu*s. Thus, his key secretaries such as Tian Jiaying and Hu Qiaomu became vital conduits for objective views to reach the Chairman, and they to some extent compensated for his increasing intolerance of the other top leaders in the system.[15]

Much of what we know about the *mishu* system comes from the memoirs of former *mishu*s of the Maoist era. Far less detail is known about the current use of *mishu*s, although confidential interviews with knowledgeable officials suggest that little in the system has changed. We will most likely be able to fill in the details of *mishu* politics of the Deng era only some time after that era has ended.

The *mishu* system exists at all levels of the Chinese hierarchy, and it works in largely the same fashion at each level. It provides key assistance to top leaders who are not well versed in some of the matters they must deal with. The *mishu*s are often well educated and quite capable of looking up needed information, or obtaining it from the *mishu*s of other leaders whom they get to know.

Only the top leaders at the Center are able to pick their *mishu*s without effective interference from the CCP Organization Department, which is normally responsible for vetting personnel appointments. At lower levels, *mishu*s must pass muster with the Organization Department before they can start work. While *mishu*s typically develop good personal networks with the *mishu*s who serve other leaders at the same level of the system, they do not deal with *mishu*s at different territorial levels.

In addition to *mishu*s, each top leader has personal guards. For at least the older generation of revolutionary leaders, these guards were truly personal: although the central guard unit under Mao's personal aegis provided overall security, each leader chose at least some guards of his own. While most of these guards have come from the PLA, the PLA has not retained operational control over them. In fact, although all the personal guards nominally belong to a single guard unit, interviews indicate that even the head of that unit has no authority over them.[16]

Personal guards render a range of services to their bosses, including advance security work for them when they travel in China. For example, if a top leader is going to a province, the provincial security forces in consultation with the Center will make numerous preparations. (When he was alive, Zhou Enlai had overall responsibility for these arrangements.) Nevertheless, the leader will not travel to the province until one of his personal guards goes to the province himself to check the preparations and make any adjustments he sees fit.

The above brief introduction to the top levels of the power elite highlights several important facets of the Chinese system: it is intensely personal, with individual relationships and therefore factional ties extremely important in determining career mobility and political decisions; power at the top is highly concentrated in a very small number of individuals, roughly twenty-five to thirty-five, who wield ultimate authority in the executive, legislative, and judicial spheres; the core leader has extraordinary authority to determine who else will be in the upper echelons of the power elite; and there are aspects of the system that do not appear on organizational charts (for example, the use of *mishu*s and the division of labor into *kou*s) but are in fact extremely important to the politics and the ordinary functioning of the system. These characteristics to some extent are evident in the Chinese political system at each level of the national political hierarchy. And at all levels, this intensely personal system among the elite exists in a dynamic tension with the very large, complex system of bureaucratic organization described in Chapter 6.

Configurations of Political Power

The actual configurations of political power are best understood by leaving behind the organization charts and instead thinking in the terms Chinese officials use when they talk among themselves about their system. In their vocabulary, the key concepts concerning the organization of power are the *kou*s, the *xitong*s, and the tensions of *tiao/kuai* relationships. These organizational arrangements and tensions encompass both the party and government sides of the system.

THE KOU

As noted above, broadly speaking the Chinese organize the top executive members of the power elite into major functional areas, each of which is referred to inside the party as a "gateway" (*kou*).[17] The number of *kou*s is not fixed, and the relative importance of different *kou*s has changed over time, depending on the importance of the people who have led them. The four broadest *kou*s are those for party affairs, government work, state security, and foreign affairs. Each of the first three have nationwide networks of bureaucracies under them and additional more narrowly defined *kou*s under them.

The party affairs (*dangwu*) gateway is the biggest and typically the most powerful *kou*. This *kou* is always headed by the preeminent person among the executive members of the power elite—Mao Zedong, then Hua Guofeng, followed by Hu Yaobang, Zhao Ziyang, and finally Jiang Zemin. The second *kou*, that for government work, is focused primarily on economic development, and it is typically headed by the numbers two and/or three people in the executive power elite. Zhou Enlai headed this while he lived. In the mid-1980s Zhao Ziyang took charge with Yao Yilin. By 1989, Li Peng and Yao Yilin shared leadership of this *kou*, and as of mid-1994 Li Peng and Zhu Rongji head it.

The state security *kou* encompasses the military, the public security (i.e., the police), and the state security (counterespionage) apparatuses. It is not clear how important this *kou* is for the military itself. In the mid-1980s, reportedly Yang Shangkun and Wan Li headed this *kou*, and as of 1994 Qiao Shi holds this position, possibly sharing some responsibility with Wei Jianxing.

The foreign affairs *kou* is rather unique in that it does not control major nationwide domestic bureaucracies. Zhou Enlai headed this *kou* while he was in power, and as of 1994 Li Peng is in charge of this.

Each *kou* has an office with some staff. Each is in charge of coordinating work in a particular sphere and of linking up the administrative bureaucracies in that sphere to the rest of the top executive power elite. Most of the above broad *kou* have what might be termed "sub-*kou*" under them in charge of more specific fields of responsibility. These sub-*kou* are also headed by members of the top executive power elite.

In each *kou*, a leadership small group, typically consisting of a Politburo Standing Committee member and several others in and outside of the Politburo, forms a bridge between the leaders at the apex of the political system and the major bureaucracies that generate information and implement policy. Each of the major leadership small groups leads an array of related party, government, and/or military bureaucracies (see Chart 7.1). In a fundamental sense, the *kou*s and their related leadership small groups define the way political power in both the party and the government is organized.

CHART 7.1 *Organization of Power*

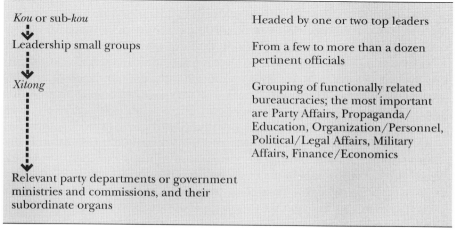

Kou or sub-*kou*	Headed by one or two top leaders
↓	
Leadership small groups	From a few to more than a dozen pertinent officials
↓	
Xitong	Grouping of functionally related bureaucracies; the most important are Party Affairs, Propaganda/Education, Organization/Personnel, Political/Legal Affairs, Military Affairs, Finance/Economics
↓	
Relevant party departments or government ministries and commissions, and their subordinate organs	

Arrows indicate direction of control.

CHART 7.2 *The* Kous

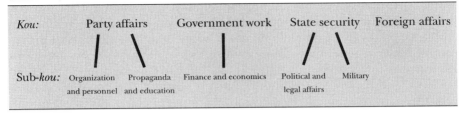

This chart does not include all *kous* and sub-*kous*. but only the most important ones.

THE XITONG

*Xitong*s are groupings of bureaucracies that together deal with a broad task the top political leaders want performed.[18] They generally are led by leadership small groups that usually are headed by the member of the Standing Committee of the Politburo in charge of that *kou* or sub-*kou*. There are many *xitong*s that cover various spheres (foreign affairs, mass work, rural work, etc.), and the boundaries of various *xitong*s have changed over the years. There are six *xitong*s that have been particularly important for concrete management of the country: Party Affairs, Organization and Personnel, Propaganda and Education, Political and Legal Affairs, Finance and Economics, and the Military. Both Organization/Personnel and Propaganda/Education are sub-*kou*s of the party affairs *kou;* Political/Legal and the Military are sub-*kou*s of the state security *kou;* and Finance/Economics falls under the government affairs *kou* (see Chart 7.2). Each includes executive agencies from the top to the bottom of the system, and each encompasses a major sphere of domestic governance within its scope.

The party/government distinction erodes in this dimension of the system, and most *danwei*s contain personnel who represent two or more of these *xitong*s. For example, a state enterprise, as noted previously, will have a party committee, a personnel department, a propaganda office, a security administration, and an enterprise manager. While specific names of these organs may vary, each in fact is part of a different hierarchical nationwide bureaucratic *xitong*. Therefore, neither the party head nor the enterprise manager has absolute control over all the activities that take place in the enterprise. The one *xitong* that stands relatively apart, as explained below, is that of the Military.

The six *xitong*s have, moreover, somewhat loose boundaries—over time specific organizations may shift from one *xitong* to another in their reporting lines if the leadership wants this to occur. As the leadership began to reconstruct the bureaucratic system after the Red Guard phase of the Cultural Revolution, the Organization/Personnel and the Propaganda/Education *xitong*s were temporarily combined under one extraordinarily powerful leadership small group. As this example suggests, political battles among top leaders have often been reflected in the changing scope of authority of the various *xitong*s, as each leader tries to expand the scope of his own *xitong* and those of his allies. During the early stages of the Cultural Revolution, for example, Mao Zedong worked with Lin Biao and Jiang Qing to first take over and then substantially expand the scope of the Military and the Propaganda/Education *xitongs* in order to weaken Mao's adversaries who headed the Party Affairs (Liu Shaoqi) and other *xitongs*. This flexibility returns us to our core theme: China's political system is awash in organizations but has few real institutions.

The six *xitongs* and their major tasks are as follows.

Party Affairs Xitong

The Party Affairs *(dangwu) xitong* is currently headed by the general secretary of the party, Jiang Zemin. Its most important personnel are the first secretaries of every territorial party committee down the hierarchy through the level of the township *(xiang)*, which is below the county. These individuals are the key leading personnel that make the Chinese system "work" on a territorial basis. They oversee implementation of political priorities sent down from above, adjudicate disputes within their territories, coordinate efforts, and lobby higher levels on behalf of their localities. They head the territorial party committees that in turn bring together the most powerful officials in each region. The first secretaries are, in short, the most important generalists at all levels of the Chinese political system.

The Party Affairs *xitong* has major participants that number in the thousands. This includes the party's general secretary, the leading secretaries of the thirty provincial party committees, the leading secretaries of more than two thousand county-level party committees, and the heads of the municipal and township party committees. (While data provided by various Chinese sources are inconsistent, it is reasonable to estimate a total of just over thirty-four hundred units above the township level and over fifty thousand townships.)

Ultimately, the people in the Party Affairs *xitong* become involved in a vast array of issues and activities. Just as the party itself tries to be the ultimate decisionmaker in all matters, the leaders of the various territorial party committees are key to the governance of the localities under their aegis. They do not have absolute power—each of the other *xitongs* slices into virtually every locality in China. But the top party secretaries of the territorial party committees and the party committees themselves bear a special responsibility for making sure that things in their area work well. Without strong territorial party committee leaders, it would be virtually impossible to coordinate adequately the work of various other *xitongs* within any given locality.

Importantly, the hierarchical relationships within the Party Affairs *xitong* are characterized by what the Chinese term "leadership ties" *(lingdao guanxi)*. That is, each territorial party committee is directly subordinate to the equivalent party committee on the next higher level. The county party committee, for example, is subordinate to the party committee of the province within which the county is located. Leadership relations mean that the upper level can dictate to the lower level, and the lower level is obligated to obey.

The Party Affairs *xitong* is thus potentially very centralized, if the Center chooses to issue detailed orders and insist on close compliance. The heads of the Party Affairs *xitong* have, over time, been Liu Shaoqi, Hua Guofeng, Hu

Yaobang, Zhao Ziyang, and Jiang Zemin. Except during and immediately after the Cultural Revolution, the Party Secretariat has typically been used to manage the Party Affairs *xitong*.

Organization Affairs Xitong

The major task of the Organization Affairs *(zuzhi)* *xitong* is to determine who should be appointed to positions of authority throughout the political system and in related bodies such as schools and hospitals. This *xitong* thus does the staff work for the party's nomenklatura (described on pp. 209–13). To a large extent, it influences who will get ahead in China and thus the types of individuals that will run the system. It does so, in the language used by pertinent books in China, so as to "organizationally guarantee implementation of the party's political line." Organization departments investigate the backgrounds of officials, and they also do studies of the PRC's personnel system itself. There is an organization leadership small group that leads this *xitong*.

This *xitong* consists primarily of the organization and personnel departments at all levels of the party and government bureaucracies. At the provincial level alone, each such department typically has from 100 to 150 officials working in it. At the Center, this *xitong* encompasses both the Central Committee's Organization Department and the government's Ministry of Labor and Personnel. The organs of the Organization *xitong* exist not only in the various territorial party committees, but also in all functional government bodies and all other state-owned enterprises and organs. The tentacles of this *xitong*, in short, reach into almost every important nook and cranny of the Chinese system.

The specific management of personnel has evolved a great deal over the years in the PRC. Indeed, as noted below, the original idea of dividing the system into broad *xitong*s itself appears to have grown out of the system for personnel assignments adopted in the early 1950s. What eventually emerged is a system of organization departments at all levels in the party that maintains personnel dossiers and does the staff work on which personnel assignments and promotions are determined. Their specific relations with related party, government, and other organs are too complex to warrant detailed examination here.

The dossiers kept by the Organization *xitong* are extremely powerful factors in the lives of Chinese.[19] They contain not only information on the individual's birth, ethnicity, education, and work history, but also the results of annual assessments and the contents of any political charges ever made against the person or other negative factors from the person's background. An individual never has the right to review his/her own dossier, yet a negative entry in the dossier can destroy the chances that a person will ever advance in their career unless they find employment in the private sector. Very likely, for example, all students who were identified on Tiananmen Square in 1989 had this unfavorable information entered into their dossiers, and this will generally keep them from holding positions of responsibility in state organizations unless the personnel system itself should change. The personnel dossiers are, not surprisingly, matters that cause great anxiety and pain in China. An individual's dossier stays with the person throughout his/her life, even if the person changes place of residence or jobs.

All organization departments in the party (and the personnel departments in other organs) are supposed to operate according to instructions peculiar to the Organization *xitong*. In this sense, this *xitong* is a power unto itself. The author, for example, once received permission from the deputy head of a large state-owned department store to examine a selection of personnel dossiers for individuals in that enterprise. But the head of the personnel department then refused to obey his "superior," citing regulations that were internal to the national Organization *xitong*.

While this *xitong* is thus extremely important and powerful, it in fact operates in a quite decentralized way. The units in this *xitong*—for example, the organization department of a county and that of the province in which the county is located—are linked by "professional relations" *(yewu guanxi),* rather than by leadership relations. Professional relations require consultation on professional issues and "guidance" from above, but they do *not* give the higher level direct body command authority over its subordinate. It is, in fact, the organization department's territorial party committee—or, in a functional organ, the party committee of that organ—that directly commands the organization department.

The party committee and its organization department in each territorial or functional unit in the system therefore form a very powerful combination. Interviewing indicates that new incumbents to the position of top secretary of a party committee typically regard placing "their" person in charge of the organization department under that committee as their highest priority. Once that is accomplished, the party committee leader adds control over appointments and careers to his arsenal of resources to use to obtain obedience from his subordinates. Western scholars call the list of positions subject to party appointment the "nomenklatura," a term that derives from Soviet usage. It is discussed in detail below, in a section devoted to the tools used by the party to control other bodies.

Propaganda and Education Xitong

The Propaganda and Education *(xuanjiao) xitong* is, like its organizational counterpart, quite decentralized. Relations between territorial administrative levels in this *xitong* are characterized by "professional" (not "leadership") ties. This has, nevertheless, been a very powerful *xitong* in the Chinese system. At its apex it is led by a Propaganda and Education Leadership Small Group, and the Central Committee has a propaganda department, too.

If the task of the Party Affairs system is to lead and coordinate on a territorial basis and the task of the Organization system is to affect career patterns, the central task of the Propaganda and Education system is to shape the values and perspectives of the entire population. Numerous units fall under the sway of this *xitong.* They include all print and broadcast media, all schools and colleges (except the specialized institutes directly run by various ministries and the party schools themselves), and virtually all research institutes (again, other than those directly under the various ministries) and cultural units such as museums and performing art troupes. For peculiar reasons, the state-run public health system also comes under the Propaganda and Education *xitong*.

The Propaganda and Education *xitong* formerly played an enormous role in mass political campaigns: the initial stage of such campaigns witnessed an upsurge in the state's propaganda effort, as the media and other resources propagated the key themes of the political mobilization effort. Even in 1994, almost all urban adult Chinese are organized into political study groups— most by their work units, but some, especially those who have retired, by their residence units. These groups meet to discuss materials dictated by the state. Many of these discussion materials are prepared by the Propaganda and Education *xitong*, and they signal the populace the directions in which the top leadership is trying to move the country.[20]

Although the Propaganda and Education *xitong* encompasses education, professional educators have played a weak role in this. The major task of this bureaucratic system has been to create people who think along socialist lines as interpreted by the top party leaders. But professional educators have tended to favor the development of knowledge that implicitly adheres to standards other than simply those of political rectitude. In addition, schools have generally been seen by officials as institutions that eat up a lot of investment, that provide no immediate profit to the state, and that often are the source of trouble because of dissident activities by students and teachers. As a consequence, the professional side of the educational system has almost constantly been under the thumb of the propaganda side of the Propaganda and Education *xitong*. This phenomenon showed up most damagingly during the Cultural Revolution, when in 1966 Mao Zedong closed all the country's schools for several years and virtually wiped the higher educational system clean of all serious scholarship for a full decade.

While Mao's Cultural Revolution extremism created a national tragedy in terms of lost educational opportunities, the bureaucratic weakness of education in China has continued to be evident even under Deng Xiaoping's reforms. These reforms demand a more educated populace to master the economic and scientific tasks necessary to be competitive in the international arena. But China's education budgets on a per capita basis remain among the lowest in the world, and the country is suffering from a severe shortage of well-educated individuals. Teachers' salaries under the reforms have not kept up with inflation, and intellectual attainment has not brought either the prestige or income that commerce and production have generated. Consequently, as of the late 1980s China found that it could not fill even the extremely limited number of graduate school places that it had available; furthermore, total enrollment in all undergraduate college and university courses represented only 2.5 percent of the population, and equaled less than the number enrolled in California alone. Generally, the low prestige and poor educational facilities reflect the dominance of those who place priority on political propaganda within the Propaganda and Education *xitong*.[21]

Mao Zedong's death and the ensuing reforms have thrown the Propaganda and Education *xitong* into malaise. The problem confronting this bureaucratic system is fundamental: in an era of substantial repudiation of Maoist values and of opening up to the international arena, what is the substance of the values that should be conveyed to the populace? Even the party elite is divided on this issue. Deng Xiaoping and other leading reformers at times called on the Propaganda and Education *xitong* to encourage people to seek money-making opportunities and to put to use their entrepreneurial talents. Chen Yun and other more conservative leaders called for stronger schooling in Marxism-Leninism Mao Zedong Thought.

With the official dominant political slogan of the early 1980s being "seek truth from facts," many in the Propaganda and Education *xitong* could not figure out what they should in fact be doing. The explicit repudiation of political campaigns as a technique of rule furthered this sense of uncertainty for those in the Propaganda and Education *xitong*. Articles even appeared in the media in the mid-1980s that held up as models Propaganda and Education *xitong* cadres in state enterprises who had become, essentially, advertising executives and public relations specialists for those firms!

The Tiananmen democracy movement of April–June 1989 revealed just how far the malaise in the Propaganda and Education *xitong* had advanced. As noted in Chapter 5, among the groups marching on Tiananmen Square on the historic day of 4 May 1989, one held up a banner declaring that it represented the Central Committee Propaganda Department and that its goal now was to tell the unvarnished truth. Another represented the *People's Daily,* the Communist party's most authoritative newspaper. The Propaganda and Education *xitong* had cracked apart right up to the top. In the wake of the repression of the democracy movement, the hard-line political leaders carried out their most thorough purges of dissidents in this *xitong.*

While the Propaganda and Education *xitong* remains powerful, therefore, the tumultuous political and economic changes China has made in the wake of Mao's death have rendered the tasks of this bureaucratic system virtually impossible. The Chinese population as of the early 1990s appears to have no consensus regarding the values that all should embrace. Also, the reach of this *xitong* into society has diminished with the extensive development of nonstate enterprises, some with foreign capital, in which the presence of the propaganda apparatus is limited. Interviews indicate, moreover, that many Chinese no longer participate seriously in the mandatory political study meetings.

Political and Legal Affairs Xitong

The *xitong* that is in charge of the civilian coercive apparatus is called the Political and Legal Affairs *(zhengfa) xitong,* which falls under the broader state security *kou.* This is headed by the Political and Legal Affairs Commission in Beijing. The highly authoritarian PRC political system has constructed an appropriately elaborate system of repression to maintain the rule of the Communist party. Part of this repressive system consists of the People's Liberation Army, which has played a major domestic garrison role. This military component of the system is discussed below.

The Chinese decided not to duplicate the KGB when they adopted major components of the Soviet political system under Stalin. That is, they decided that they would not develop a secret police apparatus that penetrated the party and government, that operated in highly centralized fashion, and that became a state within a state, answerable ultimately only to the supreme leader at the top.[22] Perhaps reflecting the lessons and operational styles developed during their long guerrilla war before 1949, the Chinese communist leaders decided to develop a somewhat more decentralized repressive apparatus with greater emphasis on political controls embedded in *danwei*s and with a taboo, broken only during the Cultural Revolution, on having the police apparatus penetrate the party itself. Thus the largest bureaucratic hierarchy within this *xitong*—the nationwide public security apparatus—utilizes a system of "dual leadership," where public security organs are under the control both of their territorial party committee and of the public security organ one level higher in the national administrative hierarchy.

The Political and Legal *xitong* that was established in the 1950s was, nevertheless, large, wide-ranging, and powerful. At one time or another it has run the court system, the prosecuting system, the labor camps, the prisons, the fire departments, the border guards, the uniformed police, the secret police, and issuance of passports, among other things. This system also provided the leadership with reports on the political attitudes of the populace, essentially substituting to an extent for the public opinion polls and a free press common to Western democracies. Reportedly the public security system employed four hundred thousand police in 1978 and twice that number by 1994. In addition, by 1994 the armed component of the civilian security forces, the People's Armed Police, numbered some six hundred thousand troops.

Various parts of this repressive empire had different histories. During the early and mid-1950s, for example, the PRC made significant efforts to develop a set of legal codes to replace the Guomindang law that had been abolished with the revolution. The court system also expanded considerably during these years. But with the Antirightist campaign of 1957 and the Great Leap Forward of 1958, this entire policy thrust disappeared[23]—so that as of 1977, the PRC still lacked any formal criminal, civilian, or other legal codes. As noted in Chapter 5, one component of the reform effort has been to develop such codes, especially to provide a firmer legal basis for the economy.

The party has always maintained its own internal bureaucratic organs, usually called Discipline Inspection Commissions, to ferret out problems and enforce party discipline.[24] When a party member has committed a serious crime, often that individual is first expelled from the party and only then turned over to the Political and Legal Affairs *xitong* organs for judgment and punishment. Powerful party figures, however, almost always escape punishment by the judicial organs.

The major government ministry under the Political and Legal Affairs *xitong* is the Ministry of Public Security. For most of the period of the PRC, this ministry and its subordinate organs have been able to investigate, arrest, prosecute, and imprison Chinese citizens without allowing them any recourse. Mao Zedong's frequent calls to intensify "class struggle" often meant, specifically, for the Political and Legal Affairs *xitong* to "ferret out" and persecute additional "class enemies." Each major political campaign of the Maoist years brought additional people into the Chinese gulag run by the public security system.[25]

Indeed, the Ministry of Public Security was the major bureaucratic unit that took charge of enforcing the class system that developed in Maoist China. People categorized as landlords during the Land Reform campaign of the early 1950s, for example, subsequently had to report as frequently as once a week to the local organ of the public security apparatus. Many were made to maintain diaries that would be turned over at these meetings for inspection by the authorities.

The Maoist leadership often expressed the principle that the Chinese should "cure the illness to save the patient" in its approach to handling those who fell out of favor. To some extent, it practiced this approach—at least more than the Soviets did under Stalin. Nevertheless, the public security system made ready use of execution, and many were put to death in public rituals designed to "educate" the rest of the population. Nobody knows the numbers of individuals executed over the years by China's public security authorities. In 1991 the number of executions announced in the public media was about one thousand, although this probably understates greatly the number of executions carried out in a typical year.

The public security system runs both prisons and "reform through labor" camps. In both instances, prisoners are forced to engage in manual labor, excepting those in the prison system held in solitary confinement or who are for other reasons restricted from working. Figures are not available on the total number of people in the Chinese gulag; the fullest study to date on the system estimates fifteen million to twenty million, but there is no way to determine whether this is accurate.[26] The value of goods produced and the range of types of labor prisoners do are also uncertain. Anecdotal evidence suggests that prisoners have played major roles in construction, in translation of works into foreign languages (many intellectuals have been put into Chinese prisons), and in production of various goods for the market.[27] Under Stalin, the Soviet Union utilized prison labor on a massive scale in mining, construction, and other areas, making slave labor a significant portion of the overall Soviet economy. Chinese prison labor very likely has played more than a trivial role in the country's economic performance, but it appears that it has not approached the significance of such labor in the Soviet system under Stalin.

The public security system ran into deep trouble in the early stages of the reforms in the late 1970s. During the Cultural Revolution, public security for the first time penetrated directly into intraparty political battles, and many of the officials who were overthrown were given over to the public security apparatus.[28] Kang Sheng, who as noted in Chapter 2 was trained by the Soviet KGB in the 1930s, gained great power in this *xitong* in the late 1960s and used it, along with extrabureaucratic "special case groups" he formed, against Mao's purported political enemies.[29]

When Deng Xiaoping and his reform-minded colleagues came into power, they took measures alarming to the public security authorities. They decreed that the public security people could no longer penetrate the party itself. They also promoted the development of laws that should affect the treatment of citizens. Most fundamentally, the reformers brought back into power those who had been purged during the Cultural Revolution, and they also declared in 1979 the end to large-scale class struggle. These two moves were profoundly disheartening to members of the public security apparatus.

Suddenly, top party leaders in power included those who had suffered grievously at the hands of the public security organs over the previous decade, and those who had carried out the repression were frightened about the possibilities of retaliation. The issue came to a head in the celebrated—and tangled—case of Zhang Zhixin. This woman was arrested early in the Cultural Revolution for the "crime" of indicating that Liu Shaoqi, Mao's chief personal target in the Cultural Revolution, had not been completely mistaken in everything he said. She was kept in harsh conditions in prison, with an inmate overseer who was promised a sentence reduction if she could make Zhang repent. Zhang, however, remained steadfast.

Finally, Zhang's obstinate support for Liu produced a decision to execute her. The provincial party leadership approved the execution (it is not clear why this case reached so high a level). The day before the execution, Zhang Zhixin's vocal chords were cut out without anesthesia "to make sure she would not shout reactionary slogans" at her public execution. She was shot the following day.

The question hotly debated in 1981 was whether those involved in this horrendous case should themselves be punished. After national attention to the issue, the reformers decided not to go after the executioners, as this would only prolong the country's agony and turmoil. But such stories, and there were many of them, diminished the prestige and shattered the confidence of many in the public security apparatus.

The 1979 decision to declare that most former members of the exploiting classes had now become members of the proletariat and peasantry—and the virtually concurrent decision to release the "rightists" from the prisons and labor camps—reduced the role of the public security apparatus. No longer would this bureaucracy intrude regularly into the lives of the dozens of millions of people who had "bad" class labels. The labor camps themselves lost inmates numbering in the millions during the rehabilitations after Mao Zedong's death.

The rise of the post-Mao reformers and the implementation of their programs not only directly hurt the bureaucratic interests of the public security apparatus, it also created a more complex situation for these people to confront. The civilian repressive apparatus is in charge of counterespionage via the State Security Ministry and of regular maintenance of public order, as well as enforcing political order. But the reforms vastly increased the contacts between Chinese and foreigners, created markets and increased the circulation of money in a fashion that nurtured more economic crimes, and encouraged the development of greater independence and resistance on the part of large sectors of the population. Rooting out crime, dealing with foreign espionage, and even maintaining control over corruption within the public security system itself became far more difficult in the more open, complex, dynamic society that the reforms produced.

Even under the reforms, however, the public security apparatus remains very large, wide-ranging, and powerful. In 1989 China published a volume that for the first time specified the number of positions in the organs of province-level units in the government.[30] This volume's data revealed that even after a decade of reforms designed to make the economic system grow, the total number of cadres at the provincial level in the civilian repressive apparatus under the Political and Legal Affairs *xitong* remained massive. According to this volume, most provinces as of 1988 had between 1,000 and 1,500 officials in this *xitong at provincial level alone.* For four localities with special security needs, the numbers at provincial level were far higher: Beijing (11,516); Shanghai (7,111); Tianjin (7,629); and Guangdong (3,953). These figures omit the far larger numbers of officials in the public security apparatus below the provincial level, in addition to uniformed police on the street, security personnel within *danwei*s, prison administrators, and the presumably huge networks of informers.

Finance and Economics Xitong

The Finance and Economics *(caijing) xitong* is charged with making the urban economy grow. Given the centrality of economic growth to the tasks of the state, each premier has taken management of the economy—especially of the urban economy—as a major area of responsibility. Concerns about the rural economy have focused more on extraction of resources than on producing new growth. Extraction is more a political task, and therefore rural economic policy has been primarily under the direct control of the CCP via its "rural work" system.

At times the Finance and Economics *xitong* has been headed by a Finance and Economics Leadership Small Group or a Finance and Economics Commission. This is a complex, multifaceted bureaucratic *xitong*. Even under Mao Zedong, different constituent parts of this *xitong* often were at loggerheads with each other. The Ministry of Finance, for example, often argued (typically unsuccessfully) with the State Planning Commission. The latter always pushed for major new projects and faster economic growth, while the former worried about the financial consequences of overly ambitious investment plans. Such tensions between finance officials and production people are typical of most political systems.

The economic reforms have been both a blessing and a bane to this *xitong*. To an extent, the priority given to economic growth under the reforms has redounded to the benefit of officials in the Finance and Economics *xitong*. Since the late 1970s, for example, this *xitong* has suffered far less interference from the interventions of the Political and Legal Affairs *xitong* and of the Propaganda and Education *xitong*, both of which had previously increased their role in economic units—typically at the cost of economic growth—during political campaigns.

In addition, more resources in general have flowed to the economic sector under the reforms, and opportunities for improvement in personal living standards for officials in this sector have grown, sometimes a great deal. Some such officials, for example, have been well-positioned to take advantage of the two-price system and of general vagueness in rules about the transition to a market economy in order to engage in large-scale corruption. Others have enjoyed many chances to have contact with foreigners and to go abroad—both of which produce increased opportunities to acquire scarce goods, foreign exchange, and new skills.

The economic reforms have also, however, sharpened contradictions within this *xitong* and have created problems for it as a whole. Insofar as the reforms progress toward a market system, the state planning officials within the Finance and Economics *xitong* lose power. As noted in Chapter 5, the reforms reduced the number of items directly planned by the Center from over six hundred in 1978 to fewer than thirty by 1988. In addition, during the course of the reforms many localities have gained substantially increased authority over making investments without the explicit approval of the planning authorities in Beijing.

In a more general sense, moreover, the long-term objective of the reforms is to move away from state administration of major portions of the urban economy. Insofar as this actually occurs, it suggests that virtually all officials working in the Finance and Economics *xitong* will see their power and resources diminish. Even short of this, moreover, the intrusion of the market is demanding new skills in economic analysis and other areas that many of the older officials in this *xitong* lack. Having gained years of experience in managing a planned economy (which operated largely without regard to—indeed, in contradistinction to—market economic principles), many of these officials find the new policy directions profoundly threatening.

The actual boundaries of the Finance and Economics *xitong* are somewhat vague. It includes the planning commission, the major production ministries, the finance ministry, the banking system, the subordinate organs of these bodies, and the state enterprises. This encompasses a huge array of bureaucratic organs and personnel. The level of centralization of decision-making varies in the different subsectors within the Finance and Economics *xitong*, but overall the reforms have encouraged greater decentralization and more of a guidance than a command role for Beijing. While this Finance and Economics bureaucratic system does not wholly encompass the nonstate urban sector or the agricultural sector, nevertheless the decisions made in the Finance and Economics *xitong* have a profound impact that reverberates throughout the economy.

Military Xitong

The final *xitong* that warrants individual treatment is that of the Military (*jun-shi xitong*). The communists' armed struggle for power lasted more than twenty years and created an almost unique, symbiotic relationship between the party and the military. The party leaders of the older generation virtually without exception had extensive pre-1949 military experience. Mao Zedong was a military strategist of the first rank. Deng Xiaoping had so much experience in warfare before 1949 that when in 1955 the PRC conferred the highest military rank (marshal) on ten individuals, it also offered this honor to Deng. He declined. To the communist leaders in China, the military has had both national security and domestic political roles.[31]

After 1949, therefore, the military retained a very special place in the new political system. As noted in Chapter 3, shortly before nationwide victory the army, air force, navy, and other military arms were combined into the People's Liberation Army (PLA). The PLA does not answer to the government, though there is a Ministry of Defense and a government Military Affairs Commission. The Ministry of Defense in reality has almost no real power in the military and is used primarily as a convenient vehicle for dealing with foreign military organizations and visitors. Likewise, the government Military Affairs Commission is a hollow shell.

The real leadership of the Chinese military is exercised through the Military Affairs Commission of the CCP, and it is a measure of party dominance of the system that the PLA is sworn to defend the Communist party rather than the state. The Military Affairs Commission has the same bureaucratic rank as does the State Council, and is thus not under government control. Rather, this commission until 1991 was headed at all times, other than during the brief Mao/Deng interregnum, by the most powerful individual in the Chinese Communist party, Mao Zedong until September 1976 and then Deng Xiaoping from June 1981. In 1991, Deng had Party General Secretary Jiang Zemin, who had no prior military experience, appointed to chair the Military Affairs Commission in order to help build up Jiang's political base for the succession, but in reality Deng has retained supreme military command authority in his own hands.

Unlike the other *xitong*s discussed above, the Military *xitong* constitutes virtually a state-within-the-state.[32] Party control is exercised at the very top via the Military Affairs Commission. Below this, there is a General Political Department that has subordinate organs at lower levels of the military hierarchy. The General Political Department is largely in charge of running party activities in the PLA. It also plays a major role in military personnel decisions and in security and counterespionage work in the PLA. Put differently, civilian party committees, the Organization *xitong,* and the public security apparatus are not allowed to penetrate the PLA itself.

The PLA also has a General Logistics Department that runs a vast network of military industries and transportation links. There are no accurate figures to indicate the size of this military sector within the country's economy, but it almost certainly has been enormous. In the transportation sector, not only were many airfields dedicated to exclusive military use, a substantial portion of the nation's rail system also was reserved for the PLA. During the 1980s reform policies were adopted to convert some military industries to civilian or to dual-use production, and in at least some instances military transportation facilities were opened to limited civilian traffic. But the notion of a tremendous system of production and transportation facilities dedicated to almost exclusive military use remains accurate as of the early 1990s. The Finance and

Economics *xitong* does not penetrate this large portion of the economy under military aegis.

The PLA has a General Staff that includes the heads of its military service arms, the army, navy, and air force. As befits a continental-sized country, the army is the most important of the three. Until the mid-1980s it had manpower levels of over four million, making it the largest ground force in the world. China as of the early 1990s is still in the very early stages of developing a blue-water navy, and its military air fleet consists of a very large number of quite outdated fighters. The PLA is, however, armed with nuclear weapons. China developed atomic and hydrogen bombs at enormous cost in the 1960s,[33] and also has missiles of intercontinental range.

The army for most of the years since 1949 retained a deep imprint of its pre-1949 existence. The PLA in the late 1940s grouped its forces into five "field armies" that swept over different parts of China. As noted previously, each field army in 1949 and 1950 "settled" into a different section of the country, depending on where the civil war had left it (Lin Biao's Fourth Field Army actually ended the war in two places: northeast China and Guangdong Province). In each instance, during the early 1950s many of the officers of the field army were assigned to civilian responsibilities, and to a large extent these civilian officials governed their regions into the 1980s. Notwithstanding the "state-within-the-state" characterization of the military system above, therefore, the personal ties between field army officers and the party and government officials of the locality often were long-standing and close. Western scholarly research strongly indicates, moreover, that field army affiliations continued to play an important role in military promotions and career patterns through the 1970s.[34]

The decade of the 1980s brought some important changes in this situation, though. Deng and the reformers sought to upgrade the quality and reduce the average age of both military officers and civilian leaders in the localities. During the mid-1980s, therefore, China experienced massive turnover of local government and party officials, with very large-scale retirements of older leaders and their replacement by generally better-educated younger people. At the same time, new military regulations required formal officer training school for promotion into the commissioned officer corps, and other measures taken to improve the quality of the officer pool further weakened field army ties.[35]

China generally divides its army in two ways. First, it separates strategic reserve forces from garrison forces.[36] The former are well-equipped, relatively highly mobile units under the direct control of the Center. These are used for national security purposes and have generally been kept out of domestic political and economic activities. The garrison forces are less well equipped and have been deployed in military regions[37] around the country. These forces play more important roles in domestic politics and economics than in protecting the country from external attack. They can be deployed to assist in emergencies such as floods and fires, to provide manpower for major construction projects and for agricultural work, to back up party and government directions with force and quell civil unrest, and in other capacities. These were the forces called upon to take over management of the society in 1968, when Red Guard battles plunged the country into virtual anarchy. Their extensive involvement in civilian activities further enhanced the ties between the military officers and officials in various localities, although competition over resources and other matters also produced tensions in many of these relationships.

More than in any other communist country, therefore, the military has been important in domestic governance in China. As further evidence of this, at all times through the early 1980s the Politburo included both individuals currently serving in the PLA and many "civilians" who had spent one to three decades in military service. Only in the late 1980s did this situation begin to change significantly. As a part of his reforms, Deng Xiaoping sought to modernize the military establishment, professionalize it, and focus its efforts more on national security than on domestic matters. These efforts were set back somewhat by the dramatic and costly use of the PLA to suppress the Tiananmen demonstrations in 1989. But the longer-term trend is in the direction Deng sought, and the continuing turnover of lower-level officers and officials due to the reforms is producing real changes in the dynamics of the military's involvement in local affairs. The passing of the elder party leaders during the 1990s should mark a very important step in the further disengagement of the military from the domestic political system. None of the potential civilian leaders has extensive military experience.

Summing Up

Overall, the Chinese political system is not divided up as neatly as the above overview of the six most important *xitong*s might suggest. Matters that seem as though they should fall completely within the boundary of one *xitong*, such as vehicle assembly under the Finance and Economics system, may in fact pop up in some instances under another, such as Propaganda and Education. This reflects the natural tendency toward empire building—and reluctance to be dependent on others—that takes place throughout the Chinese polity.

In broad terms, though, several major observations about these *xitong*s are in order:

□—All of the xitongs aim to shape the behavior of China's people. The Finance and Economics system uses primarily economic incentives, the Propaganda and Education system employs moral incentives, the Political/Legal, military, and Organization/Personnel systems utilize coercive punishments and/or career rewards, while the Party Affairs system makes use of all three types (remunerative, normative, and coercive) of incentives.

□—Generally, the Finance and Economics *xitong* played the most important role during the First Five-Year Plan (1953–57), the Party Affairs system took command of the Great Leap Forward, and the PLA surged to the fore during the Cultural Revolution. Under Deng Xiaoping's reforms, the Finance and Economics *xitong* has in relative terms done best, but even it is potentially threatened by the transition to a market economy. The interests of the other five *xitong*s have been hurt badly by Deng's reforms, and this highlights how truly remarkable the successes of Deng and his colleagues in sustaining the reforms have been, despite major setbacks.

☐—The *xitong*s as such, as noted previously, are virtually invisible on China's organization charts. Yet Chinese officials very much think in terms of these broad functional systems, and the vocabulary they use reflects this way of looking at the political system. In addition, studies of career mobility suggest that most officials tend to spend their entire careers within the bureaucratic organs of a single *xitong*.[38]

☐—Most of the organs in *xitong*s other than the military report to the territorial party committees rather than up the line within their *xitong*. Propaganda, Organization and Personnel, and Political and Legal Affairs, with the partial exception of the public security apparatus and to a still lesser extent the state security apparatus, all are characterized by only professional *(yewu)* relations up the bureaucratic hierarchy. The same is true for many, but not all, of the organs within the Finance and Economics *xitong*. The key bureaucracy that integrates the various levels of the national political system is, therefore, the *party* bureaucracy, working through its hierarchy of territorial party secretaries.

Party Control of the Government

The Communist party has a dual identity. It consists in part of the people who hold offices in the formal party apparatus—that is, who have executive positions in the party bureaucracy. The minority of party members fall into this category, but most discussions of "the party" are actually concerned with precisely this minority. The larger portion of the party consists of people who are *members* of the party but who do not have *jobs* in the party bureaucracy itself. Most officials in the government and officers in the military, for example, are party members, as are numerous workers in state enterprises, peasants, administrators in universities, and others. Party membership as of 1994 totals over fifty million people, but the party bureaucracy itself contains far fewer than ten million individuals. While the party thus defines the political elite of the country, therefore, many party members are at best very marginal members of that elite.

Concerted efforts to assure party control over the various organs of rule (the state, the military, and myriad mass organizations) dates back to 1942, when the party leadership in Yan'an first confronted this issue as the base areas grew in size and complexity.[39] The party's approaches to assuring its continuing control have evolved since 1949. In the mid-1950s, the decisions of the top party leaders in the Politburo were actually implemented through three bodies: Deng Xiaoping's Secretariat for party and mass work; the CCP's Military Affairs Commission for military affairs; and the State Council for economic and foreign affairs. In October 1955, the party's Central Committee established departments that paralleled similar bodies, called "staff offices," that had been set up under the State Council to run the economy. These new party bodies originally focused on personnel assignment work, but eventually their responsibilities broadened and they became key organs—the leadership small groups discussed above—in the party's exercise of power over the state bureaucracy.

Further evolution occurred during the Great Leap Forward, when expansion of the overall role of the party meant that the Party Secretariat assumed tremendous power at the Center and the party committees throughout the political system usurped the work of their government counterparts. The party then retreated somewhat with the collapse of the Great Leap in the early 1960s, and during the Cultural Revolution Red Guard attacks on the party rendered independent party work virtually impossible. In the late 1960s the new official organs of power, called "revolutionary committees," actually fused party and government bodies into a single unit. The party gradually was resurrected during the 1970s, and the revolutionary committees themselves were turned back into government organs in the wake of Mao Zedong's death.

As of the early 1990s, the Chinese Communist party uses four basic methods to achieve continuing control over the other bureaucracies: nomenklatura appointments and interlocking directorates, leadership small groups, party "core groups," and "party life." All four of these date back to the 1950s or before. These four practices in their totality lock government officials into such a powerful web of party interference and controls that one of the major issues confronting the Chinese political system as of the 1990s is how to establish a meaningful separation of party and government functions.

NOMENKLATURA APPOINTMENTS AND INTERLOCKING DIRECTORATES

The nomenklatura (as noted above, the term comes from usage in the former USSR) consists of lists of leading positions over which party units exercise the power of appointment and dismissal, lists of reserve candidates for those positions, and rules governing the actual processes of appointments and dismissals. Through its nomenklatura system, the CCP exercises control over who attains leading positions not only in the party, but also in the government, judicial system, schools and universities, enterprises, research establishments, religious organizations, museums, libraries, hospitals, and so forth. *All* positions of real importance in China fall under the CCP's nomenklatura— even many of those, such as the head of the National People's Congress, that are stipulated in the State Constitution as "elected" offices. Through this vehicle the party monopolizes the power to determine who will join—and who will be forced out of—the country's elite in all spheres.

Professor John P. Burns has written the most thorough analyses of China's nomenklatura system to date.[40] As Burns indicates, nomenklatura authority is actually distributed among a number of different party organs, each of which has a specific array of positions whose appointment power it controls. One significant measure of any organ's importance to the party leadership is the number of positions in that unit that is on the nomenklatura of the highest levels of the CCP. For example, the Chinese Academy of Sciences as of the late 1980s had the following positions on the Central Committee's nomenklatura list: president, vice presidents, all the members of the party core group, and the head of the discipline inspection group. For Peking University, by contrast, the Central Committee's nomenklatura at that time included only the university's president and party secretary. The central party leadership as of the late 1980s felt it was more important to control key appointments in the Chinese Academy of Sciences than in Peking University.

The actual rules governing the nomenklatura have varied over time, and little information is available in the public domain about its scope and operations. Before the Cultural Revolution, the Central Committee had permanent departments that took responsibility for various economic sectors, and these evidently exercised nomenklatura power within their domains. These specialized departments ceased to function during the Cultural Revolution and were not revived by the reformers after Mao Zedong's death. In their stead, some of the burden has been assumed by the Organization Department of the Central Committee, and part has been farmed out to other units, as explained below.

An additional consideration in China's multilayered bureaucracy is how far "down" appointment power should reach. China is such an extraordinarily bureaucratic society that virtually all organizations, whether formally part of the state or not, are assigned particular bureaucratic ranks. Table 7.1 presents the rank equivalents among government organs in somewhat simplified form.

Nonstate organs fit into this same system. The China International Trust and Investment Corporation and the Chinese Academy of Social Sciences, for example, both have the rank of State Council ministries, even though the former is an investment bank and the latter is a research organization. Enterprises, hospitals, and so forth also have assigned bureaucratic ranks that determine many aspects of their relationship to the political system.

From the mid-1950s until 1984 as a general rule the nomenklatura allowed appointments two ranks "down" in the system. The Central Committee, therefore, had on its direct nomenklatura list the leaders not only of min-

TABLE 7.1 *Rank Equivalents among Government Organs*

CENTER	PROVINCE	COUNTY
State Council		
Ministry	Province	
General bureau	Commission	
Bureau	Provincial department	
	Prefecture	
Division		County
Section		County department

Source Lieberthal and Oksenberg (1988), p. 143.

istries and provinces, but also of ministerial bureaus and provincial departments—a number of posts that extends well up into the thousands. Since the
"two rank down" system in numerous cases put the same post on two different
nomenklatura lists (e.g., of the Central Committee and of the province), it appears that both levels would participate in the final choice but that the upper
level had the final say in case of disagreement.

In August 1984, however, this system was modified in several ways to
make it more effective and more flexible, without giving up party control. The
first of the two key changes shifted from a two rank down system of appointment to a one rank down nomenklatura system. This considerably reduced
the number of positions listed on, for example, the Central Committee's
nomenklatura, dropping the total figure to about five thousand. This change
enabled the central authorities to exercise their nomenklatura powers in a
more serious fashion. The huge numbers of positions on the previous
nomenklatura lists had too often resulted in pro forma consideration and de
facto approvals of whomever the lower territorial unit nominated. At the same
time, this shift to a one rank down system meant that leaders in provincial and
lower territorial units gained almost complete control over appointments and
dismissals of officials within their territorial jurisdiction. Only the very highest
officials at each territorial level, the top party secretaries and the governor
and vice governors at the provincial level, for example, would still be appointed by the next higher level, and except in extraordinary cases even these
appointments were subject to substantial consultation with the unit affected.

The second change shifted many nomenklatura slots at the central level
from the direct control of the Central Committee to the authority of the party
core group within each ministry. As detailed below, the party core group typically consists of the top party members who are officials in the ministry, and it
almost always includes at least the minister and several vice ministers, along
with possibly one or two others. This group often will caucus separately to decide the major issues confronting the ministry. Presumably, all members of
the party core group are on the nomenklatura list of the Central Committee.
The party core group, in turn, controls the nomenklatura list for those at a
level below them in the ministry. These second-level appointments must then
be reported to the Central Committee for the record.

Both of these 1984 changes create the possibility that provinces and ministries will increasingly become in-grown, since appointments to all but the
top-level positions are controlled from within. Adequate data are lacking to
judge whether this trend has in fact appeared in the staffing of ministries
where, in any case, promotions from "in house" had been the rule for many
years. There is evidence, however, that there has been a general increase in
the percentage of provincial appointments below the top level in which the
appointee's previous position was in that same province.

The major staff organ in the nomenklatura effort at every territorial level
of the political system is the organization department under the party territorial committee. At the national level, this is the Central Committee. As noted
above, the organization departments keep extensive personnel files and have
lists of individuals that they regard as good potential appointees as posts be-

come vacant. The organization departments make the key recommendations for appointments for all positions on the nomenklatura of their parent party committee. The party committee has the final power of approval, but the organization department's dossiers and recommendations typically narrowly constrain the options of the parent committees.

Every state and collective enterprise, school, and other body also has a personnel department within it. For a unit of any size or significance, moreover, the same unit also has a party committee, under which is an organization section. Typically, all members of the personnel department are party people and most or all of them are also part of the organization section. Through this device, the party controls a huge number of positions that extend well beyond the nomenklatura for leadership positions just discussed.

In sum, the Communist party controls career mobility for all elites in China, and it exercises this control tightly. With the reforms since the late 1970s, the party has made efforts to pull back from detailed involvement in many activities, but at all times it has retained total control over appointment and dismissal of all elites. As of the late 1980s, it appears that the party's nomenklatura lists included more than eight million posts (no concrete number has been published, and this figure is Professor Burns' well-grounded extrapolation). Even outside of this "top eight million," moreover, the party intervenes massively in decisions on appointments and career opportunities. It is virtually impossible, therefore, to alienate the relevant party officials and still enjoy career success other than in a foreign-invested joint venture enterprise or a private firm. Indeed, the change to a one level down nomenklatura system in 1984 has made it almost impossible to enjoy a promotion without the support of one's immediate superior. In this sense the decentralization of personnel decisions under the reforms has increased the chances of local despotism.

Beyond using appointment and dismissal power to assure control over leaders of state organs, the party has also enhanced its leverage via "interlocking directorates"—i.e., having key party officials themselves directly take charge of state bodies. In the 1950s this practice reflected in part the scarcity of skilled individuals whom the top party leaders felt they could fully trust. It was often the case, therefore, that one individual acted as both the top party secretary and as the head of government in a territory. In 1951, for example, Huang Jing was both party secretary and mayor of Tianjin City, Peng Zhen held both positions in Beijing, Chen Yi did the same in Shanghai, Lin Ruoyu was party secretary and governor of Shandong Province, and Tan Zhenlin held both positions in Jiangsu Province, as did Ye Jianying in Guangdong. In addition, the same person often held an important post in the local military organization—typically, as political commissar of the provincial military district.

The reforms of the 1980s sought, among other things, to reduce the instances of this multiple hat-wearing. Beginning in the 1990s there are virtually no instances in which the top party secretary of a province or city simultaneously serves as governor or mayor. Yet interlocking directorates continue to be important, as many of the top officials in the government in each territorial jurisdiction typically also hold positions on the party committee that governs that jurisdiction. At the Center, as of 1994, the CCP Politburo, for example, includes the government premier (Li Peng), all four vice premiers (Li Lanqing, Qian Qichen, Zhu Rongji, Zou Jiahua),[41] and the top figures in the civilian and military security apparatuses (Jia Chunwang, Liu Huaqing, Chi Haotian).

In sum, the party's nomenklatura system gives the CCP the powerful political weapon of being able to determine who will join—and who will remain in—the elite at all levels of the system. Interlocking directorates further consolidate party control by placing many individuals who hold key government positions onto the party committee that is in charge of that territory as a whole. But even these devices understate considerably the real power of the party over the state apparatus. The core organization of this power is hidden from view in that it is sculpted around a series of secret bodies—the previously referenced leadership small groups and the party core groups—that do not appear on any organization charts.

PARTY CORE GROUPS AND PARTY LIFE

The party has formally constituted "party core groups" in the various government ministries. This form of organization evidently is not used in government bodies below the level of a ministry. In those lower-level government units, the party members are formed into party committees with branches and other subordinate divisions, depending on the number of party members in the unit. The ministerial level government bodies, however, have both a party core group and a party committee. The former is by far the more powerful body.[42]

Party core groups date back to the early days of the PRC. The initial idea was to have a separate forum for the top party members to utilize, given that in those days the CCP had visions of bringing a moderate number of nonparty individuals into positions of some authority. After the political campaigns of the 1950s, this original rationale no longer held, as virtually no individuals other than CCP members retained high positions in the ministries. The practice, nevertheless, continued.

The party core group includes the top few party members in each government ministry and commission. These individuals caucus as party members to decide issues confronting the ministry and to review appropriate directions from above. They then don their government hats as ministers and vice ministers to issue directives and carry them out. Since the actual membership of party core groups is secret, it is not clear whether some old party revolutionaries who are below the rank of vice minister participate in any of these bodies. In any case, the reporting lines for the party core groups in ministries are not known in the West, and thus it is impossible to tell the real practical effect of retaining this peculiar separate party caucus.[43]

In the late 1980s the reformers sought to phase out party core groups, arguing both that they no longer served a distinctive purpose and that nonparty individuals of talent should be allowed to hold a few top positions. This idea actually was adopted as policy in 1987, but its implementation remained incomplete and reportedly was aborted in the wake of the Tiananmen Square repression in June 1989.

In addition to the party core groups, each government body has its CCP members organized into a party committee or into smaller bodies, depending on the number of party members. The party committee, in turn, runs "party life." This is a series of activities intended to familiarize CCP members with the policies of the party and to maintain a sense of discipline and esprit de corps among party members. Party life typically includes regular meetings of the membership, at which documents are read and issues discussed. Through these channels, party members are supposed to learn about new policies or problems before their nonparty colleagues do.[44]

Party life was very important in the years before the Cultural Revolution, but it declined in vigor during and immediately after the Cultural Revolution and has suffered further erosion under the reforms. Still, party membership includes obligations to participate in these activities, and it also entails willingness to bend to party discipline on issues on which the CCP leadership demands compliance. Party life thus forms another brick—albeit a chipped and flaking one in the 1990s—in the edifice of Chinese Communist party controls over the government and other bodies.

Cadre Strategies

The picture of the Chinese political system presented in Chapters 6 and 7 to this point is one of a very strong top power elite, virtually unconstrained by law or institutions, and a highly complex organization of power beneath them that fragments authority along vertical/functional and horizontal/territorial lines. The net result, as noted in Chapter 6, is almost incessant bargaining and consensus-building among officials at most levels of the national hierarchy. In some *xitong*s, especially those dealing with the economy, bargaining is especially clear and prevalent. In others, such as those dealing with the propaganda or coercive systems, the exchanges may be more subtle and deal somewhat less in such tangible resources as price allocations and investment funds.[45]

A key question is what resources leaders of a unit seek to accrue either for themselves or for the unit in order to strike effective bargains.[46] The general answer is to develop a group of loyal followers and to nurture this group, or faction, with ongoing exchanges of resources and benefits. More particular answers to this question must vary somewhat with the motivations of the leader involved.

Some leaders seek to advance further in the system. Others give higher priority to increasing the security of their current position. Still others gain their greatest satisfaction from winning approval from their subordinates. And yet others seek primarily to feather their own nests. These various goals are, of course, somewhat overlapping, and the strategies to pursue each are not mutually exclusive. Indeed, similar choices confront middle-level managers in any bureaucratic hierarchy. But the strategies of Chinese officials to achieve varying mixes of these goals exhibit some distinctive features.

A Chinese unit leader's strategy generally must make major provision for obtaining access to scarce resources that he can distribute to individuals in his own organization; protecting his organization from the uncertainties of an external environment in which top leaders can act capriciously and bureaucratic authority is fragmented; and developing goods and services within his organization that he can use to strike his bargains with the external environment. These different components of a strategy are, moreover, to some extent interrelated. An element that is core to all three is the need to build up a collection of followers and to cultivate one or more patrons who can provide protection and benefits.

To build up a group of supporters, a successful leader must provide his followers with access to resources—including everything from improved housing to opportunities for promotion to goods that are not otherwise available. Since the start of the reforms this strategy increasingly encourages obtaining resources from the international arena, where possible, as foreign connections have become important as a way to create opportunities for supporters to obtain foreign exchange and/or to travel abroad. The ability to secure advanced study and training abroad is highly prized—often in part for the additional foreign connections it can generate—and an official who can generate these opportunities for his supporters increases his own standing not only with his followers but also with many of his peers. The foreign connection thus became a highly valued resource among Chinese officials by the mid-1980s.

There also remained ambivalence about close dealings with foreigners, who many Chinese believe may corrupt and exploit China. Close contacts with foreigners thus became simultaneously a source of strength and vulnerability for the key individuals concerned. Officials who are not successful in drawing resources from the international arena may be prepared to adopt a critical attitude toward those who do, arguing, in the vernacular used in the early 1990s, that the latter are succumbing to "peaceful evolution."[47] Many people who are able to broker relations with the international arena find, moreover, that they are under constant pressure to increase the resources they obtain so as to maintain their status by meeting the rapidly growing demands of their own constituents.

A second element of strategy—devising means to protect one's own unit from an uncertain external environment—grows out of the basic nature of the system itself. Given sharp changes in policy and the fragmentation of bureaucratic authority, it is not surprising that a demonstrated ability to protect one's own organization and its prerogatives has become a key way to generate respect.

For example, the ability to employ a large staff and to keep them working is a major ingredient of influence; it secures *guanxi* and generates loyalty. Leaders of organizations know that many of the people upon whom they depend measure their accomplishments more in terms of their success in employing and taking care of additional people than in terms of their efficiency in completing a job. The key reformers in China's current power elite want to assign efficiency a higher priority than employment. But there is ample evidence that the previous norms continue to govern the thoughts and actions of a large percentage of both cadres and workers. Indeed, the strategy of "creating a small society"—that is, of creating separate housing, health, educational, entertainment, and other facilities for one's employees—is so fundamental that it arouses comment when the leader of an important state organization chooses not to follow this approach.

Obtaining resources from the external environment and protecting the unit from the uncertainties of that environment are thus basic strategies pursued by most bureaucratic leaders to solidify their positions. But an ambitious official also wants to enhance his own and his unit's position in the system. Many tactics can contribute to meeting this goal. Leaders who want to move up almost certainly will cultivate patrons at higher levels, in which case those patrons will come under pressure to provide both protection and access to resources to their followers. In addition, successful leaders in the past have sometimes worked hard to have their own units recognized as official models for others to emulate in accomplishing one or another national task.

Given the nature of the system, which requires that units engage in an almost constant process of bargaining and exchange, an additional critical concern for an ambitious official must be to try to develop within the unit resources that can be used in bargaining with others. A major resource, in this regard, is the ability to generate revenues for the Center. At the central level, the ability of a ministry to generate funds affects its power, prestige, and, in circular fashion, its ability to obtain additional funding. The same is true at the provincial and lower levels in this increasingly decentralized system.

One component of power, of course, is the ability to oppose a policy or project. Given the nature of the Chinese system, rarely is open opposition either tolerated or effective. Indeed, when, to use a Chinese metaphor, the "wind" of a policy is blowing strongly, opponents usually quietly seek cover to ride out the tempest rather than try more overt protest actions. When a policy wind is blowing more gently, however, officials may voice dissenting views more openly.

Chinese officials have utilized a wide range of subtle strategies to lesson the impact of policies with which they disagree. Many of these strategies take advantage of the relatively self-contained nature of Chinese units to try to blunt the effects of an offending policy. One time-honored strategy of opposition, for example, has been to proclaim one's support of the offending policy while not in fact carrying it out in one's unit. When the policy eventually begins to change, the unit can then emerge as a pace-setter in support of the new policy trend. Thus, for example, in the wake of the repression at Tiananmen in 1989 the leaders of Guangdong Province did not openly protest the restrictions on the pace of further economic reforms emanating from Beijing. Rather, they moved forward without making a public show of the fact. When Deng Xiaoping sought to promote more rapid reform in 1992, however, the Guangdong provincial leaders not only hosted Deng, they also invited foreign reporters to the province and bragged openly that they had continued to march in the forefront of the efforts to open up to the international economy.

One of the factors contributing to the tendency of Chinese officials to seek to wall off their units, therefore, is connected to strategies of opposition and of self-protection. In this regard, it bears stressing that a number of reforms in the fiscal and personnel systems during the early 1980s had the effect of further encapsulating individual units, making them more opaque to observation from outside the unit. Anecdotal evidence indicates that many cadres have taken advantage of this situation to engage in corruption and to enrich themselves.

During the Maoist era, defensive strategies often also included political name-calling that sought to tarnish the reputation of an opposing unit's leaders. The post-Mao reforms generally reduced the political temperature in China to the extent that labeling opponents as class enemies and capitulationists fell out of vogue. These same reforms, however, enhanced the utility of other weapons in the arsenals available to officials. For example, the reforms generally stress technical evaluation and utilizing foreign expertise in making economic decisions, and they therefore have virtually invited officials to delay unwanted economic projects by calling for additional "feasibility studies" and using these to mobilize data and people to question the project. The rapidly growing concern over corruption in the mid-1980s also produced its own opportunities for political infighting. Whereas under Mao character assassination often took the form of questioning a person's political "stance," since the mid-1980s the more frequent charge has been that of pursuing private interests over the public good. In both cases, the object is to tarnish a policy through questioning the probity of its advocates.

Leading cadres throughout the vast communist bureaucracies thus have an arsenal of strategies they use to protect their positions and to advance their careers. Typically, these require measures of one sort or another to cultivate a patron at a higher level. (The Chinese expression used to capture this strategy is to "lean against a mountain"—*kao shan.*) Ambitious cadres also seek to increase the number of people for whom they can provide jobs.

Before the reforms, cadres in the localities had to position themselves with regard to central policies and slogans on an ongoing basis. How quickly and ambitiously one echoed a new political slogan or how much publicity one sought for the effort to implement a new policy in one's unit became vital components of a career strategy. Zhao Ziyang during the 1950s and most of the 1960s, for example, proved unusually adept at hopping on leftist bandwagons as new political campaigns cranked up—and them nimbly jumping off of them at the first sign that a period of consolidation was setting in.[48] Wu Zhipu, the party leader of Henan Province in 1958, rose to national prominence by making the province a model in mass mobilization and in the formation of people's communes at the outset of the great Leap. Wu suffered later on when the Great Leap collapsed.[49]

Since the onset of the reforms, this local sensitivity to national policy shifts has become somewhat muted, especially in China south of the Yangtze River. In part this reflects the overall decentralization in the system and the greater general stress on pragmatism over following national models. But even more it seems to be due to the overwhelming emphasis on economic results at all levels of the country's bureaucracies.

Many local officials now regard politics in Beijing as unpredictable and dangerous—and therefore as something to avoid.[50] They feel that their careers will benefit most from protecting their followers and from contributing to rapid local job creation, economic growth, and improvements in the standard of living. They therefore pay lip service to the slogans that come out of the Center and lobby the Center for resources, but they do not allow broad central policy initiatives to affect their behavior in the way that characterized the Maoist era. Put differently, as a result of the reforms and other factors, politics—and political strategies—in much of China have become more local.

8

The Succession Issue

One of the most acute flaws of Leninist party systems is that power is concentrated at the apex of the system without any means existing to assure a smooth political succession at that level. Given that China currently has an only partially reformed system, the outcome of the political succession during the 1990s will determine not only *who* will run the country but also the very *character* of the political system itself. At the top, the PRC is nearing the end of the rule of old revolutionaries. At the middle and lower rungs—i.e., from vice minister to leading county cadres, including their CCP equivalents, rapid retirement of the older generation occurred by fiat during the 1980s, and the system is currently adjusting to the new types of individuals who have assumed power. The 1990s will witness the full systemic impact of a major generation shift in the PRC's officialdom.

Succession at the Top

Despite decentralization, stability in the PRC still depends on effective leadership at the Center, but the impending succession threatens this. The PRC, like imperial China and all Leninist systems, has found it impossible to institutionalize succession. As Chapter 7 explained, among the top leaders institutions impose few real constraints on actions—and this is especially true regarding the position of "core leader." Formal succession arrangements cannot be regarded as serious constraints on the quest for power at this level of the political system.

The fundamental conundrum regarding succession is simple. Every core leader has sought to choose his successor. Because the successor-designate must at all times reassure the core leader of his continuing fidelity, it is difficult for him to build up an independent base of support to see him through the political struggles once the core leader has passed from the scene. To the extent that the designated successor does try to develop his own base, he risks losing the support of the core leader. Autocrats are notorious for suspecting that their protégés wish to unseat them, and China's autocrats have been no exception. Because power at the top in this system is not institutionalized, once the core leader dies his power dies with him; a successor therefore needs his own base of support to compete successfully for the top position.

The net result is generally predictable: either the core leader purges his protégé because of suspicions about the protégé's power and plans to assume power too soon (Liu Shaoqi, Lin Biao, Hu Yaobang, Zhao Ziyang), or the protégé assumes power after the death of the core leader, but he is unable to consolidate his position and is soon nudged aside by other contenders (Hua Guofeng). Given the extraordinary importance of the core leader to the way the Chinese system operates, though, this structural uncertainty regarding the transfer of this power constitutes a major flaw. It has been highly damaging to the system in the past and has the potential to remain extremely disruptive in the future.

DENG'S SUCCESSION STRATEGY

The PRC has suffered grievously from succession politics. During the Maoist era, the political tensions and struggles surrounding the succession issue inflicted enormous damage on the relationships among the elite. The Chairman unleashed the Cultural Revolution partly to change the succession from Liu Shaoqi to Lin Biao. With Lin's death in 1971, Mao eventually turned to Hua Guofeng, telling Hua in 1976 that, "With you in charge, I am at ease."

In the wake of Mao's death, Hua held all the top offices in the land: party chairman, premier, and chairman of the party's Military Affairs Commission. Since he owed his position solely to Mao's patronage, he insisted that China remain loyal to every word that Mao had uttered. But, as explained in Chapter 5, China in 1976–78 was ready for change. Lacking an independent base of support, Hua proved unable to consolidate his power. Deng Xiaoping, with a thick network of personal connections built up over a period of fifty years in the communist movement, effectively became the core leader in 1978. Deng eased Hua out of his major positions over the following three years, indicating once again that power resides in informal connections and command, not in formal positions.

Deng, himself twice purged by Mao, understood well the potential tragedy that struggles to succeed an all-powerful core leader can produce. He therefore almost immediately set out to put into place the building blocks of a stable, predictable succession. This produced several related initiatives: (1) he tried to keep within some bounds his own importance to the system so that his eventual retirement or death would not prove overly disruptive; (2) he chose two successors early on, built up their reputations, and gave them opportunities to construct their own political bases; (3) he tried to encourage his colleagues in his own generation to retire so that they would not interfere in the succession arrangements; and (4) he sought to enhance the importance of institutions and of regularized procedures to the politics of the top power elite so as to lay the basis for stable expectations about the transfer of power.[1]

Deng circumscribed his own role primarily by refusing to assume two of the top three positions: those of premier and the head of the party (as chairman or general secretary). He served for a number of years as a vice premier and as a member of the Standing Committee of the Politburo, but he left the top posts for his chosen successors, exercising his personal influence outside of the formal channels of authority. The one key position that Deng did assume was that of chairman of the Military Affairs Commission of the CCP. He felt that the direct control over the military was too important to entrust to others. To an extent, moreover, the military itself probably sought this arrangement, which enabled it to enjoy direct access to the party core leader.

Deng's chosen successors were Zhao Ziyang and Hu Yaobang. Zhao was a provincial official who made his early career in Guangdong province. He fell from power during the Cultural Revolution. When he returned to office, he became party secretary in Inner Mongolia (May 1971—April 1972) and in Guangdong (until 1975) before taking charge of Deng's native Sichuan Province. In Sichuan, Zhao was enormously effective in restoring the province's economy from the ravages of the Cultural Revolution through relatively bold reforms, first in agriculture and then in management of state industries. These caught Deng's attention, and Deng moved Zhao to Beijing and made him premier of the government in 1980. Deng counted on Zhao to implement a nationwide economic reform effort.

Hu Yaobang had even before 1949 been a close friend and associate of Deng's, and he served with Deng in Sichuan Province from 1949 to 1952. From then until the Cultural Revolution, Hu headed the Communist Youth League while Deng ran the party Secretariat. Both were purged early in the Cultural Revolution and rehabilitated in the early 1970s. Hu reappeared in April 1972, nearly a year before Deng's rehabilitation, then was purged again when the Gang of Four attacked Deng in early 1976. Both came back into office for a second time in 1977. Deng successively placed Hu in charge of two of the most sensitive areas of national policy, personnel (for 1978) and propaganda (for 1979). He then had Hu appointed general secretary of the CCP (February 1980) and party chairman (June 1981—until the abolition of that office in September 1982).

Deng gave both Zhao and Hu considerable leeway to propose and implement programs and to cultivate followers. Hu Yaobang focused his attention primarily on the traditional areas of party apparatus concern: propaganda, personnel, and rural policy. A remarkably impulsive and lively figure, Hu toured the countryside in the mid-1980s encouraging local officials to double economic output in the coming few years. He popularized the slogan calling for rural families to become "ten thousand–*yuan* households"—i.e., to become families whose earnings reached ten thousand Chinese dollars per year, far above the national average at that time. Politically, Hu sought to "emancipate minds" and to bring younger, more intellectually open people into office. In terms of personal political strategy, he made a concerted effort to place people who had worked closely with him during his Communist Youth League days into key positions at both the provincial and central levels.

Zhao Ziyang took charge of the Finance and Economics *kou* and focused primarily on the urban industrial economy. He strongly advocated rapid economic reform and became a champion of a coastal development strategy closely linked to the international economy. Zhao pioneered in the development, mentioned in Chapter 6, of a group of think tanks in the State Council. These focused respectively on political reform, foreign affairs, and the intersection of economics, technology, and social change, and they became impressive organizations for investigating problems and generating policy options.[2] On the whole, Zhao moved aggressively to bring up younger people who had shown some initiative and talent in the late 1970s. Many of these were individuals who had been sent to the countryside during the later stages of the Cultural Revolution and thus who had some feel for the realities of rural China as well as for the politics of the cities.

Thus, both Hu Yaobang and Zhao Ziyang sought to make their marks and to create strong political bases. Neither was simply a toady to Deng, their patron, but neither would have dared to oppose Deng when he made his position on a matter clear. Deng went some distance toward permitting them to build up the political resources necessary to see them through the succession. But both served at Deng's sufferance, and Deng protected each at various times from attacks by more conservative members of the older generation associated with Chen Yun. In addition, Deng gradually withdrew himself from day-to-day operations—in China's terminology, he "stepped back to the second line"—during the mid- and late 1980s.

Beyond setting an example for officials in general, Deng also urged the older members of the Politburo to step down voluntarily. He spoke of this as their last major contribution to the revolution, but his elderly colleagues on the Politburo resisted. Finally, Deng adopted a strategy of creating positions that permitted partial retirement. The most important of these was the founding of a Central Advisory Commission (CAC) by the Twelfth Party Congress in September 1982. Deng personally headed this commission until late 1987, even while he retained his posts on the Politburo. In November 1987 he stepped down from both the Politburo and the CAC, evidently as part of a deal he struck with Chen Yun for the latter to move from the Politburo to the be the CAC's chairman.

The CAC had no direct executive powers. It did, however, provide its members with a number of conveniences and with the right to carry out investigations and make reports to the authorities. Members of the Standing Committee of the CAC also had the right to sit in on Politburo meetings but not to cast formal votes at those meetings.

In short, the CAC provided a vehicle for old leaders to step out of their executive positions but still meddle in politics. It thus was an intermediate zone between full power and real retirement. CAC membership did not carry the potential opprobrium of retirement, but it did permit the assignment of younger officials to the top positions of formal authority in the party, government, and military. Deng conceived of the CAC as a temporary device to suit the peculiar situation in which the older revolutionaries are yielding power. He anticipated that this commission would be abolished once that generation fully retired or passed from the scene. It in fact was abolished by the Fourteenth Party Congress in late 1992.

Deng also encouraged strengthening regular institutional routines throughout the party and government, including at the upper echelons of power. Whereas in Mao's last decade nearly all institutions experienced enormous disruption, under Deng regularized meetings and procedures became more the norm. Thus, for example, the Party Congress, which is supposed to convene every five years, met in 1977, 1982, 1987, and 1992. Central Committee plenums began by the early 1980s to meet on a fairly regular basis each fall. The National People's Congress is supposed to be elected anew every four years and to hold a full plenum once each year. Under Deng, these criteria have been met, and the spring plenum of the NPC has become a key event on the annual political calendar, as has a regular summer central work conference at the seaside resort of Beidaihe. It appears that the Politburo, Secretariat, and the State Council also began to meet on a more regular basis in the 1980s, although the evidence here is thinner.

The above initiatives demonstrate that Deng Xiaoping seriously tried to reduce the chances of a destabilizing political succession. He recognized from the start that this is a dangerous flaw in the Chinese political system, and he gave considerable priority to remedying the problem. Ultimately, though, Deng failed.

THE COLLAPSE OF DENG'S SUCCESSION STRATEGY

Both the nature of the Chinese system and Deng Xiaoping's personal failings unraveled his attempt to lay the groundwork for a smooth, predictable political succession. While no single event undermined this effort, his handling of the Tiananmen democracy movement proved especially damaging. But substantial problems were evident even before Tiananmen brought them dramatically to the fore.

Deng's strategy itself proved fundamentally flawed. By denying himself the top formal positions other than in the military, from which he stepped down in 1990, yet at the same time exercising supreme power, Deng demonstrated on a daily basis that his vaunted institution building was a front and a sham. His designated successors, Zhao and Hu, held the highest positions, but those positions did not convey supreme power. As the 1980s wore on and the older generation (Deng, Chen Yun, Li Xiannian, Bo Yibo, Wang Zhen, and so forth) retired from the Politburo at the Thirteenth Party Congress in 1987, the difference between formal position and real power became even more acute. The Politburo became a committee of protégés who answered to the real powers behind the scenes, the elderly patrons whose deals among themselves determined who would serve on the party's top bodies. Even though he retired from his last formal post in 1990, for example, Deng by his bold initiatives to rekindle reform in 1992 fully demonstrated his continuing ability at age eighty-eight to affect the agenda of Chinese politics despite his near total deafness and declining health.

Deng might have rectified this situation to some degree had he personally give up power in the mid-1980s, once Zhao and Hu were firmly in place. But he refused to do so, evidently regarding himself as indispensable to protecting the reform program both from the more conservative elders and from potential excesses by his successors. But Deng ultimately proved unable to convince the other elders to retire completely while he personally remained actively involved in politics. The inevitable result has been the deep corruption of the leading institutions by the activities of a powerful, meddling group of aged revolutionaries.

To make matters worse, Deng, like Mao, purged his own designated successors when they displeased him. By 1986, Hu Yaobang felt that it was time for the successors to take over the system fully. He personally coveted the chairmanship of the Military Affairs Commission. Reportedly, at a meeting late that year where Deng proposed his own retirement, all those attending except Hu Yaobang urged Deng to stay on "in order to protect the reforms." Deng regarded Hu's position as an indication that his younger successor (Hu was seventy-one years old at the time), with whom he had worked for nearly half a century, had become too anxious to seize power. When Hu ran afoul of military leaders and of other elders later that year, therefore, Deng did not protect him. Hu's ouster itself was decided upon in January 1987 outside of the boundaries of the Politburo, the only body that had the formal right to make such a decision.

Later in 1987 Deng further damaged the institutional arrangements he himself had created. The new Party Constitution, formally known as the Party Rules, adopted in 1982 had specified that the head of the Military Affairs Commission must be a member of the Standing Committee of the Politburo. But in November 1987 Deng dropped off of the Politburo in part, as mentioned above, to bring about Chen Yun's retirement from the same body. Deng, however, retained the chairmanship of the Military Affairs Commission, thus demonstrating yet again that among the power elite the PRC remained a system of men rather than a system of law.

The Tiananmen events thus provided a body blow to an already severely weakened succession structure. But the body blow was nevertheless of enormous importance. Several aspects of the response to this challenge[3] had major repercussions for the succession, as follows:

☐—From April to June 1989, all important decisions were made by the elders rather than by the formal leaders of the party and government. Deng and/or his elderly colleagues, sometimes after heated debate, decided on the initial reaction to the April student demonstrations in the wake of Hu Yaobang's death, mapped out the strategy at each succeeding stage, decided to impose martial law and to remove Zhao Ziyang from office, and made the fateful decision to order troops to take back the streets and Tiananmen Square itself at any cost on the night of 3–4 June. Throughout this entire period the normal organizations of the leadership either did not convene or met only to hear and approve the decisions made elsewhere. Almost all political systems strain institutional boundaries at times of crisis. But the Chinese during these crucial weeks effectively set aside their institutional structure and revealed to all the locus of real power at the top—the semi-"retired" octogenarians—ten years after the reforms began.

☐—The struggles of April–May produced the purge of Zhao Ziyang, the second of Deng's two designated successors. This totally undermined Deng's effort to pick successors and to put them into position to inherit and consolidate power after he left the system. All subsequent designees would understand that they could not escape the quandary of having to retain the support of their patron even as they sought to create their own political base. People in Beijing were heard to comment in late May 1989, "The old men in their eighties are meeting to decide who in their sixties should now retire from politics."

☐—Tiananmen strengthened the harder-line leaders who opposed Deng's more radical reform activities and thus ensured a more embittered, faction ridden political environment for some years to come.

☐—Tiananmen and its immediate aftermath deeply tarnished Premier Li Peng, to the extent that it made him perhaps the most despised individual in China. This has made it difficult if not impossible for Li to compete successfully for the core leader role when Deng passes from the scene. But Li potentially has the power and skill to cause major problems for any other claimant of this position.

☐—Tiananmen produced the appointment of Jiang Zemin as general secretary and his subsequent designation by Deng as the "core leader" of the new generation. But Jiang does not have Zhao Ziyang's stature or political base of support, and Jiang has since 1989 taken great care to tack with the wind in the political currents among the elders. He has thus remained caught in the difficult situation noted above: he cannot become more independent and hold onto his current job; he cannot develop the base necessary to win the succession without becoming more independent.

More than five years after the Tiananmen massacre, therefore, the setting for a smooth succession is not good. A strong individual, Zhao Ziyang, has been replaced by a weaker man, Jiang Zemin. The 1989 events dramatized that ten years into the reforms the formal institutions still mask the real distribution of power, and thus that the formal rules cannot be counted on to constrain and decide political struggles for power at the apex. The subsequent bare-knuckled political debates and jockeying for power have made clear, moreover, that there is no consensus among either the elders or the successor generation over who should become the real core leader after Deng passes from the scene.

THE PROSPECTS FOR ELITE SUCCESSION

As the above analysis indicates, it is impossible to determine in advance either who will become the next leader(s) of China or exactly how the related political struggles will unfold. But these matters are highly consequential for China during the 1990s. The PRC remains a country where people expect strong leadership at the Center. Most Chinese firmly believe that division at the top produces paralysis or worse at lower levels, and thus that social stability and economic progress require the consolidation of power by a core leader in Beijing. Many Westerners may expect that with the reforms the leading political offices, premier and general secretary, will acquire sufficient stature and integrity that their incumbents will ride out the succession, but there seem to be few if any in China who share that hope or expectation.

A major concern of both reformers and conservatives alike, therefore, is that no individual in the successor generation—those currently in their sixties or early seventies—enjoys both the high prestige and political base necessary to be the core leader for the 1990s. Four of the members of the Standing Committee of the Politburo probably provide the initial group of key contenders. Premier Li Peng, as noted above, is so unpopular that he should be regarded more as a possible spoiler than as a potential leader. Party General Secretary Jiang Zemin is widely viewed as ineffectual, and he lacks a strong personal political base. Zhu Rongji is a Politburo Standing Committee member who works primarily on economic issues. While he spent the bulk of his post-1949 career in the central governmental apparatus dealing with the economy, he also had a highly successful stint as mayor of Shanghai from 1987 to 1990. Zhu is widely regarded as very capable and knowledgeable, but he treats his subordinates so undiplomatically that he has alienated many potential supporters. Politburo Standing Committee member Qiao Shi has a pre–Cultural Revolution background that included work both in east China and in the iron and steel industry. In the 1970s he took charge of the Central Committee's International Liaison Department. He then moved in 1985 into the Political and Legal *xitong* and became head of the Political and Legal Affairs Commission. As of 1994 he also heads the National People's Congress, a post in which he is garnering some publicity. Qiao is widely regarded as capable and a supporter of reform. His role as essentially China's top cop probably has provided him with important resources in a succession struggle.

These four are not the only potential leaders of China in the near future. There are older individuals who are most likely to play roles as brokers but who could potentially emerge as transitional leaders in their own right. These include Yang Shangkun, an octogenarian with strong ties in both the military and party apparatuses; Wan Li, who belonged to the Politburo for most of the 1980s and headed the National People's Congress from 1987 to 1993, when Qiao Shi replaced him; and Zhao Ziyang, who has quietly regained a modicum of political respectability and might reemerge to play a significant political role.

Li Ruihuan, a member of the Politburo but not of its Standing Committee, perhaps typifies the type of younger potential leader who is waiting in the wings, just beyond the first circle of power. Li, fifty-eight, has a solid political base in the province-level city of Tianjin. He is a native of Tianjin and worked there from 1981 to 1989, during the last seven years of which he ran the city as its mayor and top party secretary. While there, Li effectively facilitated the city's recovery from the devastating Tangshan earthquake of 1976 and laid the groundwork for major subsequent economic growth. Li has demonstrated initiative and organizational skills throughout his career, and he is strong willed, politically tough, and capable of assuming very reformist and somewhat conservative postures, depending on the issue and the political winds of the moment. As of 1994, however, Li is several rungs from the top spot, and he does not have the national stature expected of the party's core leader.

There are additional individuals who could be mentioned, but the above brief overview is sufficient to illustrate the general point: because no clear rules guide and constrain the process for selecting and confirming a top leader, the attendant political uncertainty and infighting could become a serious, continuing problem for the Chinese system through the mid-1990s and perhaps until late in the decade.

The military has been a powerful institution in Chinese domestic politics, and many Western scholars anticipate that the PLA may play a determining role in the next succession.[4] The basic trend in military activity, however, is away from intense involvement in elite politics. All older generation leaders almost without exception had long pre-1949 service in—and continuing very close ties with—the military. That is not true for the younger generation. Since the mid-1980s, moreover, there has been large-scale turnover in the PLA officer corps, with promotions of more professionally trained, younger individuals. The old generation of officers who moved easily between civilian politics and work in the PLA is quickly passing from the scene. Indeed, in late 1993 Deng brought two elderly military officers, Liu Huaqing and Zhang Zhen, into the Politburo, evidently to help assure military support for a reformist civilian successor leadership. Liu and Zhang are both in their late seventies, and it appears that, while both may help broker the succession, neither has pretensions for overall political power.

Very likely, during the succession struggles of the 1990s all contenders will take care to cultivate support in the PLA for fear that the military might actively intervene in favor of someone else. The development of an unstable collective leadership at the top would increase efforts to win over the military, as collective forms of leadership typically give major vested interests increased access to the political elite. But while military support will be important, a military takeover or major direct military intervention is not probable, shy of a collapse of the civilian leadership. The 1990s are more likely, in short, to see military budgets rise as a result of politicians bidding for military support than to see a coup d'état or other major forms of direct military intervention in elite politics.

The above analysis suggests several important ways in which the elite succession of the 1990s should influence the Chinese political system. Any of the following may lead to significant change in the nature of the political system itself, a possibility that is examined in the concluding chapter of this volume.

First, the succession probably will for periods of time entail the development of a more collective leadership, which is a distribution of power that tends to give major vested interests increased influence over elite decisions. The "outside" interests may be *tiao* or *kuai* organizations (institutional sectors, such as the military, or geographical locales) or some combination of the two. However, these interests almost certainly will not include independent groups or nongovernmental organizations of citizens, as their support cannot translate into political power at the top. The basic dynamics of this type of situation make it likely, on balance, that the Center will play a weaker role in the overall political system, more an adjudicator of interests and supplicant for support than a mobilizer of energies and resources. This type of political leadership may find it more difficult to discipline the bureaucracies, to call for national sacrifice, or to focus efforts on major national problems.

Second, the lack of clarity about the rules of succession means that there is a continuing risk of an open, paralyzing split among the top contenders and their supporters. This could be especially true if the leadership confronts a crisis, such as substantial social protest. This could well occur during the 1990s. As has been noted earlier in this volume, under these circumstances the possibility of rapidly escalating social disorder can grow exponentially. This danger arises from three factors.

First, the open divisions at the top create mixed signals for officials and security personnel at all levels and thus risk paralyzing these forces. This occurred during April and May of 1989 until the imposition of martial law on 20 May.

Second, in Chinese political culture there is a relatively thin line between order and chaos, a thinner line than is the case in Western political culture. Unlike Westerners, Chinese tend to see order and chaos as nesting up against each other, with a situation fairly easily slipping back and forth across that line. Westerners, by contrast, tend to assume that society is always in a state of moderate disorder. The transition from order to chaos in China can occur with astonishing speed—as can the subsequent relapse into social order. Open, paralyzing divisions at the top of the system signal that the old order is no longer certain, and the result can be large-scale social dislocation and unrest.

Third, there is massive discontent with the political system among the populace and among many officials. Relatively few can envision in concrete terms any viable substitute for the current system of fragmented authoritarianism, but many would be delighted to vent their anger and frustrations through demonstrations if they thought they could do so with impunity.[5]

The above factors combine to create a possibility of large-scale social breakdown even in the context of a rapidly growing economy. More stable succession arrangements, by ensuring the continuation of a relatively clear hierarchy of authority, would greatly diminish this prospect.

Inevitably, during the course of the 1990s the type of person leading China will change. The current generation of elders generally joined the revolution in the 1920s and hailed from peasant stock. Like Mao, many had a visceral antiurban and anti-intellectual bias, and very few had a technical education. These were individuals who risked their lives in revolutionary struggles in the belief that China's international weakness and humiliation were inextricably linked to the country's domestic social structure and culture.

In stark contrast, the likely leaders of the late 1990s will generally be individuals who chose to join the new "establishment" after 1949. Most will have had advanced technical educations, typically in engineering. Regardless of whether their origins are urban or rural, they will have lived in cities for virtually their entire adult life. Zhu Rongji is representative of this group. He joined the CCP in 1949 and graduated from the Electric Motor Engineering Department of Qinghua University in 1951. From 1952 to 1975 he served as a deputy division chief of the State Planning Commission in Beijing. He then worked for three years (1975–78) for the Ministry of Petroleum Industry and briefly (1978–79) headed the Industrial Economics Institute of the newly established Chinese Academy of Social Sciences. From 1979 to 1983 he held leading posts in the State Economic Commission, after which he moved to Shanghai where he became deputy party secretary in 1987 and mayor in 1988. In Shanghai, Zhu developed extensive contacts with foreign businessmen and proved to be a very effective, and abrasive, economic administrator. He moved to Beijing in 1990 and then assumed a variety of assignments dealing primarily with the state sector of the economy.

Men like Zhu Rongji have held provincial leadership posts and positions in the Politburo that have required that they hone their political skills. But these are not individuals with revolutionary credentials. Rather, they are skilled organization men who tend to ask how to get something done effectively rather than how policies will affect the ideological or cultural outlooks of the population. They have spent little time in the Chinese countryside, and certainly do not harbor an antiurban bias. Most worked hard in the 1980s to increase foreign involvement in the development of their respective cities.

Given their advanced ages, it is impossible to predict just when—and in what order—the current octogenarian leaders will pass from the scene. Those who remain viable will undoubtedly seek to affect politics and the succession for as long as they are able to do so. But by the late 1990s the elder statesmen still on the scene are likely to be individuals such as Zhao Ziyang who joined the revolution before 1949 but who were low-level functionaries before the communist victory and who therefore lack the legitimacy of having led the revolutionary struggle. Such individuals will more likely play the role of wise men than, as now, a shadow leadership more powerful than the group that holds formal office. Like the 1950s, therefore, the "elders" will play a weak role in the political system. Unlike the 1950s, the core leader and his top colleagues will not be revolutionaries committed to radical social change.

Fundamentally, the Chinese system is in the midst of a probable shift toward weaker central leadership overall. Mao Zedong enjoyed truly extraordinary authority because of his deep revolutionary experience, his strong commitment to ideology, his charisma, and his political ruthlessness. Deng Xiaoping has been somewhat weaker—a person with very considerable revolutionary experience and thick personal connections across the spectrum of bureaucracies, but who lacks Mao's theoretical pretensions and charisma. Deng, therefore, has had to compromise and engage in coalition-building far more than did his predecessor.

Deng's successors will be weaker still.[6] Whoever rises to the top will be an individual who has spent most of his career in one or two functional bureaucracies or locales and who lacks deep revolutionary experience. He will very likely negotiate with his colleagues more than dominate them, and officials in the provinces are unlikely to view him as charismatic. This change in leadership dynamics makes the nature and quality of cadres at the lower levels of the bureaucracies of great importance for the future performance of the PRC's political system.

Systemic Succession

Basic information about the successors below the Center, at least in aggregate, reveals that the change of leadership has already taken place throughout these lower levels of the political system.

CHANGES TO DATE

Hu Yaobang's late 1970s rehabilitation of millions of cadres led, ironically, to an effort in the early 1980s to retire many of these same individuals. These included nearly 2.5 million cadres who had joined the revolution before 1949, along with an additional 2,353,000 cadres who had been recruited from 1950 to 1952. The rehabilitations recognized the moral and political imperative to rectify the gross injustices of the Cultural Revolution. The retirement initiatives recognized that these individuals were, on the whole, not capable of implementing a program of market-oriented economic reform.

Disagreements among the leadership over actual retirement policy produced vague and conflicting instructions to lower levels, which resulted in massive rehabilitations but few retirements from 1978 to 1981. In February 1982, however, a clearer set of guidelines forced action, and throughout the 1980s large numbers of veteran cadres made way for their younger counterparts. Careful research on this process by Professor Melanie Manion highlights the reluctance of the older cadres to retire and the many side deals that they were able to cut.[7] But the overall results—in both the civilian and military sectors—are impressive. In the course of implementing this policy, moreover, a new norm—that being an official is a job from which one retires rather than the lifetime commitment of a revolutionary—began to take hold.

There have been a number of studies of leadership changes during the 1980s, and each suggests that the degree of turnover was large and that the changes reached down to every level of the administrative system.[8] In broad terms, concentrated personnel reforms from 1982 to 1984 sought four major objectives: to instill the above-mentioned new norm of retirement for officials; to reduce the number of officials overall, and especially of leading cadres; to recruit younger, better-educated cadres; and to identify yet another batch of individuals who should be cultivated to take over key positions after an additional few years. Later in the decade, particularly between 1984 and 1987, Zhao Ziyang promoted an effort to develop a civil service system for China that would govern the recruitment and promotion of individuals who hold technical staff—versus political—positions. China previously had not clearly differentiated these two groups.[9]

The results of the 1982–84 reforms at the upper levels of the system received much publicity. Summary results are presented in Tables 8.1 and 8.2.

In terms of gross statistics at a leadership level, therefore, the system moved toward a smaller number of younger, better-educated leading officials. A broader sample survey of changes among cadres of more than sixty-two hundred county-, city-, and prefecture-level units[10] provides important additional information on the real depth of the changes of 1982–84.

TABLE 8.1 *Age and Education before and after the 1982–84 Reforms*

	AVERAGE AGE		% COLLEGE-EDUCATED	
	BEFORE	AFTER	BEFORE	AFTER
Ministers and vice-ministers	64	58	38	59
Directors and deputy directors of State Council	59	54	35	52
Directors and deputy directors of central CCP organs	66	62	43	53
Heads and deputy heads of bureaus of central CCP organs	60	54	50	56
Provincial CCP secretaries, governors, and vice governors	62	55	20	44

Source Lee (1991), p. 256.

TABLE 8.2 *Reduction of Bureaucracy via the 1982–84 Reforms*

	NUMBER BEFORE	NUMBER AFTER	PERCENT REDUCTION
State Council			
Offices	98	52	47
Ministers and vice ministers	1,000	300	70
Directors and deputy directors	5,000	2,500	50
Persons in the state council	49,000	32,000	35
All cadres at the central level	600,000	400,000	33
Central party organs			
Offices			17
Directors and deputy directors			40
Heads and deputy heads of offices			14
Provincial level			
Secretaries, members of standing committee, and governors, vice governors	698	463	34
Heads of bureaus	16,658	10,604	36
Municipal-level leaders			36
District-level leaders			29
County-level leaders			25

Source Cui and Wang (n.d.).

TABLE 8.3 *Promotions, 1979–84*

Cadres in 6,262 Leading Bodies at County, City, and Prefecture Levels:
Number of cadres as of 1984: 20,732
Number of promotions, 1979–84: 20,309

Source Cui and Wang (n.d.).

Table 8.3 indicates that roughly 98 percent of the cadres in these leading bodies as of 1984 had been promoted since 1979. That almost certainly somewhat overstates the case. It is probable that in at least some instances one position on a leading body went through two or more new incumbents during this five-year period, while other positions may have been occupied continuously by one individual. Overall, however, the above figures suggest strongly that the vast majority of the positions on leading bodies at these lower levels of the Chinese leadership experienced turnover from 1979 to 1984, and other evidence supports this general picture.

Indeed, data on the average age of leaders at the lower administrative levels of the political system highlights both the timing of changes and the fact that there was a critical transition in office holders between 1982 and 1984 from those who joined the revolution before victory to those who joined the new regime after 1949 (see Table 8.4).

Table 8.4 shows the enormous continuity in generation of leadership at the subprovincial levels of the political system nationwide before the reforms. It also indicates that as of 1975 the party secretaries and deputy secretaries at the prefecture and subprovincial city levels averaged 25 to 29 years of age when the communists came to power. Most of these had probably participated in the revolution itself, many joining during the civil-war phase of the late 1940s. Their nationwide counterparts as of 1984 had been, on average, only 15 to 18 years old in 1949. These latter were very likely individuals who did not join the revolution until after it had become the "establishment."

For county-level units, including cities with the bureaucratic rank of a county, CCP secretaries and deputy secretaries throughout the country as of 1976 were on average 17 to 21 years old in 1949; for their 1984 counterparts, the equivalent average ages were 10 to 13 years old, very likely too young to have participated in the revolution. Thus, party leadership at the prefecture, county, and municipal levels passed to a predominantly postrevolution generation between 1979 and 1984.[11]

Looking at the heart of the bureaucracy at the Center, the same Chinese study investigated the bureau (*ju*) and department (*chu*) cadres in eighteen of the State Council ministries and commissions. It found that from 1982 to 1984 nearly three-quarters of the cadres were newly promoted to these positions.

TABLE 8.4 *Birth Dates of Leading Cadres at Prefectural and County Levels Nationwide, 1975–84*

	1975	1976	1977	1978	1979	1983	1984
Prefectural level							
CCP secretary	1921	1921	1922	1922	1923	1930	1931
Deputy secretary	1924	1925	1925	1925	1925	1934	1934
*Subprovincial cities**							
CCP secretary	1921	1921	1922	1921	1921	1928	1930
Deputy secretary	1924	1925	1925	1924	1924	1933	1934
Standing committee	1926	1927	1927	1926	1925	1934	1935
Counties/cities†							
CCP secretary	n.a.	1928	1929	1929	1929	1932	1936
Deputy secretary	n.a.	1931	1931	n.a.	1930	1934	1940
Standing committee	n.a.	1932	1932	n.a.	1930	1934	1941

Source Cui and Wang (n.d.).

*Cities of a bureaucratic rank below a province and above a county.

†Counties and cities with the bureaucratic rank of a county.

The study concludes that at the bureau and department levels, as of the end of 1984 "the cadres already are those who began their work after the founding of the PRC."[12]

As noted above, these changes in leadership sought to raise the educational level of cadres throughout the system. The results at the central and provincial levels are provided in Table 8.1 above. The numbers for the city and prefecture level in nine locales from very different parts of China are presented in Table 8.5.

Table 8.5 brings in locales from every major part of China, and it includes both wealthy and poor areas. Several facets of Table 8.5 warrant particular attention:

□—As of 1979 in every locale the percentage of cadres with a higher education was lower for the leading groups than for the entire group of cadres in that locale. This reflects the low educational level of the revolutionaries who seized power in 1949 and stayed in those positions in subsequent decades. Indeed, on average roughly 85 percent of the cadres in each locale's leading bodies had only a junior high school level of education or less. Only 1.5 percent, on average, had at least some higher education. Subordinate administrative personnel, by contrast, had a higher level of educational attainment.

□—In 1984, by contrast, in every locale the percentage of cadres with a higher education in the leading body had grown significantly larger than the comparable percentage for the cadre group as a whole. Clearly, higher education provided a major boost for admission to the readjusted leading bodies. Overall educational levels also rose for the cadre group as a whole in each locale, but there simply were not enough people with a higher education available to match the composition of the leading bodies in terms of educational structure.

□—In every locale but one, the number of cadres in the leading bodies declined significantly from 1979 to 1984, very much in line with the figures for higher levels presented in Table 8.2. This reflected the overall effort to cut back on the number of cadres in the bureaucracy. But, contrary to the desires of the leaders, the number of cadres *overall* shot up substantially—by an average of 35 percent—in every single locale. Reports from elsewhere, moreover, confirm that this was a general phenomenon. For example, according to the figures in one article,[13] the number of personnel in party and state institutions grew by an annual average of about 3 percent between 1966 and 1979, by about 7.7 percent between 1979 and 1989, and, within that period, by nearly 9 percent between 1984 and 1989. Administrative and management expenditures increased from 4.1 percent of the state budget in 1978 to 7.8 percent in 1985 and to 8.3 percent in 1988. Bureaucratic streamlining thus failed below the top leadership at all levels of the political system.

□—The overall numbers of city and prefecture level cadres at just these nine locations are also worthy of note. The figure totaled 403,623 cadres in 1979 and 546,162 cadres in 1984. The governing apparatus of China confronts huge problems of cadre management.

TABLE 8.5 *City and Prefecture Cadre Educational Levels, 1979 and 1984*

| CITY OR PREFECTURE | NUMBER OF CADRES | LEVEL OF EDUCATION | | | YEAR |
		HIGHER (%)	HIGH SCHOOL OR POLYTECHNIC (%)	JR. HIGH OR LOWER (%)	
Dezhou	242	0.00	13.22	90.08	1979
	184	45.70	21.70	32.60	1984
	53640	9.48	33.09	57.43	1979
	72048	12.70	48.00	39.90	1984
Weifang	257	3.5	8.17	88.33	1979
	188	53.7	23.90	22.30	1984
	78426	10.3	32.20	57.50	1979
	96658	13.4	47.70	38.90	1984
Anyang	186	2.69	6.45	90.86	1979
	120	51.70	30.00	18.30	1984
	32747	11.3	24.5	64.02	1979
	50943	13.7	37.2	49.00	1984
Zhumadian	255	1.18	6.27	92.55	1979
	139	52.50	23.70	23.70	1984
	48951	9.4	27.22	63.43	1979
	67417	12.0	44.00	44.00	1984
Baotou	126	2.38	15.87	81.75	1979
	104	58.70	26.90	13.50	1984
	39579	6.2	22.6	71.2	1979
	48716	44.0	38.0	18.0	1984
Wulumuqi	82	1.22	28.05	70.73	1979
	88	28.40	29.70	41.50	1984
	21308	13.6	35.0	51.4	1979
	27898	15.2	43.8	41.0	1984
Foshan	141	0.71	7.8	91.40	1979
	107	28.80	29.7	41.50	1984
	46372	11.39	24.5	64.0	1979
	64729	17.00	37.0	47.0	1984
Sanming	199	1.5	14.57	83.92	1979
	160	60.0	30.00	10.00	1984
	35613	15.11	39.75	45.14	1979
	48731	20.20	49.60	30.20	1984
Ningbo	159	0.63	8.18	91.40	1979
	124	57.30	20.20	22.60	1984
	46987	13.16	35.0	51.4	1979
	69022	20.90	42.7	36.4	1984

Source Cui and Wang (n.d.).

For each locale, the first two lines of figures represent cadres in the "leading bodies" of the locale, and the second two lines represent all the party and government cadres at the municipal and prefecture levels within the given local. Weifang, Anyang, Baotou, Wulumuqi (Urumqi), Foshan, Sanming, and Ningbo are cities; Dezhou and Zhumadian are prefectures.

The above figures are unusual in that they include detailed information on the middle and lower levels of the bureaucratic system. In broad terms, though, the picture they portray is largely consistent with the generalizations often found in the Chinese media about changes in the political administration staffing since the start of the reforms.

A final condition for promotion—that the individual be committed to economic development and reform while retaining loyalty to the CCP—is not possible to measure directly with objective numbers. Interviews by scholars have tended to support the notion that, especially at local levels in the political system, the new cadres are highly oriented toward rapid economic growth but that their level of enthusiasm for a revolutionary party is uncertain.

Hong Yong Lee's analysis of the prior work experience of those who held leading positions in 1982 (before the cadre reforms) and in 1987 (after the first wave of these reforms) lends indirect support to these observations. Lee looked at the previous work experience of ministers, provincial CCP secretaries, governors, and Central Committee members. In most categories—economics and management, functional bureau, Youth League, military, and mass organizations—the numbers involved were small and little change occurred. But in two categories, engineering and "CCP secretary and political fields," the numbers and the amount of change were telling (see Table 8.6).

Put simply, before the reforms most of the incumbents (except for Central Committee members) came from backgrounds in political work. After the reform wave, the balance tipped toward positions in which they did engineering—that is, practical problem-solving—work.

A Chinese analyst writing for the *Guangming ribao* (*Brightness Daily*) in 1991 summed up these changes and the issues they pose.[14] He observed that,

It should be . . . noted that with the replacement of old cadres by new ones, the main bulk of the cadres' ranks has now shifted from cadres who began working before the birth of the PRC and who were tested in the blood and fires of revolutionary struggles to those who started working after the birth of the PRC and who grew up in an environment of peace. A considerable number of them are university and technical school graduates of the 1980s. These young cadres possess a higher level of scientific and cul-

TABLE 8.6 *Leaders' Work Experience, 1982 and 1987*

	YEAR	MINISTERS NO.	MINISTERS %	SECRETARIES NO.	SECRETARIES %	GOVERNORS NO.	GOVERNORS %	CENTRAL COMM. MEMBERS NO.	CENTRAL COMM. MEMBERS %
Engineering	1982	1	2	0	0	0	0	4	2
	1987	17	45	7	25	8	33	34	26
Sec'ty and	1982	26	60	24	83	23	84	91	48
pol. work	1987	2	5	10	36	7	30	38	29

Source Lee (1991), p. 268.

tural knowledge as well as active minds and can accept new things more easily. However, most of them . . . still have some weaknesses and shortcomings in terms of ideology and politics.

In short, once the party leaders convinced old officials to retire, they faced the problem of recruiting younger individuals who had better training, a more open mind toward reform, *and loyalty to the party*. Many of the older leaders at both the central and lower levels believed, moreover, that the ones who best met these criteria were their own offspring.

The sons and daughters of the communist elite have generally enjoyed privileged educational experiences. They also have an intimate knowledge of the norms, style, and expectations of their parents' generation, and they know quite a bit about the history of the party and of major issues confronting the country. They can be counted on, in addition, not to repudiate their parents' work. Among the older offspring, moreover, many suffered grievously when their parents came under attack during the Cultural Revolution, and a parental desire to make up for this past suffering adds further impetus to maneuvering sons and daughters into top positions in either politics or in business as a condition of their own retirement.

The struggles over the roles of offspring of the elite seem to have been occurring at all levels of the political system since the mid-1980s. For obvious reasons, these are most visible at the very top. Even though the official Chinese press does not discuss the positions of offspring of national leaders, the little that is known makes two things clear: there is a power elite in China that is, in many cases, passing on political and economic power to the next generation within the family; and there have been deep disagreements over this effort at the top and strong resentment of it among the population.[15]

The evidence of the interplay of social networking and of political power at the top is clear and compelling. Many of the offspring of the elite attended the same special schools, where they both received a good education and mingled with each other—producing a fair amount of intermarriage later on. Several examples illustrate the result.

□—Deng Xiaoping's daughters are Deng Rong and Deng Nan. Deng Nan is a bureau chief of the powerful National Defense Science, Technology, and Industry Commission. Her husband He Ping, the son of former top party member He Long, who was killed during the Cultural Revolution, is deputy director of the Equipment Department under the PLA General Staff Department. He was formerly the manager of the Polytechnologies Corporation, a major firm in China's weapons business.[16] Deng Rong is the director of the National People's Congress Standing Committee's Research Office.

□—Bo Yibo, another octogenarian, has sons who are, respectively, the mayor of Dalian City (Bo Xilai) and a major Beijing businessman in the tourism industry. The latter, Bo Xicheng, until 1993 was the director of the Tourism Bureau for the city of Beijing. This position carries the rank of a bureau chief in a ministry.

□—Peng Zhen has one son who is in the political and legal affairs *xitong*, a daughter who is chair of the State Family Planning Commission, a son-in-law who is a party secretary on the Shanxi provincial party committee, and, reportedly, a son-in-law (Chen Xitong) who is mayor of Beijing. Peng hails from Shanxi Province, played a major role in the political and legal affairs system, and was for years before the Cultural Revolution the political boss of Beijing municipality.

□—Deceased PLA marshal Ye Jianying hailed from Guangdong Province. When he retired, his son Ye Xuanping took over Guangdong for about a decade in the 1980s. The younger Ye is now a member of the Standing Committee of the National People's Congress, and he has put his own choice into place to head Guangdong Province.

Along similar lines, a look at the Politburo as of 1994 shows that Li Peng is the adopted son of Zhou Enlai and Deng Yingchao, Li Tieying is the son of former head of the United Front Work Department Li Weihan (whose wife had earlier been married to Deng Xiaoping), and Li Ruihuan is rumored to be the son-in-law of former National People's Congress chairman Wan Li.[17]

The rapid rise of the offspring of leading officials became a political issue by the late 1980s. Many of these individuals are leaping over others who would appear to be at least as well qualified for the work. Rumors have circulated in recent years, also, about large-scale corrupt activities of many of these figures, both in business and through official profiteering. Many are thought to have large, secret bank accounts abroad. Whether these rumors are true or not, they have fed resentment among other officials and the population at large.

Both Hu Yaobang and Zhao Ziyang had children who reached high positions in politics and business during the 1980s. Nevertheless, Hu and Zhao recognized the political price the regime was paying for this practice and made several efforts to put a stop to it. In 1986 Hu directed an anticorruption campaign that targeted, among others, the offspring of some of his leading conservative critics, such as Mao's former *mishu* Hu Qiaomu. Hu Qiaomu played a very active role later that year in bringing down Hu Yaobang. At the peak of the Tiananmen crisis in mid-May 1989, Zhao Ziyang proposed that the leaders adopt a series of conciliatory policies, including investigating corruption among their own offspring and barring their relatives from office.[18] This suggestion contributed to sealing Zhao's fate with the octogenarians.

As the Chinese identify the individuals who should take over major positions throughout the system, therefore, one of the underlying issues is that of nepotism. The above comments focus on the more visible top layer of the political system, but interviews in China indicate that the problem is pervasive. Many of the offspring are quite competent, pragmatic individuals who are ardent reformers. The issue in most cases is not, therefore, one of officials appointing their relatives to power in order to block all changes in the system.

But in a situation in which elite turnover is producing major opportunities for rapid upward mobility, there is keen popular sensitivity to the possibility that a hereditary power elite is forming that will dominate others and reap the rewards of economic development disproportionately for themselves.

THE POLITICAL IMPLICATIONS

As the above sections detail, China in the early 1990s is ruled at the top by a generation of revolutionary gerontocrats that is all powerful but is fading from the scene, while the system over which they rule has already shed its revolutionary essence. In systemic terms, the Center is becoming weaker, and the dynamics and results of the succession at the top should continue this trend. In a political regime that is increasingly decentralized in its operations, consequently, the initiative now in many instances lies in the hands of a new generation that came to power under the reforms. Indeed, many Chinese view the key decision-making level of the current system as that of the cities and counties. At all higher levels, officials deal only with other officials. At these basic levels, people deal with real resources in a dynamically growing economy in the context of a rapidly changing society.

Those promoted to leadership under this new regime tend to be people with good educations (primarily in engineering) who are strongly committed to rapid economic growth. Even though many of the new leaders have close personal ties with the older generation officials, this is not, on the whole, an ideologically oriented political apparatus. They are, rather, problem-solvers who give the impression of seeing economic development as the best way to solve the most important problems they confront.

There is a natural tendency among Westerners to assume that individuals with technical educations who profess little commitment to ideology must be democrats and nascent capitalists. But in fact these are individuals whose education and background do not necessarily strongly predispose them toward any particular set of values and preferences. Most grew up in the Maoist system and became thoroughly disillusioned with the excesses of radical socialism. They have not had sustained exposure, however, to Western democratic values, as opposed to Western standards of production and consumption.

This is, indeed, on the whole a nonphilosophical group. If given choices of bureaucratic administration versus market forces, personal corruption versus selfless service, government power versus individual rights, and economic growth versus environmental protection, there is little likelihood that most would systematically choose the latter option in each pair. The choices, rather, would likely depend on the specific pressing problems the individual officials confront and the options available for dealing with them quickly. In this most basic sense, the Chinese revolution has ended and a more technocratic successor generation has taken over at all levels but the very top of the system.[19]

How the new elite will act, therefore, requires understanding the interplay between changes occurring in the way the political system operates and the key domestic and transnational problems with which it must grapple in the 1990s. The following chapters examine this interplay in three contexts— economic challenges; the problems raised by environmental degradation; and the evolving relations between the state and society. The final chapter will pull together these various parts and factor in transnational issues to preview the evolution of the PRC during the coming years.

Part Four

THE
CHALLENGES
AHEAD

9
Economic Development

Developing a more efficient economy that can produce technological change, raise China's living standards, and bolster international security has been at the core of the Deng-era reforms. These policies have in fact improved the standard of living of the vast majority of Chinese at a remarkable rate since 1979. But these very successes inevitably have produced related changes—in popular attitudes, social stratification, population mobility, and so forth—that during the 1990s at least affect and perhaps even threaten the political system itself.

History since the start of the industrial revolution shows that rapid industrial development entails enormous domestic and international consequences. This process literally alters the way people live, think, and produce. It changes the internal distribution of wealth as well as a country's ability to project power beyond its borders. At best, this is an unsettling process, producing enormous social strain and requiring substantial political accommodation. When the industrial revolution takes place simultaneously with the electronics revolution, including sudden participation in international telecommunications, the repercussions are all the more unsettling.

While quick economic growth may help to satisfy escalating popular demands, rapid growth can also contribute to tension and instability. Extremely rapid economic development in most cases means that people's lives in the aggregate are changing faster than are the normative systems that sustain a society and give it meaning. The dislocations always associated with urbanization and the shift to factory labor are, therefore, exacerbated by confusion in values and sharp generational conflicts.

China during the 1980s and early 1990s has been the world's fastest growing major industrial economy. Overall per capita gross national product (GNP) in constant *yuan* nearly doubled between 1978 and 1988. It should double again by about 1995. From 1978 to 1988, the number of Chinese with direct access to television increased from roughly eleven million to approximately 595 million,[1] and the content of television itself has changed from dull state-sponsored programming to, in many cases, uncensored international satellite broadcasts. As a result, despite its enormous economic successes—indeed, in part *because* of these successes—China during the 1990s confronts potentially destabilizing challenges to its political order. The incentives to maintain extremely rapid growth are, moreover, almost overpowering.

Incentives for High Growth

As explained in Chapter 5, Deng Xiaoping started China's economic reforms at the end of the 1970s largely because he recognized the dangers to China of falling so dramatically behind the growth rates being achieved elsewhere in East Asia. He saw that Mao Zedong's highly collectivist approach to development could not produce adequate results, and he realized that China had to find a way to generate technological change, a goal that had eluded all of the socialist economies of the era.

In 1983 and 1984 Premier Zhao Ziyang read and became enamored of Alvin Toffler's book, *The Third Wave.*[2] This volume argues that the technological revolution is key to growth at the end of the twentieth century and that countries that had yet to undergo the industrial revolution might actually skip much of that process and leap into the economic forefront through technological advancement. Zhao invited Toffler to Beijing, and Toffler's writings became required reading for China's top politicians and officials in economic organs.[3] The net effect was to increase awareness overall of the country's need to develop a system that could produce technological change.

In the most fundamental sense, therefore, China's economic reform strategy has been guided by an international strategic vision at the top of the political system. This vision links China's security and global influence to the state of its economy, and it asserts that China's growth must proceed at least at the overall speed of that of its neighbors in East Asia. While this vision recognizes that in the short-term China's fastest growth can only come from utilizing its relatively cheap labor force in the international division of labor, it also views technological change as an integral part of maintaining a rapidly growing economy over the long run. It is premised on the notion that a centrally administered, planned economy is inimicable to such technological dynamism.

While this grand strategic vision has provided incentives for economic reform and rapid growth, however, it is the effect at the grassroots level of economic decentralization and demographic pressures that during the 1990s provides the greatest structural imperative to *sustain* a growth-oriented economic strategy. Put simply, local leaders as of 1994 feel they must create new jobs rapidly to maintain social stability as hundreds of millions of people either enter the urban labor force for the first time or seek to shift from farm to nonfarm jobs. The Center is thus threatened with social and political upheaval if it tries to apply the brakes to rapid economic growth.

Much that occurs in China reflects the underlying need of the political system to accommodate the largest population in the world (see Table 9.1). China's population of over 1.17 billion people is greater than the *combined* populations of the United States, Canada, Western Europe, and the fifteen countries that formerly made up the Soviet Union. Even with a highly effective birth-control program in place, the PRC's net population increase (that is, births minus deaths) as of the early 1990s is about fourteen million people per year (that is, twenty-seven people *per minute*). China thus adds nearly as many people as live in Texas or Australia to its demographic base every year. It adds a population equal to Taiwan's every nineteen months.

China has, moreover, a double danger in its population pyramid: improvements in public health threaten the country with substantial increases in the number of older people beyond retirement age (fifty years old for women and fifty-five years old for men in most urban jobs) that the society must support; and earlier population growth burdens the society with many new entrants into the labor force during the 1990s. The older group makes some contributions but on balance saps resources from the system; the younger people are a potential source of instability if job aspirations are not met.

Urban employment problems potentially affect stability far more than do employment difficulties in the countryside. How many new urban jobs China must create during the 1990s, however, can only be roughly estimated because the rate of future migration from rural to urban areas is unknown. The reforms make such migration easier. Chinese experts believe that the real surplus population in agriculture by the end of the century may amount to 310 million working-age adults, of whom rural enterprises will be able to absorb perhaps 180 million, leaving another 130 million as potential migrants to the cities. Not all of these will actually migrate but, combined with natural population increase in the cities, the need to create one hundred million new urban jobs during the 1990s appears to be a quite conservative estimate.[4] Interviews with county and municipal leaders reveal that their actions are strongly motivated by the resulting pressures for job creation.

"On the ground," therefore, most of China's front-line officials—those in charge of the townships, counties, and cities—want to maximize the speed of

TABLE 9.1 *Population Size, 1970–92 (in millions)*

YEAR	POPULATION
1970	829.92
1971	852.29
1972	871.77
1973	892.11
1974	908.59
1975	924.20
1976	937.17
1977	949.74
1978	962.59
1979	975.42
1980	987.05
1981	1,000.72
1982	1,016.54
1983	1,030.08
1984	1,043.57
1985	1,058.51
1986	1,075.07
1987	1,093.00
1988	1,110.26
1989	1,127.04
1990	1,143.33
1991	1,158.80
1992	1,172.50
1993	1,185.50

Sources 1970–91: State Statistical Bureau of the People's Republic of China, *China Statistical Yearbook, 1991* (Beijing: China Statistical Information and Consultancy Service, 1991), p. 61; 1992–93: Calculated from the world population data sheets.

the country's economic expansion simply to meet the tremendous pressures for new jobs. When given a choice, these local political leaders use their power to accelerate growth. The basic reform strategy has vastly increased the power of precisely those individuals at the front line of the system.

The fact that the profits of local industries provide the major source of income for the local levels of the state also fuels growth pressures by linking the self-interest of local officials with a rapid expansion of the township and city economies. Because industry and commerce are taxed at a far higher rate than is agriculture, local officials are encouraged to favor development of the urban over the agricultural economies.[5] The resulting combination of enormous demographic pressure, exacerbated by some of the market-oriented reform measures, along with the devolution of considerable decision-making to the basic levels, has created tremendous momentum behind policies aimed at rapid short-term growth throughout most of China.

Reform Trends

The Maoist system maximized the control national leaders had over resource allocations sectorally, geographically, and socially.[6] At the same time, it prevented the free flow of information and factors of production, market-determined prices, and the competition necessary to gain economic efficiency and technological dynamism. It also prevented China from fully exercising its comparative advantage of cheap labor in the international economy.

The reforms over time have significantly affected every dimension of this system. The major trends of change have been as follows.

The system of national planning buttressed by direct administrative control over the economy by the planners has been gradually abandoned. Initially, many items shifted from "mandatory" plans to "indicative" plans. This meant that specific targets were set by local authorities; the Center would provide only broad-brush indications of the allocations it preferred. Through the mid-1980s the economy still operated overwhelmingly according to government set plans, but the role of locales increased substantially in this process.[7]

Gradually, though, the planners at all levels have reduced their direct administrative controls over the economy. By the early 1990s, most small commodities for daily use are produced totally outside of the planning system. Even many larger items are produced at the initiative of local authorities in order to satisfy local needs and larger markets.[8] By 1994, the percentage of the economy under direct national plan controls as measured by the percent of GNP produced by state-owned firms is lower than is that for such nonsocialist countries as France, Italy, and Singapore.

Under a planning system prices are set administratively to suit the needs of the planners. Such prices bear no necessary relationship to real supply-and-demand relationships, and thus they provide extremely poor guides to activities once a country has moved toward a market system. The pricing of coal, on which China depends for 76 percent of its energy, illustrates to point. Coal prices were set in the 1950s at levels that by the 1980s were well below the real costs of mining the coal. All attempts by the coal industry to have the prices raised were blocked by the powerful metallurgical industry, for which coal is a key input.

As China's reformers have tried to shift toward greater use of market forces, they have gradually moved away from the state-fixed prices on coal in several ways. In the early 1980s, they permitted the rapid expansion of production by "local" coal mines—generally, poorly equipped mines operated by individuals or local authorities that produced poor-quality coal for local consumption. Coal from these mines could sell at a price higher than the coal produced in the larger state mines that operated under the national plan.

Beijing then used its administrative power to raise the prices for some types of coal produced by the state mines. It also permitted provinces to sell a part of this coal on their own at higher prices. From the initial situation of having the vast majority of coal produced in state mines and sold at one fixed price, therefore, by the early 1990s a far more complex situation had developed. About half of all coal output came from "local" mines and sold for market-driven prices. Part of the coal from state mines could be sold by provincial officials for a price that was influenced by market forces. The remainder of the coal from state mines (a shrinking proportion of overall production) sold at state-fixed prices.

But even for that portion of state coal that sold at a fixed price, further differences were introduced. Coal sold to state enterprises to support production of goods still on the national economic plan had to be sold at a quite low, state-determined price. Coal from the state mines sold to enterprises for production of items "off" the plan could sell at a considerably higher—albeit still state-determined—price.[9]

Finally, Beijing announced in December 1993 that as of 1 January 1994 it would sell all coal from state mines at market prices.[10] The state would still intervene in distribution decisions but would let the price float freely. The upshot of this evolution is that as of early 1994 the coal sector is not totally free, though it has moved considerably in the direction of being responsive to market forces.

In broad terms, by the early 1990s the state had set up a dual-price system for most major goods. That portion, if any, of the production of an enterprise that was fixed on the economic plan would sell at a state-determined "plan" price, generally well below the market price for the item. The enterprise was rewarded by being guaranteed access to cheap inputs to produce its "planned" output. All production above the plan target could be sold at either a free-market price or within a price band set at near a free-market level. Reportedly, as of 1994 the state would retain fixed prices for thirty-three commodities including, but not limited to, many coal products, electric power, petroleum products, chemical industry products, metallurgical products, and transportation charges.[11]

This dual-system strategy sought to retain some controls while moving toward a free-market price system. Gradually, Beijing's leaders felt, the percentage of goods produced for the "above-plan" prices would grow, and thus the system would over time move to a market-based price system without suffering from the cataclysmic inflationary jolt that freeing up prices all at once would have produced. This approach has left China, though, with multiple prices for exactly the same items over a protracted period of time.

The reformers also began to experiment with various systems of taxation and budget allocation. Under the Maoist system, the profits of state enterprises provided the major source of revenue for the national authorities. The Deng reforms, however, have sharply reduced the revenues available from this traditional source, as the most rapid economic growth since the early 1980s has taken place in the local collective and private sectors in the townships and cities, outside of the official state sector.[12]

In addition, the state enterprises still bear enormous burdens, overstaffing, retirement obligations, and so forth, growing out of their Maoist past. As a result, state enterprises themselves generally have not competed successfully in the reformed economy, and their profits have declined. As of the early 1990s Beijing admits that some one-third of all state enterprises operate at substantial losses and another one-third barely break even. This has deprived the Center of a major traditional source of revenue and required that it develop new revenue streams.

The Center thus began experimenting with various types of revenue systems during the 1980s. By the end of the decade, Beijing actually was implementing about six distinctly different types of tax systems, varying by province. Changes in the particulars of these systems have occurred so frequently that any detailed description would quickly be dated. Essentially, most of these are variants on the theme of providing provinces with financial incentives to pursue economic development.

The Guangdong model during most of the 1980s, for example, required the province to pay Beijing one billion *yuan* in taxes per year, regardless of growth in the Guangdong economy. That economy in fact grew at an average of over 20 percent per year after 1984 and, as a result, its effective rate of taxation plummeted to very low levels during the latter half of the decade.[13] Other provinces did not receive as favorable treatment, but many negotiated tax deals that allowed them to retain substantial portions of any new economic growth in the province.[14]

At the heart of each of these arrangements is a fundamental weakness of China's national political system: the PRC, like imperial China, has no central tax collection agency like America's Internal Revenue Service to reach directly into locales all around the country. Rather, all taxes in China are collected and recorded locally, and then certain portions are passed up, level by level, through the national hierarchy. Each level of revenue collection is thus largely dependent on the integrity and efficiency of the level(s) below it.[15]

Not surprisingly, now that profits from state enterprises are insufficient to satisfy the bulk of the Center's revenue needs, this tax system has proven grossly inadequate. Localities regularly collect revenues beyond those they are authorized to take. Underreporting and other abuses are rife. As a consequence, Beijing's share of total tax revenue has declined from well over half to 38.6 percent in 1992.[16] Moreover, punishment for tax evasion is not normally severe in China.

The tax system is thus an inadequate vehicle for allocating revenues between the Center and lower levels. While tax rates and regulations are adopted and given rhetorical authority, the amounts actually turned over to the Center by the provinces typically have been settled by central-provincial negotiations each year and determined as a lump sum amount. This makes tax collection an almost totally ineffective means of affecting such local economic decisions as, for example, the sectoral allocation of investments. It instead creates incentives for massive tax evasion at each level and for local governments to direct their investments to locales that have been given especially light tax burdens (e.g., special economic zones such as the Pudong area in Shanghai).

Since 1978 the Center generally has agreed to increase the amount of money it leaves in the hands of lower-level officials. This reflects the reformers' fundamental assessment that a country of China's size requires substantial local initiative if it is to develop rapidly. In broad terms, therefore, the reform era has seen control over funds shift markedly from Beijing to provincial and lower levels. Local levels, especially in the wealthy coastal provinces, are far less dependent than before on Beijing's financial largesse. Indeed, the Center now runs substantial budget deficits each year (see Table 9.2). Even in the

TABLE 9.2 *Central Level Budget Deficits, 1979–92 (in billions yuan)*

YEAR	DEFICIT
1979	−17.06
1980	−12.75
1981	−2.55
1982	−2.93
1983	−4.35
1984	−4.45
1985	2.16
1986	−7.05
1987	−7.96
1988	−7.86
1989	−9.23
1990	−13.96
1991	−20.27
1992	−23.75

Sources 1979–90: State Statistical Bureau of the People's Republic of China, *China Statistical Yearbook, 1991* (Beijing: China Statistical Information and Consultancy Service, 1991), p. 183; 1991–92: International Monetary Fund, *International Financial Statistics*, 46 (July–August 1993), p. 162.

poorer provinces in the northern and western parts of the country, which remain dependent on net transfers of funds from Central coffers, Beijing has decentralized control by giving the lower levels far more leeway than before regarding how to spend their money.[17]

In theory, China's fiscal system has shifted from one of relying on profits of state enterprises to one that depends on a myriad of taxes on various types of economic activity. In reality, a massive shift of resources in favor of local levels occurred, and Beijing failed to develop a revenue bureaucracy that could use taxation as a finely honed tool of economic policy.

At the end of 1993 Beijing decided to try to recoup some of its fiscal losses by establishing a truly national tax system that would directly collect taxes due to the Center. It also adopted new tax regulations to assure the Center adequate revenue flows. A new value added tax of 17 percent, of which 75 percent is to go to the Center, is a major component of the new system.[18] To make these changes, Beijing negotiated with the provinces in late 1993 and promised to phase in the adjustments in a way that would not take any current income away from the provinces. In the longer-term, the Center seeks to capture 60 percent of all tax revenues. As of 1994, it is not clear whether the new plans will be implemented in a meaningful way.

The reformers have also sought to change the banking system so that it can become a more flexible instrument of economic policy. Under the Maoist socialist system, the banks served merely as vehicles for economic transactions.[19] They did not impose real costs on capital, did not independently evaluate the economic prospects of potential borrowers, and often did not collect the loans they made. They simply provided a means of handling money and of keeping track of the flow of funds.

Changes in the banking system are intended to make the banks function more like their Western counterparts. Increasingly, for example, investment funds are supposed to come from banks and be loaned out on the basis of the economic returns that can be expected from the project borrowing the money. Banks try to attract funds through offering realistic interest rates, and they try to control investment, at least in part, by changing the interest rate structure. Since 1978, moreover, a number of specialized banks have been established to focus on the needs of particular economic sectors.

The overall changes in the banking system until 1994, however, remained relatively modest. There is still no independent central bank. Rather, the People's Bank of China (nominally the central bank) is headed by a government minister and subject to the whims of the national political leadership. As explained below, moreover, the structure of power at local levels has often made it very difficult for local banks to make their loans only to the projects and activities that promise a reasonable return on the money. While the banking system moved in the direction of becoming a key vehicle for deciding how to allocate capital efficiently, therefore, it did not achieve the degree of independence from the political system necessary to play this role effectively.

An important meeting of the CCP Central Committee in late 1993 called for basic restructuring of this system along the lines of converting the People's Bank of China into a truly independent central bank, establishing three specialized "policy" banks (for policy loans, long-term investment, and rural development, respectively) that would direct funds to projects high on the leaders' priority list, and making all other banks function as real commercial banking enterprises responsible for their own profits and losses. For technical reasons, this grand restructuring will undoubtedly take years to bring about. The banks designated to become real profit-and-loss units, for example, will require massive recapitalization before they can be viable economically. In addition, a truly independent central bank runs so counter to the dynamics of power at the apex of the system that it seems highly improbable in the near term. But these changes reflect the reformers' desire to move the country decisively onto a market-driven path.

The terms of citizen participation in the economic system have also changed very substantially since 1978. From 1979 to 1984 rural communes were abandoned and the land was allocated to families (often extended rather than nuclear families) to farm. This process involved a great deal of trial and error and took several years to gel.[20] The new system is called the "responsibility system" because farmers contract for the use of the land on the basis of assuming particular financial and production obligations. Farmers do not outright own their land; the collective retains formal title to it.

Because experience in the early 1980s showed that short-term contracts created incentives to use the land but not to maintain it, many of these land contracts are now written for periods of up to fifty years. To further encourage maximum output from the land, since the mid-1980s the land contracts can, within limits, be bought and sold, and people with larger holdings can hire others to help them work the land; more efficient farmers are now able to expand their land holdings, while others can sell their land contracts and seek other employment. The overall trend has thus been from communes to the responsibility system to commercialization of land.

Other related changes have given the farmers far greater leeway in deciding which crops to plant, and much of what is grown is sold at free-market rates (though the bulk of China's agricultural output is consumed directly by the farm families that grow it). The state still determines the acreage that must be sown with some key crops such as grain and sets procurement prices for at least a portion of the crop.[21]

While this is thus by no means a total free-market system, farmers have considerable choice and incentive to maximize income. Social differentiation has increased in the villages, as have regional inequalities in the distribution of rural wealth. Many farm families have adopted a risk-averse strategy of sending one or two members of the family into the township or urban labor force, while others stay behind to work the land. The results have included wide-ranging changes in land use and in the economic dynamics of the country.[22]

The terms of participation in the urban economy have also changed, albeit not as dramatically. Since the mid-1980s new entrants into the urban labor force are no longer guaranteed a job by the state. The former "unified allocation of labor" that provided a state-determined job for urban workers has been abandoned for all but those university graduates who find jobs in the state sector or in the state administration.

In the state-sector enterprises it is still very difficult for management to fire workers, but workers can leave the enterprise with the permission of the manager if they have a better job offer. Such things rarely occur, though, given the current labor surplus. For state-enterprise employees who entered the labor force before the mid-1980s, therefore, a system of lifetime employment with little labor mobility remains largely intact.

Increasingly, though, state enterprises are hiring on a fixed-term basis, either by contract or by promising only short-term employment without fringe benefits. The latter is usually offered to the members of the "floating population," many of whom are hired for one day at a time from groups of "floaters" who gather each morning at particular spots around the city. Short-term contracts may be renewed repeatedly, but always without incurring either longer-term employment obligations or the need to provide fringe benefits, which are a large part of the real compensation of regular state-enterprise employees in China.

The most striking changes in urban employment grow out of the rapid expansion of the nonstate sector. Under the reforms, vast numbers of enterprises started at local initiative have sprung up. These are generally small-scale, but some have grown quite large. Many feed their products into the state sector. Others provide various services, such as machinery and vehicle repair. Still others produce finished products, such as clothing, for the domestic and international markets. Local working conditions in these firms vary greatly, but in general the jobs are not obtained through state allocations, people do not expect lifetime employment, and the fringe benefits do not match those of the major state enterprises. In some of these small nonstate firms the income (especially of managers) can be very considerably higher than that of the state enterprise employees; in numerous others, working conditions are wretched.[23]

The reforms have not opened up major new ways of employing people in the governing apparatus itself, even though standards of performance evaluation have changed considerably. Despite repeated discussion of reforms to professionalize the civil service very little progress has been made toward this goal.[24] A draft civil-service statute was adopted on a trial basis in 1993. Also in 1992 and 1993, the national leaders tried to reduce the scale of the governing bureaucracies by encouraging officials at all levels of the political system to abandon their official positions and seek employment opportunities in the market.[25] The resulting activities produced a spate of official entrepreneurship that further blurred the distinction between the state administration and the economy.

Almost across the board, then, the reformers have sought to create greater flexibility and room for individual initiative in employment. They have combined this with changes that have somewhat increased the geographical mobility allowed to individuals. As noted in Chapter 4, under the Maoist system one of the most effective means of preventing personal geographic mobility was to ration nearly all urban food and consumer goods and to distribute ration coupons that were valid only for the purchase of stipulated goods in specified localities over a particular period of time. Peasants who sought to work in a city would have to gain access to black-market ration coupons. Relatively few, therefore, could sustain themselves in the city. The same was true for people who wished to move from one city to another, as their ration coupons were not usable in the new locale.[26]

The most notable change in this respect pertains not to formal policy governing mobility, which has loosened up somewhat but remains very restrictive, but rather to the substantial reduction in the use of rationing to allocate scarce goods in the urban economy. Ration coupons have given way to prices on the consumer level. Where ration coupons still exist, they generally permit purchase of items at subsidized prices rather than governing access to the items themselves. Now people who drift into a city in search of work can purchase foods and goods on open markets without governmental interference. Those who shift their regular employment to new cities can do the same, even if their employer is not a state enterprise. The overall level of geographic mobility has thus increased, and this change is very much in tune with the demands of an economy that relies increasingly on market transactions to function.

In addition to promoting the importance of making money, the authorities have thus created "space" for individuals to devise ways to do so. They have hoped thereby to increase the quality and intensity of individual efforts to produce beneficent system-wide results.

The reforms also have sought to integrate the domestic economy more fully into the international economy. This has involved encouraging foreign businesses, many owned by overseas Chinese, to invest in China or to import goods from the PRC. The trend has been toward ever-widening foreign access to the Chinese market, and away from Beijing's 1979 Joint Venture Law, which restricted foreigners to less than 50 percent of the equity in any joint venture and stipulated that all ventures be self-liquidating over a specified period of time. Since 1979, China has increased the array of localities that may accept foreign investment and accord preferential treatment to foreign capital, added to the sectors that may welcome foreign capital, lengthened the time that joint ventures may exist, and increased the percentage of foreign equity permitted in a venture.

These reforms have progressed fitfully, but the results thus far are striking. China has opened up virtually its entire coast and the inland areas on both sides of the Yangtze River to preferential treatment for foreign capital. Many additional localities, morover, have on their own given tax breaks to foreign investors, and the list of places officially authorized to do so is growing rapidly. In the early 1990s Beijing decided to permit foreign participation in China's service sector, including retail commerce, insurance, and law. Though foreign access to this sector is regulated, this decision does create opportunities for foreign capital beyond manufacturing primarily for export. By the end of the 1980s, moreover, Beijing had removed percentage restrictions on foreign ownership in firms and dropped its insistence that all joint ventures be self-liquidating over a specified period of time.

With the rapid development since 1992 of the stock and real estate markets—both partially open to foreign participation—China has by 1994 become one of the more open economies in East Asia to foreign direct investment, with foreign capital making up a significant proportion of the new investment capital available in the PRC (see Table 9.3). A large portion of this capital is coming from Hong Kong and Taiwan (see Table 9.4).

The above selective overview indicates some of the ways in which the economy has changed since 1978. The system of central planning has given way increasingly to indicative planning, which in turn has yielded increasingly to market allocation of goods and services. The practice of fixing prices administratively for all goods has been replaced by a dual-price system for many items and a market-based system for many others. The highly centralized budget based on state-enterprise profits has shifted to a quite decentralized budgetary system, which has left the leaders facing a chronic structural budget deficit at the national level. The banking system, once a vehicle to hand out funds, is beginning to itself concentrate capital and make decisions on its allocation. The commune system in agriculture gave way to the family-based "responsibility system," and land has increasingly become a commodity. In urban areas, the former system of unified allocation of labor has nearly been abandoned, and the younger generation enjoys more room for individual initiative and fewer employment guarantees than did their elders. Strict residential controls have been eased, largely through the reduction in urban rationing, which permits greater personal geographic mobility. And China has shifted from its Mao-era posture of isolationism to one that seeks to be involved in the

TABLE 9.3 *Direct Foreign Investment by Region (in millions US $)*

PROVINCE	1983	1984	1985	1986	1987	1988	1989	1990	1991	1992
Beijing	29.34	118.73	88.82	139.94	95.34	502.78	318.46	276.95	244.82	349.85
Tianjin	2.14	105.70	55.87	29.31	127.41	31.85	28.01	34.93	132.16	107.24
Hebei	2.58	11.24	8.24	6.85	7.44	16.73	26.86	39.35	44.37	110.19
Shanxi	n.a.	1.11	0.52	0.15	2.27	6.52	8.82	3.40	3.80	53.84
I. Mongolia	2.98	2.99	2.62	0.98	1.09	3.37	0.24	10.64	1.10	5.20
Liaoning	17.63	44.08	24.58	41.28	64.50	115.25	118.57	243.73	348.88	489.56
Jilin	0.75	1.37	4.87	0.57	0.18	6.20	3.35	17.60	18.00	65.97
Heilongjiang	n.a.	5.23	3.95	17.42	11.32	40.09	22.41	24.49	9.43	70.50
Shanghai	46.01	430.81	107.54	147.65	213.66	233.17	422.12	174.01	145.19	481.10
Jiangsu	3.41	56.48	33.47	18.11	46.51	103.03	93.58	124.16	212.32	1460.00
Zhejiang	7.39	31.54	26.63	18.53	23.37	29.57	51.81	48.43	91.62	232.38
Anhui	n.a.	3.55	3.03	7.94	1.39	11.51	4.78	9.61	9.54	50.02
Fujian	39.17	236.19	118.60	61.49	51.39	130.17	328.80	290.02	466.29	1416.34
Jiangxi	n.a.	6.92	10.49	4.58	3.93	5.18	5.87	6.21	19.49	96.53
Shandong	21.95	104.94	35.63	19.39	23.81	43.09	131.32	150.84	179.50	973.35
Henan	0.05	5.97	8.27	6.05	4.50	64.18	42.66	10.49	37.91	52.15
Hubei	n.a.	9.86	8.00	12.41	11.90	22.31	22.95	29.00	46.43	203.08
Hunan	n.a.	34.64	27.48	9.48	2.35	7.71	6.43	11.16	22.76	128.53

TABLE 9.3 (*continued*)

PROVINCE	1983	1984	1985	1986	1987	1988	1989	1990	1991	1992
Guangdong	581.50	1409.34	651.31	722.68	602.99	957.86	1156.44	1460.00	1822.86	3551.50
Guangxi	16.22	26.71	30.73	36.95	37.74	20.65	45.94	28.66	25.32	178.33
Hainan						114.21	94.97	103.02	176.16	452.55
Sichuan	4.57	28.88	28.72	15.23	21.23	23.61	8.01	16.04	24.39	101.85
Guizhou	n.a.	2.88	9.78	2.20	n.a.	4.40	7.47	4.68	7.34	19.79
Yunnan	n.a.	1.51	1.63	3.54	4.80	37.10	7.40	2.61	2.96	23.13
Tibet	n.a.	n.a.	n.a.	n.a.	n.a.	0.03	n.a.	n.a.	n.a.	n.a.
Shaanxi	10.25	1.59	15.55	37.16	72.78	111.73	97.19	41.91	31.59	45.53
Gansu	n.a.	0.32	0.57	0.42	0.21	2.00	1.11	0.85	0.93	0.35
Qinghai	n.a.	23.52	0.15	n.a.	n.a.	2.70	n.a.	n.a.	n.a.	0.68
Ningxia	n.a.	3.00	0.28	0.05	0.03	0.30	n.a.	0.25	0.18	3.52
Xinjiang	n.a.	3.29	10.91	12.81	17.51	5.04	0.88	5.37	0.22	n.a.

Sources Annual issues of *Almanac of China's Foreign Relations and Trade* (Hong Kong: China Resources Trade Consultancy Co., Ltd.), 1984: pp. 1097–98; 1985: pp. 1070–71; 1987: p. 620; 1988: p. 594; 1989/90: p. 612; 1990/91: p. 554; 1991: p. 654; 1992: p. 615; 1993/94: pp. 723–24. 1986: State Statistical Bureau of the People's Republic of China, *China Statistical Yearbook, 1986* (Beijing: China Statistical Information and Consultancy Service, 1987), pp. 501–2.

Note Figures for 1983/84 are for contracted investment. Those for 1985–92 are for utilized investment.

TABLE 9.4 *Direct Foreign Investment by Source (in millions US $)*

YEAR	HONG KONG		JAPAN		US	
	CONTRACTED	UTILIZED	CONTRACTED	UTILIZED	CONTRACTED	UTILIZED
1985	4,134.32	955.68	470.68	315.07	1152.02	357.19
1986	1,449.39	1,328.71	210.42	263.35	527.35	326.17
1987	1,946.61	1,598.21	301.36	219.70	342.19	262.80
1988	3,466.58	2,095.20	275.79	514.53	370.40	235.96
1989	3,159.66	2,077.59	438.61	356.34	640.52	284.27
1990	3,833.34	1,913.42	457.00	503.38	357.82	455.99
1991	7,215.10	2,486.87	812.20	532.50	548.08	323.20
1992	40,043.80	7,507.10	2,172.50	709.80	3,121.30	511.05

Sources China Newsletter, 105 (July–August 1993), pp. 20–21; State Statistical Bureau of the People's Republic of China, *China Statistical Yearbook, 1986* (Beijing: China Statistical Information and Consultancy Service), p. 500; *China Statistical Yearbook, 1987*, p. 532; *China Statistical Yearbook, 1988*, p. 734; *China Statistical Yearbook, 1989*, p. 646; *China Statistical Yearbook, 1991*, p. 568; *China Statistical Yearbook, 1993*, p. 587; *Almanac of China's Foreign Relations and Trade 1993/94* (Hong Kong: China Resources Trade Consultancy Company, Ltd., 1994), p. 720.

international market, and to combine its vast labor supply with foreign investment to sustain growth.

These changes are interactive and, taken together, have profoundly affected the way the Chinese economic system works. Generally, they have produced the types of results the leaders have desired. China's overall economic growth averaged 9 percent per year in real terms from 1978 to 1991 and accelerated to over 12 percent in 1992 and 1993. As noted above, the PRC had the fastest growing major industrial economy in the world over that period. Almost every year, moreover, China's foreign trade grew at an even faster rate than did its GNP, reflecting the steadily increasing extent to which the PRC's economy is effectively integrating itself into the global economy (see Table 9.5). This foreign-trade record is particularly impressive in view of two additional elements: for all but a few years, China's exports have exceeded its imports, and the country has maintained both low foreign debt (US $73 billion as of the end of 1993)[27] relative to its export volume and the rate of growth of its exports, and substantial foreign-exchange reserves; and this record oc-

TABLE 9.5 *GNP and Foreign Trade*

YEAR	GNP (BILLIONS 1987 CONSTANT YUAN)	EXPORTS (BILLIONS US $)	IMPORTS (BILLIONS US $)	TOTAL FOREIGN DEBT (BILLIONS US $)
1978	506.24	9.75	10.89	0.62
1979	544.71	13.66	15.67	2.18
1980	587.20	18.12	20.02	4.50
1981	613.62	22.01	22.02	5.80
1982	667.01	22.32	19.29	8.36
1983	735.74	22.23	21.39	9.61
1984	842.71	26.14	27.41	12.08
1985	944.36	27.35	42.25	16.72
1986	1,020.77	30.94	42.90	23.75
1987	1,130.10	39.44	43.22	35.30
1988	1,252.42	47.52	55.30	42.36
1989	1,305.24	52.54	59.14	44.81
1990	1,379.93	62.09	53.35	52.55
1991	1,475.13	71.91	63.79	60.85
1992	1,677.55	84.94	80.59	69.32
1993	1,902.34	91.80	104.00	77.00

Sources GNP: World Bank, *World Tables 1993* (Baltimore: Johns Hopkins University Press, 1993), pp. 186–87; Exports and imports, 1978–92: State Statistical Bureau of the People's Republic of China, *China Statistical Abstracts, 1993* (Beijing: Statistical Publishing House, 1993), p. 101; Total foreign debt, 1978–84: World Bank, *World Tables 1994* (Baltimore: Johns Hopkins University Press, 1994), pp. 206–207. All figures for 1993: The Economist Intelligence Unit, *Country Report: China and North Korea* (London: second quarter, 1994), p. 4.

curred in the 1980s and early 1990s, during which period the overall rate of growth in global international trade was low.[28]

As of 1994, China has, in sum, sufficiently modified its economy that it is able to play an important role in the very dynamic Asia-Pacific economic region. This economic growth has stayed far ahead of population increase and has produced real improvements in the standard of living for most of its people. This is an impressive record, especially because it has been achieved during a period when the national leaders were forcing significant changes in the way the economic system operates.

But as China faces the remainder of the 1990s, it confronts serious problems that stem from the changes detailed above. For the reality of the situation is that the PRC has not yet established a market economy that is subject merely to the types of government interference that characterize almost all other market economies. Rather, China has as of 1994 crafted a *semireformed* system, one that is no longer subject to disciplined planning but one in which state officials continue to drive almost all significant decisions. This mixed economy, which has made many state officials into business people, might best be termed a *negotiated* economy, in that economic outcomes are determined through negotiations involving local officials, who act without instruction from the Center. While some of the major issues detailed in the following section reflect the types of concerns that would affect any Chinese economy at this point in time, most are integrally tied to the semireformed status of the current PRC economic system with its symbiotic relationship between state officials and the market.

Economic Issues of the 1990s

The following discussion divides the economic issues confronting China during the remainder of the 1990s into two broad groups: those that must be resolved in order to produce the internationally competitive, rapidly growing economy that China seeks; and those that have major repercussions for the stability and evolution of the political and social systems. Note, though, that the issues of the first group have at least some resonance with those in the second.

ISSUES OF EFFICIENCY

China has pursued an export-led growth strategy since the reforms got well under way. It has developed labor-intensive industries, primarily along its eastern coast, to process items that are then sent into the international market. The profits from this export sector have paid for the technology and other imports that have played a major role in accelerating the country's economic growth.

China during the remainder of the 1990s confronts significant difficulties in sustaining this posture, though its need to export will remain very strong.

By the mid-1990s the PRC should become a regular net importer of both food and energy, something it has avoided for almost all of the reform period to date. This will not only remove the export earnings from petroleum that have played a significant role in China's foreign-trade picture, but it will actually increase substantially the country's import bill simply to maintain basic resources. China therefore *must* find ways to sustain and increase its export drive in the years to come.[29]

But international trends suggest a strong possibility that Chinese exports will face greater trade barriers in the North American and European markets during the remainder of the decade. China in the early 1990s is fighting these trends. Maintaining access to the huge US market is especially important for its economic well-being.

Politically, the PRC must, therefore, support the General Agreement on Tariffs and Trade (GATT) to reduce barriers to international trade. (As of 1995, GATT is to be formally abolished and a new World Trade Organization established. These comments apply to that new organization as well.) But for China to play an effective role in this process, it must itself greatly increase foreign access to the Chinese home market. As of 1994, that market is still highly protected. China utilizes high tariff rates, secret quota and licensing requirements, political controls over foreign-exchange availability, and other administrative means to restrict the locales and sectors that may import goods from abroad. This is done in order to protect less competitive Chinese enterprises, especially those in the state sector of the economy.

Beijing recognizes and has formally accepted the notion that it must dismantle the major part of this protectionist system if it is to promote and participate in a freer world-trade system. China signed a market-access agreement with the United States in October 1992 that specifies the steps Beijing should take between 1993 and 1996 to make its market more open.[30] China's entry into the GATT hinges on its progress in taking these steps.

The market-access effort will inevitably create serious problems for many enterprises in the PRC's state sector. Throughout the reform era, these enterprises have remained largely coddled and inefficient, protected from foreign competition and partly buffered from internal competition. Relatively few of these are economically competitive without subsidies and protection.[31] Yet the regular workers in these firms expect lifetime employment—dubbed the "iron rice bowl"—and secure pensions after retirement. As of 1994 these workers still number some seventy million. They are politically an important group.

The need to maintain access to export markets is thus creating pressures to open up China's own domestic market, and this during the mid-1990s confronts the Beijing leadership with the nightmare of throwing large numbers of state-enterprise employees out of work. The fact that this occurs just as the country is trying to create jobs for new urban labor force entrants adds to the distress.

Beijing may in the final analysis fudge this issue through a number of ameliorative measures. For example, some state enterprises are setting up new service facilities and assigning redundant workers to them. After a period of support from the home enterprise, these new facilities may be expected to make a profit on their own, thus somewhat buffering the state enterprise from the onus of directly firing workers. In other instances, the state will retain majority ownership of these firms but will sell minority shares to others and contract out management functions. Foreign capital is also being invited to link up with state enterprises through stock purchases and joint ventures. Foreign management may then be blamed for measures that reduce employment. In addition, China hopes to be admitted to the GATT as a "developing country," which will allow the PRC to shield some infant industries behind high tariffs for quite a few years. Beijing is pursuing this strategy for the chemical and automotive industries and possibly for large parts of the machinery industry.[32]

In any case, during the remainder of the 1990s the Chinese will have to carry out the rationalization of their state-enterprise production, and this will give the entire system a painful jolt. Reportedly, when local officials in Dalian laid off a small number of true shirkers in state enterprises in 1993, other workers physically attacked managers and staged angry protests. The municipal officials quickly rehired the workers they had let go.[33] Managing this issue will be one of the key economic tasks of the central leadership.

A second broad economic problem China will confront is the need to march up a technology ladder in the international division of labor. China entered the East Asian economy during the 1980s primarily by becoming a major center for low-cost labor. It has absorbed a great deal of investment from elsewhere in Asia, primarily from Hong Kong but in the 1990s also increasingly from Taiwan, South Korea, and Japan, in the form of assembly operations (see Table 9.4). In these, the Chinese import most parts and components, use their own advantages in available land and low-skilled labor to assemble the final product at a comparative advantage, and then export the resulting commodity.

This practice has put pressure on Hong Kong, Taiwan, and South Korea, which formerly occupied the niche that China now dominates. In each of these other locales, land and labor have become more expensive, thus giving the Chinese mainland a distinct advantage. Since about 1980, therefore, each has had to develop new means to compete. Hong Kong, for example, lost virtually all of its manufacturing firms to China during the 1980s; as of 1994 over 83 percent of the factory workers employed by Hong Kong nationals live and work in Guangdong Province. Consequently, Hong Kong has shifted primarily to a service-based economy, and is now a finance, insurance, and shipping center. It also provides the headquarters facilities for many of the firms that have their production operations on the Chinese side of the border.

Taiwan has also adjusted in a very deliberate fashion. In the early 1980s it created a new high-technology zone in the town of Hsin-chu (in pinyin, Xinzhu) to develop new, more competitive production processes. South Korea proved slower to react to this competitive situation, but in the early 1990s began to take concerted efforts to meet the challenge.[34]

For China, the problem is that its own position as the low-cost producer is not secure over the long-run. Wage rates along the Chinese coast have increased considerably since the late 1980s, and land prices are rising rapidly with a burgeoning real-estate market. Inland transportation deficiencies make shifting production to the interior a not-wholly-satisfactory solution. And "new" low-cost production platforms in places like Vietnam will become increasingly competitive during the mid- and late 1990s.[35] Global experience since the 1970s has demonstrated that production capital—especially for low-skilled, low-value-added work—has become quite mobile. Investment quickly shifts to the low-cost producer of the moment.

China thus must follow the examples of its East Asian neighbors and begin marching up a technology ladder. This requires developing the proper incentives for higher education and producing a research community that is closely tied to production processes. As of 1994 China is lagging in both of these areas. The number of youths completing higher education is small, and the country cannot fill the fewer than five thousand places in its tiny graduate education system. Even the number of students finishing primary and secondary schooling has gone down since the reforms began. This surprising decline reflects the desire to make money as quickly as possible. Young people find it more lucrative to go into business than to stay in school. As a result, the country as a whole is not producing a solid base of skilled labor and technical scientific manpower.

Given China's huge population base, this problem should be relatively manageable. However, it requires that the central and local authorities recognize the nature of the challenge and give priority to it. So far, despite the development of several "technology zones" in Beijing and elsewhere, that action is not sufficiently in evidence. For reasons examined in Chapter 7, the educational *xitong* lacks the ability to attract resources in the PRC's bureaucratic state system.

China must also devise ways to overcome the widespread problem of local protectionism. This phenomenon has very deep roots in the structure of the Chinese political economy that the reforms have produced, and thus it will not be easy to handle.

The reforms envisioned a gradual decentralization of decision-making in the urban economy stage by stage from the Center to the provinces, then to the cities and counties, then to the enterprises. Once major decisions could be made at the enterprise level, the basis for a real market economy would have been laid.

In actuality, the decentralization for the most part has not given the enterprises full decision-making authority in economic matters. Most of this power devolved to the city/county/township level and then effectively stopped right there. The sociopolitical realities of China that have created this situation are a legacy of the Maoist system.

During the Maoist era, the top managerial positions in large enterprises required no entrepreneurial talent. Enterprise leaders did not have to figure out their costs of production and how to make production more efficient, seek out markets and maximize sales potential, decide on rates of return from various investment options, or in other ways take risks to increase production and market share. Rather, they functioned more as *middle-level* managers in capitalist societies perform: they received orders from above and worked on coordinating their implementation; they summarized developments below and reported them to higher levels; and so forth.

In addition, enterprises by the mid-1960s not only produced goods but also provided their employees with health care, housing, social activities, schooling, and so forth. In interviews, state enterprise managers have estimated that they spent an average of 85 percent of their time on these non-production-related issues.[36] They thus functioned in many ways as mayors of small communities rather than as entrepreneurs trying to maximize profit. Given that state enterprises employed workers for life, moreover, successful managers placed a premium on maintaining basic harmony within their "community."

The market-oriented reforms proved very unsettling to individuals who had achieved their positions in this Maoist system. The reforms essentially demanded skills in market behavior and enterprise management and attitudes toward risk-taking that these people lacked. Not surprisingly, many of these enterprise managers preferred to base their success, as they had before, on their ability to cultivate good ties with their administrative superiors at the municipal or county level.

The officials at the municipal and county levels who had previously taken charge of the local economy also desired to retain this control. This both made their jobs more interesting and, in an increasingly corrupt environment, provided substantial opportunities to increase their personal wealth. On both sides of the relationship between local officials and enterprise managers, therefore, there were incentives to maintain the old relationships in some form rather than to allow the market to sever them.[37]

The natural result is that under the reforms municipalities and counties (and now, townships) have become extremely powerful in the economy. Within these locales, the local state officials have remained very important in determining economic outcomes even as the central planning mechanism has declined dramatically. China has thus, as noted above, developed a "negotiated" economy rather than a market economy—that is, key economic outcomes are determined more through negotiations involving local officials than by purely market forces.

These local state administrations have tended to try to protect their own economic units against competition from other localities. They are thus adopting measures that to an extent break up China's national market into a number of smaller spheres that might be called "Tianjin, Inc.," "Shanghai, Inc.," "Wuhan, Inc.," and so forth. Cities, counties, and townships have become bureaucratic entrepreneurs that interfere in the activities of their own enterprises and try to promote the economic growth of their particular local economy.

Such behavior has had important consequences for the Chinese economy. Many cities, for example, protect local parts and components manufacturers by barring their large factories from procuring these goods from elsewhere. As a result, the country is unable to benefit from economies of scale and from appropriate levels of standardization, and thus costs remain far higher than necessary. Major enterprises often cannot expand because their products are effectively barred from markets protected by other locales.

In addition, areas that have been traditional sources of low-priced raw materials have begun constructing their own downstream facilities to capture profits from the higher value-added stages of production. As a result, for example, Shanghai's textile mills must import much of their cotton from abroad, as Shandong Province to the north now insists on producing finished textiles from its own local cotton. Not surprisingly, Shandong textiles lack the quality and style of their Shanghai counterparts.

But one of China's greatest long-term advantages lies in the enormous size of its potential market. To be sure, in a continent-sized country with poor transportation facilities, that market would always be far less than a seamless web. But the extent of local protectionism that has developed under the reforms is slowing the rationalization of production that should be occurring, at long-term cost to the economy's efficiency and competitiveness. This protectionism is creating artificial obstacles to the smooth circulation of goods even within each of the nine macroregions identified by G. William Skinner.

This situation has such deep roots in the dynamics of the reform effort that it will be very difficult to eradicate. A fundamental solution would require China to develop an independent legal system that would permit effective implementation of laws to bar administrative interference with the movement of goods and services across political boundaries. Such a system is far from being a reality as of the mid-1990s.

To some extent the problem may be alleviated by changes of incumbents in the key positions over a period of years. The managerial holdovers from the Maoist era are being replaced. In addition, if China takes forceful measures to rationalize its state enterprises as indicated above, this will change at least some of the incentives that have produced the extensive local protectionism currently characterizing the economy.

But experience in the most rapidly growing "new" sector of the economy suggests that the problems created by links between bureaucrats and firms, with inevitable protectionist ramifications, may prove intractable. The most vibrant sector under the reforms has been that of manufacturing and services in the various townships to which farmers who leave the land have been moving. The firms in these townships typically are small scale, and many in the West have mistakenly regarded them as private enterprises.

Detailed studies,[38] however, reveal that the state in most of these towns plays a dominant role in the enterprises. Officials appoint the managers, determine the size and composition of the labor force, provide investment capital, promote production, and protect from competition. In many instances, the compensation of the head of the township government is actually tied to the average rate of profitability of the township enterprises. Township officials thus often themselves become entrepreneurial, promoting the sale of local products in other markets, facilitating access to long-distance transportation, pleading with higher administrative levels for more investment capital, and so forth. While collecting large sums in taxes and fees from local enterprises, moreover, they typically turn over only a small portion of this to the higher levels.

The upshot is that in the semireformed system both the major cities and the small townships are developing more a negotiated economy than a competitive market-driven system. Over the long run, this situation is reducing competition and restricting the size of real markets for many goods and services. This system is also creating powerful vested interests at local levels in which local officials and enterprises collude to take resources out of the larger system to serve their own interests. This starves both the central government and the agricultural sector for necessary funds and amounts to a major change in the PRC's overall political economy. Wrestling with this problem without reimposing centralized administrative controls over the economy will be one of the difficult issues confronting Beijing during the coming years.

ISSUES FOR THE POLITICAL SYSTEM

The issue of local protectionism is also part of a serious conundrum facing China during the 1990s: how to strike a viable balance between the powers of the Center and those of the localities. The Maoist system tried to impose a degree of uniformity on the PRC that proved highly dysfunctional. In the 1950s, for example, Mao ordered the entire country to use one type of plow that was in fact unsuited to soil conditions in many areas.

The reformers under Deng Xiaoping, by contrast, want the Center to encourage local initiative and diversity; retain sufficient economic resources to shape the macroeconomy through, for example, controls over the growth in the money supply and leverage over decisions by means of tax regulations; provide resources that permit adequate levels of investment in basic infrastructure; and funnel money to poorer inland areas to maintain a politically equitable balance between the richer coast and the poorer interior. But this type of role for the Center has been hard to develop, as the decline in ideological discipline, administrative controls, and budgetary resources has produced a series of political as well as economic challenges to its effectiveness.

Foreign Economic Ties and National Unity

The regional growth strategy under the reforms has favored the coastal areas. These locales have superior human resources in terms of average skill levels, reflecting in turn their better educational endowments. They also enjoy better infrastructure, and geographic accessibility. These factors combine to make the coastal areas attractive to foreign investers and traders. National policy has been to capitalize on these advantages by designating some of these areas as special economic zones, and otherwise granting them preferential status.

Many areas along the Chinese coast have thus grown rapidly since the early 1980s, and this growth typically came on top of a substantial existing economic base. The interior areas lag far behind and have been told, in essence, to wait their turn—over time, a national form of trickle-down economics will bring them increasing prosperity. The absolute gap in the per capita wealth of the coastal versus the inland provinces has increased substantially under the reforms.

The telecommunications revolution is bringing home this immense gap to the population in the interior. Through television, most inland residents have seen the level of coastal prosperity. This is stoking resentment in the interior and creating rising expectations that cannot possibly be satisfied. One consequence is the "floating population" phenomenon noted earlier, as millions upon millions of inland people seek to participate in the opportunities available along the coast.[39] The pressures on the Center to keep the gap from becoming too wide are great but, as noted above, the resources available to the Center fall far short under the reforms. Local protectionism, moreover, is limiting the trickle-down effects sought by the reformers.

There is also differentiation taking place among the coastal regions themselves. Guangdong Province has benefited more than any other from the reforms, perhaps reflecting in part the fact that Zhao Ziyang (who in the 1950s, most of the 1960s, and part of the 1970s was posted to Guangdong) substantially shaped the reform effort as premier and then as general secretary during the 1980s until his removal in 1989. Guangdong as of 1992 had alone absorbed nearly two-thirds of all foreign investment in China, the vast majority of this coming from Hong Kong (see Table 9.4). Guangdong's special economic zone of Shenzhen, on the Hong Kong border, in the 1980s was transformed from a sleepy rural village area with approximately seventy thousand residents to a thriving metropolis that by 1993 had a population of over three million.[40]

In the late 1980s Beijing agreed to permit Hainan Island, which had been a part of Guangdong Province, to split off and become a separate province. Hainan was given extraordinary flexibility in economic regulations to attract foreign capital for its development. This flexibility included allowing foreign currency to circulate and leasing out large swatches of land for up to seventy years at a time. Not surprisingly, within a few years ambitious young Chinese from all over the country were swarming to Hainan to make their fortune.

The foreign links into Guangdong and Hainan are, for geographical reasons, largely centered on Hong Kong. Indeed, the Hong Kong economy has become so fully integrated with the Guangdong economy that changes in either are immediately felt in the other. Not surprisingly, a public opinion survey in 1992 in Guangdong found that more Guangdong residents knew the name of the governor of Hong Kong than that of the governor of Guangdong itself. But the close tie-ups of China's border areas with foreign countries are not limited to Hong Kong and the adjacent PRC areas.

Taiwan since about 1987 has been rapidly increasing its links with the Xiamen area of Fujian Province, directly across the Taiwan Strait. This locality shares a common dialect with Taiwan natives, most of whose ancestors hail from this part of China. By 1994 it had become questionable whether Xiamen's and Fujian's leaders were more sensitive to concerns of Taiwan's investors than they were to Beijing's agenda, just as similar questions were being raised about the sensibilities of Shenzhen's and Guangdong's leaders.[41]

South Korea in the early 1990s began energetically establishing close ties with the Shandong Peninsula. Japan began to pour large amounts of investment capital into Dalian on the Liaodong Peninsula in northeast China, a traditional area of Japanese concern.[42] All of this is occurring with the full blessing of Beijing, but all of it is also creating potential concerns about national unity.

None of the above developments necessarily portend major challenges to the territorial integrity and unity of the PRC. If a dynamic, unified national leadership holds office in Beijing, these various trends simply mean that the country will look increasingly diverse, with different styles in evidence in various parts of China, different identities in terms of external regions with which local people are concerned, and very different standards of living and career prospects. There is nothing particularly alarming about such a situation; indeed, it is quite natural.

A problem in terms of national unity could arise, however, if the central leadership were to be weakened by severe political infighting. Under those circumstances, the fault lines described above could become more salient. To an extent, China's economic trends during the early 1990s are leading in the direction of the formation of various regional economies, each coastal region other than the lower Yangtze linked primarily to the economy of one major outside power. In addition, bitter jealousies and resentments are forming between those areas benefiting from current policies and those that are falling behind. Fears of immigration may prompt some wealthier localities to raise protective barriers against population movements from the interior, while inland leaders may seek to retaliate by withholding raw materials needed by coastal industries.

Underneath China's overall strong economic performance, therefore, are trends that challenge its sense of national identity and purpose. There remain powerful mutual interests and identities that should under most circumstances hold the country together, while allowing a great deal of local variation. But the national government is constrained by the increasing willingness of local authorities to pursue local interests in violation of central directives. These realities present major challenges to reformers who wish the national government to be able to control macroeconomic outcomes, balance coastal versus inland resources, and develop needed national infrastructure.

Corruption

There are no objective ways to measure the overall level of corruption in China, but the reform era has by all accounts increased corruption significantly.[43] The reasons are partly economic and partly grounded in other facets of the reform experience. Corruption has by the mid-1990s reached such an extent that it is seriously eroding the basic legitimacy of the political system.

The nature of China's negotiated economy has created situations in which corruption carries few risks and pays large dividends, because government officials at all levels can use their offices to affect economic outcomes and have considerable discretion available in doing so. The dividing line between public and private, government and market, is blurred, and legal and moral systems to define permissible behavior rigorously are lacking. Granting licenses and loans, forgiving debts, allowing tax breaks, and providing access to needed electricity, water, telephones, and transportation are only a few of the types of decisions for which PRC officials now expect "tea money," or bribes.

The dual-price system created to help ease the way from administratively fixed prices to market prices adds to the corruption quotient. Many officials use their power to acquire "plan" goods and then turn around and sell these as market products at the far higher market price. There have been moments, for example, when the "plan" price for a ton of steel in Beijing was roughly one thousand *yuan,* while the market price for the same ton of steel was twenty-eight hundred *yuan.* Corrupt officials could use a part of their phenomenal profits on such deals to assure the cooperation of everyone who might expose their illegal activities.

It is important during the 1990s for China to give up completely the dual-price system, which invites corruption of a major order. But far more must be done to reduce the level of corruption in the system. Given the poorly defined boundaries between permissible and corrupt behavior, the spread of corruption has substantially weakened the ability of the central leadership to secure discipline from its own political apparatus.

The problem is exacerbated by the fact that Deng Xiaoping has sought to maintain support among top officials for the reform effort in part by permitting their families to benefit disproportionately from it. The key group of officials includes those who held roughly the rank of minister and above on the eve of the Cultural Revolution in 1966. Deng's policies have given extraordinary opportunities to the offspring of these same individuals. During the 1980s they became the heads of key trading firms or assumed other positions from which they could derive enormous profits. They used their connections to gain inside information, secure scarce goods and licenses, and protect themselves from legal retribution when they stepped over the line. For example, in the early 1990s, with the opening of China's basically unregulated stock markets in Shenzhen and Shanghai and with the creation of real-estate markets, they used their influence to purchase stock shares and to close lucrative real-estate deals. As a consequence, the relatives and offspring of several thousand officials—including those of almost every top Communist party member—have become wealthy. Collectively, this group is popularly called the "princes' party" (*taizidang*), although they are not an organized political group.

At the end of 1992, China's government admitted that about US $8 billion that had left the country could not be accounted for. Not all of this reflected the machinations of the *taizidang* members, but the amounts of capital being put abroad by wealthy individuals without legal authorization are becoming significant.[44]

Corruption is a function of both opportunity and lack of restraint. The restraints on such activities have eroded as the guiding ideology of the country has shifted from one of social purification to one of unvarnished pursuit of income. Essentially, the reformers have created a situation in which a rising standard of living provides the political underpinning of the regime, and thus the government has itself become a major supporter of the notion that to get rich is glorious.[45]

The money made by corruption is not being put to use to integrate the polity. In this, China's corruption differs greatly from that characteristic of, for example, the big-city political machines in the United States in the late 1800s and early 1900s. Those machines worked hard to win people's votes by solving problems that poor citizens faced. That they used the resulting political power to make a great deal of money does not mitigate the importance of the political integration role that they played at a time when American cities were being inundated by new immigrants.

Corrupt Chinese tend instead to engage in conspicuous consumption with little evident regard for those being left behind. This increasingly obvious differentiation of urban society is breeding widespread resentment, as workers and regular office staff feel that the wealthy individuals have earned their outlandish sums of money through position rather than through their contributions to the general social fabric. Social tensions in China's cities and countryside have been rising accordingly.

Given the Chinese Communist party's monopoly on political power, it is hard to envision effective measures against the corruption that is so tightly interwoven with the interests of the leading families of the party. The party has made repeated efforts since the mid-1980s to clean up its act, in each instance affirming that corruption is costing it the allegiance of the populace.[46] But none of these efforts has made a serious dent in the amount of corrupt activity, and virtually no member of the *taizidang* has felt the whip of legal punishment for lawbreaking activity. The one or two exceptions—including the arrest of Hu Qiaomu's son, mentioned in Chapter 8—have reflected political infighting among the leaders at the top more than any comprehensive effort to bring the relatives of powerholders to heel.

The economic reform effort has thus led to deeply rooted corruption of the political system. This very corruption, moreover, thrives on the fact that the Chinese system is currently semireformed, neither subject to a disciplined plan nor driven primarily by the market via activities constrained by law. The results include widespread social resentments and decline in the legitimacy of the political system. In this fashion, even the marked successes of the economic reforms to date have weakened the political base of the system. The resulting situation provides very strong incentives for the top leaders to continue to do all they can to keep the economy growing at a very rapid pace to try to buy off political upheaval.

Inflation

As Chapter 3 detailed, the Communist party gained enormous good will in the aftermath of its 1949 victory by its successful effort to rein in the ruinous and demoralizing inflation that wracked the Nationalist polity in the late 1940s. Ever since, many top officials have viewed holding the line on inflation as necessary for maintaining social stability. In the late 1980s Zhao Ziyang's economic reform strategy, including price reform, entailed substantial levels of inflation. The resulting social unrest in 1989 further solidified official fear of the damaging effects of inflation.

But the reforms themselves create conditions conducive to inflationary surges. Perhaps the most fundamental is the Center's loss of tight control over the money supply. Virtually every year the government ends up expanding the money supply far more rapidly than it had planned. This curious phenomenon results in major part from the political economy of local government under the reforms.

Local branches of the People's Bank and of other specialized banks (of Agriculture, of Industry and Commerce, etc.) are in theory subject to lending limits imposed by their superiors in the banking system. Many Chinese enterprises use bank loans both as operating funds and as the major source of capital investment. As part of the reform effort, during the 1980s the Center relaxed the previous system under which it had directly specified the amounts of investment permitted and the firms that would receive new investment capital. In all but a few cases of national priorities, these decisions were delegated to local levels.

Local officials have, however, used their power to turn local bank branches into money machines for the local economy. They lean heavily on bank officials to lend money to their favored projects, more than a few of which are of personal benefit, such as new office buildings and residential complexes for local officials. When bank officers prove reluctant, the local Communist party committee uses its powers to secure compliance. While the bank as a financial institution is under the jurisdiction of the next higher level bank, the bank's Communist party committee is directly under the authority of the Communist party committee of the locality in which the bank is located. The local party committee is not supposed to dictate business decisions to the bank. But since the party committee via its organization department determines who will head the bank, its influence over lending decisions is enormous.

Because local officials have an overriding concern to expand the local job base and to feather their own nests, they tend systematically to abuse the local banking system and cause it to lend funds beyond its prescribed quotas. Since much of this money is given out on a political rather than strictly economic basis, resulting rates of default are high. Local bank branches then turn to the Center to provide the funds to keep them solvent and enable them to meet the obligations they continue to assume.

The Center presumably could put a stop to this abuse of the system simply by refusing to cover the commitments of local banks and permitting those banks to fold. But local officials are quick to remind the Center of the potential price to be paid as payrolls are not met, workers are put on the street, and social unrest looms large. Because of these political considerations, the Center has for years opted on balance to print new money to meet obligations rather than to risk widespread bank and enterprise failures.

This constant pumping of new funds into the system at an excessive rate (often increasing China's money supply by 20 to 30 percent per year) creates the conditions for chronic inflation, as too much money is available to chase too few goods (see Table 9.6). The problems are often most evident in the construction industry, as much of the new money is given to enterprises to expand their production capabilities. New orders for cement, bricks, reinforced concrete, and so forth vastly outstrip the ability of the economy to produce these goods, with several undesirable results: bottlenecks occur, often bringing construction to a halt in mid project; prices of inputs soar; and the country's import bill goes up as desperate firms try to bring in the scarce goods from Japan and elsewhere.

But inflation is not limited to the capital construction sector. A portion of the new funds is paid out in wages and benefits, thus fueling demand in the consumer sector, including demand for better housing and transportation. With inflationary pressures building, moreover, the government has an increasingly difficult time convincing the populace to put money into bank and bond savings, as people feel they must convert their funds into physical goods before inflation erodes their value.

As the reforms have matured, some new outlets to absorb excess funds in a noninflationary way have developed. The real-estate market presents one

TABLE 9.6 *Money Supply (in billions 1987 constant yuan) and Inflation Rates*

YEAR	MONEY SUPPLY*	INFLATION (%)
1979		2.00
1980	188.37	6.00
1981	205.73	2.40
1982	228.60	1.90
1983	260.07	1.50
1984	321.57	2.80
1985	353.80	8.80
1986	410.42	6.00
1987	457.40	7.30
1988	495.89	18.50
1989	502.63	17.80
1990	539.94	1.60
1991	613.83	3.00
1992	738.51	5.60
1993		14.50

Sources Money supply: World Bank, *World Tables 1994* (Baltimore: Johns Hopkins University Press, 1994), pp. 204–05; Inflation, 1979–89: Jia-Dong Shea, Tzung-Ta-Yen, "Comparative Experience of Financial Reform in Taiwan and Korea: Implications for the Mainland of China," in Ross Garnaut, Liu Guoguang (eds.), *Economic Reform and Internationalization: China and the Pacific Region* (St. Leonards, NSW: Allen and Unwin, 1992), p. 242; 1990–92: The Economist Intelligence Unit (EIU), *Country Report China, Mongolia* (fourth quarter, 1993), p. 4; 1993: Edward G. Hinkelman (ed.), *China Business* (San Rafael, Calif.: World Trade Press, 1994), p. 173.

*Money supplied is adjusted using World Bank deflator.

possibility for soaking up large amounts of money without sparking inflation in other sectors. The stock markets that opened in Shenzhen and Shanghai in the early 1990s—with probably more on the way in other areas in the near future—also provide potentially productive outlets for excess funds. But as of 1994 these various outlets remain largely unregulated and have been subject to such abuse that they themselves amount to little more than speculative bubbles liable to burst.[47]

Periodically, the magnitude of concern about inflation makes it possible politically for the Center to take a firm set of measures to rein in the economy. This was done in the wake of the Tiananmen massacre, and it began again in July 1993. These measures include firm caps on growth in the money supply, demands that banks call in bad loans and cease lending beyond their capacity, tolerance of the collapse of many small firms (but no large ones), especially in the townships, and new incentives via higher interest rates pegged to the rate of inflation for long-term savings. The Center may also issue government bonds and force localities to purchase them. Both parties to the transaction know that the Center has a history of later reneging on payment of these obligations.

In short, the Center has demonstrated that it is able to bring down inflation rapidly by throwing the country into a recession on short notice. This has created a damaging boom-and-bust cycle that is politically demoralizing. This cycle encourages individuals and units to take full advantage of loose money periods to maximize their investment and consumption, knowing that the boom will fail at some point in the future. The downswing in each cycle, moreover, diminishes foreign confidence in the Chinese economy and risks large-scale social unrest.

Attempts to modify the structure of the local political economy that encourage this inflationary cycle have to date been unsuccessful. This cycle has, like corruption, become deeply rooted in the core dynamics of the semireformed Chinese economic system. Controlling inflation to smooth out the peaks and troughs of business cycles is a major economic and political challenge facing Beijing.

Beijing largely abandoned the mid-1993 clampdown shortly after it began. It retreated for several reasons that reflect the underlying difficulties created by the reforms: southern provinces and state industries objected to the credit squeeze, raising the specter of economic slowdown and social unrest; and local banks, ordered to recall improper loans they had made, failed in most cases to heed the order. Only one-third of such loans were called back in, more often from the large-scale state enterprises whose profits went to the higher levels of the state than from the small-scale collective enterprises whose profits fund the local level of the state administration.

The Third plenum of the Fourteenth Party Congress therefore adopted wide-ranging measures to break this boom-and-bust cycle. It essentially conceded that such cycles continue as long as the economy remained only semi-reformed. It therefore called for the measures described above: to further limit the role of state planning; convert most banks to real profit-and-loss firms; and develop a more regularized national taxation system.[48]

Many of the same structural factors that limit the leaders' ability to deal with corruption also are likely to reduce their capacity to make these major economic changes. The mid-1990s will test the ability of the Chinese system to break out of a semireformed mode and become a truly market-driven economy. The results of that test are quite uncertain as of 1994.

Rural Problems

China's farmers are suffering from an economy that increasingly is geared toward meeting the demands of the urban population. As explained in Chapter 5, the reformers began their efforts in the late 1970s by pumping considerably more money into the agricultural sector via price increases for procurement of agricultural commodities, among other measures, and then dismantled the commune system that had stifled individual incentives in the countryside. As a result of these and other measures, the country's agricultural output surged from 1980 to 1984, and in that period the reforms became very closely associated with the enormous successes taking place in the agricultural sector.

The payoffs from giving the peasants more capital, establishing better incentive systems, allowing greater freedom of crop selection, and other related changes in the structure of the administration of agriculture were almost wholly realized during these initial years. After 1984, future increases in farm production required substantial new investment. But the government instead turned its attention to the urban economy, counting on the peasants to spend much of their new income on making the investments necessary to keep output growing rapidly. Official government investment in agriculture fell off dramatically.

The government guessed wrong. Peasants instead put their money into new housing and the purchase of consumer goods to improve their quality of life. Lacking confidence that state policy would remain unchanged, they proved reluctant to improve the land they managed under the responsibility system. In addition, the new housing they built and the expansion of townships via movement of some younger laborers off the land took additional acreage out of agricultural production.

With the national level leaders paying little attention to agriculture, moreover, a price scissors began to open up to the disadvantage of the farmers—that is, the prices farmers had to pay for inputs such as fertilizer and farm machinery went up faster than the increases in prices for the farmers' crops. Perhaps more importantly, the interests of township and county officials became intricately tied up with the expansion of production of local urban collective enterprises, as indicated above. They therefore increasingly resorted to such tactics as diverting money allocated by the Center for crop procurement to investment in new township enterprises, giving the peasants IOU's instead of cash for their produce. They also levied a dismaying variety of local taxes and fees on the countryside to support rapid township development.[49] The political system effectively placed no obstacles in the path of local officials who wished to exploit the rural areas under their control.

These policies and practices have by 1994 produced a deeply disgruntled countryside, especially among those who do not live near lucrative major urban markets. Peasant revolts have occasionally been reported in locations as diverse as Sichuan in the southwest and Jilin in the northeast. More ominously, national production of basic grains, including rice, has not kept up with the rate of increase in the population. Only in 1989 did the farm output again reach that of 1984. Since then, harvests have been higher but continue to fluctuate without showing any steady upward trend (see Table 9.7).

China will encounter both economic and political problems if the agricultural sector continues to be badly shortchanged during the remainder of this decade. The PRC's economic miracle has reached the rural townships but in a form that has produced increasing frustration for the villages in vast stretches of the country.

CONCLUSION

As the above sections suggest, many forces stemming directly from the semi-reformed nature of China's economy are riling social order in 1990s. Demographic pressures create problems of urban unemployment, which are exacerbated by the numbers of people moving off the farm and looking for jobs in townships and cities. Agricultural problems are serious and growing. China's geographically uneven economic growth—combined with the knowledge revolution based on the spread of telecommunications—is producing a burgeoning floating population that presents an additional potential source of

TABLE 9.7 *Agricultural Harvest, 1979–92*

YEAR	FOODGRAIN OUTPUT (MILLION TONS)
1979	332.12
1980	320.56
1981	325.02
1982	354.50
1983	387.28
1984	407.31
1985	379.11
1986	391.51
1987	402.98
1988	394.08
1989	407.55
1990	446.24
1991	435.29
1992	442.29

Sources 1979–91: State Statistical Bureau of the People's Republic of China, *China Statistical Yearbook, 1992* (Beijing: China Statistical Information and Consultancy Service, 1992), pp. 321, 328; 1992: Seiichi Nakajima, "Obstacles to Growth of the Chinese Economy," *China Newsletter* (September–October 1993), p. 3.

social disorder in the major cities. China's need to rationalize state enterprises is creating pressures to trim dramatically the pervasive featherbedding that has historically characterized these firms. And the widespread corruption and boom-and-bust cycles in the economy are adding to social discontent.

Thus, despite the fact that the PRC's reforms have produced extraordinary economic results, China faces a daunting set of problems linked to its economy during the remainder of the 1990s. Some of these involve the imperatives, such as rationalization of state enterprises, of meeting the demands for economic efficiency to continue to benefit from participation in the international economy. Others relate directly to the country's semireformed, "negotiated" economy, with its social, economic, and political consequences. Together, these factors create seemingly irresistible pressures for local officials—those who have acquired the greatest increase in power under the reforms—to maximize short-term economic growth almost regardless of the country's macroeconomic conditions. And a great deal of power has shifted via the reforms to precisely these local officials.

In sum, China's economic development has created a substantially new distribution of wealth, skills, and attitudes in the country's population. The political system must make important accommodations beyond those already in place to maintain social stability in view of these developments.

10

The Environment

One of the major challenges China faces currently is the decline of its environment. Such factors as a large population, rapid economic growth, an industrial structure geared to heavy industry, and limited natural resources combine to spell severe environmental trouble for the PRC. China now has more extensive environmental degradation, for example, than did today's industrialized countries at comparable stages in their economic development.[1] How the PRC manages the tensions between maximizing growth and longer-term environmental protection to achieve what is termed "sustainable development" will have major consequences both for the citizens of China and, in some dimensions, for the global community. The *New York Times* concluded in late 1993, for instance, that "The world's ability to head off [global warming] may depend on China."[2]

Gaining control over China's environmental problems will require Beijing's concentrated attention and the commitment of massive funds. Unfortu-

nately, the science of environmental protection is not very precise. The interactions of the many processes that contribute to various environmental phenomena are extremely complex, and the effects of changing one or several of
these processes are often impossible to determine. In China as elsewhere, it is
difficult to persuade political leaders to commit resources where uncertainty
clouds the scientific picture.

Concerns about human health might spur environmental initiatives, but
the consequences of environmental degradation on human health have been
the subject of much debate. For example, the rates of suspended particulate
matter in China's air have been shown to be very high. The World Health Organization considers 60 to 90 micrograms per cubic meter (mcg/m^3) of suspended particulate matter an acceptable range. The average total of suspended particulate matter in north China in the 1980s, however, was 520
mcg/m^3, and in south China the figure was 318 mcg/m^3. These are among
the highest reading in the world.[3] International environmental monitoring of
Guangzhou and Shanghai from 1981 to 1989 never found a mean value per
year as low as 90 mcg/m^3. For Beijing, Shenyang, and Xi'an, the figure never
dipped below 220 mcg/m^3. This almost certainly bears some relation to the
incidence of chronic pulmonary disease. In 1988, the only recent year for
which such figures are available, 26 percent of all deaths in the PRC were
caused by lung disease. This was more than five times the rate in the United
States that year.[4]

But while the increasing rates of death from chronic pulmonary disease
do correspond with increasing levels of suspended particulate matter in the
air, they probably also result to some extent from increased use of tobacco
products over a longer period of time by a population that is growing older
because of basic improvements in the health delivery system and diet. The actual extent of each contribution to the outcome—and the interaction between the various causes—requires considerable additional study.

Besides there being controversy about what ill effects may be attributed
to environmental degradation, and how widespread those effects may be, expensive measures to remedy environmental insults are often politically unat-
tractive because they pay off only over the long term, at best. Few leaders in
any country are willing to depress current standards of living to benefit their
successors. This is especially true when popular attitudes do not give priority
to environmental issues. Such is the case in China.

Many environmental issues are, thus, politically difficult to manage. The
underlying science contains large gray areas, remedies are uncertain and expensive, payoffs are long-term, and—to add to the difficulties—the problems
often do not fall neatly within existing political jurisdictions. On a worldwide
level there are, therefore, few governments that have acted preemptively to
head off environmental insults or that have developed rigorous, comprehensive programs to reverse environmental degradation.

Given these difficulties, why look at the PRC's environmental situation
in the 1990s? Because conditions in China have in many regards reached a
critical stage. Vast populated areas are desperately short of water. Beijing is so
water-short, for example, that many Chinese scientists advocate building an

860-mile-long aqueduct to bring water from the Han River in central China to the capital.[5] Deserts are spreading, old-growth forest cover is being destroyed, cancer and lung disease are increasing, and significant parts of the country may deteriorate environmentally to the point where millions will be forced to go elsewhere to earn a living. Given China's political dependence on rapid economic growth to maintain social stability, these are unsettling trends. And, as the *New York Times* quote above indicates, they can have major consequences for the international community. Unfortunately, the structure and dynamics of China's political system create serious obstacles to its dealing with these environmental problems.

Environmental Problems Originating before 1978

The PRC currently suffers from major environmental problems along two axes: the availability and distribution of natural resources; and effects of the political system created after 1949. Each of these facets warrants brief consideration.

NATURAL RESOURCE ENDOWMENTS

Although the PRC in area is 2 percent larger than the United States, its per capita availability of productive land is modest by world standards. Fully 20 percent of the country consists of mountains, and huge deserts claim much of the rest. China is usefully seen as divided into three major topographical regions: the northwest, which is arid and suffers from wind erosion; the southwest, which is cold and contains high plateaus and some of the world's tallest peaks; and the east, with extensive rivers that have created valleys and alluvial plains.[6] About 95 percent of China's nearly 1.2 billion people live in this eastern region, which constitutes about half of the land area of the entire country.

Given this topography, it is not surprising that China has relatively little useful terrain. With some 22 percent of the globe's population, the PRC contains only 7 percent of the world's arable land. Per capita, it has less than 30 percent of the worldwide average of croplands, less than half the average of grasslands, about 16 percent of the average of forest cover, and about 17 percent of the average of wilderness areas.[7]

The pressure exerted on these small areas by China's large population is great. Every available inch is cleared for cultivation, housing, and other human uses, as the country struggles to feed a population whose expectations about diet are rising with its average income and its exposure through the media to living standards elsewhere. The results of this population pressure are starkly evident in major areas of the country. For example:

□—The loess region of north China's Shanxi Province has seen its population double since 1949, and intensive cultivation there has totally removed the ground cover and accelerated erosion to the point where 30 to 50 percent of the land, scarred by deep gullies and ravines, is unusable.

□—The hills in the red soil region of south China's Guangxi Province have been deforested and cultivated, resulting in siltation that has reduced the irrigation system to 30 percent of its capacity, and severely depleting the upland soils.

□—The mountains of southwest China's Sichuan Province have been substantially denuded, releasing large quantities of silt into the Yangtze River, vastly increasing the danger of flooding in the densely populated central China region and greatly complicating efforts to harness the river for hydropower.

□—The country's major lakes are being filled in to expand the availability of arable land, so that huge lakes like Taihu in east China and Dongting in central China have lost about half their water surface area since 1949.

□—Wetlands along the coast are being drained and planted to the extent that within a matter of years they may be totally eliminated, along with the pollution-control, fish-spawning, and biodiversity contributions they make.

China also suffers from the maldistribution of its natural resources. The energy situation is especially striking in this regard. Most of the country's population lives in the east, where most of its industry is concentrated. But most of the available oil as of the 1990s is concentrated in the inaccessible regions of the northwest. The major oil fields in the eastern half of the PRC, such as Daqing, are past their peak production. The search for commercially viable offshore oil in the 1980s produced very modest results. Yet bringing vast amounts of oil from the promising fields in northwest China's Caidam Basin and Tarim Basin presents daunting technical and financial problems.

China has natural gas, but not in sufficient quantities to make it a major source of energy. In addition, the largest proven gas reserves are in Sichuan Province, far away from the centers of industry.

The fact that the country's topography generally slopes down from west to east, from the high Himalayas and Pamirs to the coast of the East China Sea, creates substantial hydropower potential. But the major changes in altitude occur before the topography flattens out in the eastern half of the country. The bulk of the hydropower potential therefore is located in the mountainous regions of southwest China, far from the country's major consumers of electricity. Hydropower, in any case, requires dam construction that may severely damage the environment, as debates over the huge Three Gorges Dam on the Yangtze have shown.[8] In addition, deforestation in the southwest has increased the silt content of the major rivers and vastly complicated the prospect of hydropower development.

Solar power potential also is not great, given the country's weather and population distribution. The sunny western desert areas are sparsely populated, while much of the eastern part of the country traditionally has many days of cloud cover. High concentrations of suspended particulate matter in the air of the eastern sections further diminishes solar power potential, especially near the major industrial cities where power needs are greatest.

The above locational issues mean that for now and a long time into the future coal will provide the basic source of fuel for China.[9] As of 1994, approximately 75 percent of the country's energy consumption comes from burning coal. Coal is used extensively for household cooking and heating, as well as for electricity and industrial power production. The burning of coal is relatively harmful to the environment, and much of China's coal has a high sulfur content, which adds to the damage it does. Nevertheless, China's basic distribution of energy resources dictates that it will rely on coal as its major source of power.[10]

MAOISM AND THE ENVIRONMENT

The nature of the political system established in 1949 has in some ways exacerbated the country's environmental problems. On balance, the Maoist system contributed in the following dimensions to the damage the Chinese environment has suffered.

Maoist China placed primary stress on development of heavy industry as a means to achieve great power status. Heavy industry in general consumes more resources per unit of output than does light industry. Mao invested state funds in heavy industrial development even more than had Stalin during the Soviet forced industrialization of the 1930s.[11] During the First Five-Year Plan of 1953–57, for example, 80 percent of state investment went into industry, and 80 percent of this industrial investment went into development of heavy industry.

In giving priority to heavy industry development, the PRC under Mao created a system of strong industrial ministries and central planning. Each of these powerful central organs stressed physical output targets, and environmental repercussions received no attention. (To be fair, the Western industrialized countries generally became environmentally conscious only since the 1960s.) In addition, each ministry looked to its own interests and paid little if any attention to the externalities—that is, the effects on other issues—of its decisions.[12] As a result, decisions that made sense strictly in terms of development of a particular industry often had very harmful effects on major population centers.

For example, the industrial ministries and the State Planning Commission did not consider the environmental consequences of where they built new plants. As a consequence, heavily polluting steel and chemical industries were developed in Beijing's suburbs to the west and north—precisely the directions from which the Gobi Desert's winds wash over the most populated areas of the city. In Shanghai, the city's major effluent discharge pipe was placed right alongside the major intake pipe that provided the bulk of the city's water supply. This may have been the result of having different bureaucratic depart-ments take charge of the supply of water to the city on the one hand and of disposal of waste water on the other hand. In any case, this situation went un-corrected until a foreign expert noticed the problem in the 1980s.[13]

The Maoist system of administered prices consistently undervalued basic natural resource inputs such as coal and water, while overvaluing the indus-trial products produced. This fundamental approach provides incentives to factory managers and consumers to be profligate in their use of natural re-sources.

In addition, industrial enterprise managers under the Maoist system, like those under all Stalinist-type systems, were motivated to meet the physical out-put targets specified in their production plans, but they had virtually no in-centives to increase efficiency through technological upgrading, thereby pro-ducing more products with fewer inputs. Without the competition generated by market forces and without a national political leadership sensitive to envi-ronmental concerns, there was little consideration of preservation of re-sources at the level of the production enterprise. The resulting industrial sys-tem contained deep structural biases against environmental factors.

Development efforts in the countryside also wreaked environmental havoc. Perhaps the most devastating was the series of initiatives bound up with the Great Leap Forward. The water conservancy campaign during the winter of 1957–58, for example, mobilized peasants to dig new wells on a massive scale. This was done without consideration of groundwater levels, potential capillary action, and future salinization of soils. Since this campaign, the water table on the north China plain has been dropping precipitously, and exten-sive salinization of soils has occurred. The resulting zones of ground depres-sion now cover an area as large as Hungary. The groundwater level in the Bei-jing area drops nearly six feet per year.[14]

Other campaigns forced the peasants to bring every possible inch of land under cultivation. This resulted, especially during the Cultural Revolution, in extensive terracing of marginal lands and reclamation of poor-quality spaces. The efforts during the 1960s and 1970s to make each region of the country self-sufficient in grains to better prepare to fight a prolonged war produced the conversion of many grasslands to cultivated fields. In many instances, these efforts damaged the land to the point where its productivity has de-clined, soil erosion has increased, and extensive work is now required simply to restore the previous situation.

Indirectly, the fact that Mao's economic strategy kept the countryside poor also contributed to environmental damage. Obtaining adequate fuel is one of the major problems Chinese peasants confront. Most peasants, where possible, resort to gleaning forest floors for twigs, leaves, and other com-bustibles for cooking and heating. Such activities reduce the quality of forests by preventing the cycles of decay and nourishment of the soil that would nor-mally occur. Peasant incentives to cut down forests and overwork land to alle-viate their poverty are also high.

Not all aspects of the Maoist system were inimical to the environment, however. Generally speaking, urban-dwellers consume more resources and contribute more pollution to the environment than do rural residents. China's rigorous post-1961 efforts to curtail urbanization thus had the unintended side effect of saving the country from some environmental damage. Mao's policies of very low personal consumption also produced an ethos of conserving materials in a fashion that had even urban residents doing relatively little damage to the environment. The prohibition on private cars similarly reduced potential environmental insults. In addition, Maoist China devoted some efforts consciously to environmental rehabilitation, such as frequent afforestation campaigns. China lost much of its forest cover during the half century before the communist revolution.[15]

On balance, though, the Maoist system sowed the seeds of tremendous environmental injury through its emphasis on heavy industry, its adoption of wasteful technologies for production, its pricing policies that systematically encouraged waste of natural resources, and its conscious focus on maximizing industrial output without regard for environmental impact. Mao's pronatalist policies also, despite the famine in the early 1960s, increased the country's population rapidly, further stressing the natural environment. These factors set the environmental stage on which Deng's reforms have played out.

Post-1978 Reforms and the Environment

The post-1978 reforms have had a mixed impact on the environment. Some have increased the incentives to utilize resources wisely, thus limiting environmental damage; others have sharply escalated environmental damage. On balance, China as of the mid-1990s faces environmental problems that have worsened significantly since the start of the reforms. From 1982 to 1989, for example, the country lost one-third of its mature forests. Arable land diminishes by 0.5 percent per year.[16]

Some basic reform thrusts should mitigate damage done to the environment by continuing economic growth. The reforms, for example, have specifically sought to alter the mix of investment to provide more funding for light industry at the expense of heavy industry. This change in the sectoral allocation of investment—and thus over time in the sectoral balance in China's economy—should have a basically beneficent effect on use of resources per unit of output.

China's move away from centralized planning should also prove environmentally helpful. The industrial ministries do not have the clout they formerly claimed, and the State Planning Commission is far less powerful than it was at the start of the reform era. Increased stress on profitability, with some movement of natural resource prices in the direction of their true market values, should also increase incentives at the enterprise level to adopt resource-saving technologies.

The reform era's steps toward greater intercourse with the international arena should also contribute in some ways to environmental health in China.[17] Environmental consciousness abroad in the 1980s exceeded that in the PRC, and thus outside experts both sought to heighten Chinese awareness of these issues and to provide needed expertise to analyze the problems and provide solutions to specific issues.[18] The World Bank, for example, did both general and specific studies on the environmental problems China confronted, and began to insist on environmental impact statements as a part of the documentation for all projects in which it was involved. This reflected an increasing environmental awareness within the World Bank itself.

Other aspects of the reform era have, however, accelerated the deterioration of the PRC's environment. The most fundamental short-term adverse force has been the reforms' very success in promoting China's overall economic growth. With the economy expanding at a real rate of approximately 9 percent per year from 1979 to 1991 and over 12 percent per year for 1992 and 1993, even considerably greater efficiency in production is unlikely to prevent additional massive insults to the environment. Assuming China's per capita needs increase by a relatively modest 2 percent per year, for example, its production from 1990 to 2000 must increase by the *total* 1990 production of India and Brazil combined for primary energy; India and South Africa combined for coal; Japan for cement; all of Africa for grain; and Japan for nitrogen. Its direct environmental impacts sustained over the same period would be loss of arable land equivalent to Vietnam's total arable land in 1990 (Vietnam's population is about seventy million); loss of water equivalent to Mexico's 1990 water use; and increase in particulate emissions equivalent to the total 1990 particulate emissions of the United States.[19]

The breakup of people's communes and resulting movement of large numbers of farmers off the land has had various negative environmental consequences. Rural townships have expanded very rapidly, encroaching on the surrounding arable land. Large numbers of individuals have moved into urban environments, where they are consuming more resources and producing more waste than previously.

Within cities, proconsumption policies are beginning to produce the consequences of a consumer society. The number of vehicles—motor scooters, cars, and trucks—is expanding rapidly, with related contributions to air and noise pollution.[20] The state's sustained effort since the early 1980s to expand the grossly inadequate urban housing stock is rapidly expanding urban areas, which are absorbing the generally fertile suburban agricultural lands. Even in the countryside, high consumption policies have produced an enormous surge in home building. New transportation networks, including the construction of multilane highways across the country, are also taking up former agricultural areas, further depleting the pool of arable land and increasing the population pressures on the land.

Those remaining on the farm have reacted to these changes in part by seeking to bring more new land under the plow. They have not, in general, transformed marginal lands on hillsides and in remote, barren places, as the cost of doing so is too high and the rewards are too low. Rather, where possible they are instead encroaching on the rich soils around lakes and streams and in the coastal wetlands. These areas are being filled in and either cultivated or used for new housing at an alarming rate. The payoffs from increased agricultural production in highly populated areas are so great under the reforms that peasants are even planting areas that are in severe danger of flooding, such as the small flatlands inside the dikes along stretches in the lower reaches of the Yangtze River.[21]

In many ways, therefore, the reform era has brought with it behaviors that stress the environment, even as some changes in the system should provide the vehicles for more efficient, environmentally less-damaging production. As in the Maoist era, the most fundamental policy affecting the environment is the underlying emphasis on maximizing growth of GNP. It is hard to fault China's reform leaders for pursuing this goal, though.

One of the most telling measures of the quality of life of a population is the inanimate energy available per capita to that society. Such calculations are inevitably affected by basic features of the country, such as its size and its natural weather conditions. Nevertheless, other things being equal, this figure reveals a great deal about the ability of the population to control the temperatures in which they work, to enjoy different experiences, to eat and dress well, to light their dwellings, to travel, and so forth.

The United States and China are reasonable countries to compare in terms of per capita energy availability because both are about the same size, and they share roughly comparable temperature distributions. While precise comparisons are not warranted, it is significant that the typical Chinese has available per year only about 3 percent of the inanimate energy that the average American can use. Put differently, the typical American during the first two weeks of January each year utilizes more inanimate energy than the typical Chinese has available for the entire year. Given this magnitude of discrepancy, it is little wonder that China's leaders insist on the need to raise the output of the economy as their highest priority!

The Political Economy of Environmental Management

China's leaders now accept the notion that the country will pay dearly in the future if it does not pay attention to the environment now.[22] There are critical shortages of safe water: surveys show that virtually every major body of water in the country is severely polluted, just one in seven rural residents and only half the city-dwellers have access to safe water, many water-storage areas and rivers in north China have dried up, and some 60 percent of all Chinese drink water with a higher fecal coliform count than World Health Organization guidelines recommend.[23] The PRC also suffers from soaring rates of pulmonary diseases such as asthma, heavy smog that descends regularly over many urban areas, and widespread damage due to acid rain in southwest China. In the 1980s a fire burned for four days on a major river that runs through the center of Shanghai, and a later hepatitis outbreak there that felled three hundred thousand people. These and other startling indicators of environmental degradation have brought home the fact that the country faces serious problems.

As a consequence, China by the early 1990s has become an active participant in international environmental discussions, and Beijing has hosted major international conferences on environmental topics. The country set up an Environmental Commission, a National Environmental Protection Administration, local administration branches, and environmental bureaus in all ministries and many other units during the 1980s. It is gradually building up a cadre of experts on environmental issues, and it has adopted numerous environmental laws and regulations. These establish rules, for example, for moving highly polluting industries away from major cities, for payment of fees for polluting water resources, and for prohibiting the adoption of certain highly polluting technologies in new plants. China has also established a system for monitoring air quality in major cities.[24]

The structure and dynamics of China's semireformed system will determine the results to be achieved by environmental efforts during the remainder of the 1990s. This is a highly complex issue, but in broad terms the basic structural issues are the following.

Despite reforms that seek to increase the role of market forces, administrative boundaries remain extremely important in determining economic outcomes. At the lower levels of the system, as explained in Chapter 9, the major net gainers from the reforms have been the municipal, county, and township governments, which have greatly increased their wealth and decision-making power. These governments retain very substantial leverage over the firms in their jurisdiction, as by their actions regarding taxes, investment funds, access to electricity and water, and so forth, they can make or break any enterprise with which they deal. But these governments generally wish to maximize the growth of local industry and commerce, both to fill their own coffers and to expand the employment base for the growing working-age population. This presents several serious problems for environmental issues.

One complication is that very few environmental insults occur strictly within the administrative boundaries of one local political authority. Take, for example, China's fee system for contributing to water pollution.[25] Water is an ambient commodity and thus does not "belong" to any single place or authority (the same, of course, is true of air). China has developed a water pollution fee system that makes an enterprise pay for polluting the water. The basic fee system itself has flaws. For instance, it requires charges only for the single pollutant the enterprise adds to the water that *most* exceeds official standards—all other water pollutants disgorged from the same enterprise are "free" and need not be controlled. In addition, the fee levied is often considerably less than would be the cost of reducing the offending discharge, and thus a rational enterprise manager in most instances simply builds the fee into the cost of production, rather than abating the environmental offense itself.

These flaws can, at least in principle, be resolved through appropriate changes in the fee regulations. Other difficulties with the fee system are more deeply grounded in China's current political economy and thus are less easily remedied. While a fee system should in theory produce enterprise-level efforts to reduce pollution, for example, its efficacy in the context of China's system is actually sharply reduced by two additional factors.

First, the local government has an overriding interest in maintaining maximum production. In most countries, indeed, local governments are not the most effective units for remedying the environmental damage done by local industry, as at this level the industry is typically an extremely powerful political actor, due to its employment and financial contributions. Where the fee system threatens to impinge on the enterprise's operations, local governments in China have been known to find offsetting means—such as grants or tax abatements—to enable the industry to pay the fee without cutting back on production and employment.

Second, the fee system does not allow payments across administrative boundaries. Counties and cities, therefore, are locating their most polluting enterprises near the downstream boundaries of their jurisdictions so that the pollution dumped into the water becomes a problem for the next government farther downstream. The pollution fees collected are retained by the local government that collected them—or are funneled back to the offending industry via the tax abatements and grants noted above. Attacking the problem, therefore, requires that power be in the hands of regional or national authorities. The reforms in China have fragmented power geographically to too great a degree in this regard. For day-to-day management of environmental issues such as the water pollution fee system, local level governments are the key units—and they are not the optimal units to use.

Even where higher-level administrative units exist, the old systemic bias in favor of production organizations remains. The National Environmental Protection Administration, for example, has a lower bureaucratic rank than that of the various production ministries (it is an "administration" rather than a "ministry"). While it can raise issues and draft regulations, it cannot issue binding orders either to the ministries or to the provinces, which have ministry rank, and thus lacks the authority to force their compliance.[26]

In somewhat similar fashion, China has long had seven river valley commissions to work on the integrated development of entire river basins. Such commissions exist for all the major rivers, such as the Yangtze, the Yellow, and the Hai rivers. But these commissions are only advisory to the Ministry of Water Resources, and they do not have the authority to issue orders to the provinces that fall within their jurisdiction. Since each province has the same rank as does the Ministry of Water Resources, moreover, the commissions lack any direct route for exercising executive authority in their respective river basins. As a result, it is virtually impossible to implement integrated plans for river-basin development, especially as most basins cross through parts of a number of counties, cities, prefectures, and provinces.[27]

The resulting problems for water policy are evident everywhere. Downstream locales are seeing their water become truly hazardous. Foreign scholars doing research in Zouping County in Shandong Province in the late 1980s found that the local water sources had been astonishingly defiled by wastes from the upstream capital city of Jinan. That county had, consequently, developed plans to tap directly into the Yellow River, which flows through a part of the county. But other investigators who queried county officials along a vast stretch of the middle and lower reaches of the Yellow River found that many counties had developed their own plans to tap the Yellow River's water.

Should all of these be implemented, by 1996 the mighty Yellow River would be totally dry before it ever reached Zouping County!

Administrative jurisdictional boundaries are not the only source of problems in dealing with contemporary environmental issues in the PRC. The partial nature of price reform combines with the nature of a "negotiated" economy to reduce many of the benefits that a competitive market would normally be expected to produce.

Prices for coal, as explained in Chapter 9, have risen somewhat under the reforms, but they have not yet reached a full market level. Water charges have also been raised, but they remain far below the costs at which price might impose real constraints on water usage. Most other raw material inputs are similarly still selling at far below their real market values, with prices restrained by a combination of the leaders' fears of inflation and of the power of the entrenched production interests that utilize these resources. Consequently, there is still enormous waste in the use of such resources, with substantial adverse environmental consequences.

China, for example, is only half as energy-efficient as the United States, which is only half as efficient as Japan.[28] Chinese boilers burn far too much coal per unit of energy output. While some efforts have been made to improve the efficiency of these boilers, the market has not compelled improvements and thus relatively few have been made. The result is that the PRC consumes far more coal—with far greater resulting pollution—than readily available technologies require. Indeed, the energy intensity (energy used per unit of output) of China's industrial sector is higher than that for any other developing country.[29]

Water is short in many of China's major cities. A survey that covered 434 cities found that 188 are short of water and in 40 the water shortages are severe.[30] But enormous waste still occurs. Very few users pay directly for their water, and very few consumers have water meters. The incentives to put in the necessary equipment have been minimized by the extraordinarily low prices charged for water use. In agriculture, nearly half the arable land is irrigated, and many of the types of irrigation systems used pay little attention to water conservation.[31] Again, underpricing produces waste of a scarce resource.

Even where price ratios should encourage conservation, the close ties between local industries and local governments often reduce the incentive effect to near zero. The reforms are aimed primarily at increasing output, and local governments typically have ample means within their jurisdictions to maintain incentives that favor production rather than conservation. Naturally, there are individual local leaders who have become environmentalists and who strongly support sustainable development within their localities.[32] But they are more the exceptions than the norm. The market does not yet work with sufficient rigor to make a serious difference in the areas where the local political leadership wants to see the economy grow at virtually all costs. Because most enterprises are either state or collective bodies, their profits still depend more on negotiations with the state administration for favorable policies than on maximizing efficiency and improving technology in production.[33]

This dynamic has mitigated the potential environmental benefits from the development of a large number of township enterprises. These firms are generally small and presumably should be more sensitive than large state enterprises to the cost structures they confront. Environmentalists have hoped that the proliferation of these enterprises would produce a somewhat less environmentally damaging way of increasing overall GNP growth. To some extent this has occurred. Because these enterprises are concentrated in less polluting industries, they (as of 1988) produced 25 percent of industrial output but less than 10 percent of air emissions. Overall, however, environmentalists have been disappointed for three reasons. First, the above-noted nexus between the township enterprises and the local governments—these enterprises often account for up to 80 percent of the revenues of localities—have meant that real opportunity costs for the enterprises have typically not favored environmentally conscious decisions; second, the small size and low capitalization of these enterprises means that they often adopt relatively low-technology production processes that are not particularly environmentally friendly; and third, the very large number of such enterprises means that it is very difficult for governments to monitor their performance in terms of air, water, and ground pollution.

To some extent, the resulting behavior conforms to what is termed a "free-rider problem." That is, while all counties, for example, have an interest in environmental protection throughout China, it is in the specific interest of each county for all *other* counties to sacrifice in order to achieve that collective interest. In this instance, the noncomplying county can "free ride" on the environmental cleanup effected by the efforts of others. The fact that under the current system no county can impose its will on any other county simply enhances the power of this logic. Why clean up the local water supply when one cannot affect the polluting actions of the offending counties upstream? Why do so when there is no way to receive reciprocal help from the counties that benefit downstream? The logical county in this situation adds pollution to the system in the process of maximizing its own employment and financial gains. This basically describes the behavior of a very large number of Chinese township, county, and city leaders.

Upper levels of the bureaucratic system are constrained in their ability to intervene to force local leaders to take account of the larger environmental costs of their actions. The most important constraint is simply the fact that a core thrust of the reforms is to accelerate GNP growth through decentralization. Administrative demands from the Center to slow down growth in favor of broad environmental goals are out of step with this basic reform impetus. Such higher level interference is not impossible—and it does occasionally occur. But on balance the system is now geared in a different direction, and this limits the overall rigor with which national environmental regulations are implemented at the local level.

Even China's greater openness to the international arena under the reforms is not an unmixed blessing for the PRC's environment. Among the industrialized countries, many firms whose home governments have tightened their environmental regulations seek to invest in poorer countries where they are freer to pollute. Internationally, quite a few environmentalists take a dim view of regional trade agreements that facilitate cross-border investments, precisely because they see these as cloaks to permit polluting industries to shift their damaging production processes elsewhere rather than clean up their acts.[34] Japan, South Korea, and Taiwan have all by 1994 adopted environmental policies that are making some of their more polluting firms look abroad, and investment in the PRC has become a potentially attractive prospect for many of these enterprises. China generally welcomes such investment.

The largest company in Taiwan, for example, is the Taiwan Plastics Company. This huge firm seriously contemplated investing upwards of US $7 billion in a petrochemical facility across the Taiwan Strait in China's Fujian Province. According to the head of this firm, Y. C. Wang, investment in Fujian made sense because the corruption and lack of enforcement of environmental standards on the Chinese mainland bore greater similarity to the situation in Taiwan of the 1950s than to that of the 1990s. Eventually, only concerted efforts by the Taiwan government, which did not want to see that large an investment made on the mainland, prevented Taiwan Plastics from making this move.

China's environmental difficulties will cause problems outside of the PRC, too. Specifically, China's policies are likely to increase worldwide levels of greenhouse gases (the gases that contribute to global warming). Within twenty years, China will likely be the world's largest emitter of greenhouse gases.[35] China's carbon dioxide component of greenhouse-gas emissions originates primarily in coal burning. But, China also releases a great deal of methane, another greenhouse gas, into the atmosphere. This results from the country's extensive wet paddy field cultivation of rice, which releases methane as a by-product.

Beyond greenhouse gases, China is also a source of acid rain that is producing problems for the Korean peninsula and Japan. Somewhat ironically, many of the pollutants that cause acid rain do not create a problem in northeast China itself because the Gobi Desert dust that mixes with the air over that region is sufficiently alkaline to neutralize the acidity of that air. But the dust settles out, and the pollution that reaches the Korean peninsula and Japan produces acid rains there.

China's increasing standard of living and greater urbanization under the reforms also contribute to transnational environmental problems in a broader sense. As noted above, arable land is being taken for urban development, and the land available for grain production has been shrinking rapidly. Since 1981, global land planted to grains has gone down almost every year, and developments in China are increasing the resulting stress on the remaining arable land. China's citizens, with their growing wealth, are becoming net importers of food, thus increasing overall pressures on global food stocks.

In other ways, China is actually and potentially a contributor to improved global environmental outcomes. Perhaps its major contribution results from its very strict birth-control program. This program itself has a significant impact on world population growth and thus on the level of stress on the environment. If Chinese reproductive behavior were instead at the levels of, for example, India or Indonesia, the global environment would be in more difficult shape.

China can also help the international environment simply by becoming more energy efficient. This is in China's national interest even if it is not in the interests of each of the country's ministries and localities, and the technology for greatly increasing energy efficiency is already known. Beijing might thus, if given proper incentives, significantly reduce the additional strains that the PRC's economic development will place on the environment during the remainder of this decade. It is unlikely, however, that the dynamics of the reforms will permit the Center to act very effectively in this sphere in the near future.

Prognoses

Environmental issues, as noted above, are so complex that precise statements generally are not warranted. In broad terms, though, China's reform effort should, over a considerable period of time, lead to more environmentally friendly approaches to development there. The changes being introduced hold out the prospects for greater production efficiency, a smaller percentage of resources devoted to heavy industry, more rational pricing of raw materials and of pollution-control technologies, closer links with the international arena and its environmental resources, and so forth. Eventually, moreover, the reforms should vastly increase China's wealth and in the process should create a substantial number of people who will begin to demand more pleasant, less hazardous living environments. At that point, very likely China—like Taiwan in the 1990s and Japan in the 1970s—will start devoting serious resources to the abatement of environmental insults.

But this transition point almost certainly will not arrive before the turn of the century. China's per capita incomes are still so extraordinarily low that the drive for increasing industrial output will remain overwhelming for years into the future.[36] While markets will gradually play an increasing role, the "negotiated" economy is so deeply entrenched that it is very unlikely to change in any fundamental way before the year 2000. The prognosis therefore, is for *sharply increasing* environmental damage for the remainder of the decade, as fast GNP growth, rapid urbanization, and growing use of environmentally damaging conveniences such as personal motor scooters produce escalating environmental degradation. Such damage may become severe enough to limit sharply the country's ability to sustain rapid economic growth.[37] Such an adverse development would increase greatly both national and interregional tensions in the PRC.

This prognosis might be somewhat mitigated if the Chinese increase public education on environmental issues and permit the formation of politically oriented "green" movements among the populace. Precisely because environmental issues rarely coincide with existing political boundaries, green movements from below can be especially important in creating a constituency for targeted action. These movements can pull together affected people from various political jurisdictions and create a unified front of information, opinion, and visibility. In both the Soviet Union and Eastern Europe, such movements became important to the political evolution of the regimes during the 1980s. China's strict practice of prohibiting the formation of such organizations from "below" inevitably consigns environmental concerns to a subsidiary position in the present structure of power.

The PRC government is in fact promoting some environmental awareness, and local people's congresses have in some instances heard popular pleas for greater attention to environmental protection. Official fears of any type of autonomous political organization, however, make it very unlikely that real autonomous green movements will be tolerated any time soon.

In all probability, therefore, only as Chinese citizens in large numbers acquire enough resources and leverage on the system to begin to make officials more responsive to impulses from below will environmental conservation assume a far larger role on the national agenda. This should begin—but almost certainly will not go very far—during the remainder of the 1990s.

In sum, the reforms to date have not changed the system to the extent that pressures from below will put environmental issues high on the national agenda or market forces will increase substantially the attention paid to efficient, environmentally friendly production. The semireformed nature of the Chinese economy has unleashed vast initiatives at local levels for rapid economic growth, but it has also created a nexus of state/economic ties that should inhibit vigorously addressing environmental problems. The 1990s, therefore, are likely in retrospect to be seen as the Decade of Accelerated Environmental Degradation in China's overall development experience. Ironically, environmental degradation, in turn, could conceivably force serious declines in the anticipated growth rate for the country's economy.

11
The State and Society

We have focused to this point primarily on the state. Our analysis has portrayed the Chinese system as basically top-down, where the priorities and politics of the top political leadership and the bureaucratic maze through which the leadership deals with society are central to understanding the country. "Society," in this analysis, has been more the target of state action than the source of ideas and initiatives that impact on the state. To be sure, this view notes the limits of the state's ability to reshape society and the disastrous consequences when the state oversteps these limits, such as the famine that resulted from the unrealistic policies of the Great Leap Forward. It recognizes as well that segments of society may resist the state; nevertheless the overall framework has been that society does not see itself apart from the state, or as having any means to make demands upon it. Has this framework captured the essential elements of state/society relations in the past? Does it need serious modification in view of the semireformed system that exists as of 1994?

There is no question that Chinese society under the reforms has acquired a liveliness and pulse that are very different from the surface conformity of the Maoist era. It is now difficult to find citizens who voice enthusiasm for the state administration or a commitment to socialism. But how has this obvious evolution of society changed the nature of the ties that connect the society to the state? The Tiananmen mass movement in April–June 1989 and the downfall of communist regimes in Eastern Europe and the USSR between 1989 and 1991, due largely to the initiative of the populations living there, highlight the importance of this question to any discussion of China's current political system and its future. Analysis of this issue must take into account the evolution of state/society relations to date, with particular attention to the cadres at the basic levels of the state who broker these relations and to the changes in society itself.

The Maoist State and Chinese Society

After an initial decade of promoting wholesale social, economic, and political change in the countryside, the CCP in the wake of the Great Leap famine shifted its priorities. While rhetorically continuing to tout the countryside as a seedbed of revolutionary fervor, in reality it sought to extract grain, limit state-financed rural investment, bottle up rural problems in the countryside, elicit protestations of peasant loyalty, and prevent rural-based rebellion. This amounted to a significant retreat from the original revolutionary agenda in the countryside. Even the Cultural Revolution intruded only superficially into most rural villages.

The major devices utilized to cut the countryside off from the cities and to isolate rural communities have already been discussed: the *hukou* residence-registration system that inhibited geographical mobility, especially from the villages to the cities; the Cultural Revolution–era stress on local self-sufficiency in agriculture; fiscal policies that largely restricted state subsidies for food, health care, education, housing, and welfare to the urban areas; indirect levies on the peasants through such measures as forcing cotton producers to sell all their output to the state at cheap prices, while forcing peasants to purchase all cotton goods from the state at high prices; and directing the major part of state investment funds into the urban economy.

There is little question that during the Maoist era the state succeeded in acting *on* the peasants and limiting peasant initiative. The structure of state control over the countryside after the Great Leap Forward created relatively isolated, inward-looking rural villages. One small group of people provided political, economic, and cultural leadership in each village. These local cadres thus had to balance the demands from higher levels—for grain and other resources such as corvée labor, for public order, and for professions of loyalty—against the need to develop local resources and protect the village from excessive exploitation by the state. The local cadres' income depended on the production of the villages they supervised, and they therefore had a self-interest in keeping resources from flowing out of the locality.

The resulting cadre behavior undoubtedly served both to protect the locality from state demands and as a tool of the state to exploit local resources. Cadre behavior probably included understating local production, overstating the losses from natural disasters, and altering other information where possible to deceive the higher levels, though the actual balance between state and local interests struck by village-level cadres must have varied by the individual. It is possible, in addition, that grain-surplus areas witnessed more local protection than did localities that relied on subsidies from the state. There is a lively literature that has begun to examine the extent of state penetration into the villages during the late Mao era;[1] more empirical work is needed before closure is reached on this issue, though no author has asserted that the peasants actually sought to change state policy rather than to obtain exemptions from relevant policies for themselves.

The urban population under Mao also experienced major social, political, and economic change during the 1950s, but the pressures for urban change did not end with the failure of the Great Leap Forward. During the PRC's first decade, the CCP transformed the relations between the state and urban enterprises through the Three Anti Five Anti campaign in 1951–52, the Socialist Transformation of Industry and Commerce campaign in 1955–56, and the formation of a socialist system of economic planning that substituted for the forces of the market in shaping the nature of relations between the state, the managers, and the workers. Virtually all urbanities, moreover, were encouraged to join state-sponsored mass organizations such as the women's federation, youth league, trade unions, residents' committees, sports federations, and patriotic associations. These state-supported organizations professed to represent the true interests of their members, and therefore participation in politics had to be channeled through such state-controlled outlets.[2]

In the immediate aftermath of the Great Leap, the urban populace became, like their rural counterparts, fully locked into relatively isolated cells, the units (*danwei*) described in Chapter 6. The work units and residents' committees (for those without a work unit) brokered relations between the state and the citizenry. Again, there are debates about the posture assumed by the local cadres, whether they dominated their underlings on behalf of the state or protected their charges from excessive state demands. The former notion maintains that local cadres created cultures of dependence through clientelist networks, while the latter stresses the tension between the power of the state and the "immovable permanence of work unit membership."[3] It has also been suggested that the Maoist state did not wholly succeed in its attempts to restructure social cleavages along the lines dictated by Maoist politics.[4] While the state was largely able to break up solidarity among, e.g., workers as a class, incidents of popular protest nevertheless occurred when the state itself created space for such activities, such as during the Hundred Flowers campaign of 1957 or the early stages of the Cultural Revolution from 1966 to 1968.

The intellectuals warrant particular attention due to their strategic importance in traditional and contemporary China. In the traditional Chinese state the scholar officials were the high priests of the Confucian political/moral philosophy, who combined moral authority with political power.[5] With the demise of the Qing dynasty, which marked the end not only of the imperial Chinese state but of basic ideas about civilization that had been sustained for millenia, Chinese intellectuals cast about furiously in search of a new moral foundation for state power. This search led to the patriotic fervor of the May Fourth movement and to numerous experiments with different forms of state-building in various parts of China during the Republican era.

Mao Zedong built his communist movement after 1937 by utilizing both peasant power and the skills of intellectuals. In his Yan'an Talks on Literature and Art in 1942, Mao declared that the intellectuals must serve the communist cause and could not provide their own moral critique of the communist movement.[6] Wang Shiwei, an intellectual who joined the communist forces in Yan'an and then wrote critically about the growth of corruption and other problems there, was thrown in prison, where he was held until he was beheaded in 1947.

After 1949 intellectuals flocked to the communist cause. While they accepted the legitimacy of party rule, many also sought to be guardians of the new political orthodoxy. This resonated with the position of intellectuals in imperial times and coexisted, sometimes uneasily, with their ardent patriotism and desire to see a strong state succeed.

The Hundred Flowers and Antirightist campaigns in 1957 largely destroyed the role of intellectuals as guardians of orthodoxy. The party, still composed largely of peasant cadres, first invited constructive criticism and then harshly persecuted all who had accepted this invitation. While the party sought to improve relations with intellectuals as the Great Leap Forward collapsed, the Cultural Revolution crushed all semblance of intellectual input and prestige. Very few, if any, intellectuals survived the Cultural Revolution without having suffered physical and psychological abuse.[7]

For the intellectuals especially, Antirightist and Cultural Revolution political violence resulted in prolonged separation of family members.[8] Many children watched their parents cowed by mobs and, literally, beaten and spat upon. Quite a few had to join in these orgies of humiliation. Even in the 1950s spouses were pressured to divorce those who had run into political trouble,[9] and such pressures escalated to murderous proportions during the Cultural Revolution. It is difficult to know the emotional and intellectual residues such experiences left on the millions whose lives were touched by them.[10] Undoubtedly, they created a great deal of anguish about political authority, obligations to the state, social ends, and the goals of personal existence.

The Cultural Revolution had a wider-ranging effect on urban than rural society. For the middle-aged and older generations, it probably reconfirmed a long-standing belief that the young are not to be trusted with power and initiative. Many argue that Chinese more than most people fear chaos *(luan)*,[11] and the destructiveness of the Cultural Revolution probably reconfirmed the importance attached to order as well.

But the Cultural Revolution's impact was especially powerful on the urban youths who responded to Mao Zedong's call to spearhead this political movement. Primarily as a consequence of the Cultural Revolution, China's younger people as of 1976 were in general profoundly ignorant of the outside world, as Mao cut off nearly all contact abroad. Even individual older Chinese who had spent time abroad or who had foreign contacts were isolated, attacked, and cowed into silence. The populace as a whole received no uncensored information about the international arena.

History became a handmaiden to politics during this period. From 1974 to 1976 major factional political battles were fought out partly through historical allegories in the media. Eyewitness accounts of party events written by foreign-educated Chinese scholars were considered to be of no historical value.[12] Chinese education during this period intentionally neglected the country's history and traditional culture, except as tools in the constant political battles of the period.[13] Very few students were even taught the classical Chinese in which most materials were written until the late 1910s.

Political participation consisted largely of acting on the latest "supreme instructions" that emanated from Beijing. The Cultural Revolution's destruction of much of the administrative apparatus led to bloodshed over the proper interpretation of these "instructions." Many younger people and workers gained experience in promoting their own interests through manipulation of ideological slogans and through street-level political and quasimilitary organization. Political issues were regarded in black and white, with "correct" and "incorrect" views and opinions, and no gray areas or notions of contingency.

The true attitudes that resulted from such pressures are hard to judge, given the danger of expressing thoughts that were considered politically unacceptable,[14] but it appears that widely accepted notions included the following:

    □—Intellectuals are unworthy. They are inherently elitist, of doubtful loyalty, and out of touch with China's real needs. They also fear political struggle. It is better to be a worker or peasant than an intellectual.[15]

    □—Classes and class struggle are important. Members of pariah classes—those designated as capitalists, landlords, rich and upper-middle-class peasants, rightists, traitors, and others—should suffer greatly, as should those closely associated with them.

    □—Violence is a perfectly acceptable, even a necessary, form of political struggle. Without violence, enemies cannot be subdued and the society cannot be purified. This was summed up in the popular slogan that, "It is necessary to beat a mad dog in the water," meaning that an enemy should never be treated leniently, even when he has been knocked down.

    □—Plain living and basic egalitarianism are virtuous. Pursuit of personal whims and any form of ostentation reflect a "bourgeois" spirit that makes one suspect. It is right to struggle against those who seem to get ahead of the pack.

    □—The core leader guides the nation. Politics consists of implementing the spirit of directives from the Center, not of pressing for representation of individual or group interests in the political system. The objective is to obtain organic unity based on ideological purification as dictated by the leader.

☐—Political cadres other than the core leader are suspect. They may try to twist the infallible commands of the leader to suit the interests of their own factions. One should be prepared to attack even high-ranking cadres if the instructions of the core leader call for such actions. Few can be trusted to be correct.

☐—Foreigners are suspect. They seek to exploit the Chinese and possibly carve up the country.

It is impossible to know just how widespread the above attitudes were, but anecdotal evidence suggests that many urban-dwellers—not only youths—accepted and acted on them. Chinese society in 1976 was unstable, prone to political upheaval, violent, anti-intellectual, poor, anticonsumer, and contained castelike divisions in social structure. Both peasants and especially urban-dwellers had been taught to sever ties, to demonize those who ran afoul of political strictures, and to commit violence in the name of purification and as a form of self-identification with the correct political line.

In the final analysis, the Maoist state did not penetrate into every nook and cranny of its citizens' lives. Nevertheless, by the end of the Mao's life every social action was regarded as politically significant and thus could evoke a response from the political authorities. Despite severe disruptions of the political apparatus caused by the Cultural Revolution, people continued to be *politically vulnerable.* The urban personnel system of individual dossiers meant that any recorded political transgression would never be shaken off.[16] Because no urban jobs existed outside of those assigned by the state personnel system, and peasants could not leave their collective without permission, there was no escape for those who ran afoul of a political judgment. The very comprehensiveness of this political blanket—ironically, even during periods of politically induced anarchy—was one of the most distinctive characteristics of state/society relations in the era of Mao Zedong.

State/Society Relations under Deng's Reforms

Chapter 5 introduced the many sharp reversals the reforms produced in Maoist policy. The reformers sought to permit a nonpolitical sphere of activity for individuals, drop class labels, use inegalitarian distribution systems and conspicuous consumption as incentives for more work and creativity, rekindle interest in knowledge and technical skills, revive agriculture through a return to family-based farming, open the country to the international arena, and sharply reduce the overall level of political violence. These initiatives created the political space for Chinese society to bestir itself, and raise the question of the extent to which in the 1990s the state/society relationship has changed.

On the surface, Chinese life has changed greatly during the reform period. Even cities like Beijing, Shanghai, or Guangzhou in Mao's last years presented images of dull conformity—millions of people dressed in similar blue "Mao jackets," uniform hair styles among women, no advertising, and no sense of liveliness or entrepreneurship. In 1994, varied clothing, huge traffic jams, vibrant consumer culture, karaoke bars and other entertainment centers, and the seemingly unending construction of modern buildings are the norm. The near-total isolationism of the late Maoist era has been cast aside; calling cards of important Chinese now boast both telephone and fax numbers, and few urban families lack a television set.[17] Large areas of China receive "Star TV" by satellite. Its five channels of programming include Asian MTV and international sports, news, and films, all of which give the people of China images of the outside world uncensored by the Chinese authorities.

Visitors are constantly astonished at the get-rich-quick mood of the populace. Every unit and every person, it seems, is trying to find new ways to make money. The venerable Peking University, for example, in 1993 tore down a wall bordering one end of campus to put up a row of university-run shops. Military units run hotels, speculate in real estate, and sell weapons. At least one military unit in northeast China earns extra money by selling military license plates to those fencing luxury cars stolen in Hong Kong and transported to Dalian. These plates make it easier to avoid the road checks to which civilian vehicles are subject. The number of schemes and scams is, it seems, almost unlimited. A county Communist party secretary in Jilin Province boasted to a foreign visitor that the Communist party secretary of Xiaoxing, a village that had done particularly well in developing local industry under the reforms, is "a big capitalist." The county secretary made the comment while giving the "thumbs up" sign in approval. The village secretary drives a new Cadillac.[18]

How has all this commercial ebullience and exposure to the outside world affected the nature of relations between the state and society? China's society has become so variegated and career paths for many urban-dwellers so numerous that no single generalization can answer this. Also, a great deal of pertinent activity is hidden behind various facades, as explained below. The data on issues such as attitudes and even behaviors, moreover, tend to be anecdotal rather than systematic. With these caveats in mind, some broad observations are nevertheless possible.

The state no longer provides a moral compass for the population. Indeed, one of the striking features of contemporary Chinese society is the growth of nonstate sources of moral authority and spiritual well-being. There have, for example, been resurgences of Buddhism and Daoism. Almost all cities contain active temples as well as street vendors hawking spirit money, joss sticks, and the other accoutrements necessary to appease the gods and improve one's fortunes. Some traditional secret societies have reemerged, and many local sects of various kinds have sprung up in the countryside. Christian church attendance has rapidly expanded, and there are likely more Christians in China today than at any time before the revolution, though they still constitute only a tiny sliver of the population.

Some practitioners of spiritual renewal have developed nationwide reputations and mass followings. One school of restorative breathing, called *qigong*, has become particularly popular, perhaps because many of the gerontocrats in the party are said to benefit from *qigong* exercises. Some *qigong* mass meetings generate all the fervor of the most ardent revival meeting in the

West, and in some instances such gatherings conclude with an emotional intensity that is overpowering. Even many state-run book stores now contain shelves of volumes that advocate and explain *qigong* and other such approaches.[19]

Many affinity groups are forming, such as professional associations, sports clubs, and charitable organizations. Generally, these groups have not done much to create a social consciousness independent of the state. The vast majority are local in character, and all are obligated to register with the government in their locality. Authorities have not hesitated to disband such associations and groups if they become suspicious of them, and in many, such as the professional associations, the state typically plays a major role in determining who will hold the top offices.[20]

There have been some reports of local officials who have joined societal groups and then used their official position to protect the group's activities from higher-level scrutiny. Most such cases have involved rural cadres who joined secret societies or even underground Christian churches. When exposed, these officials generally claim that joining such organizations makes governing easier and assures social order. These instances suggest the possibility that potentially threatening nonstate organizations exist in China that are concealed by local state officials.[21]

There are many individuals, moreover, who manage to skirt the state's authority to pursue their own personal agendas. The huge size of the floating population demonstrates the gaps in the system's tight control over individual activities, and such problems as urban crime are increasingly blamed on these people who fend for themselves rather than belong to a unit. As of 1994, however, the floating population appears to be politically quiescent. They seek to earn a living in the cities, not to change the political system. The police have on numerous occasions cracked down on particular groups of floaters, sending them back to the countryside or subjecting them to other punishments, all without overt resistance. At this point, therefore, the floaters reflect more the current laxity of the control system than a movement toward conscious, organized social and political activity.[22] However, people who do seek change in the system may eventually be able to take advantage of this loosening of the reins as well.

BASIC-LEVEL CADRES TO THE FORE

Perhaps most important, many local unit leaders remain firmly in command but are increasingly pursuing their own political and economic agendas rather than following orders from Beijing. Numerous basic-level cadres are not sympathetic to policies emanating from above. For example, in the summer of 1989 the Center ordered rigorous reviews of the activities of people during the Tiananmen protest movement, and that appropriate notations be made in the personal dossiers of those who had defied the leaders. Throughout China, however, almost all units subverted this policy by going through the motions without really seeking to determine how their members had acted. It appears that in the final analysis very few had the dreaded notation on political unreliability put into their dossiers. In this instance, millions of citizens acting in a disaggregated way sent a quiet message to the top leadership that the Center could no longer set Chinese against Chinese at the unit level as a way to enhance Beijing's leverage. This tactic had been a hallmark of the Maoist era.

A meeting of a major research institute in Beijing, many of whose members had taken part in the demonstrations during May and early June 1989, typifies what took place. The party head in the institute called a "study meeting" to review materials on the Tiananmen massacre sent by the Central Committee propaganda department. The participants were supposed to discuss the materials in detail and then criticize each other's behavior and attitudes in accordance with the "spirit" of these documents. But in reality, the party head had everyone take a seat, passed out the documents, and asked if anyone wanted to say anything. Nobody responded. The party head then declared the meeting had served its purpose and asked that everyone give these materials full consideration on their own. Next, he adjourned the meeting and ostentatiously threw the propaganda department materials into the waste basket as he left the room. Every participant in the meeting did the same. Higher levels were told that the meeting had a lively discussion but that no "serious problems" were uncovered.[23]

Some basic-level cadres take in political dissenters or those who have political black marks in their dossiers. For example, a private Dalian-based import-export company, spun off from a state trading corporation that wanted to slim down its ranks, has actively sought to recruit outcasts, including students who received damaging entries in their personal dossiers due to Tiananmen protest activities, perhaps in the belief that such individuals would work especially hard for the firm.[24] In another instance, the Stone Corporation, a high-technology collective enterprise in Beijing, became active in the Tiananmen movement. The Stone Corporation had also set up its own research firm whose activities promoted a democratic transition in China.[25]

Local territorial leaders—especially those far from Beijing and not dependent on subsidies from the Center—have also begun to pursue their own interests, sometimes in open defiance of the top CCP leadership. During the austerity effort dictated by Beijing in July 1993, for example, Su Zhiming boasted to a reporter for the *Asian Wall Street Journal* that, "A business talent like mine is worth more than one million *yuan* in Hong Kong. My brains are 100 percent occupied by ideas for making money." Su is both the Communist party boss and mayor of Shiji, a town southeast of Guangzhou in China's booming Guangdong Province. That town already had more than one hundred imported cars when Beijing ordered a halt to new car imports. Nevertheless, Su ordered forty-two more, including a Rolls Royce. He had the money to do this because the incomes of the town's officials depend on the profits of the three dozen local companies operated by the town government. These companies are engaged in property development, import-export trading, and light industry, including electronics and garments. With business going strong during 1993, local officials stood to receive bonuses amounting to six times their salary, which would make Su's income considerably higher than that of CCP General Secretary Jiang Zemin.[26]

As these examples suggest, the Center's authority has eroded significantly under the impact of the reforms. Many individuals seek to realize their own ambitions, vigorously when the opportunity permits and surreptitiously when the "wind" blowing out of Beijing is against them. The semireformed political and economic systems provide substantial space for such activities to occur in the normal course of events. Though more of this space is available to local cadres than to ordinary citizens, the higher-level authorities do maintain considerable leverage over local officials under certain conditions.

Specifically, when the local levels would rather not follow their superiors' lead, the upper levels can assure compliance if, first, they are united in their views on the matter. Chinese officials are extremely sensitive to the existence of disagreement among the upper ranks and recognize that tactics of delay may be rewarded by a change in policy. Second, the higher levels must give the issue priority. So many orders cascade down the Chinese state administration that failure by the leadership to prioritize gives subordinates considerable room to maneuver. Finally, the results of any directive must be easy to measure. Compliance with birth-control policies, for example, is more readily determined than is implementation of an order to do spring planting well.

Where these three conditions are met, few local leaders are willing to cross their superiors, and the state is able to function in a very determined, forceful fashion. But the entire reform strategy seeks to elicit local initiative and promote local flexibility, and therefore the national leaders rarely issue directives that require disciplined implementation. In addition, the contending groups that make up the national leadership, as explained in Chapter 5, find it difficult to show complete unity on major issues.

Despite the political leeway that currently exists in China, it is notable that few anecdotes reveal substantial social activity that is wholly independent of the state. Unit-level and territorial leaders have seized far more initiative than was previously feasible, but ordinary citizens have done so to a much lesser degree. Indeed, tales abound of despotic actions by local officials toward their own constituents, some of whom feel more vulnerable to demands of their bosses than ever before.

One incident in Jilin Province in the summer of 1993 illustrates this. A village party chief confronted a peasant and demanded that he pay a tax for owning a bicycle. The peasant objected, and secretly wrote a letter to the head of the county party committee to complain of the village chief's exploitative activities. The county head admonished the village chief for dereliction because he had not intercepted the letter before it was sent, noting that they would all have been in trouble if the peasant had written to the provincial level. At the county head's suggestion, the village chief made an example of the peasant. He had the local police beat the peasant to death in front of a meeting of the entire village.

Of course, not all local cadres are despotic. There is great variation in their activities and attitudes. Some, as noted above, have linked up with local social forces, whose activities they have shielded from view of the higher ranks. In an attempt to deal with this and related problems, the National People's Congress in November 1987 adopted an Organic Law, which stipulates that village committees should be elected locally to run the villages. The law set up incentives both for responsiveness to the villagers' desires and for disciplined implementation of tasks handed down from the townships. The law sought, in short, to generate peasants' enthusiasm and curb local despotism via real elections at the village level while simultaneously making village cadres responsible for implementing tasks, such as tax collection and implementation of the birth control program, assigned from above. The results of the Organic Law have been mixed, however, and the current situation varies greatly from village to village.[27]

Generally, in urban areas, increments in labor mobility are lessening the controls that many managers can exercise over their workers. But on balance, the anecdotal evidence strongly suggests that more power in the hands of local cadres has not meant a comparable increase in the opportunities for independent social forces to coalesce. Even the strongest social groups and organizations typically must establish close relations with the local levels of the state to survive.

The possibility that in the PRC nonstate social forces are acquiring a sufficient sense of identity and critical mass to challenge the state, as such forces did in the Eastern bloc and the Soviet Union, has been given substantial attention in the recent scholarly literature on China. This literature focuses on the issue of civil society, which leads to the question of whether a "public" sphere is developing that is not essentially a part of the state. The literature traces back some of the origins of such a nonstate "public" to the development and growth in the West of a market economy.[28]

Scattered evidence indicates that this Western model does not apply to China's evolving situation in the 1990s, which, rather, seems to be characterized by two major developments. First, the basic levels of the state are increasingly seizing the initiative, and in many cases limiting the ability of the higher levels to penetrate the locale and extract support and resources from it. Individuals outside of the state administration must develop complex, wide-ranging ties with local state officials as a condition for their exercising much initiative.[29] Second, the state is sharing management of many activities with nonstate groups it has allowed to form. This duplicates a pattern seen in imperial and Republican China, before the Maoists destroyed all such groups and extended the direct power of the state.[30] While these developments do not suggest the formation of a civil society in the classic sense, they do qualify the idea, accurate in Mao's day, that China's state apparatus completely dominates its society (a situation characterized in the literature as a "strong state, weak society").[31] The national state administration is no longer tightly disciplined, and the local officials negotiate their relations with the higher authorities and, sometimes, with the citizenry as well. For its part, society at large is stirring but still tightly locked in the embrace of local officialdom, including local unit leaders of state organizations and enterprises.

The reforms are, nevertheless, affecting the very structure of the state's mechanisms to deal with the society. As stressed repeatedly throughout this volume, after the completion of the revolutionary changes wrought during the 1950s, the state adopted an approach that made state units—rural communes, state enterprises and social organizations, and state offices—the key vehicles to engage society. The unit both funneled state services to the population and performed a wide array of political and security functions. Appropriately, most of the *xitong*s described in Chapter 7 penetrated each such unit.

But the reforms are casting very large numbers of people adrift from the state units. Communes no longer exist in the countryside, and perhaps one hundred million peasants have become members of the floating population in the cities. Private enterprises, joint ventures, private schools, and so forth are providing employment opportunities for an increasing percentage of the population, and the state, for reasons discussed in Chapter 9, is trying to reduce the number of people it employs. To the extent labor mobility develops, the former system of brokering state society relations through the work unit must change.

This set of pressures is producing efforts by the state to shift services from units to city-wide or county-wide bases of delivery. Gradually, the state is trying to develop social security, insurance, public health, housing, and other resources that will be distributed by means other than the work units.[32] Detaching such resources from the work unit will eventually change the patterns of social activity and social dependence that have characterized China to date, and may force the state to develop a legal system with a serious role to play in regulating social behavior and adjudicating disputes over resource allocation. But these developments are taking place fitfully, and their future scope and pace remain uncertain as of 1994.

It also remains to be seen whether the local cadres, as their circumstances improve, will seek to develop institutionalized means to protect their prerogatives and life-style. It is possible that, over time, such attempts will create a system in China somewhat like those produced in South Korea and Taiwan by the middle classes that have emerged in those countries since the early 1980s. But the situation in China, where many of those acquiring wealth are a part the state itself, differs greatly from that of the autocratic South Korean and Taiwan states and their economic entrepreneurs. There is, therefore, little certainty that the PRC will follow the democratizing path of its East Asian counterparts.[33]

HUMAN RIGHTS

The above developments provide a framework for discussing human rights in China. Few issues are as complex and emotional as that of human rights in the 1990s. Complicating matters, the term "human rights" has different meanings to different people. To some, it means above all the freedom to express one's political views without being persecuted for doing so. This view typically also holds that no state has the right to torture its citizens or to subject them to inhumane conditions. For others "human rights" acquires a broader meaning that includes protections afforded by due process in both political and civil matters; it means, in other words, "the rule of law." And for still others, "human rights" encompass what might be termed "social rights"—access to health care, decent housing, job opportunities, education, and so forth.

Reforms have improved the human rights situation in China, almost regardless of which definition of human rights is applied. Average levels of consumption have improved dramatically, and citizens are much freer of political persecution and political violence than they were in the Maoist era. It is not at all unusual, at least in the major cities, to hear individuals complain about the Communist party leaders and such issues as corruption. Many do so in public, seemingly without fear of arrest or punishment.

But generally these very substantial, concrete improvements in the well-being of most citizens have not been accompanied by real improvement in their "rights." That is, their degree of freedom and range of opportunity remain dependent on decisions made by state officials. That such decisions are less repressive and persecution is less widely practiced is a major step forward, but still falls short of giving citizens reliable protections against the depredations of the state.

China maintains large labor-camp and prison systems, and reports of mistreatment and torture are common. Pressures on penal officials to elicit confessions before cases come to trial open the door to abuse of suspects, who have no way to protect themselves from their interrogators. In addition, China retains a form of punishment called "reform through education" that permits the state to incarcerate any citizen for up to three years without trial or formal accusation, merely on the grounds that the citizen requires "reeducation." Reports indicate little difference between the "reform through labor" camps for those convicted of crimes and the "reform through education" camps for those incarcerated by administrative order.[34]

Thus, "human rights" in China in the sense of protection against arbitrary action by the state are barely in evidence. China's leaders argue that to guarantee the citizens' rights to agitate and organize against the state would risk throwing the country into social chaos and civil war, which twentieth-century China has suffered enough of already. They point, instead, to the rapidly rising per capita GNP as a more significant indicator by which to judge human rights in the country.[35] Popular views on this issue seem to be deeply informed by China's long history of authoritarian government and its related notions of society as an organic whole.[36] But the country is changing in unprecedented ways and is more exposed to alternative views and images through telecommunications from the international arena than ever before in its history. It is difficult, therefore, to measure with confidence how ideas about human rights are changing in the PRC or how the actual situation with respect to those rights will evolve. What is without question is that in a country as large, complex, and poor as China, major violations of human rights will form at least a part of the political landscape for many years to come.

CHANGES IN SOCIAL RELATIONSHIPS AND CLEAVAGES

The above sections focus on the changes that the reforms have wrought in the ties between the state and society. What changes, though, have occurred within the society itself? Specifically, how have the reform policies altered the contours of socioeconomic inequality, and how have they affected the types of cleavages that characterize Chinese society?

Urban-Rural Incomes

The largest single cleavage in Maoist China divided urban from rural residents. The former had higher real incomes and many nonmonetary benefits. They also lived at lower risk of suffering the full brunt of economic catastrophe when Mao's policies went awry. The peasants, by contrast, bore the burdens imposed by the economic system and were less protected than their urban counterparts when national economic difficulties became severe.

Studies of urban and rural incomes in China must account adequately for urban subsidies and the value of rural housing. These elements play a large role in the Chinese scheme of compensation. Most studies have failed to account for these items and thus have tended to present false statistical pictures.

An investigation of household income conducted by a team of researchers and published in the *China Quarterly*,[37] took pains to develop accurate estimates of these missing components and to factor them into the overall analysis. This project used a survey of 10,258 rural households in twenty-eight provinces and 9,009 urban households in ten provinces to determine the composition of various types of household income as of 1988, ten years after the start of the reforms. While lack of comparable data for 1978 makes it impossible to specify the exact impact of the reforms on the types of inequality discussed below, some of the findings provide at least a good general sense of likely trends over the first reform decade.

Two findings stand out: that the net effect of the reforms in the rural areas has been to increase rural inequality in general and to exacerbate gender differences in rural income; and that urban/rural inequality even in 1988 remained very large and continued to be aggravated by state intervention in favor of urban residents. The survey provides less clear results concerning changes in regional distribution of household income, for reasons explained below.

The reforms have aggravated rural income inequality in several dimensions. Most fundamentally, rural nonfarming sources of income, including wages, entrepreneurship, and property, are far higher than farm income. In addition, the government has not developed a progressive personal income tax system to tax this nonfarm income effectively, while farm production is fully taxed. Therefore, those engaged in rural nonfarming occupations have significantly increased their incomes compared to those who rely on farming.

This difference shows up in rural income distribution figures. In 1988, 62 percent of the income from wages, including other forms of labor compensation in both cash and kind, was received by the richest 10 percent of rural individuals. Only 1 percent of the income of the poorest 20 percent of the rural population, by contrast, came from wages. Poor residents received the overwhelming portion of their income from family production of farm and nonfarm products, a very high proportion of which was retained for their own consumption. But nearly all of this is taxed, whereas the higher income of the richer rural residents includes substantial portions of nonfarm income from wages and business that escapes taxation. Overall, the richest quintile in the countryside in 1988 had a total income 5.9 times that of the poorest quintile.[38]

The ability to move into nonfarm work thus has a marked effect on income potential, and this opportunity expanded tremendously under the reforms. The data make clear, moreover, that men far more than women have been able to take advantage of the opportunity to earn nonfarm income. Where women do participate in nonfarm work, they earn less at it than do their male counterparts.

Specifically, women in 1988 constituted only 15 percent of rural technical workers, 26 percent of leading officials of state and collective enterprises, 6 percent of township or town cadres, 9 percent of township or village enterprise cadres, 15 percent of ordinary cadres in party and government institutions, 25 percent of ordinary workers, 32 percent of contract workers, and 21 percent of owners of private enterprises. Women were, however, 51 percent of all farmers. For those women who do earn a wage income, their mean regular monthly wage was only 81 percent of men's wages. Rural women thus, overall, as of 1988 had lower per capita incomes than did rural men.[39]

Rural China is also less commercialized than much of the reform rhetoric might suggest. Altogether, according to the survey data, some 41 percent of rural household income in 1988 went toward food produced by the household itself. As the authors comment, this is "the same proportion as in other extremely poor and economically backward Asian economies."[40] The high percentage of overall rural income that continues to derive from basic farm production means that, on balance, the state taxes on rural income exceed state subsidies to the countryside by an average of 2 percent of total household income.[41]

The state's posture toward urban income is strikingly different. For urban residents, the state subsidizes income; even taking taxes into account, the average urban household in 1988 received a net subsidy that amounted to 39 percent of its total income. The overall ratio of urban to rural incomes as of 1988 was thus 2.42. According to Khan et al., "This is an extraordinarily high [urban/rural] income differential by the standards of other developing countries of Asia." Had the state not intervened with net taxes in the countryside and net subsidies in the cities, the urban/rural income ratio would have been 1.45 instead of 2.42.[42]

While the survey data do not permit tracking over time of income distribution within the cities, the overall ratio of the income of the top urban quintile to that of the bottom urban quintile was a relatively modest 3.2, as compared with the 5.9 of the countryside. This makes China the only Asian country for which figures are available in which rural inequality vastly outstrips urban inequality. Relative urban equality seems to result primarily from the extraordinarily large portions of income that derive from subsidies rather than earned income. Real household income in China's cities is more equally distributed than it is in cities of other Asian countries. In addition in cities, as in the countryside, men fared better. Their average income was 20 percent higher than that of urban women.[43]

A final issue concerns changes in regional income distribution. Inequalities, both urban and rural, across regions are very substantial. Rural per capita incomes in Shanghai in 1988, for example, were about 2.95 times as large of those of the mountainous southwest province of Guizhou. Urban per capita incomes in Guangdong were nearly 2.2 times as large as those of Shanxi. But these data do not yield sufficiently precise figures to be very useful. The data, for example, are presented by province, but many provinces contain very large differences in income distribution. Some individual provinces are, after all, as large and populous as some European countries. Overall provincial averages of per capita income would also be skewed by the level of urbanization of the province, since urbanites generally make far more money than do their rural counterparts.[44] The available data, moreover, do not provide a good baseline from which to measure the changes in distribution of real per capita incomes on a regional basis since the start of the reforms.

Thus, the overall effects of the reforms on income distribution as of 1988 were complex. Quite likely, income distribution in the countryside had become less equal, as new opportunities to earn nonfarm income were unevenly distributed. Men received the larger share of this rapidly expanding part of the pie, and thus rural men seem to have benefited more from the reforms than have rural women in terms of per capita income.[45] In addition, as under Mao, the state has continued to intervene in favor of enhancing rural/urban inequalities in per capita income, although some studies suggest that it does so less than it did under the Maoist system. The bottom line is that as of 1988 the state took 2 percent of per capita income in the form of taxes in the countryside, while it provided subsidies that on average enhanced urban earned per capita income by 64 percent, producing a net subsidy component of total urban per capita income of 39 percent.

The situation as of 1993 probably has not changed dramatically from that of 1988, but some intervening trends warrant mention. This five-year period witnessed considerable migration to the larger towns and cities, but the migrants, the floating population, are not entitled to the subsidies that benefit regular employees of urban enterprises who have urban residence certificates. The net effect of this in-migration is probably to reduce somewhat the role of subsidies in the average income of urban-dwellers. In similar fashion, efforts have been made in some cities in the early 1990s to develop real-estate markets and in other ways to increase rents and cost of housing so that it better approximates real market values. Also, urban grain subsidies were considerably reduced—and in a number of places totally abolished—during the early 1990s, and grain prices have been allowed to rise closer to market levels.

These changes have probably somewhat evened out urban/rural income differentials. But this equalizing effect may itself have been swamped by corruption and malfeasance among local rural officials, combined with a widening price scissors[46] that works to the disadvantage of farmers. There were many reports in 1992 and 1993 of rural discontent because local officials had misappropriated crop procurement funds and had paid the peasants IOUs instead of cash.[47] In the inflationary economy of those years, postponement of cash payment amounted to imposing an additional tax on the farmers. The rural/urban income gap thus probably remains the greatest single source of inequality in China, and the government's pertinent policies generally exacerbate rather than reduce this differential.

Perceptions

Income does not fully capture the perceptual side of social equality and cleavages. To what extent do people feel they are holding their own with respect to social standing? Do they feel that others are advancing faster than they are, and do they feel that such changes are taking place on an equitable basis? The data to deal with such questions systematically is not available. But impressionistically, important changes have been occurring in this dimension of social stratification.

At the start of the reforms in the late 1970s there was widespread urban support for improving the lot of the peasants. By about 1983, urban moods had changed. Increasingly, people expressed dissatisfaction over their personal status, feeling that almost every other sector of society was advancing more rapidly than they. Discussions in people's homes produced a constant litany of complaints about falling behind the advances of others. The Chinese press began to talk about the spread of what was termed the "red-eye disease" (a Chinese expression for jealousy).

This shift did not reflect real changes in income distribution. It probably did reflect the fact that the government increasingly encouraged people to use their new income to purchase consumer goods and improve their standard of living. By using material incentives to spur greater effort, the government made people more conscious of how their material situation compared to that of others.

Perhaps the most disgruntled urban group as of 1994 is the intellectuals. Many feel that market opportunities are not available to them, and they are acutely aware that many street vendors earn more than do professors at leading universities. Unlike government and party officials, moreover, most intellectuals do not wield the power that would provide opportunities for corruption.

Overall, one's sense in Chinese society as of 1994 is that wealth has become the key to status and that very few people feel the system is providing them with the wealth they deserve—or, more accurately, many feel that too many others are acquiring wealth they do not deserve. Empathy for other groups—like that the urbanites had for peasants at the end of the 1970s—is notably lacking. A niggardly mood prevails even in the midst of rapid economic growth. The absence of systematic survey data on these topics, however, makes all such observations highly impressionistic—and undoubtedly skewed to the views of the better-educated residents of coastal cities.

The reforms themselves appear to have opened up many new channels of political and social mobility, creating opportunities for former outcasts and average people to change their incomes and the ways they live. In this sense, the reforms have at least as of the early 1990s increased personal mobility and blurred class lines.

One glaring exception to the blurring of class lines, as noted in Chapter 8, involves the offspring and relatives of the top officials who were rehabilitated after the Cultural Revolution. These individuals have on the whole been able to utilize their political connections to build economic empires and to insulate themselves from the normal risks of economic failure. While the hard data necessary to make a firm determination are not available, it seems as of the early 1990s that the families of the communist elite from the prereform era have adapted well to the reform environment. This relatively small group still combines political and economic power, and the members of this group tend to intermarry. An elite class appears to have sustained itself across the Maoist and Deng eras.

In sum, China's cities may still be among the most egalitarian in the world, but the new ethos of flaunting one's wealth and of paying close attention to income inequalities has created a sense of substantial and growing social stratification among the populace, even if real social mobility for most people is increasing. Large parts of the countryside are not faring well, and access to television, along with increased travel opportunities, is driving home to poor rural residents the great differences between their own standard of living and that of their urban counterparts.

Gender

Based on Confucian values, one of the most oppressed groups in traditional society had been women. After 1949, the PRC quickly adopted a new marriage law that made divorce easier to obtain, and adopted other measures, such as generous maternity leaves, to meet women's needs. More fundamentally, the collective structures created by the Maoist system significantly weakened the extended families, which had been bastions of male domination. In addition, employment practices that brought women into the labor force—where their wages were paid directly to them rather than to the male head of the household—tended to increase the leverage women had in the family.

These changes did not mean full equality for women. Male chauvinism remained deeply embedded in the Chinese psyche. An American leftist delegation that visited China in 1971 was astonished, for example, to find that when they had dinner at the home of Chen Yonggui, the former leader of Dazhai Brigade[48] and a model peasant member of the Politburo, Chen's wife stayed in a corner, not daring to sit at the table. When several female members of the delegation urged her to join them, she demurred, obviously discomfited by the suggestion. Even during the Cultural Revolution, a time of extreme egalitarianism, all female Politburo members had husbands (Mao Zedong, Zhou Enlai, Lin Biao) who were the real leaders of China.

Generally women received lower compensation than men—sometimes because they were shunted into lower-paying jobs; at other times, especially in the countryside, because it was assumed they could not do the quantity and quality of work that their male counterparts could accomplish. Women also were generally expected to take care of the household chores, in addition to holding a job.[49]

It appears that urban women as well as rural women are not faring as well as men under the reforms. In urban areas, the Maoist system accorded women a number of benefits, including earlier retirement with pension rights, extended maternity leave with pay (with options for longer leaves without pay), and crèches and nurseries at the work place. Because managers did not particularly focus on making profits, they did not begrudge female employees these benefits.

The reforms have changed the calculus, especially for the increasing number of urban firms that are not protected from market competition by state subsidies. Stories abound in the Chinese press about reluctance of managers to hire female employees because of the financial burdens of these mandated benefits. Female university graduates find that they have trouble finding work, whereas their male counterparts are snapped up by firms in the export sector and elsewhere.[50]

In the countryside, the restitution of family farming has probably strengthened the role of male heads of households. Studies show that, as was the case before collectivization of agriculture, rural household incomes from farming are generally allocated among members by the family head. Often, this is the head of an extended, rather than a nuclear, family. Women typically do not fare well under such conditions. As noted above, moreover, females have been less able to take advantage of the higher paying opportunities outside of farm labor that the reforms have opened up.[51]

Women also bear the brunt of the birth-control effort, which has been enforced vigorously under the reforms. The PRC's extraordinarily strict and successful birth-control program places the responsibility for limiting births overwhelmingly on women.[52] Policy as of the early 1990s permits each urban couple only one child. Many rural couples are allowed to have a second child if the first is a female. With the dissolution of the collectives, the financial advantage of a male child in the countryside—who will remain with his parents and will bring in a spouse to the household rather than move to another family upon marriage—has grown.

Experience in other countries such as India demonstrates that such pressures may lead to tragic consequences for wives who bear female offspring. They often assume "blame" for the sex of the child, and may suffer terrible abuse at the hands of the husband's family as a consequence. Female infanticide is another expected result and one that statistics indicate is occurring in rural China.[53]

In addition, reports from China indicate that the old practice of kidnapping women and selling them to men who want a spouse has revived and is spreading. Gangs operate across provincial boundaries and deal in ten of thousands of victims. Some of these are urban women, but most are from rural households. Because this trade in human traffic is illegal, it is impossible to know its scale.[54]

In sum, it appears that on balance women's positions in society have suffered under the reforms. Like men, of course, women enjoy an improved overall standard of living as the economy grows; nevertheless, their position *relative* to men has in some important ways deteriorated.

Political Equality

One of the most important aspects of equality in the PRC is the notion of *political* equality. The Maoist system rested on permanent discrimination against people who received "bad" class labels. These became outcasts, subjected always to the violence inherent in political campaigns, denied career and educational opportunities, required to report regularly to local police officials, and unable to free their spouses and children from the opprobrium of class discrimination. Class enemies also had no right to equal treatment in the courts, as law was itself assumed to have a class nature.[55]

Nobody knows the number of individuals who suffered from these types of discrimination. Mao Zedong preached the importance of uniting 95 percent of the people to struggle against 5 percent at any given time. This 95:5 ratio probably provides a very inexact measure of the actual numbers involved. And it very likely omits consideration of the family members of the victims, who also suffered. But as of 1976, 5 percent of the Chinese population amounted to nearly fifty million people. Regardless of the precise numbers, class discrimination was a significant, large-scale source of social inequality in the PRC on the eve of the reforms.[56]

The reform era has dramatically reduced this political source of inequality. Class labels were removed for almost all those designated as class enemies at the start of the reforms. No such labels have subsequently been pinned on people. The legal system no longer recognizes class as a pertinent consideration in determining guilt and imposing sentences. This does not mean that people are no longer imprisoned for political offenses. Laws against "counterrevolutionary" activities still provide the government with ample "legal" flexibility to incarcerate those who cause political trouble. But no class of people is *automatically* presumed guilty and subject to harsher treatment simply by virtue of their political position. This is one of the most important social changes of the reform era, in part because it permits individuals of talent, regardless of their parentage, a chance to do well in the contemporary PRC.

Generations

Despite enormous economic growth, then, contemporary Chinese society is under great strain, with social tensions pervasive in both urban and rural life. An additional concern is generational fractiousness. People generally form their basic political ideas and identity when they are in their teens and twenties. The turbulance of twentieth-century Chinese history has afforded different generations with very different socialization experiences, producing a society that is now deeply marked by strong generational cleavages.

One man, for example, who was young during the 1920s and 1930s, became a prominent banker in pre-1949 China and was initially embraced by the communists in the early 1950s. But he fell victim to the Antirightist campaign in 1957 and then suffered tremendously during the Cultural Revolution. Nevertheless, in the early 1990s he is deeply chagrined that Mao Zedong is not accorded greater respect. Even though Mao destroyed his life, he still regards the former Chairman as a true hero of the Chinese nation. Why? Because Mao led a political movement that united China after decades of warlordism and foreign invasion. In the words of this man, "That was not easy, and it took a hero to accomplish this. I will always respect Chairman Mao. No contemporary leader is his equal."

Many of those who joined the urban work force during the early and mid-1950s believe deeply in the kind of system that accorded them serious job opportunities, on-the-job training, and financial security. Recent studies show that these early job entrants after 1949 generally experienced substantial upward mobility. Many, now in retirement or nearing that age, find the new economics of the Deng era profoundly unsettling.[57] The socialist system served many in this generation well, and they see its virtues as well as—or more than—its faults.

The Cultural Revolution generation is China's lost generation. People whose education was cut short as they were told to take to the streets to "make revolution" then found, when it was all over, that real opportunities would go to those with better educations. Those who were encouraged to attack the power elite in the party then found that these same officials came back with a vengeance and that their offspring form the new ruling class. Those who in the political heat of the times killed fellow students, tortured teachers, beat elderly people, and in some cases denounced their own family members must now live with the haunting memories of their own deeds. And for the most part, they lack the skills to succeed in the new society.

Those growing up in the 1980s and 1990s are having very different experiences. Where the previous generation was raised on a diet of political struggle and personal sacrifice, the present generation includes many pampered offspring of single-child households. Raised during the consumer revolution, television has become a natural part of their environment. They are taught to worship money rather than politics and not to cause trouble, lest it become more difficult for them to get ahead. This generation is, overall, materialistic, pampered, and politically agnostic. It is a postrevolutionary generation.

Each generation is more complex than indicated here, and this layering is also imprecise. Still, it may be said that in China there are no fundamental political and social values that are widely accepted across generations. There are sharp generational differences over the role government should play in shaping the economy and society, whether people should seek broad social engagement, and what types of careers and behaviors are respectable. Even views of the country's own past vary by generation. The post-Cultural Revolution urban generation, moreover, has no understanding of—and very little respect for—the majority of the population that toils in the countryside.

Conclusion

Chinese society has, in sum, become far more variegated under the reforms than it had been at any time since the socialist transformation of the mid-1950s. But this is not a united society. It is beset by discord and lacks a moral compass. This is, in short, a society under great strain, where massive movements of people off the land, changes in the terms and structure of urban employment, new exposure to international media, and rapidly changing income structures have exacerbated already existing generational cleavages to produce fundamental confusion over such basic social issues as status and rules of behavior. It is also a society whose members have a complex relationship with local-level officials—cadres who themselves increasingly have a negotiated relationship with higher levels of the state.

The only idea that seems to be widely accepted among Chinese now is that making money and improving one's standard of living are important. Scholars of traditional China and of the Maoist era have typically felt, though, that Chinese society was almost unique in the extent to which the political leadership was expected to provide and nurture a compelling moral framework, which in turn was an absolute prerequisite to social and economic well-being. A core issue confronting students of China in the 1990s is, therefore, whether this major facet of the conventional wisdom is still valid. If it is, one must now judge Chinese society—including the cadres at the basic level of the Chinese state—to be a potential source of major instability. There being few even among basic-level officials who view the political leadership as providing moral authority, the ability of that leadership to buy social peace with economic success must be deemed quite limited.

But the Chinese societies of Taiwan, Hong Kong, and Singapore have, each in their own way, achieved basic social stability primarily through economic progress since the 1960s. Their experience at least raises the possibility that Chinese in the PRC at the end of the twentieth century might permit the continuing modernization of the economy without substantial political upheaval. Chapter 12 takes up this and related questions about China's evolution in the 1990s.

12

China Faces the Future

Even though China has the world's largest population and most rapidly growing major industrial economy, it faces an uncertain future. Knowledgeable observers have predicted everything from system collapse,[1] to the development of a federal system,[2] to a fundamental renegotiation of the country's dominant cultural ethos from a northern, inward-looking, anti-imperialist world view to a southern, outward-looking, cosmopolitan world view.[3]

These uncertainties emerge from the inconsistencies in China's current situation. Officials outside Beijing regularly circumvent—and frustrate—orders from the Center. Party cadres themselves, it seems, no longer take communism seriously. The fastest growing parts of the country are along the coastal regions in the south, and their enormously rapid development has been spurred by creative tie-ins with foreign capital, especially with overseas Chinese businesses. This is no longer a country that gives even an outward appearance of the regimentation and mechanical obedience associated with Leninist party systems.

The Tiananmen protest movement in April–June 1989 revealed massive disaffection just beneath the surface, which suggests the fragility of the Chinese political system. The collapse of the Soviet Union in 1991 seems to raise the possibility that China, too, could experience huge systemic change in the near future.[4]

China's sheer complexity magnifies the uncertainties. This huge society confronts simultaneously the problems of managing teeming urban centers and scattered peasant masses. Its political system has more officials than many countries have citizens. And it is experiencing a process of urbanization that involves more people leaving the land in a shorter period than at any previous time in human history. So much seems to be changing simultaneously—the dynamics of the political system, the economy, and the society—that it is little wonder that observers cannot agree on China's future path. There is evidence to support seemingly any scenario; firm predictions are not warranted.

This concluding chapter begins by reviewing the dynamics of the Chinese political system from the apex to the relations between leaders and society. On this basis, it assesses the future evolution of the domestic system. It then turns to China's relations with the international arena. International developments have affected China's domestic agenda from the late Qing dynasty to the present. What type of international milieu does Beijing face in the 1990s? Given China's recent commitment to openness and active international engagement, what kind of international identity will it have? Will the PRC become assertive? Will it be disciplined and responsible? As explained below, the evolution of China's domestic system will play a role in shaping the answers to these questions.

Understanding Domestic Developments

The Chinese state is now driven by the need to provide higher living standards for its huge, growing population. The structures of state control constructed by Mao Zedong froze people into place, distorted information, wasted technical talent, and forced economic enterprises to assume responsibilities for nonproductive tasks, which eventually made creating enough new jobs and satisfying material wants impossible. It was not so much enlightened beneficence as calculated fear that drove the leaders of China in the late 1970s to restructure the system. The reforms have altered not only the Chinese economy but the political system as well, making it less ideological, less reliant on mass mobilization, less coercive, and less enveloping for the average citizen. It is also, notably, far less centralized.

DECENTRALIZATION AND STABILITY

One of the most important and most confusing aspects of political change during the reforms has been the decentralization of decision-making. Market-based economic development required that the locus of economic decision-making shift to lower levels of the state. For economic growth and rising living standards to provide the key to stability, localities needed the flexibility to tap their resources for local economic success. Localities have therefore gained the ability to initiate policies and adopt strategies that differ significantly from those being articulated in Beijing. In return, Beijing demands that they maintain political stability.

There is, thus, an implicit national political bargain that has been struck in China: political stability is based on rapid economic growth, which in turn requires greater flexibility at all levels of the political system. The Center allows such flexibility, as long as growth and stability are the outcomes. Localities raise the specter of instability whenever Beijing tells them to rein in economic expansion.

This national political compact has made economic success an important part of the performance evaluation of local party and government officials. Party cadres no longer must enforce political priorities such as egalitarianism; they now join fully in the effort to maximize local economic growth, as illustrated by the example of Su Zhiming in Chapter 11. This gives both party and government cadres strong incentives to circumvent those policies adopted in Beijing that might constrain local growth.

This local orientation of cadres marks a significant change from the Maoist era, when the incentives pointed up to higher levels more than down to the locality. The new local focus is strengthened by the reform strategy that seeks rapid development of collective and private enterprises. These are under local rather than central control, and their profits fund much of the local state budget.

Real decentralization has thus occurred in China under the reforms. The territorial governing bodies at provincial, municipal, county, and township levels have gained enormous initiative at the expense of the vertical functional bureaucracies that reach to Beijing—the *kuai* has gained at the expense of the *tiao,* in Chinese bureaucratic parlance. The spirit of state activity has also changed. The state no longer promotes either revolution or ideological orthodoxy. Rather, it promotes economic growth by any means that do not produce massive social and political instability.

Measured against the criteria of the Maoist system, these changes appear to weaken China's state system. If one expects conformity to central directives and uniformity in outlook and behavior, then every sign of nonconformity and local initiative seems to testify to the failures of the Center and to the potential for regime collapse. But the reforms have made this a misleading test of system resilience. The Center has come to rely on local initiative and flexibility to strengthen the regime as a whole.[5] To a certain extent, therefore, diversity now indicates adaptability, dynamism, and strength.

But where does power lie in this more decentralized system? To read the most recent empirical studies, it appears to lie almost wherever one looks. Jean Oi and Susan Whiting, for example, find that township and county level officials have become key political and economic actors. Many are highly entrepreneurial in promoting their local interests.[6] Yongnian Zheng finds that much the same is true on the provincial level.[7] How can these observations be reconciled?

Perhaps the most useful way to think about the overall Chinese system at this point is to see it as a nested system of territorial administrations, with substantial policy initiative at each territorial level: the township, county, city, province, and Center. At each level, there is much attention to garnering resources and striking deals that will benefit the locality governed by that level of state administration. Each is willing to allow lower levels to do what they wish so long as this does not upset their own plans. In the absence of formal institutional mechanisms and a legitimate constitutional framework to give this system regularity and predictability, much is sorted out in practice through consensus building and bargaining.

The result is a dynamic, variegated set of relationships that combine bargaining, organizational routines, and regulations in determining the actual behavior of officials. The particulars of this mix vary greatly across issues, locations, levels of the political system, and time periods.

THE CENTER

Despite substantial decentralization, the upper levels have by no means relinquished all power to local leaders. The Center retains important powers. The nomenklatura system assures that all provincial leaders serve at the pleasure of Beijing. Indeed, leaders at every level of the Chinese hierarchy are appointed by those at the next higher territorial level, providing a measure of discipline throughout the system.

The Center also controls substantial coercive resources. The PLA includes crack units that are loyal to Beijing and can be called in if necessary. These units receive better equipment, higher pay, and superior training, and their officers are trusted by the central leaders. Two civilian security agencies reach down to the basic levels. The public security system is by far the larger, but it is quite decentralized. The state security system, which became a separate agency in the 1980s as a vehicle to fight espionage, has remained highly centralized but has developed a nationwide "reach." In short, the leaders still enjoy the powerful organizational resources they developed to govern a communist system: control over official appointments, and armed forces that are not constrained by the niceties of law when issues of political power are at stake.

But Beijing does not rely on force alone. Despite reform, the Center retains significant leverage over the country's economy, which it exercises in part through the management of scarce resources. China's economic progress, for example, has outstripped its infrastructure development. The PRC produces only enough electricity to run less than 80 percent of its industrial capacity at any given moment. Its railways operate beyond full capacity, and coal transport takes up so much freight space that other goods have a hard time getting to distant markets. The roads are extremely poor, and the Center has just recently initiated a program to develop a national highway system. Provincial and subprovincial levels, especially in the poorer interior of the country, desperately need funds from the Center to relieve these bottlenecks in energy and transportation. Indeed, interviews with provincial officials indicate that one of Beijing's major levers is its ability to allocate scarce electric power and petroleum among the various provinces, thereby largely determining the extent of economic prosperity that any province will be able to achieve each year. These allocations are determined during negotiations that may include many other issues in central-provincial relations.

In addition to funds, the Center also is a source of expertise on economic development issues.[8] Localities have plunged into expansion of their service sectors and light industries, as these provide the most rapid returns on investment. But pressures are mounting for many locations to develop higher technology industries in the face of international and domestic competition. The Center still has a significant edge in areas of advanced research, and thus many local authorities seek technical and other assistance from the Center as they try to march up the technology ladder.

The Center can also wield some more conventional macroeconomic tools. Although now at the risk of higher degrees of popular discontent, Beijing can control growth by cutting back sharply on the money supply, as it did in 1989. It also establishes the regulatory environment by manipulating, for example, import tariffs, nontariff trade barriers, exchange-rate rules, taxation of state enterprises, and rules governing foreign direct investment. Although there is considerable slippage in the enforcement of many of these policies, they nevertheless on balance substantially influence the economy.

If all else fails, the Center can also dispatch special work teams to particular places to investigate problems and rectify local actions. These teams may conduct investigations that result in the imposition of fines, dismissal of officials, and the prosecution of offenders. Localities conduct their business with an eye to avoiding actions that might trigger a work-team investigation.[9]

Outside of the economic sphere, the degree of central authority varies by issue area.[10] Where the Center chooses to take a strong stand, such as in limiting population growth, it can produce impressive results. China's population is growing at an average rate of roughly 1.2 percent, or about fourteen million people, per year. This compares very favorably with the record of other countries at China's per capita GDP and level of urbanization. Without its birth-control effort, the PRC's population would likely grow at roughly 2.2 percent per year, producing a net population increase of over eleven million more people than currently occurs. Enforcing a stringent policy of birth control in the face of the desire of almost all peasants to have male children requires that local officials intervene in the most private activities of spouses throughout the countryside. The Center has time and again since the 1970s demonstrated its seriousness in punishing officials whose jurisdictions run afoul of birth control quotas.

Moreover the weight of Chinese history plays an intangible but significant role in enhancing the Center's role in the system. China's culture continues to instill habits of obedience and the desire for a strong, virtuous state, values that differ from the political attitudes and actions of those socialized in Western liberal societies. The political "line" emanating from the Center thus has force, not in dictating every detail of behavior but in creating a policy atmosphere that affects popular attitudes and actions. Deng Xiaoping's early 1992 "southern tour" in which he advocated faster growth, more openness, and more rapid movement toward markets, for example, had a marked effect on the activities of many officials throughout the political apparatus.

These resources combine to provide the Center with strong leverage in the system. Provincial and lower-level leaders devote great time and energy to dealing with the Center, both in seeking new resources and asking for exemptions from various centrally dictated obligations. Every provincial leader tries to balance the demands of the Center with the needs of the province, and none can afford to let the balance tip too far in either direction without paying dearly for this error.

It is at its apex that this system has changed least under the reforms. Among the top leaders, institutions do little to constrain actions, and political contention drives the system. The means available for dispute resolution are highly personalized and therefore subject to breakdown. The personal, factional nature of elite politics makes instability an ever-present possibility.

Since the Chinese system has not developed an institutional means of succession at the top, an ongoing struggle over leadership may characterize the politics of much of the 1990s. It may be difficult for any single individual to consolidate personal power during much of the decade. The struggle for power may stay within boundaries that allow continued political stability, or it may break the system apart. In either case, it is probable that, after years of political infighting and possibly a parade of leaders, by late in the decade a more stable leadership will prevail.

Regardless of the particulars of the succession struggle, two basic changes are likely to occur at the apex. First, there will be a move away from the current structure in which party elders, almost all formally retired from their executive posts, hold ultimate power of appointments and decision-making on basic strategies. This arrangement derives from the longevity of key members of the revolutionary generation, whose personal prestige, ties to the military and other power centers, and political will will not be replicated by future generations of leaders.

Second, it is likely that more highly trained people who are less committed to socialist ideology and who have greater knowledge of the international arena will lead China by the latter part of this decade. Once they achieve power, these individuals are likely to analyze and attack problems with less concern than is now seen for the ideological consequences of their policies. This does not necessarily mean that they will make wise choices or prove to be effective leaders; it also does not preclude the possibility that they will seek to whip up ardent nationalism as a vehicle for mobilizing the country's resources.

The present situation at the apex differs from the usual Western categories of political process, such as legislative, executive, and judicial powers. The same small body of leaders dominates all three sectors, and the division of labor between them results from interpersonal dynamics and the contention for power. Some institutional development at the Center has occurred, but progress remains limited. Greater professionalism and specialization in the staffing of the National People's Congress may provide the basis for a more independent legislature later in the decade.[11] The importance of that legislative body today, however, is still determined more by elite politics than by constitutional mandate.

The more fruitful questions to ask presently about the Center, therefore, are those concerning organizational capacity. Under the reforms, these capacities on balance have grown. Beijing's leaders have lost the leverage over subordinate levels that ideological commitment formerly gave them. But the changes they have made in the political system have enhanced their ability to gather information and to analyze it, through better-trained professional staffs. Because political battle at the Center is no longer a matter of life and death, the views of most participants are now allowed to be more openly aired.

The array of activities the Maoist system seemed to control from the top, in short, was illusory. Too few people with too little information and too many ideological constraints meant that, very often, broad pronouncements from the Center left considerable room for local adaptation, even as the verbal affirmations of ideological loyalty created the impression of disciplined conformity. Now the mask is off, producing a superficial impression of greater disarray, but actually strengthening the capacities of the Center for realistic decision-making.

BELOW THE CENTER

With the exception of control over the PLA, almost all the resources available to the Center are also available to each lower territorial level of the system as it deals with its subordinates. The situation regarding electricity is typical. The Center allocates provincial quotas. Provinces allocate quotas among cities and counties. Counties allocate them among townships. Townships and cities do the same among enterprises. This system allows each level to control its subordinates. Each territorial level also retains control over nomenklatura appointments, certain police and security functions, aspects of the local regulatory environment, and so forth. Generally, all want their constituent localities to prosper and to maintain stability. But this remains a system characterized by what the Chinese call powerful, interfering "mothers-in-law."

Systemic analytical capacities and information flows have improved greatly in many provinces and lower-level administrative bodies of the state. The political successions at these levels have, as detailed in Chapter 8, already taken place, and ideological blinders generally no longer preclude realistic discussion of issues. The increased flexibility resulting from the decentralization described above has probably made the system, on balance, more adaptive to local peculiarities and responsive to local strengths and weaknesses. In sum, the system capacities of the state have in many ways grown overall since the reforms began, even as the state itself has become less disciplined internally.

But society has also become more vibrant and less malleable to state initiatives since 1978. The Maoist state penetrated deep into the urban and rural social structures. By the beginning of the 1960s, it locked people into units (*danwei*) in a way that prevented them from either expressing their ideas or changing their places of work or residence. Since 1978 the state has retreated significantly from this "forward" engagement and subjugation of society. Moreover the system of all-purpose work units quickly proved incompatible with the requirements of market-oriented economic growth.

The unit system not only provided the major vehicle for the state to indoctrinate its citizens: it also kept citizens from communicating with each other. The systems of unit-based study groups, activists, informers, and party members made people careful in their remarks, and the encapsulated nature of units prevented ideas from spreading through other than official channels.[12] The erosion of the unit system, therefore, carries with it major implications: the state can no longer tightly combine control over political thought with control over the work environment and access to social welfare;[13] and ideas can now spread horizontally among the populace to an extent not experienced since the 1950s. The further erosion of ideology as a tool to encourage social conformity thus appears to be likely as these underlying changes in the way the state manages the economy and society continue.

THE PERIPHERY

Regional differentiation will continue during the course of the decade. The fastest advancing regions will probably be coastal southeast China and the lower Yangtze, from Nanjing to Shanghai, especially if the latter can maintain adequate access to electric power and clean water to support its industrial expansion. Other areas of relatively rapid expansion should include the Shandong peninsula, the Beijing-Tianjin conurbation, and the corridor from the Liaodong peninsula to Shenyang. For the most part, distinctively different foreign economic links will characterize each of these various rapid growth regions: Hong Kong with the southeast, especially Guangdong; Taiwan with the southeast, especially Fujian; Korea with Shandong; and Japan/Korea with the Liaodong/Shenyang corridor. The Beijing/Tianjin and the lower Yangtze regions will feature more of a mix.

Some observers have suggested that this growing regional differentiation may produce either fundamental changes in the nature of the country or an actual division of China into separate smaller countries.[14] One variant of this analysis has southeastern China developing such strong economic ties with Hong Kong and Taiwan that it pulls away from the mainland, becoming a dynamic economic force on its own. Very extensive economic relations have in fact developed across the Hong Kong/Guangdong border and on both sides of the Taiwan Strait. But for reasons assessed on pp. 323–27 below, barring some cataclysmic national crisis that produces a collapse of the entire national political apparatus, there is little prospect that this economic phenomenon will lead to the development of a fully integrated Hong Kong/Taiwan/southeast China entity or that such an entity would divide off from the rest of the country.

China nevertheless does have serious concerns about some of its western territories. Roughly 95 percent of the country's population lives in the southeast half of its territory. The northwest half is populated primarily with minorities, some of whom are only poorly integrated into the national culture.[15]

In this context, the recent growth of Islamic fundamentalism in western Asia concerns Beijing. The most critical area is the former Soviet central Asia—Kazakhstan, Tadzhikistan, Kirghizistan, Uzbekistan, and Turkmenistan, of which the first three border China's Xinjiang Province. With the collapse of the USSR, the future religious and political currents within this region are unknown. Beijing fears that Islamic fundamentalism will take root in one or more of these locales and, from there, will spread across the border into Xinjiang, a province with millions of Muslims who have only weak allegiances to China. Afghanistan, which has become a training ground for Islamic fundamentalist groups, also worries Beijing. Xinjiang's Muslims inhabit a vast, sparsely populated area that contains large deposits of oil and minerals. China does not wish to see this region unsettled by ethnic strife and violence.

Tibet is also located in this sparsely populated northwest half of the PRC. High in the Himalayas, the Tibet Autonomous Region is far from Han Chinese areas both geographically and culturally. Beijing took control of this area in 1951 through an agreement that the Dalai Lama, Tibet's spiritual leader, signed under pressure. In 1959 a Tibetan revolt against Chinese rule failed, and the Dalai Lama fled into India, where he has ever since maintained an exile movement.

The Dalai Lama has traveled the world in search of support for efforts to maintain Tibet's indigenous Buddhist culture and distinct identity. In the 1990s he has achieved some measure of success: Presidents Bush and Clinton spoke with him in the White House compound, although neither gathering was designated an "official" meeting; he has been welcomed by governments in several countries in Western Europe; and he has received the Nobel Peace Prize.

Within Tibet, there is virtually universal support among native inhabitants for the return of the Dalai Lama as leader of a highly autonomous or fully independent nation. No foreign country recognizes Tibet as an independent entity, however, and all Chinese, including those on Taiwan, claim it as an integral part of China. Beijing's fear is that the Dalai Lama's quasidiplomatic successes may cause the Tibetan people to increase their proindependence activities and possibly to gain greater sympathy from abroad. To be sure, Beijing will not relinquish its control over Tibet peacefully. But the costs of maintaining that control may grow significantly.

Developments in the Mongolian People's Republic (MPR, often called Outer Mongolia) also worry Beijing. The border between China's Inner Mongolian Autonomous Region (IMAR) and the MPR is almost literally a line in the sand across the Gobi Desert. In 1991 the MPR conducted its first democratic elections. The economic conditions in the MPR have subsequently deteriorated. China worries, nevertheless, that political dynamics in the MPR could spill over the border and influence the thinking of ethnic Mongols in the IMAR. Given Beijing's strong opposition to real democratic movements, it would regard this as a security threat.

The reforms have thus encouraged centripetal forces in China. Beijing itself has promoted greater regional diversity, supporting cross-border tie-ins with the various countries around the PRC's periphery. But these developments are sharpening separate regional identities and thus potentially threaten the nation's territorial integrity. Perhaps because the Han Chinese make up the overwhelming majority of the populace and are concentrated in the eastern part of China, China often seems to be an ethnically homogenous country. But there are considerable regional differences among the Han. In addition, the PRC is in reality a multinational empire with extensive, sparsely settled border regions. It faces a challenge in the 1990s of maintaining national cohesion while permitting reform to continue to go forward.

THE NEAR ABROAD

The term "near abroad" is sometimes used in Russia to refer to those countries that until 1991 were joined with Russia to form the Soviet Union. Many regard these newly independent countries as less than sovereign entities, even as they recognize that they are no longer under Moscow's direct rule. We borrow the term to describe China's unusual relations with Hong Kong and Taiwan.

Throughout this volume, we have discussed post-1949 "China" as the territory under the direct administrative control of the leadership in Beijing. In the early 1990s, there is increasing discussion of a "Greater China," larger than the current PRC. This is a term without a precise meaning; analysts have used it in different ways.[16] Broadly though, it calls attention to the increasing interaction among the economies of the PRC, Hong Kong, and Taiwan, and the increasing role of overseas Chinese capital from throughout Southeast Asia in the development of the PRC.

Speaking of a Greater China that brings together the PRC and its "near abroad," Hong Kong and Taiwan, one author argues that, "Early in the twenty-first century the combined gross domestic product of Greater China will surpass those of the European Community and the United States; . . . it will be the world's largest consumer; it will garrison the world's largest military establishment; and it may be the preeminent member of the Group of Nine nations (including Russia)."[17]

There is little question that a country that successfully merged the resources, skills, and wealth currently resident in the PRC, Hong Kong, and Taiwan would be a major power on the world stage. The increasing movement of capital and people between Hong Kong and Taiwan and between both and the PRC,[18] combined with the fact that Hong Kong will revert to PRC sovereignty in mid-1997, appears to make the prospect of a country that encompasses all three locales increasingly realistic. But appearances may be deceiving.

China and Hong Kong

Hong Kong basically consists of two parts: the island and a small area of the mainland, which Britain obtained in the settlement of the Opium War in the 1840s, and a substantial adjacent area of the mainland that Britain leased in the 1890s for ninety-nine years. Britain has run both parts as a Crown Colony throughout the twentieth century. But the lease on the major part of Hong Kong's territory expires in 1997, and Britain has determined that the remainder is not viable as a separate entity. The entire domain will, therefore, revert to China on 1 July 1997 and will become the Hong Kong Special Administrative Region. During the 1980s Beijing and London negotiated the terms of the transfer, including stipulations for the period leading up to and following 1997.

The political relationship between the British and Beijing over Hong Kong is tense as of 1994. Broadly speaking, Hong Kong governor Chris Patten is seeking to increase the extent to which democracy is practiced there before 1997, while Beijing prefers to take over a less democratic political system. Even in the midst of the resulting political fracas, though, Hong Kong's entrepreneurs have continued to develop extensive economic ties with southeast China. As of 1994, indeed, Hong Kong's economic health is integrally tied to the economic growth of the Guangdong region, and Guangdong itself would suffer grievously if Hong Kong's economy were to collapse. There is extensive capital investment in both directions. The area that will become the Hong Kong Special Administrative Region provides China with critical expertise, wonderful harbor facilities, and numerous economic opportunities.

But domestic developments in China could spell trouble for Hong Kong. The Hong Kong-Guangdong border is becoming increasingly porous, and corruption in China is spilling across the border and affecting economic practices in Hong Kong. Corruption is hardly a new phenomenon in the colony. But starting in 1971 the British government took strong measures to tamp it down, especially as regards the police establishment. Those police forces will revert to Chinese control in 1997, though; evidence suggests that the forces on the Guangdong side of the border are already deeply tainted by corruption.

In broad terms, Hong Kong will operate in a more Chinese fashion after 1997. This probably means that its legal system, currently one of the pillars of Hong Kong's economic success, will become less independent and reliable. It may also mean that its press will become less free. And it is quite possible that Chinese firms with extensive investments in Hong Kong will enjoy major economic advantages that damage the local economy's competitive position.

Indeed, one of the keys to Hong Kong's economic success has been the extent to which it has been willing to let the market determine winners and losers in most fields. Failure to compete effectively generally means quick bankruptcy, and this market discipline has been important for keeping Hong Kong's economy vibrant even though the colony itself has virtually no natural resources and a population of over six million people.

If by 1997 the PRC still has not learned to permit the failure of politically powerful noncompetitive enterprises, this might spill over into Beijing's treatment of Hong Kong's economy. After 1997 Hong Kong's governor will be appointed directly by Beijing and will not be under the Guangdong provincial authorities. A strong government role in the economy could, over time, reduce Hong Kong's economic prospects.

Finally, domestic unrest in China could have profound repercussions in Hong Kong after reversion. Chinese fleeing unrest could stream into the Special Administrative Region. Hong Kong residents with foreign passports and foreign businesses could quickly abandon the region and move their capital abroad, producing severe economic shocks. Beijing's plan to station troops in the middle of Hong Kong's core business areas will in all likelihood heighten tensions.

There are high stakes riding on China's handling of Hong Kong. Japan and the United States have a great deal of money invested there; major unrest would quickly involve those countries in some fashion. America in particular will be sensitive to any human rights violations, such as political arrests and suppression of press freedom. Finally, Taiwan will closely watch the developments in Hong Kong after reversion. Should the process go seriously awry, the chances of Taiwan's and the PRC's peaceful reunification, already small, would diminish greatly, and the chances of Taiwan's declaring itself formally independent would grow. Such a development would almost certainly lead to some sort of diplomatic and military response from Beijing, sharply escalating tensions throughout the region.

Hong Kong's reversion thus holds both opportunity and danger for Beijing. Successful management of this issue will reassure foreign investors, contribute to the Chinese economy, potentially improve the prospects of eventual reunification with Taiwan, and build additional bridges to the United States and Japan. But domestic developments in China, both nationally and in the Guangdong region, could spill over into Hong Kong in highly unsettling fashion, with unfavorable consequences for China's foreign relations and participation in the global economy.[19]

China and Taiwan

Since 1987, Taiwan's economic ties with the mainland have proliferated, most visibly in the Xiamen region of Fujian Province, just across the hundred-mile wide strait from Taiwan.[20] Investors from Taiwan are using the mainland much as their Hong Kong counterparts use Guangdong: they are shifting the labor-intensive portions of their operations to China, where land and labor are still relatively cheap. This division of resources efficiently utilizes the endowments of both sides. But as in Hong Kong, political developments may limit the scope of economic complementarity.

After Chiang Kai-shek and his closest followers retreated to Taiwan in 1949, they continued to proclaim that theirs was the only legitimate government of all of China, with the rule over the mainland "temporarily usurped by communist bandits." Although Beijing rejected this claim, it nevertheless shared Taiwan's commitment to one China. During these years, Taiwan refused formal relations with any country that also recognized Beijing. Beijing, for its part, adopted the same attitude. Indeed, into the 1970s, the GMD firmly asserted its commitment to "gloriously retake the mainland."

But the GMD faced a fundamental political problem in Taiwan: the 90 percent of the population that is Taiwanese resented political domination by the other 10 percent who had fled there from the mainland. Chiang Kai-shek proved willing to permit the Taiwanese full participation in the economy, but he maintained a highly authoritarian political system that excluded them from power. The Guomindang thus insisted that people on Taiwan could vote only for provincial positions on the island. All "national" positions would remain in the hands of those elected in the 1947 election on the mainland until a new election in all provinces could be held. The ravages of age alone made such a posture increasingly untenable, as the original mainlanders died off.

To accommodate to these changing political conditions, in the 1980s Chiang Ching-kuo, the son of and successor to Chiang Kai-shek, began a process of "Taiwanization" in which he elevated native Taiwanese to key positions. One of these, Lee Teng-hui, eventually succeeded Chiang as head of the GMD and president of Republic of China on Taiwan.

Lee pursued not only further Taiwanization but also real democratization of Taiwan. He lifted the martial law that had been imposed for three decades, permitted a free press to develop, and allowed non-GMD candidates to campaign and contest elections. Lee felt that Taiwan's population had achieved a level of wealth, education, and sophistication such that long-term political stability would require greater democratization. It will be many years before citizens in the PRC match the per capita levels of wealth, urbanization, and education that encouraged Lee to nurture democratic competition.

In the early stages of Taiwan's electoral competition, the opposition identified itself simply as "outside the party" *(dangwai),* as formal opposition parties were still banned. The GMD eventually legalized other political party organizations, though, and the major opposition to the Guomindang in 1994 comes from a party called the Democratic Progressive party *(Minjindang).* The Democratic Progressive party has a strong Taiwanese identification and might declare the island's independence should it assume power.

The development of an increasingly vibrant democracy on Taiwan and the Taiwanization of the Guomindang since the late 1980s have Beijing worried. Because the vast majority of Taiwan's voters are Taiwanese, the Guomindang has had to make itself more attractive to Taiwanese as it has permitted expansion of the number of offices directly subject to the vote. By 1996 at the latest, all positions on Taiwan, including the presidency, should be subject to direct or indirect election by the people living on the island.

In line with these domestic changes, the Guomindang has sought ways to integrate Taiwan into the international arena. It has wrestled with various names by which it might identify Taiwan in international organizations and has, especially since the late 1980s, made diplomatic gains in various bilateral ties by pursuing a policy of what it terms "flexible diplomacy." This policy encourages development of all types of ties regardless of the other country's relations with Beijing.[21]

The internal political dynamics on Taiwan might lead over time to a formal declaration of Taiwan's independence. The Democratic Progressive party already embraces such a declaration in its party platform. The GMD recognizes that Taiwan is de facto independent and encourages other countries to treat it as such. Eventually the GMD may feel that for electoral reasons it must announce Taiwan's de jure independence. Any such move would create a crisis with Beijing. At a minimum this would disrupt the growing economic cooperation on both sides of the Taiwan Strait. At worst there is the risk of open conflict over clashing nationalist claims.

In both Taiwan and Hong Kong, in sum, although economic and technological trends strongly encourage growing integration, political uncertainties cloud the picture.[22] The component parts of a "Greater China" may act cohesively to exert great influence in the global economy of the late 1990s, but as of 1994 that outcome remains very much in doubt.

TENSIONS

China's implicit national political bargain is based on a flawed premise: that rapid economic growth will largely suffice to maintain political and social stability. Rapid growth can be a palliative by enlarging the national pie and demonstrating that governmental policies can produce results. But many of China's current problems have been created by a system that has become an almost unstoppable engine for growth. Among the strains generated by growth are massive movements of people off the land, internal migration, reductions in job security, and growing regional inequalities. Growth, moreover, may run up against environmental constraints, especially in the water shortages that plague so many Chinese cities. China is not likely, in short, to find rapid economic expansion an adequate device to dampen social tensions as this decade wears on.

The current transition from a command economy to a market economy will add its own set of problems. Unemployment will increase, at least in the short run, and corruption will likely spread. In abandoning the *danwei* as the vehicle for meeting state goals in health care, housing, pensions, job security, recreation, dispute mediation, rationing, and security, severe social and economic stresses will result from the inevitable missteps. The creation of a commercial housing market, for example, will raise nettlesome and contentious issues of equity in the distribution of the current housing stock.

The current transitional nature of the economy adds further complications. Major swings in the business cycle will continue, producing the strains of inflation during expansionary times and job loss during consolidation periods. The negotiated economy that characterizes partial reform, moreover, will continue to produce conditions that feed corruption.

China in the mid-1990s, in short, cannot avoid confronting the severe strains of transition from one type of system to another. The leaders' fear of instability will remain well grounded under even the best of circumstances.

CONCLUSION

China likely faces a tumultuous period during the remainder of the 1990s. If political contention at the apex of the system provides the necessary "space," tens of millions of people may voice their frustrations in the only way the system provides for mass political participation: through street demonstrations and protests. In the 1930s Mao Zedong popularized the phrase that, "A single spark can ignite a prairie fire." Open political stalemate at the apex of the system could provide that spark. But the resulting firestorm of discontent would probably not force a collapse of the national political system. It would probably instead quickly die down, quelled by the state's repressive response.

The system, nevertheless, will change. Some significant new policies should accompany the political succession. Policies favoring greater social welfare typically accompany successions in communist countries,[23] and the policy changes that are driven by succession politics may be more wide ranging than that. Rising incomes, at least in major cities in the coastal regions, will produce greater pressures for meaningful political participation, especially as China's telecommunications services expand with this growth. As market forces take hold, it will be surprising if efforts to form independent trade unions do not appear—efforts that will almost certainly trigger repression, at least at the start, by the political authorities.

The state can and probably will employ a range of strategies to fend off challenges from a developing society. It is likely, for example, to recognize and support social organizations, on the condition that those organizations do not challenge the state itself. With an increasingly sophisticated and differentiated society, the state will need to find creative ways to give people some voice in the system.

In other Asian countries this problem has led to the development of what might be called "dominant party authoritarian systems." In such systems, only one political party has a realistic possibility of holding political power, but one or more other parties are allowed to organize support, contest elections, and articulate the views of discontented groups. This approach enhances political stability by giving dissatisfied groups a vehicle for participating in the system itself. It also gives the ruling authorities important additional information about attitudes and trends in society with which they must cope. Dominant party authoritarian systems existed in Japan from the mid-1950s to 1993 and in South Korea, Taiwan, and Singapore during the 1980s and into the early 1990s. Eventually, such systems tend to evolve toward more truly democratic multiparty polities, but the evolution may take decades. It would likely be a drawn-out process in China.

Any shift toward a dominant party or a "one-and-a-half party" authoritarian system would require the CCP to drop its claim to monopoly power based on communist ideology. There is some precedent for this, since the PRC has all along permitted more than a half-dozen minor parties to exist under the "leadership" of the CCP. None of these has ever exercised power, but their role in the 1980s and early 1990s has grown slightly.[24] The ideological underpinning of the CCP to date, the commitment to "socialism," is already a hollow slogan in the China of 1994. This term has been tarnished by past failures and tragedies, and it in any case no longer links China up with "vanguard" countries in an international political movement. Although the CCP is unlikely to repudiate socialism, it is very possible that appeals to socialist goals will fade into oblivion during the remainder of the decade. In official documents and in speeches at major party conclaves, goals will be articulated in terms of market development, modernization of the economy, and enhancing personal well being and national strength. "Socialism" may cease to serve as a term of reference.

China's new political leaders, like their predecessors, will want some moral framework to bolster their rule and energize the country during hard times. The PRC differs fundamentally from Singapore, Hong Kong, and Taiwan in its extraordinarily extensive rural areas and large regional differences; it is extremely unlikely to prove successful in maintaining stability through creating a nation of "economic animals." It will need something more as a cohesive force, and most likely China's leaders will turn to some form of nationalism to meet this need.

How they cast that nationalism will be telling. It may be open and inclusive, essentially an assertion of pride in the success of "Chinese" (*huaren* or *xiaren,* suggesting a broad cultural notion of identity) in Asian and global terms. This type of nationalism would permit the growing regional diversity that will characterize China's future and would see the successes of Hong Kong, Taiwan, and even Singapore as sources of pride and legitimacy on the Chinese mainland. There has been some movement toward this type of nationalism during the past decade. Enormous investments in the PRC by wealthy Chinese in Hong Kong, Taiwan, and elsewhere in Asia during the 1990s are strengthening this development.

But China's nationalism may also turn strident and exclusive if a strong hand is needed to control the pressures building up from the relative losers in the economic development effort: the unemployed and those whose job security is threatened; the urban poor; residents of the disadvantaged hinterland; and so forth. This type of nationalism would likely be more statist, stressing the Chinese state *(zhongguo)* as a sovereign entity and attempting to sublimate dissatisfactions over social strains into ardent affirmation of national sovereignty, indignation at the treachery of enemies, and muscular assertiveness toward the many unresolved territorial disputes around the PRC's borders. This more statist nationalism would entail increased domestic use of police methods and serious attempts to tighten discipline through strident antiforeign propaganda. Although this path would not portend a reimposition of totalitarian controls, it would prove significantly harsher than a continuation of reform and an "open" nationalism.

In sum, China is unlikely to experience either national disintegration or the full development of democracy during the 1990s. The system should, however, evolve significantly, and popular pressures for greater participation will increase. While uncertainties abound, it appears that on balance China in the late 1990s will grow more open, decentralized, corrupt, regionally and socially diverse, militarily powerful, and socially tempestuous.

The faces of Chinese nationalism remind us that China does not exist in a vacuum. It is affected in many ways by international trends, and its domestic developments reverberate beyond the PRC's borders. We conclude our analysis by looking at China and the international arena.

China and the World

China is now at an uneasy transition stage in its relations with the rest of the world. It feels deeply the scars of being looked down upon by the industrial powers for a century and a half, and many patriotic Chinese have felt angry, defiant, uncertain, discouraged, and ambivalent toward both the West and their own history. China is not currently threatened by external aggression; most countries, in fact, are courting China. Its recent trajectory of economic development has created a global perception that it will become a driving force in Asian politics and a potential great power on the world scene during the coming decade. Nevertheless, China's leaders and people are just beginning to view themselves less as victims and more as constructive, secure participants in a complex international arena.

The international arena has impinged upon China's domestic agenda since the 1800s. The political and military pressures imposed by the industrial powers were the catalyst in turning a classic dynastic decline into a revolution at the beginning of the twentieth century. The Guomindang's failure to ward off the Japanese undermined its legitimacy and strengthened the position of the communists. Once in power, the CCP argued that only a socioeconomic revolution would gird the country to withstand foreign aggression and humiliation. China's success in fighting the United Nations forces to a standstill in the Korean War (1950–53) conferred prestige on the new government domestically, giving the people hope that their long decades of humiliation by stronger foreign military forces would finally come to an end.

It is difficult to demarcate the line between domestic and foreign politics in China since 1949. As a continent-sized country ruled by revolutionary leaders who hailed mostly from the interior, China remained largely cut off from the outside world. By the mid-1950s the new government had set up bureaucratic bodies that monopolized China's limited foreign trade. Domestic upheavals consumed the time and attention of leaders and led alike through the 1950s and 1960s. But a large question of international import remained: how could China achieve the wealth, power, and moral stature to stand tall among nations?

There have been deep connections between China's views of itself and the world throughout its history. Imperial China, convinced of its superior civilization, was content to stand above the world. During China's years of humiliation in the nineteenth and early twentieth centuries, many Chinese traced the country's weakness to the nature of its civilization.[25] After 1949, the domestic and the international remained intertwined. Thus Mao announced that with the formation of the PRC, "China has stood up." The domestic and the international aspects of policy became fused at the core of Chinese politics.

China nevertheless had to play a difficult diplomatic game (see Table 12.1). When the CCP won nationwide power, the new revolutionary government faced a bipolar world entrenched in a Cold War.[26] Mao quickly sealed an alliance with the USSR and sought both development with Soviet aid and security under the Soviet Union's nuclear umbrella. By late 1950 the PRC's forces faced US-lead United Nations troops on the Korean peninsula.[27] The Sino-Soviet alliance frayed in the late 1950s, and broke by the early 1960s, in part because of severe disagreements concerning how best to handle the threat posed by the United States.[28]

During most of the 1960s, China was the only major country in the world that dared to challenge both the Soviet Union and the United States. Mao's estimation of the resulting security threat was such that he felt China had to prepare to lose massive territory to invading foreign military forces. He therefore ordered the military to make plans to fight from bases in the southwest, much as the Guomindang had done to hold out against the Japanese. To this end, Mao had the PRC carry out a large-scale "third front" investment drive to build military-related industries in the hinterlands of Yunnan, Guizhou, and Sichuan from 1964 to 1971, even as the Cultural Revolution tore the country apart.[29]

The Soviet threat to China probably peaked in 1969–71, when border clashes took hundreds of lives and Moscow orchestrated a nuclear war scare against Beijing. Mao quickly improved relations with the US so as to fend off this looming Soviet threat. The Nixon administration, itself anxious to box in the Russians and to put pressure on Hanoi to allow an honorable end to the Vietnam war, proved willing to nurture a rapprochement with Beijing in the early 1970s. Triangular US-USSR-PRC politics became the order of the day, with China by far the weakest of the three players in this diplomatic and strategic game.

The accession of Mikhail Gorbachev to power in Moscow in 1985 and his reform initiatives—including determined efforts to reduce tensions with the US and to dampen the arms race—substantially scaled back whatever benefits

TABLE 12.1 *China's Great Power Enemies*

PRIMARY ADVERSARIAL RELATIONSHIP	APPROX. YEARS
USA	1950s
USA and USSR	1960s
USSR	1970s–mid-1980s
None	Since late 1980s

Beijing could derive from the political logic of the "strategic triangle." But during this period China's own reforms began to provide it with a new source of international prestige as the leading reformist country among the world's communist regimes. As a result leaders such as Deng Xiaoping achieved global reputations as visionaries and boldly effective pragmatists who were changing the future trends of the world.

But then came 1989. The highly visible repression in and around Beijing's Tiananmen Square in June of that year dashed China's reformist image and brought sanctions from most industrialized countries. Damaging Beijing's position still more, during the last half of 1989 virtually every communist regime in East Europe collapsed without bloodshed,[30] and the USSR began the slide toward its own eventual dissolution in 1991. Suddenly, China's international position had changed. Whereas in early 1989 it still enjoyed the prestige of being the most boldly reforming communist country, by early 1990 it was widely regarded as an international outlaw, ruled by retrograde communists who would massacre their own citizens in order to maintain their outmoded grip on power.

Beijing made a slow climb back to respectability in 1990 and 1991, based primarily on moderate, astute diplomacy. In 1992 there came another turning point. Deng Xiaoping's "southern tour" and the burst of economic activity it sparked catapulted the PRC into a far more prominent position in the international arena. As the successor states to the former Soviet Union experienced economic decline and social disorder, China seemed to stand out for its rapid growth, basic social stability, and steady approach to international issues. Increasingly, the international media began to refer to China as a looming superpower whose growth potential defied imagination.

CURRENT POSTURE AND FUTURE CHALLENGES

The PRC already possesses some of the trappings of a global power. It is a member of the United Nations' Permanent Five (the US, Russia, France, England, and China), each of whom has a veto over decisions by the UN Security Council; it possesses its own nuclear arsenal and the means to deliver it by missile and aircraft; and it is treated as an important participant in most major international financial institutions, including the World Bank, the International Monetary Fund (IMF), and the Asian Development Bank. In 1993, moreover, the IMF determined that the PRC has, in terms of real purchasing power, the third largest economy in the world, after the United States and Japan. China also has the world's largest armed forces.

The PRC is considered a major regional power in East Asia, which is in turn the most rapidly advancing global region. Other Asian countries regard China, with its expanding economy, as an engine of growth for the entire area. They also recognize that in the future China may dominate the region militarily. All other governments in the region take great care in their dealings with the Chinese. They recognize its growing potential for good and for mischief.

Within Asia, China has played a constructive role on key issues during the early 1990s. In 1993, for example, it helped bring about a stable settlement of the civil war in Cambodia, and Beijing has tried to dissuade North Korea from acquiring nuclear weapons. But China may also be disruptive. It still has territorial disputes with many of its neighbors, and its handling of these disputes could have a substantial influence on the levels of tension throughout the region. The Spratly Islands in the South China Sea is one of the most sensitive of these disputed areas, as the PRC, Taiwan, the Philippines, Malaysia, Brunei, and Vietnam all have overlapping and competing claims. China's assertive posture here, supported by its development of relevant naval and air capabilities, is increasing tension considerably throughout the area and could spark a reactive arms race in the region.[31]

In this first post–Cold War decade, China remains too weak to play the role of a superpower capable of shaping its international environment to its own interests. But in the currently fragmented international arena Beijing does control the material and military resources to significantly affect particular issues and their outcomes. Moreover, with its security council veto, China is pivotal in determining the role the UN will play in the post–Cold War world. It is a country to be reckoned with.

And Asia—at least East Asia—is a region of considerable importance. The weight of Asia in the international arena has grown to be largely coequal with North America and Western Europe. This marks the first time since the start of the industrial revolution that non-Western countries sit at the table of global politics as equals with the great powers of the West. Tensions will follow as adjustments are made and a new balance struck.

China's strength and prestige have soared in recent years along with its rate of growth. When a country with 22 percent of the globe's population achieves real rates of economic expansion of more than 12 percent per year, everybody takes notice and accommodates to the changes underway. The recent reforms have elevated China to a stronger international position than at any earlier time in the twentieth century.

Looking to the future, China probably faces a reasonably benign security environment for the remainder of the decade. Beijing periodically voices fears of Japanese rearmament, Russian disintegration, and American bullying, but none of these is likely to confront China with a major military challenge during the 1990s. The longer term situation, however, may prove more dangerous for the PRC, whose neighbors are beginning to respond to China's burgeoning defense budgets with their own military build-ups. Besides the general sense of instability that such a trend may create, there are two more immediate issues that could compromise regional security.

The first is North Korea's attempt to build a nuclear bomb. If Pyongyang is successful, South Korea, Japan, and perhaps even Taiwan might respond by developing their own nuclear capabilities. This increases the danger of military conflict on the Korean peninsula, a prospect deeply worrying to everyone in the region, including Beijing.

A second unsettling possibility is a declaration of independence by Taiwan. If Taiwan should make such a declaration, Beijing would likely feel obligated to respond. It could impose a military blockade through use of submarines, which may, in turn, elicit a diplomatic or military response by the United States. Although both the North Korean and Taiwan scenarios are highly speculative, it is noteworthy that prognoses of a benign security environment for China in the last half of the 1990s presume that neither will reach the crisis stage.

Domestic unrest may also upset China's international position in this decade. Major political instability would be met with repression, which could sour China's diplomatic ties in Asia and elsewhere. More fundamentally, domestic troubles could turn China's leaders toward the inward looking, state-oriented nationalism noted above. Such a development would greatly increase the regional fears of a resurgent China, and might accelerate an arms build-up throughout the area. It would also increase the chances of major disruption accompanying the 1997 takeover of Hong Kong, and of Taiwan's choosing to distance itself still more from the mainland.

Should China's security situation remain nonthreatening and its domestic situation basically stable, Beijing is likely to pursue a reasonably constructive diplomatic game for the remainder of the 1990s. It has already proven that it can be a good citizen in international organizations. The World Bank considers China a model borrower, while at the United Nations Beijing has cast its votes with care. China will want to continue to attract foreign investment and to prevent the emergence of trading blocks that might reduce its economic access to North America and Western Europe. Within Asia, it will place high priority on maintaining good relations with Tokyo, especially as Japan is the major contributor of foreign aid to China and is also the major economic power in Asia with which Beijing must both cooperate and compete.

There is, thus, a reasonable possibility—albeit far short of certainty—that the rest of the 1990s will see China play a constructive role in the international arena, based on its desire to give economic development top priority. But how disciplined will the PRC be as an international actor? Put differently, how effectively will Beijing be able to control the actions of China's localities and citizens? To what extent will the erosion of internal discipline that has occurred since the late 1970s affect the PRC's international performance? We take up this issue in three specific contexts: adherence to economic agreements; military developments; and international crime. In each of these arenas, China's domestic developments threaten to cast a shadow over at least some of Beijing's international policies.

International Economic Issues

The history of the PRC clearly shows that China must develop strong, wide-ranging ties to the international economic arena in order to prosper. During the 1950s the USSR provided China some aid, gave the PRC valuable technology, and served as a political and economic model for China's own forced-draft industrial development. China's real debt to the Soviets was enormous, and its economy developed rapidly with Soviet tutelage and assistance.[32]

For most of the 1960s, China proceeded on its own and its economic performance was unimpressive.[33] The PRC's strategic opening to the West and Japan in the 1970s expanded by the end of that decade to include imports of goods, know-how, and ideas. These have made a substantial contribution toward the improvements in productivity since the start of the reforms in 1978.[34] In sum, the PRC's economy has done well when it has utilized foreign inputs, and it has fared poorly when it has cut itself off from the international arena.

Beijing now seeks fully to join the international trade system as a component of its reform strategy for economic development. It has already taken important steps, and made major progress, in pursuing this goal. As previously mentioned, China has become an active participant in the major multinational financial institutions (World Bank, IMF, Asian Development Bank).[35] It has also accepted international conventions on copyrights and patents. And it has negotiated numerous bilateral trade agreements that provide for standard tariff treatments, labeling and other standards, and so forth. The most comprehensive of these is the October 1992 "market access" Memorandum of Understanding with the United States. Beijing seeks to join the General Agreement on Trade and Tariffs (GATT) by 1995, which should provide China with some protections against discriminatory tariff treatment.[36]

Somewhat ironically, while China's reforms provide the impetus for Beijing to seek these agreements, these same reforms limit Beijing's ability to assure that China will comply fully with the agreements it signs. As of 1994, despite orders from Beijing, for example, various Chinese localities are permitting some of their industries to put false labels of origin on their products. Thus, textiles produced in Shanghai may be labeled as if they were made in Honduras and then shipped to Honduras for reexport to the US as a "Honduran" product. In this way, the Chinese manufacturer can avoid the limits on Chinese textile exports to the US agreed upon by Beijing and Washington. Such false labeling is illegal but is also difficult for Beijing to police.

A similar problem arises with exports of products made by prison labor. China uses forced labor as a means of punishment for various types of offenders. American law prohibits imports of such products, and Beijing has agreed to ban their export. But as of 1994 various provinces and locales still actively connive in such exports from their own prisons, despite Beijing's disapproval.

China's economic decentralization and its attendant corruption thus call into question Beijing's future ability to abide by trade agreements. The offending activities by local authorities are properly laid at Beijing's door by the injured foreign country. Such problems are likely to grow during the remainder of the 1990s, upsetting China's bilateral trade relationships and possibly troubling the PRC's entry into the GATT/World Trade Organization and its participation in some other multilateral trade regimes.

On the other hand, the opportunities China's economic growth create for foreign sales and investment (both via exports to the PRC and via production by foreign-invested firms there) make the PRC an alluring market and add to its clout as it seeks to engage the international economy more fully. In 1993 foreign investment in China was five times larger than such investment in the United States; indeed, China became the world's largest absorber of foreign direct investment for that year.

The PRC is developing an immense country from the ground up and is doing so at a time of predicted slow-to-moderate economic growth among the economies of the industrialized countries. Overall this should make China a highly sought-after participant in the international economy of the 1990s, and it should make available to the PRC the kinds of technology and levels of capital investment needed to sustain rapid growth and productivity gains. As China grows, its economic performance and levels of trade will become significant factors, both positive and negative, in the global economy; by the year 2000, for example, there may be a 1.8 million barrel per day increase in China's drain on international oil markets.[37] Beijing will as a consequence have to become a regular participant in the various multinational consultative forums to reduce the inevitable frictions and concerns produced by its growing ability to affect the economic prosperity of others.

The Security Environment

From the 1950s to the 1970s, China became an important player in the great power politics of the Cold War, with all its attendant risks. The United States directly or indirectly threatened China with nuclear attack in 1953 and again in 1958. Taiwan, Beijing felt, threatened invasion in 1962. And the USSR orchestrated a nuclear scare in 1969. Then in the 1980s, Deng Xiaoping gradually shifted China to a position of reasonably good relations with both Moscow and Washington.[38] In 1984, Deng declared that the PRC could achieve peace for the rest of the century through astute diplomacy, and he then cut back substantially on the size of the armed forces and the defense budget. Defense expenditure trends since 1989 have, however, been upward, with an increase in real defense spending of roughly 70 percent from 1988 to 1994.

Despite its relatively favorable current military security environment, the PRC as of 1994 maintains the largest armed forces in the world. The collapse of the Soviet Union has, moreover, enabled Beijing to purchase key military technologies from a cash-strapped Russia, and China is taking advantage of that opportunity. Some of this military buildup likely reflects no more than an outgrowth of China's increasing wealth. But with military spending growing at a pace that far outstrips the PRC's overall economic growth, several additional factors must be playing a role: civilian politicians may fear refusing military requests when the PLA leadership could play an important role in the succession to Deng Xiaoping; the PLA itself wants to acquire expensive high-technology weaponry after seeing the ease with which advanced Western weapons overpowered their more numerous but low-technology Iraqi counterparts during Operation Desert Storm in 1991; and China may envision itself as playing a larger political role in Asian and global affairs and seeks the force projection capability to undergird this new position.

Other countries in Asia have watched these developments closely and see a more powerful China with which they will have to contend. In turn almost all other countries in the region have become anxious to see the United States maintain good ties with China and a strong military posture in the area so as to limit potential security problems with the PRC.

One of America's most important global foreign-policy concerns in the post–Cold War era is the proliferation of weapons of mass destruction and their means of delivery. This has become an increasingly important source of friction between the US and China in recent years, with Washington periodically accusing Beijing of selling technology and components for missiles, nuclear weapons, and chemical weaponry to other nations, destabilizing regional relations. Ironically, just as China's growing overall international importance stems from the successes of its reforms, many of its problems with the US over proliferation stem from the dynamics of precisely these same reform initiatives.[39]

China's stance on the sale of weapons and military technology is influenced by three aspects of reform politics: changes in national priorities and the distribution of authority; changes in the funding of military development; and the emergence of a "princes' party" (previously described in Chapter 9).

International attention first focused on Chinese foreign military sales in October 1987 when Iran fired Chinese Silkworm missiles at oil tankers in the Persian Gulf. Before the reforms, China had sold only small amounts of weapons abroad, roughly US $114 million in 1977. During the 1980s, though, military sales abroad became an important source of income, totaling about US $3.5 billion in 1988. China had become one of the world's leading arms merchants. A substantial portion of China's arms sales from 1983 to 1987 went to both sides in the Iran-Iraq war. But the end of that conflict, combined with the poor showing of Iraq's Chinese- and Soviet-supplied weapons against advanced American technology in the 1991 Gulf War (the liberation of Kuwait from Iraqi occupation), sharply decreased demand for China's military exports. Approaching the mid-1990s, China's foreign military sales seem to total roughly US $2 billion per year, a small fraction of comparable US sales.[40]

China's international military transfers are at times geopolitically risky. Its sale of Silkworm missiles to Iran is one example of Beijing's willingness to arm potentially aggressive regimes. By 1988 it had sold Saudi Arabia twenty-five to fifty CSS-2 missiles, which, with a range of almost sixteen hundred miles, can hit Israel. There have also been repeated accusations that China has directly contributed to Pakistan's development of a nuclear capability and the means to deliver nuclear weapons with medium-range guided missiles. Syria has received Chinese rocket fuel and perhaps related technologies. And China has begun military sales into Latin America and Southeast Asia.

The reforms themselves facilitated these sales. Deng's initiatives encouraged ministries to become more aggressive in marketing their goods, and freed up export channels through which such sales could take place. In so doing, the national leaders purposefully reduced their control over ministerial sales in order to stimulate the initiative of the ministries. In one result, six military-related ministries quickly set up their own sales companies and began directly marketing weapons and military technologies abroad.[41]

The "four modernizations" that became the centerpiece of the reform effort in 1978 placed defense modernization at the bottom of the priority list. China's defense budgets shrunk, especially after the 1984 decision to reduce men in uniform by one million and to hold down military spending. CIA estimates of the Chinese defense budget indicate that defense spending dropped from 6 to 8 percent of GNP before 1985 to about 4 percent by 1988, but then began to regain lost ground in 1989. This general decline in defense sector budgets provided another incentive to the six ministries to develop their own export markets. These ministries, though, all operate under the overall direction of the State Council, and their sales generally conform to guidelines set down by that body.

The same cannot be said of the People's Liberation Army. As noted previously, with a bureaucratic rank fully equivalent to that of the State Council, the PLA operates outside of direct State Council control. Like the ministries, the PLA "went commercial" during the 1980s. Cutbacks in defense spending virtually dictated this change. By 1988 the PLA estimated that it had to raise about 30 percent of the funds needed to cover its annual expenditures.

The PLA itself has thus become a major provider of military equipment and technologies abroad, and it is doing so largely independently of the PRC's formal foreign policy as negotiated by the Ministry of Foreign Affairs. The purpose of these sales is profit, not strategic positioning, and often those most willing to pay high prices are those who cannot purchase arms elsewhere because of the dangers they pose to international peace and security.

The PLA has also turned to many other profit-making activities, such as investing in hotels and producing air conditioners, to cover its expenses. But foreign military sales bring in by far the largest sums, much of which is in hard currency.

The relative independence of the PLA sales effort results in part from the bureaucratic rank of the PLA. But this independence also reflects the development of the "princes' party." The top executives of Polytechnologies, the most aggressive commercial arm of the PLA, can be considered members of the "princes' party."[42] He Pengfei, the son of the legendary communist He Long, is in charge of the Armaments Department that created Polytechnologies. The executive vice president of the company in 1992 was the son-in-law of then–PRC President Yang Shangkun (Yang at the time was also executive secretary of the CCP's Central Military Commission). The marketing office was headed by sons-in-law of former CCP general secretary Zhao Ziyang and Deng Xiaoping. With such figures in command, this firm could operate largely outside normal channels of authority. Persistent rumors indicate that these key figures have built up personal fortunes, partly held in foreign bank accounts, through the sales of Polytechnologies Inc.

American sanctions against direct contacts with the PLA following the Tiananmen massacre, not lifted until 1994, forced the US to address its concerns about Chinese proliferation activities to the Foreign Ministry. But the Foreign Ministry could not control, either directly or via the State Council, weapons sales the PLA was making on its own. Moreover, there are indications that some in the uniformed military sought to use such sales in part to signal to Washington the necessity of dealing directly with the PLA on such issues. They would not restrain profitable foreign sales as long as the US considered the PLA morally unfit to contact directly.

In sum, a wide array of essentially domestic factors has presented many military-related units in China with the means and incentives to export goods and technology. Some of the most active of these units are not necessarily disciplined by the international agreements reached by the Foreign Ministry and the State Council. The widespread corruption and cupidity that are products of the reforms further weaken efforts to bring China fully into compliance with post–Cold War efforts to limit transfers of certain weapons and military technologies. Effective approaches to China on proliferation issues will have to take account of these underlying domestic forces and trends. Such trends may make China a major source of destabilizing military transfers during the 1990s.

International Crime

International criminal activities pose a new type of global security threat in the wake of the Cold War. The collapse of governmental authority in much of the former Soviet Union is providing fertile ground for almost unprecedented growth of such activities. Russian, Ukrainian, and other gangs already engaged in extortion, prostitution, and other rackets are linking up with mobsters in Western Europe and elsewhere to sell drugs, supply weapons, participate in terrorism, provide safe havens, launder money, and so forth.

The situation in China is far more stable and less worrisome than is the case for the successor countries to the old Soviet Union. But some localities in China warrant concern about the development of organized crime.

The most sensitive area is the border between Guangdong province and Hong Kong. The reforms have encouraged a huge increase in traffic across this border. The volume of people, goods, and money moving between Hong Kong and Guangdong each day is large and growing rapidly. Already highly porous, this border is being penetrated in support of criminal activities in both directions. As of 1992, roughly twenty luxury cars a day, for example, were stolen in Hong Kong and transported by fast boat to Guangdong. Triads, which are a form of criminal society somewhat less tightly structured than the Sicilian mafia, operate on both sides of this border in coordinated fashion, and they have in the early 1990s extended their organized criminal activities to the United States. Although they focus primarily on protection and prostitution, they are also involved in smuggling drugs and people across international frontiers.

The decline in discipline along the Hong Kong border reflects a larger phenomenon. Local authorities in a number of PRC border locations are beginning to engage in profit-making criminal activities—or at least to turn a blind eye to such cross-border activities in return for payments. A substantial portion of the drugs produced in the Golden Triangle area of northern Thailand and Burma and destined for the US market, for example, as of 1994 no longer flows out through southern Thailand, Cambodia, and Burma. Rather, the cheapest route crosses China and exits through either Guangdong or Shanghai. The major cost in determining the economics of these routes is not transportation but the sums that must be paid local authorities to assure safe passage.

The shift in the routing of Golden Triangle drugs suggests that parts of

China may become relatively safe havens for various types of international criminal activity. This drug trafficking is evidently taking place against the wishes of national leaders. China has cooperated with Interpol, the international police organization, to stop international criminal activity since the 1980s. And Beijing has ordered severe crackdowns on drug trafficking that periodically produce public executions of dozens of "mules," the individuals caught actually carrying the illicit drugs. But local complicity with the trade has sharply limited Beijing's ability to put a stop to this activity.[43]

In the past the PRC has successfully held to a minimum the transnational criminal activities based in its territory. But state control over China's borders is weakening as a consequence of the decentralization, commercialization, and corruption produced by the reforms. Other countries will now have to pay more attention to criminal activity based in Chinese localities.

Conclusion

Despite the PRC's rapid economic growth and generally constructive foreign policy during recent years, there are significant unknowns about China's future activities in the international arena. These uncertainties arise from the possibilities of:

☐—Domestic unrest, growing out of some combination of a political stalemate at the apex, major economic setbacks (due to either a sharp downturn in the business cycle or some environmental catastrophe), tensions over corruption and inflation, fears of unemployment, a ballooning of the "floating population," and rural discontent, resulting in widespread social upheaval that in turn produces a violent, repressive political response. This combustible mixture might also produce an officially inspired surge in state-centered nationalism.

☐—A foreign policy crisis that upsets China's ability to maintain a steady, constructive international stance. A declaration of independence by Taiwan after the upcoming presidential election would present the greatest challenge to China's overall foreign policy posture because Beijing would find it difficult to avoid military steps that might bring it into confrontation with the United States. Destabilization on the Korean peninsula or proliferation of nuclear weapons throughout northeast Asia are other serious potential challenges.

The above two challenges are interrelated. If domestic unrest produces a chain reaction leading to conservative Chinese nationalism, for example, Beijing might increase pressures on Taiwan for reunification. At a minimum, Beijing's sensitivities to Taiwan's assertions of independence would grow. Yet, these same developments might make leaders in Taiwan all the more reluctant to strengthen their links with the mainland and may even lead to a declaration of independence while Beijing's relations with the industrialized countries are strained. Such a sequence would immediately draw the United States and Japan into the fray and would put at risk the healthy Sino-American and

Sino-Japanese ties on which current projections of Beijing's foreign policy behavior are based.

China's desire to assure domestic growth can, moreover, lead it to act in muscular fashion where its access to critical natural resources is at stake. Most prominently, it may engage in resource diplomacy. It is already using its diplomatic leverage and its military might to assert its claims to the Spratly island area in the South China sea, where many believe that substantial offshore oil resources are to be found. As of 1994, this is the one area in which the PRC has recently taken a very hard line, and it may portend trouble for the future.

Barring the above major upsetting developments, Beijing will likely pursue a realpolitik approach to international affairs during the 1990s that will give priority to supporting domestic economic development. Specifically, China will seek to sustain access to international capital and markets. It should thus continue to take a relatively serious and sophisticated approach to international organizations and issues, eschewing where possible commitments that might embroil it in military engagements or that might sap its resources for unproductive causes. Maintaining good working relations with both the US and Japan would be a basic component of any such foreign policy, and China would have a major interest in reducing the chances of the development of separate North American and Asian trading blocks that are relatively closed to each other's products.

Even in the best of circumstances, though, coping with China's rise in international importance will present some difficult issues. As noted above, in a fundamental sense the world is now for the first time confronting the implications of Asia's phenomenal economic success. Asian perspectives are now integral to the consideration of virtually all major global issues. In areas such as human rights, these perspectives differ very substantially from those of the industrialized West. It will take years for Western countries and their Asian counterparts to adjust both psychologically and substantively to this new reality, and China will play a very important role in this global adjustment. The extent of China's internal stability, the degree of its cultural confidence, and the nature of its resulting nationalism will be significant factors in determining how difficult this adjustment will be to make.

Even if things go relatively smoothly, however, China is unlikely to become a highly disciplined member of the international community. As illustrated by the above brief reviews of the impact of China's domestic evolution on its international activities in the economic, military, and criminal spheres, the very reforms that the world applauds are creating unintended international problems. Beijing's ability to discipline its own localities and citizens to obey its international agreements and to abstain from opportunities for illegal gain has significantly eroded. Substantial improvement in this situation probably must await the development of a system of law in China that is independent of corrupt local officials. That is unlikely to occur to a sufficient extent during the remainder of this decade.

In sum, China's reforms have brought an opening to the outside world and an effort to join fully in the international community. The vast economic gains under the reforms have greatly increased the PRC's prestige and importance abroad. In recent years, Beijing has pursued a diplomatic posture that is sober and generally constructive, both in Asia and globally. But the reforms have also created conditions where illegal economic activities, proliferation of weapons and military technologies, and other nettlesome behaviors are difficult to stop. And the future holds great uncertainties, both domestically and in international behavior.

More than fifteen years ago, Deng Xiaoping set the PRC onto a course of major change in order to accelerate economic growth while maintaining political stability. In so doing, he and his colleagues, in the Chinese phrase, "mounted a tiger." As China enters the post-Deng era, the forces Deng unleashed continue to propel China forward, but with great risks and dangers. The tiger, in short, has not yet been tamed.

Glossary of Selected Individuals Cited in the Text

Bo Yibo (1908–   ): Born in Shanxi Province, Bo joined the Communist party in the 1920s and after 1949 was a long-time member of the Politburo. He played a major role in economic decision-making, rising to the rank of vice premier in the government. As of the 1990s, Bo is one of the octogenarians who retains influence even though he holds no formal office.

Mikhail Borodin (1923–?): A Russian Jew (his real name was Mikhail Gruzenberg) who was raised in Latvia and began secretly working for Lenin in 1903, Borodin spent most of 1905–1917 in exile in the United States, teaching in Chicago. He returned to Russia after the Bolshevik Revolution and thereafter took on revolutionary assignments in Europe, Central America, and in 1923, China.

Chen Xilian (1913–   ): Born in Hubei Province, Chen became an important military figure in post-1949 China. He commanded the PLA artillery forces from 1952 to 1959 and belonged to the Politburo from 1969 to 1980. From a base in Liaoning Province in northeast China, Chen played an active role in national politics during the Cultural Revolution.

Chen Yi (1901–1972): Born in Sichuan Province, Chen commanded the forces of the Third Field Army just prior to 1949, served as mayor of Shanghai and the leading CCP figure in the city in the early 1950s, then moved to Beijing, where in 1958 he became the minister of foreign affairs. A colorful figure and strong personality, Chen was cruelly persecuted during the Cultural Revolution.

Chen Yun (1905–   ): Born near Shanghai municipality, Chen was unique among the surviving leaders of the CCP in having been a member of the urban proletariat. Chen at various times played key roles in organization/personnel work and, especially, in economic decision-making. Mao typically turned to Chen to bail out the urban economy when it ran into trouble in the 1950s. Chen strongly supported Deng Xiaoping's reforms initially but by the late 1980s led the conservative critics of Deng's efforts. As of the 1990s he is the most influential octogenarian other than Deng himself.

Chi Haotian (1928–   ): Born in Shandong Province, Chi has pursued a military career and as of 1994 is the minister of defense and a member of the Military Affairs Commission of the CCP.

Chiang Ching-kuo (Jiang Jingguo) (1909–1988): Born in Zhejiang Province, Chiang was the eldest son of Chiang Kai-shek. He took power on Taiwan after the death of his father in 1975 and played a key role in laying the basis for democratic reform there during the ensuing years.

Chiang Kai-shek (Jiang Jieshi) (1887–1975): Born in Zhejiang Province, Chiang was the dominant political figure of the Republic of China after 1926. He headed the Guomindang, with only brief and insignificant interruptions, from the mid-1920s until his death. As such, he was China's national leader from 1927 to 1949. A graduate of the Whampoa Military Academy, Chiang's political base was strongest in the military, and he was an authoritarian ruler.

Ci Xi (1835–1908):   Yehe Nara (Ci Xi) served as the Empress Dowager in the last decades of the Qing dynasty. A highly capable and ruthless leader, she exercised power through control over the last few Qing emperors. She sided with conservatives during the 1898 Hundred Days of Reform and during the Boxer Rebellion two years later. In her final years, she began grudgingly to introduce some reforms into China, but not enough to save the dynasty.

Deng Xiaoping (1904–   ):   Born in Sichuan Province, Deng throughout his career has demonstrated extraordinary leadership capabilities. He was a leading figure in the Second Field Army before 1949, and by the mid-1950s had become one of the top six leaders in the CCP. He headed the party Secretariat from the mid-1950s to the Cultural Revolution. Purged in 1966 and again in 1976, Deng surged back after Mao Zedong's death to become the architect of China's post-Mao reforms. In the 1990s, he remains the most powerful of the party elders and is referred to as the "core leader."

Deng Yingchao (1904–1992):   Born in Henan Province, Deng early on joined the communist revolution. She married Zhou Enlai. After 1949, she worked primarily in the Women's Federation and achieved independent political influence only after Zhou's death in 1976.

Deng Zihui (1896–1972):   Born in Fujian Province, Deng joined the CCP in the mid-1920s. After 1949 he served as the key figure in the central-south administrative region. He transferred to Beijing in 1954 and thereafter played an important role in economic policy, especially regarding agriculture. He clashed with Mao Zedong several times in the 1950s over the cooperativization of agriculture.

Feng Yuxiang (1882–1948):   Born in Hebei Province, Feng was a major north China warlord.

Fu Zuoyi (1895–1974):   Born in Shanxi Province, Fu was a key Guomindang general who effected the peaceful surrender of Beijing to the communists in January 1949. He thereafter became a figurehead minister of water conservancy in the PRC.

Gao Gang (1905–1954):   Born in Shaanxi Province, Gao was the leader in northeast China from 1949 to 1952, when he moved to Beijing. He was accused of maneuvering to replace Liu Shaoqi in 1953, as a consequence of which he was purged. He committed suicide in prison in 1954.

Guangxu emperor (1871–1908):   The Guangxu emperor nominally reigned from 1875 to 1908. In reality, he assumed the throne as a minor at the age of four. His mother, the Empress Dowager Ci Xi, exercised real power. When he reached maturity he determined that the Qing dynasty needed to reform, and in 1898 he launched the wide-ranging Hundred Days of Reform. The Empress Dowager allied with court conservatives to cut short this effort and effectively held the emperor under house arrest from then until his death in 1908. Many believe the emperor was poisoned on the orders of his mother, who knew her own death was imminent.

Heshen (1750–1799):   An imperial bodyguard, Heshen caught the eye of the aging Qianlong emperor, who elevated Heshen to the post of grand councillor. He remained a confidant of the Qianlong emperor for the rest of his reign. But Heshen became enormously corrupt and was forced to commit suicide in 1799, shortly after the death of the Qianlong emperor.

Hu Qiaomu (1912–1993): Born in Jiangsu Province, Hu caught Mao Zedong's attention through articles he wrote while in Yan'an in the early 1940s. After 1949 Hu at various times was a leading figure in the propaganda sphere, worked as an assistant to Mao, and served on the CCP Politburo. He became a conservative critic of Deng Xiaoping by the mid-1980s.

Hu Shi (1891–1962): Born in Shanghai municipality, Hu Shi was a prominent advocate of Western ideas in Republican China. He played a major role in promoting use of the vernacular in the written language, thereby facilitating the development of mass political propaganda. Hu went to Taiwan when the Guomindang took control there.

Hu Yaobang (1915–1989): Born in Hunan Province, Hu joined the revolution as a teenager. He spent his career until the Cultural Revolution focused on youth work and developed close ties with Deng Xiaoping. Hu served as official head of the CCP from 1981 to 1987 and, along with Zhao Ziyang, was a major architect of the reforms and prospective successor to Deng. A lively individual, Hu was purged in January 1987. His death from a heart attack in April 1989 provided the initial momentum for what became the Tiananmen student movement, leading to the Tiananmen massacre on 4 June 1989.

Hua Guofeng (1921–   ): Born in Shanxi Province, Hua made his pre–Cultural Revolution career in Mao Zedong's native Hunan Province. Hua moved to Beijing early in the 1970s and served as a transitional leader between Mao's death in 1976 and Deng Xiaoping's consolidation of power in late 1978. Loyal to Mao, Hua lost his last political posts in 1981.

Huang Jing (1911–1958): Born in Zhejiang Province, Huang is reported to have been married to Jiang Qing in the 1930s, before Jiang met and married Mao Zedong. From 1949 to 1953, Huang was the top political figure in Tianjin municipality. He subsequently led the State Technology Commission until his death from illness in 1958.

Ji Dengkui (1923–1988): Born in Shanxi Province, Ji's political career soared during the Cultural Revolution, when he jumped from the Henan provincial apparatus to become an alternate, and then later a full, member of the Politburo. Loyal to Mao Zedong's ideas, Ji lost power in 1980 as Deng Xiaoping consolidated his own position.

Jia Chunwang (1938–   ): Born in Beijing municipality, Jia has served as minister of state security since 1985. He is the son-in-law of Bo Yibo.

Jiaqing emperor (1760–1820): The Jiaqing emperor ruled from 1796 to 1820, taking over from the great Qianlong emperor, who abdicated in 1796 after a reign of sixty years. The Jiaqing emperor inherited a system that had begun to decline from corruption and rebellion in peripheral areas.

Jiang Qing (1913–1991): Born in Shandong Province, Jiang Qing had been an actress in Shanghai in the 1930s before moving to Yan'an, where she met and married Mao Zedong. She played a leading radical role in the Cultural Revolution. She particularly focused on policy toward culture, over which she assumed ultimate control in the late 1960s. Jiang chafed for many years under restrictions on her activities imposed by the CCP leaders, who had opposed her marriage to Mao. She used the Cultural Revolution, in part, to settle these numerous scores. She was imprisoned in 1976 as a member of the Gang of Four, which also included Wang Hongwen, Yao Wenyuan, and Zhang Chunqiao. She reportedly committed suicide while still incarcerated.

Jiang Zemin (1926–   ):   Born in Jiangsu Province, Jiang held a wide array of posts in the automotive, machine building, and electronics industries from the 1950s to the mid-1980s. He became mayor of Shanghai in 1986 and secretary of the Shanghai municipal party committee in 1987. In 1989 he moved to Beijing, where as of 1994 he holds the posts of general secretary of the Communist party, chairman of the CCP Military Affairs Commission, and president of the PRC. Deng Xiaoping has indicated he expects Jiang to succeed him as "core leader" after his own demise.

Kang Sheng (1898–1975):   Born in Shandong Province, Kang sponsored Jiang Qing's membership in the CCP in 1931 and remained close to her thereafter. Kang trained in Moscow in the 1930s and became a key figure both before and after 1949 in using brutal tactics to purge suspected enemies in the CCP. He played a prominent role in the Cultural Revolution. Kang was known both for his fine artistic sensibilities and for his sadism in torturing his victims.

Kangxi emperor (1654–1722):   The first of the two great Qing dynasty emperors (the other was the Qianlong emperor), the Kangxi emperor reigned from 1661 to 1722. He stabilized the northern and western borders of the new dynasty and in 1689 signed the Treaty of Nerchinsk with Russia.

Lee Teng-hui (Li Denghui) (1929–   ):   Born in Taiwan, Lee assumed the presidency of the Republic of China on Taiwan upon the death of Chiang Ching-kuo. Lee continued Chiang's efforts to Taiwanize the Guomindang and to democratize Taiwan.

Li Fuchun (1900–1975):   Born in Hunan Province, Li by the mid-1950s had become a vice premier of the State Council and head of the State Planning Commission, positions that he held until the 1970s. He was a key economic decision-maker in Beijing.

Li Lanqing (1932–   ):   Born in Jiangsu Province, Li as of 1994 is an urbane vice premier, Politburo member, and head of the commission in charge of foreign economic relations.

Li Peng (1928–   ):   An adopted son of Zhou Enlai and Deng Yingchao, Li received part of his education in Moscow in the late 1940s and early 1950s. He spent his subsequent career in the power industry until the 1980s, when he began to assume broader political responsibilities. Li became premier in 1988, a position he retains as of 1994. A Standing Committee member of the Politburo, he is widely regarded as a conservative and took a hard-line public stance against the democracy demonstrators in 1989 and in support of the June 1989 Tiananmen massacre.

Li Ruihuan (1934–   ):   Born in Tianjin municipality, Li first achieved fame as a key leader in the construction of the Great Hall of the People in 1958–59. He had a highly successful tenure as head of Tianjin from 1983 through the end of the decade. He has been a member of the Politburo and its Standing Committee and of the CCP Secretariat. A carpenter by training, Li has risen by dint of his great organizational and problem solving skills and keen political sensibilities.

Li Ssu (?–208 B.C.):   Born in the Ch'u state, Li was a ruthless minister under the first emperor of the Qin dynasty. Li advocated use of vicious punishments, including torture and mutilation, to maintain order among the populace. Accused of treason after

Qin Shi Huang Di's death, Li was sawed in two in the marketplace, a punishment in keeping with his own approach to discipline.

Li Xiannian (1909–1992): Born in Hubei Province, Li was a political leader in his native province until 1954. He then spent more than two decades as vice premier of the State Council and minister of finance. Li served on the CCP Politburo from 1956 to 1987 and held the largely honorific post of president of the PRC for 1983 to 1988. He was a key economic decision-maker from the 1950s to the 1980s. From 1981 to 1988, Li also headed the Leading Group for Foreign Affairs.

Li Zongren (1890–?): Born in Guangxi Province, Li served in the National Revolutionary Army before 1949 and briefly became the president of the Republic of China in 1949.

Lin Biao (1907–1971): Born in Hubei Province, Lin was one of the Chinese communists' greatest military strategists during the years before 1949. After 1949, he suffered from real or imagined illnesses that kept him inactive for years at a time. He nevertheless became a leading Politburo member in 1958 and the operational head of the military in 1959. Lin fostered the Mao Zedong personality cult and played a key role in the Cultural Revolution, becoming Mao's designated successor in 1969. Lin died in a plane crash in Outer Mongolia in 1971, purportedly while fleeing after a botched attempt to assassinate Mao.

Liu Bocheng (1892–1986): Born in Sichuan Province, Liu had a distinguished military career, working closely with Deng Xiaoping, before 1949. He became a marshal (the highest military rank) in the PLA, one of only ten individuals to be accorded this honor, when the PLA established ranks in 1955. Liu's post-1949 career focused on military training and policy, and he was a leading member of the Military Affairs Commission. Although a member of the Politburo from 1956 to 1982, Liu in fact was largely inactive in his later years due to illness.

Liu Huaqing (1916–   ): Born in Hubei Province, General Liu is a career military man who fought in many of the key battles during the 1930s and 1940s. He attended the Voroshilov Naval Academy in the USSR in the mid-1950s and thereafter played a central role in developing the naval arm of the PLA. As of 1994 he has come out of retirement to serve on the Politburo.

Liu Shaoqi (1898–1969): Born in Hunan Province, Liu became a strong supporter of Mao Zedong in the early 1940s. He was widely regarded as Mao's likely successor but was purged and vilified during the Cultural Revolution. Liu concentrated on running the CCP organization and he believed strongly in organizational discipline. Starting in 1959 he served in the honorific post of president of the PRC. Liu died of the severe treatment he received during the Cultural Revolution, when he was branded as the "number one person in authority taking the capitalist road" and as "China's Khrushchev."

Liu Zhidan (1903–1936): Born in Shaanxi Province, Liu was one of the founders of the north China guerrilla base that later became the final destination of the Long March.

Mao Zedong (1893–1976): Born in Hunan Province, Mao was one of the founders of the CCP and led the party from 1935 until his death. He was the charismatic leader of the communist revolution and the dominant political figure from 1949 to 1976. His personal views and proclivities affected the lives of millions, given the extraordinary concentration of power in his hands.

Peng Dehuai (1898–1974): Born in Hunan Province, Peng was one of China's top communist military figures both before and after 1949. He commanded the Chinese forces in Korea and for most of the 1950s took charge of the day-to-day operations of the CCP's Military Affairs Commission. Peng clashed with Mao over various issues from the early 1940s through the 1950s. In what proved to be a turning point in the politics of the Mao era, Peng was purged at the Lushan plenum in August 1959 after delivering a strong critique of the mistakes of the Great Leap Forward. Peng received very rough treatment during the Cultural Revolution and died as a result of this persecution.

Peng Zhen (1902?–   ): Born in Shanxi Province, Peng Zhen played key roles in the Beijing municipal Communist party leadership and in the political and legal affairs system until the Cultural Revolution. He was also a member of the CCP Politburo and Secretariat. Peng was one of the first victims of the Cultural Revolution. He was rehabilitated after Mao Zedong's death and for a period in the 1980s headed the legislature, the National People's Congress. Peng retains considerable informal influence, especially in the security apparatus.

Pu Yi (1906–1967): The last emperor of the Qing dynasty, Pu Yi was only five years old when the dynasty fell. In 1932 he became the head of the puppet government the Japanese established in Manchuria (Manchukuo).

Qianlong emperor (1711–1799): The greatest Chinese emperor after the Kangxi emperor, the Qianlong emperor occupied the dragon throne from 1736 to 1796, when he abdicated due to age. He expanded the empire through the conquests of Ili and Turkestan. The Qing reached its zenith and began to decline under the rule of the Qianlong emperor.

Qiao Shi (1924–   ): Born in Zhejiang Province, during the 1950s Qiao worked primarily in economic administration. From 1963 to 1983 he worked in the International Liaison Department of the CCP, concerned with foreign policy and contacts with the international communist movement. During the remainder of the 1980s Qiao held posts as head of the Organization Department of the CCP, as head of the General Office of the CCP, and as head of the political and legal affairs system. As of 1994, he heads the legislature, the National People's Congress. He is a member of the Standing Committee of the Politburo and is a vice premier of the State Council. He is known as a politically astute and very capable individual.

Qin Shi Huang Di (259–210 B.C.): The first emperor of the short-lived Qin dynasty, Qin Shi Huang Di is widely regarded as China's first real emperor. A ruthless man, millions died under the exactions of his rule. He standardized weights and measures, created a national communications system, constructed major stretches of the Great Wall, and built a tomb of legendary grandeur. He also created the country's first nationwide bureaucracy. Mao Zedong occasionally remarked that he regarded himself as a modern Qin Shi Huang Di.

Rao Shushi (1903–1975): Born in Jiangxi Province, Rao was one of the major leaders of east China during 1949 to 1952. Rao then moved to Beijing, where he took charge of the CCP Organization Department. He was purged with Gao Gang in 1954, with whom he had allegedly conspired to obtain the top state and party posts under Mao Zedong.

Song Ping (1917–   ):   Born in Shandong Province, Song's post-1949 career has included a number of posts involved primarily with state economic planning. He headed the State Planning Commission from 1983 to 1987, at which time he became head of the CCP Organization Department. He is considered a conservative supporter of Chen Yun. Song became a Politburo member in the late 1980s. As of 1994 he is retired but retains influence as a party elder.

Sun Yat-sen (Sun Zhongshan) (1866–1925):   Born in Guangdong Province, Sun organized the Guomindang and is generally regarded as the founding father of Republican China. Sun was the first Chinese revolutionary of international reputation. He served briefly, for only six weeks, as the first president of the Republic of China. Sun's political thought in the form of the "Three People's Principles" has been the official guiding ideology of the Guomindang.

Tan Zhenlin (1902–1983):   Born in Hunan Province, Tan served as party secretary in Zhejiang Province from 1949 to 1955 and then moved to Beijing, where he joined the CCP Secretariat in 1956 and the Politburo in 1958. He lost both memberships during the Cultural Revolution.

Tang Shengzhi (1890–?):   Born in Hunan Province, Tang was a Guomindang military commander who in 1929 went to battle against forces loyal to Chiang Kai-shek. He was pardoned in 1931 but remained in the PRC after 1949, where he held minor government posts.

Tian Jiaying (?–1966):   Tian served in Mao Zedong's personal office from the 1950s to the early 1960s. A disagreement with Mao over agricultural policy during the Great Leap Forward led to his dismissal. He committed suicide early in the Cultural Revolution.

Tian Jiyun (1929–   ):   Born in Shandong Province, Tian has spent his career primarily in financial administration, first in Guizhou Province, then in Sichuan Province, and finally at the national level. He has held the posts of vice premier, member of the CCP Secretariat, and member of the Politburo.

Tongzhi emperor (1856–1875):   On the throne from 1861 until his death in 1875, the Tongzhi emperor was too young to exercise real power. But during his reign, talented government officials brought the Taiping, Nian, Northwest Moslem, and Southwest Moslem rebellions to an end and sought to revitalize the Confucian base of the dynasty. This effort, partially successful, has been dubbed the Tongzhi Restoration.

Wan Li (1916–   ):   Born in Shandong Province, Wan served on the Beijing municipal CCP committee from 1958 to 1966 and 1974 to 1975. After terms as minister of railways and minister of agriculture, he joined the CCP Secretariat in 1980 and the Politburo in 1982. He then served as chairman of the legislature, the National People's Congress, from 1987 to 1993.

Wang Dongxing (1916–   ):   Born in Jiangxi Province, Wang pursued a career in the security services, most notably as the man in charge of Mao Zedong's personal security detachment and then as the leader of the 8341 Division, which provided security for the entire top leadership. Wang served on the Politburo from 1977 to 1980. Generally considered a hard-liner loyal to Mao, he was removed by Deng Xiaoping as part of Deng's effort to sustain his reform initiatives.

Wang Guangmei (1922–   ):   Born in the United States, Wang came from a prominent Tianjin family. Liu Shaoqi married her in 1948, shortly before the communist victory. Jiang Qing resented Wang's upper-class background and when Jiang gained power with the onset of the Cultural Revolution, she had Wang thrown in prison, where she languished in solitary confinement for nearly twelve years.

Wang Hongwen (1935–   ):   Born in Jilin Province, Wang worked in security at an enterprise in Shanghai and catapulted to political power through his early leadership of one of the most prominent Shanghai Red Guard units in the initial stages of the Cultural Revolution. Wang served on the Politburo Standing Committee from 1973 to 1976, when he was arrested as a member of the Gang of Four, which also included Jiang Qing, Yao Wenyuan, and Zhang Chunqiao. He is serving a life sentence in prison.

Wang Jingwei (1883–1944):   Born in Guangdong Province, Wang headed the "left Guomindang" during the Northern Expedition but later defected to the Japanese and headed one of their regional puppet governments in China.

Wang Zhen (1908–1993):   Born in Hunan Province, Wang was a military man of peasant origin who delighted in discomfiting intellectuals with his crude manners and ready resort to violence. During the 1980s he became an important member of the conservative opposition to Deng Xiaoping's reform effort.

Wei Jianxing (1931–   ):   Born in Zhejiang Province, Wei rose to national prominence in the 1980s, when he moved from Harbin municipality and became head of the CCP Organization Department (1984 to 1985). He then assumed leadership of the Ministry of Supervision and in 1992 became secretary of the CCP Central Discipline Inspection Commission. He also gained positions on the CCP Secretariat and the Politburo in 1992.

Wei Jingsheng (1950–   ):   Born in Beijing municipality, Wei was a worker who became prominent during the Democracy Wall movement in 1978–79, when he wrote an essay calling for a "fifth modernization," democracy. He was sentenced in 1979 to fifteen years in prison for revealing state secrets to foreigners. Released six months early in 1993, he immediately began to criticize the government over human-rights issues. Widely regarded as China's Sakharov, as of mid-1994 Wei is again in prison.

Wu De (1914–   ):   Born in Hebei Province, Wu headed Beijing's municipal party committee from 1973 to 1978. On 5 April 1976, he ordered the forcible expulsion of thousands of demonstrators from Tiananmen Square. He held Politburo membership from 1973 to 1980, when he was removed as part of Deng Xiaoping's effort to sweep out conservative opposition to his reform initiatives.

Wu Peifu (1874–1939):   Born in Shandong Province, Wu was an important northern warlord in the 1920s, and he largely controlled the Beijing government until 1922. He suppressed railway workers on strike on the Beijing-Hankow railway in 1923, dealing a major blow to communist efforts to instigate revolution through worker organizations.

Wu Zetian (625–705):   Through talent, intrigue, and ruthlessness, the only woman in Chinese history to become empress.

Wu Zhipu (1906?–Cultural Revolution):   Wu was a key leader in Henan Province for the 1950s and a secretary of the CCP's central–south bureau from 1962 to 1967. He played a significant role in the movement toward communes in 1958 and encouraged Mao Zedong's most radical economic and political inclinations at the beginning of the Great Leap Forward.

Xianfeng emperor (1831–1861): The Xianfeng emperor ruled China from 1851 to 1861. During this time the country was plagued by the Taiping, Nian, Southwest Moslem, and Northwest Moslem rebellions, as well as by foreign pressures to implement fully the treaties signed at the conclusion of the Opium War.

Yan Xishan (1881–1960): Born in Shaanxi Province and a major warlord there, Yan joined with other northern warlords against Chiang Kai-shek at the end of the 1920s. Thereafter, he joined the Guomindang, serving in its National Military Council and other organs, and he eventually became a presidential advisor to Chiang.

Yao Wenyuan (1931–): Born in Zhejiang Province, Yao was an editor in Shanghai who achieved fame as a member of the Cultural Revolution Small Group in the late 1960s. His critique of Wu Han's play, *Hai Rui Dismissed from Office,* in late 1965 may be seen as the opening shot in the Cultural Revolution. He was purged and arrested in October 1976 as a member of the Gang of Four, which also included Jiang Qing, Wang Hongwen, and Zhang Chunqiao.

Ye Jianying (1897–1986): Born in Guangdong Province, Ye was one of China's ten military marshals. He held high PLA and party posts, at various times serving as the operational head of the CCP Military Affairs Commission and as a member of the Politburo. Ye was one of the very few top leaders to survive the Cultural Revolution unscathed. He protected Deng Xiaoping when Deng was purged in 1976, and he played key roles in the October 1976 arrest of the Gang of Four and in Deng's 1977–78 political comeback.

Ye Qun (?–1971): Ye was Lin Biao's wife. A powerful personality, she achieved considerable influence in the military during the Cultural Revolution years. Ye died in the plane crash in Outer Mongolia that also killed her husband, allegedly while both were fleeing to the Soviet Union in the wake of a failed attempt to assassinate Mao Zedong.

Ye Xuanping (1924–): Born in Guangdong Province, Ye is the son of Marshal Ye Jianying. Ye became a powerful leader of Guangdong Province in the mid-1980s and continues in 1994 to exercise great informal influence over the province's political affairs.

Yuan Shikai (1859–1916): Born in Henan Province, Yuan developed the most modern military forces in the late Qing dynasty. His machinations when rebellion broke out against the Qing in 1911 brought about the abdication of the emperor and the end of the dynastic system. Yuan soon became the president the Republic of China, and within a few years attempted to have himself declared emperor. The attempt failed, and Yuan died soon after.

Zhang Chunqiao (1917–): Born in Shandong Province, Zhang was a municipal official involved in cultural affairs in Shanghai at the start of the Cultural Revolution. He became a key figure in the radical group during the Cultural Revolution and was purged and arrested in October 1976 as a member of the Gang of Four, which also included Jiang Qing, Wang Hongwen, and Yao Wenyuan.

Zhang Xueliang (1898–): Born in Liaoning Province, Zhang was the son of warlord Zhang Zuolin. Zhang engineered the December 1936 kidnapping of Chiang Kai-shek in order to force Chiang to focus his energies on stopping the Japanese encroachments into China. Zhang was placed under house arrest upon his release of Chiang, and he remains under a loose form of house arrest in Taiwan as of the 1990s.

Zhang Zhen (1914–): Born in Hunan Province, Zhang is a career military officer who joined the Communist party in 1930. He fought in the Korean War, and held numerous military posts, including leadership of the PLA Military Academy and of the National Defense University. As of 1994, he is a member of the Politburo of the CCP.

Zhang Zuolin (1873–1928):   Born in Liaoning Province, Zhang Zuolin was a powerful warlord in the 1920s. He was assassinated by the Japanese, who blew up the train on which he was riding.

Zhao Ziyang (1919–   ):   Born in Henan Province, Zhao spent most of his pre–Cultural Revolution career in Guangdong Province. He suffered during the Cultural Revolution but then took command of Sichuan Province in the late 1970s. His successes in Sichuan catapulted him to national power, first as premier and then as general secretary of the CCP during the 1980s. In these positions, Zhao became a major architect of Deng Xiaoping's economic reforms. Zhao was purged in mid-1989. He was a political casualty of the Tiananmen movement and its suppression.

Zhou Enlai (1898–1976):   Born in Jiangsu Province, Zhou was one of the outstanding figures in the Chinese communist leadership. He served as premier and, until 1958, as the PRC's foreign minister. His actual activities were varied, encompassing security as well as economics and foreign affairs. Chinese often liken Zhou to a willow tree—extremely durable but able to bend easily with the wind. Zhou was Mao Zedong's key colleague. He never frontally challenged Mao. Rather, he played an essential role in turning Mao's wide-ranging ideas into actual programs and activities. In some instances, he used his power to tone down the excesses of Mao's initiatives.

Zhou Xiaozhou (1912–1966):   Born in Hunan Province, Zhou spent his career during the 1950s in posts in Hunan. He had served as assistant to Mao Zedong for a period in Yan'an. Zhou was purged along with Peng Dehuai at the Lushan plenum in August 1959 for opposing the way the Great Leap Forward was being carried out.

Zhu De (1886–1976):   Born in Sichuan Province, Zhu was, along with Mao Zedong, the most important military commander of the revolution before 1949. Considered the "grand old man" of the revolution, Zhu did not exercise great power after 1949, although he served as a member of the Politburo from 1934 until his death in 1976.

Zhu Rongji (1928–   ):   Born in Hunan Province, Zhu had a career in the State Planning Commission and State Economic Commission. He was Shanghai's mayor from 1988 to 1992, during which time he established a reputation as an effective, open-minded economic administrator. As of 1994, Zhu is a member of the Standing Committee of the Politburo and is a vice premier who exercises enormous authority over economic policy. He is considered very capable and very hard-nosed.

Zou Jiahua (1927–   ):   Born in Shanghai municipality, Zou studied in Moscow in the early 1950s with Li Peng. He then had a career primarily engaged in the machine building and related military ordnance industries through the mid-1980s. Zou has been a Politburo member since 1987, and is currently also a vice premier of the State Council. He headed the State Planning Commission from 1989 to 1993. He is a son-in-law of the late Marshal Ye Jianying.

APPENDIXES

APPENDIX 1

Constitution of the People's Republic of China

(Adopted at the Fifth Session of the Fifth National People's Congress and Promulgated for Implementation by the Proclamation of the National People's Congress on 4 December 1982)

CONTENTS

Preamble

China is a country with one of the longest histories in the world. The people of all of China's nationalities have jointly created a culture of grandeur and have a glorious revolutionary tradition.

After 1840, feudal China was gradually turned into a semi-colonial and semi-feudal country. The Chinese people waged many successive heroic struggles for national independence and liberation and for democracy and freedom.

Great and earthshaking historical changes have taken place in China in the 20th century.

The Revolution of 1911, led by Dr. Sun Yat-sen, abolished the feudal monarchy and gave birth to the Republic of China. But the historic mission of the Chinese people to overthrow imperialism and feudalism remained unaccomplished.

After waging protracted and arduous struggles, armed and otherwise, along a zigzag course, the Chinese people of all nationalities led by the Communist Party of China with Chairman Mao Zedong as its leader ultimately, in 1949, overthrew the rule of imperialism, feudalism and bureaucrat-capitalism, won a great victory in the New Democratic Revolution and founded the People's Republic of China. Since then the Chinese people have taken control of state power and become masters of the country.

After the founding of the People's Republic, China gradually achieved its transition from a New Democratic to a socialist society. The socialist transformation of the private ownership of the means of production has been completed, the system of exploitation of man by man abolished and the socialist system established. The people's democratic dictatorship led by the working class and based on the alliance of workers and peasants, which is in essence the dictatorship of the proletariat, has been consolidated and developed. The Chinese people and the Chinese People's Liberation Army have defeated imperialist and hegemonist aggression, sabotage and armed provocations and have thereby safeguarded China's national independence and security and strengthened its national defence. Major successes have been achieved in economic development. An independent and relatively comprehensive socialist system of industry has basically been established. There has been a marked increase in agricultural production. Significant advances have been made in educational, scientific and cultural undertakings, while education in socialist ideology has produced noteworthy results. The life of the people has improved considerably.

Both the victory in China's New-Democratic Revolution and the successes in its socialist cause have been achieved by the Chinese people of all nationalities, under the leadership of the Communist Party of China and the guidance of Marxism-Leninism and Mao Zedong Thought, by upholding truth, correcting errors and surmounting numerous difficulties and hardships. The basic task of the nation in the years to come is to concentrate its effort on socialist modernization. Under the leadership of the Communist Party of China and the guidance of Marxism-Leninism and Mao Zedong Thought, the Chinese people of all nationalities will continue to adhere to the people's democratic dictatorship and the socialist road, steadily improve socialist institutions, develop socialist democracy, improve the socialist legal system, and work hard and self-reliantly to modernize the country's industry, agriculture, national defence and science and technology step by step to turn China into a socialist country with a high level of culture and democracy.

The exploiting classes as such have been abolished in our country. However, class struggle will continue to exist within certain bounds for a long time to come. The Chinese people must fight against those forces and elements, both at home and abroad, that are hostile to China's socialist system and try to undermine it.

Taiwan is part of the sacred territory of the People's Republic of China. It is the inviolable duty of all Chinese people, including our compatriots in Taiwan, to accomplish the great task of reunifying the motherland.

In building socialism it is essential to rely on workers, peasants and intellectuals and to unite all forces that can be united. In the long years of revolution and construction, there has been formed under the leadership of the Communist Party of China a broad patriotic united front which is composed of the democratic parties and people's organizations and which embraces all socialist working people, all patriots who support socialism and all patriots who stand for the reunification of the motherland. This united front will continue to be consolidated and developed. The Chinese People's Political Consultative Conference, a broadly based representative organization of the united front which has played a significant historical role, will play a still more important role in the country's political and social life, in promoting friendship with other countries and in the struggle for socialist modernization and for the reunification and unity of the country.

The People's Republic of China is a unitary multinational state created jointly by the people of all its nationalities. Socialist relations of equality, unity and mutual assistance have been established among the nationalities and will continue to be strengthened. In the struggle to safeguard the unity of the nationalities, it is necessary to combat big-nation chauvinism, mainly Han chauvinism, and to combat local national chauvinism. The state will do its utmost to promote the common prosperity of all the nationalities.

China's achievements in revolution and construction are inseparable from the support of the people of the world. The future of China is closely linked to the future of the world. China consistently carries out an independent foreign policy and adheres to the five principles of mutual respect for sovereignty and territorial integrity, mutual non-aggression, non interference in each other's internal affairs, equality and mutual benefit, and peaceful coexistence in developing diplomatic relations and economic and cultural exchanges with other countries. China consistently opposes imperialism, hegemonism and colonialism, works to strengthen unity with the people of other countries, supports the oppressed nations and the developing countries in their just struggle to win and preserve national independence and develop their national economies, and strives to safeguard world peace and promote the cause of human progress.

This Constitution, in legal form, affirms the achievements of the struggles of the Chinese people of all nationalities and defines the basic system and basic tasks of the state; it is the fundamental law of the state and has supreme legal authority. The people of all nationalities, all state organs, the armed forces, all political parties and public organizations and all enterprises and institutions in the country must take the Constitution as the basic standard of conduct, and they have the duty to uphold the dignity of the Constitution and ensure its implementation.

CHAPTER ONE

General Principles

ARTICLE 1

The People's Republic of China is a socialist state under the people's democratic dictatorship led by the working class and based on the alliance of workers and peasants.

The socialist system is the basic system of the People's Republic of China. Disruption of the socialist system by any organization or individual is prohibited.

ARTICLE 2

All power in the People's Republic of China belongs to the people.

The National People's Congress and the local people's congresses at various levels are the organs through which the people exercise state power.

The people administer state affairs and manage economic, cultural and social affairs through various channels and in various ways in accordance with the law.

ARTICLE 3

The state organs of the People's Republic of China apply the principle of democratic centralism.

The National People's Congress and the local people's congresses at various levels are constituted through democratic elections. They are responsible to the people and subject to their supervision.

All administrative, judicial and procuratorial organs of the state are created by the people's congresses to which they are responsible and by which they are supervised.

The division of functions and powers between the central and local state organs is guided by the principle of giving full scope to the initiative and enthusiasm of the local authorities under the unified leadership of the central authorities.

ARTICLE 4

All nationalities in the People's Republic of China are equal. The state protects the lawful rights and interests of the minority nationalities and upholds and develops a relationship of equality, unity and mutual assistance among all of China's nationalities. Discrimination against and oppression of any nationality are prohibited; any act which undermines the unity of the nationalities or instigates division is prohibited.

The state assists areas inhabited by minority nationalities in accelerating their economic and cultural development according to the characteristics and needs of the various minority nationalities.

Regional autonomy is practised in areas where people of minority nationalities live in concentrated communities; in these areas organs of self-government are established to exercise the power of autonomy. All national autonomous areas are integral parts of the People's Republic of China.

All nationalities have the freedom to use and develop their own spoken and written languages and to preserve or reform their own folkways and customs.

ARTICLE 5

The state upholds the uniformity and dignity of the socialist legal system.

No laws or administrative or local rules and regulations may contravene the Constitution.

All state organs, the armed forces, all political parties and public organizations and all enterprises and institutions must abide by the Constitution and the law. All acts in violation of the Constitution or the law must be investigated.

No organization or individual is privileged to be beyond the Constitution or the law.

ARTICLE 6

The basis of the socialist economic system of the People's Republic of China is socialist public ownership of the means of production, namely, ownership by the whole people and collective ownership by the working people.

The system of socialist public ownership supersedes the system of exploitation of man by man; it applies the principle of "from each according to his ability, to each according to his work."

ARTICLE 7

The state economy is the sector of socialist economy under ownership by the whole people; it is the leading force in the national economy. The state ensures the consolidation and growth of the state economy.

ARTICLE 8

Rural people's communes, agricultural producers' cooperatives and other forms of co-operative economy, such as producers', supply and marketing, credit and consumers' co-operatives, belong to the sector of socialist economy under collective ownership by the working people. Working people who are members of rural economic collectives have the right, within the limits prescribed by law, to farm plots of cropland and hilly land allotted for their private use, engage in household sideline production and raise privately owned livestock.

The various forms of cooperative economy in the cities and towns, such as those in the handicraft, industrial, building, transport, commercial and service trades, all belong to the sector of socialist economy under collective ownership by the working people.

The state protects the lawful rights and interests of the urban and rural economic collectives and encourages, guides and helps the growth of the collective economy.

ARTICLE 9

All mineral resources, waters, forests, mountains, grasslands, unreclaimed land, beaches and other natural resources are owned by the state, that is, by the whole people, with the exception of the forests, mountains, grasslands, unreclaimed land and beaches that are owned by collectives in accordance with the law.

The state ensures the rational use of natural resources and protects rare animals and plants. Appropriation or damaging of natural resources by any organization or individual by whatever means is prohibited.

ARTICLE 10

Land in the cities is owned by the state.

Land in the rural and suburban areas is owned by collectives except for those portions which belong to the state in accordance with the law; house sites and privately farmed plots of cropland and hilly land are also owned by collectives.

The state may, in the public interest, requisition land for its use in accordance with the law.

No organization or individual may appropriate, buy, sell or lease land or otherwise engage in the transfer of land by unlawful means.

All organizations and individuals using land must ensure its rational use.

ARTICLE 11

The individual economy of urban and rural working people, operating within the limits prescribed by law, is a complement to the socialist public economy. The state protects the lawful rights and interests of the individual economy.

The state guides, assists and supervises the individual economy by administrative control.

ARTICLE 12

Socialist public property is inviolable.

The state protects socialist public property. Appropriation or damaging of state or collective property by any organization or individual by whatever means is prohibited.

ARTICLE 13

The state protects the right of citizens to own lawfully earned income, savings, houses and other lawful property.

The state protects according to law the right of citizens to inherit private property.

ARTICLE 14

The state continuously raises labour productivity, improves economic results and develops the productive forces by enhancing the enthusiasm of the working people, raising the level of their technical skill, disseminating advanced science and technology, improving the systems of economic administration and enterprise operation and management, instituting the socialist system of responsibility in various forms and improving the organization of work.

The state practises strict economy and combats waste.

The state properly apportions accumulation and consumption, concerns itself with the interests of the collective and the individual as well as of the state and, on the basis of expanded production, gradually improves the material and cultural life of the people.

ARTICLE 15

The state practises planned economy on the basis of socialist public ownership. It ensures the proportionate and coordinated growth of the national economy through overall balancing by economic planning and the supplementary role of regulation by the market.

Disturbance of the socioeconomic order or disruption of the state economic plan by any organization or individual is prohibited.

ARTICLE 16

State enterprises have decision-making power with regard to operation and management within the limits prescribed by law, on condition that they submit to unified leadership by the state and fulfill all their obligations under the state plan.

State enterprises practise democratic management through congresses of workers and staff and in other ways in accordance with the law.

ARTICLE 17

Collective economic organizations have decision-making power in conducting independent economic activities, on condition that they accept the guidance of the state plan and abide by the relevant laws.

Collective economic organizations practise democratic management in accordance with the law. The entire body of their workers elects or removes their managerial personnel and decides on major issues concerning operation and management.

ARTICLE 18

The People's Republic of China permits foreign enterprises, other foreign economic organizations and individual foreigners to invest in China and to enter into various forms of economic cooperation with Chinese enterprises and other Chinese economic organizations in accordance with the law of the People's Republic of China.

All foreign enterprises, other foreign economic organizations as well as Chinese-foreign joint ventures within Chinese territory shall abide by the law of the People's Republic of China. Their lawful rights and interests are protected by the law of the People's Republic of China.

ARTICLE 19

The state undertakes the development of socialist education and works to raise the scientific and cultural level of the whole nation.

The state establishes and administers schools of various types, universalizes compulsory primary education and promotes secondary, vocational and higher education as well as pre-school education.

The state develops educational facilities in order to eliminate iliteracy and provide political, scientific, technical and professional education as well as general education for workers, peasants, state functionaries and other working people. It encourages people to become educated through independent study.

The state encourages the collective economic organizations, state enterprises and institutions and other sectors of society to establish educational institutions of various types in accordance with the law.

The state promotes the nationwide use of Putonghua (common speech based on Beijing pronunciation).

ARTICLE 20

The state promotes the development of the natural and social sciences, disseminates knowledge of science and technology, and commends and rewards achievements in scientific research as well as technological innovations and inventions.

ARTICLE 21

The state develops medical and health services, promotes modern medicine and traditional Chinese medicine, encourages and supports the setting up of various medical and health facilities by the rural economic collectives, state enterprises and institutions and neighbourhood organizations, and promotes health and sanitation activities of a mass character, all for the protection of the people's health.

The state develops physical culture and promotes mass sports activities to improve the people's physical fitness.

ARTICLE 22

The state promotes the development of art and literature, the press, radio and television broadcasting, publishing and distribution services, libraries, museums, cultural centres and other cultural undertakings that serve the people and socialism, and it sponsors mass cultural activities.

The state protects sites of scenic and historical interest, valuable cultural monuments and relics and other significant items of China's historical and cultural heritage.

ARTICLE 23

The state trains specialized personnel in all fields who serve socialism, expands the ranks of intellectuals and creates conditions to give full scope to their role in socialist modernization.

ARTICLE 24

The state strenghtens the building of a socialist society with an advanced culture and ideology by promoting education in high ideals, ethics, general knowledge, discipline and legality, and by promoting the formulation and observance of rules of conduct and common pledges by various sections of the people in urban and rural areas.

The state advocates the civic virtues of love of the motherland, of the people, of labour, of science and of socialism. It conducts education among the people in patriotism and collectivism, in internationalism and communism and in dialectical and historical materialism, to combat capitalist, feudal and other decadent ideas.

ARTICLE 25

The state promotes family planning so that population growth may fit the plans for economic and social development.

ARTICLE 26

The state protects and improves the environment in which people live and the ecological environment. It prevents and controls pollution and other public hazards.

The state organizes and encourages afforestation and the protection of forests.

ARTICLE 27

All state organs carry out the principle of simple and efficient administration, the system of responsibility for work and the system of training functionaries and appraising their performance in order constantly to improve the quality of work and efficiency and combat bureaucratism.

All state organs and functionaries must rely on the support of the people, keep in close touch with them, heed their opinions and suggestions, accept their supervision and do their best to serve them.

ARTICLE 28

The state maintains public order and suppresses treasonable and other counter-revolutionary activities; it penalizes criminal activities that endanger public security and disrupt the socialist economy as well as other criminal activities; and it punishes and reforms criminals.

ARTICLE 29

The armed forces of the People's Republic of China belong to the people. Their tasks are to strengthen national defence, resist aggression, defend the motherland, safeguard the people's peaceful labour, participate in national reconstruction and do their best to serve the people.

The state strengthens the revolutionalization, modernization and regularization of the armed forces in order to increase national defence capability.

ARTICLE 30

The administrative division of the People's Republic of China is as follows:

(1)   The country is divided into provinces, autonomous regions and municipalities directly under the Central Government;

(2)   Provinces and autonomous regions are divided into autonomous prefectures, counties, autonomous counties, and cities;

(3)   Counties and autonomous counties are divided into townships, nationality townships, and towns.

Municipalities directly under the Central Government and other large cities are divided into districts and counties. Autonomous prefectures are divided into counties, autonomous counties, and cities.

All autonomous regions, autonomous prefectures and autonomous counties are national autonomous areas.

ARTICLE 31

The state may establish special administrative regions when necessary. The systems to be instituted in special administrative regions shall be prescribed by law enacted by the National People's Congress in the light of specific conditions.

ARTICLE 32

The People's Republic of China protects the lawful rights and interests of foreigners within Chinese territory; foreigners on Chinese territory must abide by the laws of the People's Republic of China.

The People's Republic of China may grant asylum to foreigners who request it for political reasons.

CHAPTER TWO

The Fundamental Rights and Duties of Citizens

ARTICLE 33

All persons holding the nationality of the People's Republic of China are citizens of the People's Republic of China.

All citizens of the People's Republic of China are equal before the law.

Every citizen is entitled to the rights and at the same time must perform the duties prescribed by the Constitution and the law.

ARTICLE 34

All citizens of the People's Republic of China who have reached the age of 18 have the right to vote and stand for election, regardless of ethnic status, race, sex, occupation, family background, religious belief, education, property status or length of residence, except persons deprived of political rights according to law.

ARTICLE 35

Citizens of the People's Republic of China enjoy freedom of speech, of the press, of assembly, of association, of procession and of demonstration.

ARTICLE 36

Citizens of the People's Republic of China enjoy freedom of religious belief.

No state organ, public organization or individual may compel citizens to believe in, or not to believe in, any religion; nor may they discriminate against citizens who believe in, or do not believe in, any religion.

The state protects normal religious activities. No one may make use of religion to engage in activities that disrupt public order, impair the health of citizens or interfere with the educational system of the state.

Religious bodies and religious affairs are not subject to any foreign domination.

ARTICLE 37

Freedom of the person of citizens of the People's Republic of China is inviolable.

No citizen may be arrested except with the approval or by decision of a people's procuratorate or by decision of a people's court, and arrests must be made by a public security organ.

Unlawful detention or deprivation or restriction of citizens' freedom of the person by other means is prohibited, and unlawful search of the person of citizens is prohibited.

ARTICLE 38

The personal dignity of citizens of the People's Republic of China is inviolable. Insult, libel, false accusation or false incrimination directed against citizens by any means is prohibited.

ARTICLE 39

The residences of citizens of the People's Republic of China are inviolable. Unlawful search of, or intrusion into, a citizen's residence is prohibited.

ARTICLE 40

Freedom and privacy of correspondence of citizens of the People's Republic of China are protected by law. No organization or individual may, on any ground, infringe upon citizens' freedom and privacy of correspondence, except in cases where, to meet the needs of state security or of criminal investigation, public security or procuratorial organs are permitted to censor correspondence in accordance with procedures prescribed by law.

ARTICLE 41

Citizens of the People's Republic of China have the right to criticize and make suggestions regarding any state organ or functionary. Citizens have the right to make to relevant state organs complaints or charges against, or exposures of, any state organ or functionary for violation of the law or dereliction of duty; but fabrication or distortion of facts for purposes of libel or false incrimination is prohibited.

The state organ concerned must deal with complaints, charges or exposures made by citizens in a responsible manner after ascertaining the facts. No one may suppress such complaints, charges and exposures or retaliate against the citizens making them.

Citizens who have suffered losses as a result of infringement of their civic rights by any state organ or functionary have the right to compensation in accordance with the law.

ARTICLE 42

Citizens of the People's Republic of China have the right as well as the duty to work.

Through various channels, the state creates conditions for employment, enhances occupational safety and health, improves working conditions and, on the basis of expanded production, increases remuneration for work and welfare benefits.

Work is a matter of honour for every citizen who is able to work. All working people in state enterprises and in urban and rural economic collectives should approach their work as the masters of the country that they are. The state promotes socialist labour emulation, and commends and rewards model and advanced workers. The state encourages citizens to take part in voluntary labour.

The state provides necessary vocational training for citizens before they are employed.

ARTICLE 43

Working people in the People's Republic of China have the right to rest.

The state expands facilities for the rest and recuperation of the working people and prescribes working hours and vacations for workers and staff.

ARTICLE 44

The state applies the system of retirement for workers and staff of enterprises and institutions and for functionaries of organs of state according to law. The livelihood of retired personnel is ensured by the state and society.

ARTICLE 45

Citizens of the People's Republic of China have the right to material assistance from the state and society when they are old, ill or disabled. The state develops social insurance, social relief and medical and health services that are required for citizens to enjoy this right.

The state and society ensure the livelihood of disabled members of the armed forces, provide pensions to the families of martyrs and give preferential treatment to the families of military personnel.

The state and society help make arrangements for the work, livelihood and education of the blind, deaf-mutes and other handicapped citizens.

ARTICLE 46

Citizens of the People's Republic of China have the duty as well as the right to receive education.

The state promotes the all-round development of children and young people, morally, intellectually and physically.

ARTICLE 47

Citizens of the People's Republic of China have the freedom to engage in scientific research, literary and artistic creation and other cultural pursuits. The state encourages and assists creative endeavours conducive to the interests of the people that are made by citizens engaged in education, science, technology, literature, art and other cultural work.

ARTICLE 48

Women in the People's Republic of China enjoy equal rights with men in all spheres of life, in political, economic, cultural, social and family life.

The state protects the rights and interests of women, applies the principle of equal pay for equal work to men and women alike and trains and selects cadres from among women.

ARTICLE 49

Marriage, the family and mother and child are protected by the state.

Both husband and wife have the duty to practise family planning.

Parents have the duty to rear and educate their children who are minors, and children who have come of age have the duty to support and assist their parents.

Violation of the freedom of marriage is prohibited. Maltreatment of old people, women and children is prohibited.

ARTICLE 50

The People's Republic of China protects the legitimate rights and interests of Chinese nationals residing abroad and protects the lawful rights and interests of returned overseas Chinese and of the family members of Chinese nationals residing abroad.

ARTICLE 51

Citizens of the People's Republic of China, in exercising their freedoms and rights, may not infringe upon the interests of the state, of society or of the collective, or upon the lawful freedoms and rights of other citizens.

ARTICLE 52

It is the duty of citizens of the People's Republic of China to safeguard the unification of the country and the unity of all its nationalities.

ARTICLE 53

Citizens of the People's Republic of China must abide by the Constitution and the law, keep state secrets, protect public property, observe labour discipline and public order and respect social ethics.

ARTICLE 54

It is the duty of citizens of the People's Republic of China to safeguard the security, honour and interests of the motherland; they must not commit acts detrimental to the security, honour and interests of the motherland.

ARTICLE 55

It is the sacred duty of every citizen of the People's Republic of China to defend the motherland and resist aggression.

It is the honourable duty of citizens of the People's Republic of China to perform military service and join the militia in accordance with the law.

ARTICLE 56

It is the duty of citizens of the People's Republic of China to pay taxes in accordance with the law.

CHAPTER THREE

The Structure of the State

SECTION I *The National People's Congress*

ARTICLE 57

The National People's Congress of the People's Republic of China is the highest organ of state power. Its permanent body is the Standing Committee of the National People's Congress.

ARTICLE 58

The National People's Congress and its Standing Committee exercise the legislative power of the state.

ARTICLE 59

The National People's Congress is composed of deputies elected from the provinces, autonomous regions and municipalities directly under the Central Government and of deputies elected from the armed forces. All the minority nationalities are entitled to appropriate representation.

Election of deputies to the National People's Congress is conducted by the Standing Committee of the National People's Congress.

The number of deputies to the National People's Congress and the procedure of their election are prescribed by law.

ARTICLE 60

The National People's Congress is elected for a term of five years.

The Standing Committee of the National People's Congress must ensure the completion of election of deputies to the succeeding National People's Congress two months prior to the expiration of the term of office of the current National People's Congress. Should extraordinary circumstances prevent such an election, it may be postponed and the term of office of the current National People's Congress extended by the decision of a vote of more than two-thirds of all those on the Standing Committee of the current National People's Congress. The election of deputies to the succeeding National People's Congress must be completed within one year after the termination of such extraordinary circumstances.

ARTICLE 61

The National People's Congress meets in session once a year and is convened by its Standing Committee. A session of the National People's Congress may be convened at any time the Standing Committee deems it necessary or when more than one-fifth of the deputies to the National People's Congress so propose.

When the National People's Congress meets, it elects a Presidium to conduct its session.

ARTICLE 62

The National People's Congress exercises the following functions and powers:

(1) to amend the Constitution;

(2) to supervise the enforcement of the Constitution;

(3) to enact and amend basic laws governing criminal offences, civil affairs, the state organs and other matters;

(4) to elect the President and the Vice-President of the People's Republic of China;

(5) to decide on the choice of the Premier of the State Council upon nomination by the President of the People's Republic of China, and on the choice of the Vice-Premiers, State Councillors, Ministers in charge of ministries or commissions, the Auditor-General and the Secretary-General of the State Council upon nomination by the Premier;

(6) to elect the Chairman of the Central Military Commission and, upon nomination by the Chairman, to decide on the choice of all other members of the Central Military Commission;

(7) to elect the President of the Supreme People's Court;

(8) to elect the Procurator-General of the Supreme People's Procuratorate;

(9) to examine and approve the plan for national economic and social development and the report on its implementation;

(10) to examine and approve the state budget and the report on its implementation;

(11) to alter or annul inappropriate decisions of the Standing Committee of the National People's Congress;

(12) to approve the establishment of provinces, autonomous regions, and municipalities directly under the Central Government;

(13) to decide on the establishment of special administrative regions and the systems to be instituted there;

(14) to decide on questions of war and peace; and

(15) to exercise such other functions and powers as the highest organ of state power should exercise.

ARTICLE 63

The National People's Congress has the power to remove from office the following persons:

(1) the President and the Vice-President of the People's Republic of China;

(2) the Premier, Vice-Premiers, State Councillors, Ministers in charge of ministries or commissions, the Auditor-General and the Secretary-General of the State Council;

(3) the Chairman of the Central Military Commission and other members of the Commission;

(4) the President of the Supreme People's Court; and

(5) the Procurator-General of the Supreme People's Procuratorate.

ARTICLE 64

Amendments to the Constitution are to be proposed by the Standing Committee of the National People's Congress or by more than one-fifth of the deputies to the National People's Congress and adopted by a vote of more than two-thirds of all the deputies to the Congress.

Laws and resolutions are to be adopted by a majority vote of all the deputies to the National People's Congress.

ARTICLE 65

The Standing Committee of the National People's Congress is composed of the following:

the Chairman;
the Vice-Chairmen;
the Secretary-General; and
the members.

Minority nationalities are entitled to appropriate representation on the Standing Committee of the National People's Congress.

The National People's Congress elects, and has the power to recall, members of its Standing Committee.

No one on the Standing Committee of the National People's Congress shall hold office in any of the administrative, judicial or procuratorial organs of the state.

ARTICLE 66

The Standing Committee of the National People's Congress is elected for the same term as the National People's Congress; it shall exercise its functions and powers until a new Standing Committee is elected by the succeeding National People's Congress.

The Chairman and Vice-Chairman of the Standing Committee shall serve no more than two consecutive terms.

ARTICLE 67

The Standing Committee of the National People's Congress exercises the following functions and powers:

(1) to interpret the Constitution and supervise its enforcement;

(2) to enact and amend laws, with the exception of those which should be enacted by the National People's Congress;

(3) to partially supplement and amend, when the National People's Congress is not in session, laws enacted by the National People's Congress provided that the basic principles of these laws are not contravened;

(4) to interpret laws;

(5) to review and approve, when the National People's Congress is not in session, partial adjustments to the plan for national economic and social development or to the state budget that prove necessary in the course of their implementation;

(6) to supervise the work of the State Council, the Central Military Commission, the Supreme People's Court and the Supreme People's Procuratorate;

(7) to annul those administrative rules and regulations, decisions or orders of the State Council that contravene the Constitution or the law;

(8) to annul those local regulations or decisions of the organs of state power of provinces, autonomous regions, and municipalities directly under the Central Govern-

ment that contravene the Constitution, the law or the administrative rules and regulations;

(9) to decide, when the National People's Congress is not in session, on the choice of Ministers in charge of ministries or commissions, the Auditor-General or the Secretary-General of the State Council upon nomination by the Premier of the State Council;

(10) to decide, upon nomination by the Chairman of the Central Military Commission, on the choice of other members of the Commission, when the National People's Congress is not in session;

(11) to appoint or remove, at the recommendation of the President of the Supreme People's Court, the Vice-Presidents and Judges of the Supreme People's Court, members of its Judicial Committee and the President of the Military Court;

(12) to appoint or remove, at the recommendation of the Procurator-General of the Supreme People's Procuratorate, the Deputy Procurators-General and procurators of the Supreme People's Procuratorate, members of its Procuratorial Committee and the Chief Procurator of the Military Procuratorate, and to approve the appointment or removal of the chief procurators of the people's procuratorates of provinces, autonomous regions and municipalities directly under the Central Government;

(13) to decide on the appointment or recall of plenipotentiary representatives abroad;

(14) to decide on the ratification or abrogation of treaties and important agreements concluded with foreign states;

(15) to institute systems of titles and ranks for military and diplomatic personnel and of other specific titles and ranks;

(16) to institute state medals and titles of honour and decide on their conferment;

(17) to decide on the granting of special pardons;

(18) to decide, when the National People's Congress is not in session, on the proclamation of a state of war in the event of an armed attack on the country or in fulfilment of international treaty obligations concerning common defence against aggression;

(19) to decide on general mobilization or partial mobilization;

(20) to decide on the imposition of martial law throughout the country or in particular provinces, autonomous regions, or municipalities directly under the Central Government; and

(21) to exercise such other functions and powers as the National People's Congress may assign to it.

ARTICLE 68

The Chairman of the Standing Committee of the National People's Congress directs the work of the Standing Committee and convenes its meetings. The Vice-Chairmen and the Secretary-General assist the Chairman in his work.

The Chairman, the Vice-Chairmen and the Secretary-General constitute the Council of Chairmen which handles the important day-to-day work of the Standing Committee of the National People's Congress.

ARTICLE 69

The Standing Committee of the National People's Congress is responsible to the National People's Congress and reports on its work to the Congress.

ARTICLE 70

The National People's Congress establishes a Nationalities Committee, a Law Committee, a Finance and Economic Committee, an Education, Science, Culture and Public

Health Committee, a Foreign Affairs Committee, an Overseas Chinese Committee and such other special committees as are necessary. These special committees work under the direction of the Standing Committee of the National People's Congress when the Congress is not in session.

The special committees examine, discuss and draw up relevant bills and draft resolutions under the direction of the National People's Congress and its Standing Committee.

ARTICLE 71

The National People's Congress and its Standing Committee may, when they deem it necessary, appoint committees of inquiry into specific questions and adopt relevant resolutions in the light of their reports.

All organs of state, public organizations and citizens concerned are obliged to furnish necessary information to the committees of inquiry when they conduct investigations.

ARTICLE 72

Deputies to the National People's Congress and members of its Standing Committee have the right, in accordance with procedures prescribed by law, to submit bills and proposals within the scope of the respective functions and powers of the National People's Congress and its Standing Committee.

ARTICLE 73

Deputies to the National People's Congress and members of the Standing Committee have the right, during the sessions of the Congress and the meetings of the Committee, to address questions, in accordance with procedures prescribed by law, to the State Council or the ministries and commissions under the State Council, which must answer the questions in a responsible manner.

ARTICLE 74

No deputy to the National People's Congress may be arrested or placed on criminal trial without the consent of the Presidium of the current session of the National People's Congress or, when the National People's Congress is not in session, without the consent of its Standing Committee.

ARTICLE 75

Deputies to the National People's Congress may not be held legally liable for their speeches or votes at its meetings.

ARTICLE 76

Deputies to the National People's Congress must play an exemplary role in abiding by the Constitution and the law and keeping state secrets and, in public activities, production and other work, assist in the enforcement of the Constitution and the law.

Deputies to the National People's Congress should maintain close contact with the units which elected them and with the people, heed and convey the opinions and demands of the people and work hard to serve them.

ARTICLE 77

Deputies to the National People's Congress are subject to supervision by the units which elected them. The electoral units have the power, through procedures prescribed by law, to recall deputies they elected.

ARTICLE 78

The organization and working procedures of the National People's Congress and its Standing Committee are prescribed by law.

SECTION II *The President of the People's Republic of China*

ARTICLE 79

The President and Vice-President of the People's Republic of China are elected by the National People's Congress.

Citizens of the People's Republic of China who have the right to vote and to stand for election and who have reached the age of 45 are eligible for election as President or Vice-President of the People's Republic of China.

The term of office of the President and Vice-President of the People's Republic of China is the same as that of the National People's Congress, and they shall serve no more than two consecutive terms.

ARTICLE 80

The President of the People's Republic of China, in pursuance of the decisions of the National People's Congress and its Standing Committee, promulgates statutes, appoints or removes the Premier, Vice-Premiers, State Councillors, Ministers in charge of ministries or commissions, the Auditor-General and the Secretary-General of the State Council; confers state medals and titles of honour; issues orders of special pardons; proclaims martial law; proclaims a state of war; and issues mobilization orders.

ARTICLE 81

The President of the People's Republic of China receives foreign diplomatic representatives on behalf of the People's Republic of China and, in pursuance of the decisions of the Standing Committee of the National People's Congress, appoints or recalls plenipotentiary representatives abroad, and ratifies or abrogates treaties and important agreements concluded with foreign states.

ARTICLE 82

The Vice-President of the People's Republic of China assists the President in his work.

The Vice-President of the People's Republic of China may exercise such functions and powers of the President as the President may entrust to him.

ARTICLE 83

The President and Vice-President of the People's Republic of China exercise their functions and powers until the new President and Vice-President elected by the succeeding National People's Congress assume office.

ARTICLE 84

In the event that the office of the President of the People's Republic of China falls vacant, the Vice-President succeeds to the office of the President.

In the event that the office of the Vice-President of the People's Republic of China falls vacant, the National People's Congress shall elect a new Vice-President to fill the vacancy.

In the event that the offices of both the President and the Vice-President of the People's Republic of China fall vacant, the National People's Congress shall elect a new

President and a new Vice-President. Prior to such election, the Chairman of the Standing Committee of the National People's Congress shall temporarily act as the President of the People's Republic of China.

SECTION III *The State Council*

ARTICLE 85

The State Council, that is, the Central People's Government, of the People's Republic of China is the executive body of the highest organ of state power; it is the highest organ of state administration.

ARTICLE 86

The State Council is composed of the following:

the Premier;
the Vice-Premiers;
the State Councillors;
the Ministers in charge of ministries;
the Ministers in charge of commissions;
the Auditor-General; and
the Secretary-General

The Premier assumes overall responsibility for the work of the State Council. The Ministers assume overall responsibility for the work of the ministries and commissions.

The organization of the State Council is prescribed by law.

ARTICLE 87

The term of office of the State Council is the same as that of the National People's Congress.

The Premier, Vice-Premiers and State Councillors shall serve no more than two consecutive terms.

ARTICLE 88

The Premier directs the work of the State Council. The Vice-Premiers and State Councillors assist the Premier in his work.

Executive meetings of the State Council are to be attended by the Premier, the Vice-Premiers, the State Councillors and the Secretary-General of the State Council.

The Premier convenes and presides over the executive meetings and plenary meetings of the State Council.

ARTICLE 89

The State Council exercises the following functions and powers:

(1) to adopt administrative measures, enact administrative rules and regulations and issue decisions and orders in accordance with the Constitution and the law;

(2) to submit proposals to the National People's Congress or its Standing Committee;

(3) to formulate the tasks and responsibilities of the ministries and commissions of the State Council, to exercise unified leadership over the work of the ministries and commissions and to direct all other administrative work of a national character that does not fall within the jurisdiction of the ministries and commissions;

(4) to exercise unified leadership over the work of local organs of state administration at various levels throughout the country, and to formulate the detailed division of functions and powers between the Central Government and the organs of state administration of provinces, autonomous regions, and municipalities directly under the Central Government;

(5) to draw up and implement the plan for national economic and social development and the state budget;

(6) to direct and administer economic affairs and urban and rural development;

(7) to direct and administer the affairs of education, science, culture, public health, physical culture and family planning;

(8) to direct and administer civil affairs, public security, judicial administration, supervision and other related matters;

(9) to conduct foreign affairs and conclude treaties and agreements with foreign states;

(10) to direct and administer the building of national defence;

(11) to direct and administer affairs concerning the nationalities and to safeguard the equal rights of minority nationalities and the right to autonomy of the national autonomous areas;

(12) to protect the legitimate rights and interests of Chinese nationals residing abroad and protect the lawful rights and interests of returned overseas Chinese and of the family members of Chinese nationals residing abroad;

(13) to alter or annul inappropriate orders, directives and regulations issued by the ministries or commissions;

(14) to alter or annul inappropriate decisions and orders issued by local organs of state administration at various levels;

(15) to approve the geographic division of provinces, autonomous regions and municipalities directly under the Central Government, and to approve the establishment and geographic division of autonomous prefectures, counties, autonomous counties, and cities;

(16) to decide on the imposition of martial law in parts of provinces, autonomous regions, and municipalities directly under the Central Government;

(17) to examine and decide on the size of administrative organs and, in accordance with the law, to appoint or remove administrative officials, train them, appraise their performance and reward or punish them; and

(18) to exercise such other functions and powers as the National People's Congress or its Standing Committee may assign to it.

ARTICLE 90

Ministers in charge of the ministries or commissions of the State Council are responsible for the work of their respective departments and they convene and preside over ministerial meetings or general and executive meetings of the commissions to discuss and decide on major issues in the work of their respective departments.

The ministries and commissions issue orders, directives and regulations within the jurisdiction of their respective departments and in accordance with the law and the administrative rules and regulations, decisions and orders issued by the State Council.

ARTICLE 91

The State Council establishes an auditing body to supervise through auditing the revenue and expenditure of all departments under the State Council and of the local governments at various levels, and the revenue and expenditure of all financial and monetary organizations, enterprises and institutions of the state.

Under the direction of the Premier of the State Council, the auditing body independently exercises its power of supervision through auditing in accordance with the law, subject to no interference by any other administrative organ or any public organization or individual.

ARTICLE 92

The State Council is responsible and reports on its work to the National People's Congress or, when the National People's Congress is not in session, to its Standing Committee.

SECTION IV *The Central Military Commission*

ARTICLE 93

The Central Military Commission of the People's Republic of China directs the armed forces of the country.

The Central Military Commission is composed of the following:

The Chairman;
the Vice-Chairmen; and
the members.

The Chairman assumes overall responsibility for the work of the Central Military Commission.

The term of office of the Central Military Commission is the same as that of the National People's Congress.

ARTICLE 94

The Chairman of the Central Military Commission is responsible to the National People's Congress and its Standing Committee.

SECTION V *The Local People's Congresses and Local People's Governments at Various Levels*

ARTICLE 95

People's congresses and people's governments are established in provinces, municipalities directly under the Central Government, counties, cities, municipal districts, townships, nationality townships, and towns.

The organization of local people's congresses and local people's governments at various levels is prescribed by law.

Organs of self-government are established in autonomous regions, autonomous prefectures and autonomous counties. The organization and working procedures of organs of self-government are prescribed by law in accordance with the basic principles laid down in Sections V and VI of Chapter Three of the Constitution.

ARTICLE 96

Local people's congresses at various levels are local organs of state power.

Local people's congresses at and above the county level establish standing committees.

ARTICLE 97

Deputies to the people's congresses of provinces, municipalities directly under the Central Government and cities divided into districts are elected by the people's congresses at the next lower level; deputies to the people's congresses of counties, cities not divided into districts, municipal districts, townships, nationality townships, and towns are elected directly by their constituencies.

The number of deputies to local people's congresses at various levels and the manner of their election are prescribed by law.

ARTICLE 98

The term of office of the people's congresses of provinces, municipalities directly under the Central Government and cities divided into districts is five years. The term of office of the people's congresses of counties, cities not divided into districts, municipal districts, townships, nationality townships, and towns is three years.

ARTICLE 99

Local people's congresses at various levels ensure the observance and implementation of the Constitution and the law and the administrative rules and regulations in their respective administrative areas. Within the limits of their authority as prescribed by law, they adopt and issue resolutions and examine and decide on plans for local economic and cultural development and for the development of public services.

Local people's congresses at and above the county level shall examine and approve the plans for economic and social development and the budgets of their respective administrative areas and examine and approve the reports on their implementation. They have the power to alter or annul inappropriate decisions of their own standing committees.

The people's congresses of nationality townships may, within the limits of their authority as prescribed by law, take specific measures suited to the characteristics of the nationalities concerned.

ARTICLE 100

The people's congresses of provinces and municipalities directly under the Central Government and their standing committees may adopt local regulations, which must not contravene the Constitution and the law and administrative rules and regulations, and they shall report such local regulations to the Standing Committee of the National People's Congress for the record.

ARTICLE 101

Local people's congresses at their respective levels elect and have the power to recall governors and deputy governors, or mayors and deputy mayors, or heads and deputy heads of counties, districts, townships and towns.

Local people's congresses at and above the county level elect, and have the power to recall, presidents of people's courts and chief procurators of people's procuratorates at the corresponding level. The election or recall of chief procurators of people's procuratorates shall be reported to the chief procurators of the people's procuratorates at the next higher level for submission to the standing committees of the people's congresses at the corresponding level for approval.

ARTICLE 102

Deputies to the people's congresses of provinces, municipalities directly under the Central Government and cities divided into districts are subject to supervision by the units which elected them; deputies to the people's congresses of counties, cities not divided into districts, municipal districts, townships, nationality townships, and towns are subject to supervision by their constituencies.

The electoral units and constituencies which elect deputies to local people's congresses at various levels have the power to recall the deputies according to procedures prescribed by law.

ARTICLE 103

The standing committee of a local people's congress at and above the county level is composed of a chairman, vice-chairmen and members, and is responsible and reports on its work to the people's congress at the corresponding level.

A local people's congress at or above the county level elects, and has the power to recall, members of its standing committee.

No one on the standing committee of a local people's congress at or above the county level shall hold office in state administrative, judicial and procuratorial organs.

ARTICLE 104

The standing committee of a local people's congress at or above the county level discusses and decides on major issues in all fields of work in its administrative area; supervises the work of the people's government, people's court and people's procuratorate at the corresponding level; annuls inappropriate decisions and orders of the people's government at the corresponding level; annuls inappropriate resolutions of the people's congress at the next lower level; decides on the appointment or removal of functionaries of state organs within the limits of its authority as prescribed by law; and, when the people's congress at the corresponding level is not in session, recalls individual deputies to the people's congress at the next higher level and elects individual deputies to fill vacancies in that people's congress.

ARTICLE 105

Local people's governments at various levels are the executive bodies of local organs of state power as well as the local organs of state administration at the corresponding levels.

Governors, mayors and heads of counties, districts, townships and towns assume overall responsibility for local people's governments at various levels.

ARTICLE 106

The term of office of local people's governments at various levels is the same as that of the people's congresses at the corresponding levels.

ARTICLE 107

Local people's governments at and above the county level, within the limits of their authority as prescribed by law, conduct administrative work concerning the economy, education, science, culture, public health, physical culture, urban and rural development, finance, civil affairs, public security, nationalities affairs, judicial administration, supervision and family planning in their respective administrative areas; issue decisions and orders; appoint or remove administrative functionaries, train them, appraise their performance and reward or punish them.

People's governments of townships, nationality townships, and towns execute the resolutions of the people's congress at the corresponding level as well as the decisions and orders of the state administrative organs at the next higher level and conduct administrative work in their respective administrative areas.

People's governments of provinces and municipalities directly under the Central Government decide on the establishment and geographic division of townships, nationality townships, and towns.

ARTICLE 108

Local people's governments at and above the county level direct the work of their subordinate departments and of people's governments at lower levels, and have the power to alter or annul inappropriate decisions of their subordinate departments and of the people's governments at lower levels.

ARTICLE 109

Auditing bodies are established by local people's governments at and above the county level. Local auditing bodies at various levels independently exercise their power of supervision through auditing in accordance with the law and are responsible to the people's government at the corresponding level and to the auditing body at the next higher level.

ARTICLE 110

Local people's governments at various levels are responsible and report on their work to people's congresses at the corresponding levels. Local people's governments at and above the county level are responsible and report on their work to the standing committees of the people's congresses at the corresponding levels when the congresses are not in session.

Local people's governments at various levels are responsible and report on their work to the state administrative organs at the next higher level. Local people's governments at various levels throughout the country are state administrative organs under the unified leadership of the State Council and are subordinate to it.

ARTICLE 111

The residents' committees and villagers' committees established among urban and rural residents on the basis of their place of residence are mass organizations of self-management at the grass roots level. The chairman, vice-chairman and members of each residents' or villagers' committee are elected by the residents. The relationship between the residents' and villagers' committees and the grass roots organs of state power is prescribed by law.

The residents' and villagers' committees establish sub-committees for people's mediation, public security, public health and other matters in order to manage public affairs and social services in their areas, mediate civil disputes, help maintain public order and convey residents' opinions and demands and make suggestions to the people's government.

SECTION VI *The Organs of Self-Government of National Autonomous Areas*

ARTICLE 112

The organs of self-government of national autonomous areas are the people's congresses and people's governments of autonomous regions, autonomous prefectures and autonomous counties.

ARTICLE 113

In the people's congress of an autonomous region, prefecture or county, in addition to the deputies of the nationality exercising regional autonomy in the administrative area, the other nationalities inhabiting the area are also entitled to appropriate representation.

Among the chairman and vice-chairmen of the standing committee of the people's congress of an autonomous region, prefecture or county there shall be one or more citizens of the nationality or nationalities exercising regional autonomy in the area concerned.

ARTICLE 114

The chairman of an autonomous region, the prefect of an autonomous prefecture or the head of an autonomous county shall be a citizen of the nationality exercising regional autonomy in the area concerned.

ARTICLE 115

The organs of self-government of autonomous regions, prefectures and counties exercise the functions and powers of local organs of state as specified in Section V of Chapter Three of the Constitution. At the same time, they exercise the power of autonomy within the limits of their authority as prescribed by the Constitution, the Law of the People's Republic of China on Regional National Autonomy and other laws and implement the laws and policies of the state in the light of the existing local situation.

ARTICLE 116

The people's congresses of national autonomous areas have the power to enact regulations on the exercise of autonomy and other separate regulations in the light of the political, economic and cultural characteristics of the nationality or nationalities in the areas concerned. The regulations on the exercise of autonomy and other separate regulations of autonomous regions shall be submitted to the Standing Committee of the National People's Congress for approval before they go into effect. Those of autonomous prefectures and counties shall be submitted to the standing committees of the people's congresses of provinces or autonomous regions for approval before they go into effect, and they shall be reported to the Standing Committee of the National People's Congress for the record.

ARTICLE 117

The organs of self-government of the national autonomous areas have the power of autonomy in administering the finances of their areas. All revenues accruing to the national autonomous areas under the financial system of the state shall be managed and used by the organs of self-government of those areas on their own.

ARTICLE 118

The organs of self-government of the national autonomous areas independently arrange for and administer local economic development under the guidance of state plans.

In exploiting natural resources and building enterprises in the national autonomous areas, the state shall give due consideration to the interests of those areas.

ARTICLE 119

The organs of self-government of the national autonomous areas independently administer educational, scientific, cultural, public health and physical culture affairs in their respective areas, protect and sift through the cultural heritage of the nationalities and work for a vigorous development of their cultures.

ARTICLE 120

The organs of self-government of the national autonomous areas may, in accordance with the military system of the state and practical local needs and with the approval of the State Council, organize local public security forces for the maintenance of public order.

ARTICLE 121

In performing their functions, the organs of self-government of the national autonomous areas, in accordance with the regulations on the exercise of autonomy in those areas, employ the spoken and written language or languages in common use in the locality.

ARTICLE 122

The state provides financial, material and technical assistance to the minority nationalities to accelerate their economic and cultural development.

The state helps the national autonomous areas train large numbers of cadres at various levels and specialized personnel and skilled workers of various professions and trades from among the nationality or nationalities in those areas.

SECTION VII *The People's Courts and the People's Procuratorates*

ARTICLE 123

The people's courts of the People's Republic of China are the judicial organs of the state.

ARTICLE 124

The People's Republic of China establishes the Supreme People's Court and the people's courts at various local levels, military courts and other special people's courts.

The term of office of the President of the Supreme People's Court is the same as that of the National People's Congress. The President shall serve no more than two consecutive terms.

The organization of the people's courts is prescribed by law.

ARTICLE 125

Except in special circumstances as specified by law, all cases in the people's courts are heard in public. The accused has the right to defence.

ARTICLE 126

The people's courts exercise judicial power independently, in accordance with the provisions of the law, and are not subject to interference by any administrative organ, public organization or individual.

ARTICLE 127

The Supreme People's Court is the highest judicial organ.

The Supreme People's Court supervises the administration of justice by the people's courts at various local levels and by the special people's courts. People's courts at higher levels supervise the administration of justice by those at lower levels.

ARTICLE 128

The Supreme People's Court is responsible to the National People's Congress and its Standing Committee. Local people's courts at various levels are responsible to the organs of state power which created them.

ARTICLE 129

The people's procuratorates of the People's Republic of China are state organs for legal supervision.

ARTICLE 130

The People's Republic of China establishes the Supreme People's Procuratorate and the people's procuratorates at various local levels, military procuratorates and other special people's procuratorates.

The term of office of the Procurator-General of the Supreme People's Procuratorate is the same as that of the National People's Congress; the Procurator-General shall serve no more than two consecutive terms.

The organization of the people's procuratorates is prescribed by law.

ARTICLE 131

The people's procuratorates exercise procuratorial power independently, in accordance with the provisions of the law, and are not subject to interference by any administrative organ, public organization or individual.

ARTICLE 132

The Supreme People's Procuratorate is the highest procuratorial organ.

The Supreme People's Procuratorate directs the work of the people's procuratorates at various local levels and of the special people's procuratorates. People's procuratorates at higher levels direct the work of those at lower levels.

ARTICLE 133

The Supreme People's Procuratorate is responsible to the National People's Congress and its Standing Committee. People's procuratorates at various local levels are responsible to the organs of state power which created them and to the people's procuratorates at higher levels.

ARTICLE 134

Citizens of all nationalities have the right to use the spoken and written languages of their own nationalities in court proceedings. The people's courts and people's procuratorates should provide translation for any party to the court proceedings who is not familiar with the spoken or written languages commonly used in the locality.

In an area where people of a minority nationality live in a concentrated community or where a number of nationalities live together, court hearings should be conducted in the language or languages commonly used in the locality; indictments, judgments, notices and other documents should be written, according to actual needs, in the language or languages commonly used in the locality.

ARTICLE 135

The people's courts, the people's procuratorates and the public security organs shall, in handling criminal cases, divide their functions, each taking responsibility for its own work, and they shall coordinate their efforts and check each other to ensure the correct and effective enforcement of the law.

CHAPTER FOUR

The National Flag, the National Emblem and the Capital

ARTICLE 136

The national flag of the People's Republic of China is a red flag with five stars.

ARTICLE 137

The national emblem of the People's Republic of China consists of an image of Tiananmen in its centre illuminated by five stars and encircled by ears of grain and a cogwheel.

ARTICLE 138

The capital of the People's Republic of China is Beijing.

Amendments to the Constitution of the People's Republic of China

(Adopted by the Seventh National People's Congress at Its First Session, 12 April 1988)

1. Article 11 of the Constitution shall include a new paragraph, which reads: "The state permits the private sector of the economy to exist and develop within the limits prescribed by law. The private sector of the economy is a complement to the socialist public economy. The state protects the lawful rights and interests of the private sector of the economy, and exercises guidance, supervision and control over the private sector of the economy."

2. The fourth paragraph of Article 10 of the Constitution, which provides that "no organization or individual may appropriate, buy, sell or lease land, or unlawfully transfer land in other ways," shall be amended as: "No organization or individual may appropriate, buy, sell or unlawfully transfer land in other ways. The right to the use of land may be transferred in accordance with the law."

APPENDIX 2

Constitution of the Communist Party of China

(Adopted by the Fourteenth National Party Congress, 18 October 1992)

The Communist Party of China is the vanguard of the Chinese working class, the faithful representative of the interests of the people of all nationalities in China, and the force at the core leading China's cause of socialism. The party's ultimate goal is the creation of a communist social system.

The CPC takes Marxism-Leninism-Mao Zedong Thought as its guide to action.

Marxism-Leninism has revealed the universal law on the history of social development of mankind and analyzed the insurmountable contradictions inherent in the capitalist system, pointing out that the socialist society is bound to replace capitalist society, and ultimately develop into a communist society. The history of more than a century since the publication of the *Communist Manifesto* proves the correctness of the theory on scientific socialism and the strong vitality of socialism. Socialism essentially means to emancipate and develop productive forces, to eliminate exploitation and polarization, and to ultimately realize common prosperity. The development and perfection of the socialist system is a protracted historical process. Despite twists and turns, and relapses in the course of development, the inevitable replacement of capitalism by socialism is an irreversible general trend in the history of social development. Socialism is bound to gradually triumph along paths that are suited to the specific conditions of each country and are chosen by its people of their own free will. The Chinese Communists, with Comrade Mao Zedong as their chief representative, created Mao Zedong Thought by integrating the universal principles of Marxism-Leninism with the concrete practice of the Chinese revolution. Mao Zedong Thought is Marxism-Leninism applied and developed in China; it consists of a body of theoretical principles concerning the revolution and construction in China, and a summary of experience therein, both of which have been proved correct by practice; it represents the crystallized, collective wisdom of the CPC.

The CPC led the people of all nationalities in waging their prolonged revolutionary struggle against imperialism, feudalism, and bureaucrat-capitalism, winning victory in the new democratic revolution and establishing the PRC, a people's democratic dictatorship. After the founding of the People's Republic, it led them in smoothly carrying out socialist transformation, completing the transition from New Democracy to socialism, establishing the socialist system, and developing socialism in its economic, political, and cultural aspects. Since the Third Plenary Session of the 11th CPC Central Committee was convened, the party, after summarizing both positive and negative experiences and by emancipating the mind and seeking truth from facts, has shifted the focus of the whole party's work to economic construction, and implemented reform and opening up. It has gradually formed the theory, line, principles, and policies on building socialism with Chinese characteristics by integrating the basic tenets of Marxism with the practice of socialist construction in contemporary China, thereby opening up a new era in the development of the socialist cause. The theory on building socialism with Chinese characteristics, which expounds on the fundamental issues related to building, consolidating, and developing socialism in China, and which inherits and develops Marxism, is a guide for the socialist cause to advance continuously in China.

Our country is now in the initial stage of socialism. This is an impassable stage for economically and culturally backward China in the drive for socialist modernization, which may take up to a hundred years. Socialist construction in our country must proceed from its own conditions and follows the road of socialism with Chinese characteristics. At the present stage, the principal contradiction in our country is that between the people's growing material and cultural needs, and the backward level of our social production. However, because of domestic circumstances and foreign influences, class struggle will continue to exist within certain limits for a long time, and may even sharpen under certain conditions, but class struggle is no longer the principal contradiction. The basic tasks of socialist construction in our country are to further liberate and develop the productive forces, to realize socialist modernization step by step, and, to this end, to reform the aspects of and links in the relations of production and in the superstructure that are not suited to the development of the productive forces. It is imperative to uphold an ownership structure embracing diverse economic sectors with the public ownership of means of production as the main one; to apply the system of distribution with "to each according to his work" as the mainstay, supplemented by other modes of distribution; to encourage some people and areas to prosper before others; to reach common prosperity by eliminating poverty step by step; and to continuously satisfy the people's growing material and cultural needs on the basis of developed production and increased social wealth. The general starting point of and the criteria for appraising all our work should be conducive to developing the productive forces of our socialist society, increasing our socialist country's overall strength, and raising the people's living standards. The strategic objective of our country's economic development is to quadruple the gross national product [GNP] of 1980 by the end of this century and to have our per capita GNP reach the level of a moderately developed country by the middle of next century.

The CPC's basic line for the initial stage of socialism is to lead and unite the people of all nationalities throughout the country to carry out economic construction as the central task, to uphold the four cardinal principles, to persevere in reform and opening to the outside world, and to strive to build our country into a prosperous, powerful, democratic, and civilized socialist modern country through our own arduous efforts.

In leading the socialist cause, the CPC must persist in regarding economic construction as its central task, and all other work must be subordinated to and serve the central task. It is necessary to seize the opportunity to speed up development; to give full play to the role of science and technology as the primary productive force; to raise efficiency, quality, and speed by relying on scientific and technological progress and improving workers' quality; and to strive to push economic construction forward.

The foundation for our country is to uphold the four cardinal principles—upholding the socialist road, the people's democratic dictatorship, leadership of the CPC, and Marxism-Leninism-Mao Zedong Thought. In the whole process of socialist modernization, it is imperative to uphold the four cardinal principles and oppose bourgeois liberalization.

Reform and opening to the outside world are the only way to liberate and develop the productive forces. It is necessary to fundamentally reform the economic structure impeding the development of the productive forces and to institute a system of socialist market economy. Corresponding to this, reform should be carried out in the political structure and other fields. Opening includes opening to the outside and inside in an all-around way. Efforts should be made to develop economic and technological exchanges and cooperation with foreign countries; use more foreign funds, resources, and technology; and draw on and assimilate all the achievements of civilization created by mankind, including developed Western countries' advanced methods of operation and management reflecting the law of modern production. In carrying out reform and opening to the outside, we should boldly explore, do pioneering work, and blaze new trails in practice. The CPC leads the people, as they build a material civilization, and in striving to build a socialist spiritual civilization. The building of socialist spiritual civilization provides the powerful mental impetus and intellectual support for economic construction, reform, and opening to the outside world, and helps create a favorable social environment; Major efforts should be made to promote education, science, and culture, and it is necessary to respect knowledge and trained personnel; to raise the ideological, moral, scientific, and cultural quality of the whole nation; to develop fine traditional national culture; and to bring about a thriving and developed socialist culture. It is essential to educate party members and the masses of people in the party's basic line, patriotism, collectivism, and socialist ideology, and to enhance their spirit of national dignity, confidence, and self-improvement. Efforts should also be made to educate party members in lofty communist ideals, to resist the corrosive influence of decadent capitalist and feudalist ideas, to eliminate all ugly social phenomena, and to encourage the Chinese people to have lofty ideals, moral integrity, education, and a sense of discipline.

The CPC leads the people in promoting socialist democracy, perfecting the socialist legal system, and consolidating the people's democratic dictatorship. It upholds the system of people's congresses, the system of multiparty cooperation under the leadership of the Communist Party, and the system of political consultation. It greatly supports the people in becoming masters of their own country and takes concrete steps to protect the people's right to run the affairs of state and society, and to manage economic and cultural undertakings. It encourages the free airing of views. It establishes a sound system and process for democratic decisionmaking and democratic supervision. It strengthens state legislation and improves the implementation of the state law, to gradually incorporate all state undertakings into a legal framework. It enhances comprehensive control of public security and strives to maintain long-term social stability. It firmly cracks down on criminal acts and criminal elements who jeopardize state security and interests, and who endanger social stability and economic development. It makes a strict distinction between, and correctly handles the nature of, two different contradictions, namely, the contradiction between ourselves and the enemy and the contradictions among the people.

The CPC upholds its leadership over the People's Liberation Army [PLA] and the other people's armed forces; strives to strengthen the building of the PLA; and fully gives play to the PLA's role in consolidating national defense, in defending the motherland, and in taking part in socialist modernization construction. The CPC upholds and promotes relations of equality, unity, and mutual assistance among all nationalities in the country. It persists in implementing and improving the system of regional autonomy for minority nationalities. It makes great efforts to train and promote minority cadres, and assists in the development of the economy and culture in areas inhabited by minority nationalities with a view to bringing about common prosperity and progress for all nationalities.

The CPC unites with all workers, peasants, and intellectuals, and with all the democratic parties, nonparty democrats, and patriotic forces of all nationalities in China in further expanding and fortifying the broadest possible patriotic united front embracing all socialist working people and all patriots who support socialism, or who support the reunification of the motherland. It is necessary to constantly strengthen the unity of all people in the nation, including the unity of our compatriots in Taiwan, Xianggang (Hong Kong), and Aomen (Macao) and Overseas Chinese, and accomplish the great task of reunifying the motherland according to the policy of "one country, two systems." The CPC stands for the vigorous development of relations with foreign countries and exerts efforts to create a favorable international environment for our country's reform, opening to the outside world, and modernization construction. In international affairs, it adheres to the peaceful foreign policy of independence, maintains our country's independence and sovereignty, opposes hegemonism and power politics, safeguards world peace, and promotes human progress. It stands for the development of state relations between China and other countries on the basis of the five principles of mutual respect for sovereignty and territorial integrity, mutual non-aggression, non-interference in each other's internal affairs, equality and mutual benefit, and peaceful coexistence. It constantly develops our country's good-neighborly and friendly relations with peripheral countries, and enhances unity and cooperation with developing countries. It also develops relations with communist parties and other political parties in other countries on the basis of the principle of independence, complete equality, mutual respect, and non-interference in each other's internal affairs.

In order to lead Chinese people of all nationalities in attaining the great goal of socialist modernization, the CPC must closely follow the party's basic line, strengthen party building, persist in strict management of the party, carry forward its fine traditions and work style, enhance its fighting capacity, and build the party into a strong core that leads all people in the nation to constantly advance along the road of socialism with Chinese characteristics. The following four basic requirements must be met in party building:

First, it is necessary to adhere to the party's basic line. The entire party should unswervingly and always persist in unifying thinking and actions in line with the theory of building socialism with Chinese characteristics, and the party's basic line. We should unify reform and opening with the four cardinal principles, comprehensively implement the party's basic line, and oppose all erroneous tendencies of "leftist" and rightist deviation; while keeping vigilance against rightist deviation, main attention should be paid to guarding against "leftist" deviation. Building of various levels of leading bodies should be stepped up. Cadres who have done outstanding jobs and are trusted by the masses in the course of reform, opening, and socialist modernization construction should be promoted. Hundreds and millions of successors to the cause of socialism should be trained and nurtured. All party organizations must ensure the implementation of the party's basic line.

Second, it is necessary to persist in emancipating the mind and seeking truth from facts. The party's ideological line is to proceed from reality in all things, to integrate theory with practice, to seek truth from facts, and to verify and develop truth through practice. In accordance with this ideological line, the entire party must make vigorous explorations, conduct bold experiments, work creatively, constantly study the new situation, sum up new experiences, solve new problems, and enrich and develop Marxism through practice.

Third, it is necessary to serve the people wholeheartedly. The party has no special interests of its own apart from the interests of the working class and the broadest masses of the people. It always gives first priority to the masses' interests, shares weal and woe with them, maintains the closest ties with them, and never allows party members to deviate and ride roughshod over them. The party practices the mass line in its work. While it does all things for the masses, it also relies on all things from the masses. As the party springs from the masses, it must return to the fold. It also converts its correct policy into the masses' voluntary actions. The issues of party style and the ties between the party and the masses are two issues that concern the life and death of the party. The party steadfastly opposes corruption and always works to improve party style and build a clean government.

Fourth, adherence to democratic centralism. Democratic centralism is the integration of centralism based on democracy and democracy under the guidance of centralism. It is the party's basic organizational principle as well as the application of the mass line in the conduct of party activities. Full play should be given to democracy within the party, and the initiative and creativity of party organizations at all levels and the broad ranks of party members should be brought into full play. It is necessary to exercise correct centralism to ensure unity of action throughout the ranks, and the prompt and effective implantation of decisions. It is necessary to strengthen a sense of organization and discipline, and see to it that everyone is equal before party discipline. In its internal political life, the party conducts criticism and self-criticism in the correct way, waging ideological struggles over matters of principle, upholding truth, and rectifying mistakes. It is necessary to work to develop a political situation in which we have both centralism and democracy, both discipline and freedom, both unity of will and personal ease of mind and liveliness.

Party leadership consists mainly of political, ideological, and organizational leadership. The party must adapt to the needs of reform, opening up, and socialist modernization, and step up and improve its leadership. It must concentrate on leadership over economic construction, and organize and coordinate the forces of all quarters to carry out its work around economic construction with concerted efforts. The party must practice democratic and scientific decisionmaking; formulate and implement correct lines, principles, and policies; do its organizational, propaganda, and educational work well; and ensure that all party members play their exemplary vanguard role. It must conduct its activities within the limits permitted by the Constitution and the law. It must see to it that the legislative, judicial, and administrative organs of the state and the economic, cultural, and people's organizations work actively and with initiative, independently, responsibly, and in harmony. It must strengthen leadership over the trade unions, the Communist Youth League, the Women's Federation, and other mass organizations, and give full scope to their roles. The party must adapt to the developments and changes of the situation, constantly improve its leadership style and method, and raise its leadership level. Its members must work in close cooperation with the masses of nonparty people in the common effort to build socialism with Chinese characteristics.

CHAPTER I *Membership*

ARTICLE 1

Any Chinese worker, peasant, member of the Armed Forces, intellectual or any other revolutionary who has reached the age of 18; who accepts the party's program and constitution; and is willing to join and work actively in one of the party organizations, carry out the party's decisions, and pay membership dues regularly may apply for membership of the CPC.

ARTICLE 2

Members of the CPC are vanguard fighters of the Chinese working class imbued with communist consciousness.

Members of the CPC must serve the people wholeheartedly, dedicate their whole lives to the realization of communism, and be ready to make any personal sacrifices.

Members of the CPC are at all times ordinary members of the working people. Communist Party members must not seek personal gain or privileges beyond the personal benefits, job functions, and powers as provided for by the relevant laws and policies.

ARTICLE 3

Party members must fulfill the following duties:

(1) Conscientiously study Marxism-Leninism-Mao Zedong Thought; study the theory on building socialism with Chinese characteristics and the party's line, principles, and policies; study essential knowledge concerning the party; and acquire general, scientific, and professional knowledge.

(2) Unswervingly implement the party's basic line, principles, and policies; take the lead in participating in reform, opening up, and socialist modernization; encourage the masses to work hard for economic development and social progress; and play an exemplary vanguard role in production and other work, study, and social activities.

(3) Adhere to the principle that the interests of the party and people stand above everything, subordinate their personal interests to the interests of the party and people; be the first to bear hardships and the last to enjoy comforts; and work selflessly for the public interests and make more contributions.

(4) Conscientiously observe party discipline and the laws of the state, rigorously guard party and state secrets, execute the party's decisions, accept any job, and actively fulfill any task assigned them by the party.

(5) Uphold the party's solidarity and unity; be loyal to and honest with the party and match words with deeds; and firmly oppose all factional organizations and small-group activities, and oppose double-dealing and scheming of any kind.

(6) Earnestly practice criticism and self-criticism, be bold in exposing and correcting shortcomings and mistakes in work, and resolutely fight negative and decadent phenomena.

(7) Maintain close ties with the masses, propagate the party's views among them, consult with them when problems arise, keep the party informed of their views and demands in good time, and defend their legitimate interests.

(8) Develop new socialist habits; advocate communist ethics; and, as required by the defense of the country and the interests of the people, step forward in times of difficulty and danger, fighting bravely and defying death.

ARTICLE 4

Party members enjoy the following rights:

(1) To attend pertinent party meetings and read pertinent party documents, and to benefit from the party's education and training.

(2) To participate in discussion at party meetings and in party newspapers and journals on questions concerning the party's policies.

(3) To make suggestions and proposals regarding the work of the party.

(4) To make well-grounded criticism of any party organization or member at party meetings; to present information or charges against any party organization or member

concerning violation of discipline and of the law to the party in a responsible way, and to demand disciplinary measures against such a member, or to demand the dismissal or replacement of any cadre who is incompetent.

(5) To vote, elect, and stand for election.

(6) To attend, with the right of self-defense, discussions held by party organizations to decide on disciplinary measures to be taken against themselves or to appraise their work and behavior, while other party members may also bear witness or argue on their behalf.

(7) In case of disagreement with a party decision or policy, to make reservations and present their views to party organizations at higher levels up to and including the Central Committee, provided that they resolutely carry out the decision or policy while it is in force.

(8) To put forward any request, appeal or complaint to a higher party organization up to and including the Central Committee, and ask the organization concerned for a responsible reply.

No party organization, up to and including the Central Committee, has the right to deprive any party member of the above-mentioned rights.

ARTICLE 5

New party members must be admitted through a party branch and the principle of individual admission must be adhered to.

An applicant for party membership must fill in an application form and must be recommended by two full party members. The application must be accepted by a general membership meeting of the party branch concerned and approved by the next higher party organization, and the applicant should undergo observation for a probationary period before being transferred to full membership.

Party members who recommend an applicant must make genuine efforts to acquaint themselves with the latter's ideology, character, personal history, and work performance; must explain to each applicant the party's program and constitution, qualifications for membership and the duties and rights of members; and must make a responsible report to the party organization on the matter. The party branch committee must canvass the opinions of persons concerned, inside and outside the party, about an applicant for party membership and, after establishing the latter's qualifications following a rigorous examination, submit the application to a general membership meeting for discussion.

Before approving the admission of applicants for party membership, the next higher party organization concerned must appoint people to talk with them, so as to get to know them better and help deepen their understanding of the party.

In special circumstances, the Central Committee of the party or the party committee of a province, an autonomous region, or a municipality directly under the central government has the power to admit new party members directly.

ARTICLE 6

A probational party member must take an admission oath in front of the party flag. The oath reads: It is my will to join the Communist Party of China, uphold the party's program, observe the provisions of the party constitution, fulfill a party member's duties, carry out the party's decisions, strictly observe party discipline, guard party secrets, be loyal to the party, work hard, fight for communism throughout my life, be ready at all times to sacrifice my all for the party and the people, and never betray the party.

ARTICLE 7

Probationary members have the same duties as full members. They enjoy the rights of full members except those of voting, electing, or standing for election.

When the probationary period of a probationary member has expired, the party branch concerned should promptly discuss whether he is qualified to be transferred to full membership. A probationary member who conscientiously performs his duties and is qualified for membership should be transferred to full membership as scheduled; if continued observation and education are needed, the probationary period may be prolonged, but by no more than one year; if a probationary member fails to perform his duties and is found to be unqualified for membership, his probationary membership shall be annulled. Any decision to transfer a probationary member to full membership, prolong a probationary period, or annul a probationary membership must be made through discussion by the general membership meeting of the party branch concerned and approved by the next higher party organization.

The probationary period of a probationary member begins from the day of the general membership meeting of the party branch, which admits him as a probationary member. The party standing of a member begins from the day he is transferred to full membership on the expiration of the probationary period.

ARTICLE 8

Every party member, irrespective of position, must be organized into a branch, cell, or other specific unit of the party to participate in the regular activities of the party organization and accept supervision by the masses inside and outside the party. Leading cadres of the party must also participate in democratic discussions at meetings of party committees or units. There shall be no privileged party members who do not participate in the regular activities of the party organization, and do not accept supervision by the masses inside and outside the party.

ARTICLE 9

Party members are free to withdraw from the party. When a party member asks to withdraw, the party branch concerned shall, after discussion by its general membership meeting, remove his name from the party rolls, make the removal publicly known, and report it to the next higher party organization for the record.

The party branch concerned should educate a party member who lacks revolutionary will, fails to fulfill the duties of a party member, and is not qualified for membership, and should set a time limit by which the member must correct his mistakes; if he remains incorrigible after repeated education, he should be persuaded to withdraw from the party. The case shall be discussed and decided by the general membership meeting of the party branch concerned and submitted to the next higher party organization for approval. If the party member being persuaded to withdraw refuses to do so, the case shall be submitted to the general membership meeting of the party branch concerned for discussion and decision on the removal of his name from party rolls, and the decision shall be submitted to the next higher party organization for approval.

A party member who fails to take part in regular party activities, pay membership dues or do work assigned by the party for six successive months without proper reason is regarded as having given up membership. The general membership meeting of the party branch concerned shall decided on the removal of such a person's name from the party rolls and report the removal to the next higher party organization for approval.

CHAPTER II *Organizational System of the Party*

ARTICLE 10

The party is an integral body organized under its program and constitution, and on the principle of democratic centralism. The basic principles of democratic centralism as practiced by the party are as follows:

(1) Individual party members are subordinate to the party organization, the minority is subordinate to the majority, the lower party organizations are subordinate to the higher party organizations and members of the party are subordinate to the national congress and the Central Committee of the party.

(2) The party's leading bodies of all levels are elected except for the representative organs dispatched by them and the leading party members' groups in nonparty organizations.

(3) The highest leading body of the party is the national congress and the central committee elected by it. The leading bodies of local party organizations are the party congresses at their respective levels and the party committees elected by them. Party committees are responsible, and report their work, to the party congresses at their respective levels.

(4) Higher party organizations shall pay constant attention to the views of the lower organizations and the rank-and-file party members and solve in good time the problems they raise. Lower party organizations shall report on their work to and request instructions from higher party organizations; at the same time, they shall handle, independently and in a responsible manner, matters within their jurisdiction. Higher and lower party organizations should exchange information and support and supervise each other. Party organizations at all levels shall make it possible for party members to have a better understanding of and more participation in the party's affairs.

(5) Party committees at all levels function on the principle of combining collective leadership with individual responsibility based on division of labor. All major issues shall be decided upon by the party committee after democratic discussion. Members of the party committee shall effectively perform their duties according to collective decisions and division of labor.

(6) The party forbids all forms of personality cult. It is necessary to ensure that the activities of party leaders be subject to supervision by the party and the people, while at the same time to uphold the prestige of all leaders who represent the interests of the party and the people.

ARTICLE 11

The election of delegates to party congresses and of members of party committees at all levels should reflect the will of the voters. Elections shall be held by secret ballot. The lists of candidates shall be submitted to party organizations and voters for full deliberation and discussion. The election procedure of nominating a larger number of candidates than the number of persons to be elected may be used in a formal election. Or this procedure may be used first in a preliminary election in order to draw up a list of candidates for the formal election. The voters have the right to inquire into the candidates, demand a change, or reject one in favor of another. No organization or individual shall in any way compel voters to elect or not elect any candidate.

If any violation of the party constitution occurs in the election of delegates to a local party congress, the party committee at the next higher level shall, after investigation and verification, decide to invalidate the election and take appropriate measures. The decision shall be reported to the party committee at the next higher level for checking and approval before it is formally announced and implemented.

ARTICLE 12

When necessary, party committees at the central and local levels may convene conferences of delegates to discuss and decide on major problems that require timely solution. The number of delegates to such conferences and the procedure governing their election shall be determined by the party committees convening them.

ARTICLE 13

The formation of a new party organization or the dissolution of an existing one shall be decided upon by the higher party organizations.

Party committees at the central and locals may send out their representative organs. When the congress of a local party organization at any level, including the grass-roots level, is not in session, the next higher party organization may, when it deems it necessary, transfer or appoint responsible members of that organization.

ARTICLE 14

When making decisions on important questions affecting the lower organizations, the leading bodies of the party at all levels should, in ordinary circumstances, solicit the opinions of the lower organizations. Measures should be taken to ensure that the lower organizations can exercise their functions and powers normally. Except in special circumstances, higher leading bodies should not interfere with matters that ought to be handled by lower organizations.

ARTICLE 15

Only the Central Committee of the party has the power to make decisions on major policies of a nationwide character. Party organizations of various departments and localities may make suggestions with regard to such policies to the Central Committee, but shall not make any decisions or publicize their views outside the party without authorization.

Lower party organizations must firmly implement the decisions of higher party organizations. If lower organizations consider that any decisions of higher organizations do not suit actual conditions in their localities or departments, they may request modification. If the higher organizations insist on their original decisions, the lower organizations must carry out such decisions and refrain from publicly voicing their differences, but have the right to report it to the next higher party organization.

Newspapers, journals, and other means of publicity run by party organizations at all levels must propagate the line, principles, policies, and resolutions of the party.

ARTICLE 16

When discussing and making decisions on any matter, party organizations must keep to the principle of subordination of the minority to the majority. A vote must be taken when major issues are decided on. Serious consideration should be given to the differing views of a minority. In case of controversy over major issues in which supporters of two opposing views are nearly equal in number—except in emergencies where action must be taken in accordance with the majority view—the decision should be put off to allow for further investigation, study, and exchange of opinions followed by another vote. Under special circumstances, the controversy may be reported to the next higher party organization for ruling.

When, on behalf of the party organization, an individual party member is to express views on major issues beyond the scope of existing decisions of the party organization, the content must be referred to the party organization to which the party member is affiliated for prior discussion and decision, or must be referred to the next higher party organization for instructions. No party member, whatever his position, is allowed to make decisions on major issues on his own. In an emergency, when a decision by an individual is unavoidable, the matter must be reported to the party organization immediately afterward. No leader is allowed to decide matters arbitrarily on his own or to place himself above the party organization.

ARTICLE 17

The central, local, and primary organizations of the party must all pay great attention to party building. They shall regularly discuss and check up on the party's work in propaganda, education, organization, discipline inspection, mass work, and united front work. They must carefully study ideological and political developments inside and outside the party.

CHAPTER III *Central Organizations of the Party*

ARTICLE 18

The national congress of the party is held once every five years and convened by the Central Committee. It may be convened before the due date if the Central Committee deems it necessary or if more than one-third of the organizations at the provincial level so request. Except under extraordinary circumstances, the congress may not be postponed. The number of delegates to a national congress and the procedure governing their election shall be determined by the Central Committee.

ARTICLE 19

The functions and powers of the national congress of the party are as follows: 1) to hear and examine the report of the Central Committee; 2) to hear and examine the report of the Central Commission for Discipline Inspection; 3) to discuss and decide on major questions concerning the party; 4) to revise the constitution of the party, 5) to elect the Central Committee; and 6) to elect the Central Commission for Discipline Inspection.

ARTICLE 20

The authority and functions of the national congress of party delegates are to discuss and decide on major issues, and to readjust and elect through by-election some members of the Central Committee and Central Discipline Inspection Commission. However, the number of members and alternate members of the Central Committee obtained through readjustment and by-election must not exceed one-fifth of the total number of Central Committee members and alternate members who were elected at the national party congress.

ARTICLE 21

Each term of the party's Central Committee is five years. In case of the advancement or postponement of the convening of the national party congress, the Central Committee's term shall be correspondingly shortened or extended. Members and alternate members of the Central Committee must have a party standing of five years or more. The number of members and alternate members of the Central Committee shall be determined by the national congress. Vacancies on the Central Committee shall be filled by its alternate members in the order of the number of votes by which they were elected. The Central Committee meets in plenary session at least once a year, and such sessions are convened by its Political Bureau. When the national congress is not in session, the Central Committee carries out its decisions, directs the entire work of the party, and represents the CPC in its external relations.

ARTICLE 22

The Political Bureau, the Standing Committee of the Political Bureau, and the general secretary of the Central Committee are elected by the Central Committee in plenary session. The general secretary of the Central Committee must be a member of the Standing Committee of the Political Bureau.

When the plenary session of the Central Committee is not in session, the Political Bureau of the Central Committee and its Standing Committee exercise the functions and powers of the Central Committee. The Secretariat of the Central Committee is an organization that runs day-to-day work for the Political Bureau of the Central Committee and its Standing Committee. Members of the Secretariat are nominated by the Standing Committee of the Political Bureau of the Central Committee and approved by the Central Committee in plenary session. The general secretary of the Central Committee is responsible for convening the meetings of the Political Bureau and its Standing Committee, and presides over the work of the Secretariat.

Members of the Military Commission of the Central Committee are decided by the Central Committee.

The central leading bodies and leaders elected by each Central Committee shall, when the next national congress is in session, continue to preside over the party's day-to-day work until the new central leading bodies and leaders are elected by the next Central Committee.

ARTICLE 23

Party organizations in the Chinese PLA carry out their work in accordance with the instructions of the Central Committee. The General Political Department of the Chinese PLA is the political work organ of the military commission; it directs party and political work in the army. The organizational system and organs of the party in the armed forces will be prescribed by the Military Commission.

CHAPTER IV *Local Organizations of the Party*

ARTICLE 24

A party congress of a province, autonomous region, municipality directly under the central government, city divided into districts, or autonomous prefecture is held once every five years.

A party congress of a county (banner), autonomous county, city not divided into districts, or municipal district is held once every five years. Local party congresses are convened by the party committees at the corresponding levels. Under extraordinary circumstances, they may be held before or after their due dates upon approval by the next higher party committees. The number of delegates to the local party congresses at any level and the procedure governing their election are determined by the party committees at the corresponding levels and should be reported to the next higher party committees for approval.

ARTICLE 25

The functions and powers of the local party congresses at all levels are as follows: 1) To hear and examine the reports of the party committees at the corresponding levels; 2) to hear and examine the reports of the commissions for discipline inspection at the corresponding levels; 3) to discuss and decide on major issues in the given areas; and 4) to elect the party committees and commissions for discipline inspection at the corresponding levels.

ARTICLE 26

The party committee of the province, autonomous region, municipality directly under the central government, city divided into districts, or autonomous prefecture is elected for a term of five years. The members and alternate members of such a committee must have a party standing of five years or more. The party committee of a county (banner), autonomous county, city not divided into districts, or municipal district is elected for a term of five years. The members and alternate members of such a committee must have a party standing of three years or more. When local party congresses at various levels are convened before or after their due dates, the terms of the committees elected by the previous congresses shall be correspondingly shortened or extended. The number of members and alternate members of the local party committees at various levels shall be determined by the next higher committees. Vacancies on the local party committees at various levels shall be filled by their alternate members in the order of the number of votes by which they were elected.

The local party committees at various levels meet in plenary session at least twice a year.

Local party committees at various levels shall, when the party congresses of the given areas are not in session, carry out the directives of the next higher party organizations and the decisions of the party congresses at the corresponding levels, direct work in their own areas, and report on it to the next higher party committees at regular intervals.

ARTICLE 27

Local party committees at various levels elect, at their plenary sessions, their standing committees, secretaries, and deputy secretaries, and report the results to the higher party committees for approval. The standing committees at various levels exercise the powers and functions of local party committees when the latter are not in session. They continue to handle the day-to-day work when the next party congresses at their levels are in session, until the new standing committees are elected.

ARTICLE 28

A prefectural party committee, or an organization analogous to it, is the representative organ dispatched by a provincial or an autonomous regional party committee to a prefecture embracing several counties, autonomous counties or cities. It exercises leadership over the work in the given region as authorized by the provincial or autonomous regional party committee.

CHAPTER V *Primary Organizations of the Party*

ARTICLE 29

Primary party organizations are formed in enterprises, rural villages, offices, schools, scientific research institutions, city neighborhoods, PLA companies, and other basic units where there are three or more full party members.

In primary party organizations, the primary party committees or committees of general party branches and party branches are set up as the work requires and according to the number of party members, subject to approval by the higher party organizations. A primary party committee is elected by a general membership meeting or a meeting of delegates. The committee of a general party branch or a party branch is elected by a general membership meeting.

ARTICLE 30

A primary party committee is elected for a term of three or four years, while a general party branch committee or a party branch committee is elected for a term of two or three years. Results of the election of a secretary and deputies secretaries by a primary party committee, general party branch committee, or party branch committee shall be reported to the higher party organization for approval.

ARTICLE 31

The primary party organizations are militant bastions of the party in the basic units of society. Their main tasks are:

(1) To propagate and carry out the party's line, principles, and policies, and decisions of the party Central Committee and other higher party organizations, and their own party organizations; to give full play to the exemplary vanguard role of party members; and to unite and organize the cadres and the rank and file inside and outside the party in fulfilling the tasks of their own units.

(2) To organize party members to conscientiously study Marxism-Leninism-Mao Zedong Thought; study the theory of building socialism with Chinese characteristics and the party's line, principles, policies, and decisions; study essential knowledge concerning the party; and study scientific, cultural, and professional knowledge.

(3) To educate and supervise party members, improve their quality, enhance their party spirit, ensure their regular participation in the activities of the party organization, promote criticism and self-criticism, safeguard and enforce party discipline, see that party members truly fulfill their duties, and protect their rights from encroachment.

(4) To maintain close ties with the masses, constantly seek their criticisms and opinions regarding party members and the party's work, protect their legitimate rights and interests, and ensure good ideological and political work among them.

(5) To give full scope to the initiative and creativeness of party members and the masses; discover, train, and make recommendations for talented people; encourage them to contribute their wisdom and talent to reform, opening up, and the modernization drive; and support them in these efforts.

(6) To educate and train activists asking to be admitted into the party; recruit party members on a regular basis; and attach importance to recruiting outstanding workers, peasants, and intellectuals working on the forefront of production and other fields of endeavor.

(7) To see that party and other nonparty functionaries strictly observe the state laws and administration discipline, and the financial and economic regulations and personnel system, and that none of them infringe upon the interests of the state, the collective, and the masses.

(8) To educate party members and the masses to conscientiously resist unhealthy tendencies and wage resolute struggles against various lawbreaking activities.

ARTICLE 32

Neighborhood, township and town primary party organizations, and village party branches lead the work of their areas; support administrative, economic, and mass self-management organizations; and ensure that such organizations fully exercise their functions and powers.

In a state-owned enterprise, the primary party organization shall give full play to its role as the political nucleus, and perform its work around enterprise production and management. It shall ensure and supervise the implementation of party and state principles and policies in the enterprise; support the factory director (or manager) in performing his duties according to the law, and uphold and improve the system of full responsibility for factory directors; rely wholeheartedly on the masses of workers and staff members, and support the workers congress in performing its work; participate in making major decisions for the enterprise; strengthen itself; and lead ideological and political work as well as trade union and Communist Youth League organizations.

In an institution implementing the system of full responsibility for administrative leaders, the primary party organization shall give full play to its role as the political nucleus. In an institution where the system of full responsibility for administrative leaders is implemented under the leadership of the party committee, the primary party organization shall discuss major issues and decide on them, and ensure that the administrative leader fully exercise his functions and powers.

In party and state offices at all levels, the primary party organizations shall assist the head of these offices in fulfilling their tasks, improving their work, and in exercising supervision over all party members, including the heads of these offices who are party members. However, they shall not lead the work of these offices.

CHAPTER VI *Party Cadres*

ARTICLE 33

Party cadres are the backbone of the party's cause and public servants of the people. The party selects its cadres according to the principle that they should possess both political integrity and professional competence, persists in the practice of appointing people on their merit and opposes favoritism; it calls for genuine efforts to make the ranks of cadres more revolutionary, younger in average age, better educated, and more professionally competent. The party should attach importance to the education, training, promotion, and appraisal of cadres, especially the training and promotion of outstanding young cadres. Vigorous efforts should be made to reform the cadre system. The party should attach importance to the training and promotion of women cadres and cadres from among the minority nationalities.

ARTICLE 34

Leading party cadres at all levels must perform in their duties as party members in an exemplary way prescribed in Article 3 of this Constitution and must meet the following basic requirements:

(1) Have a knowledge of the theories of Marxism-Leninism-Mao Zedong Thought and of the policies based on them that are needed to perform their duties; grasp the theory of building socialism with Chinese characteristics; and strive to use the Marxist stand, viewpoint, and method to solve practical problems.

(2) Resolutely implement the party's basic line, principles, and policies; be determined to carry out reform and opening to the outside world; devote themselves to the cause of modernization; and work hard to blaze new trails and make actual achievements in socialist construction.

(3) Persevere in seeking truth from facts, conscientiously make investigations and study, combine the party's principles and policies with the realities of their areas or departments, tell the truth, do practical work, work for actual results, and oppose formalism.

(4) Be fervently dedicated to the revolutionary cause and imbued with a strong sense of political responsibility and be qualified for their leading posts in organizational ability, general education, and professional knowledge.

(5) Correctly exercise the powers entrusted to them by the people, be honest and upright, work hard for the people, make themselves an example, carry forward the style of hard work and plain living, forge close ties with the masses, uphold the party's mass line, conscientiously accept criticism and supervision by the masses, oppose bureaucratism, and oppose the unhealthy trend of abusing one's power for personal gain.

(6) Uphold the party's democratic centralism, have a democratic work style, take the overall situation into account, and be good at uniting and working with comrades, including those holding differing opinions.

ARTICLE 35

Party cadres should be able to cooperate with nonparty cadres, respect them, and learn open-mindedly from their strong points. Party organizations at all levels must be bold in discovering and recommending talented and knowledgeable nonparty cadres for leading posts, and ensure that the latter enjoy authority commensurate with their posts and can play their roles to the full.

ARTICLE 36

Leading party cadres at all levels, whether elected through democratic procedure or appointed by a leading body are not entitled to lifelong tenure, and they can be transferred from or relieved of their posts.

Cadres no longer fit to continue work due to old age or poor health should retire according to state regulations.

CHAPTER VII *Party Discipline*

ARTICLE 37

Party discipline is the code of conduct that party organizations at all levels and all party members must observe; it is a guarantee for safeguarding the party's solidarity and unity, and the accomplishment of the party's tasks. Party organizations shall strictly enforce and safeguard party discipline. A Communist Party member must consciously act within the bounds of party discipline.

ARTICLE 38

Party organizations shall criticize, educate, or take disciplinary measures against members who violate party discipline, depending on the nature and seriousness of their mistakes and in the spirit of learning from past mistakes to avoid future ones, and curing the sickness to save the patient.

Party members who have seriously violated criminal law shall be expelled from the party.

It is strictly forbidden, within the party, to take any measures against a member that contravene the party constitution or the laws of the state, or to retaliate against or frame comrades. Any offending organization or individual must be dealt with according to party discipline or the laws of the state.

ARTICLE 39

There are five measures of party discipline: Warning, serious warning, removal from party posts, placement on probation within the party, and expulsion from the party.

The period for which a party member is placed on probation shall not exceed two years. During this period, the party member concerned has no right to vote, elect or stand for election. A party member who proves during this time that he has corrected his mistake shall have his rights as a party member restored. Party members who refuse to mend their ways shall be expelled from the party.

Expulsion is the ultimate party disciplinary measure. In deciding on or approving an expulsion, party organizations at all levels should study all the relevant facts and opinions, and exercise extreme caution.

ARTICLE 40

Any disciplinary measure against a party member must be discussed and decided on at a general membership meeting of the party branch concerned, and reported to the primary party committee concerned for approval. If the case is relatively important or complicated, or involves the expulsion of a member, it shall be reported, on the merit of that case, to a party commission for discipline inspection at or above the county level for examination and approval. Under special circumstances, a party committee or a commission for discipline inspection at or above the county level has the authority to decide directly on disciplinary measures against a party member.

Any decision to remove a member or alternate member of the Central Committee or a local committee at any level from posts within the party, to place such a person on probation within the party or to expel him from the party, must be taken by a two-thirds majority vote at a plenary meeting of the party committee to which he belongs. Under special circumstances, the Political Bureau of the CPC Central Committee or the standing committees of local party committees at all levels may adopt a decision on disciplinary measures, which has to be confirmed when the committees meet in plenary session. Such a disciplinary measure against a member or alternate member of local committees at all levels is subject to approval by the higher party committees.

Members or alternate members of the Central Committee who have seriously violated criminal law shall be expelled from the party on the decision of the Political Bureau of the Central Committee; members and alternate members of local party committees who have seriously violated criminal law shall be expelled from the party on the decision of the standing committees of the party committees at the corresponding levels.

ARTICLE 41

When a party organization decides on a disciplinary measure against a party member, it should investigate and verify the facts in an objective way. The party member in question must be informed of the decision to be made and of the facts on which it is based. He must be given a chance to account for himself and speak in his own defense. If the member does not accept the decision that has been adopted, he can appeal; the party organization concerned must promptly deal with or forward his appeal and must not withhold or suppress it. Those who cling to erroneous views and unjustifiable demands shall be educated by criticism.

ARTICLE 42

Failure of a party organization to uphold party discipline must be investigated.

In the case of a party organization which seriously violates party discipline and is unable to rectify the mistake on its own, the next higher party committee should, after verifying the facts and considering the seriousness of the case, decide on the reorganization or dissolution of the organization, report the decision to the party committee higher up for examination and approval, and then formally announce and carry out the decision.

CHAPTER VIII *Party Organs for Discipline Inspection*

ARTICLE 43

The party's Central Commission for Discipline Inspection functions under the leadership of the Central Committee of the party. Local commissions for discipline inspection at all levels function under the dual leadership of the party committees at the corresponding levels and the next higher commissions for discipline inspection. The local commissions for discipline inspection serve a term of the same duration as the party committees at the corresponding levels. The Central Commission for Discipline Inspection elects, in plenary session, its Standing Committee, and secretary and deputy secretaries, and reports the results to the Central Committee for approval. Local commissions for discipline inspection at all levels elect, at their plenary sessions, their respective standing committees, and secretaries and deputy secretaries. The results of the elections are subject to endorsement by the party committees at the corresponding levels and should be reported to the higher party committees for approval. The question of whether a grass-roots party committee should set up a commission for discipline inspection or simply appoint a discipline inspection commissioner shall be determined by the next higher party organization in light of the specific circumstances. The committees of general party branches and party branches shall have discipline inspection commissioners.

The party's Central Commission for Discipline Inspection shall, when its work so requires, accredit discipline inspection groups or commissioners to party or state organs at the central level. Leaders of the discipline inspection groups or discipline inspection commissioners may attend relevant meetings of the leading party organizations in the said organs as non-voting participants. The leading party organizations in the organs concerned must support their work.

ARTICLE 44

The main tasks of the central and local commissions for discipline inspection are as follows: To uphold the Constitution and the other important rules and regulations of the party; to assist the respective party committees in rectifying party style; and to check up on the implementation of the line, principles, policies, and decisions of the party.

The central and local commissions for discipline inspection shall carry out constant education among party members on their duty to observe party discipline. They shall adopt decisions for the upholding of party discipline, examine and deal with relatively important or complicated cases of violation of the constitution and discipline of the party or the laws and decrees of the state by party organizations or party members, decide on or cancel disciplinary measures against party members involved in such cases, and deal with complaints and appeals made by party members.

The central and local commissions for discipline inspection should report to the party committees at the corresponding levels on the results of their handling of cases of special importance or complexity, as well as on the problems encountered. Local commissions for discipline inspection should also present such reports to the higher commissions.

If a discipline inspection commission discovers a violation of party discipline by any member of a party committee at the corresponding levels, it may conduct an initial verification of facts; if the case requires setting up of a file for investigation, it should report to the party committee at the corresponding level for approval; if the case involves a standing committee member of the party committee, the commission should report such an offense to the party committee at the corresponding level and to the higher discipline inspection commission for approval.

ARTICLE 45

Higher commissions for discipline inspection have the power to check up on the work of the lower commissions and to approve or modify their decision on any case. If decisions so modified have already been ratified by the party committee at the corresponding level, the modification must be approved by the next higher party committee.

If a local commission for discipline inspection or such a commission at the basic level does not agree with a decision made by the party committee at the corresponding level in dealing with a case, it may request the commission at the next higher level to reexamine the case; if a local commission discovers cases of violation of party discipline by the party committee at the corresponding level or by its members, and if that party committee fails to deal with them properly or at all, it has the right to appeal to the higher commissions for assistance in dealing with such cases.

CHAPTER IX *Leading Party Members' Groups*

ARTICLE 46

A leading party members' group shall be formed in the leading body of a central or local state organ, people's organization, economic or cultural institution or other non-party unit. The main tasks of such a group are: To see to it that the party's line, principles, and policies are implemented; discuss and make decisions on major issues in their respective units; to unite with the nonparty cadres and masses in fulfilling the tasks assigned by the party and the state; and to guide the work of the party organizations of the department and those in the units directly under it.

ARTICLE 47

The members of a leading party members' group are appointed by the party committee that approves its establishment. The group shall have a secretary and deputy secretaries.

The leading party members' group shall subject itself to the leadership of the party committee that approves its establishment.

ARTICLE 48

Party committees may be set up in those government departments which need to exercise centralized and unified leadership over subordinate units. Procedures for electing such a committee and its functions, powers, and tasks shall be provided separately by the Central Committee of the party.

CHAPTER X *Relationship between the Party and the Communist Youth League*

ARTICLE 49

The Communist Youth League of China [CYL] is a mass organization of advanced young people under the leadership of the CPC; it is a school where large numbers of young people will learn about communism through practice; it is the party's assistant and reserve force. The CYL Central Committee functions under the leadership of the Central Committee of the party. Local CYL organizations are under the leadership of the party committees at the corresponding levels and of the higher organizations of the League itself.

ARTICLE 50

Party committees at all levels must strengthen their leadership over the CYL organizations, and pay attention to the selection and training of league cadres. The party must firmly support the CYL in the lively and creative performance of its work to suit the characteristics and needs of young people, and give full play to the league's role as a shock force and as a bridge linking the party with the broad masses of young people.

Those secretaries of league committees, at or below the county level or in enterprise and institutions, who are party members may attend meetings of party committees at the corresponding levels and of their standing committees as nonvoting participants.

APPENDIX 3

On the Ten Major Relationships*

(25 April 1956)

In recent months the Political Bureau of the Central Committee has heard reports on the work of thirty-four industrial, agricultural, transport, commercial, financial and other departments under the central authorities and from these reports has identified a number of problems concerning socialist construction and socialist transformation. In all, they boil down to ten problems, or ten major relationships.

It is to focus on one basic policy that these ten problems are being raised, the basic policy of mobilizing all positive factors, internal and external, to serve the cause of socialism. In the past we followed this policy of mobilizing all positive factors in order to put an end to the rule of imperialism, feudalism and bureaucrat-capitalism and to win victory for the people's democratic revolution. We are now following the same policy in order to carry on the socialist revolution and build a socialist country. Nevertheless, there are some problems in our work that need discussion. Particularly worthy of attention is the fact that in the Soviet Union certain defects and errors that occurred in the course of their building socialism have lately come to light. Do you want to follow the detours they have made? It was by drawing lessons from their experience that we were able to avoid certain detours in the past, and there is all the more reason for us to do so now.

What are the positive factors, internal and external? Internally, the workers and the peasants are the basic force. The middle forces are forces that can be won over. The reactionary forces are a negative factor, but even so we should do our work well and turn this negative factor as far as possible into a positive one. Internationally, all the forces that can be united with must be united, the forces that are not neutral can be neutralized through our efforts, and even the reactionary forces can be split and made use of. In short, we should mobilize all forces, whether direct or indirect, and strive to make China a powerful socialist country.

I will now discuss the ten problems.

I The Relationship between Heavy Industry on the One Hand and Light Industry and Agriculture on the Other

The emphasis in our country's construction is on heavy industry. The production of

Speech at an enlarged meeting of the Political Bureau of the Central Committee of the Chinese Communist Party. Bearing in mind lessons drawn from the Soviet Union, Comrade Mao Tsetung summed up China's experience, dealt with ten major relationships in socialist revolution and socialist construction and set forth the ideas underlying the general line of building socialism with greater, faster, better and more economical results, a line suited to the conditions of our country.

*Text from Mao (1977).

the means of production must be given priority, that's settled. But it definitely does not follow that the production of the means of subsistence, especially grain, can be neglected. Without enough food and other daily necessities, it would be impossible to provide for the workers in the first place, and then what sense would it make to talk about developing heavy industry? Therefore, the relationship between heavy industry on the one hand and light industry and agriculture on the other must be properly handled.

In dealing with this relationship we have not made mistakes of principle. We have done better than the Soviet Union and a number of East European countries. The prolonged failure of the Soviet Union to reach the highest pre-October Revolution level in grain output, the grave problems arising from the glaring disequilibrium between the development of heavy industry and that of light industry in some East European countries—such problems do not exist in our country. Their lop-sided stress on heavy industry to the neglect of agriculture and light industry results in a shortage of goods on the market and an unstable currency. We, on the other hand, attach more importance to agriculture and light industry. We have all along attended to and developed agriculture and have to a considerable degree ensured the supply of grain and raw materials necessary for the development of industry. Our daily necessities are in fairly good supply and our prices and currency are stable.

The problem now facing us is that of continuing to adjust properly the ratio between investment in heavy industry on the one hand and in agriculture and light industry on the other in order to bring about a greater development of the latter. Does this mean that heavy industry is no longer primary? No. It still is, it still claims the emphasis in our investment. But the proportion for agriculture and light industry must be somewhat increased.

What will be the results of this increase? First, the daily needs of the people will be better satisfied, and, second, the accumulation of capital will be speeded up so that we can develop heavy industry with greater and better results. Heavy industry can also accumulate capital, but, given our present economic conditions, light industry and agriculture can accumulate more and faster.

Here the question arises: Is your desire to develop heavy industry genuine or feigned, strong or weak? If your desire is feigned or weak, then you will hit agriculture and light industry and invest less in them. If your desire is genuine or strong, then you will attach importance to agriculture and light industry so that there will be more grain and more raw materials for light industry and a greater accumulation of capital. And there will be more funds in the future to invest in heavy industry.

There are now two possible approaches to our development of heavy industry: one is to develop agriculture and light industry less, and the other is to develop them more. In the long run, the first approach will lead to a smaller and slower development of heavy industry, or at least will put it on a less solid foundation, and when the over-all account is added up a few decades hence, it will not prove to have paid. The second approach will lead to a greater and faster development of heavy industry and, since it ensures the livelihood of the people, it will lay a more solid foundation for the development of heavy industry.

II The Relationship between Industry in the Coastal Regions and Industry in the Interior

In the past our industry was concentrated in the coastal regions. By coastal regions we mean Liaoning, Hebei, Beijing, Tianjin, eastern Henan, Shandong, Anhui, Jiangsu, Shanghai, Zhejiang, Fujian, Guangdong and Guangxi. About 70 per cent of all our industry, both light and heavy, is to be found in the coastal regions and only 30 per cent in the interior. This irrational situation is a product of history. The coastal industrial base must be put to full use, but to even out the distribution of industry as it develops we must strive to promote industry in the interior. We have not made any major mistakes on the relationship between the two. However, in recent years we have underestimated coastal industry to some extent and have not given great enough attention to its development. This must change.

Not so long ago, there was still fighting in Korea and the international situation was quite tense; this could not but affect our attitude towards coastal industry. Now, it seems unlikely that there will be a new war of aggression against China or another world war in the near future, and there will probably be a period of peace for a decade or more. It would therefore be wrong if we still fail to make full use of the plant capacity and technical forces of coastal industry. If we are to have only five years, not to say ten, we should still work hard to develop industries in the coastal regions for four years and evacuate them when war breaks out in the fifth. According to available information, in light industry the construction of a plant and its accumulation of capital generally proceed quite rapidly. After the whole plant goes into production, it can earn enough in four years to build three new factories, or two, or one or at least half of one, in addition to recouping its capital outlay. Why shouldn't we do such profitable things? The notion that the atom bomb is already overhead and about to fall on us in a matter of seconds is a calculation at variance with reality, and it would be wrong to take a negative attitude towards coastal industry on this account.

It does not follow that all new factories should be built in the coastal regions. Without doubt, the greater part of the new industry should be located in the interior so that industry may gradually become evenly distributed; moreover, this will help our preparations against war. But a number of new factories and mines, even some large ones, may also be built in the coastal regions. As for the expansion and reconstruction of the light and heavy industries already in the coastal regions, we have done a fair amount of work in the past and will do much more in the future.

Making good use of the old industries in the coastal regions and developing their capacities will put us in a stronger position to promote and support industry in the interior. To adopt a negative attitude would be to hinder the latter's speedy growth. So it is likewise a question of whether the desire to develop industry in the interior is genuine or not. If it is genuine and not feigned, we must more actively use and promote industry in the coastal regions, especially light industry.

III The Relationship between Economic Construction and Defence Construction

National defence is indispensable. Our defence capabilities have attained a certain level. As a result of the war to resist U.S. aggression and aid Korea and of several years of training and consolidation, our armed forces have grown more powerful and are now stronger than was the Soviet Red Army before the Second World War; also, there have been improvements in armaments. Our defence industry is being built up. Ever since Pan Ku separated heaven and earth, we have never been able to make planes and cars, and now we are beginning to make them.

We do not have the atom bomb yet. But neither did we have planes and artillery in the past. We defeated the Japanese imperialists and Chiang Kai-shek with millet plus rifles. We are stronger than before and will be stronger still in the future. We will have not only more planes and artillery but atom bombs too. If we are not to be bullied in the present-day world, we cannot do without the bomb. Then what is to be done about it? One reliable way is to cut military and administrative expenditures down to appropriate proportions and increase expenditures on economic construction. Only with the faster growth of economic construction can there be greater progress in defence construction.

At the Third Plenary Session of the Seventh Central Committee of our Party in 1950, we already raised the question of streamlining the state apparatus and reducing military and administrative expenditures and considered this measure to be one of the three prerequisites for achieving a fundamental turn for the better in our financial and economic situation. In the period of the First Five-Year Plan, military and administrative expenditures accounted for 30 per cent of the total expenditures in the state budget. This proportion is much too high. In the period of the Second Five-Year Plan, we must reduce it to around 20 per cent, so that more funds can be released for building more factories and turning out more machines. After a time, we shall not only have plenty of planes and artillery but probably have our own atom bombs as well.

Here again the question arises: Is your desire for the atom bomb genuine and very keen? Or is it only lukewarm and not so very keen? If your desire is genuine and very keen, then you will reduce the proportion of military and administrative expenditures and spend more on economic construction. If your desire is not genuine or not so very keen, you will stay in the old rut. This is a matter of strategic policy, and I hope the Military Commission will discuss it.

Would it be all right to demobilize all our troops now? No, it would not. For enemies are still around, and we are being bullied and encircled by them. We must strengthen our national defence, and for that purpose we must first of all strengthen our work in economic construction.

IV The Relationship between the State, the Units of Production and the Producers

The relationship between the state on the one hand and factories and agricultural co-operatives on the other and the relationship between factories and agricultural co-operatives on the one hand and the producers on the other should both be handled well. To this end we should consider not just one side but all three, the state, the collective and the individual, or, as we used to say, "take into consideration both the army and the people" and "take into consideration both the public and the private interest." In view of the experience of the Soviet Union as well as our own, we must see to it that from now on this problem is solved much better.

Take the workers for example. As their labour productivity rises, there should be a gradual improvement in their working conditions and collective welfare. We have always advocated plain living and hard work and opposed putting personal material benefits above everything else; at the same time we have always advocated concern for the livelihood of the masses and opposed bureaucracy, which is callous to their well-being. With the growth of our economy as a whole, wages should be appropriately adjusted. We have recently decided to increase wages to some extent, mainly the wages of those at the lower levels, the wages of the workers, in order to narrow the wage gap between them and the upper levels. Generally speaking, our wages are not high, but compared with the past the life of our workers has greatly improved because, among other things, more people are employed and prices remain low and stable. Under the regime of the proletariat, our workers have unfailingly displayed high political consciousness and enthusiasm for labour. When at the end of last year the Central Committee called for a fight against Right conservatism, the masses of workers warmly responded and, what was exceptional, overfulfilled the plan for the first quarter of the year by working all out for three months. We must strive to encourage this zeal for hard work and at the same time pay still greater attention to solving the pressing problems in their work and everyday life.

Here I would like to touch on the question of the independence of the factories under unified leadership. It's not right, I'm afraid, to place everything in the hands of the central or the provincial and municipal authorities without leaving the factories any power of their own, any room for independent action, any benefits. We don't have much experience on how to share power and returns properly among the central authorities, the provincial and municipal authorities and the factories, and we should study the subject. As a matter of principle, centralization and independence form a unity of opposites, and there must be both centralization and independence. For instance, we are now having a meeting, which is centralization; after the meeting, some of us will go for a walk, some will read books, some will go to eat, which is independence. If we don't adjourn the meeting and give everyone some independence but let it go on and on, wouldn't it be the death of us all? This is true of individuals, and no less true of factories and other units of production. Every unit of production must enjoy independence as the correlative of centralization if it is to develop more vigorously.

Now about the peasants. Our relations with the peasants have always been good, but we did make a mistake on the question of grain. In 1954 floods caused a decrease in production in some parts of our country, and yet we purchased 7,000 million more catties of grain. A decrease in production and an increase in purchasing—this made grain the topic on almost everyone's lips in many places last spring, and nearly every household talked about the state monopoly for marketing grain. The peasants were disgruntled, and there were a lot of complaints both inside and outside the Party. Although quite a few people indulged in deliberate exaggeration and exploited the opportunity to attack us, it cannot be said that we had no shortcomings. Inadequate investigation and failure to size up the situation resulted in the purchase of 7,000 million catties more; that was a shortcoming. After discovering it, we purchased 7,000 million catties less in 1955 and introduced a system of fixed quotas for grain production, purchasing and marketing[1] and, what's more, there was a good harvest. With a decrease in purchasing and an increase in production, the peasants had over 20,000 million more catties of grain at their disposal. Thus even those peasants who had complaints before said, "The Communist Party is really good." This lesson the whole Party must bear in mind.

The Soviet Union has adopted measures which squeeze the peasants very hard. It takes away too much from the peasants at too low a price through its system of so-called obligatory sales[2] and other measures. This method of capital accumulation has seriously dampened the peasants' enthusiasm for production. You want the hen to lay more eggs and yet you don't feed it, you want the horse to run fast and yet you don't let it graze. What kind of logic is that!

Our policies towards the peasants differ from those of the Soviet Union and take into account the interests of both the state and the peasants. Our agricultural tax has always been relatively low. In the exchange of industrial and agricultural products we follow a policy of narrowing the price scissors, a policy of exchanging equal or roughly equal values. The state buys agricultural products at standard prices while the peasants suffer no loss, and, what is more, our purchase prices are gradually being raised. In supplying the peasants with manufactured goods we follow a policy of larger sales at a small profit and of stabilizing or appropriately reducing their prices; in supplying grain to the peasants in grain-deficient areas we generally subsidize such sales to a certain extent. Even so, mistakes of one kind or another will occur if we are not careful. In view of the grave mistakes made by the Soviet Union on this question, we must take greater care and handle the relationship between the state and the peasants well.

Similarly, the relationship between the co-operative and the peasants should be well handled. What proportion of the earnings of a co-operative should go to the state, to the co-operative and to the peasants respectively and in what form should be determined properly. The amount that goes to the co-operative is used directly to serve the peasants. Production expenses need no explanation, management expenses are also necessary, the accumulation fund is for expanded reproduction and the public welfare fund is for the peasants' well-being. However, together with the peasants, we should work out equitable ratios among these items. We must strictly economize on production and management expenses. The accumulation fund and the public welfare fund must also be kept within limits, and one shouldn't expect all good things to be done in a single year.

Except in case of extraordinary natural disasters, we must see to it that, given increased agricultural production, 90 per cent of the co-operative members get some increase in their income and the other 10 per cent break even each year, and if the latter's income should fall, ways must be found to solve the problem in good time.

In short, consideration must be given to both sides, not to just one, whether they are the state and the factory, the state and the worker, the factory and the worker, the state and the co-operative, the state and the peasant, or the co-operative and the peasant. To give consideration to only one side, whichever it may be, is harmful to socialism and to the dictatorship of the proletariat. This is a big question which concerns 600 million people, and it calls for repeated education in the whole Party and the whole nation.

V The Relationship between the Central and the Local Authorities

The relationship between the central and the local authorities constitutes another contradiction. To resolve this contradiction, our attention should now be focussed on how to enlarge the powers of the local authorities to some extent, give them greater independence and let them do more, all on the premise that the unified leadership of the central authorities is to be strengthened. This will be advantageous to our task of building a powerful socialist country. Our territory is so vast, our population is so large and the conditions are so complex that it is far better to have the initiative come from both the central and the local authorities than from one source alone. We must not follow the example of the Soviet Union in concentrating everything in the hands of the central authorities, shackling the local authorities and denying them the right to independent action.

The central authorities want to develop industry, and so do the local authorities. Even industries directly under the central authorities need assistance from the local authorities. And all the more so for agriculture and commerce. In short, if we are to promote socialist construction, we must bring the initiative of the local authorities into play. If we are to strengthen the central authorities, we must attend to the interests of the localities.

At present scores of hands are reaching out to the localities, making things difficult for them. Once a ministry is set up, it wants to have a revolution and so it issues orders. Since the ministries don't think it proper to issue orders to the Party committees and people's councils at the provincial level, they establish direct contact with the relevant departments and bureaus in the provinces and municipalities and give them orders every day. These orders are all supposed to come from the central authorities, even though neither the Central Committee of the Party nor the State Council knows anything about them, and they put a great strain on the local authorities. There is such a flood of statistical forms that they become a scourge. This state of affairs must be changed.

We should encourage the style of work in which the local authorities are consulted on the matters to be taken up. It is the practice of the Central Committee of the Party to consult the local authorities; it never hastily issues orders without prior consultation. We hope that the ministries and departments under the central authorities will pay due attention to this and will first confer with the localities on all matters concerning them and issue no order without full consultation.

The central departments fall into two categories. Those in the first category exercise leadership right down to the enterprises, but their administrative offices and enterprises in the localities are also subject to supervision by the local authorities. Those in the second have the task of laying down guiding principles and mapping out work plans, while the local authorities assume the responsibility for putting them into operation.

For a large country like ours and a big Party like ours the proper handling of the relationship between the central and local authorities is of vital importance. Some capitalist countries pay great attention to this too. Although their social system is fundamentally different from ours, the experience of their growth is nevertheless worth studying. Take our own experience; the system of the greater administrative area instituted in the early days of our People's Republic was a necessity at that time, and yet it had shortcomings which were later exploited to a certain extent by the anti-Party alliance of Guo Gang and Rao Shushi. It was subsequently decided to abolish the greater administrative areas and put the various provinces directly under the central authorities; that was a correct decision. But neither was the outcome so satisfactory when matters went to the length of depriving the localities of their necessary independence. According to our Constitution, the legislative powers are all vested in the central authorities. But, provided that the policies of the central authorities are not violated, the local authorities may work out rules, regulations and measures in the light of their specific conditions and the needs of their work, and this is in no way prohibited by the Constitution. We want both unity and particularity. To build a powerful socialist country it is imperative to have a strong and unified central leadership and unified planning and discipline throughout the country; disruption of this indispensable unity is impermissible. At the same time, it is essential to bring the initiative of the local authorities into full play and let each locality enjoy the particularity suited to its local conditions. This particularity is not the Kao Kang type of particularity but one that is necessary for the interest of the whole and for the strengthening of national unity.

There is also the relationship between different local authorities, and here I refer chiefly to the relationship between the higher and lower local authorities. Since the provinces and municipalities have their own complaints about the central departments, can it be that the prefectures, counties, districts and townships have no complaints about the provinces and municipalities? The central authorities should take care to give scope to the initiative of the provinces and municipalities, and the latter in their turn should do the same for the prefectures, counties, districts and townships; in neither case should the lower levels be put in a strait-jacket. Of course comrades at the lower levels must be informed of the matters on which centralization is necessary and they must not act as they please. In short, centralization must be enforced where it is possible and necessary, otherwise it should not be imposed at all. The provinces and municipalities, prefectures, counties, districts and townships should all enjoy their own proper independence and rights and should fight for them. To fight for such rights in the interest of the whole nation and not of the locality cannot be called localism or an undue assertion of independence.

The relationship between different provinces and municipalities is also a kind of relationship between different local authorities, and it should be properly handled too. It is our consistent principle to advocate consideration for the general interest and mutual help and accommodation.

Our experience is still insufficient and immature on the question of handling the relationship between the central and local authorities and that between different local authorities. We hope that you will consider and discuss it in earnest and sum up your experience from time to time so as to enhance achievements and overcome shortcomings.

VI The Relationship between the Han Nationality and the Minority Nationalities

Comparatively speaking, our policy on the relationship between the Han nationality and the minority nationalities is sound and has won the favour of the minority nationalities. We put the emphasis on opposing Han chauvinism. Local-nationality chauvinism must be opposed too, but generally that is not where our emphasis lies.

The population of the minority nationalities in our country is small, but the area they inhabit is large. The Han people comprise 94 per cent of the total population, an overwhelming majority. If they practised Han chauvinism and discriminated against the minority peoples, that would be very bad. And who has more land? The minority nationalities, who occupy 50 to 60 per cent of the territory. We say China is a country vast in territory, rich in resources and large in population; as a matter of fact, it is the Han nationality whose population is large and the minority nationalities whose territory is vast and whose resources are rich, or at least in all probability their resources under the soil are rich.

The minority nationalities have all contributed to the making of China's history. The huge Han population is the result of the intermingling of many nationalities over a long time. All through the ages, the reactionary rulers, chiefly from the Han nationality, sowed feelings of estrangement among our various nationalities and bullied the minority peoples. Even among the working people it is not easy to eliminate the resultant influences in a short time. So we have to make extensive and sustained efforts to educate both the cadres and the masses in our proletarian nationality policy and make a point of frequently reviewing the relationship between the Han nationality and the minority nationalities. One such review was made two years ago and there should be another now. If the relationship is found to be abnormal, then we must deal with it in earnest and not just in words.

We need to make a thorough study of what systems of economic management and finance will suit the minority nationality areas.

We must sincerely and actively help the minority nationalities to develop their economy and culture. In the Soviet Union the relationship between the Russian nationality and the minority nationalities is very abnormal; we should draw lessons from this. The air in the atmosphere, the forests on the earth and the riches under the soil are all important factors needed for the building of socialism, but no material factor can be exploited and utilized without the human factor. We must foster good relations between the Han nationality and the minority nationalities and strengthen the unity of all the nationalities in the common endeavour to build our great socialist motherland.

VII The Relationship between Party and Non-Party

Which is better, to have just one party or several? As we see it now, it's perhaps better to have several parties. This has been true in the past and may well be so for the future; it means long-term coexistence and mutual supervision.

In our country the various democratic parties, consisting primarily of the national bourgeoisie and its intellectuals, emerged during the resistance to Japan and the struggle against Chiang Kai-shek, and they continue to exist to this day. In this respect, China is different from the Soviet Union. We have purposely let the democratic parties remain, giving them opportunities to express their views and adopting a policy of both unity and struggle towards them. We unite with all those democratic personages who offer us well-intentioned criticisms. We should go on activating the enthusiasm of such people from the Guomindang army and government as Wei Lihuang and Wen Wenhao, who are patriotic. We should even provide for such abusive types as Long Yun, Liang Shuming and Peng Yihu and allow them to rail at us, while refuting their nonsense and accepting what makes sense in their rebukes. This is better for the Party, for the people and for socialism.

Since classes and class struggle still exist in China, there is bound to be opposition in one form or another. Although all the democratic parties and democrats without party affiliation have professed their acceptance of the leadership of the Chinese Communist Party, many of them are actually in opposition in varying degrees. On such matters as "carrying the revolution through to the end," the movement to resist U.S. aggression and aid Korea and the agrarian reform, they were against us and yet not against us. To this very day they have reservations about the suppression of counter-revolutionaries. They didn't want to have a constitution of the socialist type, for, as they said, the Common Programme was just perfect, and yet when the Draft Constitution came out, their hands all went up in favour. Things often turn into their opposites, and this is also true of the attitude of the democratic parties on many questions. They are in opposition, and yet not in opposition, often proceeding from being in opposition to not being in opposition.

The Communist Party and the democratic parties are all products of history. What emerges in history disappears in history. Therefore, the Communist Party will disappear one day, and so will the democratic parties. Is this disappearance so unpleasant? In my opinion, it will be very pleasant. I think it is just fine that one day we will be able to do away with the Communist Party and the dictatorship of the proletariat. Our task is to hasten their extinction. We have spoken about this point many times.

But at present we cannot do without the proletarian party and the dictatorship of the proletariat and, what is more, it is imperative that they should be made still more powerful. Otherwise, we would not be able to suppress the counter-revolutionaries, resist the imperialists and build socialism, or consolidate it when it is built. Lenin's theory on the proletarian party and the dictatorship of the proletariat is by no means "outmoded," as alleged by certain people. The dictatorship of the proletariat cannot but be highly coercive. Still, we must oppose bureaucracy and a cumbersome apparatus. I propose that the Party and government organs should be thoroughly streamlined and cut by two-thirds provided that no person dies and no work stops.

However, streamlining the Party and government organs does not mean getting rid of the democratic parties. I suggest you give attention to our united front work so as to improve our relations with them and make every possible effort to mobilize their enthusiasm for the cause of socialism.

VIII The Relationship between Revolution and Counter-revolution

What kind of factor are counter-revolutionaries? They are a negative factor, a destructive factor, they are forces opposed to the positive factors. Is it possible for counter-revolutionaries to change? The die-hards will undoubtedly never change. However, given the conditions in our country, most of the counter-revolutionaries will eventually change to a greater or lesser extent. Thanks to the correct policy we adopted, many have been transformed into persons no longer opposed to the revolution, and a few have even done some good.

The following points should be affirmed:

First, it should be affirmed that the suppression of counter-revolutionaries in 1951–52 was necessary. There is a view that this campaign needn't have been launched. This is wrong.

Counter-revolutionaries may be dealt with in these ways: execution, imprisonment, supervision and leaving at large. Execution—everybody knows what that means. By imprisonment we mean putting counter-revolutionaries in jail and reforming them through labour. By supervision we mean leaving them in society to be reformed under the supervision of the masses. By leaving at large we mean that generally no arrest is made in those cases where it is marginal whether to make an arrest, or that those arrested are set free for good behaviour. It is essential that different counter-revolutionaries should be dealt with differently on the merits of each case.

Now let's take execution in particular. True, we executed a number of people during the above-mentioned campaign to suppress counter-revolutionaries. But what sort of people were they? They were counter-revolutionaries who owed the masses many blood debts and were bitterly hated. In a great revolution embracing 600 million people, the masses would not have been able to rise if we had not killed off such local despots as the "Tyrant of the East" and the "Tyrant of the West." Had it not been for that campaign of suppression, the people would not have approved our present policy of leniency. Now that some people have heard that Stalin wrongly put a number of people to death, they jump to the conclusion that we too were wrong in putting those counter-revolutionaries to death. This is a wrong view. It is of immediate significance today to affirm that it was absolutely right to execute those counter-revolutionaries.

Second, it should be affirmed that counter-revolutionaries still exist, although their number has greatly diminished. After the Hu Feng case surfaced, it was necessary to ferret out the counter-revolutionaries. The effort to clear out those who remain hidden must go on. It should be affirmed that there are still a small number of counter-revolutionaries carrying out counter-revolutionary sabotage of one kind or another. For example, they kill cattle, set fire to granaries, wreck factories, steal information and put up reactionary posters. Consequently, it is wrong to say that counter-revolutionaries have been completely eliminated and that we can therefore lay our heads on our pillows and just drop off to sleep. As long as class struggle exists in China and in the world, we should never relax our vigilance. Nevertheless, it would be equally wrong to assert that there are still large numbers of counter-revolutionaries.

Third, from now on there should be fewer arrests and executions in the suppression of counter-revolutionaries in society at large. They are the mortal and immediate enemies of the people and are deeply hated by them, and therefore a small number should be executed. But most of them should be handed over to the agricultural co-operatives and made to work under supervision and be reformed through labour. All the same, we cannot announce that there will be no more executions, and we must not abolish the death penalty.

Fourth, in clearing out counter-revolutionaries in Party and government organs, schools and army units, we must adhere to the policy started in Yan'an of killing none and arresting few. Confirmed counter-revolutionaries are to be screened by the organizations concerned, but they are not to be arrested by the public security bureaus, prosecuted by the procuratorial organs or tried by the law courts. Well over ninety out of every hundred of these counter-revolutionaries should be dealt with in this way. This is what we mean by arresting few. As for executions, kill none.

What kind of people are those we don't execute? We don't execute people like Hu Feng, Pan Hannian, Rao Shushi, or even captured war criminals such as Emperor Pu Yi and Kang Ze. We don't have them executed, not because their crimes don't deserve capital punishment but because such executions would yield no advantage. If one such criminal is executed, a second and a third will be compared with him in their crimes, and then many heads will begin to roll. This is my first point. Second, people may be wrongly executed. Once a head is chopped off, history shows it can't be restored, nor can it grow again as chives do, after being cut. If you cut off a head by mistake, there is no way to rectify the mistake, even if you want to. The third point is that you will have destroyed a source of evidence. You need evidence in order to suppress counter-revolutionaries. Often one counter-revolutionary serves as a living witness against another, and there will be cases where you may want to consult him. If you have got rid of him, you may not be able to get evidence any more. And this will be to the advantage of counter-revolution, not of revolution. The fourth point is that killing these counter-revolutionaries won't (1) raise production, (2) raise the country's scientific level, (3) help do away with the four pests, (4) strengthen national defence, or (5) help recover Taiwan. It will only earn you the reputation of killing captives, and killing captives has always given one a bad name. Another point is that counter-revolutionaries inside Party and government organs are different from those in society at large. The latter lord it over the masses while the former are somewhat removed from the masses, and therefore make enemies in general but seldom enemies in particular. What harm is there in killing none of them? Those who are physically fit for manual labour should be reformed through labour, and those who are not should be provided for. Counter-revolutionaries are trash, they are vermin, but once in your hands, you can make them perform some kind of service for the people.

But shall we enact a law stipulating that no counter-revolutionary in Party and government organs is to be executed? Ours is a policy for internal observance which need not be made public, and all we need do is carry it out as far as possible in practice. Supposing someone should throw a bomb into this building, killing everybody here, or half or one-third of the people present, what would you say—execute him or not execute him? Certainly he must be executed.

Adopting the policy of killing none when eliminating counter-revolutionaries from Party and government organs in no way prevents us from being strict with them. Instead, it serves as a safeguard against irretrievable mistakes, and if mistakes are made, it gives us an opportunity to correct them. In this way many people will be put at ease and distrust among comrades inside the Party avoided. If counter-revolutionaries are not executed, they have to be fed. All counter-revolutionaries should be given a chance to earn a living, so that they can start anew. This will be good for the cause of the people and be well received abroad.

The suppression of counter-revolutionaries still calls for hard work. We must not relax. In future not only must the suppression of counter-revolutionaries in society continue, but we must also uncover all the hidden counter-revolutionaries in Party and government organs, schools and army units. We must draw a clear distinction between ourselves and the enemy. If the enemy is allowed to worm his way into our ranks and even into our organs of leadership, we know only too well how serious a threat this will be to the cause of socialism and to the dictatorship of the proletariat.

IX The Relationship between Right and Wrong

A clear distinction must be made between right and wrong, whether inside or outside the Party. How to deal with people who have made mistakes is an important question. The correct attitude towards them should be to adopt a policy of "learning from past mistakes to avoid future ones and curing the sickness to save the patient," help them correct their mistakes and allow them to go on taking part in the revolution. In those days when the dogmatists headed by Wang Ming were in the saddle, our Party erred on this question, picking up the bad aspect of Stalin's style of work. In society the dogmatists rejected the middle forces and inside the Party they did not allow people to correct their mistakes; they barred both from the revolution.

The True Story of Ah Q is a fine story. I would recommend comrades who have read it before to reread it and those who haven't to read it carefully. In this story Lu Xun writes mainly about a peasant who is backward and politically unawakened. He devotes a whole chapter, "Barred from the Revolution," to describing how a bogus foreign devil bars Ah Q from the revolution. Actually, all Ah Q understands by revolution is helping himself to a few things just like some others. But even this kind of revolution is denied him by the bogus foreign devil. It seems to me that in this respect some people are quite like that bogus foreign devil. They barred from the revolution those who had committed errors, drawing no distinction between the making of mistakes and counter-revolution, and went so far as to kill a number of people who were guilty only of mistakes. We must take this lesson to heart. It is bad either to bar people outside the Party from the revolution or to prohibit erring comrades inside the Party from making amends.

With regard to comrades who have erred, some people say we must observe them and see if they are going to correct their mistakes. I would say just observing them will not do, we must help them correct their mistakes. That is to say, first we must observe and second we must give help. Everybody needs help; those who have not done wrong need it and those who have need it still more. Probably no one is free from mistakes, only some make more and some less, and once they do they need help. It is passive just to observe; conditions must be created to help those who have erred to mend their ways. A clear distinction must be drawn between right and wrong, for inner-Party controversies over principle are a reflection inside the Party of the class struggle in society, and no equivocation is to be tolerated. It is normal, in accordance with the merits of the case, to mete out appropriate and well grounded criticism to comrades who have erred, and even to conduct necessary struggle against them; this is to help them correct mistakes. To deny them help and, what is worse, to gloat over their mistakes, is sectarianism.

For revolution, it is always better to have more people. Except for a few who cling to their mistakes and fail to mend their ways after repeated admonition, the majority of those who have erred can correct their mistakes. People who have had typhoid become immune to it; similarly, people who have made mistakes will make fewer ones provided they are good at drawing lessons. On the other hand, since it is easier for those who have not erred to become cocky, they are prone to make mistakes. Let us be careful, for those who fix people guilty of mistakes will more often than not end up finding themselves in a fix. Gao Gang started out to lift a rock to hurl at others only to find himself being knocked down. Treating with good will those who have erred will win general approval and unite people. A helpful attitude or a hostile attitude towards comrades who have erred—this is a criterion for judging whether one is well-intentioned or ill-intentioned.

The policy of "learning from past mistakes to avoid future ones and curing the sickness to save the patient" is a policy for uniting the whole Party. We must stick to this policy.

X The Relationship between China and Other Countries

We have put forward the slogan of learning from other countries. I think we have been right. At present, the leaders of some countries are chary and even afraid of advancing this slogan. It takes some courage to do so, because theatrical pretensions have to be discarded.

It must be admitted that every nation has its strong points. If not, how can it survive? How can it progress? On the other hand, every nation has its weak points. Some believe that socialism is just perfect, without a single flaw. How can that be true? It must be recognized that there are always two aspects, the strong points and the weak points. The secretaries of our Party branches, the company commanders and platoon leaders of our army have all learned to jot down both aspects in their pocket notebooks, the weak points as well as the strong ones, when summing up their experience. They all know there are two aspects to everything, why do we mention only one? There will always be two aspects, even ten thousand years from now. Each age, whether the future or the present, has its own two aspects, and each individual has his own two aspects. In short, there are two aspects, not just one. To say there is only one is to be aware of one aspect and to be ignorant of the other.

Our policy is to learn from the strong points of all nations and all countries, learn all that is genuinely good in the political, economic, scientific and technological fields and in literature and art. But we must learn with an analytical and critical eye, not blindly, and we mustn't copy everything indiscriminately and transplant mechanically. Naturally, we mustn't pick up their shortcomings and weak points.

We should adopt the same attitude in learning from the experience of the Soviet Union and other socialist countries. Some of our people were not clear about this before and even picked up their weaknesses. While they were swelling with pride over what they had picked up, it was already being discarded in those countries; as a result, they had to do a somersault like the Monkey Sun Wigong. For instance, there were people who accused us of making a mistake of principle in setting up a Ministry of Culture and a Bureau of Cinematography rather than a Ministry of Cinematography and a Bureau of Culture, as was the case in the Soviet Union. They did not anticipate that shortly afterwards the Soviet Union would make a change and set up a Ministry of Culture as we had done. Some people never take the trouble to analyse, they simply follow the "wind." Today, when the north wind is blowing, they join the "north wind" school; tomorrow, when there is a west wind, they switch to the "west wind" school; afterwards when the north wind blows again, they switch back to the "north wind" school. They hold no independent opinion of their own and often go from one extreme to the other.

In the Soviet Union, those who once extolled Stalin to the skies have now in one swoop consigned him to purgatory. Here in China some people are following their example. It is the opinion of the Central Committee that Stalin's mistakes amounted to only 30 per cent of the whole and his achievements to 70 per cent, and that all things considered Stalin was nonetheless a great Marxist. We wrote "On the Historical Experience of the Dictatorship of the Proletariat" on the basis of this evaluation. This assessment of 30 per cent for mistakes and 70 per cent for achievements is just about right. Stalin did a number of wrong things in connection with China. The "Left" adventurism pursued by Wang Ming in the latter part of the Second Revolutionary Civil War period and his Right opportunism in the early days of the War of Resistance

Against Japan can both be traced to Stalin. At the time of the War of Liberation, Stalin first enjoined us not to press on with the revolution, maintaining that if civil war flared up, the Chinese nation would run the risk of destroying itself. Then when fighting did erupt, he took us half seriously, half sceptically. When we won the war, Stalin suspected that ours was a victory of the Tito type, and in 1949 and 1950 the pressure on us was very strong indeed. Even so, we maintain the estimate of 30 per cent for his mistakes and 70 per cent for his achievements. This is only fair.

In the social sciences and in Marxism-Leninism, we must continue to study Stalin diligently wherever he is right. What we must study is all that is universally true and we must make sure that this study is linked with Chinese reality. It would lead to a mess if every single sentence, even of Marx's, were followed. Our theory is an integration of the universal truth of Marxism-Leninism with the concrete practice of the Chinese revolution. At one time some people in the Party went in for dogmatism, and this came under our criticism. Nevertheless, there is still dogmatism today. It still exists in academic circles and in economic circles too.

In the natural sciences we are rather backward, and here we should make a special effort to learn from foreign countries. And yet we must learn critically, not blindly. In technology I think first we have to follow others in most cases, and it is better for us to do so, since that is what we are lacking at present and know little about. However, in those cases where we already have clear knowledge, we must not follow others in every detail.

We must firmly reject and criticize all the decadent bourgeois systems, ideologies and ways of life of foreign countries. But this should in no way prevent us from learning the advanced sciences and technologies of capitalist countries and whatever is scientific in the management of their enterprises. In the industrially developed countries they run their enterprises with fewer people and greater efficiency and they know how to do business. All this should be learned well in accordance with our own principles in order to improve our work. Nowadays, those who make English their study no longer work hard at it, and research papers are no longer translated into English, French, German or Japanese for exchange with other countries. This too is a kind of blind prejudice. Neither the indiscriminate rejection of everything foreign, whether scientific, technological or cultural, nor the indiscriminate imitation of everything foreign as noted above, has anything in common with the Marxist attitude, and neither in any way benefits our cause.

In my opinion, China has two weaknesses, which are at the same time two strong points.

First, in the past China was a colonial and semi-colonial country, not an imperialist power, and was always bullied by others. Its industry and agriculture are not developed and its scientific and technological level is low, and except for its vast territory, rich resources, large population, long history, *The Dream of the Red Chamber* in literature, and so on, China is inferior to other countries in many respects, and so has no reason to feel conceited. However, there are people who, having been slaves too long, feel inferior in everything and don't stand up straight in the presence of foreigners. They are just like Jia Gui[3] in the opera *The Famen Temple* who, when asked to take a seat, refuses to do so, giving the excuse that he is used to standing in attendance. Here we need to bestir ourselves, enhance our national confidence and encourage the spirit typified by "scorn U.S. imperialism," which was fostered during the movement to resist U.S. aggression and aid Korea.

Second, our revolution came late. Although the Revolution of 1911 which overthrew the Qing emperor preceded the Russian revolution, there was no Communist Party at that time and the revolution failed. Victory in the people's revolution came only in 1949, some thirty years later than the October Revolution. On this account too, we are not in a position to feel conceited. The Soviet Union differs from our country in that, firstly, tsarist Russia was an imperialist power and, secondly, it had the October Revolution. As a result, many people in the Soviet Union are conceited and very arrogant.

Our two weaknesses are also strong points. As I have said elsewhere, we are first "poor" and second "blank." By "poor" I mean we do not have much industry and our agriculture is underdeveloped. By "blank" I mean we are like a blank sheet of paper and our cultural and scientific level is not high. From the developmental point of view, this is not bad. The poor want revolution, whereas it is difficult for the rich to want revolution. Countries with a high scientific and technological level are overblown with arrogance. We are like a blank sheet of paper, which is good for writing on.

Being "poor" and "blank" is therefore all to our good. Even when one day our country becomes strong and prosperous, we must still adhere to the revolutionary stand, remain modest and prudent, learn from other countries and not allow ourselves to become swollen with conceit. We must not only learn from other countries during the period of our First Five-Year Plan, but must go on doing so after the completion of scores of five-year plans. We must be ready to learn even ten thousand years from now. Is there anything bad about that?

I have taken up ten topics altogether. These ten relationships are all contradictions. The world consists of contradictions. Without contradictions the world would cease to exist. Our task is to handle these contradictions correctly. As to whether or not they can be resolved entirely to our satisfaction in practice, we must be prepared for either possibility; furthermore, in the course of resolving these contradictions we are bound to come up against new ones, new problems. But as we have often said, while the road ahead is tortuous, the future is bright. We must do our best to mobilize all positive factors, both inside and outside the Party, both at home and abroad, both direct and indirect, and make China a powerful socialist country.

NOTES

[1]The system of fixed quotas for the production, purchase and marketing of grain was instituted in the spring of 1955. The quotas for production fixed in that year were based on the grain yield per *mou* in normal years, and increases in production were not to entail extra sales of grain to the state for three years. The fixed quota for purchase refers to the purchase by the state of a fixed proportion of surplus grain from peasant households having a surplus. The fixed quota for marketing refers to the quota for the state's supply of grain to grain-deficient households. The system was adopted in order to raise the peasants' enthusiasm for increasing production.

[2]The system of obligatory sales enforced in the Soviet Union from 1933 to 1957 was the principal measure by which the state bought agricultural products. Under it the collective farms and individual peasant households were required to sell their agricultural products annually to the state in quantities and at prices fixed by the state.

[3]In the Peking opera *The Famen Temple,* Jia Gui is a trusted lackey of Liu Qin, a Ming Dynasty eunuch.

APPENDIX 4

Decision of the CPC Central Committee on Some Issues Concerning the Establishment of a Socialist Market Economic Structure

(Adopted on 14 November 1993 by the Third Plenary Session of the Fourteenth Central Committee of the Chinese Communist Party)

In order to fulfil the task of reforming the economic structure put forward at the 14th National Congress of the Chinese Communist Party and to accelerate reform, opening to the outside world and the socialist modernization drive, the Third Plenary Session of the 14th Central Committee of the Communist Party of China has discussed some major issues concerning the establishment of a socialist market economic structure, and has adopted the following decision.

I The New Situation and New Tasks In China's Efforts to Reform Its Economic Structure

1. Great changes have occurred in China's economic structure through reforms over the past 10-odd years guided by the theory of building socialism with Chinese characteristics put forward by Comrade Deng Xiaoping. A situation with the publicly owned economic sector constituting the mainstay while various other economic sectors develop simultaneously has taken initial shape. The economic restructuring in the rural areas continues to develop in depth; state-owned enterprises are shifting to new management mechanisms; the role of the market in the allocation of resources is rapidly expanding; economic and technological exchanges and cooperation with other countries are conducted widely; and the structure of a planned economy is gradually being replaced by the socialist market economic structure. Reform has emancipated and developed the social productive forces, and promoted to a new height the country's economic construction, the people's living standards and overall national strength. China's socialist system has shown great vitality in a situation marked by abrupt changes in the international arena. The reform and opening to the outside world which have been adopted by the Party and people on the basis of a conscientious summing up of historical experiences constitute a strategic policy decision that conforms with the law of social and economic development and is the necessary path for China to achieve modernization.

Marked by Comrade Deng Xiaoping's important speeches in early 1992 and the 14th National Congress of the Chinese Communist Party, China's reform, opening to the outside world and the drive for socialist modernization have developed to a new stage. The 14th National Congress explicitly laid down the task of establishing a socialist market economic structure, which is an important component of the theory of building socialism with Chinese characteristics and is of profound and far-reaching significance for China's modernization drive. To establish a new economic structure by the end of this century is a great historic task of the whole Party and people of all nationalities in China during the new period.

2. The socialist market economic structure is linked with the basic system of socialism. The establishment of this structure aims at enabling the market to play the fundamental role in resource allocations under macro-economic control by the state. To turn this goal into reality, it is necessary to uphold the principle of taking the publicly owned sector as the mainstay, while striving for a simultaneous development of all economic sectors, to further transform the management mechanism of state-owned enterprises, and to establish a modern enterprise system which meets the requirements of the market economy and in which the property rights as well as the rights and responsibilities of enterprises are clearly defined, government administration and enterprise management are separated and scientific management is established. It is necessary to establish a nationwide integrated and open market system to closely combine the urban market with the rural market and link the domestic market with the international market, so as to optimize the allocation of resources. It is necessary to transform the government's functions in economic management and establish a sound macro-economic control system which chiefly relies on indirect means so as to ensure the healthy operation of the national economy. It is necessary to establish an income distribution system which takes the principle of "to each according to his work" as its mainstay, gives priority to efficiency while taking fairness into account so as to encourage some localities and people to become prosperous first while adhering to the road to common prosperity. It is also necessary to establish a multi-layered social security system and provide both urban and rural people with a degree of security commensurate to China's reality so as to promote economic development and social stability. All these major links comprise an organic entity, interrelated and mutually conditioning, together forming the basic framework of the socialist market economy. It is necessary to establish a legal system in line with and corresponding to these major links, and to adopt down-to-earth measures to push the overall reform forward actively step by step and promote the development of the social productive forces.

3. The establishment of a socialist market economic structure is a pioneering undertaking unprecedented in history; it requires tackling many extremely complicated problems. In the past 15 years, we have blazed a fruitful trail in reform and accumulated rich experiences. Practice has proved that so long as we unswervingly adhere to Comrade Deng Xiaoping's theory of building socialism with Chinese characteristics and the basic line of the Party at the primary stage of socialism, we can withstand all kinds of tests and successfully achieve the great goals of reform, opening to the outside world and modernization.

In the process of establishing the socialist market economic structure, we must, under the guidance of the Party's basic theory and line, decide on the various steps of reform and judge their success or failure by always adhering to the basic criterion of whether they help develop the productive forces of the socialist society, enhance the overall strength of the socialist state and improve the people's living standards. Attention should be paid to the following points:

—Emancipating the mind and seeking truth from facts. It is necessary to change the traditional concepts of planned economy and advocate active exploration and bold experiment. Therefore, it is necessary, on the one hand, to inherit our fine traditions and, on the other, to break away from outmoded conventions and, proceeding from the realities of China, learn from those experiences of all countries, including the developed capitalist countries, that reflect the general laws of social production and market economy. It is necessary to be on the alert against Right tendencies, but mainly to guard against "Left" tendencies.

—With economic construction as the central link, reform and opening to the outside world, economic development and social stability promote one another and form a single entity. Development is an essential criterion. Only by seizing the favorable opportunities, conducting reform in depth, expanding the opening to the outside world and accelerating the pace of development, can we consolidate China's political stability and unity. Only by upholding the four cardinal principles, fostering both material progress and cultural and ideological progress, and maintaining social and political stability can we effectively guarantee the smooth progress of reform and opening to the outside world and the development of China's economy. In making active efforts to develop the economy and implementing reform and opening to the outside world, we should take care to be steady and discreet and steer clear of massive losses and social upheavals.

—Respecting the pioneering spirit of the masses and attaching importance to their personal interests. It is necessary to sum up in time the experience the masses create in practice, show respect for the wishes of the people and to properly guide and protect their initiative so as to give it full play. In the process of deepening the reform and developing the economy, it is necessary to properly handle the relationship between accumulation and consumption, between overall and partial situations and between long-term and short-term interests, and to effect continuous improvement in the people's living standards, so as to establish a broad and deep popular basis for our reform.

—Combining package reform with breakthroughs in key areas. It is a correct policy decision conforming to China's realities to start the reform from the countryside and gradually extend it to the cities, to combine urban reform with rural reform, keep micro-economic reform in step with macro-economic reform, and ensure that the enlivening of the domestic economy and the opening to the outside world are closely related to and promote each other. In accordance with differing situations, for some major reform measures, plans can be drawn up first and conducted coordinately in related areas of the economic system, while some others should be tried out first in selected localities or areas and then extended after experience has been gained. It is necessary both to pay attention to the gradual progress of the reform as a whole and to miss no opportunity of making breakthroughs in key areas that spur the overall reform.

II Changing the Operation Mechanism of State-Owned Enterprises and Establishing a Modern Enterprise System

4. A modern enterprise system with public ownership as its mainstay is the foundation of the socialist market economic structure. Over the past dozen years or more, state-owned enterprises have been invigorated through such measures as expanding their power to make decisions regarding management and changing the mode of management, thus laying the initial foundation for their entry into the market. To continu-

ously deepen enterprise reform, it is necessary to tackle some deep-seated contradictions, focus on innovations of the enterprise system, further emancipate and develop the productive forces and bring the superiority of the socialist system into full play.

Establishing a modern enterprise system is a necessary requisite for developing socialized mass production and the market economy; and it represents the orientation of reform of China's state-owned enterprises. Its basic features are: First, the property rights relationships are clearly defined; the ownership of state-owned assets in the enterprises belongs to the state; the enterprises, as legal entities, possess all rights over the assets formulated by investments from various sources, including the state, and become legal entities that enjoy rights and shoulder responsibilities under civil law. Second, the enterprises use all the resources to which legal entities are entitled to conduct management independently and shoulder sole responsibility for gains and losses according to law, pay taxes in line with related stipulations, and assume the responsibility of maintaining and increasing the value of the assets in the interests of the investors. Third, the investors enjoy, commensurate with their shares of capital investment, their rights and interests as part owners of the enterprises, that is, the right of dividend and the right to take part in strategic decisions and choice of managers. Should the enterprises go bankrupt, the investors only shoulder limited liability for the debts of such enterprises according to the amount of their capital investment. Fourth, the enterprises organize production and management according to market demand and aim at raising the productivity of labor and the economic returns of the enterprises. The government does not directly interfere with the managerial activities of enterprises. Those which have been in losses for a long time and whose assets cannot cover the debts should apply for bankruptcy according to law; the successful enterprises prosper and those which fail are eliminated in the market competition. Fifth, it is necessary to establish a scientific enterprise leadership structure and organizational management system, regulate the relations between the owners, managers, and the workers and staff, and build a management mechanism which combines incentives and restraints. All enterprises should work hard toward this direction.

5. To establish a modern enterprise system is an arduous and complicated undertaking; it requires the accumulation of experience and creation of the necessary conditions and should be conducted step by step. At present, it is necessary to continue to implement the Law Concerning Industrial Enterprises Owned by the Whole People and Regulations on Changing the Management Mechanism of Industrial Enterprises Owned by the Whole People, and to really unreservedly extend to the enterprises the various rights and responsibilities pertaining to their own management. It is necessary to strengthen supervision and control over the state-owned assets possessed by enterprises and reach the aim of maintaining and increasing the value of the state-owned assets. It is necessary to quicken the pace of the change of the management mechanism and readjustment of the organizational structure of state-owned enterprises. Unwarranted pooling of funds, arbitrary requisition of donations and exaction of fees from enterprises must be resolutely stopped. It is necessary to reduce the financial burden the enterprises have to bear in supporting social undertakings. It is necessary to, step by step, make an inventory of and check of the stockpiles and capital of enterprises, define the property rights, clarify debts receivable and debts payable, evaluate the assets to verify the amount possessed by the enterprise legal entities. It is necessary to create conditions in all respects for state-owned enterprises to shift steadily to the modern enterprise system.

6. Large and medium-sized state-owned enterprises are the mainstay of the national economy; to introduce the modern enterprise system is of great importance for heightening their managerial expertise and competitiveness, and for enabling them to better

play their leading role. Modern enterprises may have varying organizational patterns according to the composition of their assets. For state-owned enterprises, it is useful to experiment with the corporate system. Standardized corporations can effectively accomplish separation between the ownership of the investors and the rights of enterprises, as legal entities, over their assets; this is conducive to separating government administration from enterprise management, changing the management mechanism, and enabling the enterprises to get rid of reliance on administrative organizations and enabling the state to get away from its unlimited responsibility for enterprises; and it is also conducive to raising funds and diversifying risks. The corporations can be of various types. Among large and medium-sized state-owned enterprises with the necessary conditions, those whose investments come from a single source can be reorganized into wholly owned companies according to law, and those with investments from several sources can be turned into limited-liability companies or limited-liability stock companies according to law. Limited-liability stock companies whose shares are listed should be a small number and they must be strictly examined and approved beforehand. What amount of shares in the companies should be suitably held by the state can vary according to the different industries and the different degrees of distribution of the shares. Companies that turn out special-category products and those producing armaments should be held by the state alone. In key enterprises in "backbone" and basic industries, the state should have controlling shares and at the same time bring in nonstate capital, so as to expand the leading role and scope of influence of the state sector of the economy. Introduction of the corporate system does not simply mean a change of names, neither is its aim simply the pooling of funds; the important thing is the shifting of mechanism. It should be adopted in a gradual manner after experiments; it must not be done for show, or rashly on a mass scale. It is necessary to guard against indiscriminately changing enterprises without the necessary conditions into companies. The existing companies should be reshuffled to conform to required norms.

In line with the demands of the modern enterprise system, existing national corporations covering entire industries should be changed step by step into holding companies. It is necessary to establish a number of large enterprise groups "trans-regional and embracing several trades" that have public ownership as their mainstay and are linked mainly by property rights, and to bring into play their important role in promoting structural readjustment, raising returns through an economy of scale, accelerating the development of new technology and new products and enhancing competitiveness in the international market.

As for the small state-owned enterprises, the management of some can be contracted out or leased; others can be shifted to the partnership system in the form of stock sharing, or sold to collectives or individuals. Incomes from selling such enterprises or equity in them can be diverted by the state to industries which are urgent to develop.

7. Reforming and perfecting the organizational and managerial systems of enterprises. It is necessary to adhere to and improve the system of responsibility of factory director (manager), and to ensure that the directors (managers) enjoy their rights and carry out their responsibilities according to law. Enterprises which adopt the corporate system must establish internal organizations that accord with related laws and regulations. Party organizations in enterprises should play the role of the political core and supervise and guarantee the implementation of the principles and policies of the Party and state. We should wholeheartedly rely on the working class. The trade unions and workers' congresses should organize the workers and staff to take part in democratic management of the enterprises, and uphold the legitimate rights and interests of the workers and staff. It is necessary to improve the competence of the ranks of the work-

ers and staff, and create a contingent of entrepreneurs. It is also necessary to set up a mechanism of clearly delineated rights and responsibilities inside enterprises which promotes unity and cooperation as well as provides mutual restraint and can mobilize the initiative of all groups.

The enterprises should, in line with the requirements of the market economy, improve and straighten out their internal management, enforce labor discipline, strengthen their work in technological development, quality control, marketing, finance and information, raise their decision-making ability and improve their quality and economic returns. It is necessary to elevate enterprise culture and foster fine professional ethics and the spirit of love for one's own profession and factory, observance of law, faithfulness to one's word, and readiness for new explorations and innovations.

8. Strengthening control over state-owned property in enterprises. For state-owned property in enterprises, the system will be for unitary ownership by the state, supervision by governments at various levels and independent management by the enterprises. In line with the principle of separating the socio-economic control function of the government from its function as the owner of state-owned property, appropriate channels will be actively sought to control and manage state-owned assets. It is necessary to strengthen organizations specializing in the control of state-owned assets both by the central authorities and by the governments of various provinces, autonomous regions and municipalities directly under the central government. The current defective control over state-owned assets and serious losses of state-owned assets warrant serious attention. The departments in charge of supervising state-owned assets in enterprises should assume their responsibility and perform their duty; when necessary, they may set up boards of supervisors and send their members to enforce supervision over the work of maintaining and increasing the value of state-owned assets in enterprises. It is strictly forbidden to convert state-owned assets into shares and sell them at low prices, still less distribute them to individuals without compensation. It is necessary to improve the system to plug the loopholes in all respects, so as to ensure that the state-owned assets and their rights and interests are not infringed upon.

9. Adhering to the principle of taking public ownership as the mainstay and effecting a simultaneous development of all economic sectors. While striving actively to promote the development of the state and collective economy, it is necessary to encourage the development of the individually owned, privately owned and foreign-invested economic sectors, and to strengthen control over them according to law. With the fluidity and reshuffling of property rights, there are more and more economic entities with mixed ownership; this will bring forth a new structure of ownership. Nationwide, public ownership should be the mainstay in the national economy but it may vary in different places and trades. The position of public ownership as the mainstay in the national economy manifests itself chiefly in the advantageous position the state-owned and collectively owned sectors occupy in the totality of social assets, and in the fact that the state-owned economy controls the lifeline of the national economy and plays the leading role in economic development. The publicly owned sector, and especially the state-owned sector, must take an active part in market competition and grow and develop in the competition. The state should create conditions for economic sectors under different kinds of ownership to compete in the market on equal terms, and should deal with the various types of enterprises without discrimination. It is also necessary to strengthen the property rights in existing urban collective enterprises, and they may be turned into shareholding cooperatives or partnership enterprises as indicated by different conditions. Those with the necessary conditions can also be organized into limited-liability companies. A small number of them, which are large in size and have good economic returns, can also be turned into limited-liability stock companies or enterprise groups.

III Cultivating and Expanding the Market System

10. Giving effect to the basic role of the market mechanism in the allocation of resources requires the cultivation and expansion of the market system. Currently, the emphasis should be on developing the production-factors market, standardizing market activities, breaking the barriers and blockades between regions or departments, opposing unfair competition and creating an environment for competition on equal terms, so as to form a unified, open, competitive and orderly integrated market.

11. Pushing forward price reform and establishing a mechanism in which the prices are formed mainly by the market. Although the prices of most commodities have already been decontrolled, the double-track price system still exists for some capital goods, the degree of application of market prices for production factors is relatively low, and the mechanisms for price formation and regulation are still not completely sound. The main tasks in deepening price reform are: On the premise of keeping the general price level relatively stable, to decontrol the prices of competitive commodities and services, adjust government-set prices for some commodities and services to reasonable levels; abolish the dual-pricing system for capital goods as quickly as possible; accelerate the marketization of prices of production factors; and establish and improve a sound system of stockpiling a small number of important commodities that have a great bearing on the national economy and people's livelihood, thereby stabilizing market prices.

12. Reforming the existing commodity circulation system and further developing the commodity market. Wholesale markets will be set up for bulk agricultural produce, industrially produced consumer goods and capital goods in major commodity-producing, marketing and distributing areas. Experimentation with a few commodity futures markets will be strictly standardized. State-owned enterprises in the sphere of circulation should transform their management mechanism, participate actively in market competition, improve economic efficiency and give play to their leading role in the process of improving and expanding the wholesale market. To meet the needs of commodity circulation, a commodity market network comprehensive in its functions "characterized by the combination of large, medium and small markets, and the coexistence of various economic modes and forms" should be established to push forward the modernization of circulation.

13. The present cultivation of the market system should focus on the development of markets for finance, labor, real estate, technology and information.

Developing and perfecting the financial market focused on bank loans. Capital markets should actively but steadily expand financing activities in the form of bonds and stocks. It is necessary to establish a rating system for bond-issuing agencies and bond credits, so as to bring about the healthy development of the bond market. It is necessary to standardize and gradually expand the scale of the issue and listing of stocks. The money market should develop standard inter-bank lending and bill discount; the central bank should develop trading in government bonds. Illegal raising of funds, money-lending and other such financing activities should be resolutely checked and corrected.

Reforming the labor system and gradually forming a labor market. China's abundant labor force is advantageous for economic development, but also brings pressure on employment. The development, utilization and rational allocation of human resources should be the starting point of developing the labor market. We should create more job opportunities in order to employ more urban labor forces. We should encourage and guide the surplus rural labor force to shift gradually to non-agricultural fields, and effect orderly labor mobility between regions. We should develop various forms of employment, and use economic measures to adjust the employment structure, so as to form an employment mechanism for the two-way choice between the employing units and the employees and rational labor mobility.

Standardizing and developing the real estate market. With scarcity of land and a large population, we in China have to value and make rational use of land resources, and strengthen land management. We should conscientiously protect cultivated land and strictly control the transfer of land from agricultural to non-agricultural use. The state monopolizes the primary urban land market. We should implement a system for the transfer of land-use rights with compensation and within a time limit. With regard to the sale of land-use rights for commercial purposes, we should change the method of negotiated lease into one of public bidding and auctioning. At the same time, we should strengthen the management of secondary markets and establish a normal market mechanism for the formation of prices for land-use rights. By starting to levy and adjust real estate taxes and other fees, we should forestall any attempt to reap excessive profits in real estate transactions and prevent the loss of state profits. We should control the rapid growth of luxury housing and high-consumption recreational facilities. We should accelerate reform of the urban housing system, control the land price for housing and promote the commercialization of housing and the development of housing construction.

Further developing the technological and information markets. We should introduce a mechanism of competition in these spheres, protect intellectual property rights, carry on transfers of technological achievements with compensation and promote commercialization and industrialization of technological research results and information.

14. Actively developing professional intermediate organizations of market and giving play to their services, such as their linking, notarial and supervisory role. Currently, emphasis should be placed on increasing the number of accountants', auditors' and lawyers' firms, notarial and arbitration organizations, organizations for measurement and quality inspecting certification, information and consultant organizations and organizations for asset evaluating and credit rating. We should bring into play the role of trade associations and chambers of commerce. Professional intermediate organizations should, following the law and through competence confirmation and observance of market rules, set up self-regulatory operational mechanisms. They should undertake appropriate legal and economic responsibilities and accept administration and supervision from the government departments concerned.

15. Improving and strengthening management and supervision of the markets. We should set up a normal procedure for market access, market competition and market transactions, guarantee fair exchange and competition on equal terms, and protect the lawful rights and interests of traders and consumers. We should resolutely punish, according to law, such illegal acts as producing and selling faked and shoddy goods and the manipulation of markets. We should raise the rate of open market transactions, establish authoritative organizations for law enforcement and supervision in the markets, strengthen management of the markets and give play to the mass media's role in supervising the markets.

IV Transforming Government Functions, Establishing a Sound Macro-economic Control System

16. The establishment of a socialist market economy urgently requires the transformation of government functions and reform of government organizations. Government functions in economic management consist mainly of devising and implementing

macro-economic control policies, appropriate construction of infrastructure facilities and creation of a favorable environment for economic development. At the same time as we cultivate the market system, supervise the operation of markets and safeguard competition on equal terms, we should regulate social distribution and organize social security, curb population growth and protect natural resources and the ecological environment; also we should control state assets and supervise their operation so as to achieve national goals of economic and social development. The government manages the national economy by economic, legal and necessary administrative means, but it does not directly interfere in the production and management of enterprises.

At present, over-staffing, overlapping of functions and inefficient organization, prevalent at all levels of government, are seriously retarding the process of transforming the operational mechanism of enterprises and the establishment of a new structure. In line with the principles of separating the functions of the government from those of enterprises, simplifying structures and promoting unity and efficiency, we should continue to reform government organizations and seek to complete this task at the earliest possible date. The economic management departments of the government should transform their functions; specialized economic departments should gradually reduce their size; and comprehensive economic departments should properly perform their work of overall coordination. At the same time, the government's social management functions should be strengthened to ensure the normal operation of the national economy and good order in society.

17. The socialist market economy must have a sound macro-economic control system. The main tasks of macro-economic control are: to maintain a basic balance between total supply and total demand in the economy, promote the optimization of the economic structure, guide the national economy in sustained, rapid and healthy development and bring about all-round social progress. In macro-economic control, we should primarily use economic measures; we should, in the near future, take significant steps in the reform of the systems of taxation, financing, investment and planning, and establish a mechanism in which planning, banking and public finance are coordinated and mutually check each other while strengthening the overall coordination of economic operations. The plan sets forth the objectives and tasks for national economic and social development and the necessary coordinated economic policies; the central bank whose primary objective is to stabilize currency value, regulates the aggregate money supply and maintains balance of international payments; the fiscal departments regulate the economic structure and social distribution primarily by budgeting and taxation. Monetary and fiscal policies should be used to adjust and achieve a basic balance between overall demand and overall supply, which, in coordination with industrial policies, in turn promotes the coordinated development of the national economy and society.

18. Actively pressing ahead the reform of the fiscal and taxation systems. Reform in the near future should focus on: First, changing from the current fiscal contractual responsibility system of local authorities to a tax assignment system on the basis of a rational division of power between central and local authorities, and establishing separated central and local taxation systems. The categories of taxes required for safeguarding national rights and interests and the exercise of macro-economic control are assigned as the central tax; the main categories of taxes directly related to economic development are assigned as the sharing taxes; the range of items subject to local tax should be broadened to increase local revenue. Through developing the economy, improving efficiency and opening up more sources of revenue, we should gradually increase the percentage of fiscal income in the gross national product (GNP) and rationally determine the proportion between central and local fiscal income. We should implement a system

wherein the central fiscal authority returns and transfers payments to local authorities in order to adjust the distribution pattern and regional structure, and in particular to support the development of economically underdeveloped regions and the transformation of the old industrial bases. Second, it is necessary to reform and improve the taxation system in line with the principles of unifying tax laws, fairness of tax burden, simplification of the tax system and rational division of power. We should implement an indirect tax system based mainly on the value-added tax, levy consumption taxes on a small number of goods and continue to levy the turnover tax on most non-product businesses. On the basis of reducing the rate of the income tax imposed on state-owned enterprises, and of discontinuing construction funds for key energy and communications projects and budgetary regulatory funds, enterprises should pay taxes according to law, and the ratio of profit distribution between the state and state-owned enterprises can be straightened out. We should introduce uniformity in enterprise income tax and personal income tax, standardize tax rates and expand the tax base. We should levy and readjust taxes of certain categories, check up on tax reductions and exemptions, strictly enforce the levying and management of taxes and block the loss of tax income. Third, we should improve and standardize the double budget system. We can set up a government public budget and a budget for management of state assets and, when necessary, establish a social security budget and other budgets. We should strictly control fiscal deficits. The fiscal deficits of the central authorities should be met by issuing long- and short-term government bonds rather than by overdrafts from the bank. The government's domestic and external debts should be centrally managed.

19. Accelerating reform of the financial system. As the central bank, the People's Bank of China, under the leadership of the State Council, should implement monetary policies independently; it should control the money supply and stabilize currency value by changing from relying mainly on the control over the scale of credit to using such means as reserve ratio on deposits, the central bank's lending rates and open market operations; it should supervise and control various types of financial institutions and maintain financial order, and no longer handle business with non-financial institutions. Banking business and securities business should be managed along separate lines. A monetary policy committee should be organized for the timely adjustment of monetary and credit policies. To meet the needs of the nationwide circulation of money and the requirements of centralized and unified regulations, the branches of the People's Bank of China are clarified as agencies of its head office, and active efforts should be made to create conditions for setting up trans-regional branches.

We should establish policy-lending banks, and should separate policy-lending banking from commercial banking. We should organize the National Development Bank and the Import and Export Credit Bank, and reorganize the Agricultural Bank of China, all of them handling strictly defined policy-related business.

We should develop commercial banks. Existing specialized banks should gradually change into commercial banks and, when necessary, rural and urban co-operative banks should be set up step by step. The commercial banks should engage in the management of the proportions of assets and liabilities and in management of risks. We should standardize and develop non-banking financial institutions.

In light of the changes in the monetary supply and demand, the central bank should make timely readjustments of the benchmark interest rate and allow the deposit and loan interest rates of commercial banks to float freely within a specified range. We should reform the foreign exchange control system, set up a market-based manageable floating exchange rate system, and set up an integrated and standardized foreign exchange market. Renminbi (People's Currency) should gradually become a convertible currency.

We should set up computer networks for the banking system, expand the use of such payment instruments as commercial bills of exchange and checks, enforce strict settlement discipline, improve settlement efficiency, and actively popularize the use of credit cards so as to reduce the amount of cash in circulation.

20. Deepening reform of the investment system. We should gradually establish risk liabilities for corporate investment and bank credits. Competitive project investment should be decided by the enterprises themselves which also bear any risk that may be involved, granting of needed loans is to be decided by the commercial banks, assuming sole responsibility for profits and losses. A project registration system for the record should be set up in place of the current system of administrative examination and approval. Such financial investment activities should be carried on in the market and guided by the state's industrial policies. Construction of infrastructure projects should be encouraged and investments from various sources should be drawn into this work. Local governments are to be responsible for construction of infrastructure facilities within their areas. The capital of major state construction projects should be furnished by policy-related banks, such as the National Development Bank, by raising funds through financial investment and financial bonds and through a variety of other forms including the holding and buying of shares and the granting of preferential loans allowed by policies. As legal entities, enterprises are to be responsible for the whole process from planning, fund-raising and construction to production, management, and the repayment of loans and interest, and the maintenance and increase of asset values. Funds from various strata of the society should be absorbed for the construction of public welfare projects, and overall financial arrangements should be made by government departments in accordance with the division of power over central and local affairs.

21. Speeding up reform of the planning system and further transforming planning management functions. State plans should be based on the market, on the whole they should be guidance plans. The tasks of planning are: to rationally define strategies for the development of the national economy and society and the objectives of macro-economic control and industrial policies, make good economic forecasts, plan major economic structures, plan the distribution of productive forces, and plan the conservation of national territories and the construction of key projects. Planning work should concentrate on the overall situation, strategies and policies, with emphasis on drafting medium- and long-term plans, and on the comprehensive and coordinated use of macro-economic policies and economic levers. We should establish a new national economic accounting system and improve the macro-economic monitoring and warning systems.

22. The powers of the central and local authorities over economic administration should be rationally delineated and the initiative of both the central and local authorities should be brought into play. Powers of macro-economic control, which include power over the issuance of currency, the determination of benchmark interest rates, regulation of exchange rates and readjustment of the rates of major tax items, must be concentrated in the hands of the central government. This is necessary for maintaining the balance of economic aggregates, optimizing the economic structure and unifying the national market. As China is a big country with a large population, the various provinces, autonomous regions and municipalities directly under the central government should be invested with the necessary powers so that they can, in accordance with state laws and regulations and macro-economic policies, formulate regional regulations, policies and plans, regulate the economic activities in areas under their jurisdictions by local taxation and budgetary measures, and make full use of local resources to promote economic and social development in their respective areas.

V Establishing a Rational System of Income Distribution to Individuals and a Social Security System

23. In the distribution of incomes to individuals, it is necessary to adhere to the system which takes the principle of "to each according to his work" as its mainstay and facilitates the coexistence of multiple distribution methods, and to implement the principle of giving priority to efficiency while taking fairness into account. It is necessary to introduce competitive mechanisms for rewarding individual labor and break away from egalitarianism, so as to implement the principle of more pay for more work and rationally widen the income gap. The policy of encouraging some localities and people to become prosperous first through honest labor and legal operation should be adhered to, and those who have become well-off should be encouraged to lead forward and support those lagging behind, so as to achieve common prosperity step by step.

24. Establishing a wage system suited to the characteristics of enterprises, institutions and administrative organizations and introducing regular wage increase mechanisms. On the premise that the growth rate of the gross payroll of an enterprise is below than that of its economic returns and that the average wage of its workers and staff increases at a rate below that of its labor productivity, any state-owned enterprise may decide on its wage rates and internal distribution methods for itself according to changes in the supply of labor and demand for jobs and according to the government's relevant policies and stipulations. Administrative organizations are to adopt the system of public service, and the salaries of public servants are to be set and readjusted by the state in accordance with national economic development while taking into consideration the average wage standards in the enterprises. Regular promotion and salary rise mechanisms are to be established. Institutions will practice different wage systems and methods of distribution, and those with appropriate conditions may adopt the wage system for enterprises. The government will set the minimum wage scale; and all enterprises and institutions must follow it strictly. Monetization and standardization in rewarding individuals should be actively promoted.

25. The state protects the legitimate incomes and property of all legal entities and residents according to the law, encourages urban and rural residents to deposit their money in banks and make investments, and permits the distribution of earnings by capital and other production factors belonging to individuals. The system of the declaration of individual incomes for tax payment should be gradually established, and the collection and management of the individual income tax strengthened according to law. Taxes on inheritance and gifts will be levied in due course. We should prevent polarization arising from abnormally high incomes of a small minority through the enforcement of distribution policies and regulation of the income taxes. Persons who embezzle public property and seek gain through tax evasion and tax resistance, offering and accepting bribes and other illegal means will be punished according to law.

26. The establishment of a multi-layered social security system is of great importance to the deepening of the reform of enterprises and institutions, maintaining social stability and the smooth establishment of a socialist market economic structure. The social security system covers social insurance, social relief, social welfare, special care to disabled servicemen and family members of revolutionary martyrs and servicemen, jobs for demobilized soldiers, social mutual help, and security based on accumulation of individual accounts. We should unify social security policies and legalize their management. The level of social security should suit the development of China's social productive forces and acceptability to all concerned. Social security practices for urban and rural residents should be different. Mutual help in society should be encouraged. Commercial insurance will be developed as a supplement to social insurance.

27. Defining sources of funds and methods of guarantee suited to the different types of social security. Priority will be given to perfecting old-age pension and unemployment insurance systems in enterprises, strengthening social service functions and reducing the burden of enterprises, promoting readjustment of the organizational structures of enterprises, and enhancing their economic returns and competitive capacity. Expenditures for old-age pensions and health care insurance for workers and staff in cities and towns are to be shared by work units and individuals, and by combining mutual assistance funds with individual accounts. The unemployment insurance system will be further improved, and premiums will be paid by enterprises in a unified way on the basis of a fixed percentage of their gross payrolls. An enterprise industrial injury insurance system will be universally established. The support of the aged in rural areas will be shouldered chiefly by their families and supplemented by community assistance. Where possible, old-age insurance derived from accumulation of individual accounts may be introduced among farmers on a voluntary basis. The rural cooperative health care system will be developed and perfected.

28. Establishing unified social security management organizations. The level of management of social security will be enhanced, and sound circulation mechanisms will be formed for the collection and management of social insurance funds. The administration of social security and the management of social insurance funds should be separated. Social security management organizations will perform chiefly administrative functions. Supervisory organs for social insurance funds will be set up with the participation of relevant government departments and representatives from the public to supervise the revenue, expenditure and management of social insurance funds. On the premise of ensuring the normal payment and safe circulation of the funds, organizations handling social insurance funds may use them to purchase state treasury bonds according to law, in order to maintain and add to the value of the funds.

VI Deepening Rural Economic Structural Reform

29. Agriculture, rural areas and the farmers are fundamental issues concerning China's economic development and modernization drive. The reform in China's rural areas over the past decade and more has brought historic changes to the socio-economic outlook of rural areas, and laid a foundation for the reform and development of the entire national economy. In recent years, the rural areas have been facing new problems which call for immediate solution, the chief ones being the decline of the comparative returns of agriculture, particularly grain and cotton production, the widening of the scissors gap between the prices of industrial and agricultural products, and the slow growth of the incomes of farmers. We should stabilize the Party's basic policies in the rural areas, deepen rural reform, expedite rural economic growth, increase the incomes of farmers, and further strengthen the role of agriculture as the foundation of the national economy, so as to ensure that agricultural production will reach a new height by the end of this century and the living standards of the masses of farmers shall be raised from the current level of sufficient food and clothing to a better-off level of moderate prosperity.

30. The development of China's rural economy is entering a new stage mainly characterized by structural readjustment and improved efficiency. Agricultural production should be adapted to changes in the consumption of farm produce on the market, and the product-mix should be optimized to enable agriculture to develop towards a pattern of high yields, high quality and high efficiency. On the premise of maintaining the stable increase of grain, cotton and other basic farm produce, we will readjust the industrial structure of the rural areas, and expedite the development of township en-

terprises and other non-agriculture sectors, so as to provide more job opportunities for surplus rural labor. To accomplish the readjustment of the structure of farm products and rural industry, we will enliven rural markets, remove the barriers between different regions, reduce the separation of city and countryside, further invigorate circulation, broaden the development of rural economy, and promote the deployment and circulation of all economic resources. This is the basic way to speed up the development of the rural economy and increase the incomes of farmers.

31. The double-layered management system in the countryside, in which the main form is the contracted responsibility system based on the household with remuneration linked to output, together with the combination of unified management and independent management, is the basic economic system in the rural areas; it should be stabilized for a long time to come and constantly improved. On the premise of adhering to the collective land ownership, the term for contracting cultivated land may be extended, and we allow the inheritance of contracts for the management of explorative undertakings and the compensated transfer of the land-use rights according to law. Operations adapted to scaled economy may be developed in a few economically developed areas through varied forms such as the transfer of contracts and the purchase of shares on a voluntary basis, in order to raise the productivity of agricultural labor and of the land. Rural collective economic organizations must actively set up economic entities to provide services to household operations, gradually accumulate collective assets and enhance the economic strength of the collectives.

32. Developing the rural social service system, and promoting the specialization, commercialization and socialization of agricultural production. We will develop diversified service organizations in line with the practical needs of the farmers, and form a service network composed of rural collective economic organizations, state economic and technological departments, and associations of the farmers themselves, such as specialized and technical societies. The supply and marketing cooperatives at all levels must continue to deepen reforms, strive to transform themselves into genuine cooperative economic organizations of the farmers, and actively explore new ways to develop themselves into comprehensive service organizations. We will gradually de-control the management of farm produce to the fullest extent, and change the current situation characterized by departmental segmentation and the divorce of production from marketing. Efforts will be pooled to develop all forms of integrated management of trade, industry and agriculture, and to closely combine production and processing with marketing. The reform and development of education in rural areas will be expedited. We will actively promote the combination of agriculture, science and education, strengthen research in agro-science and technology, strive to popularize advanced and applicable technologies, and use modern science and technology to transform traditional agriculture. Active efforts should be made to gear agricultural production to the international market, and energetically develop products with high added value and promote export-oriented and foreign-exchange-earning agriculture.

33. Township enterprises are an important pillar of the rural economy. We will perfect the contracted responsibility system, develop the cooperative share-holding system, make innovations in their property rights system and methods of management, and further invigorate township enterprises. On the basis of clearly defined property rights, it is necessary to promote trans-community mobility and the combination of production factors, so as to form a more rational layout of enterprises. We should strengthen planning and guide township enterprises to concentrate appropriately, make full use of the existing small cities and townships and transform them, build up new ones, gradually reform the residence registration system there, allow farmers to work in factories or do business in small cities and towns, develop rural tertiary industries and promote the transfer of rural surplus labor force to other fields of endeavor.

34. Strengthening government support to agricultural production and protecting the interests of farmers. Governments at all levels must gradually increase their investment in agriculture, actively encourage farmers and collectives to increase their input of labor and capital, constantly improve the conditions for farm production, and strengthen the material and technological foundation of agriculture. We should take care to establish and perfect of a system of reserves to regulate prices and of market risk funds for grain and other basic farm produce, introduce a price-protection purchasing system to prevent major fluctuation of market prices. The development of agriculture-oriented industries should be supported. The government will set standards for, and regulate by law, all contributions of funds and labor required of farmers, in order to genuinely protect their economic interests.

35. Assisting the economic development of poor areas, particularly former revolutionary base areas, areas inhabited by minority nationalities, and remote and border areas. The central and local authorities should be concerned for and support the socio-economic development in these areas, further strengthen the work of aiding the poor through developing production, give priority to agricultural capital construction, and improve transport facilities and postal and telecommunications services there. The exchange of cadres between developed and undeveloped areas and economic and technological cooperation between them will be expanded. The masses will be encouraged to enhance their sense of a market economy, make full use of the advantages offered by local resources, and gradually develop ways and means to overcome poverty and achieve prosperity by relying on their own efforts.

VII Deepening the Reform of the System of Foreign Economic Relations, Opening Wider to the Outside World

36. Firmly carrying out the policy of opening to the outside world, expediting the opening-up effort, making full use of the international and domestic markets and resources both at home and abroad, and optimizing the allocation of resources. We should actively participate in international competition and economic cooperation, give play to the comparative advantages of our economy, develop an open economy, and allow the domestic economy to dovetail with and supplement the international economy. We should standardize our foreign economic activities in line with our national conditions and the norms of international economic life, correctly handle our foreign economic relations, and constantly increase our competitiveness in international markets.

37. Practicing multi-directional opening. We will continue to promote the opening of special economic zones, coastal open cities and areas, cities along the country's borders, cities along the Yangtze River, and inland central cities, and give full play to the radiating and promoting role of the open areas; expedite the development and opening of areas along major transport trunk lines; encourage areas in central and western China to absorb foreign capital to develop and use their natural resources, so as to invigorate their economy; work out comprehensive plans to run economic and technological development zones and bonded zones all to form a pattern of multi-directional opening with each layer having its own characteristics. We will widen the scope of opening to the outside world, expand the mobility and exchange of production factors, expedite the opening to abroad of other sectors on the basis of stressing international industrial and trading contacts, and develop the service trade. The work of the customs, commodity inspection and transportation at the various ports and points of entry will be improved. Management of Chinese-funded enterprises abroad will be strengthened. We will seriously sum up experiences, constantly increase our openness, and give guidance to its development to a higher level and in breadth and depth.

38. Further reforming the foreign economic and trade system, and establishing operational mechanisms suited to the rules and customs common in international economic activities. We should adhere to such principles of reform as unified policy, liberalized operation, equal competition, responsibility for one's own profits and losses, the integration of industry and trade, and the promotion of the agent system. Efforts will be made to expedite the change of the operational procedures of all enterprise in their foreign trade activities, reorganize state-owned foreign trade enterprises in the light of the modern enterprise system, grant to qualified manufacturing and scientific and technological enterprises the right to handle foreign trade, and develop a number of internationalized, industrialized and comprehensive trading companies. The state will regulate foreign economic activities mainly by such economic means as the exchange rate, taxation and credit. In the reform of the import and export management system, mandatory plans will be abandoned and administrative intervention reduced. In handling the few commodities whose import and export are subject to the quota system, the bidding, auction and formula allocation of quotas will be run in accordance with the principle of ensuring economic returns, fairness and openness. The import and export chambers of commerce should perform to the full their functions of coordinative guidance and consulting service. A market diversification strategy, with product quality as a top concern, will be actively promoted. Border trade will be better handled. The system of reimbursement of indirect tax to the exporters will be perfected. With regard to tariffs, we will lower their general level, rationally readjust their structure, tighten up their collection and administration and crack down on smuggling. The reform of the system of foreign economic and technological cooperation will be deepened, and efforts will be made to enhance comprehensive management and increase overall returns. We should unify and perfect legislation concerning foreign economic relations and safeguard the interests of the state.

39. Actively introducing capital, technology, professional personnel and management expertise from the outside. We will improve our investment environment and methods of management, expand the introducing scale, widen the area of investment and further open the domestic market. Conditions will be created to grant foreign-funded enterprises national treatment, and management over foreign-funded enterprises will be improved according to law. Foreign investment will be channelled into such key areas as infrastructure facilities, basic industries, new and high-tech industries and the technological transformation of old enterprises. The establishment of export-oriented enterprises will be encouraged. We should give play to the comparative advantages of China's resources and markets to attract foreign funds and technology so as to promote China's economic development.

VIII Further Revamping Scientific, Technological and Educational Systems

40. Science and technology constitute a prime productive force. Economic development cannot do without science and technology, and scientific and technological work must be geared to economic construction. The reform of scientific and technological work is designed to establish a new system which fits the development of the socialist market economy, complies with the laws governing scientific and technological development and integrates science and technology closely with the economic development—all for the purpose of promoting progress in science and technology, scaling new scientific and technological heights and effecting comprehensive and well-coordinated economic, scientific and technical and social development. It is imperative for

the central authorities and various localities and enterprises to increase their input into science and technology in order to formulate, step by step, a well-structured, rationally distributed and highly efficient system of research and development, promote the development of exploratory research, new and high technology and their related industries, and basic research, and more quickly transform new scientific findings and technological achievements into actual productive forces. It is necessary to abolish the old practice in which departments are segmented, restructure the system for scientific and technological work and rationally distribute human resources. In this regard the policy is to "hold fast to one end and leave the whole field open," that is to say, while redoubling research efforts in basic science and for the development of new and high technology, we should give free rein to research, development and business activities of organizations engaged in developing technology or providing scientific and technical services. Great efforts should be made to develop scientific and technological enterprises under varied types of ownership and management. Institutes engaged in the application of science and in exploratory research, and organizations which provide consulting and information services, should adapt themselves to the needs of the market, gradually introduce entrepreneurial management, and build up their self-development ability and competitiveness on the market.

41. Actively promoting the integration of science and technology with the economy. First, it is necessary to coordinate the deployment of scientific research resources for the purpose of solving knotty technological problems which have an important bearing on the national economy. Second, in order to do good work in importing advanced technology and in technical upgrading, it is necessary to establish a new framework under which the developmental efforts of research institutes are dovetailed to the introduction of imported technology. High-tech industrial development zones should be well run so as to promote the commercialization and industrialization of their research results. Third, scientific research institutes, institutions of higher learning and enterprises should be encouraged to cooperate in developing new technologies; research institutes engaged in technical development should be encouraged to work together with large enterprises and enterprise groups in establishing research organizations for the task of developing new products and new technologies to speed progress in upgrading traditional industries by arming them with new and high technology; and it is also necessary to establish a mechanism for technical progress within each enterprise to handle the task of developing new technology by integrating scientific research with production and the market and turn the enterprises into the mainstay of China's technological development. Fourth, intermediary organizations and intermediate and industrial experiments should be developed so as to promote technological transfers; it is also necessary to form regional and professional organizations for technical renovation and a network for the diffusion of technology. Fifth, it is imperative for national defence and military research institutes to further carry out the principle of integrating military and civilian industries, deepen their reform and transform their managerial mechanism, and, on the premise of strengthening national defence, step up research and development in technology that can be used for both military and civil purposes, and energetically promote the transfer of military technology to civilian use.

42. In the final analysis, the establishment of the socialist market economic structure and the realization of modernization hinge on raising the quality of the entire population and on the training of competent professionals. Party committees and governments at various levels should make it a strategic task to give priority to education and tighten up their leadership over educational work. Concrete steps should be taken to implement the Outline Program for the Reform and Development of Education in

China and accelerate the restructuring of the educational system. Investment in education should be ensured, and both teaching quality and educational efficacy increased. The situation in which the government runs all schools should be changed to give rise to a new system in which the government plays the central role in running schools, and all walks of life pool their efforts to expand education. Compulsory education should be strengthened, vocational and adult education vigorously developed, and the structure of education optimized. In running schools for compulsory education, the government should contribute the lion's share of the investment but encouragement should simultaneously be given to the running of nongovernmental schools as well as to other forms of schools run with funds raised through various channels from different walks of social life. Vocational and adult education and other forms of social education should better meet market needs, and various fields of endeavor should play a role in this regard. In higher education, it is necessary to change the way institutions of higher learning are run and remove the barriers between regions and government departments; with the exception of certain special academic disciplines and by dealing with each college or university on its own merits, higher education should be gradually placed under a two-level administrative system, central and local, under which the decision-making powers of localities in running schools and of colleges and universities in running their own affairs are expanded. Institutions of higher learning should step up their reform in enrollment, curricula, teaching materials and methods, employment system for graduates, etc. All schools should work to strengthen their teaching staff, upgrade their professional proficiency and improve education in socialist morality.

43. Respecting knowledge, respecting talents and creating the necessary environment and conditions for talents to emerge and play their full role. It is imperative to train, through various forms and channels, a large contingent of skilled workers and professionals in various fields and to nurture a team of academic and technical leaders who will be in the van of scientific and technological development in the coming century. Training should be combined with the rational use of the intellectual resources, and for this purpose both the labor and personnel systems and the procedures for screening and selecting leaders should be overhauled. Each trade or profession should work out its own qualification and employment standards and introduce its own licensing system based on academic diplomas and job qualification certificates, and steps should be taken to encourage fair competition and promote the rational flow of talent by putting up jobs for public application. Talented people studying or residing in foreign countries should be encouraged in various ways to return and serve their motherland; in this regard the state policy is to "support students studying overseas, encourage them to return and let them decide for themselves whether to come or go."

IX Tightening Up the Legal System

44. The establishment and improvement of the socialist market economic structure should be codified and guaranteed by an all-inclusive legal system. We must pay due attention to tightening up the legal system, bringing the effort of reform and opening up to the outside world within the framework of the legal system, and learning how to manage the economy by legal means. In building up a well-developed legal system, the goals are: first, following the principles prescribed in the Constitution to speed up economic legislation, further improve civil, commercial and criminal laws and the legislation associated with state organizations and administrative affairs, and initially establish a legal system adapted to the socialist market economy by the turn of the

century; second, reforming and improving the judicial and administrative law-enforcement mechanism and heightening proficiency in judicial and administrative law-enforcement work; and third, establishing a sound law-enforcement supervisory mechanism, improving legal service organizations, deepening education in the legal system, and enhancing the sense of law and awareness of the legal system throughout society.

45. Persisting in the unification of the socialist legal system. The decision-making process in reform should be closely integrated with that in legislation. Legislation should embody the spirit of reform, and the law should be applied to guide, promote and ensure the smooth progress of reform. It is necessary to map out a well-conceived legislative plan, and enact, without delay, laws designed to standardize norms for the market, keep the market in order, tighten macro-economic control, improve social security and speed up opening up to the outside world. Laws and regulations which prove inappropriate to the establishment of the socialist market economic structure should be promptly amended or abolished. It is imperative to strengthen Party leadership over legislative work, perfect the law-making system, improve the legislative procedures, quicken the law-making process and provide legal norms of conduct for the socialist market economy.

Judicial and administrative law enforcement should be strengthened and improved, and so should supervision over the way law is enforced, in order to maintain social stability, guarantee economic growth and safeguard the legitimate rights and interests of the citizens. Criminal and economic offenders should be brought to justice according to law, and economic and civil disputes dealt with promptly. Governments at various levels should abide by law in administrative and other matters. In economic and other activities, it is essential to resolutely correct violations of law such as failure to abide by the law, lax law enforcement, letting law-breakers go free, the abuse of power and position, and seeking the interests for a department or locality by illegal means. Redoubled effort is called for to build up the law-enforcement departments and raise the quality and law-enforcing ability of their personnel. A system should be devised for bringing to account law-enforcement officers who have broken the law, and to grant compensation to victims of such abuses.

46. We should act promptly and unfailingly to build clean government and combat corruption, for this is not only an essential condition and important guarantee for the establishment of the socialist market economic structure but also has great bearing on the destiny of the ongoing reform and on the destiny of the Party and the country. The fight against corruption is a long-term and arduous task and should be carried out with unremitting effort. It is necessary to tighten up the legal provisions for the building of a corruption-free government and improve the mechanism under which Party and state organizations, their staff in general, and leading officials in particular, have criteria by which to discipline themselves, and by which supervision against corruption can be carried out. Law enforcement, judicial, economic management and other departments must establish workable supervisory mechanisms to prevent their personnel from abusing power for personal gain, and to stamp out fraudulent practices among various departments, professions and trades. On no account should we allow the principle governing commodity exchange to penetrate inner-Party political life and the administrative activities of the state organs. On no account should we allow power to be traded for money. Serious measures should be taken under the law against major offenses, including crimes perpetrated by legal entities, and those found guilty of corruption should be sternly punished. The work of Party discipline inspection organs and the judicial, supervisory and auditing departments should be strengthened, and

the supervisory role of the law, the relevant organizations, the public and public opinion should be given full play.

X Strengthening and Improving Party Leadership and Striving to Initiate a Socialist Market Economic Structure by the End of the 20th Century

47. To build up the socialist market economic structure and speed up the modernization drive, we should strengthen and improve leadership by the Party. We should also build up the Party's own strength in order to fulfill the great historical task for the new period. In Party building the present emphasis should be on work in the following fields: First, we should persist in arming the entire Party with Comrade Deng Xiaoping's theory on building socialism with Chinese characteristics. We should, in studying Marxism-Leninism and Mao Zedong Thought, stress the theory on building socialism the Chinese way, carry out more firmly and consciously the Party's basic line and the series of principles and policies designed to develop the socialist market economy, and be at one ideologically and politically with the Party. Second, we should adhere to the cardinal principle of serving the people wholeheartedly, carrying forward the Party's fine traditions and style of work and fostering even closer ties between the Party and the masses. Third, we should be strict in carrying out the Party's system of democratic centralism, foster a healthy atmosphere for inner-Party political life, safeguard the Party's unity, tighten Party discipline and enhance our awareness of the overall interest, so that the entire Party membership will act in unison and all the laws and regulations will be effectively carried out. Fourth, we should redouble efforts to strengthen the leading bodies at all levels, go deep into reality to see how things really are, unhesitatingly overcome bureaucratism and formalism, conscientiously learn the basics of the socialist market economy and modern scientific and technological knowledge, and strive to increase our leadership ability in the modernization drive. Fifth, we should work in a down-to-earth way to build up the Party's grass-roots organizations, work hard to deliver some Party organizations from their state of incompetence and slackened morale, and give full play to the role of the grass-roots Party organizations as combat bastions and to the exemplary vanguard role of the vast numbers of Party members.

48. To keep pace with the growth of the socialist market economic structure and economic development, active work should be done to promote the reform of the political structure and strengthen the political construction of socialist democracy. It is necessary to uphold and improve the People's Congress system, multi-party cooperation and the system of political consultation under the leadership of the Communist Party. It is also important to give full scope to the role of trade unions, the Communist Youth League, women's federations and other mass organizations as bridges and channels in maintaining the Party's close relations with the masses. The construction of a sound decision-making system on a democratic and scientific footing should be speeded up and the decision-making ability improved. The Party's policy concerning the nationalities should be implemented in an all-round way, and the system of regional autonomy in areas inhabited by ethnic minority peoples in compact communities should be improved so as to promote the economic and cultural development in these areas, consolidate and develop socialist inter-ethnic relations of equality, mutual assistance, unity and cooperation, and steer a course toward common prosperity, unity and progress among all nationalities. It is necessary to conscientiously carry out the Party's policies concerning religion and concerning the overseas Chinese to rally them

around the cause of socialist modernization. Democracy at the grass-roots level should be strengthened and the various supervisory systems should be improved to solidly guarantee the citizens' democratic rights in running state, economic and social affairs according to law.

49. We should stick to the principle that both material progress and cultural and ideological progress should be promoted in real earnest and neither aspect should be neglected. We should also work well in promoting socialist culture and ethics for the purpose of cultivating a new generation of well-educated, well-disciplined people imbued with lofty ideals and socialist moral values. Party committees and governments at all levels should give priority to ideological and political work and strengthen their leadership in the fields of publicity, ideology and culture. We should spare no effort in our research in Comrade Deng Xiaoping's theory on building socialism with Chinese characteristics and in philosophy and other branches of social sciences under the guidance of Marxism. It is necessary to carry on education in patriotism, collectivism and socialism in a broad and deep-going way and in vivid forms, and to conduct education in Chinese history, particularly in modern and contemporary history and in the fine traditions of the Chinese nation "so as to heighten the Chinese people's self-respect, self-confidence and sense of pride, carry forward their hard-working spirit and concentrate the tremendous creativity of hundreds of millions on the great cause of building socialism with Chinese characteristics." In the condition of a socialist market economy, we should actively propagate the necessity of persisting in the correct outlook on life and a civilized, healthy lifestyle, work to promote public and professional ethics, and combat money worship, extreme individualism and decadent lifestyles. We should persevere in cracking down on pornography and other social evils, and comprehensively consolidate public security and order. We should adhere to the principles of serving the people and socialism and of "letting a hundred flowers bloom and a hundred schools of thought contend," and encourage the creation of progressive, and uplifting literary and art works that both entertain and enlighten the people, so as to enrich the people's spiritual life. It is necessary to deepen the reform of the cultural structure, improve economic policies linked with the cultural field, and tighten up the management of the cultural market according to law. It is necessary to properly handle the relationship between the social effect and economic results of cultural products by making their social effect the paramount standard. Where necessary, the state will provide financial support for selected fine works of literature and art that call for such assistance.

50. The reform of the economic structure entails a profound revolution in the economic base and many aspects of the superstructure. It is bound to change the various irrational relationships of interest that either were inherent in the old structure or have resulted from the process of transition from the old to the new. Difficulties and obstructions of one kind or another are unavoidable. Therefore, we should, with the overall situation in mind, properly handle the relationship between reform, development and stability and the relationships of interest between various quarters, mobilize all positive factors, and create favorable conditions for the healthy development of the national economy. Fundamentally speaking, some of the contradictions and problems that have arisen in the high-speed growth of the Chinese economy stem from the fact that the drawbacks of the old structure have not been thoroughly eradicated and the new structure has yet to take shape. For this reason, Party committees and governments at all levels should redouble their efforts to speed up the reform. We should push forward in real earnest with the reform in key fields, work out detailed plans, be bold in exploration and practice, sum up our experience conscientiously, and never stop breaking new ground in our march forward.

The Third Plenary Session of the 14th Party Central Committee calls on the entire Party membership and the people of all nationalities throughout the country to rally more closely around the Party Central Committee with Comrade Jiang Zemin as its nucleus. Under the guidance of Comrade Deng Xiaoping's theory on building socialism with Chinese characteristics and following the course charted by the 14th Party Congress, let us unite as one and dedicate ourselves heart and soul to the cause of reform, and, by relying on our own efforts and working diligently, strive to initially build up the structure of socialist market economy and realize the strategic goals for the second phase of the nation's socio-economic development by the end of this century!

Notes

PREFACE

1. "Blue" because of the color of the clothing most Chinese of the time wore.

CHAPTER 1

1. According to Wood (1991), chap. 1, for example, attitudes and mores of American society in the early seventeenth century paralleled to a remarkable extent those of Chinese society of the same period.

2. Quoted from the "Debate on Salt and Iron," as excerpted in Ebrey (1981), pp. 24–25.

3. Siu (1990).

4. Translation from Cranmer-Byng (1962), pp. 338–40. The most complete examination of the Macartney mission is in Peyrefitte (1992).

5. Hymes (1966) tries to determine the actual mobility into the elite through careful study of Fu-chou in the Sung dynasty. He demonstrates that there was somewhat less upward mobility than is commonly asserted.

6. Watson (1988).

7. Link (1992).

8. The only female ruler in Chinese history was the Empress Wu Cetian (r. 690–705).

9. Fairbank (1953); Fairbank (1968).

10. Peyrefitte (1992) conveys the practical consequences of this in vivid detail.

11. Waldron (1989).

12. An extraordinary sense of the life and times of Qin Shi Huangdi is provided in a novel: Levi (1985). Western punishments of that era were equally cruel.

13. See, for example, Balazs (1964).

14. See, for example, Wright (1964). Bartlett (1991) uses a different definition of "inner" and "outer" court.

15. Two books highlight different views on this issue during the Qing dynasty. Bartlett (1991) argues that the administrative system carved out substantial independence from the emperor's control; Kuhn (1990) argues in favor of more unbounded imperial power.

16. Morse (1966) presents both the formal system and its warts.

17. This practice, called the *xiangyue* system, is described in Hsiao (1960).

18. On government administration, see Ch'u (1969).

19. Naquin and Rawski (1987).

20. Naquin and Rawski (1987).

21. On the gentry, see Ch'u (1969), chap. 10, and Ho (1962).

22. Ho (1962).

23. Wolf contribution to Wolf and Witke (1975).

24. Fried (1953).

25. See, for example, Melby (1968), the Chinese civil war memoir of an American diplomat.

26. Nathan (1985).

27. Rowe (1984); Rowe (1989).

28. See, e.g., the travel accounts as late as the 1920s of Franck (1923).

29. Detailed in Naquin and Rawski (1987).

30. Elvin (1973).

31. The two key studies in this debate are Kang (1986) and Perkins (1969).

32. These questions are reviewed and evaluated in Little (1989).

33. Skinner (1964–65); Skinner (1977).

34. Actually, eight fully formed regions and one, the northeast, that was only partially in evidence. By the period of the PRC, the ninth region is also fully formed.

35. For the scholar, the major difficulty is that the historical data available are presented in terms of administrative boundaries, and for most issues it is extremely difficult to reconstitute all information according to the boundaries of regional systems.

36. Naquin and Rawski (1987).

37. Skinner has developed his argument in a series of publications. The one most pertinent to this point is Skinner (1977), pp. 275–352.

38. Shue (1988); Balazs (1964).

39. Balazs (1964).

40. Wittfogel (1957).

41. Tong (1991).

42. Naquin and Rawski (1987), p. 25.

43. Hummel (1967).

44. For a fascinating self-portrait of this great figure, see Spence (1974).

45. Perry (1980).

46. Michael (1966–71); Chu (1966); Jen (1973).

47. More broadly on this, see Kuhn (1970).

48. Wright (1966).

49. Kennedy (1987); Barraclough (1967).

50. These products included opium, imported primarily by the British, who grew it in Bengal, India, and shipped it to China to earn money to pay for tea, silks, and other items destined for the British market. By 1820 annual opium shipments to China totaled about 10,000 chests (one chest contained 133 pounds of opium). The figure grew to 40,000 chests by 1838 and 50,000–60,000 by 1860.

51. This cycle is detailed in Teng and Fairbank (1963).

52. Classic studies of this dynamic include Fairbank (1953) and Teng and Fairbank (1963).

53. Smith (1978).

54. Teng and Fairbank (1963).

55. A magisterial treatment that carries the story forward well into the twentieth century is given by Wang (1966).

56. Fairbank (1953); Murphey (1970).

57. Fairbank, Reischauer, and Craig (1973); Beckmann (1962).

58. Oksenberg and Goldstein (1974); Lieberthal chapter in Harding (1984).

59. Lieberthal (1977).

60. See the discussions of this in Wright (1966), Eastman (1974), and Dirlik (1975).

61. Cf. Kuo essay in Fairbank and Liu (1978).

62. Hao essay in Twitchett and Fairbank (1978).

63. Tan (1955).

64. For a wide-ranging, excellent series of essays on this reform decade, see Wright (1968).

65. Young (1977).

CHAPTER 2

1. Young (1977).

2. Gillin (1967).

3. Wang (1966).

4. Young (1977).

5. Wang (1966).

6. Spence (1981); Witke chapter in Young (1973).

7. Chow (1960) presents a magisterial treatment of this movement.

8. North (1952).

9. Chu (1992); Tine (1989).

10. Schiffrin (1970).

11. Schwartz (1964).

12. Harrison (1972).

13. Eastman (1974).

14. A vivid dramatization is provided by Malraux (1934). Differing analytical frameworks are provided in Isaacs (1938) and Schwartz (1964).

15. For differing interpretations of this period, see Wilbur (1984) and Isaacs (1938).

16. Young (1977). On the anticommunist terror and the CCP's counterefforts, see Byron and Pack (1992).

17. Bergere in Howe (1981); Lieberthal (1980).

18. Eastman (1974).

19. Some held on in the cities until 1932–33, and a very few remained after that. Byron and Pack (1992) provide a vivid description of the increasingly difficult threat those in Shanghai faced.

20. Pu Yi (1979).

21. One of the most important resulting developments was the student-led December Ninth movement in 1936: Klein (1976).

22. Byron and Pack (1992) attribute the CCP's stance to pressures from Moscow, where Stalin was worried about Japanese advances on the Asian mainland.

23. Chi (1982).

24. Tuchman (1970).

25. Vivid portrayals are provided in the accounts of two eye witnesses: Fairbank. (1982); and T. H. White (1978).

26. Details are provided in Whitson (1973).

27. Lieberthal (1980).

28. On the politics of this period, see Pepper (1978). See also Tien (1972) and Bianco (1971).

29. There are numerous histories of the Chinese communist movement before 1949. Two of the more complete are Harrison (1972) and Guillermaz (1972).

30. Bennett (1976).

31. Skocpol (1979) emphasizes this central idea.

32. On Peng Pai, another key figure, see Hofheinz (1977).

33. See, for example, Schram (1963) and Schram (1966).

34. Mao, (1965a), pp. 24, 28 (quotation changes sequence of sentences in the original).

35. Schwartz (1964) and Isaacs (1938) give differing assessments, with Isaacs feeling that the CCP would have been wise to break with the GMD and form its own organs of power before April 1927.

36. Urban uprisings, encouraged by Moscow, continued into 1930. All of them failed.

37. Erbaugh (1992) analyzes the role of the Hakka minority in the Chinese communist movement.

38. Byron and Pack (1992).

39. Kim chapter in Barnett (1969).

40. A detailed explanation of the communists' 1950 land-reform law that embodies these distinctions is provided in *Renmin shouce* (1951), pp. *ch'en* 32–43.

41. Belden (1949) provides first-hand accounts of these types of efforts in the 1940s.

42. Details are provided in Van Slyke (1967).

43. Mao (1965b), pp. 79–194.

44. Erbaugh (1992).

45. Salisbury (1985) provides a detailed and vivid account of the rigors of the Long March.

46. Barnett (1967) discusses the special stature of the Long March cadres.

47. Snow (1961), pp. 215–16. See also Salisbury (1985), among many sources on the Long March.

48. Braun's Chinese name was Li De.

49. Byron and Pack (1992) provide information on Wang's stay in Moscow and his initial efforts once he returned to China.

50. Both sides of this equation are presented in Peck (1967).

51. Van Slyke (1967).

52. The final straw was a GMD attack on Communist New Fourth Army forces that had penetrated south of the Yangtze River: Harrison (1972).

53. Belden (1949); Selden (1971); Van Slyke (1968).

54. Lifton (1961).

55. Belden (1949) describes life in several of these base areas.

56. Selden (1971).

57. Byron and Pack (1992) and Vladimirov (1975) provide good details.

58. Levine (1987) details developments in this region from 1945 to 1948.

59. Pepper (1978).

60. Lieberthal (1980).

61. Lieberthal (1971).

62. E.g., Guillermaz (1972).

63. Pepper (1978) provides detailed information on the "third force" possibilities.

64. See, e.g., Solinger (1977).

65. The author has heard this statement made by various high-ranking PRC officials.

66. A. Goldstein (1991); Teiwes (1990).

67. Teiwes (1990).

CHAPTER 3

1. Anarchism, though, had been an early influence on the communist movement: Dirlik (1991).

2. See, e.g., MacFarquhar, Cheek, and Wu (1989).

3. Li (1994).

4. Bernstein (1984).

5. Lieberthal (1971).

6. Lardy and Lieberthal (1983).

7. Bennett (1976) provides a systematic overview of this phenomenon.

8. Schram (1966).

9. Siu (1990).

10. *Mao Zedong sixiang wan sui!* (1969), p. 195.

11. Van Slyke (1967).

12. Van Slyke (1968).

13. Pepper (1978).

14. Coble (1980).

15. For this reason, sources for the information provided in this brief description generally are given in Chapters 6 and 7, rather than here.

16. Wu (1992).

CHAPTER 4

1. A. Goldstein (1991).

2. Teiwes (1990) makes this case in detail with respect to the first major purge of top officials after 1949: the 1953–54 Gao Gang/Rao Shushi affair.

3. Central work conferences are detailed in Chang (1970) and Lieberthal and Dickson (1989).

4. Mao (1977).

5. Text of this speech is in Mao (1965c), pp. 361–75.

6. Riskin (1987).

7. On Sino-Soviet relations see Barnett (1977), Clubb (1971), and Dittmer (1992); on Mao's trip see Goncharov, Lewis, and Xue (1993).

8. Cohen (1990).

9. On the Korean War and Sino-US relations, see *inter alia:* Cohen (1990), Gaddis (1978), Grasso (1987), Hoyt (1990), Hunt (1987), Hunt (1992), Kalicki (1975), Stueck (1981), Zhang (1992), and Goncharov, Lewis, and Xue (1993).

10. Whiting (1960); Goncharov, Lewis, and Xue (1993).

11. Barnett (1964); Lieberthal (1980).

12. Teiwes chapter in MacFarquhar and Fairbank (1987), reprinted in MacFarquhar (1993).

13. Friedman, Pickowicz, and Selden (1991).

14. Friedman, Pickowicz, and Selden (1991); Schurmann (1971).

15. Lieberthal (1980).

16. Lieberthal (1980); Montell (1954); Barnett (1964); Teiwes in MacFarquhar (1993); Teiwes (1979).

17. Lieberthal (1980).

18. Wu (1993); on thought reform during these early post-1949 years more generally, see Lifton (1961).

19. Borisov and Koloskov (1975); Naughton chapter in Lieberthal and Lampton (1992); Perkins (1966). The Naughton essay explains the enormous importance of the technology transfers involved in this Soviet aid program. On the economic planning system in China, see Lyons (1987).

20. Shue (1980).

21. Yeh chapter in Treadgold (1967).

22. Teiwes chapter in MacFarquhar and Fairbank (1987), reprinted in MacFarquhar (1993); Schurmann (1971).

23. Li (1994); Salisbury (1992).

24. Teiwes chapter in MacFarquhar (1993).

25. For details of this process in the southwest, see Solinger (1977).

26. The definitive study to date is Teiwes (1990).

27. On field armies and their relations to civilian politics, see Whitson with Huang (1973), Whitson (1973), and Swaine (1992).

28. Oksenberg (1974).

29. The most complete analysis of this tension is Lee (1991).

30. On the reasons for launching the Great Leap, see Lieberthal chapter in MacFarquhar and Fairbank (1987), reprinted in MacFarquhar (1993); and MacFarquhar (1983).

31. Text in Mao (1977).

32. The text of Khrushchev's speech is available in Khrushchev (1970), pp. 559–618.

33. The text of the "Ten Major Relationships" is provided in Appendix 3, pp. 403–17.

34. The second session met in May 1958. This is the only CCP Congress to have met in two sessions.

35. The officially released version of this speech is in Mao (1977).

36. MacFarquhar (1974).

37. For examples in various units, see Chang (1991), Wu (1993), and Yue and Wakeman (1985).

38. Their experience in the camps, from which many of the survivors did not emerge until 1979, is typified by Wu (1993).

39. Donnithorne (1967); Lardy (1978); Schurmann (1971).

40. Schurmann (1971).

41. *Mao Zedong sixiang wan sui!* (1969).

42. Joffe (1971).

43. L. T. White III (1978) details this phenomenon in Shanghai.

44. Skinner (1965).

45. There are numerous accounts of the Lushan conference and plenum. See, e.g., MacFarquhar (1983), Li (1989), and Domes (1985).

46. See the plenum communique in Bowie and Fairbank (1962), pp. 533–35.

47. America suffered just under fifty-five thousand combat deaths during the Vietnam war.

48. Numerous writings describe and analyze the Great Leap Forward. See, e.g., Bachman (1991), Lieberthal chapter in MacFarquhar (1993), MacFarquhar (1983), and Solomon (1971).

49. Walder (1986) analyzes the resulting situation in the urban state enterprises.

50. Specifically, Mao engaged in polemics with Moscow via letters exchanged by the respective central committees that China published. The texts of these are available in Griffith (1967).

51. Naughton (1988).

52. Baum and Teiwes (1968).

53. Lewis and Xue (1988) provide the best available account of China's development of the atomic bomb.

54. Lee (1991).

55. Harding (1981); Joffe (1971).

56. See, e.g., Harding in MacFarquhar and Fairbank (1991), reprinted in MacFarquhar (1993).

57. Kang's control over the civilian security forces is suggested in Byron and Pack (1992).

58. Andrew Walder examines this policy and its effects within the factory in Walder (1986).

59. Lampton (1977).

60. Nelsen (1981).

61. See, e.g., Yue and Wakeman (1985), and Chang (1991).

62. Salisbury (1992), among other sources.

63. Chinese and foreign scholars have never fully been able to explain the extent to which Mao was able to provoke sadistic violence among the population. One of the more serious attempts at explanation is in White (1989). See also Thurston (1988).

64. Dittmer (1974).

65. Numerous accounts by former Red Guards detail the horrors they inflicted. See,

e.g., Liang and Shapiro (1983), Yue and Wakeman (1985), Chang (1991), and Thurston (1991).

66. Text available in *Chinese Communist Party Documents* (1968), pp. 33–54.

67. Chang (1970); Lieberthal and Dickson (1989).

68. Walder (1978).

69. Bernstein (1977).

70. Gottlieb (1977); Lieberthal (1978).

71. Text of the 1969 Party Constitution is available in *Peking Review,* 30 April 1969, pp. 36–39.

72. For details, see Naughton chapter in Lieberthal et al., (1991).

73. Nelsen (1981).

74. There are numerous accounts of the Cultural Revolution in various localities and schools. For details of developments at Peking University, see Yue and Wakeman (1985); for Qinhua University, see Hinton (1972); for the high school level, see Bennett and Montaperto (1972).

75. Bernstein (1977).

76. Whitson and Huang (1973).

77. MacFarquhar chapter in MacFarquhar and Fairbank (1991), reprinted in MacFarquhar (1993).

78. There is no certainty about the actual events leading to Lin's demise. The view presented here is the official Beijing version, but it may not be accurate. See MacFarquhar chapter in MacFarquhar (1993).

79. Detailed in Li (1994).

80. MacFarquhar provides a good overview in his chapter in MacFarquhar (1993).

81. Lieberthal (1977).

82. MacFarquhar chapter in MacFarquhar (1993).

83. Harding (1993); Solomon (1981).

84. On Mao's tactics, see Oksenberg chapter in Wilson (1977); on Mao's dealings with those in Group One (as his personal office was designated), see Li (1994).

85. For systematic analysis of this issue, see Harding (1981).

86. For various thoughts about the encapsulation of peasant society, see Oi (1989), Shue (1988), and Siu (1989).

87. Walder (1986).

88. The first eight categories referred to negative class labels such as landlords and rightists.

CHAPTER 5

1. Oksenberg and Yeung (1977).

2. On this period, see MacFarquhar chapter in MacFarquhar (1993), Garside (1981), Lieberthal (1978), and Fingar (1980).

3. Lampton (1986) focused on Ji and Chen as possible successors to Mao.

4. Text of the communique announcing these appointments is in *FBIS,* 22 August 1977, pp. D2–10.

5. Sources provided in Lieberthal and Dickson (1989), p. 246.

6. In March 1978 Deng also assumed his former government post as a vice premier of the State Council.

7. Text of Hua's speech is available in *FBIS*, 22 August 1977, pp. D11–46.

8. This, for example, occurred in rural policy during the shift from people's communes to family farming in 1979–84: Kelliher (1992).

9. Bonavia (1989); Franz (1988).

10. The major sources for Deng's political tactics from 1977 through the 1980s are Harding (1987), Hamrin (1990), MacFarquhar chapter in MacFarquhar (1993), Baum (1993), and Fewsmith (1994).

11. Ruan (1994); Schoenhals (1991).

12. Yang Zhong Mei (1988).

13. Ho and Hueneman (1984).

14. Pepper (1990).

15. Text of Hua's proposal is in *Peking Review*, 7 March 1978, pp. D1–38.

16. Yang Zhong Mei (1988).

17. Seymour (1980).

18. The "communique" of the plenum is available in *Peking Review*, 9 December 1978, pp. 6–16.

19. The positions are the major ones held before their respective purges.

20. The full text of Wei's declaration is available in Seymour (1980), pp. 47–69.

21. Wei was eventually paroled in late 1993, just six months shy of serving his full sentence. He did not change his views while in prison, and his outspoken comments after his release led to his rearrest in early 1994.

22. Bachman (1985); Lardy and Lieberthal (1983).

23. Ruan (1994) provides an insider's account of the politics of this period.

24. Yang Zhong Mei (1988) provides a political biography of Hu.

25. For graphic details, see Chang (1991).

26. Shambaugh (1984) provides a political biography of Zhao.

27. Fewsmith (1994).

28. On the retrenchment policy in the urban sector, see Solinger (1991).

29. Toffler (1980).

30. The reform effort is analyzed in terms of policy cycles in Baum (1993) and Hamrin (1990). Fewsmith (1994) views the oscillations in the reforms more as a function of the struggle for power at the top of the system, given the rules of the game there.

31. A voluminous literature exists on the Tiananmen demonstrations and their aftermath. Perhaps the best documentary collection in English on this movement and its background is Oksenberg, Sullivan, and Lambert (1990).

32. For three interesting interpretations of this dynamic, see Manion's Introduction in Oksenberg, Sullivan, and Lambert (1990); Pye (1990); and Esherick and Wasserstrom (1990).

33. Manion's Introduction to Oksenberg, Sullivan, and Lambert (1990).

34. Representative documents are in Oksenberg, Sullivan, and Lambert (1990).

35. Text of Deng's remarks appear in Oksenberg, Sullivan, and Lambert (1990), pp. 376–82.

36. Baum (1993) provides information on Deng's "southern journey" and its aftermath through mid-1993.

37. Manion (1993); Manion (1984).

38. Deng's speech to the March 1978 National Science Conference was a key step in developing this argument; the text appears in Deng (1984), pp. 101–06.

39. On bonuses and pay raises, see Shirk (1981) and Walder (1986).

40. Solinger (1991).

41. Kelliher (1992) examines the interplay of peasant initiatives and policy responses in the shift from collectivized to family-based farming.

42. On the agricultural reforms and their effects, see Kelliher (1992), Zweig (1989), Shue (1988), and Oi (1989).

43. This became official at the Thirteenth Party Congress in 1987.

44. Details are in Oksenberg and Tong (1991).

45. Wong (1991).

46. There is an enormous literature on the development experiences of these other countries. See, e.g., Vogel (1980) and Vogel (1991).

47. Ho and Hueneman (1984) detail the policies for opening up to the international arena in the late 1970s through the early 1980s.

48. On Shenzhen and Zhuhai in Guangdong Province, see Vogel (1989).

49. But the actual leverage of each side in these transactions is a complex issue. See Pearson (1991).

50. Cohen (1968).

51. Jacobson and Oksenberg (1990) detail the process and its repercussions.

52. Eckstein (1966) analyzes the very limited role of foreign trade in the Maoist system.

53. Lieberthal and Prahalad (1989).

54. The United States attracted more Chinese students than did any other country. For details, see Lampton (1986).

CHAPTER 6

1. Related in Salisbury (1992).

2. Two very good analyses of the Stalinist system are in Bialer (1980) and Fainsod (1965).

3. At times, various other levels have also existed, such as communes and townships. These, too, are omitted from this discussion of the four enduring bureaucratic levels.

4. The boundaries of at least some of the units at all levels below the Center have changed at various times since 1949.

5. All known meetings through 1986 of the national bodies discussed in this chapter are detailed in Lieberthal and Dickson (1989).

6. This body is also called the Military Commission in some sources. On this commission, see Nelsen (1981) and Swaine (1992).

7. Li (1993).

8. Tanner in Potter (1993); Tanner (1994).

9. On Discipline Inspection until the Cultural Revolution, see Schurmann (1971); on the situation under Deng, see Sullivan (1984).

10. Lieberthal and Oksenberg (1988).

11. All "autonomous regions" have large ethnic minorities, whose names are usually included in the title of the autonomous region.

12. Teiwes (1979).

13. Decisions adopted at the end of 1993 (see Appendix 4) anticipated the establishment of a truly national revenue system in 1994. This large a change, however, will take years to implement fully.

14. Banners are a traditional name held over from Qing dynasty times. These are county-level administrative units in the Inner Mongolian Autonomous Region.

15. Walder (1986).

16. Lieberthal and Oksenberg (1988). This was less the case in the countryside, where the village head played a key broker role between the village and the higher levels of the commune organization: Oi (1989); Shue (1988).

17. The "floating" population refers to individuals who are in a city without formal permission to be there.

18. Lieberthal chapter in Lieberthal and Lampton (1992).

19. Lieberthal and Oksenberg (1988).

20. Shirk chapter in Lieberthal and Lampton (1992).

21. The official position on Mao's "mistakes" is contained in the "Resolution on Certain Questions in the History of Our Party . . ." adopted in June 1981: "Resolution on Certain Questions . . ." (1981).

22. Schell (1984).

23. Watson chapter in Lieberthal et al. (1991).

24. Wong (1991).

25. For the history of the negotiations over this dam project, see Lieberthal and Oksenberg (1988).

26. Salisbury (1992).

27. Bernstein (1984).

28. As of the late 1950s, roughly 70 percent of the Chinese Communist party members were illiterate: Dickson (1994).

29. On central work conferences, see Chang (1970) and Lieberthal and Dickson (1989).

30. Partial documentation is in MacFarquhar, Cheek, and Wu (1989).

31. Lieberthal (1978); Wu (1970).

32. Lee (1991).

33. Halpern chapter in Lieberthal and Lampton (1992).

34. Jacobson and Oksenberg (1990).

35. Halpern chapter in Lieberthal and Lampton (1992).

36. Liu Binyan, one of China's best known investigative reporters, provides details on this dynamic in Liu (1992).

37. Harding (1981).

38. Sullivan (1984)

39. Lieberthal and Oksenberg (1988).

CHAPTER 7

1. There is a massive literature on various aspects of the Qing governing structure and practice. See Morse (1966) for an interesting description of the dynamics of the overall Qing governmental system.

2. This conceptualization comes from Lieberthal and Oksenberg (1988).

3. Mao, for example, attacked Bo Yibo early in the Cultural Revolution in part by criticizing how much meat Bo's family consumed during the famine of the early 1960s.

4. Mao, (1977).

5. Li (1994) provides numerous examples of this attitude.

6. Li (1994).

7. Salisbury (1992).

8. Salisbury (1992).

9. Li (1994) provides a powerful, detailed description of Mao in his last days.

10. Chen Yun, Li Xiannian, and Bo Yibo had worked primarily in economic policy-making; Peng Zhen had headed the Beijing municipal party apparatus and, more important, had held the top post in the "political and legal system" (described in the text below), which coordinated work in the civilian coercive bureaucracies such as the police, court system, and prison labor system; Wang Zhen's ties were primarily to the military.

11. Hamrin chapter in Lieberthal and Lampton (1992) provides an insightful analysis of the dynamics of appointments in the top power elite.

12. Pye (1980).

13. Swaine (1992).

14. Discussion of the *mishu* system is based on Li and Pye (1992) and numerous interviews on the topic with Chinese officials.

15. Mao's tolerance of even these individuals had its limits, though. He became disillusioned with Tian Jiaying and persecuted him. Tian committed suicide early in the Cultural Revolution.

16. Li (1994) provides the best available overview of the security system for China's leaders.

17. The most extensive available analysis of the *kou* and "leadership small group" structure is the Hamrin chapter in Lieberthal and Lampton (1992). This section draws from Hamrin and from interviews the author has conducted with Chinese officials.

18. Barnett first introduced Western scholars to the notion of the *xitong*. As Barnett notes, Chinese officials use this term in two ways: to refer to a group of functionally related bureaucracies (e.g., the "finance and economics *xitong*"); and to refer to the bureaucratic hierarchy under one ministry or commission (e.g., the "machine building ministry *xitong*"): Barnett (1967). The discussion here refers only to the former use of the term.

19. Barnett (1967) provides details of the personnel dossier system. White (1989) analyzes the tensions this system engendered.

20. Whyte (1974).

21. Paine chapter in Lieberthal and Lampton (1992); Pepper (1990).

22. Fainsod (1965).

23. Cohen (1968).

24. Schurmann (1971).

25. The most complete description of the Chinese gulag is in Wu (1992).

26. Wu (1992).

27. See, e.g., Bao (1973).

28. Wang Ruowang (1991) provides a graphic account of the fate of a leading Shanghai official arrested by the Public Security Bureau.

29. Byron and Pack (1992).

30. *Zhonghua Renmin Gongheguo sheng. . . .* (1989).

31. Good analyses of various dimensions of the military system and its connections with the civilian apparatus include Joffe (1971), Joffe (1987), Nelson (1981), Swaine (1992), Whitson (1973), and Whitson with Huang (1973).

32. This conceptualization is explored in the Pollack chapter in Lieberthal and Lampton (1992).

33. Lewis and Xue (1988) tells the story of the Chinese bomb in detail.

34. The fullest statement of this argument is Whitson with Huang (1973).

35. Swaine (1992) carries the analysis up to the early 1990s, detailing the changes in the field armies and their role in the system under the reforms.

36. Nelsen (1981).

37. The number of military regions has varied from thirteen before the Cultural Revolution to eleven in the 1970s and early 1980s, to seven since the mid-1980s.

38. Barnett (1967).

39. This story is traced in the Hamrin chapter in Lieberthal and Lampton (1992).

40. Burns (1987); Burns (1989b).

41. Li Lanqing heads the ministry in charge of foreign trade: Qian Qichen heads the Foreign Ministry; Zhu Rongji heads the People's Bank and an office that assumes major responsibility for domestic economic performance.

42. Lieberthal and Oksenberg (1988).

43. Lieberthal chapter in Lieberthal and Lampton (1992).

44. Barnett provides an extensive description of "Party life" in Barnett (1967); see also Townsend (1969).

45. Lieberthal and Lampton (1992) examines this variance by *xitong*. The Lampton chapter in *ibid.* focuses on the elements in the Chinese system that produce extensive bargaining.

46. Much of the remainder of this section is drawn from Lieberthal and Oksenberg (1988).

47. Chinese conservatives assert that John Foster Dulles first used this term in the 1950s to describe a strategy of bringing about the gradual evolution of communist systems by peaceful means. The term, as used by conservatives, suggests that the West is purposely using its ties with China to undermine the political system of the PRC.

48. Shambaugh (1984).

49. Teiwes (1979).

50. Based on author's interviews with Chinese officials.

CHAPTER 8

1. Because the political history of the Deng era is detailed in Baum (1993), Hamrin (1990), Harding (1987), and Fewsmith (1994) and is summed up in Chapter 5, the specific political events of this period are not footnoted in this chapter.

2. Halpern chapter in Lieberthal and Lampton (1992).

3. Oksenberg, Sullivan, and Lambert (1990), among many other sources, provide details of the Tiananmen developments.

4. The most detailed and sophisticated analysis is Swaine (1992).

5. This underlying anger is captured well in Lord (1990).

6. See also Bachman (1992) and Nathan (1993A).

7. Manion (1993) presents the most comprehensive analysis of the 1980s efforts to retire revolutionary cadres. See also the Manion chapter in Lieberthal and Lampton (1992).

8. Chinese figures in different sources on the number of "state and party cadres," the number of "leading officials," and the number of "people in leading bodies" seem to vary by large numbers. Very likely, there are definitional issues at play that are producing these seemingly large variances, but the net result is that gross statistics are difficult to compare across different studies.

9. Burns (1989).

10. Cui and Wang (n.d.). This volume, published on the mainland, provides no date and place of publication. It also, like virtually all such volumes published in China, provides no information on the methodology used to generate the numbers.

11. Cui and Wang (n.d.), p. 25.

12. Cui and Wang (n.d.), p. 24.

13. Yang (1991).

14. Liu (1991), p. 31.

15. See, e.g., Tanner and Feder (1993).

16. See Hyer (1992).

17. The above connections are drawn from Tanner and Feder (1993). Tanner and Feder provide many other examples of the placement of offspring of high officials into elite jobs. The three Li's here are not related to each other.

18. Oksenberg, Sullivan, and Lambert (1990).

19. Li and White (1991); White and Li (1990).

CHAPTER 9

1. State Statistical Bureau (1991), p. 277. The direct audience probably reached 675 million by the end of 1989 and has grown very rapidly since then.

2. Toffler (1980).

3. Hamrin (1990).

4. Tien et al., (1992).

5. Oi (1994); Whiting (1994).

6. These facets of the Maoist system are explained variously in Eckstein (1966), Oi (1989), Riskin (1987), and Walder (1986).

7. Naughton (1990).

8. World Bank (1990a).

9. Lieberthal and Oksenberg (1988).

10. *Renmin ribao (People's Daily)*, 23 December 1993.

11. *Ching Chi Tao Pao*, 13 December 1993, p. 28 (translated in *FBIS/China*, 17 December 1993, pp. 28–29).

12. Oksenberg and Tong (1991); Wong (1991); World Bank (1990b).

13. Maruya (1992).

14. Oksenberg and Tong (1991).

15. Wong (1991).

16. World Bank Transition Economics Division (December 1993), p. 7.

17. On interprovincial financial transfers via the Center under Mao, see Lyons (1990).

18. World Bank Transition Economics Division (December 1993), p. 7. For the changes adopted in late 1993, the original text of the overall policy statement is presented in Appendix 4 at the end of this volume.

19. Donnithorne (1967).

20. Kelliher (1992) describes the process.

21. Kelliher (1992).

22. Findlay (1993); Hinton (1990); Kelliher (1992); Powell (1992).

23. On labor market issues, see Davis (1992), Granick (1991), Jefferson and Rawski (1992), Korzec (1992), and White (1988).

24. Burns (1989a).

25. The number of state officials and party officials had grown from 5.05 million in 1979 to 10.79 million in 1990: State Statistical Bureau (1991), p. 77.

26. Goldstein and Goldstein (1984).

27. *Wall Street Journal*, January 24, 1994.

28. Lardy (1992a); Lardy (1992b); Lardy (1994).

29. Lardy (1992a); Lardy (1994); Riskin (1987).

30. Massey (1992).

31. D. Li (1993).

32. Professor Nicholas Lardy, private communication with the author.

33. Private communication to the author.

34. On these changes, see Bernard (1992), Goldstein (1991), Haggard (1990), Vogel (1991), and Vogel (1989).

35. Karp (1991).

36. Lieberthal and Prahalad (1989).

37. Huang (1990); Walder chapter in Lieberthal and Lampton (1992).

38. Zweig chapter in Lieberthal and Lampton (1992); Whiting (1994); Oi (1994).

39. Solinger (1993).

40. The best treatment of Guangdong's growth and development of relations with Hong Kong under the reforms is Vogel (1989).

41. Howellpearson (1992); Pearson (1991).

42. Sander and Friedland (1993); Kristof (1993); Cheesman (1992).

43. Sun (1991); "Rotten to the Core . . ." (1993); Lo (1993).

44. Thurston (1993).

45. This in fact became the title of a book that tried to capture the spirit of the early reform era in China: Schell (1984).

46. "Corrupt Officials Expelled . . ." (1993); "Disciplining Party Members" (1990); "Jiang Declares War . . ." (1993); Wu (1990).

47. "Alongside China's Official Exchanges . . ." (1993); "Irrational Rationing . . ." (1992); "Through the Roof . . ." (1991).

48. Summarized in World Bank Transition Economics Division (December 1993).

49. Ash (1992).

CHAPTER 10

1. Vaclav Smil provides an overview of the parlous state of China's environment in Smil (1993).

2. *New York Times* Editorial Notebook, 8 December 1993.

3. World Bank (1991).

4. Biers (1994).

5. *New York Times,* 19 July 1994.

6. Cannon and Jenkins (1990).

7. Yi (1989).

8. Luk and Whitney (1993); Lieberthal and Oksenberg (1988).

9. Nuclear power is not discussed here because it does not depend on natural resource distribution. China has a very modest civilian nuclear power effort, with one plant coming on line at Daya Bay in Guangdong and another near Shanghai. No other nuclear power plants will be completed in the near future, and China has no plans to make nuclear power a major component of its energy system. This distinguishes the PRC from Japan, South Korea, and Taiwan, all of which make extensive use of nuclear power.

10. World Bank (1985).

11. Yeh chapter in Treadgold (1967).

12. The Halpern chapter in Lieberthal and Lampton (1992) discusses the externality issue. See also Donnithorne (1967). This is a well-known phenomenon in socialist economic systems.

13. Personal communication from the foreign expert to the author.

14. *New York Times,* 19 July 1994; Ross (1988); "Scientists Warn of Resource Shortages" (1992); "New Strategy for Environmental Protection" (1988).

15. Ross (1980).

16. Smil (1993).

17. This played a role in raising environmental consciousness in the USSR in the 1980s: Economy (1994).

18. Jahiel (1994).

19. Smil (1993).

20. Vehicle production doubled to over a million units per year between 1987 and 1993.

21. Personal observation by the author.

22. "Environment and Development" (1992); Jahiel (1994); Ross (1988); Smil (1993).

23. Qu and Li (1990).

24. Jahiel (1994); Ross (1987); Ross (1988).

25. Jahiel (1994) provides a detailed analysis of the fee system and its consequences.

26. Jahiel (1994).

27. Lieberthal and Oksenberg (1988).

28. Smil (1993).

29. Smil (1993).

30. Qu and Li (1990).

31. This is true even in very water-short areas of North China: Smil (1993).

32. Jahiel (1994) provides examples.

33. D. Li (1993).

34. This formed a major plank of the opposition to the North American Free Trade Agreement during the national debate on ratifying that agreement in the United States in late 1993.

35. Smil (1993).

36. There are no agreed upon figures for China's per capita income in dollar terms. Estimates range from a low of about $460 per person to a high, estimated by the International Monetary Fund on the basis of a calculation of purchasing parity, of over $2,000 per person. The real figure is probably somewhere around $1,000 per person. For a sensible discussion of this issue, see Lardy (1994).

37. Smil (1993).

CHAPTER 11

1. See, for example Friedman, Pickowicz, and Selden (1991), Oi (1989), Shue (1988), and Siu (1989).

2. Townsend (1969) provides details.

3. See the exchange between Walder and Womack: Walder (1991) and Womack (1991) (quotation in text is from Womack, p. 314) for a discussion of this issue in state enterprises. The discussion grows out of Walder (1986).

4. E.g., Perry (1993).

5. The Cheek chapter in Wasserstrom and Perry (1992), uses the notion of traditional intellectuals as priests.

6. Mao (1965c), pp. 69–98.

7. Siu (1990) presents a nuanced treatment of the changing role of intellectuals from the imperial era to the present in her introductory essay.

8. See, e.g., Wu (1993).

9. Liang and Shapiro (1983).

10. For an extensive treatment of this and related issues, see Thurston (1988).

11. E.g., Pye (1980), Pye (1988), and Pye (1992); Solomon (1971). Nathan (1993) questions the empirical validity of such statements about the distinctiveness of China's political culture.

12. For example, when the author in 1976 visited the site of the first Chinese Communist Party Congress in Shanghai, he offered to provide a copy of a master's thesis writ-

ten about that Congress by Chen Gongbo, who had been in attendance and later went to Columbia University. The exhibit guide responded curtly that Chen had become a renegade and therefore that his writings were of no historical interest.

13. The most striking example is the 1974 campaign to "criticize Lin Biao and Confucius," during which many younger Chinese learned about the rudiments of Confucian teachings.

14. Link (1992) provides a subtle, sensitive explication of this phenomenon.

15. One intellectual commented to the author in 1980 that, "I can forgive the communists anything else, but I can never forgive them for making my children despise intellectuals."

16. White (1989); Barnett (1967).

17. Black and white TV is considered a sign of poverty in China of 1994, even in many villages.

18. These examples are obtained from interviews.

19. "New Qigong Film" (1991); Lou and Huang (1990); Cui (1989); "Qigong—Popularity Is Rising" (1988).

20. The Shue chapter in Migdad, Kohli, and Shue (1994) examines this in several rural locations.

21. Kaye (1993); "Hong Kong: Secret Societies Rampant . . ." (1992); "Wang Zhen Decries Loss of Party Influence" (1991); Cheung (1990); "Nanjing Paper . . ." (1987); "Threat from Secret Societies . . ." (1986).

22. Solinger (1993).

23. Based on author's interviews with participants in the meeting.

24. Interview with the author.

25. Background details are provided in the Solinger chapter in Rosenbaum (1992).

26. Leung (1993).

27. The incident in Jilin came to the attention of higher officials and then received local publicity. Based on the author's interview of a foreign visitor who read the local press reporting on this incident. On the Organic Law and its implementation, see O'Brien (1994) and Lawrence (1994). Rozelle (1994) details how extensive the authority of government officials remains in many Chinese villages.

28. Madsen (1993); Solinger (1993); Zhou (1993); Perry (1993); Rosenbaum (1992); Wasserstrom and Perry (1992); Wakeman (1993); Rowe (1993); Shen (1992); McCormick, Su, and Xiao (1992), among others.

29. The Solinger chapter in Rosenbaum (1992) explores this interaction regarding the state and merchants in a nuanced way.

30. Huang (1993).

31. China differed from most third-world countries in that it had a strong state and a weak society: Migdal (1988). On the application of this idea to Maoist China, see Kelliher (1992).

32. "State Instituting Social Services . . ." (1993); "New Achievements in Social Services . . ." (1993); "Jiangsu Province Social Services . . ." (1990); Davis (1989) provides a review of China's social welfare policies and outcomes.

33. Haggard (1990); Chu (1992); Vogel (1991).

34. Wu (1992) describes the reform through labor system.

35. "Human Rights in China" (1991).

36. Nathan (1985).

37. Khan et al. (1992).

38. Khan et al. (1992), pp. 1040–41.

39. Khan et al. (1992), pp. 1041–42.

40. Khan et al. (1992), p. 1036.

41. Khan et al. (1992), p. 1037.

42. Khan et al. (1992), p. 1037.

43. Khan et al. (1992), pp. 1042, 1044, 1059.

44. Khan et al. (1992), pp. 1047–50.

45. For an excellent treatment of the impact of the rural reforms on women, see the Kelkar chapter in Agarwal (1988).

46. "Price scissors" refers to the differences in relative prices between what the farmers pay for agricultural inputs and items they consume and what they receive for the agricultural products they sell.

47. Goodspeed (1993); Swain (1993); Lam (1993).

48. During the Cultural Revolution, this brigade became a widely heralded model of the spirit of hard struggle and self-reliance, based on its success in springing back from natural disaster without relying on government assistance. Salisbury (1992) provides behind-the-scenes information on the politics of the Dazhai model.

49. Good sources on the position of women under the Chinese communists during the Maoist era include: Andors (1983); Johnson (1983), and Davin's chapter in Afshar (1991).

50. See Bauer et al. (1992).

51. "Symposium on Rural Family Change." (1992); Judd (1990); Bridges (1991).

52. On the birth-control program, see Zhang (1992); Yang and Zhang (1992); Peng (1990).

53. Norman (1993); "Slaughtering the Innocents" (1993); Andersen (1993).

54. "Four Sentenced to Death" (1993); Kahn (1993); Mirsky (1992); "Hong Kong: Officials Fight . . ." (1991).

55. Cohen (1965).

56. On the issue of class in Maoist China, see Kraus (1981).

57. Davis (1992).

CHAPTER 12

1. MacFarquhar (1991).

2. Yan (1992).

3. Friedman (1994).

4. Whyte's chapter in Rosenbaum (1992), for example, traces the seeds of potentially rapid democratic transition in China's society.

5. This is a central thesis of Zheng (1994).

6. Oi (1994); Whiting (1994).

7. Zheng (1994).

8. Naughton explores this in his chapter in Lieberthal and Lampton (1992).

9. Oi (1994) details this at the township level.

10. Lieberthal and Lampton (1992) explores this issue systematically.

11. Tanner (1994).

12. Walder (1986); Whyte (1974).

13. Walder (1986); Oi (1989).

14. E.g., Friedman (1994).

15. Dreyer (1976); Harris (1993).

16. Harding (1993a) details this terminological confusion.

17. Shambaugh (1993), p. 654.

18. Ash and Kueh (1993).

19. Lieberthal (1992); Overholt (1993); Vogel (1989).

20. Luo and Howe (1993).

21. Dickson (1994); Tien (1989).

22. Watson (1993) gives technological and economic forces the edge, while Johnston (1993) highlights the political factors.

23. Bunce (1981).

24. Seymour (1987).

25. This is captured, *inter alia,* in a wonderful short story by Lu Xun called "The Story of Ah Q." See Lu (1971).

26. Garver (1993) provides a solid overview of the history of the PRC's foreign affairs.

27. Hoyt (1990); Hunt (1992); Stueck (1981); Whiting (1960).

28. Barnett (1977); Borisov and Koloskov (1975); Chang (1990); Griffith (1967); Dittmer (1992); Jones (1985); Zagoria (1962).

29. Naughton (1988).

30. Only Romania's December 1989 political upheaval produced substantial carnage.

31. Garver (1992); *New York Times,* 21 July 1994.

32. See the sources on the Sino-Soviet relationship cited in Note 21 above.

33. See the Naughton chapter in Lieberthal, Kalgren, MacFarquhar, and Wakeman (1991).

34. See, e.g., D. Li (1993).

35. Jacobsen and Oksenberg (1990).

36. As of 1995 the World Trade Organization is to replace the former General Agreement on Tariffs and Trade, with somewhat different rules taking effect. The comments in the text refer equally to the time after this transition.

37. *New York Times* "Week in Review" section, 3 April 1994, p. 3.

38. Gottlieb (1977); Kissinger (1979); Lieberthal (1978c); Solomon (1981); Wich (1980).

39. The best analytical pieces on the domestic pressures feeding China's military exports are Lewis, Hua, and Xue (1991) and Hyer (1992). This section draws primarily from these two sources.

40. Hyer (1992).

41. For details, see Hyer (1992).

42. For details, see Hyer (1992).

43. Beijing's *Fazhi Bao (Legal Gazette)* on 16 January 1994 (trans. in *FBIS China Daily Report,* 2 February 1994, pp. 10–17) decried the extent to which international criminal gangs have penetrated China for gun running and narcotics operations and provided a brief overview of the government's efforts to control these activities. The *South China Morning Post* of 2 February 1994 reported that "ice," the drug of choice in the Philippines and Japan, is typically produced in laboratories in South China and transshipped by gangs through Hong Kong to the Philippines, Japan, Taiwan, South Korea, and Hawaii.

Bibliography of Sources Cited in the Text

Afshar, Haleh, ed. *Women, Development, and Survival in the Third World.* London: Longman, 1991.

Agarwal, Bina, ed. *Structures of State Patriarchy: State, Community, and Household in Modernizing Asia.* London: Zed Books, 1988.

"Alongside China's Official Exchanges, Booming Illegal Stock Market Operates." *Wall Street Journal* (Eastern edition). 2 June 1993, p. A11.

Andersen, John W. and Molly Moore. "Murdered at Birth for Being Female." *Toronto Star.* 4 April 1993, p. A1.

Amnesty International. *Political Imprisonment in the People's Republic of China.* London: Amnesty International, 1978.

———. *China: Violations of Human Rights.* London: Amnesty International, 1984.

Andors, Phyllis. *The Unfinished Liberation of Chinese Women, 1949–1980.* Bloomington: Indiana University Press, 1983.

Armstrong, Tony. *Breaking the Ice: Rapprochement between East and West Germany, the United States and China, and Israel and Egypt.* Washington, D.C.: United States Institute of Peace Press, 1993.

Ash, Robert. "The Agricultural Sector in China: Performance and Policy Dilemmas during the 1990s." *China Quarterly* 131 (September 1992): 545–76.

Ash, Robert, and Y. Y. Kueh. "Economic Integration within Greater China: Trade and Investment Flows between China, Hong Kong, and Taiwan." *China Quarterly* 136 (December 1993): 711–45.

Atlantic Council and National Committee on US-China Relations. *United States and China Relations at a Crossroads.* Washington, D.C., and New York: Atlantic Council and National Committee on US-China Relations, 1993.

Bachman, David M. *Chen Yun and the Chinese Political System.* Berkeley and Los Angeles: University of California Press, 1985.

———. *Bureaucracy, Economy, and Leadership in China: The Institutional Origins of the Great Leap Forward.* New York: Cambridge University Press, 1991.

———. "The Limits to Leadership in China." In *The Future of China,* 23–35. Seattle: National Bureau of Asian Research, 1992.

Balazs, Etienne. *Chinese Civilization and Bureaucracy.* New Haven: Yale University Press, 1964.

Bao, Ruo-wang. *Prisoner of Mao.* New York: Coward, McCann and Geoghegan, 1973.

Barnett, A. Doak. *Communist China: The Early Years, 1949–55.* New York: Praeger, 1964.

———. *Cadres, Bureaucracy, and Political Power in Communist China.* New York: Columbia University Press, 1967.

————. *China and the Major Powers in East Asia.* Washington, D.C.: Brookings Institution, 1977.

————, ed. *Chinese Communist Politics in Action.* Seattle: University of Washington Press, 1969.

Barraclough, Geoffrey. *An Introduction to Contemporary History.* New York: Penguin, 1967.

Bartlett, Beatrice. *Monarchs and Ministers.* Berkeley and Los Angeles: University of California Press, 1991.

Bauer, John, Wang Feng, Nancy Riley, and Xiaohua Zhao. "Gender and Inequality in Urban China." *Modern China* (July 1992): 333–70.

Baum, Richard. *Prelude to Revolution: Mao, the Party, and the Peasant Question, 1962–66.* New York: Columbia University Press, 1975.

————. *Chinese Politics in the Age of Deng Xiaoping: The Cycles of Reform.* Princeton: Princeton University Press, 1994.

Baum, Richard, and Frederick Teiwes. *Ssu-Ch'ing: The Socialist Education Movement of 1962–1966.* Berkeley and Los Angeles: University of California Press, 1968.

Beckman, George M. *The Modernization of China and Japan.* New York: Harper and Row, 1962.

Belden, Jack. *China Shakes the World.* New York: Monthly Review Press, 1949.

Bennett, Gordon A. *Yundong: Mass Campaigns in Chinese Communist Leadership.* Berkeley: Center for Chinese Studies, University of California, 1976.

Bennett, Gordon A., and Ronald Montaperto. *Red Guard: The Political Biography of Dai Hsiao-Ai.* Garden City, N.Y.: Anchor, 1972.

Bernstein, Thomas P. *Up to the Mountains and Down to the Villages: The Transfer of Youth from Urban to Rural China.* New Haven: Yale University Press, 1977.

————. "Stalinism, Famine, and Chinese Peasants—Grain Procurement during the Great Leap Forward." *Theory and Society* 13, no. 3 (1984): 339–77.

Bialer, Seweryn. *Stalin's Successors: Leadership, Stability, and Change in the Soviet Union.* Cambridge: Cambridge University Press, 1980.

Bianco, Lucien. *Origins of the Chinese Revolution, 1915–1949.* Stanford: Stanford University Press, 1971.

Biers, Dan, "China's Rush to Boost Industry Causing Disastrous Pollution." Associated Press, 28 April 1994.

Bonavia, David. *Deng.* Hong Kong: Longman, 1989.

Borisov, O. B., and B. Y. Koloskov. *Sino-Soviet Relations, 1945–1970.* Translated by Yuri Shirokov. Moscow: Progress Publishers, 1975.

Bowie, Robert K., and John K. Fairbank. *Communist China, 1955–1959.* Cambridge: Harvard University Press, 1962.

Bridges, William P., Moshe Semoyonov, and Richard E. Barret. "Female Labor Participation in Urban and Rural China." *Rural Sociology* 56 (Spring 1991): 1–21.

Bunce, Valerie. *Do Leaders Make a Difference?* Princeton: Princeton University Press, 1981.

Burns, John P. "China's Nomenklatura System." *Problems of Communism* 36 (September–October 1987): 36–51.

————. "Chinese Civil Service Reform: The 13th Party Congress Proposals." *China Quarterly* 120 (December 1989a): 739–70.

————. *The Chinese Communist Party Nomenklatura System: A Documentary Study of Party Control of Leadership Selection*. Armonk, N.Y.: M. E. Sharpe, 1989b.

Byron, John, and Robert Pack. *Claws of the Dragon*. New York: Simon and Schuster, 1992.

Cannon, Terry, and Alan Jenkins. *The Geography of Contemporary China: The Impact of Deng Xiaoping's Decade*. New York: Routledge, 1990.

Chan, Anita, Richard Madsen, and Jonathan Unger. *Chen Village: The Recent History of a Peasant community in Mao's China*. Berkeley and Los Angeles: University of California Press, 1984.

Chang, Gordon H. *Friends and Enemies: The United States, China, and the Soviet Union, 1948–72*. Stanford: Stanford University Press, 1990.

Chang, Jung. *Wild Swans: Three Daughters of China*. New York: Simon and Schuster, 1991.

Chang, Parris. "Research Notes on the Changing Loci of Decision in the CCP." *China Quarterly* 44 (October–December 1970): 169–94.

Cheesman, Bruce. "China—South Korea: A Case of Pure Mathematics." *Asian Business* 28 (October 1992): 16.

Chen, Jie. *Ideology in US Foreign Policy*. Westport, Conn.: Praeger, 1992.

Chesneaux, Jean. *The Chinese Labor Movement, 1919–1927*. Stanford: Stanford University Press, 1968.

Cheung, Tai Ming. "Fighting the Good Fight: Underground Church Reaps the Fruits of Religious Boom." *Far Eastern Economic Review* 149 (5 July 1990): 39–41.

Chi, Hsi-sheng. *Nationalist China at War: Military Defeats and Political Collapse, 1937–45*. Ann Arbor: University of Michigan Press, 1982.

China Statistical Information and Consultancy Service. *China Statistical Yearbook, 1991*. Beijing: China Statistical Information and Consultancy Service, 1991.

Chow, Ts'e-tung. *The May Fourth Movement: Intellectual Revolution in Modern China*. Cambridge: Harvard University Press, 1960.

Ch'u, Tung-tsu. *Local Government in China Under the Ch'ing*. Stanford: Stanford University Press, 1969.

Chu, Yun-han. *Crafting Democracy in Taiwan*. Taipei: Institute for National Policy Research, 1992.

Chu, Wen-djang. *The Moslem Rebellions in Northwest China*. Paris: Mouton, 1966.

Clubb, O. Edmund. *China and Russia: The Great 'Game.'* New York: Columbia University Press, 1971.

Coble, Parks M. *The Shanghai Capitalists and the Nationalist Government, 1927–1937*. Cambridge: Council on East Asian Studies, Harvard University, 1980.

Cohen, Jerome A. *The Criminal Process in the People's Republic of China, 1949–1963: An Introduction*. Cambridge: Harvard University Press, 1968.

Cohen, Paul. *Reform in Nineteenth-Century China*. Cambridge: East Asian Research Center, Harvard University, 1976.

Cohen, Warren I. *America's Response to China: A History of Sino-American Relations*. New York: Columbia University Press, 1990.

"Corrupt Officials Expelled from Party." *Beijing Review* 36 (12 July 1993): 5.

Cranmer-Byng, J. L., ed. *An Embassy to China*. London: Longman, 1962.

Cui, Lili. "Qigong on Qinghua Campus." *Beijing Review* 32 (24 April 1989): 24–26.

Cui, Wunian and Wang Junxian. *Zhongguo ganbu jiegou di bianqian* (Changes in the structure of China's cadres). No city of publication, publisher, or date of publication provided.

Davis, Deborah. "China's Social Welfare: Policies and Outcomes." *China Quarterly* 119 (September 1989): 577–97.

———. "Job Mobility in Post-Mao Cities: Increases in the Margins." *China Quarterly* 132 (December 1992): 1062–85.

Deng, Xiaoping. *Selected Works of Deng Xiaoping, 1975–1982,* vol. 2. Beijing: Foreign Languages Press, 1984.

———. *Selected Works of Deng Xiaoping, 1983–1992,* vol. 3. Beijing: Foreign Languages Press, 1993.

Dickson, Bruce. *The Adaptability of Leninist Parties: A Comparison of the Chinese Communist Party and the Kuomintang.* Ph.D. diss., University of Michigan, 1994.

Dirlik, Arif. "The Ideological Foundations of the New Life Movement." *Journal of Asian Studies* 34, no. 4 (August 1975): 945–80.

———. *Anarchism in the Chinese Revolution.* Berkeley and Los Angeles: University of California Press, 1991.

"Disciplining Party Members." *Beijing Review* 33 (29 January 1990): 6–7.

Dittmer, Lowell. *Liu Shao-ch'i and the Chinese Cultural Revolution.* Berkeley and Los Angeles: University of California Press, 1974.

———. *Sino-Soviet Normalization and Its International Implications 1945–90.* Seattle: University of Washington Press, 1992.

Dittmer, Lowell, and Samuel S. Kim, eds. *China's Quest for National Identity.* Ithaca, N.Y.: Cornell University Press, 1993.

Domes, Jurgen. *Peng Te-huai: The Man and the Image.* London: C. Hurst and Co., 1985.

Donnithorne, Audrey. *China's Economic System.* New York: Praeger, 1967.

Dreyer, June T. *China's Forty Millions.* Cambridge: Harvard University Press, 1976.

Eastman, Lloyd E. *The Abortive Revolution: China under Nationalist Rule, 1927–1937.* Cambridge: Harvard University Press, 1974.

Ebrey, Patricia, ed. *Chinese Civilization and Society.* New York: The Free Press, 1981.

Eckstein, Alexander. *Communist China's Economic Growth and Foreign Trade: Implications for US Policy.* New York: McGraw-Hill, 1966.

———. *China's Economic Revolution.* Cambridge: Cambridge University Press, 1977.

Economy, Elizabeth. *Domestic Reforms and International Regime Formation: China, the USSR, and Global Climate Change.* Ph.D. diss., University of Michigan, 1994.

Elvin, Mark. *The Pattern of the Chinese Past.* Stanford: Stanford University Press, 1973.

"Environment and Development: A World Issue." *Beijing Review* 35 (8 June 1992): 18–20.

Erbaugh, Mary S. "The Secret History of The Hakkas: The Chinese Revolution as a Hakka Enterprise," *China Quarterly* 132 (December 1992): 937–68.

Esherick, Joseph W. *Lost Chance in China: The World War II Despatches of John S. Service.* New York: Vintage, 1974.

Esherick, Joseph W., and Jeffrey N. Wasserstrom. "Acting Out Democracy: Political Theater in Modern China." *Journal of Asian Studies* 49 (November 1990): 835–65.

Fainsod, Merle. *How Russia Is Ruled*. Cambridge: Harvard University Press, 1965.

Fairbank, John K. *Trade and Diplomacy on the China Coast: The Opening of the Treaty Ports, 1842–1854*. Stanford: Stanford University Press, 1953.

———. *Chinabound: A Fifty Year Memoir*. New York: Harper and Row, 1982.

———, ed. *The Chinese World Order*. Cambridge: Harvard University Press, 1968.

Fairbank, John K. and Kwang-ching Liu, eds. *The Cambridge History of China*. Vol. 10. New York: Cambridge University Press, 1978.

Fairbank, John K., Edwin O. Reischauer, and Albert M. Craig. *East Asia*. Boston: Houghton Mifflin, 1973.

FBIS [Foreign Broadcast Information Service]. *China Daily Report*. Arlington, Va.

Fewsmith, Joseph. *Dilemmas of Reform in China: Political Conflict and Economic Debate*. Armonk, N.Y.: M. E. Sharpe, 1994.

Findlay, Christopher C. *Policy Reform, Economic Growth and China's Agriculture*. Paris: Development Centre, Organization for Economic Cooperation and Development, 1993.

Fingar, Thomas. *China's Quest for Independence: Policy Evolution in the 1970s*. Boulder: Westview Press, 1980.

"Four Sentenced to Death for Women, Children Racket." Agence France Press, 15 November 1993.

Franck, Harry A. *Wondering in North China*. New York: The Century Co., 1923.

Franz, Uli. *Deng Xiaoping*. Boston: Harcourt Brace Jovanovich, 1988.

Fried, Morton. *The Fabric of Chinese Society*. New York: Praeger, 1953.

Friedman, Edward. "Reconstructing China's National Identity: A Southern Alternative to Mao-era Anti-imperialist Nationalism." *Journal of Asian Studies* (February 1994): 67–91.

Friedman, Edward, Paul G. Pickowicz, and Mark Selden. *Chinese Village, Socialist State*. New Haven: Yale University Press, 1991.

Gaddis, John L. *Containment: Documents on American Policy and Strategy, 1945–50*. New York: Columbia University Press, 1978.

Gamble, Sidney D. *Ting Hsien: A North China Rural Community*. Stanford: Stanford University Press, 1954.

Gao, Yuan. *Born Red: A Chronicle of the Cultural Revolution*. Stanford: Stanford University Press, 1987.

Garside, Roger. *Coming Alive: China after Mao*. New York: McGraw-Hill, 1981.

Garver, John W. *China's Decision for Rapprochement with the United States, 1968–74*. Boulder: Westview Press, 1982.

———. "China's Push through the South China Sea: The Interaction of Bureaucratic and National Interests." *China Quarterly* 132 (December 1992): 999–1028.

———. *Foreign Relations of the People's Republic of China*. Englewood Cliffs, N.J.: Prentice Hall, 1993.

Gillin, Donald G. *Warlord: Yen Hsi-shan in Shansi Province 1911–1949*. Princeton: Princeton University Press, 1967.

Goldman, Merle. *Literary Dissent in Communist China.* New York: Atheneum, 1971.

———. *China's Intellectuals: Advise and Dissent.* Cambridge: Harvard University Press, 1981.

Goldstein, Alice, and Sidney Goldstein. "Population Movement, Labor Force Absorption, and Urbanization in China." *Annals of the American Academy of Political and Social Science* 476 (November 1984): 90–110.

Goldstein, Avery. *From Bandwagon to Balance-of-Power Politics.* Stanford: Stanford University Press, 1991.

Goldstein, Steven M. *Minidragons: Fragile Economic Miracles in the Pacific.* Boulder: Westview Press, 1991.

Goncharov, Sergei N., John W. Lewis, and Litai Xue. *Uncertain Partners.* Stanford: Stanford University Press, 1993.

Goodspeed, Peter. "China's Peasants Get Restless; Rural Protests Send Shock Waves through Beijing Urbanized Elite." *Toronto Star.* 11 July 1993, p. F2.

Gottlieb, Thomas M. *Chinese Foreign Policy: Factionalism and the Origins of the Strategic Triangle.* Santa Monica, Ca.: Rand Corporation, 1977.

Granick, David. "Multiple Labor Markets in the Industrial State Enterprise Sector." *China Quarterly* 126 (June 1991): 269–89.

Grasso, June. *Truman's Two China Policy: 1948–50.* Armonk, N.Y.: M. E. Sharpe, 1987.

Grieder, Jerome B. *Hu Shih and the Chinese Renaissance: Liberalism in the Chinese Revolution, 1917–1937.* Cambridge: Harvard University Press, 1970.

Griffith, William E. *Sino-Soviet Relations, 1964–1965.* Cambridge: MIT Press, 1967.

Guillermaz, Jacques. *A History of the Chinese Communist Party.* New York: Random House, 1972.

Haggard, Stephen. *Pathways from the Periphery: The Politics of Growth in the Newly Industrializing Countries.* Ithaca, N.Y.: Cornell University Press, 1990.

Hallenberg, Jan. *Foreign Policy Change: United States Foreign Policy toward the Soviet Union and the People's Republic of China, 1961–80.* Stockholm: University of Stockholm, 1984.

Hamrin, Carol Lee. *China and the Challenge of the Future: Changing Political Patterns.* Boulder: Westview Press, 1990.

Harding, Harry. *Organizing China: The Problem of Bureaucracy 1949–1976.* Stanford: Stanford University Press, 1981.

———. *China's Second Revolution: Reform after Mao.* Washington, D.C.: Brookings Institution, 1987.

———. "The Concept of 'Greater China': Themes, Variations, and Reservations." *China Quarterly* 136 (December 1993a): 660–86.

———. *A Fragile Relationship: The United States and China Since 1972.* Washington, D.C.: Brookings Institution, 1993b.

———, ed. *China's Foreign Relations in the 1980s.* New Haven: Yale University Press, 1984.

Harris, Lillian Craig. "Xinjiang, Central Asia, and the Implications for China's Policy in the Islamic World." *China Quarterly* 133 (March 1993): 111–29.

Harrison, James Pinckney. *The Long March to Power.* New York: Praeger, 1972.

Hinton, William. *Hundred Day War: The Cultural Revolution at Tsinghua University.* New York: Monthly Review Press, 1972.

————. *The Great Reversal: The Privatization of China*. New York: Monthly Review Press, 1990.

Ho, Ping-ti. *The Ladder of Success in Imperial China: Aspects of Social Mobility, 1368–1911*. New York: Science Editions, 1964.

Ho, Sam P., and Ralph W. Hueneman. *China's Open Door Policy: The Quest for Foreign Technology and Capital*. Vancouver: University of British Columbia Press, 1984.

Hofheinz, Roy, Jr. *The Broken Wave*. Cambridge: Harvard University Press, 1977.

"Hong Kong: Officials Fight 'Losing War' against Slave Trade." *FBIS* (12 December 1991): 29.

"Hong Kong: Secret Societies 'Rampant' Throughout." *FBIS* (14 May 1992): 29.

Howe, Christopher, ed. *Shanghai: Revolution and Development in an Asian Metropolis*. Cambridge: Cambridge University Press, 1981.

Howellpearson, Martin. "The New Chinese Superstate." *Global Finance*, 6, no. 2 (February 1992): 56–59.

Hoyt, Edwin Palmer. *The Day the Chinese Attacked: Korea 1950; The Story of the Failure of America's China Policy*. New York: McGraw-Hill, 1990.

Hsiao, Kung-Chuan. *Rural China: Imperial Control in the Nineteenth Century*. Seattle: University of Washington Press, 1960.

Huang, Philip. " 'Public Sphere'/'Civil Society' in China? The Third Realm Between State and Society." *Modern China* (April 1993): 216–40.

Huang, Yasheng. "Web of Interests and Patterns of Behavior of Chinese Local Economic Bureaucracies and Enterprises during the Reforms." *China Quarterly* 123 (September 1990): 431–58.

Hucker, Charles O. *China's Imperial Past: An Introduction to Chinese History and Culture*. Stanford: Stanford University Press, 1975.

"Human Rights in China." *Beijing Review* 34, no. 44 (4–10 November 1991): 8–45.

Hummel, Arthur W. *Eminent Chinese of the Ch'ing Period*. Taipei: Ch'eng-Wen Publishing Company, 1967.

Hunt, Michael H. *Ideology and US Foreign Policy*. New Haven: Yale University Press, 1987.

————. "Beijing and the Korean Crisis, June 1950–June 1951." *Political Science Quarterly* 107 (Fall 1992): 453–78.

Hyer, Eric. "China's Arms Merchants: Profits in Command." *China Quarterly* 132 (December 1992): 1101–18.

Hymes, Robert. *Statesmen and Gentlemen: The Elite of Fu-chou, Chiang-hsi, in Northern and Southern Sung*. New York: Cambridge University Press, 1966.

"Irrational Rationing: Chaotic Shenzhen Share Issue Reveals Basic Flaws." *Far Eastern Economic Review* 155 (20 August 1992): 65.

Isaacs, Harold R. *The Tragedy of the Chinese Revolution*. London: Secker and Warburg, 1938.

Jacobson, Harold K., and Michel Oksenberg. *China's Participation in the IMF, the World Bank, and the GATT: Toward a Global Economic Order*. Ann Arbor: University of Michigan Press, 1990.

Jahiel, Abigail. *Policy Implementation under "Socialist Reform": The Case of Water Pollution Management in the People's Republic of China*. Ph.D. diss., University of Michigan, 1994.

Jefferson, Gary H., and Thomas G. Rawski. "Unemployment, Underemployment, and Employment Policy in China's Cities." *Modern China* 18 (January 1992): 42–71.

Jen, Yu-wen. *The Taiping Revolutionary Movement*. New Haven: Yale University Press, 1973.

"Jiang Declares War on Corruption." *Beijing Review* 36 (6 September 1993): 5–6.

"Jiangsu Province Social Services Aid Agriculture." *FBIS* (12 December 1990): 45.

Joffe, Ellis. *Party and Army Professionalism and Political Control in the Chinese Officer Corps, 1949–1964*. Cambridge: Harvard University Press, 1971.

————. *The Chinese Army after Mao*. Cambridge: Harvard University Press, 1987.

Johnson, Kay. *Women, the Family, and Peasant Revolution in China*. Chicago: University of Chicago Press, 1983.

Johnston, Alastair I. "Independence through Unification: On the Correct Handling of Contradictons across the Taiwan Straits." *Contemporary Issues 2*. Cambridge: Fairbank Center for East Asian Research, May 1993.

Jones, Peter. *China and the Soviet Union*. London: Longwan, 1985.

Judd, Ellen R. " 'Men Are More Able': Rural Women's Conceptions of Gender and Agency." *Pacific Affairs* 63 (Spring 1990): 40–61.

Kahn, Joseph. "Buying, Selling of Women on Rise in China." *The Vancouver Sun*. 30 May 1993, p. B3.

Kalicki, J. H. *The Pattern of Sino-American Crises: Political-Military Interactions in the 1950s*. London: Cambridge University Press, 1975.

Kang, Chao. *Man and Land in China*. Stanford: Stanford University Press, 1986.

Karp, Jonathan. "The Vietnam Option: Taiwan Directs Investment Flows Away from China." *Far Eastern Economic Review* 154 (31 October 1991): 70–71.

Kaye, Lincoln. "Religious Groundswell: Underground Churches Lead Christian Revival." *Far Eastern Economic Review* 156 (21 January 1993): 13.

Khan, Azizur Rahman, Keith Griffin, Carl Riskin, and Renwei Zhao. "Household Income and Its Distribution in China." *China Quarterly* 132 (December 1992): 1029–61.

Khrushchev, Nikita S. *Khrushchev Remembers*. Boston: Little, Brown, 1970.

Kelliher, Daniel. *Peasant Power in China: The Era of Rural Reform, 1979–1989*. New Haven: Yale University Press, 1992.

Kennedy, Paul. *The Rise and Fall of the Great Powers*. New York: Random House, 1987.

Kirby, William. *Germany and Republican China*. Stanford: Stanford University Press, 1984.

Kissinger, Henry. *White House Years*. Boston: Little, Brown, 1979.

Klein, Donald. *Rebels and Bureaucrats: China's December 9ers*. Berkeley and Los Angeles: University of California Press, 1976.

Korzec, Michael. *Labour and the Failure of Reform in China*. New York: St. Martin's, 1992.

Kraus, Richard. *Class Conflict in Chinese Socialism*. New York: Columbia University Press, 1981.

Kristof, Nicholas D. "China's Newest Partner: South Korea." *New York Times*. 5 April 1993, pp. D1–D2.

Kuhn, Philip A. *Rebellion and Its Enemies in Late Imperial China*. Cambridge: Harvard University Press, 1970.

————. *Soulstealers: The Chinese Sorcery Scare of 1768*. Cambridge: Harvard University Press, 1990.

Lam, Willy Wo-Lap. "Jiang Urges Huge Grain Store System." *South China Morning Post.* 16 June 1993, p. 10.

Lampton, David M. *The Politics of Medicine in China: The Policy Process, 1949–1977.* Boulder: Westview Press, 1977.

———. *Paths to Power: Elite Mobility in Contemporary China.* Ann Arbor: Center for Chinese Studies, University of Michigan, 1986a.

———. *A Relationship Restored: Trends in US-China Educational Exchanges, 1978–1984.* Washington, D.C.: National Academy Press, 1986b.

Lardy, Nicholas R. *Economic Growth and Distribution in China.* Cambridge: Cambridge University Press, 1978.

———. "China's Growing Economic Role in Asia." In *The Future of China,* 5–12. Seattle: National Bureau of Asian Research, 1992a.

———. *Foreign Trade and Economic Reform in China, 1978–1990.* New York: Cambridge University Press, 1992b.

———. *China in the World Economy.* Washington, D.C.: Institute for International Economics, 1994.

Lardy, Nicholas R., and Kenneth Lieberthal. *Chen Yun's Strategy for China's Development: A Non-Maoist Alternative.* Armonk, N.Y.: M. E. Sharpe, 1983.

Lawrence, Susan V. "Democracy, Chinese Style." *Australian Journal of Chinese Affairs* 32 (July 1994): 61–70.

Lee, Hong Yung. *From Revolutionary Cadres to Technocrats in Socialist China.* Berkeley and Los Angeles: University of California Press, 1991.

Leung, Julia. "As Zhu Preaches Austerity, Boom Town Throws a Party." *Asian Wall Street Journal.* 3 January 1994.

Levi, Jean. *The Chinese Emperor.* New York: Harcourt Brace Jovanovich, 1985.

Levine, Steven I. *Anvil of Victory: The Communist Revolution in Manchuria, 1945–1948.* New York: Columbia University Press, 1987.

Lewis, John W., Di Hua, and Litai Xue. "Beijing's Defense Establishment: Solving the Arms Export Enigma." *International Security* 15, no. 4 (Spring 1991).

Lewis, John W., and Litai Xue. *China Builds the Bomb.* Stanford: Stanford University Press, 1988.

Li, Cheng, and Lynn T. White III. "China's Technocratic Movement and the World Economic Herald." *Modern China* 17 (July 1991), 342–88.

Li, David D. "The Chinese State-Owned Enterprise Under Reform." Unpublished paper presented at the American Economic Association Annual Meeting, Boston, December 1993.

Li, Rui. *Lushan Huiyi Shilu.* Beijing: Chunqiu Chubanshe, 1989.

Li, Wei. "The General Office System: A Crucial Integrative Mechanism of China's Bureaucracy." Unpublished manuscript, 1993.

———. "The Security Service for Chinese Central Leaders." Unpublished manuscript, 1994.

Li, Wei, and Lucian Pye. "The Ubiquitous Role of the *Mishu* in Chinese Politics." *China Quarterly* 132 (December 1992): 913–36.

Li, Zhisui, with Anne Thurston. *The Private Life of Chairman Mao.* New York: Random House, 1994.

Liang, Heng, and Judith Shapiro. *Son of the Revolution.* New York: Alfred A. Knopf, 1983.

Lieberthal, Kenneth. "Mao vs. Liu? Policy Toward Industry and Commerce, 1946–194," *China Quarterly* 47 (July/September 1971).

———. "The Foreign Policy Debate in Peking as Seen through the Allegorical Articles." *China Quarterly* 71 (September 1977): 528–54.

———. *Central Documents and Politburo Politics in China.* Ann Arbor: Center for Chinese Studies, University of Michigan, 1978a.

———. "The Politics of Modernization." *Problems of Communism* 27, no. 3 (May–June 1978b): 1–17.

———. *Sino-Soviet Conflict in the 1970s: Its Evolution and Implications for the Strategic Triangle* (Rand report R-2342-NA). Santa Monica, Ca.: Rand Corporation, 1978c

———. *Revolution and Tradition in Tientsin, 1949–1952.* Stanford: Stanford University Press, 1980.

———. "The Future of Hong Kong." *Asian Survey* (July 1992): 666–82.

Lieberthal, Kenneth, and Bruce J. Dickson. *A Research Guide to Central Party and Government Meetings in China, 1949–1986.* Armonk, N.Y.: M. E. Sharpe, 1989.

Lieberthal, Kenneth, Joyce Kalgren, Roderick MacFarquhar, and Frederic Wakeman, Jr., eds. *Perspectives on Modern China: Four Anniversaries.* Armonk, N.Y.: M. E. Sharpe, 1991.

Lieberthal, Kenneth, and David M. Lampton, eds. *Bureaucracy, Politics and Decision Making in Post-Mao China.* Berkeley and Los Angeles: University of California Press, 1992.

Lieberthal, Kenneth, and Michel Oksenberg. *Policy Making in China: Leaders, Structures, and Processes.* Princeton: Princeton University Press, 1988.

Lieberthal, Kenneth, and C.K. Prahalad. "Multinational Corporate Investment in China." *China Business Review* 16, no.2 (March–April 1989): 47–49.

Lifton, Robert Jay. *Thought Reform and the Psychology of Totalism.* New York: W. W. Norton, 1961.

Link, Perry. *Evening Chats in Beijing: Probing China's Predicament.* New York: W. W. Norton, 1992.

Little, Daniel. *Understanding Peasant China: Case Studies in the Philosophy of Social Science.* New Haven: Yale University Press, 1989.

Liu, Binyan. *People or Monsters and Other Stories and Reportage from China after Mao.* Bloomington: Indiana University Press, 1992.

Liu, Junlin. "Make Efforts to Strengthen Further Building of Cadres' Ranks." *Guangming ribao.* 14 July 1991 (translated in *FBIS/China Daily Report* (30 July 1991): 31–33).

Lo, T. Wing. *Corruption and Politics in Hong Kong and China.* Philadelphia: Open University Press, 1993.

Lord, Bette Bao. *Legacies: A Chinese Mosaic.* New York: Alfred A. Knopf; distributed by Random House, 1990.

Lou, Xinya, and Junjie Huang. "Qigong Series Off the Press." *Beijing Review* 33 (8 January 1990): 46.

Lu, Hsün, *Ah Q and Other Selected Stories.* Westport, Ct. Greenwood, 1971.

Luk, Shiu-hung, and Joseph Whitney, eds. *Megaproject: A Case Study of China's Three Gorges Project.* Armonk, N.Y.: M. E. Sharpe, 1993.

Luo, Qi, and Christopher Howe. "Direct Investment and Economic Integration in the Asia Pacific: The Case of Taiwanese Investment in Xiamen." *China Quarterly* 136 (December 1993): 746–69.

Lyons, Thomas. *Economic Integration and Planning in Maoist China*. New York: Columbia University Press, 1987.

———. "Planning and Interprovincial Coordination in Maoist China." *China Quarterly* 121 (March 1990): 36–60.

MacFarquhar, Roderick. *The Origins of the Cultural Revolution 1: Contradictions among the People, 1956–57*. New York: Columbia University Press, 1974.

———. *The Origins of the Cultural Revolution 2: The Great Leap Forward 1958–1960*. New York: Columbia University Press, 1983.

———. "The Anatomy of Collapse." *New York Review of Books*, 26 September 1991.

———, ed. *The Politics of China, 1949–1989*. New York: Cambridge University Press, 1993.

MacFarquhar, Roderick, Timothy Cheek, and Eugene Wu. *The Secret Speeches of Chairman Mao*. Cambridge: Harvard University Press, 1989.

MacFarquhar, Roderick, and John K. Fairbank, eds. *Cambridge History of China*, vol. 14. New York: Cambridge University Press, 1987.

———, eds. *Cambridge History of China*, vol. 15. New York: Cambridge University Press, 1991.

Madsen, Richard. "The Public Sphere, Civil Society and Moral Community: A Research Agenda for Contemporary Chinese Studies." *Modern China* 19 (April 1993): 183–98.

Malraux, Andre. *Man's Fate*. New York: Vintage, 1934.

Manion, Melanie. "Cadre Recruitment and Management in the People's Republic of China." *Chinese Law and Government* 17:3, (Fall 1984): 3–128.

———. *Retirement of Revolutionaries in China: Public Policies, Social Norms, Private Interests*. Princeton: Princeton University Press, 1993.

Mann, Susan. *Local Merchants and the Chinese Bureaucracy, 1750–1950*. Stanford: Stanford University Press, 1987.

Mao, Zedong. *Selected Works of Mao Zedong*, vol. 1. Beijing: Foreign Languages Press, 1965a.

———. *Selected Works of Mao Zedong*, vol. 2. Beijing: Foreign Languages Press, 1965b.

———. *Selected Works of Mao Zedong*, vol. 4. Beijing: Foreign Languages Press, 1967.

———. *Selected Works of Mao Zedong*, vol. 5. Peking: Foreign Languages Press, 1977.

———. *Writings of Mao Zedong: 1949–1976*, vol. I. Armonk, N.Y.: M. E. Sharpe, 1986.

Mao Zedong sixiang wan sui! (Long live Mao Zedong Thought!). No city of publication or publisher provided. 1969.

Marshall's Mission to China, December 1945–1947: The Report and Appended Documents. Arlington, Va.: University Publications of America, 1976.

Maruya, Toyojiro. "The Development of the Guangdong Economy and Its Ties with Beijing." *China Newsletter* 96 (January–February 1992): 2–10.

Massey, Joseph. "301: The Successful Resolution." *China Business Review* 19, no. 6 (November–December 1992): 9–11.

McCormick, Barret L., Shaozhi Su, and Xiaoming Xiao. "The 1989 Democracy Movement: A Review of the Prospects for Civil Society in China." *Pacific Affairs* 65 (Summer 1992): 182–202.

McCullough, David G. *Truman*. New York: Simon and Schuster, 1992.

Melby, John F. *Mandate of Heaven*. Toronto: University of Toronto Press, 1968.

Michael, Franz. *The Taiping Rebellion*. 3 vols. Seattle: University of Washington Press, 1966–71.

Migdal, Joel. *Strong Societies and Weak States*. Princeton: Princeton University Press, 1988.

———, Atul Kohli, and Vivienne Shue, eds. *State Power and Social Forces: Domination and Transformation in Asia, Africa, and Latin America*. New York: Cambridge University Press, 1994.

Mirsky, Jonathan. "China: Bartered Brides." *The Ottawa Citizen*. 5 October 1992, p. D12.

Montell, Sherwin. "The San-fan Wu-fan Movement in China." In *Papers on China* vol. 8. Cambridge: Harvard University, 1954.

Morse, Hosea Ballou. *The Trade and Administration of the Chinese Empire*. Taipei: Ch'eng-Wen Publishing Company, 1966.

Murphey, Rhoads. *The Treaty Ports and China's Modernization: What Went Wrong*. Ann Arbor: Center for Chinese Studies, University of Michigan, 1970.

"Nanjing Paper Attacks Secret Societies, Sects." *FBIS* (18 February 1987): 5.

Naquin, Susan, and Evelyn Rawski. *Chinese Society in the Eighteenth Century*. New Haven: Yale University Press, 1987.

Nathan, Andrew J. *Chinese Democracy*. New York: Alfred A. Knopf, 1985.

———. "China's Path from Communism." *Journal of Democracy* 4, no. 2 (April 1993a): 30–42.

———. "Is Chinese Culture Distinctive?" *Journal of Asian Studies* 52 (November 1993b): 923–36.

Naughton, Barry. "The Third Front: Defense Industrialization in the Chinese Interior." *China Quarterly* 115 (September 1988): 351–86.

———. "China's Experience with Guidance Planning." *Journal of Comparative Economics* 14 (1990): 743–67.

Nelsen, Harvey W. *The Chinese Military System: An Organizational Study of the Chinese People's Liberation Army*. 2nd ed. Boulder: Westview Press, 1981.

"New Achievements in Social Services in 1992." *FBIS* (3 February 1993): 18.

"New Qigong Film." *Beijing Review* 34 (1 July 1991): 41–42.

"New Strategy for Environmental Protection: Putting a Price on Resources." *Beijing Review* 31 (22 August 1988): 32–34.

Norman, Matthew. "When Being Female Is a Deadly Crime." *Evening Standard*. 26 September 1993, p. 55.

North, Robert C. *Kuomintang and Chinese Communist Elites*. Stanford: Stanford University Press, 1952.

O'Brien, Kevin. "Implementing Political Reform in China's Villages." *Australian Journal of Chinese Affairs* 32 (July 1994): 33–60.

Ogata, Sadako M. *Normalization with China: A Comparative Study of US and Japanese Processes*. Berkeley: Institute of East Asian Studies, University of California, 1988.

Oi, Jean. *State and Peasant in Contemporary China: The Political Economy of Village Government.* Berkeley and Los Angeles: University of California Press, 1989.

————. *Rural China Takes Off: Incentives for Reform.* Unpublished manuscript, 1994.

Oksenberg, Michel, and Steven Goldstein. "China's Political Spectrum." *Problems of Communism* 23 (March–April 1974): 1–13.

Oksenberg, Michel, and James Tong. "The Evolution of Central-Provincial Fiscal Relations in China, 1971–1984: The Formal System." *China Quarterly* 125 (March 1991): 1–32.

Oksenberg, Michel and S.C. Yeung. "Hua Kuo-feng's Pre-Cultural Revolution Hunan Years, 1949–66: The Making of a Political Generalist." *China Quarterly* 69 (March 1977): 3–54.

Oksenberg, Michel, Lawrence Sullivan, and Marc Lambert, eds., with an introduction by Melanie Manion. *Beijing Spring, 1989.* Armonk, N.Y.: M. E. Sharpe, 1990.

Overholt, William H. *The Rise of China.* New York: W. W. Norton, 1993.

Pearson, Margaret. *Joint Ventures in the People's Republic of China: The Control of Foreign Direct Investment Under Socialism.* Princeton: Princeton University Press, 1991.

Peck, Graham. *Two Kinds of Time.* Boston: Houghton Mifflin, 1967.

Peng, Peiyun. "Population Problems and Countermeasures." *Beijing Review* 33 (7 May 1990): 20–24.

Pepper, Suzanne. *Civil War in China.* Berkeley and Los Angeles: University of California Press, 1978.

————. *China's Education Reform in the 1980s: Policies, Issues and Historical Perspectives.* Berkeley: Center for Chinese Studies, University of California, 1990.

Perkins, Dwight. *Market Control and Planning in Communist China.* Cambridge: Harvard University Press, 1966.

————. *Agricultural Development in China, 1368–1968.* Chicago: Aldine, 1969.

————, ed. *Rural Development in China.* Baltimore: Johns Hopkins University Press, 1984.

Perry, Elizabeth J. *Rebels and Revolutionaries in North China, 1985–1945.* Stanford: Stanford University Press, 1980.

————. "China in 1992: An Experiment in Neo-Authoritarianism." *Asian Survey* 33 (January 1993): 12–21.

————. "Shanghai's Strike Wave of 1957." *China Quarterly* 137 (March 1994): 1–27.

Petrov, Vladimir. *Soviet-Chinese Relations 1945–1970.* Bloomington: Indiana University Press, 1975.

Peyrefitte, Alain. *The Immobile Empire.* New York: Alfred A. Knopf, 1992.

Potter, Pitman B., ed. *Domestic Law Reforms in Post-Mao China.* Armonk, N.Y.: M. E. Sharpe, 1993.

Powell, Simon. *Agricultural Reform in China: From Communes to Commodity Economy, 1978–1990.* Manchester: Manchester University Press, 1992.

Pu Yi, Aisin-Gioro. *From Emperor to Citizen.* Peking: Foreign Languages Press, 1979.

Pye, Lucian W. *The Dynamics of Factions and Consensus in Chinese Politics: A Model and Some Propositions.* Santa Monica, Ca.: Rand Corporation, 1980.

————. *The Mandarin and the Cadre.* Ann Arbor: Center for Chinese Studies, University of Michigan, 1988.

———. "Tiananmen and Chinese Political Culture: The Escalation of Confrontation from Moralizing to Revenge." *Asian Survey* 30 (April 1990): 331–47.

———. *The Spirit of Chinese Politics.* Cambridge: Harvard University Press, 1992.

"Qigong—Popularity Is Rising." *Beijing Review* 31 (14 November 1988): 32–35.

Qu, Geping, and Jinchang Li. *An Outline Study on China's Population—Environmental Issues.* Beijing: National Environmental Protection Agency, 1990.

Qu, Geping, and Woyen Lee, eds. *Managing the Environment in China.* Dublin: Tycooly International, 1984.

Renmin shouce (People's Handbook). Beijing, 1951.

"Resolution on Certain Questions in the History of Our Party since the Founding of the People's Republic of China." *Beijing Review* 27 (6 July 1981): 10–39.

Riskin, Carl. *China's Political Economy: The Quest for Development Since 1949.* Oxford: Oxford University Press, 1987.

Rosenbaum, Arthur Lewis, ed. *State and Society in China.* Boulder: Westview Press, 1992.

Ross, Lester. *Forestry Policy in China.* Ph.D. diss., University of Michigan, 1980.

———. *Environmental Law and Policy in the People's Republic of China.* New York: Quorum, 1987.

———. *Environmental Policy in China.* Bloomington: Indiana University Press, 1988.

"Rotten to the Core: Monopoly of Power Leads to Rampant Corruption." *Far Eastern Economic Review* 156 (16 September 1993): 16–17.

Rowe, William T. *Hankow: Commerce and Society in a Chinese City, 1796–1889.* Stanford: Stanford University Press, 1984.

———. *Hankow: Conflict and Community in a Chinese City, 1796–1895.* Stanford: Stanford University Press, 1989.

———. "The Problem of 'Civil Society' in Late Imperial China." *Modern China* (April 1993): 139–57.

Rozelle, Scott. "Decision Making in China's Rural Economy: The Linkages Between Village Leaders and Farm Households." *China Quarterly* 137 (March 1994): 99–124.

Ruan, Ming. *The Empire of Deng.* Boulder: Westview Press, 1994.

Salisbury, Harrison E. *The Long March: The Untold Story.* New York: Harper and Row, 1985.

———. *The New Emperors: China in the Era of Mao and Deng.* Boston: Little, Brown, 1992.

Sander, Henny, and Jonathan Friedland. "Investment: Think Twice." *Far Eastern Economic Review* 156, no. 36 (9 September 1993): 46–49.

Saunders, Harold, et al. *Tibet: Issues for Americans.* New York: National Committee on US-China Relations, 1993.

Schell, Orville. *To Get Rich Is Glorious: China in the Eighties.* New York: Pantheon, 1984.

Schiffrin, Harold Z. *Sun Yat-Sen and the Origins of the Chinese Revolution.* Berkeley and Los Angeles: University of California Press, 1970.

Schoenhals, Michael. "The 1978 Truth Criterion Controversy." *China Quarterly* 126 (June 1991): 243–68.

———. "Selections from *Propaganda Trends,* Organ of the CCP Central Propaganda Department." *Chinese Law and Government,* 24, no. 4 (Winter 1991–92): 5–93.

Schram, Stuart R. *The Political Thought of Mao Tse-Tung.* Middlesex: Penguin, 1963.

————. *Political Leaders of the Twentieth Century: Mao Tse-Tung.* Baltimore: Penguin, 1966.

Schurmann, Franz. *Ideology and Organization in Communist China.* 2nd ed. Berkeley and Los Angeles: University of California Press, 1971.

"Scientists Warn of Resource Shortages." *Beijing Review* 35 (18 May 1992): 7.

Schwartz, Benjamin I. *Chinese Communism and the Rise of Mao.* Cambridge: Harvard University Press, 1964.

Selden, Mark. *The Yenan Way in Revolutionary China.* Cambridge: Harvard University Press, 1971.

Seymour, James D. *The Fifth Modernization: China's Human Rights Movement, 1978–1979.* Stanfordville, N.Y.: Human Rights Publishing Group, 1980.

————. *China's Satellite Parties.* Armonk, N.Y.: M. E. Sharpe, 1987.

Shambaugh, David. *The Making of a Premier: Zhao Ziyang's Provincial Career.* Boulder: Westview Press, 1984.

————. "Introduction: The Emergence of 'Greater China'." *China Quarterly* 136 (December 1993): 653–59.

Shen, Tong. "Will China Be Democratic?" *World Affairs* 154 (Spring 1992): 139–54.

Sheng, Kang. *The Claws of the Dragon.* New York: Simon and Schuster, 1992.

Shirk, Susan L. "Recent Chinese Labor Policies and the Transformation of Industrial Organization in China." *China Quarterly* 88 (December 1981): 575–93.

————. *The Political Logic of Economic Reform in China.* Berkeley and Los Angeles: University of California Press, 1993.

Shue, Vivienne. *Peasant China in Transition: The Dynamics of Development toward Socialism, 1949–1956.* Berkeley and Los Angeles: University of California Press, 1980.

————. *The Reach of State.* Stanford: Stanford University Press, 1988.

Siu, Helen F. *Agents and Victims in South China: Accomplices in Rural Revolution.* New Haven: Yale University Press, 1989.

————, ed. *Furrows: Peasants, Intellectuals, and the State.* Stanford: Stanford University Press, 1990.

Skinner, G. W. "Marketing and Social Structure in Rural China," *Journal of Asian Studies* Nov., 1964; Feb., 1965; May, 1965.

————. *The City in Late Imperial China.* Stanford: Stanford University Press, 1977.

Skocpol, Theda. *States and Social Revolutions.* Cambridge: Cambridge University Press, 1979.

"Slaughtering the Innocents." *South China Morning Post,* 26 September 1993, p. 54.

Smil, Vaclav. *The Bad Earth: Environmental Degradation in China.* Armonk, N.Y.: M. E. Sharpe, 1984.

————. *China's Environmental Crisis.* Armonk, N.Y.: M. E. Sharpe, 1993.

Smith, Richard. *Mercenaries and Mandarins: The Ever Victorious Army in Nineteenth Century China.* Millwood, N.Y.: KTO, 1978.

Snow, Edgar. *Red Star over China.* New York: Grove, 1961.

Solinger, Dorothy J. *Regional Government and Political Integration in Southwest China, 1949–1954: A Case Study.* Berkeley and Los Angeles: University of California Press, 1977.

————. *From Lathes to Looms: China's Industrial Policy in Comparative Perspective, 1979–1982.* Stanford: Stanford University Press, 1991.

————. "China's Transients and the State: A Form of Civil Society." *Politics and Society* 21 (March 1993): 91–122.

Solomon, Richard H. *Mao's Revolution and the Chinese Political Culture.* Berkeley and Los Angeles: University of California Press, 1971.

————. ed. *The China Factor: Sino-American Relations and the Global Scene.* Englewood Cliffs, N.J.: Prentice Hall, 1981.

Spector, Stanley. *Li Hung-Chang and the Huai Army: A Study in Nineteenth-Century Chinese Regionalism.* Seattle: University of Washington Press, 1964.

Spence, Jonathan. *Emperor of China: Self Portrait of K'ang Hsi.* New York: Alfred A. Knopf, 1974.

————. *Death of Woman Wang.* New York: Viking, 1978.

————. *The Gate of Heavenly Peace.* New York: Penguin, 1981.

Starr, John Bryan, and Nancy Anne Dyer. *Post-Liberation Works of Mao Zedong: A Bibliography and Index.* Berkeley and Los Angeles: University of California Press, 1976.

"State Instituting Social Services for Retirees." *FBIS* (27 October 1993): 40.

State Statistical Bureau. *China Statistical Yearbook, 1990.* New York: Praeger, 1991.

Stueck, William Whitney. *The Road to Confrontation: American Policy Toward China and Korea, 1947–50.* Chapel Hill: University of North Carolina Press, 1981.

Sullivan, Lawrence R. "The Role of Control Organs in the Chinese Communist Party, 1977–83." *Asian Survey* 24 (June 1984): 597–617.

Sun, Yan. "Chinese Protests of 1989: The Issue of Corruption." *Asian Survey* 31 (August 1991): 762–82.

Sutter, Robert G. *China Watch: Sino-American Reconciliation.* Baltimore: Johns Hopkins University Press, 1978.

Swain, Jon. "Beijing Reasserts Control as Economic Unrest Mounts." *Sunday Times.* 4 July 1993.

Swaine, Michael. *The Military and Political Succession in China* (Rand Report R-4254-AF). Santa Monica, Ca.: Rand Corporation, 1992.

"Symposium on Rural Family Change." *China Quarterly* 130 (June 1992): 317–91.

T'an, Chester C. *The Boxer Catastrophe.* New York: Columbia University Press, 1955.

Tanner, Murray Scot. "CCP Central Document Number Eight [1991] and the Erosion of Central Party Control of Lawmaking." *China Quarterly* 137 (March 1994).

Tanner, Murray Scot, and Michael J. Feder. " 'Family Politics,' Elite Recruitment and Succession in Post-Mao China." *Australian Journal of Chinese Affairs* 30 (July 1993): 89–120.

Tawney, R. H. *Land and Labor in China.* Boston: Beacon, 1966.

Teiwes, Frederick C. *Elite Discipline in China: Coercive and Persuasive Approaches 1950–1953.* Canberra: Australian National University Press, 1978.

————. *Politics and Purges in China.* White Plains, N.Y.: M. E. Sharpe, 1979.

————. *Politics at Mao's Court: Gao Gang and Party Factionalism in the Early 1950s.* Armonk, N.Y.: M. E. Sharpe, 1990.

Teng, Ssu-Yu, and John K. Fairbank. *China's Response to the West: A Documentary Survey 1839–1923*. New York: Atheneum, 1963.

Terrill, Ross. *A Biography: Mao*. New York: Harper and Row, 1980.

"Text of the 14th CPC Congress Political Report." *FBIS* (8 October 1992): 1–20.

"Threat From 'Secret Societies' Examined." *FBIS* (16 July 1986): K1.

"Through the Roof: Shenzhen Takes Steps to Curb Property Speculation." *Far Eastern Economic Review* 154 (24 October 1991): 75–76.

Thurston, Anne F. *Enemies of the People*. Cambridge: Harvard University Press, 1988.

———. *A Chinese Odyssey: The Life and Times of a Chinese Dissident*. New York: Charles Scribners Sons, 1991.

———. "The Dragon Stirs." *Wilson Quarterly* (Spring 1993): 10–15.

Tien, Hung-Mao. *Government and Politics in Kuomintang China 1927–1937*. Stanford: Stanford University Press, 1972.

———. *The Great Transition: Political and Social Change in the Republic of China*. Stanford: Stanford University Press, 1989.

Tien, H. Yuan, Tianlu Zhang, Yu Ping, Jingneng Li, and Zhongtang Liang. "China's Demographic Dilemmas." *Population Bulletin* 47 (June 1992): 1–44.

Toffler, Alvin. *The Third Wave*. New York: Morrow, 1980.

Tong, James. *Disorder Under Heaven: Collective Violence in the Ming Dynasty*. Stanford: Stanford University Press, 1991.

Townsend, James R. *Political Participation in Communist China*. Berkeley and Los Angeles: University of California Press, 1969.

Treadgold, Donald W., ed. *Soviet and Chinese Communism: Similarities and Differences*. Seattle: University of Washington Press, 1967.

Tsou, Tang. *America's Failure in China, 1949–50*, vol. 1. Chicago: University of Chicago Press, 1963a.

———. *America's Failure in China, 1949–50*, vol. 2. Chicago: University of Chicago Press, 1963b.

Tuchman, Barbara. *Stilwell and the American Experience in China 1911–1945*. New York: Macmillan, 1970.

Twitchett, Denis, and John K. Fairbank, eds. *Cambridge History of China*, vol. 11. New York: Cambridge University Press, 1978.

Van Slyke, Lyman P. *The United Front in Chinese Communist History*. Stanford: Stanford University Press, 1967.

———. *The Chinese Communist Movement*. Stanford: Stanford University Press, 1968.

Vladimirov, Petr P. *The Vladimirov Diaries: Yenan, China, 1942–45*. Garden City, N.Y.: Doubleday, 1975.

Vogel, Ezra F. *Japan as Number One: Lessons for America*. New York: Harper and Row, 1980.

———. *One Step Ahead in China: Guangdong under Reform*. Cambridge: Harvard University Press, 1989.

———. *The Four Little Dragons: The Spread of Industrialization in East Asia*. Cambridge: Harvard University Press, 1991.

Wakeman, Frederic, Jr. "The Civil Society and Public Sphere Debate." *Modern China* (April 1993): 108–38.

Walder, Andrew G. *Chang Ch'un-Ch'iao and Shanghai's January Revolution.* Ann Arbor: University of Michigan, 1978.

———. *Communist Neo-Traditionalism: Work and Authority in Chinese Industry.* Berkeley and Los Angeles: University of California Press, 1986.

———. "Reply to Womack." *China Quarterly* 126 (June 1991): 333–39.

Waldron, Arthur. *The Great Wall of China: From History to Myth.* New York: Cambridge University Press, 1989.

Wang, Ruowang. *Hunger Trilogy.* Armonk, N.Y.: M. E. Sharpe, 1991.

Wang, Y. C. *Chinese Intellectuals and the West, 1872–1949.* Chapel Hill: University of North Carolina Press, 1966.

"Wang Zhen Decries Loss of Party Influence." *FBIS* (12 March 1991): 32.

Wasserstrom, Jeffrey, and Elizabeth Perry, eds. *Popular Protest and Political Culture in Modern China.* Boulder: Westview Press, 1992.

Watson, James L. *Death Ritual in Late Imperial and Modern China.* Berkeley and Los Angeles: University of California Press, 1988.

———. "Hong Kong, 1997, and the Transformation of South China: An Anthropological Perspective." *Contemporary Issues 1.* Cambridge: Fairbank Center for East Asian Research, May 1993.

White, Gordon. "State and Market in China's Labour Reforms." *Journal of Developmental Studies* 24 (July 1988): 180–202.

White, Lynn T., III. *Careers in Shanghai.* Berkeley and Los Angeles: University of California Press, 1978.

———. *Policies of Chaos: The Organizational Causes of Violence in China's Cultural Revolution.* Princeton: Princeton University Press, 1989.

White, Lynn T., III, and Cheng Li. "Elite Transformation and Modern Change in Mainland China and Taiwan: Empirical Data and the Theory of Technocracy." *China Quarterly* 121 (March 1990): 1–35.

White, Theodore H. *In Search of History.* New York: Harper and Row, 1978.

Whiting, Allen S. *China Crosses the Yalu.* Stanford: Stanford University Press, 1960.

Whiting, Susan. *The Political Economy of Rural Enterprises in Shanghai, Wuxi, and Wenzhou.* Ph.D. diss., University of Michigan, 1994.

Whitson, William W. *The Military and Political Power in China in the 1970s.* New York: Praeger, 1972.

———. *Chinese Military and Political Leaders and the Distribution of Power in China, 1956–71* (Rand report R-1091-DOS/ARPA). Santa Monica, Ca.: Rand Corporation, 1973.

Whitson, William W., with Chen-hsia Huang. *The Chinese High Command: A History of Communist Military Politics, 1927–1971.* New York: Praeger, 1973.

Whyte, Martin King. *Small Groups and Political Rituals in China.* Berkeley and Los Angeles: University of California Press, 1974.

Wich, Richard. *Sino-Soviet Crisis Politics.* Cambridge: Harvard University Council on East Asian Studies, 1980.

Wilbur, C. Martin. *The Nationalist Revolution in China, 1923–1928.* New York: Cambridge University Press, 1984.

Wilson, Dick, ed. *Mao Tse-tung in the Scales of History: A Preliminary Assessment.* Cambridge: Harvard University Press, 1977.

Wittfogel, Karl A. *Oriental Despotism: A Comparative Study of Total Power.* New Haven: Yale University Press, 1957.

Wolf, Margery, and Roxanne Witke, eds. *Women in Chinese Society.* Stanford: Stanford University Press, 1975.

Womack, Brantly. "Transfigured Community: Neo-traditionalism and Work Unit Socialism in China." *China Quarterly* 126 (June 1991): 313–32.

Wong, Christine. "Central-Local Relations in an Era of Fiscal Decline: The Paradox of Fiscal Decentralization in China." *China Quarterly* 128 (December 1991): 691–715.

Wood, Gordon. *The Radicalism of the American Revolution.* New York: Random House, 1991.

World Bank. *China: The Energy Sector.* Washington, D.C.: World Bank, 1985.

———. *China: Between Plan and Market.* Washington, D.C.: World Bank, 1990a.

———. *Revenue Mobilization and Tax Policy.* Washington, D.C.: World Bank, 1990b.

———. *Efficiency and Environmental Impact of Coal Use in China.* Washington, D.C.: World Bank, 1991.

———. *China Updating Economic Memorandum: Managing Rapid Growth and Transition.* Washington, D.C.: World Bank, 1993.

World Bank Transition Economics Division. *Transition.* Washington, D.C.: World Bank Transition Economics Division.

Wright, Arthur. *Confucianism and Chinese Civilization.* New York: Atheneum, 1964.

Wright, Mary C. *The Last Stand of Chinese Conservatism: The T'ung-chih Restoration, 1862–1874,* rev. ed. Stanford: Stanford University Press, 1966.

———, ed. *China in Revolution: The First Phase, 1900–1913.* New Haven: Yale University Press, 1968.

Wu, Hongda Harry. *Laogai—The Chinese Gulag.* Boulder: Westview Press, 1992.

Wu, Naitao. "An Open System: Ensuring An Honest Government." *Beijing Review* 33 (29 January 1990): 6–7.

Wu, Ningkun. *A Single Tear: A Family's Persecution, Love, and Endurance in Communist China.* New York: Atlantic Monthly Press, 1993.

Wu, Silas H. L. *Communication and Imperial Control in China: Evolution of the Palace Memorial System, 1693–1735.* Cambridge: Harvard University Press, 1970.

Yan, Jiaqi. *Lianbang Zhongguo gouxiang* (Conception of a federal China). Hong Kong: Mingbao Publishing Company, 1992.

Yang, C. K. *Chinese Communist Society: The Family and the Village.* Cambridge: MIT Press, 1959.

Yang, Jisheng. "Bloated State Administrative Institutions," in *Qunyan* 8 (7 August 1991): 23–34; translated in *FBIS/China Daily Report* (29 August 1991): 39–31.

Yang, Xiaobing. "Taiwan Steps Up Mainland Investment." *Beijing Review* 31 (24 October 1988): 42.

Yang, Xiaobing, and Lei Zhang. "China's Population Policy." *Beijing Review* 35 (13 April 1992): 17–20.

Yang, Zhong Mei. *Hu Yao Bang: A Chinese Biography.* Armonk, N.Y.: M. E. Sharpe, 1988.

Yi, Z. "Population Policies in China: New Challenge and Strategies." In *An Aging World: Dilemmas and Challenges for Law and Social Policy,* edited by J. M. Eekelaar and D. Pearl. Oxford: Clarendon, 1989.

Young, Earnest. *The Presidency of Yuan Shih-Kai.* Ann Arbor: University of Michigan, 1977.

Young, Marilyn B., ed. *Women in China.* Ann Arbor: Center for Chinese Studies, University of Michigan, 1973.

Yue, Daiyun, and Carolyn Wakeman. *To the Storm: The Odyssey of a Revolutionary Chinese Woman.* Berkeley and Los Angeles: University of California Press, 1985.

Zagoria, Donald. *The Sino-Soviet Conflict 1956–61.* Princeton: Princeton University Press, 1962.

Zhang, Shu Guang. *Deterrence and Strategic Culture: Chinese-American Confrontations, 1949–58.* Ithaca, N.Y.: Cornell University Press, 1992.

Zheng, Yongnian. *The Making of a Federal System: Quasi Corporatism and the Rise of Local Power in China.* Ph.D. diss., Princeton University, 1994.

Zhonghua Renmin Gongheguo sheng zizhiqu zhishushi dang zheng chun jiguan zuzhi jigou, gai yao (Outline of the organizational structure of the Party, government, and mass organizations of the provinces, autonomous regions, and directly-administered cities of the PRC). Beijing: China Personnel Publishing Company, 1989.

Zhou, Xuegang. "Unorganized Interest and Collective Action in Communist China." *American Sociological Review* 58 (February 1993): 54–73.

Zweig, David. *Agrarian Radicalism in China, 1968–1981.* Cambridge: Harvard University Press, 1989.

Index